PAT CHAPMAN was born in London's Blitz, with an addiction to curry inherited from his family's six-generation connection with India, the story of which is told in Pat's new book *Pat Chapman's Taste of the Raj* (*see* page 2). Virtually weaned on his grandmother's curries, he was taken to his first curry houses – Veeraswamy in Piccadilly, and Shafi's in Gerrard Street – at the age of six, at a time when there were only three such establishments in London, and six in the whole of the UK. Visits became a regular treat and confirmed in Pat a passion and a curiosity about the food of India. He was already a curryholic! Following education at Bedales and Cambridge, he did a short stint in the RAF, flying fast jets, then spent several years in industry.

He founded the now world-renowned Curry Club in 1982, at a time when the curry was just beginning to become nationally important, as the means to share information about recipes, restaurants and all things to do with spicy food. Soon a national network of curry restaurant reporters was established, whose voluntary contributions led to the publication of the first edition of this highly successful *Good Curry Restaurant Guide* in 1984, and its prestigious awards to restaurants.

Assisted by his wife, Dominique, Pat frequently demonstrates at major food shows and appears on TV and radio, and they regularly stage cookery courses and events. His pioneering Gourmet Tours to India are now well-established holidays for *aficionados*.

With book sales exceeding 1 million, Pat is best known as a writer of easy-to-follow recipes. His succession of popular curry titles, some of which are listed on page 2, are published by Hodder & Stoughton, Piatkus, Sainsbury's and the BBC.

Some of Pat Chapman's Best-sellers

PAT CHAPMAN'S CURRY BIBLE
The big definitive book about curry and spices. Lavishly illustrated.

PAT CHAPMAN'S TASTE OF THE RAJ
Fascinating history, funny family anecdotes, 100 spicy recipes.

PAT CHAPMAN'S THAI RESTAURANT COOKBOOK
Over 100 fabulous recipes with fabulous background information.

THE CURRY CLUB INDIAN RESTAURANT COOKBOOK
Hints, tips and 150 recipes. All your restaurant favourites.

THE CURRY CLUB BALTI CURRY COOKBOOK
All Balti's secrets are revealed in this best-selling 100-recipe book.

THE CURRY CLUB BANGLADESHI CURRY COOKBOOK
The curry house operators ... the real authentic background.

THE CURRY CLUB INDIAN VEGETARIAN COOKBOOK
150 vegetarian recipes, all authentic to the curry lands.

CURRY CLUB 250 FAVOURITE CURRIES AND ACCOMPANIMENTS
A well-illustrated mix of authentic and restaurant recipes.

PAT CHAPMAN'S BBC QUICK AND EASY CURRIES
Over 100 recipes prepared in half an hour, with plenty of tips.

THE 1998 GOOD CURRY GUIDE

EDITED BY
PAT CHAPMAN

In association with
Cobra Indian Lager & The Taj Group of Hotels

CORONET BOOKS
Hodder & Stoughton

Assistant Editor: Dominique Chapman (D.B.A.C.)
Contributors: David Wolfe, Iqbal Wahhab, Andy Mitchell
Designer: Peter Ward
Fact verification: David Mackenzie
Text verification: Jane Struthers
Statistics: Taylor Nelson, Sub Continent Publishing
Disc conversion: Tex Swan
Certification: Louise Paul
Researchers: Karan, Arjay, Arjun, Samson and Bobbi

Good Curry Guide Reporters of the Year:
Hilary Chapchal of London
Melinda and Graham Paine of Coventry
Brian George of Milton Keynes
Plus many hundreds of others, without whom
this Guide would not exist

Copyright © 1997 by Pat Chapman

First published in Great Britain in 1997 by Hodder & Stoughton
A division of Hodder Headline PLC

A Coronet paperback

1   3   5   7   9   8   6   4   2

All rights reserved. No part of this publication may be reproduced,
stored in a retrieval system, or transmitted, in any form or by any means
without the prior written permission of the publisher, nor be otherwise
circulated in any form of binding or cover other than that in which
it is published and without similar condition being imposed on
the subsequent purchaser.

ISBN 0 340 68032 6

Printed and bound in Great Britain by
Mackays of Chatham PLC, Chatham, Kent

A catalogue recommendation for this book is available
from the British Library

Hodder and Stoughton
A division of Hodder Headline PLC
338 Euston Road
London NW1 3BH

Author's Note

Sponsorship The continuing sponsorship of Cobra Lager and Taj Hotels enables the author to finance the considerable costs of operating and producing this Guide, which are over and above the normal costs involved in producing a book. These include: maintaining the restaurant database on computer; subscribing to a press-cutting service and other information suppliers; printing a detailed questionnaire; mailing it to all 8300 restaurants on two occasions; mail-shotting the 1200-plus restaurants that are selected to appear in this Guide; telephoning many for verification of information; producing, supplying and mailing the selected restaurants (free of charge) their wall certificates and window stickers; printing restaurant report forms for interested parties and mailing them; collating and recording the information received (some 5000 reports per annum); operating the Awards Ceremony.

Accuracy The contents of this Guide are as up to date and accurate as possible, but we cannot be held responsible for changes regarding quality, price, menu details, decor, ownership, health offences or even closure, since our report details were processed.

Connections Pat Chapman, the publishers of this Guide and the proprietors of The Curry Club wish to make it quite clear that they have absolutely no financial or ownership connections with any restaurants, including those mentioned in this Guide.

False representation Restaurant reports are welcomed from members of The Curry Club and others. We do not pay for reports – they are sent in spontaneously and voluntarily. Our own research and restaurant testing is normally done anonymously, the bill is paid, and often no disclosure is made as to our presence. On some occasions, such as openings, we accept invitations to visit restaurants as 'guests of the house'. We point out that in no circumstances do we tout for free hospitality, and anyone doing so in the name of The Curry Club is an impostor. We have heard of cases where people claiming to be members of The Curry Club, or *Good Curry Guide* 'inspectors', request payment and/or free meals in return for entry into this Guide. In such a case, we earnestly advise restaurants to threaten to call the police, for this is attempting to obtain goods and services by false pretences. We would also like to be informed of the names and addresses of such fraudsters. We will not hesitate to take action against such people acting illicitly or illegally in the name of The Curry Club or *The Good Curry Guide*.

Discounts We invite all restaurants selected to appear in this Guide to participate in a discount scheme for members of The Curry Club. Some agree to do so, and are indicated by the symbol © on their entry. The terms of this scheme are clearly spelled out to all parties. We cannot be held responsible if, at any time, the restaurant declines the offered discount.

CONTENTS

Detailed County Index

Introduction

The *Good Curry Guide* (GCG) is now in its fourteenth year and this, its fifth edition, marks its coming of age. Not only does it have a new title or, to be exact, its original title, with the dropping of the word 'Restaurant', it has, we hope, a friendlier look, and it also has a new publisher, Coronet. And with that comes two things, one of which has been long-awaited, and much-demanded by its followers: annual publication. The other is the dropping of advertising which, though it never gave the advertising restaurants rights, nor immunity from criticism, does now make the Guide a much better publication. We are pleased to keep our two previous sponsors, Cobra Indian Lager and Taj Hotels of India, and our reason for needing them is explained on page 5.

In a recent letter, M.W. Smith of Woldingham introduced himself as a new Guide reporter, with my favourite one-liner of the year. Having been an enthusiastic reader of the *Good Curry Guide* since being given a copy last Christmas, he says: 'It is the best appetite-inducer I know.'

It sure is! And as one who labours for weeks over its 200,000 words, all pertaining to curry, I can assure you it not only makes one positively salivate, it makes one rush off to the nearest curry house to satiate one's withdrawal symptoms. And that, pure and simple, is its purpose. Its title says it all – it is the *Good Curry Guide*. It enables diners to find a good curry somewhere near them.

It concentrates on nothing else. Other Guides have other remits. For example, there has been criticism of the *Michelin Guide* recently for not focusing on curry. In our view, they do not need to because that is our job. We do it by listing what you tell us are the best restaurants in your area.

That is exactly what this Guide is all about. Of course standards will vary, and the curry at The Wind of India in Puddlecome-on-the-Marsh may well be reported as the best in the world by its most ardent, youngest, novice, local fan (and I want such opinions), and it will probably not rate highly if compared blow by blow with London's Bombay Brasserie. But nevertheless, it will be a safe-bet competent curry house in that area, serving the standard formula curry. A good number of the entries in this Guide come into this category. And they are here because someone out there, maybe many more than one, has taken the trouble to write in and praise the place, and to exclude it would be wrong. Quite simply, we want to know what you know.

We rely on a number of sources of information, but by far the most important are the genuine voluntary reports (around 5000) sent in by hundreds of people every year. The report itself can be a simple short note, but we have a special form available for all who want one. (See the pages at the end of this Guide for further information.) One report may deal with just one restaurant. Another report may contain information on dozens of restaurants. Some reporters only write to us once. Other reporters write repeatedly. We read and record every report, of course, though it gets progressively harder to reply. So if I failed to do so to you, may I say thank you now for being good enough to take a little of your time to tell us where you have found the best, good, mediocre and even bad curries.

A further simple question on our form – name your favourite curry restaurant(s) – yields plenty more information. But answering this may not always be as easy as it sounds. Sutton Coldfield's John Brockingham, a retired college lecturer, puts it succinctly. He used to tell his students that he didn't answer difficult questions, only easy ones. 'So,' he wrote, 'I feel inclined to say the same to you when you ask me to tell you my favourite restaurants in descending order, when they are so varied and numerous. They range from opulent establishments, like Rajdoot, Birmingham, where I might take the family on special occasions, to cheap and cheerful places like Erdington's Balti Express, where a meal costs £2 a head. I have a favourite posh curry restaurant, when I can afford it, and a favourite posh Balti. But I have a favourite plonk version of both, and a favourite takeaway, and then there's a favourite lucky dip. Some of my favourites are good enough to tempt me in whenever I'm in the district, but could not be nominated for the highest accolade. Like the Dilshad in Wolverhampton where they serve the most delicious tikka in the business, except on one occasion mine was tepid, and I was assured by a harassed waiter that it was meant to be so. And dare I mention the Streetly Balti on the A452, which is so good, but so small, the residents have threatened a public execution of anyone found guilty of reporting it to the Curry Club?' Your secret's safe with me, John.

Before we even start to select who gets into the Guide we send every one of the nation's 8300 curry restaurants a simple questionnaire, mainly to verify our facts but also to remind them we are here. This time we did so twice, with a few weeks in between. After fourteen years of bona fide operations, you would imagine that curry house owners would clamour to be in the Guide. And indeed some do. I have said before that more than one restaurant has made veiled hints as to the benefits that would be made available to the editors if that restaurant were declared the UK's number one. To those restaurateurs who believe that they can buy this accolade, or even entry into this Guide, I politely request that they save their energy. Never in my life have I acceded to bribes. I hate the notion, and find even hints highly embarrassing. And, of course, if one did accede, word would soon get round and it would be the end of the credibility of both author and publication. The book is paid for through book sales and its support activities by sponsorship, not through bribes.

Then we make our selection. With 8300 restaurants to choose from, the task gets harder than ever (there were 7900 for the last Guide and just 3500 for our first 1984 edition). With an expanding market (see statistics on page 19) and with standards already high and getting higher, it is not surprising that our Guide contains more entries each edition. This time we have over 1300. Even so, regrettably over 7000 have not made it into this Guide.

But I'll guarantee that, as usual, we've missed someone's favourite, and as usual there will be a few *faux pas* too. Almost certainly some of them should have been included. How come they are omitted?

Such is life, of course, that we do not receive reports on every single establishment. So, yes, it is possible that we've omitted a really good one – and it's bound to be your favourite! So tell us please, and we'll know for next time. Equally, though we do our best to filter out 'good' reports on bad restaurants – particularly those written by their hopeful owners, and this time, yet again Rafu's of Swindon (who sent many) leads the field in this department, with Birmingham's Clock Tower Balti, and Worthing's Maahns, close behind. And yes, even after fourteen years in the editor's chair, it is possible that I've been conned and a bad one has slipped into the Guide. Let us know about that too, please. No doubt, we'll continue to get irate letters from people who won't have bothered to read this explanation, telling us that, because this or that restaurant was awful when they visited, 'it casts doubt on the credibility of the entire Guide'. Despite this caveat being printed every time, we did indeed receive such a complaint from a Mr Malcolm Wilkins, and coincidentally from North Devon Trading Standards asking me for information. Needless to say I sent both a copy of the Guide, highlighting this very sentence, and nothing more has been heard from the latter. But Mr Wilkins sent a decent reply; indeed, he promises to send us reports.

Of course, standards and ownership do change, increasingly so in the curry restaurant business, it seems. Equally, staff move around for numerous reasons. But I repeat, not one restaurant gets into this Guide unless we have had at least one recent good report on it, preferably several.

As I said earlier, not all our correspondence is flattering. I've had a few real snorters this year. Top of the pile is one from a Dr Ho Yen from Milton Keynes. He complained furiously that a group of his staff booked a Christmas dinner at the Jaipur. Without advising the restaurant, two of the party failed to show. The restaurant had printed on its booking form leaflet that the management reserved the right to charge for no-shows. They did charge, a residual amount of £6.66. But the group, and the good doctor, who wasn't even there, went ballistic. No amount of persuasion convinces him that his friends had entered into a contract, and that the restaurant is legally correct. He calls me pompous for suggesting it and has vowed never to return to the Jaipur, nor to buy this Guide. Seems to me he's cutting off his nose, since the Jaipur is one of the UK's top ten restaurants. And without the Guide, how will he find a replacement? Medics definitely like complaining. There are more medic complainants on my files than anyone else.

Talking of health, Durham's David Mackenzie points out that at the Corbridge Tandoori, in Northumberland, a customer who was allergic to nuts died. The menu now scrupulously lists all ingredients, and he was surprised to see how many dishes do contain nuts. Perhaps the law should oblige all restaurants to do this, in the way that food manufacturers have to.

So what of this Guide? It has more entries than ever. We give price information and list the 600 or so restaurants that have agreed to participate in our discount schemes. Peter May from St Albans wants this made brief and simple: 'I loved the detailed descriptions in the 1992 Guide, but feel too much space was taken in the 1995 edition with information about discounts. A discount symbol and the manager's name is all that's needed.' Your wish is my command, Peter. Indeed, we note the unusual points, such as vegetarian restaurants, BYO, closed days, evenings only, takeaway only, etc., rather than stating the normal, such as licensed, do takeaway, open lunch and dinner, etc.

Names get more bizarre, no more so, I suppose, than London's new Chor Bizarre, but Crawley's Ruby Murray, London's Exotikka, Kenilworth's Balti Towers and Plymouth's Veggie Perrins are still vying for attention. I am waiting for the first restaurant to call itself The Spice Girls. And with Girl Power at a peak, maybe some of the wilier Bangladeshi restaurateurs will retire gracefully and let their daughters take over – and not before time!

British Telecom never stops fiddling with codes and probably never will. It keeps printers and sign-writers busy, but it is the counties which have had more upsets this time, with the demise of Avon, Cleveland and Humberside, for example. Indian restaurant name-changes continue unabated. Whether it is just change for change's sake, or whether it is to avoid creditors, tax inspectors or the VAT person, or simply to confuse your editor, I cannot say, but we do our best to keep up. The record probably goes to Coventry's Shahi Palace, with four changes in a decade. I have said before that every village has its curry house. Central TV's Tony Francis points out that Chipping Camden, Bourton-on-the-Water and Crondal don't and never will. Someone must tell me which is the largest town without for next time.

The recession has hit hard at trade, with some desperate restaurateurs resorting to slashing prices. In some cases it worked, but it's always a dangerous policy if it is uncontrolled, as was graphically demonstrated in Bristol. There it became a price-war between certain rival restaurants, so much so that some of them wiped themselves out. But in Norwich, this dangerous game seems to fill the curry houses.

A much more positive attempt to improve trade has been the introduction of home-delivery. Such a service has been part of American culture for ever, it seems. Eventually the pond was crossed, first by pizza deliveries (them again) and now by curry houses. It is a sign of the times that we prefer the luxury of an on-the-doorstep-service to the tedious wait at the takeaway. We don't even mind paying for it. It's all a question of giving the people what they want. But not all regions do it, and some penalize you for the privilege. For examples of the good and the bad respectively, see the Shahanaz, Haslemere, Surrey and Anwar's, Bognor, Sussex.

The trend for themed mega-restaurants, which has swept around London, has not quite hit the curry trade yet, though we hear of a few speculative plans. Restaurateurs are beginning to add real, authentic Bangladeshi dishes to their menus. But it is too slow. They blame lack of demand. But how can demand evolve if the invite is not there in the first place? I still want to see a blackboard 'dish of the day' system at the standard curry house, which allows room for experimentation. But the café nomenclature is here to stay, as are blurry, out-of-focus photographs in trendy new cookbooks. *Chambers Dictionary* describes a café as 'a small inexpensive place where you can get beverages, snacks and easily prepared meals and refreshments'. Brasserie and bistro means much the same. Perhaps someone should remind the various proprietors of these places of the words 'inexpensive', 'snacks', and 'easily', not to mention 'all day'! And the latest marketing gimmick comes from Adlid – takeaway-container lids that carry advertisements.

From the new to the old. Keen readers will note that I like to know about a restaurant's pedigree. I went on a business trip to Gibraltar recently and I thought I'd found a real scoop. There in the baggage hall I spied an advert for the Star of India on Main Street, Gibraltar. Founded 1893, it said. Amazing! We all thought the first curry house appeared in 1911 in Holborn. So off I trotted up to Main Street, but no restaurant could I find. Eventually I realized that the Star was in fact a purveyor of French perfumes, beauty products, pens and sunglasses! Gib, by the way, has no less than six curry houses, a testament not just to the one-time British forces there – because there must now be more Barbary apes than troops – but to the force of the food. Curry is as big a deal with Gib's population as it is with ours. Britain's oldest curry restaurant, Piccadilly's Veeraswamy, has been saved from extinction in its seventieth year, appropriately fifty years to the day after India's Independence.

Balti has now become respectable! Last time I reported that Madhur Jaffrey denied all knowledge of it. 'It doesn't exist in India,' she had said in print. In fact, when I appeared with her in July on BBC TV (she was cooking pakoras, I was cooking chicken and mushroom Balti), I was fully expecting a lambast from her. But far from it. She pronounced my dish delicious, then asked me to take her for a Balti down the road in Brum, something I've always promised her we'd do. Her U-turn is, in part, inspired by the fact that she now endorses William Levine's range of Balti cookware but, given that there is a little hype involved, it is no worse than that which elevated pizza into prominence on the British street scene a few years ago. And if it succeeds in getting more Brits converted to curry then so much the better.

And there's more: you'll find the answers to lots of questions in this

Guide. Where can you enjoy curry and Karaoke? Or a table magician? Where can a couple enjoy a quick cuddle? Where indeed can you buy curry-flavoured condoms? Where do the toilets smell like a horse box? Which restaurateur gives his clients a lift home? Where do they call you from the pub over the road when your table's ready? Who does a 550-mile round trip for a decent curry? Where is a curry house in a former cricket pavilion? A medieval barn? A Portakabin? A converted mill? A railway carriage? A former dance hall? A warehouse? A former refreshment hut? Which has a filling-station pump in its forecourt? Whose waiters are walking football encyclopedias? Who visits his local takeaway 100 times a year? Who has been to 203 curry restaurants this year? Which owner-chef likes you to ring him on his mobile? Where can you buy a 200-year-old brandy at £35 a shot? Which restaurant serves an Indian knickerbocker glory? Which restaurant is part of an hotel? Where would an ex-London couple like the Tube to run to? Who moved house from Abingdon just to be near their favourite restaurant? Who fancies Brigitte Bardot? Which restaurant has a resident duck? Where can you still find red flock wallpaper? Which restaurant says Balti comes from Banglastan? Which restaurant shuts at 5p.m., then moves the staff down the road to run a different venue till late? And which restaurant owner has outlived twenty-two Hoovers, two recessions, several Prime Ministers and served enough naans to stretch from London to Paris?

It's all in the Guide. Indeed, we run an annual competition amongst Curry Club members each autumn to answer 50 questions, of which these are some, with the winner getting a fantastic prize. It's not too late to compete. To join, see the last page in the book.

It's all fun but Europe has put the dampeners on things a bit, recently. Can there be any people more bonkers than British politicians at election time (one recent poster read: 'BRUSSELS SPROUTS ... 100 regulations are passed every day'), except perhaps EU politicians at all times. Three ludicrous recent examples of Brussels spouting in the food business are the banning of Thai lime leaves, edible silver leaf and Bombay Duck. Lime leaves, said Brussels, are hallucinogenic and must be banned. Just how many leaves one has to take to go on a trip, or who in Brussels conducted the experiments, I do not know, but the ban is frankly bonkers. Anyway, it stopped fresh lime leaves from entering Britain for a while. Then Waitrose started selling them again and now, hopefully, everyone else will follow suit. As to silver leaf or vark, the reason given by the EU was that it is adulterated with aluminium. This is like saying that fake Gucci luggage isn't the real thing. Yes, vark has always been prone to that little scam. The answer is to use reputable suppliers. As for Bombay Duck, Brussels evidently found a consignment with a bug infestation and they blamed the processing. Well, blow me down! The greatest problem that all dry-food suppliers have is bugs! Ask Rank Hovis McDougall, the country's largest flour-millers, what they fear most. Is it strikes? Is it crop failure? Is it lack of profitability? Goodness me, no! It is the common weevil, a tiny round black bug that inhabits wheat grain and which, given a chance, over-runs the flour mill, contaminating all the product. Such infestations occur. But does that mean that all flour is banned? No, of course not.

Bombay Duck, incidentally, is an eel-like fish which is native to the Bombay area. It is processed by drying it in the sun. This is a process which has been done worldwide for thousands of years. The process is perfectly safe and sound. And since this delicious dried fish is deep-fried before being served, any chance of a problem is simply cooked away. I miss my Bombay Duck at the moment and can't wait for this piece of madness to pass on by and for supplies to be resumed.

To get into our TOP 100, the restaurant must have had many recent good reports from different people. As I said last time, I explained this rule to one Wiltshire restaurant. A few days later, and for weeks after-wards, the mail delivered a glowing report about this very restaurant, each in totally different handwriting. In normal circumstances such a volume of good reports would have catapulted the restaurant near to the top of our TOP 100. The only problem was that every report was a copy, more or less word for word, of the first. Did this earnest restau-rateur get all his clients to write in? Even the notepaper and envelopes were similar! As a regular Guide entrant, it's back but, again, not as a TOP 100. This time I'll name it – it was Rafu's of Swindon. Third time lucky, sir? I think not!

Last time we got nine reports on a Cheshire curry house, including one from a Mr Moan, all in different hands but written on the same date! As it happens this restaurant had already been selected to enter the élite TOP 100. But no Mr Moan this time. Pity!

But not all restaurants are that eager to be entered in our Guide. Some still say they have never heard of the *Good Curry Guide* nor of the Curry Club. Pick of the pack Brain-dead Award of the Year goes to Ely's Surma, whose waiter denied all knowledge of both the Club and the Guide, despite our certificate being on his wall, our sticker on his window and mention made of both facts all over his menus! Since we have been going for fifteen years, which is more than most restaurants, we take that with a pinch of masala! Some restaurants, perhaps, are busy enough not to need the extra traffic we cause. Others are downright suspicious of us, believing they will get an invoice for their entry. They never will from us, but they do from others. What we hate is the seemingly unstoppable, legal but unethical, scam of the bogus certificate syndrome. We know of fourteen different operators of such schemes. They approach all restaurants (regardless of quality) with the lure of a 'prestigious' certificate. Every restaurateur wants accolades, and many say 'yes'. They receive their certificate but, along with it, they get an invoice ranging from between £100 and £600 for the privilege. The remarkable fact is that so many, otherwise hardened, restaurateurs are actually gullible enough to cough up. We have heard of more than one who'll pay well over £1000 per annum for such services. Sadly, apart from the certificate, nothing else whatsoever is supplied.

Perhaps certificates do impress the locals, but readers of this Guide could help the situation by encouraging their favourite local restaurant to avoid paying for certificates, and to support the bona fide non-charging restaurant guides by communicating with them. We feel that the production of this Guide should be helpful not only to readers and potential customers, it should also be of use to the restaurants themselves. They have a right to be proud of their entry in this Guide. It is, after all, prestigious to a restaurant to be singled out with a one-in-nine accolade of excellence from the dining public. All restaurants nominated in this Guide are awarded a free certificate, not one they have had to pay tens or hundreds of pounds for, and a window sticker to display if they wish. The élite, highlighted in our TOP 100 list, are recognized by special awards, again at no cost to themselves.

Finally, as ever, I hope this Guide will amuse and entertain you, as well as inform you and guide you to a good curry somewhere in the 1000-plus best curry houses across the length and breadth of Great Britain and beyond.

I hope reading its contents will make your mouth water as much as it did ours when we wrote it, and that this will mean you'll just have to have a curry right now! If it's a restaurant from the Guide, I hope you will enjoy the cuisine of the sub-continent of India at the highest standards. If you think so, this Guide will have done its job.

Or it might be a restaurant that's not in the Guide. Either way, and whatever you think of it, please let us know, so we can tell everyone next time.

I hope that, like Mr M.W. Smith of Woldingham, you too will find this Guide the best appetite-inducer you know.

Pat Chapman,
Founder THE CURRY CLUB

Curry Statistics

Britons have eaten their way to the top of the European fast-food league, considerably outspending our neighbours Germany, France, Spain and Italy on hamburgers, pizzas and fried chicken. Britain spent £2.4 billion on these delights, and the surveys did not include fish and chips, Chinese or curry. In another recent survey, undertaken by Bi-so-dol to establish what the nation consumed, curry (which led the poll at 18%), it seems, has become our number one national dish, ahead of fish and chips and roasts (which polled 16%) – and this was under-taken before the BSE crisis. This, of course, will come as no surprise to those avidly reading these pages. Figures from statisticians Taylor Nelson confirm that the curry dining-out market continues to expand, while those from Mintel concur with curry ingredients and ready-meals sold at the supermarkets. Asda has opened a section called the Curry Pot where you can choose from a selection of chilled, fresh cur-ries. This has not escaped the notice of our reporters, who say that for the first time a supermarket has got it right in taste and texture. Maybe the death of the revolting packet/frozen/chilled supermarket curry is imminent?

Another phenomenon, slipping through the back door, is the rapid growth of curries served at our pubs. Realizing that they were losing trade to the ethnic restaurants because of the dire food they served, the pubs have begun to hit back. It started with Thai pub food, but now an amazing 6500 pubs serve curries and baltis and all the works, some being rated 'excellent'. True, that's only 15% of all pubs, and it may well hit some of our curry restaurants hard, but I believe there is room for both, and a reason for more growth. And what of our restaurants?

Despite new openings (700 since we last published in mid-1995), the number of UK curry restaurants has appeared to have grown only by 3% from 8000 to 8300. Some 400 closures have been recorded, as well as countless changes of ownership. Despite this, business at the Indian restaurant has never been more booming. It now accounts for 8% of all meals consumed in the entire UK restaurant/takeaway industry, making it the fourth largest sector after pubs and bars, Chinese restaurants/takeaways and burger bars. This is an increase of 2% in two years, when it came seventh, and in that time it has over taken fish and chip outlets, the steak house and Italian/pizza establishments. In the year May 1996-May 1997, meals consumed in the curry house have boomed back and are now recorded at 36% of the total (an increase of 27%), with takeaway meals accounting for 44% (no change), and home deliveries 20% (42% growth).

Still, remarkably, many restaurants do not offer this delivery service, while others have obtained off-licences so that they can deliver hot curries with cold lager or wine. One that we have recorded in this Guide goes the whole hog, delivering all this, plus cigarettes, pizzas, baked potatoes, donner kebabs, burgers, chips, coleslaw salad and gar-lic bread. He'll probably be delivering the baby next, then offer baby-sitting! Several home deliverers who have not got an off-licence give free lager or wine with an order above a certain amount. All this is cer-tainly better than price-warring and closures, and proves that positive sales techniques work.

Indian meals are still very much the preserve of the younger con-sumer, remaining just about stable from two years ago – 24% are eaten by people aged between 16 to 24, 36% by those between 25 to 34, and 23% are eaten by 35- to 44-year-olds. An interesting comparison appears with the over-65s. Curry is still not a big thing in this age group. Only 6% consume it, although this figure has increased by 4% since 1995, whereas a total of 18% eat out at other (non-ethnic) restaurants. Of curry diners, 57% are male and 43% are female. On premises the split was 61%:39% respectively, while in takeaways and home deliveries it was 54%:46%. In the Curry Club, 65% of members are male, and of the restaurant reports we receive the percentage from males is around 75%, many of whom, it seems, are teachers, medics or policemen – all used to filling out paperwork! In socio-economic terms, AB consumers accounted for 21% of the total curry market, C1s 31%, C2s 28% and DEs 18%. In the takeaway/delivery sector, it was 19%, 29%, 31% and 21% respectively.

Well over 2.5 million diners use the Indian restaurant each week. The average number of seats is 53. With an average bill of between £12-£15, the total spend is now estimated at over £2 billion. Old habits die hard, with 92% of curry house users preferring evenings. Saturday night accounts for 25% of all trade, Friday 18% and Thursday 12%. Sunday lunch only accounts for 2%. Indeed, with the curry house lunch trade amounting to only 9%, more restaurants have decided not to open at lunchtimes.

And what did these people order? Predictably, chicken remains the most popular ingredient, rising to 65% in 1997 (from 52.5% in 1991 and 60% in 1995). Surprisingly though, in the year of the BSE scare, demand for meat at the curry house has risen from 20% to 23%, with lamb accounting for 10%, beef for 9% and venison and mutton nearly 4%. (Pork and veal rarely appear.) Fish and prawns have inexplicably dropped to 4% (down 6%) while vegetables account for just 8% (down 2%). According to Gallup (mid-1997), in the last year there has been a tiny gain of vegetarians to 5.4% of the population. Until then, the national figure for vegetarians had been around 5% for some years. Gallup point out that a further 14.3% of the population avoid red meat – the reasons given are taste 24%, BSE 22% and moral grounds 8%. Cost plays a factor, too. Called demi-vegetarians, many people still eat poultry and fish. This figure has hardly changed, either, over the years. At the curry house, Chicken Tikka Masala remains the number one ordered dish (16%), with Chicken Korma next (8%) and Jalfrezi, Masala, Roghan, Karahi and Tikka/Tandoori all close behind at around 6%.

The curry scene at the supermarket continues to see an annual growth of between 15% and 20%, as it has done since 1982. Curry ingredients and ready-meal sales exceed £600 million a year, putting them ahead of the nearest ethnic cuisine (Chinese) by a wide margin. Almost 3 million households cook curry once a week or more. What they cook ranges from reheating a frozen or chilled ready-curry to cooking a fully fledged curry from a recipe book. £22 million is spent on papadoms alone. That's 440 million papadoms. Add the 205 million sold by the restaurants, and that's an astounding 645 million! Restaurants use 37,000 tonnes of rice and 1440 tonnes of pickles. Finally, good news for Cobra – 111 million pints of beer are sold at Indian restaurants each year, placing it ahead of wine. But contrary to public belief, curry house diners are not lager louts. Only 23% visit the pub before going to the restaurant.

Main source: Taylor Nelson AGB.
Subsidiary information: Tandoori Magazine Restaurateurs survey and Curry Club User Survey.

Oh La La Wahhab!

Iqbal Wahhab pokes around under the thali to reveal 1997 at the curry house

It was in 1997 that Indian restaurant owners told their designers to flock off.

Since the publication of the last edition of the Curry Club *Good Curry Restaurant Guide*, there has been an explosion of style, colour, regional tastes and restoration in the Indian sector, never before experienced on such a grand scale.

Luxury and grandness to match that of the Bombay Brasserie came in the shape of the Blue Elephant group's La Porte des Indes in London's Marble Arch, where over £2 million was spent converting a huge ballroom into a 350-seater eating extravaganza based loosely on the cuisine of Pondicherry, the former French colony of India.

Stunning surroundings also apply to the more recently launched Chor Bizarre on the site of the old Gaylord in Mayfair. Literally meaning (despite the clever spelling twist) a thieves' market, the restaurant has been fitted out with an utterly eclectic collection of Indian antiques, with no two tables looking the same. To give you a feel of the place, one of the tables is enveloped in the ornaments of an 18th-century four-poster bed from Calcutta!

More modern styles and approaches have also been in play, most notably with the high-profile launch of Amin Ali's latest venture, Soho Spice - a riot of bright colours helps to create a lively brasserie atmosphere. Over 400 people are visiting it every day and there is a definite feel-good factor to this place, unlike so many Indian restaurants where you walk in and see some sad-looking waiter and you want to ask him, 'What happened?'

Soho Spice is a virtual round-the-clock operation. It starts at 7a.m. offering Indian breakfasts, through to mid-morning and afternoon snacks, and has an à la carte menu which is astonishingly cheap at around £15 a head.

Chelsea, too, has a slick new outfit to give Chutney Mary a run for its money. This is Vama – The Indian Room, run by a slick bunch from Delhi. Such are the stakes in the London restaurant business at the moment that both Vama and Soho Spice hire not one but two PR out-

fits each to ensure that not only are the restaurants full, they are full
with the right sort of people. The new restaurants don't want too many
stuffy pinstripe types. They want the It girls – the Taras and the
Tamaras – and they're starting to get them, suggesting that the new
kids on the block intend to turn Indian food into a fashion statement.

Matching this trend has been the emergence of Indian superchefs,
with three in particular leading this race. The first is Cyrus Todiwala
of Café Spice Namaste, whose bold experimentation with all sorts of
meats (Bison Vindaloo, Kangaroo Tikka) and his gradual absorption
of oriental influences into essentially Indian cooking have meant that
his colourful restaurant in the City hardly ever has an empty table to
be seen or nabbed.

Cyrus is making a name for himself on television, having been the
star of a two-part series on BBC2's *Food and Drink* programme in which
he took a bunch of nerds and turned them into deft curry cooks. Big
money is backing Cyrus and you can expect to see many Café Spice
Namastes opening up in the next couple of years – as many as 15,
according to some reports.

Also climbing high in the PR stakes is Vineet Bhatia, currently with
the Star of India. Vineet is flavour of the month with the food critics
and, while still in his twenties, he has already individualized a cooking
style that has a lighter, perhaps more delicate, touch than Cyrus's
robust style.

Also erring towards delicacy is Sitangsu Chakravarty, who recently
came to London to head up things at The Red Fort. Sitangsu has
introduced what he calls Avant Garde Cuisine, which in essence means
that none of the dishes on the Red Fort menu are cooked with any oil
or fat. This is not just a gimmick to catch on to the apparent fad for
healthy eating (which Whitbread are trying with their first Indian
restaurant, Zujuma's, in Wimbledon). Sitangsu is a philosopher-chef
who believes that what we eat affects how we conduct our lives rather
than the other way round, which sort of makes sense.

Yet, despite so much happening at the top end of the industry, with
so much public attention and seemingly unstoppable demand, the key
accolades of the restaurant business still evade the Indian sector. Most
notably, the *Michelin Guide* has yet again failed to award even one star to
a single Indian restaurant.

The snooty French bias of the Michelin boffins would be laugh-
able if it were not for the fact that the discerning diner still pays

attention to those to whom Michelin awards stars. Those that do get them get better reviews and more business. The same respect should be applied to Indian restaurants. Those Michelin tyres need some Indian rubber on them.

On the subject of European bias, Brussels has banned another great institution – the Bombay Duck. Why? Because they don't like the way it is prepared. Notice how they don't ban fois gras which, if you ask me, is prepared in a far more unappealing manner than Bombay Duck, which is dried naturally. Whilst I am not a particular fan of Bombay Duck, I do believe that restaurants are being indirectly discriminated against by not being allowed to sell it.

One thing I am a fan of is Cobra Indian Beer, and this year Cobra took the big step of coming out on draught and improving upon its already excellent recipe. Not only have the Indians taught the Brits about food but now we have also taught you how to make decent lager. No longer is there a need to swill pints of harsh and gassy beer in the pub before going for a curry. The Indian restaurant now contains the complete experience. Nothing else matters.

LSE-trained former *Independent* journalist, Iqbal Wahhab, is Editor-in-Chief of *Tandoori Magazine*, the monthly trade journal sent to all British and European Indian restaurants, and also of *Indian and Oriental Food and Drink*, the new curry consumer magazine.

Wolfe on Wine

If you wish to drink fine wine with curry, that's fine by wine expert David Wolfe

Beer and curry go together like – lager and vindaloo? Yes, for many, but not for everyone. Some enjoy whisky and water; others prefer nimbu, home-made lemonade. Lhassi makes a good aperitif but is too rich for continued drinking. Water is boring and reacts with some spices to give a metallic twang at the back of the throat. For my taste, and that of many others, wine is best.

It must be remembered that wine, even well-chilled wine, doesn't quench thirst. On the contrary, its alcohol content makes it dehydrating. We drink wine to complement food and for the pleasure of drinking it. For my pleasure it must be red with Indian food, because the wine needs masses of flavour to stand up to the spices. No white has enough. 'No white?' Well, there are exceptions, of course. There is a case for a light, dry, crisp Sauvignon to cut through the fat or oil in curries and the yoghurt marinade of tandooris. Alsace Riesling, Pinot Blanc and Pinot Gris are wonderfully refreshing, as is Australian dry Riesling. Those with a sweeter tooth may prefer German Riesling. Then there is Gewürztraminer, often recommended with Indian food. Wrongly, I believe. The idea arises from the 'Gewürz' in the grape's name, which means 'spicy'. But its spiciness is more like that of tropical fruits than cooking spices. So the fruity Gewürztraminer may actually clash with the food. Which brings us back to the best of all drinks with Indian food - red wine. Do I hear outraged cries from the traditionalists? Don't Indian spices ruin red wine? And the chilli – doesn't that kill red wine? To which I reply, yes and no!

Red wine is not spoiled by chillies. The wine and the heat don't confront each other face to face, but slide past. As the wine flavour takes over, the palate 'forgets' the chillies; then the chillies return and the wine is forgotten. Ah, the intense pleasure of contrast! More likely to overpower red wine is the sugar in mango chutney. Try mango pickle instead. The need for a dull, rich, deep flavour rules out some favourites, such as refreshing, slightly chilled young Beaujolais, Italian Bardolino and Valpolicella. It also rules out wines made from that delicate grape, the Pinot Noir. So I regretfully shun my favourite red

Burgundies with Indian food. The grapes that work best are Cabernet Sauvignon, Merlot and Shiraz. Of these, the softest and fullest wines are made from the Merlot. It is the main grape for the clarets of St Emilion and Pomerol, and a few from the Médoc. But claret from any part of Bordeaux is normally a blend using Merlot, Cabernet Sauvignon and small amounts of several other varieties. Pure Merlot comes from southern France, Italy, Bulgaria, New Zealand and Chile. The powerful Syrah is the great grape of the Rhône and the same variety, under the name Shiraz, is one of Australia's most important reds. It seems to go best with tandooris. It may seem oddly lacking in depth with curry.

Apart from 'varietals', other wines with deep, rich flavours come from such hot climates as Argentina, California, Turkey, North Africa, Spain, southern Italy and the islands of Sicily and Sardinia. Another source is a country whose wines are rapidly improving - India. My recommendations are, of course, only for the good examples. Thin, watery wines do nothing for Indian food – or for any other. Sadly, too many house wines are like that. If you think of drinking one, taste it, if necessary by ordering a single glass first.

Finally, a piece of advice that should appear at the end of every article on something as subjective as the taste of food and wine. And that is that if you have found by experience that you disagree with this advice, ignore it. But if you have not tried these suggestions, please do so. The best combinations of food and wine, for your palate, can be found only by your own experiments.

David Wolfe writes for all the gourmet and wine magazines. He is also a specialist consultant to ethnic restaurants that need advice about their wine list selection and wine descriptions.

Cobra Beer

Now, don't get me wrong. Some of my best friends are wine critics.

Over the past couple of years, virtually every newspaper and magazine has been running articles on trying to match wines with Indian food. I have been to dozens and dozens of tastings trying to find which wines go with our cuisine and, whilst not every wine is a failure, the most telling thing happens after the poncey proceedings are over, once everyone has done their swirling and their sniffing. Everyone has a beer.

As our appreciation of Indian cuisine becomes ever more sophisticated, we seek to add new layers of sophistication onto it that otherwise aren't there. The great buzzword of the moment is 'authenticity', and the true lovers of Indian food are constantly seeking out the authentic Indian experience.

Restaurants and food manufacturers are often criticized for producing anglicized food or even, these days, Europeanized Indian food. Yet it is precisely this Europeanization process that the same critics are applying when they insist that wines should be drunk with Indian food.

But there is beer and there is beer. And there are beer-drinkers and then there are beer-drinkers. We must not confuse our disdain of the lager lout with the lager clout. The Indian restaurant industry is desperately seeking to get away from the image of being the last port of call for lads after they've been swilling harsh and gassy beer in the pub.

The typical European lager in fact goes less well with Indian food than the majority of wines. While subtle wines tend to lose their subtlety against spicy food, a lot of beers have an even more negative effect. Because they are so gassy, they tend to make you bloated. Though the thought of a long, cold glass of beer to go with an Indian meal is an appealing one, the repercussions can be quite unappealing.

Indian beer provides the solution and Cobra Indian Beer provides the best solution. Cobra was created in Bangalore in 1990 as a beer so smooth that it would go well with any Indian meal. After much research, a brew was formulated that was not just smooth, but extra smooth. A special double-filtration process helped to create a beer that was much less gassy while retaining a distinctive taste and the premium strength of 5% alcohol.

Cobra is brewed using only top-quality barley malt, hops, maize, yeast and rice, and has a clean, refreshing body and aroma, all of which make it ideal to drink with Indian food because the hoppy feel lends itself to spicy food while its smoothness means it is dangerously easy to drink. Reports abound from restaurants of the extraordinary quantities of Cobra that their customers consume.

Cobra is now the biggest-selling Indian bottled beer in the UK, and has just recently also become available in selected restaurants on draught. An image overhaul this year introduced eye-catching, bright and rich new packaging and an improved recipe, enhancing the smoothness and introducing a more refreshing taste to the beer.

The overhaul in image reflects what is happening in Indian restaurants as they sharpen up their act and command more respect as a result. A recent survey showed that for the first time only a minority of Indian restaurant-goers visit a pub beforehand, thus helping to break down the negative stereotype.

People are also visiting their Indian restaurant earlier in the evening, suggesting that they are seeking a more all-rounded Indian experience from their visit, and what they are finding is that, with Cobra, that experience is more complete. Cobra's larger bottle (660ml) is ideal for when groups go out to dinner because, just as with the food, one can share the bottles and top one another up, thus adding to the communal experience of eating Indian.

The regular 330ml bottle is increasingly becoming available outside Indian restaurants, most notably in Tesco and Waitrose. As we are now eating more Indian food at home than in the restaurant, the quest to bring the real Indian experience into our dining rooms is made that much easier and that much more pleasurable.

If you want more information about Cobra, you can call their head office on Freephone 0800 146 944. Cobra is distributed by Cobra Beer Ltd, 208 The Plaza, 535 King's Road, Chelsea, London sw10 0sz. Tel: 0171 376 3330. Fax: 0171 352 1604. E-mail: cobra-beer@cobrabeer.com. Brewed and bottled in the UK for Cobra Indian Beer Pvt. Ltd (India).

A Taste of India

---✦---

THE TAJ GROUP *of* HOTELS

Taj Hotels ask 'Why settle for a taste of India, when we can give you the whole banquet?'

Travelling India with us could make you a broader person. Because once you taste the true flavours of this mystical land, you discover that the food of India is sustenance for both body and soul. Every mouthful blends the splendours of the past with a vision for the future in an unforgettable, magical reality.

So come with us on a culinary journey through India, from palace to plate, from temple to tea party, and from one extraordinary sensation to another. Only the exquisite restaurants and the immaculately trained chefs of the Taj Group of Hotels can be trusted to take the flavours, the spirit, the magic, the pageantry, the rituals and the riches of India and blend them subtly and seductively into a feast for all the senses.

The notion is not entirely original. Travellers have been dining like kings in this ancient land long before the term 'haute cuisine' was coined. But there has never been a better way, or a better time, to savour the pleasures of this earthly paradise than at a table with the Taj. Will you, indeed, want to leave your table to see the splendid stone maidens of Khajuraho, the busy boats bobbing on the mighty Ganges, or that tear-stained, pearl-crowned mighty monument to love, the Taj Mahal? We will not blame you if you don't.

Besides, it is our proud belief that our restaurants vie for your attention with the many splendours of India. Not only are the world's finest and freshest foods used in the creation of each dish; so, too, are the long-lost arts of patience, craftsmanship and detail. From the fine filigree icing on your French pastry to the way in which flavours are woven like bright silks through your Rogan Josh Gosht, Taj cuisine is an ever-present echo of the artistic and architectural grandeur that surrounds your every step in India.

From a delicate custard apple ice-cream to a perfect Bloody Mary;

from a tropical pasta to European sacher torte; from an exquisite vegetarian thali to a magnificent array of barbecued shellfish; our restaurants, like India herself, are home to all the arts.

In your own world, you live in the here and now, but in India, we live in eternity. There has been plenty of time to perfect the gentle art of spicing, making the drip by drip decoction of coffee in south India, the catching of fresh seafood, the making of a perfect cup of tea and the creation of ethereal sweetmeats in Calcutta.

So that instead of bargaining over the brilliant brocades of Rajasthan, the land of kings, you may relax over a gin and tonic at the Polo Bar at the Rambagh Palace at Jaipur and still acquaint yourself with the fine arts of India.

In Varanasi, you can explore the world's most ancient city and its sacred river one day, and the city's most famous dish of slow-cooked potatoes with over a dozen spices at the Hotel Taj Ganges the next.

As always, it is the colours of India that you will treasure most. The turquoise and vermilion of freshly caught fish at Kerala, the brilliant jewel-like cerise and lemon of tropical fruit at Madras. And while nothing is quite as ethereal as a burnt orange sunset over the still waters of Lake Pichola, Upaidur, the colour is caught and held by every dish of delicate Kashmiri saffron-tinted rice at our world-famous Lake Palace.

Colour is everywhere, more vivid than the brilliant piles of spices at the markets and robes of the devout. You will be equally entranced by the faded salmon colours that tint the whole city of Jaipur, or the Indian ocean crab baked to perfection at the Beach Café of The Taj Holiday Village in Goa.

At bustling Bombay, you can tear yourself away from the majesty of the Gateway of India to admire the artistry and grandeur of our famous Indian banquet table at the Taj Mahal Intercontinental, or to feast on the sizzling splendours of the Chinese province of Szechwan without having to pass through the Gateway once again.

Agra means both the romance and majesty of the Taj Mahal, and the candlelight gleaming in a glass of Indian bubbly at your table for two at the Taj View Hotel. Beautiful, tropical Goa gives you brilliant sea views of freshly netted lobsters the size of your arm at the Fort Aguada Beach Resort.

At Paradise Island at the Taj West End, Bangalore, savour a Thai prawn curry over a beautiful pond.

And who could forget the sparkling treasure trove that is

Kathmandu, as you sample the authentic flavours of Nepalese cooking at the Taj Hotel De L'Annapurna, or the spicy serendipity that is
Sri Lanka at the Taj Sumandra Hotel?

From the rich Moghlai lamb dishes and tantalizing tandoori of the
north to the sensational seafood, chilli and coconut of the south, we
invite you to join us on a gastronomic adventure and to discover the
real jewels in our crown.

We will certainly feed you like royalty if you like. But we would
prefer to feed you like a god.

Taj Hotels are India's number one group of hotels, with a portfolio of some
fifty magnificent properties, ranging from tiny and large former palaces to
brand new purpose-built extravaganzas. In addition, they have a further thirty
other equally splendid hotels worldwide. Taj has its own purpose-built chef
school at Aurangabad, where novices undergo a four-year apprenticeship
before a further year of work experience in a Taj Hotel. Only then do they
become qualified.

Our Top 100 Restaurants

Only one in every eight of the nation's curry restaurants achieve entry into this Guide, so they are all top restaurants and a cut above the norm. But, naturally, we are always asked to identify the best of the best, so to speak. And it is true that there is an élite number of really excellent restaurants including, by definition, those establishments about which we receive many consistently good reports. For over a decade we have listed them as our TOP 100 restaurants. There is change from last time, of course, as you would expect after two years – thirteen have been replaced, of which only two are caused by closure, the others, sadly, due simply to a decline in performance. However, whereas last time we managed to choose exactly 100, this time, reflecting an ever-growing number of restaurants, we have expanded the list to 114. However, this needs a little explanation because eighteen of these are branches of just six restaurants (marked †). Of the 'new' entrants (indicated *), some are indeed newish, although some are long-established, and have been brought to our attention by our reporters. So if there are yet others we have missed, please report to us. For a restaurant to remain in our TOP 100 list, we also need your views.

There is a further, even more élite list, the cream of the cream, winners of our SPECIAL AWARDS (highlighted in bold type), all of whom attend the Guide's prestigious ceremony in London to receive their awards. For the record, previous winners of such an award are also indicated, since they all remain at the top of our TOP 100.

London

E1	*	Café Spice Namaste
		Lahore Kebab House
N1		Sonargaon
NW1		Diwana Bhel Poori
		Great Nepalese
NW4	*	Prince of Ceylon
NW5		Bengal Lancer
SE23		Babur Brasserie
		Dewaniam

SE26		Jehangir (Previous Award Winner)
SW1		Saloos
SW3		Tandoori of Chelsea
SW5	*	Star of India
SW6		Blue Elephant (Previous Award Winner)
SW7		Bombay Brasserie (Previous Award Winner)
SW10		Chutney Mary (Previous Award Winner)
SW12	*	**Tabaq** (BEST PAKISTANI)
SW13		Haweli (Previous Award Winner)
SW15	*	Ma Goa
SW17		Sree Krishna
W1		Caravan Seral
		Mandeer
	*	**La Porte des Indes** (BEST INDIAN)
		Ragam South Indian
	*	Soho Spice
		Tamarind (BEST INDIAN)
		Veeraswamy (MOST PROMISING NEWCOMER)
W2		Bombay Palace
		Khan's
		Old Delhi
W5	*	Gitanjli of Mayfair
		Monty's
W6		Tandoori Nights (Previous Award Winner)
W8		Malabar
W13	*	**Sigiri** (BEST SRI LANKAN)
WC1	*	Malabar Junction
WC2		The India Club (Previous Award Winner)
		Punjab

Rest of England

BERKSHIRE

Reading		Blna (Previous Award Winner)
Theale	*	**Café Blue Cobra** (BEST IN THE WEST)

BRISTOL

Bristol	†	Rajdoot (Previous Award Winner)

BUCKINGHAMSHIRE

Milton Keynes	**Jaipur** (BEST BANGLADESHI RESTAURANT)

CHESHIRE

Ellesmere Port   **Agra Fort** (BEST IN THE NORTH)

DEVON

Plymouth   Kurbani

DORSET

Poole   * Rajasthan

ESSEX

Ilford   * Curry Special

           Jalalabad

HAMPSHIRE

Fleet   * **Gurkha Square** (BEST NEPALESE)

Liss   Madhuban

Portsmouth   Palash

Southampton   Kuti's Brasserie

HERTFORDSHIRE

Abbots Langley   Viceroy of India

Royston   British Raj

St Albans   * Mumtaj

KENT

Bromley   **Tamasha** (BEST IN THE SOUTH)

Chislehurst   Bengal Lancer

Folkestone   India

Orpington   The Bombay

LANCASHIRE

Adlington   Sharju

LEICESTERSHIRE

Leicester   Curry Fever

           Friends Tandoori

LINCOLNSHIRE

Boston   Star of India

G. MANCHESTER

Manchester   * Gaylord

           † Rajdoot (Previous Award Winner)

Ramsbottom   Moghul Dynasty

MERSEYSIDE

Liverpool   * Gulshan

MIDDLESEX

Southall   **Brilliant** (BEST PUNJABI RESTAURANT)

MIDDLESEX (continued)

Southall	**Madhu's Brilliant** (*Special Award* – BIGGEST EVENT)
	Omi's
	Sagoo and Thakhar
Wembley	Chetna's Bhel Puri
	Curry Craze

NORTHUMBERLAND

Corbridge	The Valley (Previous Award Winner)

NOTTINGHAMSHIRE

Nottingham	*	Chand
		Saagar

OXFORDSHIRE

Oxford	Aziz
	Polash Tandoori

STAFFORDSHIRE

Lichfield	Eastern Eye
Stoke-on-Trent	Al Sheik's

SUFFOLK

Woodbridge	Royal Bengal

SURREY

Tolworth	*†	Jaipur
Woking	*†	Jaipur

TYNE AND WEAR

Gateshead	*	Last Days of the Raj
Newcastle		Rupali
		Sachins
		Vujon

WARWICKSHIRE

Leamington Spa	Ashoka

WEST MIDLANDS

Birmingham		Days of the Raj
		Maharajah (BEST IN THE MIDLANDS)
	†	Rajdoot (Previous Award Winner)
		Royal Naim (BEST BALTI HOUSE, SECOND TIME)
Coventry		**King William IV Pub** (BEST CURRY PUB)
	*	Rupali
Warley		Rowley Village

N. YORKSHIRE
Harrogate   *† Shabab
Skipton   † **Aagrah** (BEST RESTAURANT CHAIN)
N. YORKSHIRE (Continued)
Tadcaster   *† **Aagrah** (BEST RESTAURANT CHAIN)
S. YORKSHIRE
Doncaster   *† **Aagrah** (BEST RESTAURANT CHAIN)
W. YORKSHIRE
Bradford   † Nawaab
Garforth   † **Aagrah** (BEST RESTAURANT CHAIN)
Halifax   *† Shabab
Huddersfield † Nawaab
Leeds   Darbar
                 Hansa's Gujarati Vegetarian
              *† Shabab
Pudsey   † **Aagrah** (BEST RESTAURANT CHAIN)
Shipley   † **Aagrah** (BEST RESTAURANT CHAIN)

Scotland

FIFE
St Andrews   New Balaka Bangladeshi (Previous Award
                 Winner)
LOTHIAN
Edinburgh   Lancers Brasserie
                 Shamiana (BEST CHEF AWARD)
                 Verandah
STRATHCLYDE
Glasgow   **Balbir's** (BEST IN SCOTLAND)

Wales

CLWYD
Deeside   † **Bengal Dynasty** (BEST IN WALES, SECOND TIME)
GWYNEDD
Llandudno   † **Bengal Dynasty** (BEST IN WALES, SECOND TIME)

The Cuisine of the Sub-continent

Afghan Afghanistan's location had always held the strategic key to India until this century, for it was through the solitary mountain passes that the invaders came and possessed India from as early as 3000 BC. Located between Iran (formerly Persia) and Pakistan (formerly N.W. India), it brought the cuisine of the Middle East to India – and that of India to the Middle East. Afghan food features Kebabs and Birianis, and skewered spiced lamb over charcoal. The only Afghan restaurant in the UK is Caravan Serai, London WI.

Bangladeshi/Bengali Most of the standard curry houses in the UK are owned by Bangladeshis and nearly all of those serve standard formula curries, ranging from mild to very hot. Bangladesh, formerly East Pakistan, is located at the mouth of the River Ganges. Before Partition, the area either side of the Ganges was Bengal. Today Bengal is the Indian state that shares its border with Bangladesh. In terms of food, Bangladesh is Muslim, so pork is forbidden. The area enjoys prolific fresh and seawater fish – pomfret, boal, ruhi, hilsa and ayre, and enormous tiger prawns – and it specializes in vegetable dishes such as Shartkora and Niramish. Until recently, true Bangladeshi/Bengali cuisine was nigh on impossible to find in the UK. With the Dine Bangladeshi campaign gaining ground, we can expect to find more and more of our Bangladeshi restaurants serving the delights of their own country.

Bombay Bombay curries are mellow and light and, although a favourite restaurant dish, Bombay Potato (*see* glossary) is not found as such in Bombay but it is typical of Bombay tastes. Also in the glossary are Bombay Duck, presently banned from the UK, and Bombay Mix, re-invented under this name in Southall in the 1970s. Bhel Puri, also in the glossary, is Bombay's favourite kiosk food, most famously available at the city's Chowpatti beach. Years ago it found its way to the UK in the form of the Bhel Puri houses in Drummond Street, Westbourne Grove, Southall, Wembley and other places around London. It is served cold and is delicious. India's Parsee (*see* Persia) population, with their distinctive food, live in Bombay.

Burmese Burma, now renamed Myanmar, shares its boundaries with Bangladesh, India, China, Laos and Thailand. Its food is a combination of these styles. Rice is the staple and noodles are popular too. The curries are very hot and there are no religious objections to eating pork, beef or other meats. Duck and seafood are commonly eaten. The only Burmese restaurant in the UK is the Maymo, London SE24.

Goan Goa is on the west coast of India, about 400 miles south of Bombay. It was established in 1492 by the Portuguese who occupied it until 1962. It is now a state of India where Christianity prevails and there are no objections to eating pork or beef. The food of Goa is unique. Their most famous dish is Vindaloo, but it is not the dish from the standard curry house. The real thing is derived from the Portuguese dish Vino d'Alhos, traditionally pork marinated (the longer the better) in wine vinegar and garlic, then simmered until tender. To this the Goans added hot red chillies, creating a rich red curry gravy. Goa also has delicious seafood and fish dishes. There is only one Goan restaurant in the UK, Ma Goa in London SW15, although Goan dishes do appear at the better Indian restaurants.

Gujarati Gujarat is a sea-board state north of Bombay. Its population is largely vegetarian. Their food is the least spicy and they like adding a little sweetening to their food. Yoghurts and gram flour prevail. Their best-loved curry is Kadhai, in which gram-flour dumplings float in a turmeric- and yoghurt-based curry sauce. Equally popular are rissoles, e.g., Vada and snacks e.g., Patra (*see* glossary). Gujarati restaurants are prevalent in Leicester and Wembley, Middlesex, and they pop up elsewhere, too.

Moghul The curry from the standard curry house is based on rich, creamy dishes developed by the Moghul emperors. No one on earth was richer than the Moghuls, and it was during their time, four centuries ago, that Indian food was perfected. Authentically, this style of food should be subtly spiced. It can be found in an increasing number of 'haute cuisine' restaurants around the country, spelt variously Moghul, mogul, moglai, muglai mugal, mugul, etc.

Nawabi The Nawabs were the rich royals of the Lucknow area of India who lived over two centuries ago. Like the Moghuls before them, they perfected a style of cooking which was spicy and fragrant. Called Dum or Dum Pukt, it involves cooking the curry or Biriani in a round pot, whose lid is sealed into place with a ring of chapatti dough. The resulting dish is opened in front of the diners, releasing all those captured fragrances. This style has recently hit the better UK curry restaurant scene.

Nepalese Nepal, located to the north of India in the Himalayas, is famous for Sherpas and Gurkhas. The Nepalese enjoy curry and rice, of course, but their own specialities are perhaps less well known. Momos, for example, are dumplings with a mince curry filling. Aloo Achar are potatoes in pickle sauce, and Bhat is fragrantly cooked rice. There is an increasing, although still small, number of restaurants with Nepalese specials on the menu, particularly in west London. More menu examples will be found in the entry for The Gurkha Kitchen, Oxted, Surrey.

Pakistani Until independence in 1947, Pakistan formed the northwestern group of Indian states. Located between Afghanistan and India, it contains the famous Khyber Pass. The people are predominantly meat-eaters, favouring lamb and chicken (being Muslim, they avoid pork). Charcoal cooking is the norm, and this area is the original home of the tandoor. Breads such as Chupatti, Nan and Paratha are the staple. Balti cooking originated in the northernmost part of Pakistan and found its way to Birmingham centuries later. In general, Pakistani food is robustly spiced and savoury. The area called the Punjab was split by the formation of Pakistan, and it is the Punjabi tastes that formed the basis of the British curry house menu (*see* Punjab, London wc2). Bradford, Glasgow and Southall have sizeable Pakistani populations.

Persian It is quite common to see Persian dishes listed on the standard curry house menu. Dishes such as Biriani and Pullao did indeed originate in Persia (now called Iran). Bombay's Parsees came from there, having fled from Persia centuries ago. In India, they originated dishes of their own, such as Dhansak and Patia. The real thing is a subtle cooked-together combination of meat and vegetables and/or fruit. True Persian food is hard to find in the UK, although it is to be found at the Old Delhi, London w1. There is no Parsee restaurant in the UK but London sw's Bombay Brasserie and Chutney Mary both have Parsee chefs who cook decent Parsee dishes.

South Indian   Much of India's population is vegetarian, and the southern part of India is almost exclusively so. Until recently the extraordinary range of vegetarian specialities was virtually unknown in the UK. The introduction of more and more restaurants offering south Indian fare coincides with the increasing awareness of vegetarianism. Specialities include many types of vegetable curry including Avial, with exotic vegetables in a yoghurt base, and Sambar, a lentil-based curry. Other delights include huge, thin crisp rice- or lentil-flour pancakes called Dosas, with a curry filling (masala) and Idlis – steamed rice- or lentil-flour dumplings. Restaurants serving this type of food are slowly springing up all around the UK.

Sri Lankan   Sri Lanka is the small, pearl-shaped island, formerly Ceylon, at the southern tip of India. Its cuisine is distinctive and generally chilli hot. They eat similar fare to that of south India, i.e., vegetarian dishes, but they also enjoy very pungent meat, squid, chicken and duck curries. Good Sri Lankan restaurants include Adjay, Southall, Middlesex, Prince of Ceylon, London NW4, Jehangir, London SW26, Sigiri, London W13, and elsewhere.

The A to Z of the Curry Menu

To the first-timer, the Indian restaurant menu is a long and complex document. This glossary sets out to explain many of the standard, and some of the specialized, dishes and items that you will encounter at many a curry house. See also The Cuisine of the Sub-continent. Spellings of vowel sounds will vary vastly from restaurant to restaurant, reflecting the fifteen languages and hundreds of dialects of the sub-continent. (*See* Masala, Moglai, Papadom and Rhogan Josh Gosht for some examples.) Our spelling here is as near as possible to the standard accepted way of spelling, when translating phonetically from Delhi Hindi, Lahori Urdu or Dacca Bengali to Queen's English.

A

AAM or AM Mango.

ACHAR or ACHAAR Pickle, such as lime, mango, aubergine, etc. Achar Ghost is meat curry, curried in a pickle base, Achar Murgh is the chicken version.

AFGHANI CURRY Nuts and fruit are added for the standard curry house interpretation.

ALOO Potato.

B

BALTI Balti originated centuries ago in north Pakistan's Mirpur, Kashmir and Skardu (Baltistan). It found its way to east Birmingham in the 1970s, where any combination of ingredients was curried in a two-handled pot – the karahi (q.v.) elsewhere, but the balti there. Served to the table still cooking, the art is to eat the food – which should be spicy, herby and aromatic – Indian-style, with the bread as the scoop in the right hand. In the 1990s, Balti spread rapidly all over the UK and beyond. The Balti found at the standard Bangladeshi curry house, however, owes its flavours more to Patak's acidic Balti paste than to Mirpur, and unless it is cooked in its pan and served cutlery-free, it will (correctly) never convince the Brummy purist that it is anything other than hype.

BARFI or BURFI Indian fudge-like sweet made from reduced condensed milk (koya or khoa), in various flavours.

BATTAR Quail.

BENGAL CURRY A chicken or meat curry with chilli, sugar, potato cubes and halves of tomato.

BHAJI or BHAJEE Dryish, pan-fried mild vegetable curry.

BHAJIA Deep-fried fritter, usually with sliced onion, mixed with spiced gram flour batter, then deep-fried. Bhajia is the correct term, meaning fried. Bhaji or Bhajee is the anglicization (see above for the correct meaning). For the real thing, visit Maru's Bhajia House, Wembley, Middlesex. *See also* Pakora.

BHEL PURI This is the delicious street food snack from Bombay. It is a cold combination of those crunchy squiggles you find in Bombay Mix (q.v.), the smallest of which is called Sev. To this is added small-diced cooked potato, puffed rice (mamra), coriander leaf, onion and chilli. It is laced with brown sweet and sour tamarind (imli) sauce, yoghurt (dahi), coriander chutney (dhania) and chilli sauce, and topped with crispy puri biscuit chippings. The result is an exquisite combination of crisp, chewy and soft textures with sweet, hot, savoury and sour tastes. Variations include differing amounts of ingredients, under various similar names, such as Sev Batata Puri, Dahi Batata Puri, Chat Aloo Papri and Batata Pava. Bhel can be accompanied by Gol Goppas (q.v.). This delicious food is generally beyond the abilities of the average curry house, so is rarely found. Try it when you can (*see* London NW1's Drummond Street).

BHOONA or BHUNA Cooking process (slowly frying out all the water content) to produce a dry, usually mild curry.

BINDI A pulpy, rather sappy vegetable also known as okra or ladies fingers. Correct cooking of this dish is a good test of a chef's ability.

BIRIANI Traditionally, rice baked between layers of meat or vegetable filling, enhanced with saffron and aromatic spices, traditionally served topped with edible silver foil (vark). The restaurant interpretation is a cooked rice, artificially coloured, with filling stir-fried in. It is usually very garnished and served with a vegetable curry sauce (*see* Pullao).

BOMBAY DUCK A smallish fish native to the Bombay docks, known locally as bommaloe macchi. This was too hard for the British Raj to pronounce, so it became Bombay Duck. It is dried and appears on the table as a crispy deep-fried starter or accompaniment to a curry.

BOMBAY MIX An age-old traditional Indian snack nibble, called muruku, made from a savoury, gram-flour, spiced batter called ompadi, which is forced through a press straight into the deep-frier, to give different shapes and thicknesses of squiggly nibbles. Nuts, pulses, seeds and other ingredients are added. It should always be really crunchy and fresh. Re-invented by G.K. Noon, owner of manufacturer Royal Sweets in Southall, under the catchy name Bombay Mix, it is indispensable to keep you going at the bar.

BOMBAY POTATO A popular invention of the curry house. Potatoes in curry sauce with onions and tomato.

BOTI KEBAB Marinated cubes of lamb cooked in a tandoor oven (q.v.).

BRINJAL Aubergine, also called baigan or began. In Baigan Burtha, aubergine is smoked, spiced and mashed, in Baigan Bhaji it is chopped and curried by pan-frying.

C

CTM Chicken Tikka Masala. Invented by a British curry house chef (identity unknown) circa 1980, as a way to exploit his already popular Chicken Tikka by adding it to a creamy, pink, mild sauce made tasty by skilful blending of curry sauce, tomato purée, tandoori paste, cream, coconut, mango chutney and ground almonds. It is now ordered by 65% of all diners. Not only that, it appears in supermarket sandwiches, flavours crisps, is a pizza topping and even flavours mayonnaise. If only that chef had copyrighted it, he'd be earning millions in royalties a year. *See* Makhani and Tikka.

CEYLON CURRY At the curry house, this is usually cooked with coconut, lemon and chilli.

CHANA Chana is a yellow lentil resembling, but not identical to, the split pea, used in Dhal (q.v.) and to make gram flour. Kabli chana is the chickpea. Both can be curried or dried and deep-fried as in Bombay Mix (q.v.). *See also* Paneer.

CHAT or CHAAT Literally means 'snack'.

CHILLI Fleshy members of the capsicum family, ranging in heat from zero (the bell pepper) to incendiary. All chillies start green and, if left long enough, eventually become red, the one being no hotter than the other. The chilli normally used in Indian cooking is the narrow 7.5-cm (3-inch) cayenne. The hottest in the world are Mexican habaneros, Caribbean Scotch bonnets and Bangladeshi nagas. People build up a tolerance to chillies, coming to adore them, but they should never be inflicted upon the novice, not even in fun.

CHUPATTI A 15-cm (6-inch) flat disc of unleavened bread, cooked dry on the tava (q.v.). It should always be served hot and pan-fresh. The spelling can vary — Chupatti, Chapati, etc.

CHUTNEY The common ones are onion chutney, mango chutney and tandoori chutney. There are dozens of others that rarely appear on the standard menu. See Sambals.

CURRY The only word in this glossary to have no direct translation into any of the sub-continent's fifteen or so languages. The word was coined centuries ago by the British in India. Possible contenders for the origin of the word are: arahi or arai (Hindi) — the wok-like frying pan used all over India to prepare masala (spice mixtures); Karhi or Khadi — a soup-like dish made with spices, gram-flour dumplings and buttermilk; Kari — a spicy Tamil sauce; Turkuri — a seasoned sauce or stew; and Kari Phulia — Neem leaves, which are small and rather like bay leaves, used for flavouring.

CURRY HOUSE *See* Formula.

D

DAHI YOGHURT. Used as a chutney and in the cooking of some curries. Most curry houses make their own, and it is delicious as an accompaniment to curry, being less sharp than the shop-bought equivalent. Incidentally, Dahi, not water, is the best antidote if you eat something that's too hot for you.

DAHI VADA South Indian savoury gram-flour doughnut, deep-fried, cooled and dunked into cold, spicy yoghurt (*see* Vada).

DAL or DHAL LENTILS. There are over sixty types of lentil in the sub-continent, all packed full of nutrients. The common restaurant types are massor (red, which cooks yellow), moong (green), chana (also used to make gram flour) and urid (black).

DHANIA Coriander leaf or spice.

DHANSAK Traditional Parsee meat dish cooked in a purée of lentils, aubergine, tomato and spinach. Restaurants use dal and methi, and sometimes chilli and pineapple.

DoPIAZA Traditional meat dish. Do means two, piaza means onions. Onions appear twice in the cooking, first fried and second raw. The onions give the dish a sweetish taste.

DOSA South Indian pancake made from rice and urid (lentil) flour, which when made into a batter soon ferments to give a superb sour taste. Masala Dosa is a Dosa filled with mashed potato curry spiced with onion, chilli, turmeric and mustard seed.

DUM Cooking by steaming, invented by the Royal Nawabs (*see* Curry Cuisines of the Sub-continent), e.g., Aloo Dum, steamed potatoes.

E

ELAICHI Cardamom. Can major in curries – for example, Elaichi Murgh is chicken curried with a predominance of green cardamom.

F

FOOGATH Lightly-cooked vegetable dish

FORMULA CURRIES Many of our 'Indian' (q.v.) restaurants operate to a formula which was pioneered in the late 1940s. In those early restaurants, a way had to be found to deliver to the table a variety of curries without an unreasonable delay from order to table. Since all authentic Indian recipes require hours of cooking in individual pots, there was no guarantee that they would even be ordered. So cubed meat, chicken or potatoes, dhal and some vegetables were lightly curried and chilled, and a large pot of thick curry gravy, a kind of master stock, was brewed to medium-heat strength. To this day, portion by portion, on demand, these ingredients are reheated by pan-frying them with further spices and flavourings. At its simplest, a Medium Chicken Curry, that benchmark of middle ground, is still on many menus, though sometimes disguised as

Masala, and requires no more than a reheat of some gravy with some chicken. For instance, take a typical mixed order for a couple at a table for two. She wants Chicken Korma (fry a little turmeric, coriander and cumin, add six pieces of chicken, add a ladleful of curry gravy, plenty of creamed coconut, almonds maybe and a little cream – result, the additions make it mild and creamy-golden in colour), and with it she'll have Vegetable Dhansak (fry some cumin seeds, dry methi leaves (q.v.), chopped onions, a little sugar, tomato, red and green capsicum with the gravy, add dhal and some cooked veg – result, colourful, and still medium-strength). He wants Meat Korma (as for the chicken, using meat), and he wants Prawn Vindaloo (fry spices and chilli powder, add the gravy which at once goes red and piquant, then cooked peeled prawns, fresh tomato and potato, simmer and serve). Maybe they'll also take a Sag Paneer (fry cumin, some thawed creamed spinach and pre-made crumbled paneer together, add fresh coriander – done). One cook can knock all these up, simultaneously, in five pans, within minutes. Rice is pre-cooked, breads and tandoori items made to order by a different specialist. And, hey presto, your order, sir and madam! Thus the menu can be very long, with an almost unlimited variety of dishes, sometimes numbered, sometimes heat-graded, mild, medium and hot, hotter, hottest, and any dish is available in meat, poultry, prawn, king prawn, and most vegetables, too. That's the formula, and its perpetrator is the standard curry house. Just because this is not authentic does not make it bad. It can be, and variously is, done well. This Guide is full of many such restaurants, about which we say 'a standard curry house, doing the formula well'.

G

GARAM MASALA Literally meaning hot (roasted) mixture (of pepper and aromatic spices), it originated in Kashmir and is added towards the end of cooking in certain north Indian curries. *See also* Masala.

GHEE Clarified butter or vegetable oil used in high-quality north Indian cooking.

GOBI Cauliflower.

GOL GOPPAS Gol Goppas, or Pani Puri, are mouth-sized puffed-up crispy biscuits, served with Jeera Pani (water spiced predominantly with chilli, black salt and cumin water) and Aloo Chaat (potato curry) at Bhel Puri (q.v.) houses. To eat the correct way, gently puncture the top of the biscuit, pour in some Jeera Pani, and pop into the mouth in one. Chew and then add some Aloo Chaat.

GOSHT Lamb or mutton.

GULAB JAMAN An Indian dessert of cake-like texture. Balls of curd cheese paneer, or flour and milk-powder, are deep-fried to golden and served in light syrup.

GURDA Kidney. Gurda Kebab is marinated kidney, skewered and cooked in the tandoor.

H

HALVA Sweets made from syrup and vegetables or fruit. Served cold in small squares, it is translucent and comes in bright colours depending on the ingredients used. Orange – carrot; green – pistachio; red – mango, etc. Has a texture thicker than Turkish Delight. Sometimes garnished with edible silver leaf.

HASINA KEBAB Pieces of chicken breast, lamb or beef marinated in a yoghurt and spice (often tandoori) mixture, then skewered and barbecued/baked, interspersed with onions, capsicum and tomato. Turkish in origin. *See* Shaslik.

I

IDLI Rice- and lentil-flour steamed cake, about the size and shape of a hockey puck, served with a light but fiery curry sauce. South Indian in origin.

IMLI Tamarind. A very sour, date-like fruit used as a chutney and in cooking. Imli chutney is of purée consistency, sweetened with sugar.

INDIAN In 1947, the sub-continent of India was partitioned. To cut a long story short, in Britain and the west we still generally erroneously refer to our curry restaurants as 'Indian'. In fact, over 85% are Bangladeshi, with only around 8% run by Indians and 8% run by Pakistani. There is a smattering of Nepalese and Sri Lankan restaurants, and only a single Afghan and a single Burmese restaurant in Britain. See Formula Curries.

J

JALEBI An Indian dessert. Flour, milk-powder and yoghurt batter is squeezed through a narrow funnel into a deep-frier to produce golden, curly, crisp rings. Served in syrup.

JAL FREZI Sautéed or stir-fried meat or chicken dish, often with lightly cooked onion, garlic, ginger, green pepper and chilli.

JEERA Cumin seed or powder, hence Jeera Chicken, etc.

K

KALIA Traditional Bengali/Bangladeshi meat, poultry or fish dish in which red coloured ingredients are mandatory, especially red chillies and tomatoes. *See* Rezala.

KARAHI A two-handled Indian kitchen dish. Some restaurants reheat curries in small karahis and serve them straight to the table with the food sizzling inside. *See also* Curry and Balti.

KASHMIR CHICKEN Whole chicken stuffed with minced meat. See Kurzi.

KASHMIR CURRY Often a medium curry to which is added cream and coconut and/or lychees, pineapple or banana.

KEBAB Kebab does not mean 'skewer'. It means 'cooked meat' in ancient Turkish, traditionally cooked over charcoal, in a process over 4000 years old. It was imported to India by the Muslims centuries ago. See Boti, Hasina, Nargis, Shami and Sheek Kebab.

KEEMA Minced meat curry. *See also* Mattar.

KOFTA Minced meat or vegetable balls in batter, deep-fried and then cooked in a curry sauce.

KORMA It probably derived from the Persian Koresh, a mild stew. The Moghuls made it very rich, using cream, yoghurt and ground almonds, fragranced with saffron and aromatic spices. But, traditionally, Kormas need not be mild. In Kashmir a popular dish is the Mirchwangan Korma, red in colour because it is full of Kashmiri chillies. To the curry house, Korma is terminology for the mildest curry, sometimes made sickly by the overuse of creamed coconut block, cream and nuts.

KULCHA Small leavened bread. Can be plain or stuffed, e.g., Onion Kulcha.

KULFI Indian ice cream. Traditionally it comes cone-shaped in vanilla, pistachio or mango flavours.

KURZI Leg of lamb or whole chicken given a long marination, then a spicy stuffing, e.g., rice and/or Keema (q.v.), then slowly baked until tender. This is served with 'all the trimmings'. It is many a curry house's Special, requiring 24 hours' notice (because of the long preparation, and a deposit to make sure you turn up to eat it). Often for two or four, it is good value. Also called Khurzi, Kasi, Kozi, Kushi, etc. *See also* Murgh Masala.

L

LASSI A refreshing drink made from yoghurt and crushed ice. The savoury version is Lassi Namkeen and the sweet version is Lassi Meethi.

M

MACCI or MACHLI Fish. Today, fresh exotic fish from India and Bangladesh are readily available and, when a restaurant offers them, you have the chance of getting a truly authentic dish.

MADRAS You will not find a Madras Curry in Madras, any more than you'll find a London Pie in London. Neither exist. But the people of the south eat hot curries, firing them up with as many as three different types of chilli – dry, powdered and fresh – added to the cooking at different stages. As the Brits got used to their early formula curries, they began to demand them hotter. With no time to add chillies in the traditional way, one of the pioneer curry house chefs simply added one teaspoon of extra-hot chilli powder to his standard sauce, along with tomato and ground almonds, and ingeniously called it 'Madras'. The name stuck. *See also* Chilli, Phal and Vindaloo.

MAKHANI A traditional dish. Tandoori chicken is cooked in butter ghee and tomato sauce. Some say this was the derivation of CTM (q.v.).

MALAI Cream. So Malai Sabzi Kofta, for example, means vegetable balls in a creamy curry gravy. *See* Rasmalai.

MALAYA The curries of Malaya are traditionally cooked with plenty of coconut, chilli and ginger. In the Indian restaurant, however, they are usually based on the Korma (q.v.), to which is added pineapple and/or other fruit.

MASALA A mixture of spices which are cooked with a particular dish, e.g., Garam Masala (q.v.). It can be spelt a remarkable number of ways – Massala, Massalla, Masalam, Mosola, Moshola, Musala, etc.

MASALA DOSA *See* Dosa.

MATTAR Green peas. So Mattar Paneer is peas with Indian cheese, Keema Mattar is mince meat curry with peas, and so on.

MEDIUM CURRY *See* Formula.

METHI Fenugreek, pronounced 'maytee'. Savoury spice. The seed is important in masalas. The leaves, fresh or dried, are used particularly in Punjabi dishes. At the curry house, the flavour of these leaves predominates in their Dhansak.

MOGLAI Cooking in the style of the Moghul emperors, whose chefs took Indian cookery to the heights of gourmet cuisine centuries ago. Few restaurateurs who offer Moglai dishes come anywhere near this excellence. Authentic Moglai dishes are expensive and time-consuming to prepare. Can also be variously spelt Muglai, Mhogulai, Moghlai, etc.

MULLIGATAWNY A Tamil vegetable consommée (molegoo pepper, tunny water), adapted by the Raj to create that well-known, thick, meat-based British soup.

MURGH Chicken.

MURGH MASALA or MURGH MASSALAM Whole chicken, marinated in yoghurt and spices for hours, then stuffed and roasted. See Kurzi.

N

NAAN or NAN Pronounced 'narn', it is flat, leavened bread, usually made from plain white flour (maida) dough, but sometimes from wholemeal flour (atta). After the dough rises, it is rolled out and baked in the tandoor (q.v.). It is teardrop-shaped and about 20-25cm (8-10 inches) long. It must be served fresh and hot. As well as Plain Naan, there are many variations involving the addition of other ingredient(s). Keema Naan is stuffed with a thin layer of minced, spiced kebab meat. Peshwari Naan is stuffed with almonds and/or cashew nuts and/or raisins. Garlic, onion, pineapple, tomato, indeed anything, can be added. Double- or treble-sized Karak, Elephant or Family Naans are offered at Balti houses to share to scoop your food up with.

NARGIS KEBAB Indian scotch egg – spiced, minced meat around a hard-boiled egg.

NIRAMISH A Bangladeshi mixed vegetable, often cooked without garlic, and spiced only with Indian Five Spice mixture.

O

OOTHAPPAM *See* Uthappam.

P

PAAN Betel leaf folded, samosa-fashion, around a stuffing of aniseed, betel nut, sunflower seeds, lime paste, etc., and eaten in one mouthful, as a digestive after a meal. The leaf is bitter, the mouth-feel coarse and the taste acquired, but more acceptable (to westerners) small spices and seeds (Supari), sometimes sugar-coated in lurid colours, are often offered by the curry house after the meal.

PAKORA The true Pakora is a whole piece of vegetable, lightly coated in gram-flour batter and deep-fried, although at the curry house it is to all intents and purposes the same as the Bhajia (q.v.).

PANEER Cheese made from milk by separating the whey (liquid) from the curds (solids) which, when compressed, can be crumbled, chopped, fried, tandoori-baked and/or curried (*see* Mattar Paneer). In Bengali, Paneer is called Chhana, not to be confused with the lentil, Chana (q.v.).

PAPADOM or PAPAD Thin lentil-flour wafers. When cooked (deep-fried or baked) they expand to about 20 cm (8 inches). They must be crackling crisp and warm when served. If not, send them back to the kitchen and deduct points from that restaurant. They come either plain or spiced, with lentils, pepper, garlic or chilli. There are many ways to spell papadom, using any combination of the vowels 'a', 'o' and 'u', and double 'p' and double 'd'. But, despite many people calling it so, it should never be referred to as a Pampadom.

PASANDA Meat, usually lamb, which traditionally is thinly beaten, then cooked in a creamy curry gravy to which some chefs add red wine. The dish and wine were both true treats of Moghul emperor Jehangir who, though Muslim, blessed the wine to make it 'holy water' and thus avoided the rules of Islam, then he and his court proceeded to drink themselves legless while enjoying this dish.

PATIA Restaurant curry with a thick, dark, red sweet and sour sauce. Based on a Parsee prawn or fish dish.

PATRA A Gujarati speciality, in which colcasia (patra) leaves are rolled in gram-flour paste, like a Swiss roll, then steamed, sliced and finally deep-fried.

PESHWARI NAAN *See* Naan.

PHAL The hottest curry, also known as a Bangalore Phal, invented by the British curry house restaurateurs.

PICKLE Pungent, hot, pickled vegetables essential to an Indian meal. The most common are lime, mango, brinjal and chilli. Though rarely seen at the restaurant, meat and game are made into traditional and very delicious Rajasthani pickles

PODINA Mint. Also a fresh chutney, puréed from fresh mint, chilli and onion.

PRAWN BUTTERFLY Usually a large or giant king prawn, cut so that it opens out and flattens, marinated in spices and immersed in gram-flour batter, then deep-fried. A curry house invention, probably first called batter-fry.

PRAWN PURI Prawns in a hot sauce served on a Puri (q.v.) bread. Although sometimes described as Prawn Puree it is not a purée.

PULLAO Ancient Persia invented Pollou, with rice and meat and/or vegetables, cooked together in a pan until tender. Following Muslim invasions it evolved into Turkey's Pilav, Greece's Pilafi, Spain's Paella and, of course, India's Pullao. In many curry houses, the ingredients are mixed after cooking, to save time. (*See* Biriani.) There are many ways to spell it, e.g., Pillau, Puloa, Pillar, Pilaw, Polaw, etc.

PULLAO RICE The restaurant name for rice fried with aromatic spices, usually with rice grains coloured yellow and/or red and/or green.

PURI Unleavened wholemeal bread, rolled out flat to about 10cm (4 inches) in diameter, it puffs up when deep-fried, and should be served at once.

Q

QUAS CHAWAL or KESAR CHAVAL Rice fried in ghee (q.v.), flavoured and coloured with saffron (kesar).

R

RAITA A cooling chutney of yoghurt and vegetable, e.g., cucumber or mint (sometimes called Tandoori Sauce) to accompany papadoms, the starter or the main course.

RASGULLA Walnut-sized balls of paneer, or semolina and cream cheese, cooked in syrup (literally meaning 'juicy balls'). They are white or pale gold in colour and served cold or warm. See Rasmalai.

RASHMI KEBAB Kebab of minced meat inside an egg net or omelette.

RASMALAI Rasgullas cooked in cream, served cold. Very rich, very sweet.

REZALA Bengali/Bangladeshi speciality. Lamb cooked in evaporated milk, rich and subtly spiced, it would be milder than Korma except that green chillies are mandatory. Traditionally no red- or orange-coloured ingredients should be used. See Kalia.

RHOGAN JOSH GOSHT Literally meaning 'lamb in red gravy'. Traditionally, in Kashmir, lamb is marinated in yoghurt, then cooked with ghee, aromatic spices and natural red colorants. It should be creamy but not hot. The curry house version omits the marinade and the aromatics, and uses tomato and red pepper to create a red appearance. There are many ways of spelling it – Rogon, Roghan, Rugon, Rugin, Rowgan, Ragan, etc., Just, Joosh, Juice, Jash, etc., Goosht, Goose, Gost, etc.

ROTI Flat bread of any type.

S

SABZI Vegetable.

SAG or SAAG Spinach, also called Shak in Bengali, Palak in the Punjab and Rai, although these are mustard leaves. Lalshak is delicious red spinach.

SAMBALS A Malayan term describing the chutneys accompanying a meal. Sometimes referred to on the Indian menu.

SAMBAR A hot and spicy, runny, almost consommée-like south Indian vegetable curry made from lentils and exotic vegetables, such as the drumstick. In the Manchester/Merseyside area, the curry houses call a dish Samber. It bears no resemblance to Sambar, except that lentils and a lot of chilli powder are added to meat, chicken or prawn curry.

SAMOSA Celebrated triangular, deep-fried meat or vegetable patties, supreme as starters or snacks.

SHAMI KEBAB Round minced meat rissoles.

SHASHLIK KEBAB Shashlik in Armenia means 'to grill'. Cubes of skewered lamb or chicken are marinated (in an oil, garlic and chilli mixture) then grilled. *See* Hasina.

SHATKORA A Bangladeshi citrus fruit, the size of a grapefruit but sharper in flavour, though softer than a lemon. Can be eaten fresh or used in cooking.

SHEEK KEBAB or SEEKH Literally means (in Turkish) a skewer. Spiced minced meat, usually coloured lurid red at the curry house (from proprietary tandoori/kebab paste), is moulded onto the skewer, then baked in the tandoori and grilled.

STANDARD CURRY *See* Formula.

T

TANDOORI An ancient style of cooking, which originated in the rugged north west frontier of India (now Pakistan). It gets its name from the cylindrical clay oven, the tandoor, with its opening at the top, fired with charcoal in its base. Originally the ingredients were chicken and lamb, marinated for many hours in a spiced yoghurt-based sauce, traditionally slightly reddened with red chilli, then skewered and baked in the tandoor. Now the curry house product also includes fish, prawns, Paneer (q.v.) and vegetables. But its lurid red or orange colour is created by the unnecessary use of tartrazine food colouring in proprietary ready-to-use pastes. See Boti Kebab, Tikka, Naan Bread and Raita.

TARKA DHAL A tasty, spicy lentil dish, the Dhal being massoor (red) lentils, cooked to a purée, to which the Tarka (crispy, fried caramelized onion and/or garlic) is added as a garnish. This simple-sounding dish is a great test for the cook. It should taste very slightly burnt (from the Tarka), and be subtly, yet decisively, spiced, neither too thick nor too thin.

TAVA A heavy steel, rimless, flattish frying pan, used to cook items such as Parathas.

THALI or TALI A round tray (thali) with a low rim, averaging about 34cm (12 inches) in diameter. It is a food plate on which an entire meal is served for one person. Dry items, such as rice, bread and even dry curries, are placed directly on the thali. Wet portions, such as curries, dhals, soups and sweets, etc., are placed in matching serving bowls (tapelis) of different diameters, and they too reside on the thali. They were made of solid gold for the Moghul emperors, solid silver for the Maharajas, and stainless steel for us lot. To be found at certain restaurants serving 'special' meals.

TIKKA Literally, Tikka means a small piece. For example, Chicken Tikka is a filleted chunk of chicken, marinated (see Tandoori), skewered and baked in the tandoor. Traditionally, the marinade is identical to Tandoori marinade, and cooks a naturally russet brown colour. Proprietary Tikka paste, as used in the curry house, is lurid orange or yellow because of the tartrazine colourings it contains.

TINDALOO see Vindaloo

U

UPPUMA South Indian dish. Lightly-fried semolina with onion and spices.

UTHAPPAM A spicy south Indian pizza, made from rice flour and topped with onions, tomatoes and chilli.

URID A type of lentil, its husk is black, and it comes whole, split or polished. Available as a dhal dish in some restaurants, e.g., Maharani Dhal.

V

VADA or VADAI Lentil-flour spicy doughnut, enjoyed in Gujarat and south India. *See* Dahi Vada.

VINDALOO A fiery dish from Goa. (See Curry Cuisines of the Sub-continent.) At the restaurant scene, it now means the second hottest dish (two spoonfuls of chilli powder), usually with a chunk of potato (Aloo). Also sometimes called Bindaloo or Tindaloo (even hotter). *See also* Chilli, Madras and Phal.

Y

YAKNI Literally mutton, or a meat-based stock.

Z

ZEERA Alternatively called Jeera, which is cumin. Zeera Gosht is lamb cooked with cumin.

THE 1998
GOOD CURRY
GUIDE

THE DIRECTORY

LONDON

Before we get accused of London bias, it is worth explaining that, of the 8300 British curry restaurants on our nationwide database, over 2000 of them are in London. Naturally, with such competition, many of the country's best are in the capital. Our coverage reflects this, with a strong London section. Furthermore, the choice of regional food is total, i.e., in addition to standard Bangladeshi curry houses, you'll find examples of every one of the regional cuisines, all of which are detailed on page 37.

Greater London, established in 1965, absorbed Middlesex and parts of Essex, Hertfordshire, Kent and Surrey. For GL towns/boroughs in these areas, please see the relevant county (*see* list on page 8). For the purpose of this Guide we define London by its well-known 1870s post codes. We run alphabetically as follows: E, EC, N, NW, SE, SW, W and WC.

London E

E1 – Brick Lane

This area was once predominantly Jewish, containing tailors and cab drivers, and salt-of-the-earth street markets. Since 1971, it has become home to the country's largest Bangladeshi community. All around the area you will find small, very cheap curry restaurants and cafés. The most prolific street is the long and narrow Brick Lane, running between Shoreditch and Aldgate East Tube stations. It has become a centre for cheap and cheerful curry cafés, snack bars, restaurants and provisions shops, run by the thriving community. (To emphasize its roots you'll also find an all-night, fresh-baked bagel shop where cabbies queue for sustenance.) As for curry, most of the establishments are unlicensed, and are fairly spartan, and in some, you can BYO. The number of curry houses has grown from a couple in 1971 to 24 in 1997, reflecting exactly the growth of curry houses nationally. Here we single out several on Brick Lane.

BALTI HOUSE   NEW ENTRANT   ©

63a Brick Lane, E1   ℡ **0171 375 1696**

Pakistani Baltis cooked by Bangladeshi chef-owner Babul, in the Brick Lane Bangladeshi heartland. Whatever next, you may ask? But we hear they are good. Price check: Papadom 65p, CTM £5.75, Balti Chicken £5.95, Pullao Rice £1.75.

BENGAL CUISINE   ©

12 Brick Lane, E1   ℡ **0171 377 8405**

A. Rashid's licensed restaurant is well-established, in Brick Lane terms (1980), and operates all day between noon and midnight. 'I was tired and cold and wanted somewhere to sit in comfort. At 4p.m., I was their only customer. Food excellent,' B.G. Price check: Methi Chicken £4.95, Sag Bhaji £2.45, Papadom 40p, CTM £6.95, Pullao Rice £2.15.

BHEL POORI BRASSERIE   √ BYO

63a Brick Lane, E1   ℡ **0171 377 6412**

This is unusual for Brick Lane in that it serves Bhel Poori (*see* glossary) and south Indian dishes. Indeed, it is all vegetarian. J.T. says: 'The decor was extremely eye-catching with black chairs complementing the pink tablecloths and neatly laid-out tables. The main course, Chef's Thali, was the choice for three out of four in our party, which was exceedingly good value. Eight small pots of carefully prepared vegetable curries and side dishes surrounded a larger central dish of Pullao Rice. Although the Bhel Poori restaurant is not licensed, customers are welcome to BYO from the off-licence opposite.

CLIFTON TANDOORI

126 Brick Lane, E1

This institution is now closed. RIP!

©	Curry Club discount (see p. 607)	🍺 Unlicensed
√	Vegetarian	⊞ Home delivery
BYO	Bring your own alcohol	service available

NAZRUL   BYO

130 Brick Lane, E1   © 0171 247 2505

I guess this Guide would be incomplete without the Nazrul, and it has graced our pages since our first edition in 1983. Previously, D.M.W. told us of the loose toilet pedestal and leaky S-bends, but we never did hear more on the subject! (Although I did get a review from a W.C., which I took to be a S-end up!) For the first-timer, the delights of the toilets in such establishments are best avoided. Nazrul is an archetypal BYO, really cheap, café-style venue, with a huge following of curryholics – and fabulous food! It is for that you must go. New to the menu are Balti dishes. 'Always appears to be busy – particularly popular with students,' A.S. 'Made the kids really welcome,' H.C. Still has red banquettes and flock, long may that last … somebody get it listed! Price check: Balti Chicken £2.95, Chicken Curry £2.35. Set meal average £6. Branch: Nazrul II, 49 Hanbury Street, E1.

SHAMPAN   ©

79 Brick Lane, E1   © 0171 375 0475

It is licensed and up-market. As well as serving your typical Bangladeshi formula curries, the Shampan, unlike most Bangladeshi E1 restaurants, makes a point of serving Bangladeshi specials. So go for all your curry favourites, if you must, but why not try such specials with Betki, Rup, Ayre and Rhui (Bengali fish) and the unique Shatkora Gosht/Murgh, meat or chicken (£4.45), given a sour flavour with that lemon-like Sylheti citrus fruit, washed down with Cobra lager. Price check: Bangladeshi Thali £9.95, Papadom 35p, CTM £4.95, Pullao Rice £1.45. Branch: Baburchi, 138 Brick Lane, E1.

SWEET AND SPICY   BYO

40 Brick Lane, E1   © 0171 247 1081

'Friendly, formica-tabled, canteen-style service, with good Punjabi-style food at reasonable prices. I had Chicken Madras, Naan, Pullao Rice (delicate buttery flavour), Raita, onion salad, green chillies, a sweet red sauce and a Coke for just £5.95. Will return for more!' P.H. BYO, and little changed since it opened in 1969, though G.R. 'loved the grub' but would like a redec. (Rubbish – they'd put the prices up!)

Elsewhere in E1

CAFE INDIYA   NEW ENTRANT

30 Alie Street, E1   ℂ **0171 481 8288**

Steve Modi needed to do something dramatic to the former Namaste,
once Cyrus vacated the place (*see* next entry), and do something he did.
He gutted it, and far from being a belt factory, let alone the shabby
Namaste, it is now bright and airy, and modern in decor with a minimalist look of polished wooden floors, charcoal-coloured tables and
ladder-backed chairs, set off against cream walls. Michael Tarat (*see*
Rupee Room, EC2), was responsible for all this, and for the running of
the place. Antoinette D'Cruz, a Taj-trained Goan, does the cooking.
There is a limited but carefully-chosen menu, with items ranging from
the Tandoor-cooked Afghani Murghi Kebabish – chicken pieces marinated in vinegar, cashew paste, melon seeds and spices – to Raan –
sliced leg of lamb, from Rajasthan (£9.75) – Chicken Pista Korma
from Hyderabad (£7.95) and Chicken Pepper Fry from south India.
Goan specialities are there, including a traditional Pork Vindaloo
(£7.25) and some Goan fish dishes. Cyrus's ghost remains to haunt the
place with such things, and there's even a Parsee Lobster dish. Price
check: Papadom 60p, Pullao Rice £1.95 (no CTM). Open weekday
lunches and evenings, evenings only on Saturdays. Closed Sundays.

CAFE SPICE NAMASTE   NEW ENTRANT TOP 100   ©

16 Prescot Street, E1   ℂ **0171 488 9242**

I'm pleased to have known Chef Cyrus for many years and witnessed
his outstanding cooking in the Taj Hotels Fort Aguada complex in
Goa, when his delightful wife, Pervin, was restaurant manager. They
both came to England in 1991 and set up the Namaste. This Guide was
the first to give his talents the recognition they deserved, and now he
is virtually smothered with other food guide awards. But things move
on, and I'm pleased that I had the opportunity to bring Cyrus, Pervin
and Michael Gottlieb (of Smolenski's fame) together, to start this new
venture in 1995. It was not without trauma, with games being played
with phones by former associates, and a horrendous first week of bun-
gled operations, but Cyrus's brigade of City men and women were not
to be put off by mere trifles like that and, sensibly, they stayed loyal,

and soon Cyrus came back to full flow. The plan, I can reveal now, is for Café Spice to be the first of a larger chain, and plans are well developed for satellite branches to open elsewhere in London, with Cyrus as a partner and Executive Chef.

This restaurant will remain the flagship, and it is fascinating to see how cleverly Gottlieb and his designer brought this precious listed building back from the brink of dereliction in the hands of the DHS. The design and concept is refreshing and will be much copied. It seats 110 in two sections. Located in the City, it does a really busy lunch trade Mondays to Fridays, the service of which is supervised by Pervin. Evenings are generally quieter and are the best time to go. Against the trend, Saturdays (shut lunchtime) are often the quietest time, but book for any time. On Sunday they close completely.

The reason for the restaurant's popularity is quite simply the food. Chef Cyrus is one of the few Indian chefs prepared to innovate, making him one of the top curry chefs in the UK. He is a Parsee, trained in classical Indian cooking, particularly Goan. He seems able to take any ingredient and turn it into something magical – the hallmark of the great chef, of course. His à la carte menu simply bristles with originality. True, the unadventurous can pick Onion Bhajia, Samosa and Shami Kebab for starters and follow with Pullao Rice (£2.35), Naan bread and Chicken Tikka Masala (£8.95 with rice), and a superb meal you'd have, too although, unlike everywhere else in Britain, these items are well down on the venue's popularity list. And that's because there are so many other items on the menu competing for your choice. For example, your eye would be caught by some truly extraordinary items. Starters like Chilli Cheese Garlic Toast, for example, Shinanio Balchao (mussels in a Goan sauce) or Tangri Piri Piri (tandooried chicken drumsticks) – delicious, of course, and completely devoid of red food colouring.

For the main course you could try Kerla Nandu (crab curry), Galhina Xacutti (Goan chicken curry), Parsee Lamb Liver and Kidney Curry or Rawa Kalwa (oysters marinated in Goan Piri Piri Masala, dipped in dry semolina and crisply flash-fried, served with a hot garlic dip). Main courses include curries made from venison, goose, emu, bison, kangaroo, grouse and pheasant as well as the more conventional ingredients: chicken, duck, lamb and beef dishes, but all cooked to unusual authentic Indian recipes. One of the most popular ingredients is Wensleydale Wild Boar – in such guises as Jungli Maas Dhuanaar –

where a haunch is marinated in a masala smoked over whole spices such as cinnamon, cardamom, cloves, etc., then slowly oven-roasted. On the whole, this is Indian cuisine extraordinaire, but curry-house it is not! Our advice is that you forgo your regular standard favourite and try things new. Comments, mostly very good, are many, but M.A. (an Indian) thought the food 'disappointing'. Café Spice branches are imminent in Leman Street and Lavender Hill. Watch this space!

GULSHAN

11-13 Sandy's Row, E1   🅒 0171 247 2812

A bog-standard, licensed Bangladeshi curry house, serving all the favourites, usefully from 11.30a.m. to midnight daily except all major holidays. Price check: Papadom 50p, CTM £5.95, King Prawn Rezala £8.50, Pullao Rice £1.95. Set meal average for two £24.90.

LAHORE KEBAB HOUSE   TOP 100

2 Umberton Street, E1   🅒 0171 481 9737

For anyone who has not been to either Pakistan or to the Sparkbrook area of Birmingham, this is what it is all about. Darned good food, served without compromising it for westerners. The place is geared to local Asians, who cope with its relatively new-found glory as a lunchtime dive for the money boys and girls from the City. And despite Brum's claim to be the inventor of the currinary world, this gaff has been doing Balti, under what some say is its true name, Karahi – or Karrai (sic) – since it opened over twenty years ago. It's two floors of tat. Expect no decor, comfort or licence, and don't BYO please, it's strict Muslim. Cutlery is for wimps (they'll give you a spoon if you ask). But do it the correct way, and scoop up with a marvellous Roti in your right hand – too bad if you're left-handed. And expect limitations if you're a veggie. Halal mutton, chicken and quail are it, in the karahi, from the tandoor as tikkas or kebabs, or as steam roast (Choosa), with robust lentils and fragrant rice. Real veterans show their spurs by enjoying the celebrated, and very filling and satisfying, Paya (lamb's trotters), laced with the Hot Chilli Raita, followed by the gorgeous Kheer rice pudding. Service is swift and accurate, but don't expect pampering, and don't expect to pay more than a tenner, including tip, in cash, please ... nothing fancy like credit cards. Open noon-midnight daily, with a different atmosphere at all different times of its day, and different again at the weekend, depending on who's eating when. It remains very popular with local Asian families and well-heeled Indians and Pakistanis alike, indeed with all curry *cognoscenti*, and remains firmly in our TOP 100. Branch: 19 Upton Road, E7.

PRIDE OF ASIA   ©

207 Mile End Road, E1   ✆ 0171 780 9321

A bog-standard, licensed Bangladeshi curry house, serving all the favourites, with normal hours (closed from 2.30-6p.m.) Price check: Papadom 45p, CTM £5.50, Pullao Rice £1.50.

TAYYAB NEW ENTRANT   BYO

89 Fieldgate Street, E1   ✆ 0171 247 9543

A truck-stop, according to one reporter. Well, an unlicensed caff, anyway, which now operates daytime, serving Southall-style Pakistani/Punjabi kebabs and curries at ludicrously reasonable prices, as it has done for years. But they have recently opened a new venture with a curious operating procedure that would make any accountant faint at misused resources. The staff and cooks close down at 5p.m. and all traipse three doors up the street to ...

NEW TAYYAB NEW ENTRANT   BYO

83 Fieldgate Street, E1   ✆ 0171 247 9543

... this 65-seat venue, where they carry on currying till midnight, in rather smarter premises, where the phone number is the same. For that matter so is the food, and it's OK with our regulars, especially the prices. And since the Tayyab family are the owners, accountants and cooks, it's OK with them too! Unlicensed and BYO with discretion please, i.e., don't flash it around and offend strict Muslims who are the real regulars. Price check: Papadom 50p, CTM £3.80, Pullao Rice £1.50.

TIFFIN   ©

165 Cannon Street Road, E1   ✆ 0171 702 3832

Abdul Kalam has been going since 1992 with this up-market venue, just off the Commercial Road. We stay with our previous description – 'A refreshing haven in London's East End' – and we don't mind if the restaurants changes 'haven' to 'heaven'. But refreshing it is, with delights like Salmon Samosa (£2.95) and Bathera – quails – (£8.50) or Lebu Murghi – special chicken – (£9.95), but the Tiffin Royal Tandoori (£13) would make Meena Patak blush to the same colour red, so much of her paste is used on the ingredients. 'Good to busting, it is,' T.H. Price check: Papadom 50p, CTM £6.95, Pullao Rice £1.95. Set meal from £8.95.

E2

AL-AMIN   ©

483 Cambridge Heath Road, E2   ✆ 0171 729 7415

A previous Guide entrant, though now under the new ownership of Fazlul Haque, and as popular as ever as a standard, small (39 seats) Bangladeshi curry house with all the trimmings, including Balti. Price check: Papadom 45p, CTM £5.35, Pullao Rice £1.65.

E4 – Highams Park

PURBANI

34 The Avenue, Highams Park, E4   ✆ 0181 531 8804

'I don't visit this very often, but I am never disappointed. They have catered well for me when we have ordered special meals for large groups. It continues to be of good quality,' B.G. Price check: Papadom 50p, CTM £5.85, Pullao Rice £1.50. Minimum charge per person £7.50.

E6 – East Ham

EASTERN EYE   ©

269 High Street, East Ham, E6   ✆ 0181 470 8078

D.MCC. visits here 'many times', and she never has 'any complaints'. It's a good standard curry house run by Mabud Mussain, who also owns the Himalaya, 178 The Grove, Stratford, E15.

MOBEEN   NEW ENTRANT

229 High Street North, East Ham, E6   ✆ 0181 470 9365

New to the Guide is this chain of unlicensed Pakistani caffs, where BYO is not permitted – the owners are strict Muslims. Good, inexpensive, value-for-money, Punjabi, Southall-style food, selected from the counter is the norm. Kebabs, tandoori items and darned good curries of all sorts, with specials varying from day to day. Branches: 222 Green Street, E7; 725 High Road, Leyton, E10; 80 Ilford Lane, Ilford, Essex.

YAAL

404 Barking Road, East Ham, E6   ✆ 0181 471 6744

Sri Lankan and south Indian food, but no reports received since last time, so let's have some, please.

E10 – Leyton

RAJ BRASSERIE   ©

322 Lea Bridge Road, Leyton, E10   ✆ 0181 539 8504

Owned by Messrs Miah (manager), Musabbir and Haque (chef), the Raj has a full complement of favourite tandoori and curry dishes with a comprehensive vegetarian section at sensible prices.

TANDOORIAN RECIPES   ©

434 High Road, Leyton, E10   ✆ 0181 556 2475

Iqbal Hussain's quaintly-named Tandoorian Recipes has a large and comprehensive menu with some nice specials (Butter Chicken gets the thumbs-up from A.R.). It also has a vegetarian section, and Balti comes to E10 with some 30 dishes.

E12 – Manor Park

THE EMPRESS INDIAN CUISINE   ©

729 Romford Road, Manor Park, E12   © 0181 478 2500

The menu misses nothing. It's good formula curry house stuff, including Balti. Price check: Papadom 30p, CTM £5.20, King Prawn Korai Tandoori £6.90, Pullao Rice £1.40. Sunday buffet £6.

E17

DHAKA TANDOORI   NEW ENTRANT

103 Hoe Street, Walthamstow, E17   © 0181 520 5151

'I used to live in Walthamstow and my hall is littered with takeaway menus. But my winner, to whom I still return, is the Dhaka,' c.j.

E18 – South Woodford

MEGHNA GRILL   ©

219 High Road, South Woodford, E18   © 0181 504 0923

New entrant, but long-established (1971). Standard, competent Bangladeshi curry house stuff with no surprises from Siddiqur Rahman. Price check: Papadom 50p, CTM £6.50, Pullao Rice £1.70. Sunday buffet £6.95. Minimum charge per person £5. Takeaway-only branch down the road at no. 249.

ROSE OF INDIA   ©

65-67 High Road, South Woodford, E18   © 0181 989 8862

The Rose has been operating for 20 years now under Messrs Miah and Hoque. It offers a good range of favourite tandooris and curries at sensible prices.

London EC

EC1

BROKER'S INN NEW ENTRANT

5 Clerkenwell Road, EC1   ✆ 0171 490 4468

It's bare and modern inside, with framed share certificates on the walls, hence the un-Indian name. But Indian it is, 'discovered' by H.C. on her way to a Barbican concert. 'The menu is fairly extensive with a proper vegetarian section. Butter Murgh delicious, sprinkled with almonds and made spicier, as requested, with chilli. Our meal with Cobra was £25.'

HAWELLI NEW ENTRANT

19-21 Old Street, Barbican, EC1   ✆ 0171 490 2055

Our reporters tell of up-market, elegant decor, and standard formula food to match. C.T. loved the Chicken Tikka Korai – 'large chunks of prime chicken with a wonderful sauce, excellent Bombay Aloo and nice Sag Bhaji'. H.C. thought 'the Vegetable Dhansak outstandingly good, very spicy, and not seen on many menus'. Price check: Papadom 50p, CTM £6.65, Pullao Rice £1.75. Daily buffet lunch £5.95. Set dinner for two £23.90.

RAVI SHANKAR   √

442 St John Street, Clerkenwell, EC1   ✆ 0171 833 5849

Ravi Shankar is a regular entrant to this Guide. It delights D.R.C. with its south Indian vegetarian menu, which 'appeals to me so choosing is always agonizing. The Vegetarian Thali and a starter of yoghurt, spices, and what appeared to be small pieces of idli, was delicious, spicy, sweet and sour all at once. Our Paper Dosa, with usual relishes, was absolutely marvellous and served very eye-catchingly, vertically, curved around the back of the stainless steel platter with the relishes in front, rather than the more usual roll laid on the plate. I don't know how they got it to stand upright.'

SEMA INDIAN BALTI CUISINE   BYO ©

141 Whitecross Street, EC1   © 0171 916 1797

Abdul Chowdhury's Oxford Tandoori is a previous Guide entrant, and it is good to hear that his 1993 venture in the City is thriving. It's a regular Bangladeshi restaurant with formula curries but it's unlicensed, so BYO, and they'll supply the glasses. Price check: Papadom 50p, CTM £5.50, Pullao Rice £1.60. Set meal from £4.75.

EC2

RUPEE ROOM   NEW ENTRANT

10 Copthall Avenue, EC2   © 0171 628 1555

Michael Tarat, whose family run Bromley, Kent's Tamasha (*see* entry), has launched out with another new (1995) venture (*see* Café Indiya, E1), this one with an apt name. For rupee's the name, rupee's the decor, and rupee's the game. Its City-suit brigade, it seems, don't mind forking out mucho dinero while they fork up. The times – open daily, 11.30a.m.- 10p.m., closed Saturdays, Sundays and Bank Holidays – give the clue. And chattering chef Abdur Rob will happily boast that his magnificent food can lead to spends of over £75 a head! Tarat is more subdued, pushing Rob back where he belongs, behind stoves, and you will get away with half that, we hear. Reports, please.

London N

N1

EVA II

41 Newington Green Road, N1   © 0171 704 2279

The second of three Evas (number one is in Drummond Street, NW1, and Eva III is in Hackney Road, E2). The owners are hoping for a nationwide chain, but it has yet to materialize. Good reports continue, but we'd like to hear more.

INDIAN VEG BHEL POORI HOUSE   √ ©

92-93 Chapel Market, Angel, N1   © 0171 837 4607

T.N. says: 'Not being a veggie, I walked past this wonderful smelling restaurant, with its eighteen buffet dishes looking great in the window, for five years. I was dragged in screaming with a group from work. I gingerly helped myself from the EAMAYL (not E-Mail: eat-as-much-as-you-like) selection, and discovered that I like vegetable curries, and went back for two more platefuls! It was all excellent, especially as it was just £2.95!!!' Indeed, Nurus Safa's fixed-price buffet lunch at £3.25, and dinner at £3.50, remain outstanding value for money.

MILAN INDIAN PURE VEGETARIAN   √ ©

52 Caledonian Road, Kings Cross, N1   © 0171 278 3812

Mr and Mrs Verma (manager and chef respectively) own this good-value vegetarian eatery which is open on weekdays, noon-10p.m. (Saturday noon-2p.m. and 6-10p.m., closed Sunday). They will give a discount to Curry Club members at the eat-as-much-as-you-like buffet.

RAJMONI INDIAN CUISINE   ©

279 Upper Street, Islington, N1   © 0171 354 3821

Kalam and Jamal's Rajmoni is a standard curry house that has been operating for more than seven years and has attracted a strong local following. Branches: Rajgate, Ampthill, Beds; Villa Bombay, sw6.

SONARGAON TOP 100   ©

46 Upper Street, Islington, N1   © 0171 226 6499

'On a training course in Islington a few of my colleagues from Manchester, knowing I am a curry addict, asked if I knew any good curry restaurants in the area. I opened my *Good Curry Guide* and to my great delight found that the Sonargaon was just around the corner from the training course. Off we went and had what proved to be one of the best meals any of us had ever had. The Manchester lads know their curries, as they are regular visitors to the Rusholme area, and to a man they declared that the Sonargaon was well worth its TOP 100 rating. We were met at the door by an extremely friendly waiter who invited us in. Service and atmosphere were good and we enjoyed a variety of excellent dishes. The Pall Masala turned out to be hot enough, even for me, and the taste was out of this world. One of my colleagues had Chicken Jalfrezi and voted it one of the best ever. The Chicken Tikka starter also received wide acclaim while the Naan bread, although not particularly large, was the tastiest I've had. The Lamb Roghan Josh, Chicken Tikka Masala and the Prawn Puri starters were all well appointed. It is rare to go to a restaurant with such a large group and find that to a man everyone reckoned it to be one of the best ever,' B.G. And we are pleased to keep the Sonargaon in our TOP 100.

SURUCHI

82 Mildmay Park, N1   *©* **0171 241 5213**

Khalil Miah's Suruchi is in all respects a standard formula Bangladeshi curry house, and it has been in our Guide before. It has the bonus of a patio garden which, with Britain's new-found sub-tropical climate, is worth gold dust to its loyal clientele. Branches: Babur, 32 Mill Lane, NW6; Ruchi, 92 Kingsgate Road, NW6.

N3 – Finchley

KARAHI HUT

164 Ballards Lane, Finchley Central, N3   *©* **0181 346 5947**

Delicious food, and many tempting offers as well.

RANI   √

3 Long Lane, Finchley, N3   *©* **0181 349 2636**

Jyoti Pattni's vegetarian menu, with its mainly Gujarati specials (cooked by his wife and his mother), makes this restaurant different. 'Just had a splendid meal – yet again. The restaurant is immaculate in every respect, the staff warm and efficient. Aloo Dhai Poori (£3.60) starter great, Lentil Bhajis (£3.20) good, if a little small. Banana Methi (£5) tastes and looks glorious, Stuffed Aubergines and Potato (£5.40) exquisite, well spiced with ground nuts and coriander, and their Pullao

Rice rises well and truly above most others, cooked with vegetables, sultanas and cashews. Portions ample, but one wishes they would change the menu from time to time,' c.t. Branch: Richmond, Surrey.

N4

JAI KRISHNA   √ BYO

161 Stroud Green Road, N4   ✆ **0171 272 1680**

Unlicensed, BYO, cheap, cheerful, reliable, typically south Indian vegan food.

SUNDERBAN   ©

50 Blackstock Road, N4   ✆ **0171 359 9243**

'This is a basic, standard – but clean – curry house. Decor – flock. Service is very good if you mention Curry Club. We have been here on numerous occasions, the food is always excellent,' a.s.

N6 – Highgate

KIPLINGS   ©

2 North Hill, Highgate, N6   ✆ **0181 340 1719**

This fairly new venture (1993) is from the Stanley Krett stable (*see* Bengal Lancer, nw5). It has quickly established itself a good reputation with everything 'as it should be', J.E.

N8 – Hornsey

JALALIAH   ©

163 Priory Road, Hornsey, N8   ✆ **0181 348 4756**

The Jalaliah has been in business for 22 years under Moen Uddin's ownership. The menu follows the curry formula so you can expect to find all your favourites here. It remains 'inexpensive and very good'.

JASHAN   ©

19 Turnpike Lane, N8   ✆ 0181 340 9880

The change of ownership to Gujarati from Kenyan has already been reported by certain of our scribes, with mixed views. c.f., with his large group of fellow doctors, many Indian themselves, tried it again but were still not impressed. Others tell of 'unusual fish curry (£5.50) and the strong taste of Punjabi spices such as methi, awash with ghee. Great if you like this sort of thing,' a.n. g.g. still considers it 'the best he's been in' and others sing equal praises. Evenings only, and closed Mondays.

MEGHNA   ©

55 Topsfield Parade, Tottenham Lane,
Crouch End, N8   ✆ 0181 348 3493

Owner Omar Khan's Meghna's wedge-shaped room lends itself to a spacious, typical Indian-arch type of decor. Its menu, in the hands of chef Moynul Haque, is comprehensive and has a full complement of standard items plus specials. Lemon Chana Chicken is the usual favourite of f.s. The all-day Sunday help-yourself-to-as-much-as-you-like buffet is the favourite of several other reporters. Price check: Papadom 50p, CTM £5.95, Pullao Rice £1.95. Branch: Palace Tandoori, 42 Craven Park Road, Harlesden, nw10.

N10

TASTE OF NAWAB   NEW ENTRANT   ©

93 Colney Hatch Lane, N10   ✆ 0181 444 6146

A. Kalam took over this well-established local in 1996 to good reports. Price check: Papadom 50p, CTM £5.95, Pullao Rice £1.75.

©	Curry Club discount (see p. 607)	☕	Unlicensed
√	Vegetarian	⊞	Home delivery
BYO	Bring your own alcohol		service available

N11 – New Southgate

BEJOY   NEW ENTRANT

72 Bounds Green Road,
New Southgate, N11   © 0181 888 1268/1262

Standard Bangladeshi formula curries at A. Suker's new (1995) place.
Price check: Papadom 50p, CTM £6.30, Pullao Rice £1.60. Set meal
from £8.75. Branch: Sunderban, N4.

N12 – North Finchley

CURRY ROYAL   ©

932-4 High Road, North Finchley, N12   © 0181 445 1650

Mr Abdul Choudhury's Curry Royal opened as early as 1970 and it has
always attracted favourable reports. One regular likes the Garlic
Chicken and another asks whether Chicken or Meat Kushboo is
unique to this restaurant. It is flavoured with such herbs as fresh corinal (sic). Corinal may be unique but Kushboo isn't (*see* Days of the
Raj, NW7).

FINCHLEY PAN CENTRE   BYO

15 Woodhouse Road,
North Finchley, N12   © 0181 446 5497

A tiny, unlicensed Indian snack bar, frequented by Indians, and open
daily except Tuesdays, noon-10p.m. (Fridays, 3.30-10p.m.). Kebabs,
samosas, veg rissoles, etc., very inexpensive and with friendly service.
Cash preferred.

N14 – Southgate

ROMNA GATE TANDOORI

14 The Broadway, Southgate, N14   © 0181 882 6700

Everyone remarks on the decor – 'impressive', 'outstanding'. The room is made spectacular and intimate by the skilful use of elegant coloured glass, mini waterfalls and wrought-iron work. The little service bell on each table is a good idea. 'The glass screens each side of the table cut out cigarette smoke from other diners,' D.C.G. We do hear about it getting very busy, particularly at peak times, which is always taxing for the best-run restaurants, and occasionally leads to a less than perfect occasion. However, most reporters remain happy with all aspects of the Romna, though C.F. tells of the same red sauce appearing on several dishes and watery dhal, etc. Reports, please.

N15

GUPTA BHEL PURI   √ ©

460 West Green Road, N15   ✓ © 0181 881 8031

If you enjoy Bhel Puri (*see* glossary), Gupta's is for you. It's a vegetarian establishment and the food is inexpensive, satisfying and very moreish. It's open daily, 11a.m.-11p.m.

N16 – Stoke Newington

ANGLO ASIAN TANDOORI   NEW ENTRANT

60-62 Stoke Newington
Church Street, N16   © 0171 254 3633

New to the Guide, following good reports. C.T. finds it 'very fine with service friendly and extremely attentive. Chicken Patia outstanding, CTM very good, though far too red, Chicken Bhuna, Bindi Bhajee, and Tarka Dhal, simply superb.'

LANCERS   ©

18 Stoke Newington Church Street, N16   © 0171 254 4429

Sunawar Ali's standard curry house has been operating since 1989, and now has a regular following. We hear of a menu full of old favourites, with a good vegetable selection as well, at reasonable prices.

RASA   √

55 Stoke Newington Church Street, N16   ✆ 0171 249 0344

'Owned by Das, who was formerly the manager at Spices, on the same street. Specializes in southern Indian vegetarian cooking. Decor is very relaxing, with about fifteen tables. On my one visit so far, I had Thayir Vadal as a starter. This is fried urid bean doughnut marinated in freshly spiced yoghurt. For my main course I had Moru Kachiathu, a Travancore speciality of yoghurt curry prepared with green banana and sweet mangoes, served lukewarm (as it should be, apparently) on Lemon Rice. Both dishes were new to me and were delicious!' D.S. The 'very good' from Dr C.F. and his tribe of medics is praise indeed!

SPICE OF ASIA BALTI   ©

56 Stoke Newington Church Street, N16   ✆ 0171 923 4285

Another good Stoke Newington Church Street curry house, with a formula menu consisting of many a tandoori and curry favourite. The owner, Mr Chowdhury, has recently introduced Balti to his menu (as well as to the restaurant's name).

N19

RAJ VOGUE   ©

34 Highgate Hill, N19   ✆ 0171 272 9091

Abed Choudhury is still here with his manager, Abdur Rahman, and chef, Suruk Miah. And, yes, Ken Livingstone (who's he?) and Spurs football stars (and who are they?) are also still here, we're told. The food is still good, according to Dr C.F. and G.G. confirms it is 'excellent, including the Kebab Platter'.

N21

RAJ OF INDIA

10 Station Road, Winchmore Hill, N21   ✆ 0181 360 9543

J.S. advises us not to be 'fooled by the tatty exterior of this restaurant.

Inside is a traditional (red flock wallpaper), largish – 20 tables – Indian eatery. The food wheeled in on a wooden trolley is superbly cooked and nicely presented. There is nothing lavish or exotic about the food or surroundings but don't let that detract from a very pleasant meal. The dishes are not very spicy, so if you like the food hot you can go for the Vindaloo without ordering a gallon of water. The waiters were helpful and pleasant and did not mind waiting at least 10 minutes while we pondered and asked their advice.'

London NW

NW1 – Drummond Street

I am often asked where the best restaurants are. It's one reason for producing this Guide. As far as central London is concerned, Drummond Street is one area which I recommend. Just behind Euston Station, it is easy to get to. It is short and will not win any awards for beauty. It lacks the ethnic glamour of Southall and Wembley, and the intensity of purpose of Brick Lane, but it is a small, concentrated sector of extremely good, mainly inexpensive, Indian food. There are greengrocers and delis supplying Indian ingredients, an off-licence, and a dozen or so takeaways and restaurants. Here in alphabetical order is our Drummond Street selection:

AMBALA SWEET CENTRE

112 Drummond Street, NW1   ✆ **0171 387 3521**

Ambala started trading in 1965. It specializes in savoury snacks (Pakoras and Samosa, etc.), Indian sweets (Halva, Jalebi, Gulab Jamun, Barfi, etc.) and a few curries. All are to take away only. Established initially for the Asian trade, it now has branches in Birmingham, Bradford, Derby, East Ham, Finchley, Glasgow, Leicester, Leyton, Luton, Manchester, Slough, Southall, Tooting and Wembley. Drummond Street is the flagship. All branches serve identical items at identical prices. The quality is first-class and the prices are always reasonable. Be prepared to queue, and pay cash. Open daily, 10a.m.-11p.m.

CHUTNEYS   √

134 Drummond Street, Euston, NW1   ℂ 0171 388 0604

One of three Drummond Street restaurants in the same ownership (*see also* Haandi and Ravi Shankar). They are all licensed and this one serves only vegetarian food, including Bhel Puri (*see* next entry), but at slightly higher prices reflecting the cost of the decor and licence. Set buffet lunch, though, is still only £3.95, and 'one of the best feed-ups in central London,' C.J. Average food spend £8.

DIWANA BHEL POORI TOP 100   √ BYO

121 Drummond Street, Euston, NW1   ℂ 0171 380 0730

As is often the way, the originator of a concept (in this country at any rate) usually remains the best. Diwana pioneered Bombay pavement kiosk snack food in the UK and is now much copied. And it is undoubtedly still the best of its kind. Diwana is small (thirty-nine seats in two sections), functional, café-style, unlicensed, open all day and, above all, it's still very cheap. Bhel Puri (several types) is a must here, and is a tantalizing cold mixture of crispy, chewy textures, sweet, hot and sour tastes. Crunchy, savoury, squiggly biscuits share the bowl with diced potato, puffed rice (mamra) and fresh coriander (dhania). Lace it together with yoghurt, tamarind (imli) sauce, chilli sauce and coriander chutney, and you have it. You might continue your meal with a Dosa Pancake filled with Sambar curry, boosted with fresh coconut and mustard seed chutney. It's all vegetarian, with much vegan, it's all fabulous, and it's all authentic. Try the Diwana's legendary Kulfi. 'I recommend the Paper Dosa for its spectacular appearance. The highlight of our meal was the Falooda – an Indian knickerbocker glory – probably the best in London. You wouldn't want to linger too long over your meal at Diwana – the seats are uncomfortable wooden benches – however, the quality of the food outweighs the numbness in your backside!' D.B. 'The back of the bill has a questionnaire. I was pleased to tick excellent for everything,' H.C. Booking is hit and miss, so expect a queue (especially at peak hours). Probably the best value in London ... and don't forget to BYO (no corkage charge). Off-licence with chilled Cobra available up the street. Buffet lunch £3.95. Hard to exceed £12 for a good veggie blow-out! It remains high in our TOP 100. Open noon-11p.m.

GUPTA CONFECTIONERS

100 Drummond Street, Euston, NW1   ✆ 0171 380 1590

Overshadowed, undoubtedly, by the Ambala up the road, Gupta is nonetheless a very good, long-established snack and sweet takeaway. Vegetable-only Samosas and Pakoras, plus a delightful unique Pea Kebab, are inexpensive and often still hot, being freshly cooked in the kitchens behind. Their sweets achieve a lightness of touch, and seem to avoid the taste of tinned evaporated milk that sometimes spoils those made by others. Cash or cheques. Branch: Watford Way, Hendon.

HAANDI

161 Drummond Street, Euston, NW1   ✆ 0171 383 4557

In decor terms it's the smartest of the Chutneys, Haandi, Ravi Shankar trio. It has all the south Indian favourites but this is the only one of the three to offer meat dishes. 'Upon ordering the waiter asked if we would like a complementary glass of white wine or onion bhajia starter. A further special offer was 50% off the total bill,' J.T.

RAAVI KEBAB

125 Drummond Street, Euston, NW1   ✆ 0171 388 1780

It's very much a meat place, as its name suggests. 'Had three Roti which were freshly made, very good and moist. Main course was Haleem, which was described as a very special dish from the sub-continent cooked with meat, wheat, lentils and spices – very nice and spicy. The rest of the menu wasn't extensive with five grills, four specials, four meat, three curry, four vegetable dishes. Worth a visit and seemed to be patronized by local Asians,' G.H. Open 12.30-11p.m.

RAVI SHANKAR

133 Drummond Street, Euston, NW1   ✆ 0171 388 6458

Open all day (noon-11p.m.) and the least pretentious of the Chutneys, Haandi group (and the first), it is slightly (but only just) more up-market. Otherwise, similar in most respects to the Diwana (*see* entry) which it followed into Drummond Street. It is licensed, but prices are still very reasonable and it is usually busy. Recommended are the two

Thali set dishes – the Mysore and the Shankar – and the Shrikhan dessert. Branch: EC1.

Elsewhere in NW1

GREAT NEPALESE TOP 100   ©

48 Eversholt Street, Euston, NW1   ✆ 0171 388 6737

A regular entrant to the Guide, and justly so. It is one of London's few Nepalese restaurants but, unlike many of these, the Great actually has a Nepalese chef (Masuk) and owner (Manandhar) and, more particularly, it has a decent number of Nepalese specialities on the menu. Masco Bara (black lentil pancakes), Mamocha or Momo – steam-cooked meat pastries (£3.30) – and Kalezo Ra Chyow (chicken liver) are three such starters. Main courses include Dumba (mutton), Pork Bhutwa and Hach Ko (duck) curries. There is also a range of eleven Nepalese vegetable dishes. Add those to sixteen 'standard' curry house vegetable dishes and the vegetarian will be spoilt for choice. In addition, the Great does all the standard curries and tandooris, from Phal, 'very very hot', to Shali Korma, 'very very mild'. If you are new to Nepalese food, our advice is to go for the Nepalese set meal (£12). For consistency, reliability and for a range of choice, plus quality that is way above average, we are pleased to keep the Great in our TOP 100.

MUMTAZ

4 Park Road, NW1   ✆ 0171 706 2855

'"Very" is perhaps the keyword to describe Mumtaz. The restaurant is very smart, very clean – the food was very excellent and very expensive. I think it's worth the very extra cost. Chicken Tikka Masala was very!' D.W. A sense of humour, Lord Latif-style (*see* Rupali, Newcastle, Tyne & Wear) has crept into the menu, with a 'very' hot dish challenge: Hot Pot Chicken Chilli Masala (£8.50) is cooked with five types of chilli, including the Bangladeshi Naga incendiary – 'Finish the entire dish, and you get a free beer' ... and you'll need it! Price check: CTM (Mumtaz Masala) £7.75, Buttery King Prawns £12.50, Pullao Rice £3, Thali £12-£18. Fill-your-face Sunday buffet good value at £14.

TANDOORI NIGHTS   ©

108 Parkway, Regents Park, NW1   © 0171 482 1902

It is unusual to see a woman working in a Bangladeshi restaurant, but this does not deter the eloquent and elegant Mrs Yasmeen Rashid, who is not only to be seen here, and at her other branches, but owns them. Manager Raj is equally smooth and, coming from Goa, he might point you at a Goan dish or two (Goan Fish is £7.95). Henry Lobo has just joined as chef, hot-foot and hot spice from Veeraswamy, so it remains to be seen what he does to the menu. This change means it has to step down from our TOP 100, hopefully temporarily. Reports, please. Price check: Papadom 50p, CTM £6.95, Pullao Rice £2.30. Service charge 10%. Branches: Cockfosters, Herts; Covent Garden, WC2.

VICEROY OF INDIA

3-5 Glentworth Street, NW1   © 0171 486 3515

Following the departure of the originator, Mr Mulhotra, from this bench-mark of elegance, the Viceroy has never received the same consistent adulation from our reporters that it once did. Last time we reported that, following its change of ownership to the Gaylord, Albemarle Street group, its uneven period was over. Sadly this has not been maintained. Most of our reports tell that the food is good, but nothing special. For this reason, we have (temporarily, we hope), removed the Viceroy from its TOP 100 perch. We've had no complaints, mind, but we urge the management to inject some energy into the kitchens, and resume their rating. So why visit? The Viceroy is undoubtedly London's most elegant curry establishment. It is large (150 seats) yet has a feeling of spaciousness. Once you have found it (off Marylebone Road), the exterior, with its marble facing and copper Hindi dome, is very inviting. Inside, the marble theme continues with pillar facings, steps and counter tops, and skilful use is made of natural brick walls and York floortiles, Indian wood carvings, paintings and artefacts. Round and square tables, some in bays, are crisply adorned and plants are dotted around to provide relief. One main feature, now much copied, is the tandoori kitchen, which is on view behind glass. We point out that this is an Indian operation (rather than Bangladeshi) and the kitchens offer what at first may appear to be a small choice – just five starters, eight tandoori items and an equally careful selection of main course dishes, breads and rice with nary a Phal, Vindaloo, Madras, Dhansak or Tikka Masala in sight. Spicing is gentle and subtle but is geared up on request. Our advice is to request it or you may find tastes too subtle. The Viceroy has long been one of the regular haunts of London's well-heeled Indian diplomatic and commercial community, and prices are well above average, as you'd expect. Minimum charge £14.50. Service charge 15%. Average meal £25, plus drinks.

NW2

SHAMA   BYO ©

66 Cricklewood Broadway, NW2   © 0181 450 9052

The Shama is one of those places that local communities thrive on. It's small (50 seats) and comfortable, but not plush. Owned by Messrs Rawat (manager) and Ahmed (chef) since they started it in 1980. The food is competent and inexpensive. Two more advantages: you can BYO (despite it being licensed) and Curry Club members will be offered a discount. Price check: Papadom 25p, CTM £4.30, Karahi Chicken/Lamb £3.60, Pullao Rice £1.20.

NW3

CURRY MANJILL

34 England's Lane, Hampstead, NW3   © 0171 722 4053

A typical, long-standing (1970) family-run curry house with a typical menu boosted by some nice specials – Pomphret Mosalla (sic) and Koliza Bhuna (chicken liver in a creamy sauce). There are some Balti dishes here, too, all at reasonable prices.

CURRY PARADISE

49 South End, Green End, NW3   © 0171 794 6314

'Served us well for over ten years. Unfortunately, recent indoor redecoration has lessened seating power, increasing likelihood of sitting next to smokers. A pity. Otherwise, superb Phals – fire-eaters' dream! An excellent and extremely reliable curry house, reasonably priced,' D.McC.

FLEET TANDOORI   ©

104 Fleet Road, Hampstead, NW3   © 0171 485 6402

'A good restaurant for those seeking a dependable, quiet and inexpensive meal. The Sunday buffet is a must for those who wish a cheap alternative to meat and two veg. An additional attraction is the Special on the menu – Pomfret Fish, which comes either tandoori or, for those with a rich palate, bathed in a curry sauce flavoured with a multitude of spices. Good prices enhanced by a 10% discount to Curry Club members at any time!' A.D.

PAPADAM   NEW ENTRANT

58 Belsize Lane, NW3   © 0171 794 0717

Formerly the Guide entrant Belsize Tandoori, now with new name and new owners. D.R.C. says: 'It is a lovely, small and attractive restaurant, with charming staff. Generous quantities of food served in square, classy china dishes. Danny had huge success with the Garlic Duck, I stuck to CTM, we shared Garlic Mushrooms, Veg Dhansak, Naan, Papadoms, relishes and bhajis. Not a grand place like the B.B. (Bombay Brasserie), but one of the best. The bill, with drinks and coffee, about £49.'

NW4

PRINCE OF CEYLON   NEW TO OUR TOP 100

39 Watford Way, NW4   © 0181 202 5967

There are precious few Sri Lankan (let alone Ceylonese) restaurants in London (*see* Tooting, SW17), and while the Prince has a pretty much standard menu, with tandooris, kebabs, curries and all the business, all perfectly competently cooked, it is not those you want to go for. It is the Sri Lankan specials. Of course, these items have their own language and may be unfamiliar to many curryholics. Meanwhile, it is worth asking waiter advice, but be patient if explanations are unclear at first.

It is a rice (Buth) cuisine. Hoppers or Appas are rice and coconut-flour pancakes, String Hoppers ditto, but resembling vermicelli nests (10 for £3), or Pittu – ditto dumpling – and straight rice are accompanied by pungent watery curries, in which coconut, chillies, turmeric, tamarind and curry leaves feature. But they can be mild, too. Look out for aromatic black curries and fragrant white ones. Fish dishes, such as Ambul Thial (a Sri Lankan national dish – a sour, spicy fish dish) and the Ceylon Squid (Dhallo) curry are popular. And there are substantial curries such as Lumpri (chicken, meat and egg). Sambols, or relishes, include dried fish and chilli (Seeni Sambol is a cooked version). Our reporters find the Prince engaging: 'Service prompt and pleasant. The waiters found it hard to explain the dishes so we ended up with huge quantities which we were unable to finish as we were too full. We pronounced ourselves well satisfied with the quality of the meals,' G.G.P. We are pleased to promote the Prince to our TOP 100.

NW5

BENGAL LANCER TOP 100   ©

---

253 Kentish Town Road, NW5   ✆ **0171 485 6688**

Stanley Krett and Akram Ali's brainchild brasserie, now ten years on, pioneered a wave of Raj reminiscence-theme restaurants, including one of their own (*see* below). The Lancer soldiers on, attracting good reports a-plenty. 'This is a restaurant whose standard has remained consistently high. Always a pleasure to visit. The service is efficient, but not obtrusive, and the quality of food very high, thus guaranteeing that we will be visiting again shortly,' D.M. 'A monthly outing of the Jubilee Line Extension Project curry clan. Good food presented with some style even when faced with nine very hungry people. Service good, portions reasonable. Highlights from the menu included Potato Chat and Jeera Chicken. The Peshwari and Keema Naan were also extremely good,' P.C. 'A genuine classy restaurant with an excellent menu range. Liver Hazra, liver cooked and tossed in spices, rich and almost a meal in itself. Unusual, good and great taste. Tiger Wings are chicken drumsticks tandoori-style. Service first-class, attentive and despite a packed peak-time Saturday night they kept checking up to see if we required anything else. Food up among the best for quality, portions more than adequate and at value-for-money prices. Deserves its rating in the TOP 100,' A.S. Some criticism, though, about the service charge, the cover charge and 'lighting too intense for an intimate dinner,' D.W. It remains in our TOP 100. The discount for Curry Club members will go some way to offset these minor criticisms. Branch: Kiplings, N6.

INDIAN LANCER   ©

56 Chetwynd Road, NW5   © 0171 482 2803

A small restaurant which, under the ownership of M.Y. Hashmi, has become a very popular local offering formula curry house food at reasonable prices.

SHAHANA TANDOORI   ©

343 Kentish Town Road,
Kentish Town, NW5   © 0171 485 5566

Owner M.E. Muslim is on hand in this popular local curry house, again offering formula curry house food at reasonable prices.

NW6

GEETA SOUTH INDIAN

57 Willesden Lane, NW6   © 0171 624 1713

It's vegetarian food at which Geeta excels, and has done for two decades, with never a decline in standard. Dosas, Idlis, Upamas Karela (bitter gourds), drumsticks (long pithy marrow which you suck to extract the tender flesh), Rasams, Sambars and more. It's all fine stuff, served in less than glamorous surroundings, to a thoroughly devoted following. Actually, they do have good meat and tandoori items on their menu but, good though these are, the *aficionados* prefer the authentic vegetarian offerings, washed down with Cobra lager – and all at reasonable prices. Even with the ridiculous 10% service charge, you'll spend less than a tenner, with drink.

PANSHI   NEW ENTRANT

31 Malvern Road, NW6	© 0171 328 1226

Panshi may well have been the Bangladeshi royal barge of yore, but it is now a curry house, run by Messrs Abdul Salam and Bahar, between Maida Vale and Kilburn, so says Fay Maschler and their menu. Ms M. goes on to praise the food, which at first sight is formula, but is augmented by a small attempt by chef Adbul Hakim to offer true Bangladeshi curries, such as Rezala (a kind of korma with coconut and chilli) and Gowa, even hotter (Naga chillies?). As I'm always saying (*see* introduction), I'd like to see much more authentic Bangladeshi food, and maybe this restaurant will dare to do it, sooner rather than later. Meanwhile, it's definitely worthy of a new Guide entry. Price check: Papadom 40p, CTM £5.50, Badami Gosht £6.50, Pullao Rice £1.75.

SURYA   ©

59-61 Fortune Green Road, West Hampstead, NW6	© 0171 435 7486

This tiny, 34-seat restaurant really packs 'em in. Run by the husband and wife Tiwari team (he's front of house, she's the chef), there's no room to move, almost literally – it's always full. The dish of the day (it changes daily) excites several of our regulars at this vegetarian, licensed restaurant. We have heard well of Gujarati dishes such as Patra and Kaddu Kari and inexpensive prices. It opens daily, 6-10.30p.m., and for Sunday lunch. Branch: Shree Ganesha, 4 The Promenade, Edgwarebury Lane, Edgware, Middlesex.

VIJAY

49 Willesden Lane, NW6	© 0171 328 1087

Correct me if I'm wrong, but Vijay, founded in 1966, predated nearby Geeta (*see* above) by several years, so it can take the crown for being the earliest to provide south Indian food for NW6, and its menu contains all the vegetarian items listed in Geeta's entry, at much the same prices. Vijay has its own clan of loyal regulars who know they'll get 'very nice tasty food,' B. and w.w.

NW7

BRENT TANDOORI ©

24 High Road, Willesden Green, NW0   ✆ 0181 459 0649

This takeaway-only is reported as being clean, generous, prompt and efficient. The food is evidently well-liked and the prices reasonable. Owner Monojir Ali welcomes Curry Club members to whom he will give a discount, on his already reasonable prices, at his quieter times.

DAYS OF THE RAJ ©

123 The Broadway, Mill Hill, NW7   ✆ 0181 906 3363

The Days' extensive menu appears to be formula stuff from Kurma (sic) to Phal, etc., available in the form of chicken, lamb, beef, prawn, king prawn and vegetables. But a closer look provides a number of 'unique' dishes. What are Noorane, Sherajee, Kushboo, Dilkush and Bakhara curries, for example? Each available in the above forms (the menu explains their attributes), they are clearly house inventions. So is the dish Days of the Raj, gently cooked with pineapple, lychees and sultanas in a thick creamy sauce sprinkled with nuts. It sounds like a fruit salad but is, we're assured, 'really quite delicious, the chicken quite succulent, and mild enough for my boss who is a curry novice,' G.C. Owner Khalam Matin and his partner, chef, S. Miah, are to be applauded. We said last time that this could be just the place to offer some real Bangladeshi dishes. It hasn't happened yet, but we live in hope that the food the staff eat at home will soon be on the menu. Meanwhile, it is more than a 'safe-bet' curry house. It is very smart indeed and is a place to go for an enjoyable meal out. Price check: Papadom 40p, CTM £7.25, Duck Bakhara £7.90, Pullao Rice £1.90. Service charge 10%. Eat-your-fill lunch buffet daily £6.90.

©	Curry Club discount (see p. 607)	🍷	Unlicensed
√	Vegetarian	⊞	Home delivery
BYO	Bring your own alcohol		service available

NW10

ANN MARIE AT THE TASTE OF THE TAJ   ©

4 Norbreck Parade, off Hanger Lane,
Ealing, NW10   ℂ **0181 991 5366**

Let's get it clear, Ann Marie's Taste, which has been going since 1989, *is* in Ealing. It's also in NW10, which Ealing isn't (but it used to be W5). The North Circular Gyratory rebuild caused mayhem with Ann Marie's access, if you follow me, not to mention with her postcode. She says herself it's 'essential to phone and ask for directions, because the access to the front is now closed from the North Circular'. As in Birmingham, you can see it, but you cannot touch it. But find it you should, and avail yourself of a personalized service and advice that some of Ann Marie's regulars have known and delighted in for some 30 years, in another Ealing venue. First-timers will discover (if they listen to her) that it's the memsahib's personal touches that make this very ordinary-looking menu into a welcoming taste experience. Chef Nazrul converts it all into stimulating cuisine. We hear of a 'fabulous fresh Chicken Dapeaza [sic] floating in fresh glistening onions' from C.R. and 'a rather unexpected delicacy of touch in the Courgette Bhaji' from R.G.

KADIRI KITCHEN   ©

26 High Road, Willesden, NW10   ℂ **0181 451 5525**

It's a small place (36 seats) that has been around for a long time (since 1974). Sayed Kadiri's 150-item menu surely has something for everyone, 'including fish curries (Wednesdays only) and a great selection of Paneer dishes, e.g., Paneer Chilli Masala,' G.B. Good food, good value.

SABRAS   √

263 High Road, Willesden Green, NW10   ℂ **0181 459 0340**

Hemant and Nalinee and Mrs Desai, it appears, are still struggling with their current financial problems, but are determined to keep their baby, now nearly 25 years of age, afloat. Regulars have shown sympathy and support, and keep on going back, past the tacky shopfront (and telling us so) for really excellent, home-style vegetarian Gujarati food. The prices are still really attractive, and help is at hand if you are unfamiliar with the food. Licensed, open 6-10.30p.m., every night except Sundays. Expect to pay between £12 and £15 for a worthy meal.

NW11

GURKHA BRASSERIE   ©

756 Finchley Road, NW11   ℭ 0181 458 6163

One of the best places to go for Nepalese food. Owner-chef Hari K.C. is often on hand to explain what's what amongst the Gurkha's Nepalese specials. The regular curries are 'pretty darned good too,' s.w. Branch: Gurkha Brasserie, w1.

London SE

SE1

BENGAL CLIPPER

11-12 Cardamom Building, 31 Shad Thames,
Butlers Wharf, SE1   ℭ 0171 357 9001

Once you have found it, and found a parking space, you'll find Kenneth Lynn's interior sophisticated and expensive. The grand piano is still in evidence but was silent on our last visit, thank heavens, so we could hear each other talk. Service has become slicker and there is no doubt that everyone cares about image. Chef Azam Khan cares about his food, and the relatively short menu takes the diner on a gastronomic tour of India. Expect to pay more than average here, and please send us some reports. Price check: Papadom 75p, CTM £9.25, Dahi Dover Sole £13.95, Pullao (Pilaw – sic) Rice £2.25. Cover charge £1.50, incl. Papadoms.

CASTLE TANDOORI

200-201 Elephant and Castle
Shopping Centre, SE1   ℂ 0171 703 9130

Mr Uddin's Castle is a spirited place, and a regular entrant in our Guide. He tells us, and you, if you care to be entertained by him, that he's outlived twenty-two Hoovers, two recessions, and several prime ministers, and served enough naan bread to stretch from Waterloo to Paris. The menu is pretty much formula (135 items) but includes duck, lamb chops and trout in various curry guises. Reports tell of the value for money. Open for lunch Monday to Friday, and evenings until 1a.m. daily (extended to 2.30a.m. on Fridays and Saturdays). We know of no longer hours in London. (Tell me if you know better.) So, if you're an insomniac curryholic, or just a late-night reveller, note this place well.

IMPERIAL TANDOORI   NEW ENTRANT   ©

48 Kennington Road, SE1   ℂ 0171 928 4153

MPs love it, says Mohibad Rahman. Price check: Papadom 40p, CTM £6.45, Tandoori Shashlik £5.95, Pullao Rice £1.75. Minimum charge £7.95.

THAMES TANDOORI

79 Waterloo Road, SE1   ℂ 0171 928 3856

Still doing it under the railway bridge, but is its neighbour, the Fishcotheque, still doing it? And I'm still waiting for it to name-change to Tikkateque! H.C. still loves it – 'Brinjal Bhaji so good, we ordered a second portion!'

TOWER TANDOORI   ©

74 Tower Bridge Road, SE1   ℂ 0171 237 2247

Shab Uddin's place has been doing it well since 1978. In fact, they were in our first Guide, so welcome back, and nice to see you give the Curry Club discount on already reasonable prices. Price check: Papadom 55p, CTM £6.70, Pullao Rice £1.60. Minimum charge £10.

SE2

ABBEY WOOD TANDOORI   NEW ENTRANT   ⊞

13 Wickham Lane, Abbey Wood, SE2   ✆ 0181 310 3534

D.P. and his girlfriend have eaten in over 100 curry restaurants, but the one nearest their home is their favourite. She believes there's nothing he has not eaten on the menu over the past three years! They deliver, too. Price check: Papadom 40p, CTM £4.95, Balti Lamb £5.25, Pullao Rice £1.45.

SE4

ROYAL TANDOORI   NEW ENTRANT

387 Brockley Road, SE4   ✆ 0181 692 7260

Owner-chef Taruz Zaman's Royal, takeaway only, is new (1996), but already getting good reports. Price check: Papadom 40p, CTM £5, Chicken Royalpur £5.95, Pullao Rice £1.40.

SE5 – Camberwell

CAMBERWELL TANDOORI   ©

22 Church Street, Camberwell, SE5   ✆ 0171 252 4800

Our regular correspondents continue to vote for Chef Huda and owner-manager Sam Huda's Camberwell. They tell of some unusual items, e.g., Kebab-E-Coxbazza (sic), a fish dish from that region of Bangladesh (Cox's Bazaar!). Equally liked is their Murug-E-Makoney (sic), a type of Chicken Tandoori Masala. And there's Balti on the menu – Balthee (sic) chicken. Reasonable prices. Price check: Papadom 35p, CTM £5.95, Pullao Rice £1.35. Minimum charge £6.95.

NOGAR   ©

59 Denmark Hill, SE5   ✆ 0171 252 4846

Until 1993, this was the Akash. Now, as the Nogar, it is owned and

managed by K. Hussain, with A. Islam as chef. 'We liked the idea of
Chicken Flaming – whole breast mediumly [sic] cooked, sizzling with
a flame of Sambuca. And we liked it when it came,' B.K. We liked the
move towards Bengal fish specials (there are four); we also note a Balti
dish here.

SE9 – Eltham

JIBON SATHI   ©

52 High Street, Eltham, SE9   ℰ **0181 265 0406**

Evenings only at this curry house (6-11.30p.m.) It opened in 1979 under
owner-manager A.B. Choudhury and fairly recently changed its name
from the Luna. The food remains excellent, we hear, the service experienced and competent.

MAHATMA TANDOORI   ©

156 Bexley Road, Avery Hill, Eltham, SE9   ℰ 0181 859 7954

The Mahatma has a chatty menu, which explains fully many of chef
Miah's formula curries. A good all-rounder where you should not be
disappointed.

RUCHITA TANDOORI   NEW ENTRANT   ⊞ ©

31 Avery Hill Road, SE9   ℰ **0181 850 1202**

Miss Salma Yousuf's takeaway-only, evenings-only, Ruchita has been
going since 1975. So our scribes tell us that manager A. Karim and chef
Samad know what they're doing. Price check: Papadom 40p, CTM
£5.50, Pullao Rice £1.50. Set meal £12.90. Minimum charge £10 on
home delivery.

WELL HALL TANDOORI   ©

373 Well Hall Road, SE9   ℰ **0181 856 2334**

A competent curry house owned and managed by Tuahid (front) and
Abdul (chef) Ali and Muhan Miah.

SE13

BENGAL BRASSERIE   ©

79 Springbank Road, Hither Green, SE13   © 0181 244 2442

c.t. describes this venue, owned by Syed Ahmed, as having 'a nice lit-
tle menu, now containing a few originals'. The spinach in Lobster
Saghee (£6.95) makes this 'a fine dish', e.s. And others enjoy the Sea
Thali (£8.50) – clever name. Evenings only. Price check: Papadom 40p,
CTM £5.50, Pullao Rice £1.30. Minimum charge £15. Service charge
10%. Cover charge £1. Phew!

SPICE OF LIFE   ©

**260 Lee High Road,
Lewisham, SE13   © 0181 852 5414/473 8222**

With its owner Harris Miah, and cooking by Jilad, the extremely popular Spice of Life moved from no. 260, re-opened as the Chanpur at
no. 134, and now is back again as the Spice, in its original place, completely refurbished and redecorated. It doesn't fool us, though, thanks
to vigilant reporting by *aficionados* G. and c.m. 'Fresh, new, comfortable
and attractive,' they say. 'Some changes to the menu, but still with daily
blackboard specials, the high standard has been maintained. We were
welcomed as usual and treated to a bottle of wine. We thoroughly
enjoyed the meal.' Daily blackboard specials are so rare in the curry
business, but it's one of my bones of contention and I shall go on nag-
ging until more curry restaurants do it. Welcome back to the Guide,
though I've broken my own rules since the Spice has not returned its
questionnaire to us. Even the B.B. (Bombay Brasserie) has done that.
So, Gilian, it will have to wait for your wish – its promotion to our
TOP 100 – until it talks to us!

©	Curry Club discount (see p. 607)	🍵	Unlicensed
√	Vegetarian	⊞	Home delivery
BYO	Bring your own alcohol		service available

SE19

GOLDEN CURRY CENTRE   ©

86 Anerley Road, SE19   ℂ 0181 788 9997

Another takeaway-only, with lunchtime and evening hours (to midnight). Owned by M. Ali (front of house) and chef Johur Ali.

PASSAGE TO INDIA

232 Gipsy Road, SE19   ℂ 0181 670 7602

'I have been eating here for eight or nine years. It is still excellent. I ate there last week and had a wonderful meal,' G.G.

SE22 – East Dulwich

MIRASH

94 Grove Vale, East Dulwich, SE22   ℂ 0181 693 1640

'A crisp and smart interior,' says V.G. Formula curries include all the favourites. Value-for-money Sunday set lunch.

SURMA   ©

42 Lordship Lane, East Dulwich, SE22   ℂ 0181 693 1779

Muzahid Ali opened the popular Surma in 1976. Harun Ali's cooking is a good example of the formula. Price check: Papadom 35p, CTM £4.75, Taba Gosht £5.50, Pullao Rice £1.40. Set meal £25 for two. Branch: Joy Bangla Curry House, 39 Denmark Hill, SE5.

SE23 – Forest Hill

BABUR BRASSERIE   TOP 100   ⊞ ©

119 Brockley Rise, Forest Hill, SE23   ℂ 0181 291 2400

Babur established the Mogul Empire in 1483 through his courage and daring in capturing Delhi. This restaurant captured Forest Hill in 1985, though its ownership by the dynamic Rahmans did not occur until 1992, which got it promoted to our TOP 100 last time. Quite simply, it's in our TOP 100 because everything the Rahmans do, they do well. If you are a regular, you'll get frequent mail-shots telling you what is happening here, from festivals to their new alfresco dining outside the restaurant. Talking about outside, the front is really attractive, with white Mogul arches, each one enhanced by hanging baskets and floor tubs. The white decor continues inside, offset by 56 air-force blue chairs. Dining is intimate in a screened area or in the conservatory. While perusing the menu, you may be tempted by a range of cocktails, including Monsoon Hurricane (£4.25), making you 'hot, heavy and ready to go'. But, we presume, not too heavy to order! The menu is a careful compilation of well-known favourites, with an above-average selection of unusuals. Fish, crab, mussels and the rarely-seen Patra – a steamed, then deep-fried, Gujarati savoury swiss roll of Besan and patra leaf (£2.60). Aloo Choff (£2.75) is a Raj-style rissole of mashed potato and vegetable, rolled in chopped cashew and pan-fried. Main courses include the gorgeous traditional Parsee dish, Sali Jardaloo (£6.50). Here, lamb is slowly cooked with savoury spices, enhanced with the sweet and sour tastes of dried apricots (jardaloo) and honey. The dish is garnished with straw potatoes (sali). Goa is well represented with Chicken Cafriel (£6.95), Badak Xec Xec – pronounced 'shek-shek' – (£7.50) which is fragrant duck, Tuna Bulchao (£7.50) – hot and tangy – and the even hotter Lobster Peri Peri (£13.95). Also from the Raj is Ginger Roast Lamb (£6.95). Among a satisfactory choice of vegetables, you'll find Dum Tori (£3.25) – courgettes tossed with sour mango powder – and Shorvedar Makhani (£3.50) – involving beetroot. All co-owner chef Enam Rahman's cooking is bright and fresh. Front of house is equally bright and fresh, under the careful supervision of co-owner manager Emdad Rahman. Keep an eye out for their regular cuisine festivals and special offers. It is plentiful attention to details (such as the gold-credit-card-style member cards), good food, service and ambience which keeps this restaurant in our TOP 100. For the record, here's our standard price check: Papadom 50p, CTM £6.25, Pullao Rice £1.95. Minimum charge £7.95. But do yourself a favour and treat yourself to the works. Open for lunch and dinner every day. Branch: it's all available for takeaway, or home delivery, evenings only, closed Tuesdays, at Babur Takeaway, 443 Brockley Road, Crofton Park, SE4.

DEWANIAM   TOP 100   ⊞

133-5 Stanstead Road, Forest Hill, SE23   ℂ 0181 291 4778

It's great how one good restaurant encourages another. Forest Hill has a further TOP 100 restaurant, the Dewaniam. The name is Mogul, meaning the Hall of Public Audience. Despite a wretched arson attack reported last time (on the above Babur, too), owners Rashid Ali and Fozlu Miah (chef) fought back and rebuilt their 88-seat Dewaniam, keeping their promise that the menu and atmosphere would be the same. It's the menu that we have been extolling since it first went into our Guide in 1986. We put it in our TOP 100 when we started that category in 1991, and we keep it there because our scribes continue to report with glowing contentment. Unlike its near neighbour, the Dewaniam sticks hard and fast to the Bangladeshi curry house formula. But there are surprises throughout. There is the usual complement of tandooris and kebabs, ranging from £2.50 for Chicken Tikka to £7.95 for Tandoori King Prawn. The surprise in this section is Tandoori Sri Lanka (£7.50) augmented with hot spices! Curries range from Kurma (sic) – very mild – to Phall – extra hot – through eighteen others, including the surprise, with bamboo shoots, and all with meat. Chicken, Prawn (all around £3.20) or King Prawn (£5.20). Add the sundries and veg side dishes, and that's the formula. And we repeat what we've said previously: you can, of course, have a thoroughly good meal there, choosing nothing but these favourites. But there are some truly outstanding alternative choices. Game is represented by pheasant, quail, duck, and venison. Don't panic about Heron Tikka, however – it's not that elusive, well-loved river bird, it's 'marinated deer meat barbecued in the tandoor'. (The Hindi/Urdu word for venison is Heeran!) Chef Fozlu is an innovator. His skilful use of alcohol, unusual in Indian cooking, matches anything you'd find in the French repertoire. Mugli Batak, for example, is duck cooked with mince, egg, cream, green herbs and red wine. But it's not just red wine that appears in a number of dishes – white wine enhances the Tandoori Trout marinade, brandy is used as a flambé (for tandoori pheasant or quail) and Tia Maria as a marinade in Chicken Indropuri. There's one Bangladeshi fish dish, Fish Masallah (sic), and a no-compromise vegetable dish, Sabzi Satrang, of okra, bitter gourd, sour tinda and aubergine. I'd still like to see the Dewaniam add more really authentic Bangladeshi dishes, the real thing the families and staff eat, hot and spicy, fish and veg, perhaps as a blackboard dish of the day (without, of course, removing any of their existing dishes). Forest Hill can take it – in fact, they'd like it, I'm sure. I am retaining this restaurant high in our TOP 100. For the record, here's our standard price check: Papadom 55p, CTM £5.50, Pullao Rice £1.70. No minimum charge. Open for lunch and dinner every day. Sunday lunch eat-your-fill buffet, noon-5.30p.m., £6.95, kids £3, under-5s free. Branches: it's all available for takeaway, or home delivery, evenings only, minimum charge £7.50, at: The Dewaniam Takeaway, 3 Westdale Road, SE23. Other branch: Muglai, 61a Dartmouth Road, SE23 – reports, please.

SE25 – South Norwood

JOMUNA BRASSERIE   ©

165 Portland Road, South Norwood, SE25 ✆ 0181 654 9385

E. Ali's 44-seat standard curry house with all the good old favourites, plus some Balti dishes. Be adventurous … try the Machi Koiful – Bangladeshi fish with Sylhetti vegetables (£4.60). Price check: Papadom 45p, CTM £5.30, Pullao Rice £1.45. Minimum charge £7.50. Open for lunch and dinner, every day, Sunday eat-your-fill buffet, 1-6p.m., £5.95, kids £3.95.

SE26 – Sydenham

JEHANGIR TOP 100   ©

67 Sydenham Road, Sydenham, SE26   ✆ 0181 244 4244

I have to start by saying that Fay Maschler did not agree with my review of the Jehangir in our last Guide. She wrote to me that she rated the Prince of Ceylon (*see* NW4) better for Sri Lankan food. It shows the slight difficulty we have in relying on reports because, looking it up, I see that the reports we received on the Prince were by different people to those who wrote about the Jehangir. They are, after all, poles apart, literally – at the extreme north and south of the London postcodes. Answer: we revisited both, anonymously, and agreed with Ms M. enough to upgrade the Prince and give it our TOP 100 rating, but not to remove the Jehangir from that list. We like it, and we continue to get happy reports from its fans. Unlike the dark brown decor and dispassionate service at the Prince, the Jehangir's dining room is light and airy and gorgeously decorated, with vaulted archways, marble floors, hand-painted ceiling, complete with huge colonial fan, mahogany carvers and Wedgwood crockery. But it's the food that counts. The Jehangir's menu is astonishing. It runs to 10 pages and contains a massive 143 numbered items. The takeaway version comes as a little booklet, and even that has 87 items! Get one. It gives really good descriptions of each item. In fact, the Jehangir gives a combination of north and south Indian and Sri Lankan food, with a touch of the Maldive Islands thrown in. There are 23 starters. Hot Tempered Prawns are indeed hot, and the Gothamba Roti, a thin bread, is indeed silky. There are eight types of Dosai (urid and rice-flour pancakes), idlis and three hoppers. Main courses include thirteen chicken, twelve lamb and ten seafood dishes, many of which use imported Sri Lankan fish. Breads, rice and biriyanis (sic) are followed by one of the most remarkable vegetarian selections we've seen – over 23 dishes. And the service? Good on our visit, and we hear they are extremely good with customer care. On the special occasions, cards, flowers, cake or champagne is given by the management. Recent reports received are contented. 'Everything you say about this is correct. It is superb and I have used this restaurant many times since discovering it,' G.G. Mr T.N. liked the view into the kitchen, 'en-route to the mediocre loos. It was quite full of couples on a Sunday evening, but we were the only couple to have the Sunday buffet, which proffered a starter of papadoms, salad and two hot chutneys, followed by five curries and rice, with rice white buns (idlis), which cost £21, incl. Cokes and service.' Mrs T.N., though, found the dishes too hot. This is a problem with the food of this region, so ask manager S. Nathan for advice about mild curries, if that's your bag. Chefs Mrs Mano and Mrs Kughan will oblige so, with that proviso, our advice here, as ever, is to go at quieter times for the best food and service, and to order Sri Lankan/south Indian items, rather than north Indian. We're happy to keep the Jehangir in its TOP 100 slot. For the record, here's our standard price check: Papadom 55p, CTM £5.25, Pullao Rice £1.95. Minimum charge £10, set meal from £6.95, plus 12½% service charge, all relieved by the Curry Club discount!

London SW

SW1

KUNDAN

3 Horseferry Road, SW1	ℂ 0171 834 3434

There are 117 seats at the Kundan (and 200 or so at the House of Lords and 632 at the Commons). And like as not you'll spot many a political face in here, all enjoying right-wing-raitas with Commons seeds and red-Vindaloos or Matar Peers, perhaps. Our Honourable and Right Honourable members enjoy curry so much that they've even formed a branch of The Curry Club at their House, and are frequently seen practising at the Kundan. We've not heard of Blair Biriani, or Major Madras, Prescott Patia, or Kinnock Kebab, but I wouldn't put it past owner Nayab Abbasi, who just loves all this, of course. Given half a chance, if he's not at his San Francisco branch, he'll explain that they, and many other politirati, have been seen tucking in here, as often as not. Ask him to explain about the loud bell that rings here from time to time. And since so many of you have asked me to explain, I will: it's not the fire alarm, so don't make a move! It's an extension of the division bell. In times of tight majorities, it means a mad exodus of smart, dark Armani suits (unless it's Ken Clarke, of course), leaving half-eaten plates of curry. Standard food, with some nice specials from Chef Mohamed Aziz Khan. Not cheap, but such delights wouldn't be, and it *is* Westminster! Lunch, and dinner from 7p.m. Closed Sundays and Bank Holidays.

SALOOS   TOP 100

62-64 Kinnerton Street, Knightsbridge, SW1	ℂ 0171 235 4444

I get more reports about Saloos from my Indian friends than about any other restaurant. Curious, really, because I do mean Indian. And Saloos is very much Pakistani, owned by M. Salahuddin who wrote me a kind letter inviting me to lunch in April 1992, which I never fulfilled, then threatened to sue me, on another matter, in July 1992. Never mind – such is the price of fame. The matter was dropped. But despite such activity, and maybe because of its idiosyncrasies, of which more below,

I continue to love-hate and promote Saloos in our Guide, as I have since 1984. As I say, it is immensely popular with London's well-educated wealthy Indians, who ignore politics when it comes to good food. And in their opinion (not mine!) there is precious little good Indian, let alone good Pakistani, food in Britain. Because I have had no reports since last time, and we've not saved up enough to visit it since then, I'll stick with our report from last time: 'On the evening of our visit, we found the first-floor restaurant nearly full, its clientele composed of the aforementioned Indians, plus some Arabs and whites. Drinks orders for gin and tonic (£5.50 each) were taken promptly and delivered by a very nervous young man. The wine (Mouton Cadet £18.50) was opened with no grace and if there had been any sediment at the bottom of the bottle it was now distributed equally among the liquid. The glasses weren't even as nice as the ones you can collect with Esso vouchers. The restaurant atmosphere wasn't the usual one of diners chatting and eating, clinking of glasses. It reminded me of breakfast-time in a large hotel: eating with not much talking,' D.D. Despite the large, genial head waiter's habit of telling us what we were about to order (Chicken Shashliks were doing a roaring trade, it seemed) we were finally allowed to choose for ourselves. Seated near the back stairs – the route to the kitchen – provided us with a fair measure of cabaret. The ordering system is to throw a copy of the chit down the stairs with a screech. It is collected by an unseen minion, and later is transferred into food, carried aloft up the stairs by a seen minion, complete with long white Marigold gloves, who silently waits until the head waiter takes these offerings from him. Time after time he appeared with a 2-foot-long Chicken Shashlik skewer in each hand. These were ceremoniously carried aloft by the maitre d' who proudly delivered them to the appropriate table. Also watching these proceedings was a well-dressed gentleman who spent his time preparing bills, raising his eyes to the heavens and from time to time muttering in our direction. I took him to be Mr Salahuddin himself. And what about the food? Meat predominates. Lamb and chicken is halal, of course, and, being the major part of Pakistani repertoire, the same applies at Saloos. Vegetarians be warned! There is a comprehensive tandoori section providing succulent, natural-coloured, divinely-flavoured offerings. Our lamb chop (£9.90) and Shami Kebab (£10.50) were both lean and melt-in-the-mouth. The Chicken Shashlik looked equally good. From the select range of main courses we chose the hard-to-find (but acquired taste) Hyderabadi dish – Haleem (£10.50) – pounded meat cooked with wheat, supplied complete with a DIY spice kit of chillies, ginger, garam masala and onion tarka, which you add yourself. It was, however, rather undefined in flavour. The Chicken Jalfrezi (£10.50) was the weak link, with too much ginger and rather stringy, overcooked chicken. The Pullao Rice (£3.95) was superb and definitive. Aloo Paratha (£3.90) was fantastic. It is essential to book. The elegant Farizeh Salahuddin (daughter of the house – she can be heard out of hours on the answer machine) handles bookings with considerable aplomb. Our bill for two with an aperitif, wine, starter, main course and coffee came to £100, including a cover charge of £1.50 and 15% service charge, which makes it probably the most expensive Pakistani, Indian or Bangladeshi restaurant in the UK, if not the world. These are 1995 prices. *Time Out*'s Guy Dimond tells of a 30% price rise on some items! Perhaps it is here that Gerald Campion should do his cost analysis (*see* introduction). The place is a bizarre institution and is worth at least one visit. Open: Monday to Saturday, noon-2.30p.m. and 7-11.45p.m. We pondered whether it should remain in our TOP 100, and decided it would, at least for now. What do you think?

WOODLANDS   √

37 Panton Street, SW1   ✆ 0171 930 8200

Long-established licensed, vegetarian, south Indian restaurant, one of three Woodlands in London and several in India. Just a cat's swing from the Haymarket Theatre, this one is the tiniest, though its decor has been changed to dappled green walls with Indian wall hangings. Surviving this upgrade are the 'rocky tables, and nasty music, forgivable for Woodlands' orgasmic food, and nearly forgivable for its 12½% service charge,' R.C. 'I particularly like southern Indian food, and find the menu so appealing, it makes choice difficult. We chose one exceptionally good-value set Thali (£6.50), which was quite generous, with good variety, and the Paper Dosa (£3.95). Upma (£2.95), Lhassi (£1.25) and Channa (£3.75) are as good as ever. Also glad to have a choice of Indian desserts. Good value,' H.C. Branches: London, W1; Wembley, Middlesex.

SW2

LANCER OF BENGAL   ⊞ ©

220 Brixton Hill, Brixton, SW2   © 0181 674 4736

Akal Ali's restaurant is a small place (40 seats), but it serves the formula curry (preceded by an 'exotic' cocktail) at reasonable prices. Home delivery also available.

SW3

SHAHEEN OF KNIGHTSBRIDGE   ©

225 Brompton Road, SW3   © 0171 581 5329

Formula curries right here on Brompton Road, not a chupatti throw from Harrods. Good Bangladeshi stuff from chef Mustafa Kamal, with one or two 'unusuals'. The Maahn Dal is a Gujarati special with black lentils, ginger, tomato and chillies, and Mango Lassi is a favourite with some. Despite being prone to tourists, and therefore more expensive than average (£35 average per head, with drink, service and cover charges), it is competent and friendly, and owner A.K. Trehan will give a discount to Curry Club members.

TANDOORI OF CHELSEA TOP 100

153 Fulham Road, Chelsea, SW3   © 0171 589 7617

This elegant basement restaurant quietly goes about its business without fanfare or hype. It is, and always has been since it opened in the 1960s, a leader in style, from its carefully selected small number of dishes to its decor and wine list. It is, of course, Indian, not Bangladeshi, and owned by A. Rajan, whose conversation with us amused many last time and is worth repeating (excuse the pun) and expanding: Should one drink lager with his food, I ask. 'Certainly not, spice and gas don't mix!' he explodes. 'Good wine does go with well-cooked Indian food. It is not overpowered by subtle spicing. That is why we have Chateau Latour on the menu.' 'How much?' say I. '£100 a bottle!' 'Who the heck can afford that?' 'Arabs,' he winks knowingly. 'An indisputably smart place, where dressing up is part of the fun,' says E.B.

The food is indeed subtly spiced, but the chefs will step up both spice levels and chilli heat if requested. Here is what one of our ace reporters (Mrs H.C.) says: 'I've walked by this restaurant dozens of times and always admired the Indian-dressed doorman and imagined the basement restaurant would be attractive. This week found ourselves driving right by at the right time, wanting a quick meal, and there was a parking space right outside, so took the opportunity to find out what the interior is like. Yes, it is very attractive, elegant Indian-style, and we were made very welcome in the totally empty restaurant. Other diners soon arrived, but it was never more than half-full, which seemed a shame for such a good restaurant. The food was superb, menu fairly limited, much less for a vegetarian than is usual in Indian restaurants. Every dish we had was marvellous, service was good, prices fair for the quality and area. We were very impressed.' The restaurant remains firmly in our TOP 100.

SW4 – Clapham

BENGAL TANDOORI AND BALTI HOUSE
NEW ENTRANT   ©

31 Clapham Park Road,
Clapham Common, SW4   © 0171 622 3332

Enamul Kabir and A. Begum's new (1996) venture does the formula and the Baltis well, we hear. Price check: Papadom 45p, CTM £5.65, Murghi Khass Masala £6.95, Pullao Rice £1.65. Minimum charge £7.95. Evenings only.

GOLDEN CURRY TANDOORI

131 Clapham High Street, SW4   © 0171 720 9558

Just a newcomer compared to the Maharani (*see* below), it only opened in 1971. Joking aside, it's a pleasure to welcome Abdur Choudury's long-standing, good, formula, Bangladeshi curry house back to the Guide. Chef Siraze Ahamed has some Indo-French specials up his sleeve (£6.25-£8.95). Tell us about them, please. Price check: Papadom 55p, CTM £5.50, Pullao Rice £1.75.

MAHARANI

| 117 High Street, Clapham, SW4 | ✆ 0171 622 2530 |

I was asked recently by a television company to present a zero-budget, 30-minute programme, on the growth of the Indian restaurant in Britain, for the Foreign Office, no less, for screening in the Third World. The producer wanted me to tell the story in a very long-established suburban curry house. The Maharani immediately came to mind. It was established in 1958, at which time there were under 200 curry houses in the whole of the UK. It was not only Clapham's first curry house, opened long before Clapham became trendy, it was one of the first to open in a London suburb. It has always earned its keep by providing good, bog-standard, formula curries; indeed, owner S.U. Khan was one of the pioneers of the formula. Under the same ownership for all these years, Khan has kept up with the trends, though, and everything is as it should be. Branches: Maharani, NW4; Sonargaon, SW9; Taste of India, 334 Kennington Road, SE11.

SW5

EARLS COURT TANDOORI

| 275 Old Brompton Road, SW5 | ✆ 0171 370 3366 |

What happened to the Bharat, in the last Guide, you asked? Answer: it changed its name and didn't tell us — so out it went! Naughty old owner Abu Shidullah still hasn't told us, but we have ways! And you like his place, you tell us, so here it is with its, by now, not so new name. The clue is still on the menu. It offers Bharat Specials, including the Kuku. By the way, Abu used to offer £100 if his diners could tell him the precise geographic location of his recipes. My answer would be Earls Court, but I never did find out whether anyone got paid or not. Please tell me for next time. Or whether they still do it. Sounds Kuku to me! What, you want an explanation? All right then - it's chicken with chilli, tomato and cucumber.

NIZAM   ©

**152 Old Brompton Road,
South Kensington, SW5**   ✆ **0171 373 0024**

M. Mian's Nizam (Nizam was the former ruler of Hyderabad, once
the richest man in the world) is indeed a small (62 seats) but smart
place, 1989 vintage, with cool bamboo and plant 'outdoor' light-and-
airy, green-carpeted decor. ('Don't forget the bird paintings, Pat,' said
a reporter – OK, remembered!) The service is said to be exemplary,
with smartly waistcoated waiters, exuding expertise, but we spot a
change of manager (to Michael Hopkins). The food is still carefully
executed by new chef M. Riaz's good cooking. Reports welcomed on
both changes. Price check: Papadom 60p, CTM £7.95, Hyderabadi
Lamb £7.95, Pullao Rice £2.50. Cover charge £1.

STAR OF INDIA   NEW TO OUR TOP 100

**154 Old Brompton Road,
South Kensington, SW5**   ✆ **0171 373 2901**

I've got a bone to pick with owner Reza Mohammed. (He doesn't
know this, but I remember him when he was a schoolboy and I was a
regular at his family's Shah of India in Drummond Street – the fourth
London curry house, from about 1950, sadly long gone.) But the Star
was established as the Shah's young offspring (in 1959) and I regularly
ate at both venues in those early days. The redec, now some years old,
still has everyone talking, and we continue to get comments about the
murals, the stars, the lighting, the flora and the prices – above all, the
prices. No one talks louder or more profusely than Reza himself, so
I'll let him carry the can. 'Such luxury doesn't come cheap,' he says.
'What do you expect for the Sistine Chapel directed by Zeffirelli?'
And, as he says the 94 seats are always occupied (booking essential),
we assume Reza's investment has been amply repaid. And even if allu-
sions to Michelangelo are somewhat overstated, so what? We loudly
applaud such theatre. Dining out is supposed to be fun and escapist.
But what of the food? The cooking by chef Vineet Bahtia is a far cry
from those early formula days, good though they were. Dishes are indi-
vidually and carefully spiced, from Raan to Roti, and Baigan to Biriani.
But the formula still lurks there with CTM and other such dishes.
They're fine, but our advice is to choose the unusual. The Patrani

Maachli (pomfret with coriander wrapped in banana leaf), and the red mullet, red chilli variant are superb, with the smoky-tasting Baingan-e-Bahar (aubergine stuffed with paneer and spiced with curry leaf, mustard and sesame), an unmissable signature dish. Reza's £1 cover charge per person is irksome, particularly when the bill will average £30 plus, with drinks. But that's not the reason for picking my bone. It's well worth the visit, and the expense, and I am delighted to promote the Star into our TOP 100. No, talking about carrying the can, as I was above, is what my bone is about. Having recommended the Star to BBC-TV, as a suitable, true Indian venue at which to film their *Good Food* programme (it has screened my recipes in the past), Reza then proceeded to pour scorn on the whole Balti concept. 'It doesn't exist,' he insisted. 'It's all rubbish. Balti just means a bucket in Hindi!' And to prove it, he produced his well-used floor mop bucket with one hand while, with the other, he fanned overheated presenter Pete Macarthy (such people can never stand the heat of the kitchen!) with a papadom. Very funny, Reza. But I've got news for you. I've got some chaps who tell me they can't wait to meet you. The lads from Mirpur and Pakistan's Kashmir, a.k.a. Baltistan, now operating the Balti houses in Birmingham's Sparkbrook, were not amused, and they invite you to go there to eat your words, and their food, if not your floor bucket. I'll come too. Indeed, I'll pay your rail fare. Watch this space, folks!

SW6

THE BLUE ELEPHANT TOP 100

4-6 Fulham Broadway, SW6   ℂ 0171 386 6595

No one seems to mind, in a Guide as idiosyncratic as mine, that I delve off into Thai restaurants now and again. I'd do more, if I had more space, actually. Well, not quite everyone doesn't mind. I did get a 10 page dirge, from some git, asking why I wasted valuable space on such things, and saying that Thai food had nothing to do with Indian food, nor curry, and that he hated Thai food, and would never eat it, nor could he ever afford to go to such restaurants as the Elephant, and what did I know about Thai food anyway? (And that was *after* my Thai Cookbook was published!) Oh deary me and dreary he! Why can't I get 'Disgusted of Tunbridge Wells', whose 'why, oh whys' are written in

Parker copperplate, on crisp, perfumed, bond paper, with embossed address, and which come in a well-fitting, self-seal envelope, which is a pleasure to open – or is that just for Radio 4? No, I get 'Anarack of Acton', whose illegible, smudged scrawl covers several thin, curry-stained pages, stuffed into the smallest brown envelope he can find, which glues itself to the paper and tears the letter apart when opened, making reading it a two-hour chore – or it would have been if I'd read past line 10! Of course it went in the bin, and that's the end of another great relationship (I hope!).

OK, so Thai curries are quite different from Indian, though there is Indian influence in the south of Thailand, and Burmese in the north. Read my book for more – I've got to plug it somewhere! Alternatively, visit the country or, since that is a bit extreme, visit the best Thai restaurant in the UK. The frontage is fairly nondescript, with its blue neon competing with that of the pub next door. Go inside and you get a warm welcome from the hosts and hostesses in national costume. There's a bar and a cloakroom, and some tables. Nothing out of the ordinary here but, when you book, insist on being seated further in. Because it is then that you realize this is no ordinary place. Ahead of you is the jungle: literally hundreds of strategically-placed plants. Bamboo on the walls and ceiling, and pagodas transport you at once from Fulham to Phuket. And just when you think you've seen it all, you realize there's more. The restaurant goes on and on. Small bridges traverse ponds, inhabited by huge golden carp and lilies. Waterfalls tinkle gently down. So does your small change if you want a lucky wish. The perfumes from exotic flowers fill the air. Little Thai houses surround the walls, and different dining areas have different characteristics. Some are secluded, some communal. Yet despite being gigantic (it has a massive 250 covers) one is simply not aware of its size and it somehow manages to retain a feeling of intimacy. The blue elephant motif appears again and again – in the carpets, in the tablecloths, on the crockery, in the display cabinet among items for sale and on the menu.

What of the menu? Well, there are two, actually (three, if you count the wine list). One is the main menu, the other is the vegetarian menu. The main menu contains seventeen starters, five soups and thirty-four meat, chicken, duck and seafood dishes. Chilli heat is indicated by elephant symbols (three for hottest) on the menu, and there are a number of Thai curry dishes. For those who like to try a wide range of dishes, the Banquet for £27 without soup, £30 with, provides a massive selection of dishes although you need a large party to take advantage of this. Smaller groups, even singles, can sample a selection of starters and main-course dishes by ordering Pearls and Royal Platter. The Blue Elephant flies in fresh produce every week. Ingredients such as lemon grass, aubergines, green peppers, chillies, holy basil and banana leaves (they make disposable doilies from them), orchids and galingale combine to produce those memorable Thai fragrances. And flying in their own food ensures a freshness unmatched in rival Thai restaurants. Portions are more than ample. Service is gracious, smiling and accurate. Don't forget to book – it is always full. Parking is nigh on impossible so go by taxi. (It's opposite the Tube, but if you can't afford a taxi you might as well forget the Blue Elephant.) It's a top-price restaurant (for Indo-Thai that is, but still much less than Roux/Little/Hilton-type places). Expect to pay between £30 and £50 per head depending on how lavish your extras are, and that may not include the 15% service charge and £1.50 cover charge. If you want to carp about that, do it to the carp at the restaurant, not me! The food at the Blue Elephant is spot on, and since even three elephants is nowhere near as hot as you'd get in Bangkok, you only have to ask! The place has become an institution. For two or three hours you can escape from the world in here. It is fun and it is theatre. What more can one ask? Remains very high in our TOP 100. Indian branch: La Porte des Indes, w1.

THE EAST INDIAN RESTAURANT
NEW ENTRANT   ©

448 Fulham Road, SW6   ℂ **0171 381 2588.**

I think this was Fulham's first curry restaurant, est. 1962? And I've had my knuckles rapped for not entering it before. Ouch! Anyone trading that long knows what they're doing. Therefore, owner Habibur Rahman won't mind me saying that he's an old hand at the game. Everything smacks of it. The right formula things are here on the menu, even the spelling is 100% (so often a giveaway with the new boys). Chef Islam's cooking is 100% too, so go there and enjoy curry house cooking as it should be. Price check: Papadom 50p, CTM £6.25, Bhaja Mas (trout) £6.95, Pullao Rice £1.95. Minimum charge £9. Branch: Modern Tandoori, Stanley Road, Teddington.

MAMTA   √

692 Fulham Road, SW6   ✆ 0171 736 5914

A Gujarati vegetarian restaurant is a rarity in Fulham. Gujarati food is
based on yoghurt and gram flour, and is sweetish and quite bland and,
frankly, not to everyone's taste. And I don't just mean Brits who adore
the Bangladeshi formula. One of my Punjabi friends gets withdrawal
symptoms if expected to eat it, and not just because he's an inveterate
meat-eater – he simply finds it too bland. So if it's new to you, try it
all from the starters onwards, and enjoy the results, served on a Thali.
Ask for advice from the helpful staff and, above all, tell them to spice
it up, if that's how you like it – they're not mind-readers!

NAYAB   ©

309 New Kings Road, SW6   ✆ 0171 731 6993

We've remarked before that owner Praveen Rai is quite a wag. He'll
regale you with many a tale about his travels and his ability, both of
which, according to him, are boundless. 'There isn't a chef in India, or
indeed in Britain,' he claims, 'whose particular talents are safe from my
scrutiny.' His really quite up-market menu is full of 'some dishes you
won't recognize and some that you will'. The former include Masha –
onion skins filled with spiced cabbage, celery and black-eyed beans –
Baked Squid, and Meat Dhaba Wala Lamb cooked in bone marrow
stock and mince (ask Rai to tell you about this). A substantial quota
of interesting vegetable dishes is also on offer. If you like it hot, there
is Lasooni Lamb Rara (sharp and hot) and Hot Legs, devilled chick-
en drumsticks, but for heaven's sake don't order a Phal. Mr Rai's menu
tells us it comes from the Hindi phrase 'Bhund Phar', which, put delicately, as if Rai would, means 'bottom-ripping', and was 'invented by
chefs as a revenge against the lager lout', and he'd never serve it! Be that
as it may, chilli is addictive and adored by myself and many of my
Indian friends, so if you like it hot, as Praveen himself does, then ask
for it hot! Manager Ms N. Kapre (Naz) handles all Rai's exuberance
with grace and efficiency, making the Nayab a popular place.

TIFFIN

541a Kings Road, Chelsea, SW6   © 0171 610 6117

Tiffin is billed as the world's first 'Indian Tapas Bar and Brasserie'. It is designed to appeal to the Chelsea set. Tiffin came to mean lunch in the Raj, but the word derived from the verb, to tiff, meaning to sip. And there is a satisfying list of soft drinks including several lassis and Nimboo Pani – fresh lime and soda (try it with salt!) – and alcoholic beverages amongst which are various Indian beers. Indeed, on the one occasion I dined here, it was a coincidental meeting of the Indian brewery clans. I went with the owner of Cobra, only to find the head of La Toofan and the Kingfisher London rep already ensconced in a tête à tête. They graciously dropped their private conversation and invited us to join them, and much fun was had over a splendid beery (all types) lunch, at which the owner brought us a wide range of items from the menu. Snacks (tiffins) from the tandoor as well as old favourites such as samosas. Choley Garam is unusual – it is a Punjabi hawkers' dish with chick peas in a spicy sauce, served piping hot on a dried leaf plate. The à la carte selection of main courses is small but has a good selection of chicken, meat and fish curries. Of course, the best such occasions are always made better by good company, but this is a good watering hole at any time.

SW7 – Kensington

BOMBAY BRASSERIE   TOP 100

**Courtfield Close, Courtfield Road,
Kensington, SW7**   © 0171 370 4040

Despite talk of new openings, the Bombay Brasserie is still, amazingly, the Taj Hotel Group's only UK Indian restaurant. It opened in 1982, as an experiment. It was the brainchild of Taj director Camelia Panjabi, who explains: 'I wanted to launch regional Indian cuisine in England – home-style Bombay dishes such as Patrani Macchli, fish with green chutney, baked in a banana leaf, and streetside food. Sev Batata Puri for starters, and regional main-course dishes, such as Parsee Jardaloo Sali Boti, lamb cooked with apricot, and garnished with potato straws.' But such a venture in 1982 was by no means a safe bet. By coincidence, it was the year in which I founded the Curry Club, so I know with certainty that there were then 3500 'Indian' restaurants, and though the market was beginning to grow, there were some who felt London was already saturated. The B.B., in its out-of-the-way location, they felt, would not succeed. In those days I was too low on the Indian food chain to receive an invite to that glittering, star-studded opening night, but I soon went there and found it to be as good as the best Taj hotels in India. True to the vision, the B.B. cooking was, and still is, shared by specialist chefs from Goa, and elsewhere, doing their own regional thing. Camelia's story can be read in her book *50 Great Curries*. The current exec. chef, Udit Sharkel, has also recently written his own book, *The Bombay Brasserie Cookbook*, which, curiously, avoids any mention of Camelia in its history, though its 100-plus recipes give you B.B. cooking at home, should you want it. But the purpose of this entry is to persuade the newcomer to venture here and try Indian regional cooking that's as near to authentic as you can get out of the Indian home.

The dishes mentioned above, and many other similar authentic dishes, have remained on the menu all these years and are always in demand. It is the regional specialities that you should go for when you visit. Of course, the B.B. does some well-known Punjabi dishes too. Tikka, kebabs and tandoori come luscious and succulent and devoid of artificial food colouring. Familiar main courses include Rogan Josh, Chicken Tikka Makhani and Biriani. There are plenty of vegetarian choices and several set-meal Thalis.

In its first decade, we used to get three good reports to every bad one. The problem was that diners were quite unprepared for the difference, as explained above. Since the last Guide, though, we have had no complaints at all, which is heartening. S.T. says: 'This restaurant never fails to delight. It's pricier than many, but worth every penny for the uniqueness, quality, service and ambience. It's a special occasion place for me, but I'd be a regular if I could afford it! – the bill for the Sunday eat-your-fill buffet with wine was £65 for two.' D.M. was: 'Impressed with the service from the moment I made a telephone reservation at short notice for 20 people in the conservatory, which Rashmi Bathia arranged for me with pleasure. Our group included many curry connoisseurs, anxious to sample the delights offered by the Curry Club's "numero uno". My reputation was on the line as a known member of the Club, within our circle.' [Ours too, Derek, I guess!] 'I need not have worried.' [Phew!] 'Everybody thoroughly enjoyed their meal, including the continuous supply of fresh naans, which led to one of our group earning the nickname Nine-Naan. We were particularly impressed by the concern expressed for the two children in our party. A specially mild chicken dish was freshly cooked and brought direct to our table. It's not expensive, considering the quality of the place, the food and the service.'

General Manager Adi Modi tells me that he is currently having to turn up to 80 people away every night. That's 29,000 covers a year! So booking well ahead is essential, unless you're lucky. If you prefer the conservatory, ask for it when booking. To lessen disappointment, plans are afoot to add another 80 seats. Perhaps a more immediate, less costly, solution would be to close the weaker Chinese restaurant at St James Court Hotel and replace it with a second B.B.

The Bombay Brasserie, despite being a large machine, operates very smoothly with a very experienced team. It has the benefit of an even bigger operation and team in the form of its owners, the Taj Hotel Group. Despite the arrival of a good many new contenders on the Indian restaurant scene, none has quite managed to topple the B.B. from its position of excellence. And despite a close run from Chutney Mary, our previous Guide's overall winner, The Bombay Brasserie is at the top of our TOP 100.

CAFE LAZEEZ

23-29 Old Brompton Road,
Kensington, SW7   © **0171 581 9933**

Lazeez, meaning 'delicate and aromatic', describes itself as a 'new type of Indian restaurant'. It operates in true café mode, with unstopping opening hours between 11a.m. and 1a.m. (10.30p.m. Sunday). It has a striking frontage, with 26 outside seats in clement weather. Inside are 130 seats, on two floors. Downstairs in stark, minimalist surroundings, is a short-menu café (which changes to full menu after 7p.m.). Upstairs is decorated with an illuminated, white, tented roof, and a full menu. In fact its director of cuisine and owners are Pakistani, in the persons of the elegant Ms Sabiha Kasim and her brother Zahid. I was recently invited to come here by *Tandoori Magazine* for a Korma taste-test, with the magazine editor, Iqbal Wahhab, whose family hail from Bangladesh; Chutney Mary boss, Namita Panjabi, from Bombay;

Sabiha, from Lahore; and myself, a Londoner, born and bred, with six generations of Raj behind me – a truly international curry committee! The outcome of this irrelevant story is that we sampled five factory products, all worthy of the bin, with an excess of tomato and/or coconut, plus one home-made dish. We did not know which was which until afterwards but, not surprisingly, the home-made version won hands down. It was, as you might by now have guessed, cooked by Café Lazeez, and was mild, aromatic lamb marinated in yoghurt, with a generous, but very subtle, aromatic spicing, including a hint of garam masala. This is the true Mogul classic Korma, alive and well in the Pakistani heartlands, and at Lazeez. The point I am making is that Café Lazeez suffers criticism because its dishes try to be one of two things, authentic or evolved. Nothing wrong with either aspiration, but somehow the result just isn't quite right. We have mixed reports, though one totally reliable reporter, H.C., glows: 'Spicing different, and not necessarily Indian. A good place to take people who say they don't like Indian food. Succulent prawns, sizzling lamb chops, well-spiced vegetables, rich and creamy Korma, Lamb Sag, not enough lamb, but good flavour, Saffron Rice fantastic, firm, fresh and spicy mushrooms, star dish, aubergine – superb – and the Naan, small, round, lightest and crispest I've had. Expensive, but first class. Overall, a wonderful meal.' It's a lively place, with useful hours, and if Ms Kasim would kick-start the kitchens, it could be great. Average snack price £6, meal price £30, incl. service and cover charge.

DELHI BRASSERIE   ©

134 Cromwell Road,
South Kensington, SW7   ✆ 0171 370 7617

Opened in 1986 and now well-established and popular, this 60-seater is unusual for the area in that it's open all day, from noon-11.30p.m. Owner Mr A. Jabber says 'pop in when you've done your shopping' (it's near Sainsbury's). Chef Ram Singh's food is 'particularly tasty', says G.H. And manager K. Choudhury gives a discount to Curry Club members. Branch: London W1.

KHAN'S OF KENSINGTON

3 Harrington Road,
South Kensington, SW7   ℭ 0171 584 4114

Please don't forget to say 'of Kensington' this time, said the manager,
so I haven't. He went on: 'We are nothing to do with the one in W2.'
OK, sir, point made! Attractive pastel pinks and greens in the decor,
60 seats, and the waistcoats, make it 'Indian in a modern way. We were
made very welcome, and all the food was above average and prices very
reasonable for central London,' D.R.C. Plenty for veggies, though the
rarely-found south Indian meat dish, Narial Gosht (lamb in coconut),
and Machli Gowala (pomfret), are highlighted. Try them! Set lunch £8,
dinner from £12.

KWALITY   ©

38 Thurloe Place, SW7   ℭ 0171 589 3663

Sultan Khan's Kwality has been in operation since 1984. 'In appearance,
very old-fashioned, typical flock wallpaper, standard Indian restaurant
china, but we were pleasantly surprised. We were made very welcome
and the service from start to finish was efficient, professional and very
friendly. All the food, by chef Gafur, was above average. Gulab Jamun,
fine. Good to see it on the menu, one of my grumbles is the shortage
of Indian sweets in Indian restaurants; a selection of international-
style ice creams is a lazy way out,' reports D.R.C.

MEMORIES OF INDIA

18 Gloucester Road, SW7   ℭ 0171 589 6450

Back after one absence from our Guide. H.C. is a regular, but 'for heav-
en's sake, why the open credit card voucher, when service has already
been applied to a £75 bill for two?'

MOTI MAHAL

3 Glendower Place,
South Kensington, SW7   ℭ 0171 584 8428

An old hand, established in 1956, and it knows its business, serving,
according to D.R.C., 'food ranging from very good to excellent'.

SHEZAN   ©

16-22 Cheval Place, Knightsbridge, SW7   © 0171 584 9316

This 1966 Pakistani restaurant, in the street opposite the world's number one store, is easy to find. We left it out of the Guide last time but a change of ownership (to M. Piracha) has put it back in, because we believe an effort is being made, and it needed it. The downstairs 120-seat dining room, past the bar, is still elegantly simple, with its down-lighters, pewter plates and candlelight. Chef Khan's food is sophisticated. The service is equally sophisticated, to match the prices, which *are* Knightsbridge, but are you sitting comfortably? Price check: Papadom free, CTM (sorry, Makhni) £11.75, Karahi Kebab £12.75, Pullao Rice £4.50. Set lunch £12.95. Minimum charge dinner £25. Service charge 10%. Cover charge £1.50.

SW8

BIRAJ   ©

266 Wandsworth Road, SW8   © 0171 622 0455

Formerly the Wandsworth Tandoori, now the Biraj, it is open 6p.m.-midnight, closed Tuesdays. This reflects the fact that it is family-(Choudhury) run, and we hear of fresh home-style cooking and satisfied locals.

QUEEN'S STAR   ©

39 Queenstown Road, SW8   © 0171 622 7228

Established in 1980 and recently refurbished. Mr M. Tafader's restaurant has a comprehensive menu selection, with all your favourites, including Baltis, at realistic prices.

©	Curry Club discount (see p. 607)	🍵	Unlicensed
√	Vegetarian	🏠	Home delivery
BYO	Bring your own alcohol		service available

SW9

OLD CALCUTTA   ©

64a Brixton Road, Oval, SW9   ✆ 0171 582 1415

Owned and managed by Mrs Syed and Rafia Khatun, this restaurant is good value (try the cheap set meals) and enterprising (ask to see the publicity about Bishop Tutu among others). The wide-ranging menu serves Balti among many favourites. The restaurant will give a 10% discount to Curry Club members on takeaways.

SONARGAON   ©

260 Brixton Road, Brixton, SW9   ✆ 0171 274 5422

Named after one of Bangladesh's ancient cities, the Sonargaon is in the same ownership (Karim, Khan and Islam) as the Maharani in sw4 and nw4 and Taste of India, 334 Kennington Road, se11. Such a pedigree ensures good quality. Price check: Papadom 40p, CTM £4.50, Balti Ayre £6.95, Pullao Rice £4.50. Set lunch £3.50, dinner £5.50. Minimum charge dinner £6. Cover charge 50p.

SW10 – Chelsea

CHUTNEY MARY TOP 100

535 Kings Road, Chelsea, SW10   ✆ 0171 351 3113

It was this Guide that first nominated Chutney Mary as the number one Indian restaurant in Britain. I now have to own up that, at the time, this was a risk for me, and it ran against the tide. 'Why there? Haven't you been to the B.B. [Bombay Brasserie] or Saloos, or the Lahore Kebab House?' some of my Indian friends quipped, going on: 'Who wants to eat Anglo-Indian anyway? Got enough of that at school.' I got flack from the B.B., too. Dear Adi was not pleased – why, I don't know, when he was already fuller than full, and turning away 29,000 covers a year. Then I got flak from the Brits, at least those who expected formula Phal, and I got the usual 'too expensive' snipes. But I did get a champagne thank you from Namita, and she won't mind me saying that our accolade did help to transform C.M. from struggling to prof-

itable, and from half-empty to full-to-bursting. I'm delighted. The
more so because now my newer Indian friends ask me whether I've
tried Chutney Mary. 'It's so good, my dear!' Yes, it is, and now, so say
all of us Guides (except the sniffy G.F.G., which has noticed the B.B.
but remains obdurately blind to C.M. – ah me!) But all I did was my
job. I simply pointed everyone in the right direction. The restaurant
did the rest. I well remember Harold Pendleton, the founder of the
Marquee Club, claiming that, without him, the Rolling Stones and the
Who would never have become noticed, let alone world stars. True, he
did put them on the bill, early on in their career (for next to no money,
of course). But he did not create their talent! And he did not 'make'
their careers. But try telling him that – ask Mick Jagger! Chutney Mary
was the same. With the talent, drive and persistence of its prime mover,
now owner, Namita Panjabi, it was bound to succeed.

The front-of-house team, under General Manager Joe Mirrelson
(ex-Dorchester) and his very highly trained Indian team, have maintained a consistency of service for three years now, and Chutney Mary
is maybe even better since it went its own way from the Chez
Gerard/Bertorelli group. The place is easy enough to find, though it's
not near a Tube, so it's taxi, bike or shanks. Parking is iffy, but worth
a try. The decor is theatrical, with its Raj-style upstairs bar and short
snack tiffin menu. Count the brass cobra lamp stands – a grand apiece
from up-the-street Christopher Wray. Downstairs is gorgeous with its
murals, Indian props and conservatory. And the food? The menu is a
brief document. Nothing on it resembles formula curry house, of
course, but I believe most diners are aware of that. Chutney Mary still
alludes to being the first Anglo-Indian restaurant – indeed, I believe it
remains the only such establishment. And true, there is Kedgeree,
Country Captain and Bangalore Sausage and Mash, which my late
grandmother may or may not have been familiar with in her days in
the Raj. But that's about it. Chef Hardev Singh Bhatty and his brigade
of five chefs are very much Indian, and so is their food. And very talented they are, made all the better by the strictest quality control I
know, namely chefs face to face for a Namita kitchen taste whenever
she feels like it. 'Anyway, it's my local, so I expect it to be good', she
told me. 'Why own a restaurant if you don't dine in it?' And dine she
does, in the company of her co-owner husband Ranjit on occasions or,
on others, with friends ranging from maharaja to merchant banker.
Says A.J.M.: 'The food was good and extremely well presented, it was

difficult to compare the food with the normal local "curry house" because it would be like comparing good pub grub to the Ritz. Both are excellent in their own right. The prices are far more expensive than you normally pay (about £35 a head) but you get what you pay for!' 'A lovely restaurant, in an unimpressive location. When I booked, I asked for a larger table, for two. They told me they'd try, but couldn't promise. When we arrived, we were shown to a table for four, laid for two, in the main dining room, even though they were busy. The waiter joked that we'd have to eat twice as much! I couldn't fault the restaurant, food or service, but there was something missing from the overall experience. Maybe, like you say, we all expect just too much,' admits P.J. 'The only one, in my view, and that of many Indians, that is so professional, and maintains high standards,' M.A. Acceptance by the Indian community proves that the food is as close to Indian home cooking as you could get in any restaurant. Go for the aptly named Grand Sunday Buffet for best value, or for the food festivals that Namita stages from time to time. But I'm not promoting C.M. back to its number-one place, though it is as equally deserving of it as the B.B. Why? Because I've got another punt to take elsewhere and, believe it or not, I think Namita will be pleased. Oh, and just in case your visit to the toilet mystifies you, a Pickle John was the derogatory, arrogant term bestowed by both snooty Brits and Indians upon young Indian men who dared to wear western clothes and adopt western attitudes in the 1920s and 1930s Raj. The equivalent female was called a Chutney Mary! Pretty apt, really. This restaurant dared do its thing, and it won.

EXOTIKKA OF INDIA   NEW ENTRANT   ©

35 Stadium Street, SW10   🕾 0171 376 7542

Someone had to think of the name! And it may as well be owners Hye and Hussain. Competent formula Bangladeshi curries. Price check: Papadom 40p, CTM £5.50, Pullao Rice £1.75. Set lunch £6.95. Evenings only.

VAMA – THE INDIAN ROOM   NEW ENTRANT

438 Kings Road, London SW10   🕾 0171 351 4118

Look out for the newly-opened Vama – The Indian Room, a seriously cool new restaurant sandwiched between Conran's Bluebird on one side and Chutney Mary on the other. Slick design is matched by a clever menu which specializes in grills. Starters include Murgh Malai Kebab and Rustami Khumb Bahar – amazingly tasty tandoori mushrooms. Main courses to look out for include an aromatic Handi Gosht Biryani and Bhindi Bhoj Puri – crispy fried bhindi flavoured with dried mango powder. Open daily noon-3.30p.m. and 6-11.30p.m.

SW11 – Battersea

BALTI HOUSE

76 Northcote Road, SW11   **✆ 0171 924 2347**

Free bottle of wine with every takeaway over £15. What a great deal. Go and take them up on their offer!

BANGLES   NEW ENTRANT   √

124 Northcote Road, SW11   **✆ 0171 924 3566**

Mainly evening wine bar (lunches Saturday and Sunday) run by Kenyan Asians who put on Indian vegetarian snacks, misnamed vegan by one of our reporters. Vegan dishes there are, but vegans don't eat dairy products, such as the home-made, yoghurt-based, Garlic Lhassi (£1.25) – not the one to impress the boss with when you go for a pay rise!

BATTERSEA TANDOORI

515 Park Road, Battersea, SW11   **✆ 0171 585 0487**

'Fairly standard menu but the food is well cooked and always arrives at the table hot. Quantities are very generous and prices reasonable,' D.R.G.

BATTERSEA VILLAGE RICKSHAW

27-29 High Street, Battersea, SW11   **✆ 0171 924 2450**

'We were made welcome and service was efficient and professional. Standard menu with fair prices. Very light and crispy Onion Bhaji. Absolutely wonderful Chicken Makhani. Had to try the Kadu –

pumpkin – very good. One of the best Mutter Panir, very creamy and rich, superb. Chef very heavy-handed with the lurid red colouring,' D.C.

PANAHAR

184 Lavender Hill, SW11	✆ 0171 228 8947

'Quiet service, good menu range, very comfortable and attractive environment,' P.C.

THE RAJ PUTH   NEW ENTRANT   ©

135a St John's Hill, SW11	✆ 0171 228 9440

Ownership of this 1977 restaurant changed in 1995 to Mrs Olida Muhith, and management to M. Khan. We are now hearing of good Bangladeshi formula curries, with some interesting specials. Price check: Papadom 50p, CTM £5.70, Balti Vegetable £5.45, Tandoori Trout £6.95, Pullao Rice £1.60. Set lunch £6.95. Evenings only.

SW12

BOMBAY BICYCLE CLUB

95 Nightingale Lane, SW12	✆ 0181 673 6217

Flamboyant name, nice room, colonial Raj-style, well-liked by its loyal locals, to whom B.B.C. does not mean 'auntie'. Actually, its name is meant to evoke some kind of nostalgia in people who never sampled the snobbish attitudes that abounded for those clubs of yore that the Raj were prone to joining. Actually, my grandpa preferred riding a bike when they became army issue in Edwardian India, because he reckoned they were 'servant-free'. The army didn't agree when he became a senior officer, and so he was obliged to ride in a horse-drawn trap, requiring two servants to operate it. The B.B.C.'s been around for more than a decade, so why in one Guide and out the next? asked one of the locals (G.R.). Because no one wrote in, including the B.B.C., that's why, so on your bike! Maybe the locals really do want it kept as a secret club for themselves. Anyway, not any more. It's back! We're told by several that it's good and, yes, there is Mulligatawny Soup, but better to try the

Tellicherri Squid – a kind of Calimares Fritos-con-spice! (£4.75) – to start. Short menu includes reliable tandoor and curry items, but go for the unusual. The kitchen brigade is Nepalese, where spicing is light, so ask the cosmopolitan waiting staff for extra spice, if that's your choice. s.n. and r.a. booked the function room for a party and heartily recommend it. r.s. finds 'food so exquisitely spiced, clean, delicate flavours, and good ingredients. It never fails to delight,' he says. He also wants it promoted to our TOP 100. What do you think?

TABAQ NEW TO OUR TOP 100 BEST PAKISTANI   ©

---

47 Balham Hill, Balham, SW12   ℂ **0181 673 7820**

I hang my head in shame and in disgust with myself over the Tabaq. This is an absolute gem of a restaurant, and it is a rarity in Balham, let alone the UK. Why? Because it is Pakistani, and the food is really exquisite. And why my emotions? Because, somehow, half the Tabaq entry got wiped last time, and all we were left with was a complaint by a really sniffy doctor (T.M.B.). Can anyone tell me why medical doctors are such complainers? No, really, I get more complaints from doctors than anyone else. And they really must tell you that they are a doctor. Who cares? I want your views, good or bad, but I really don't give a damn if you're a drag artist or the dustman! But no, Dr is underlined by some of these characters, as if they believe that gives them extra authority. Perhaps my friend Dr c.f. can answer (it will be published here). And he's no easy chap to satisfy. Maybe it's because doctors nearly always seem to visit Indian restaurants in herds (or is it droves of doctors?), with some drug company rep, whose mega-rich company picks up the tab. And groups, no matter how long they've been at school, are always a pain, the worse when they get a freebie! Anyway, back to the Tabaq. Owner M.M. Ahmed wrote me a steaming letter claiming that some of my 'didactically constructed' Guide entries amounted to 'verbal diarrhoea' (who, me, Mr Ahmed? More apt for those quacks, I think) and that he'd sue me for 'deformation' if I did not apologize. Not wanting to be sued for deformation (of the computer-operating finger, I presume, because I think I wiped the good comments by mistake), nor for defamation, I apologized then in our Curry Club Magazine, and apologize now. But it got results. We got a wealth of glowing reports, and none bad. Actually, there are two M. Ahmeds. Mushtaq, we've met. He is front-of-house manager. His domain consists of pale walls giving a spacious feel, enhanced by richly embroidered tapestries of rural Lahore, and tables with pink cloths, around which are just 50 seats, so booking is necessary. The other Ahmed, his brother Manoor, is head chef, and the culinary magic emanates from him and his brigade. But don't expect quick food from him. He cooks everything freshly, and a 30-minute wait is not uncommon. The menu is pure Lahore – which means meat – the tandoor items are well spoken of. Try the Masala Machli Lahori – robustly spiced white fish – or the Quail Masala or Baby Chicken Tabaq. The daring will go for liver (but can no longer try that great Pakistani speciality, goat's brains, because it's now banned) and there are prawn and vegetable dishes too. Their Pullao Rice Masaledaar gets thumbs up. R.B. always makes a bee-line for it, often from miles away: 'I think it gives fair value for money … and fine quality. They really care about their cooking. My favourite is Gosht Ka Lazeez Masala.' C.H.C. loves the place too: 'They made us welcome.' Tabaq means large serving dish. And if you want to stage something really spectacular for your well-behaved party (of non-doctors!), order (in advance, of course) a whole baby lamb, cooked Raan-style, or even a leg or two. Hours: 6p.m.-midnight. Deservedly promoted to our TOP 100. Price check: Papadom 60p, CTM £6.50, Pullao Rice £2.75. Set lunch £6.95. Closed Sundays.

SW13 – Barnes

HAWELI TOP 100   ©

7 White Hart Lane, Barnes, SW13   ℭ **0181 876 4441**

Manju Choudhury is an energetic Bangladeshi entrepreneur, whose Haweli chain (*see* below) has been an inspiration and an example to all in the trade. From just one restaurant, he has expanded it, with the help of his extended family, to nine, and all do really excellent food with good service. Keeping it in the family helps, but so does the fact that Manju likes nothing better than hands-on cooking. In fact, the place where you are most likely to find him isn't here, the current flagship, but at his St Margarets, Twickenham, takeaway-only branch. 'It's much harder to do takeaway,' he says. 'It's faster, and it keeps you on the go for hours, non-stop.' I make no secret of the fact that I was commissioned by Manju to consult as a chef, cooking with Manju in the kitchens of this very branch. It was not the first time I have cheffed at Indian and Bangladeshi restaurants, but this was an exciting brief. Manju wanted unusual dishes. He had seen some in my cookbook, *250 Favourite Curries*, and he wanted, among other things, Balti. So together we worked out a new and exciting menu, then I trained the other chefs to use ingredients new to them. For example, Mirchwangi Korma is from Kashmir. There, a special root is used to achieve a dark red colour. Here, we use beetroot (not otherwise used in curry restaurants), with red chilli, capsicum and tomato, and it dispels the myth that all Kormas are mild! And the Harlyala Murgh is chicken, marinated with a coriander, spinach and mint purée, then baked. The Balti dishes available are herbal and aromatically spiced, and were not only the first in London but are correctly made, with specially roasted and ground spices, rather than that acidic horror paste, straight from a well-known manufacturer's bottle, as offered by most Bangladeshi restaurants. You tell us you like the Hawelis very much so, with my declaration of interest made, how could we not continue to give this restaurant a TOP 100 award? Haweli (meaning 'palace') gets very busy at the weekends so booking is advisable. Manager Nazrul (Nigel) Choudhury will give a discount to Curry Club members. Hours: 12.30-3p.m. and 6-11.30p.m. Haweli branches: Belmont; Epsom; New Malden; St Margarets, Middlesex (takeaway only); Surbiton; Sutton; Wallington; West Byfleet. Guru Express, 146 Fulham Road, sw6.

TANDOORI GRILL   ©

188 Castelnau, Barnes, SW13   © **0181 748 1515**

Regular, formula, competent curry house, with reasonable prices and no surprises. Branches: Sopna, 175 High Street, Hampton Hill, Middlesex; Bilas, 4 Broad Street, Teddington, Middlesex.

SW14

TASTE OF THE RAJ

130 Upper Richmond Road West, SW14   © **0181 876 8326**

A modern, up-market curry house, well above average, run by the articulate Shawkat Ahmed (call me Chris). 'The food came in delicious waves and the time went by easily,' P.C.

SW15 – Putney

BANGLADESH CURRY MAHAL   ©

29 Upper Richmond Road, Putney, SW15   © 0181 789 9763

Proprietor M. Nurul Islam's Mahal, or palace, is an old hand (1971), managed by Hasnath Chowdhury, and as such is popular for its no-frills, formula stuff at sensible prices. Price check: Papadom 45p, CTM £5.95, Goost Laziz £5.95, Pullao Rice £1.60. Branch: Putney Tandoori, 137 Lower Richmond Road, Putney, SW15.

GANGES   ©

205 Lower Richmond Road, Putney, SW15   © 0181 789 0357

A small and cosy restaurant seating 34 diners. Menu contains all your usual favourites such as Jalfrezi, Pasanda and Madras. Korahi (sic) dishes are also here. Owner and manager, Mr B. Ahmed, will give a discount to Curry Club members.

MA GOA   NEW TO OUR TOP 100

244 Upper Richmond Road, Putney, SW15   © 0181 780 1767

And now for something completely different. How would you like real home-cooked Goan food, cooked by the ubiquitous female chef, always called 'auntie'? (Even the B.B. [Bombay Brasserie] has an 'auntie' Goan chef — that's the way it is — the best are always women.) Well, at Ma Goa that's exactly what you get, only it's cooked by owner R. Kapoor's mum, not his auntie, so easy on the Ma Goa gags! It's a tiny place, 30 seats, with an extension dreamed of but not yet existing. Meanwhile it's the real stuff, and even Dr C.F. and his Goan doctor friends like it, so I take back a bit of what I said earlier about docs! Goan food is unique in India: with a largely Christian population, any meat goes and pork is the favourite. Try Chorizo, Goan chilli pork sausage, and, of course, chilli *aficionados* must try the Vindaloo. But this isn't the formula interpretation of standard curry gravy, with two spoons of chilli powder and a chunk of potato (aloo). This is the real thing, based on the dish Portuguese, Vinho d'alhos, or wine vinegar and garlic. In the Goan version, pork is marinated with the above and plenty of chillies. It is then slow-cooked, and that's that, with nary a potato in sight! Ma Goa serve it in traditional earthenware Handis. There are many other Goan delights, too numerous to list here. Specials are on the blackboard. Advice is forthcoming. If you ask for Goan heat, you'll get it hot! Meat, chicken, fish and veg are all authentic. There are even Goan puds. But a word of caution. Please be patient. This is not your wham-bam-and-thank-you-ma'am, multi-dish, rapid-fire curry house. Relax with their chilled Portuguese Vinho Verde, and nibble something while you wait for your order to be cooked. Think *manyana*, as they do in Goa, and plan your next holiday there. Before you can say 'goan, goan, gone', a super meal will be with you. 'Groan, groan, groan, Pat,' says fact-verifier D. MCK. 'and tomorrow is *tolice* in Portuguese.' Dinner only, Mondays to Saturdays, closed Sundays. A rarity deserving of our TOP 100 cachet.

MUNAL TANDOORI   NEW ENTRANT   ©

---

393 Upper Richmond Road,
Putney, SW15   ✆ 0181 876 3083

It's Nepalese, and although you'll find all your curry favourites here, try something different, such as Nepalese Chicken Bhutwa (£4.95). Ask owner-manager Khem Ranamagar for explanations, and enjoy chef Bijaya Thapa's good food. Price check: Papadom 40p, CTM £5.50, Pullao Rice £1.80. Set meal £7.95. Minimum charge £8. Evenings only.

PUTNEY TANDOORI

---

137 Lower Richmond Road,
Putney, SW15   ✆ 0181 788 4891

Proprietor Mr Ahmed runs a very good restaurant, serving competent curries to a famous local clientele which he'll delight in telling you about, given a chance.

SW16

ANARKALI BALTI HOUSE   ⊞ ©

229 Streatham High Road, SW16   © 0181 769 3012

'It had been some time since we had been to M. Miah's Anarkali and a takeaway menu popped through the door was enough to prompt us to order a delivery. The food standard was high and very tasty. Balti is on the menu,' S.N. and R.A.

MEMORIES OF INDIA

109 Mitcham Lane, SW16   © 0181 677 8756

A small and pleasant restaurant seating a cosy 36 diners, so booking is necessary at the weekends.

MIRCH MASALA   NEW ENTRANT   BYO

1416 London Road, SW16   © 0181 679 1828

Not far from Tooting (*see* SW17, below), Mirch Masala, meaning 'pepper mixture', is a good example of a London Balti house under another name, such as has dominated Southall for years. In this case I should say Wembley, because it is an offspring of the ever-popular Karahi King, where meat is king, cutlery is out, and BYO is in. Open kitchen cooking, with unusual Kenyan-Asian specials by owner Ali's brigade. Cassava chips (mogo) can substitute for papadoms, before you plough on into a wide selection of dechi (saucepan) or karahi dishes, kebabs and all the trimmings. Good veggie stuff, too. All at under a tenner, noon–midnight, Tuesdays to Sundays, closed Mondays. Some credit cards accepted.

SHAHEE BHEL POORI VEGAN   √ ©

145 London Road, Norbury, SW16   © 0181 679 6275

One of the few Indian restaurants to offer vegan food, and the delightful Bhel. Manager S.A. Rahim will give a discount to Curry Club members. Hours: noon–2.30p.m. and 6–11p.m.

SPICE COTTAGE

78 Streatham High Road,
Streatham, SW16   ✆ 0181 677 1719

Seating is divided over two floors. Hours: evenings only, Monday to
Saturday, 6p.m.-midnight, Sunday 5-11p.m. Price check: Papadom 50p,
CTM £5.80, King Prawn £9.90, Pullao Rice £1.60.

SW17 – Tooting

Over the last few years Tooting, and in particular Upper Tooting Road
(U.T.R.), has begun to come of age with regard to its Asian community. For years, the area has reflected the roots of its population, being
home to two of London's best south Indian restaurants – Kolam and
Sree Krishna – and one Sri Lankan, Jaffna House. More recently, there
have been Gujarati arrivals – Milan and Kastoori. These are great
havens for vegetarians. Sakoni at 204-208 U.T.R. must be the best
Asian veg shop in London and next door's Dadus, at 210 U.T.R., is one
of the best spice/grocery shops, of which more and more have opened
in the last few years, including several Sri Lankan specialists. Sweets
and samosa shops include Ambala at 48 U.T.R. and Alaudin at 98
U.T.R., with Royal beyond U.T.R. towards London. The most recent
arrivals include Muslim-Punjabi establishments, with halal meat shops
and Southall-style kebab restaurants, such as Handis, Lahore Karahi,
Masaledar at 121 U.T.R. and Garam Masala. As if that were not
enough choice, there are formula Bangladeshi curry houses of which
the pick is the Peacock. Nearby Nazim's has become a Balti house.
Unlike Southall, and now Wembley, parking has not yet reached
Sunday traffic-warden proportions but I fear it will soon happen.
Meanwhile, with such a wide diversity, U.T.R. is an evening car-park-
er's and all-day curryholic's paradise.

HANDIS   NEW ENTRANT

164 Upper Tooting Road, SW17   ✆ 0181 672 6037

It's a tiny (20 seats, bookable), licensed place, with on-view cooking
down one entire side. The Handi is a clay cooking pot, and dishes are
served either in this or in the karahi. c.t. loved it: 'The best Peshwari

Nan (£1.65) I've had, and an outstanding Chicken Zalfrezi (£5.50)
available dry or saucy, rich and fresh.' Price check: Papadom 30p, CTM
£4.50, Pullao Rice £2.50. Set lunch £6.95. From 4.30-11p.m. daily.

JAFFNA HOUSE   BYO

90 High Street, Tooting Broadway, SW17   ℂ 0181 672 7786

K. Sivalogarajah's Jaffna House built its name on its authentic Sri
Lankan dishes (and south Indian, too), with its different Friday,
Saturday and Sunday specials being particularly popular. It has recently added a range of tandoori items and north Indian curries to its
repertoire, about which we have yet to hear (please). Unlicensed, very
cheap, huge choice of good food, served noon-midnight, last sit-down
orders 11p.m. Cash preferred, cheques minimum £5. Some credit cards
accepted, minimum £15. Price check: Papadom 25p, CTM £4.25,
Mutton Kotthu £2.50, Masala Dosai £1.50, Pullao Rice £1.25.
Minimum charge £5.

KASTOORI

188 Upper Tooting Road, SW17   ℂ 0181 767 7027

Somehow Mr and Mrs Thanki's Kastoori was omitted from the last
Guide (sorry). Now it's back. This African-Asian family specialize in
both Gujarati and Kenyan vegetarian dishes. The former include Dahi
Vadas and Kadhi – yoghurt and besan sauce, with dumplings – and
Katia Wahd, a tomato-based curry. Karela Bharah is stuffed bitter
gourd. The Kenyan connection gives Cassava Chips, Kasodi – sweetcorn in a peanut and yoghurt-based sauce – and Matoki – plantain
curry. Dish of the day. Licensed. Average meal £12. Takes credit cards.
Dinner, but no lunch, on Mondays and Tuesdays. Open for lunch and
dinner all other days.

KOLAM   ©

58-60 Upper Tooting Road, SW17   ℂ 0181 767 2514

South Indian delights are the best options, in our opinion. Tamarind
Rice good. Things were quite slow when Dom and I went with Erik
on the day Harrison was born. There was only one other couple there,
and it took at least 15 minutes before anything happened, but that's just

the pace of things in south India, of which it reminded us greatly. Patience will reward you with a good inexpensive meal, and manager S. Rajakumar will give a discount to Curry Club members. Dinner, but no lunch, on Mondays. Open for lunch and dinner all other days. Price check: Papadom 40p, CTM £4.25, Pullao Rice £1.75, Veg Thali £17.90, Non-Veg Thali £19.50. Set lunch £4. Average meal £10. Credit cards accepted, and it's licensed.

LAHORE KARAHI NEW ENTRANT   BYO

1 High Street, Tooting Broadway, SW17   ⓒ **0181 767 2477**

At last, a Karahi house in Tooting! It's been open since late 1995 and was long awaited, and I bet soon the place will be crawling with them. In fact, others have opened since and we're keeping our tongues to the Karahi. As ever, watch this space! It's Southall in style and Southall in name, though, as far as we know, the owners are new to the game, having copied, not without hiccups, an established formula. For example, they originally offered a choice of dishes unlikely to be eaten by most of Tooting's Asians, such as Haleem – ground meat and wheat grains – and Raan. Not even Southall offers these, the former a central Indian Muslim speciality from Hyderabad, the latter a Kashmiri Mogul dish. So out they've gone, and sticking to kebabs, tandoori and Punjabi food is a safer bet for them for now. And it's all good stuff. Maybe a dish of the day concept, at a future date, can bring back these unusual items. Open noon-midnight every day. Unlicensed and BYO welcomed. Waiter service, with the cooking on view. 'Exceptional flavours,' C.H.C. Cash only, average meal under £10.

MILAN NEW ENTRANT   √

158 Upper Tooting Road, SW17   ⓒ **0181 767 4347**

This is just the sort of place we like to recommend. It's an unpretentious Gujarati café, unexpectedly licensed, with those subtly spiced curries, made largely from besan flour and yoghurt, spiced with turmeric and curry leaves. So, if it's robust meat you want, you're in the wrong joint, so see previous entry! But for the vegetarian, what more could you ask for? If it's new to you, ask for help, or for a Thali (from £4.75). You'll adore the fresh home-made relishes, and the dish of the day is always a good choice. One of the few places where fresh Rotla (millet bread) is served. Open 10a.m.-10p.m., takes no credit cards. Minimum charge is a ridiculous £2, average meal under £10, so cash preferred, and leave some room for the terrific Indian sweets on display!

NAZIM'S BALTI HOUSE   NEW ENTRANT   ©

398 Garratt Lane, SW17   © 0181 946 2219

S. Miah's Nazim's has been doing it (the Bangladeshi formula, that is) since 1966, but only recently have they added Balti to name and menu. Price check: Papadom 45p, CTM £5.50, Baltis from £5.95, Pullao Rice £1.60. Minimum charge £8. Licensed. Evenings only.

PEACOCK TANDOORI   ©

242 Upper Tooting Road, SW17   © 0181 672 8770

Proprietor Yogi Anand's Peacock was established in 1988 and has built up a loyal local crowd who can be sure of good formula north Indian tandoori and curries. Price check: Papadom 50p, CTM £5.60, Batair-e-Khas (quail) £7.65, Pullao Rice £1.95.

SREE KRISHNA   TOP 100

192-194 Tooting High Street, SW17   © 0181 672 4250

Sree Krishna is a revered, playful Hindi god. His picture is in this corner restaurant, which has been in our Guide since we started. The slightly tacky decor transports one straight back to Kerala, and the food transports you to heaven. It's a no-frills place. Paper tablecloths, methodical but sure service, bizarre toilet location, and plenty of regulars, Indian and white. Cobra, Kingfisher and Kaliani Indian beers are all here, and they never seem to muddle the labelled glasses. Its specialities are south Indian vegetarian food. We always go for the best Masala Dosa in town – a thin rice and urid flour pancake, wrapped around a tasty potato curry, accompanied by Rasam (pepper soup), and Sambar (thin lentil curry). Start with a Papadam and the hot red coconut chutney, and/or the hotter green one, and we are totally stuffed. We wonder how others have what we have as a starter, then migrate into meat curries with dhal, bread and rice, which we are assured are equally good, if only we had room! We must try the Chilli

Pakoras one day! Our bill for two never exceeds £20, with Cobra and service charge, but could obviously be twice that if we pigged out! Minimum charge £5. Credit cards accepted. Definitely remains in our TOP 100. Branch: Ragam, 57 Cleveland Street, w1.

SW18 – Earlsfield

NAZMIN   ⊞ ©

398 Garratt Lane, Earlsfield, SW18   © 0181 946 2219

A standard curry house serving all your favourite standard curry house food at reasonable prices. Manager A. Rashid will give a discount to Curry Club members. Home delivery service available.

SW19 – Wimbledon

NIRVANA   ©

277 Wimbledon Park Road, SW19   © 0181 780 2406

Formula curries from this much-liked establishment. Proprietor M.A. Mannan will give a discount to Curry Club members.

ZUJUMA'S NEW ENTRANT

58a Wimbledon Hill Road, SW19   © 0181 879 0916

We don't usually enter a restaurant which is so new that the ink's hardly dry on the menu. But Zujuma's isn't usual. It opened in May '97, as the brainchild of Zuju Shareef. She's a cookery writer from Hyderabad. This vibrant central Indian city is known for pearls, monuments, silver leaf, a former rich ruler (the Nizam), bad driving, a small Parsee and large Muslim population, Biriani and Haleem. But expect none of that at Zujuma's, nor your formula curries. Zuju's menu is very short. Classic Indian dishes have been modernized and evolved. An example is Murgh Adrak, meaning chicken with ginger, which is thin strips of chicken, cut and stir-fried Chinese-style, with Indian spices and chiffonaded Thai lime leaves. Other dishes use olive oil, fruit, and the lightest of spices, and many, being inventions, have unfamiliar names. 'No papadoms – rather nice!' D.W. Expect to pay £15-20 a head with wine. Open daily, noon-11p.m. (10.30 p.m. Sundays). Reports, please.

SW20

INDIAN GOSSIP

20 Leopold Road, Wimbledon, SW20   © 0181 946 0586

'Aiming at up-market-type clientele – open, airy restaurant in pastel blue. Dhansak very rich and spicy,' S.N.

NAZ   ⊞ ©

554 Kingston Road, Raynes Park, SW20   © 0181 542 1608

All your regular curries at this establishment. Set meals good value for money. Will give a discount to Curry Club members. Home delivery service available. Evenings only: 6p.m.-midnight.

London W

W1

ANWARS   BYO

64 Grafton Way, W1   © 0171 387 6664

A café, old-style, not trendy, new and flashy, open from noon-11p.m., owned by Muhammed Afzal Zahid, whose gutsy, spicy Pakistani food is redolent of Southall. Make your choice from the serving counter, from the dishes of the day (no menu as such), then carry your tray to a formica table and enjoy it. It's not licensed, BYO accepted. It has good local Asian patronage. 'Remains a star – I've been going for 25 years plus,' C.J. Price check: Papadom 30p, CTM £5, Haleem £3, Pullao Rice £1.40. Set meal, veggie £3.50, non-veggie £4.85.

CARAVAN SERAI TOP 100

50 Paddington Street, Marylebone, W1   ✆ 0171 935 1208

A very nice touch is free hot Pakoras with chutney, given at the beginning while you examine the menu. Try the Logery – leg of lamb, flavoured with spices and saffron – or the Sekonia (skewered lamb, cooked in the tandoor). Ashaks are pastries, filled with a spicy leek and mince filling, with yoghurt. Kohi is roast lamb, spiced with Char Masala and blackcurrant. Yoghurt and garlic, root vegetables and pulses are also popular. End with Carrot Kulfi or Coconut Halva. The service is exemplary, as is the presentation. The food is superb, although portions are on the small side. Remains in our TOP 100.

CHOR BIZARRE NEW ENTRANT

16 Albemarle Street, W1   ✆ 0171 629 8542

On the site of the tired-looking old Gaylord in Mayfair comes an extraordinary-looking upgrade in the shape of Chor Bizarre. Throughout India there are Chor Bazaars – literally, thieves' markets – which canny Delhi entrepreneur Rohit Khattar used as a theme when opening restaurants there, the idea being to create a restaurant where everything was brought in from these markets and no two items were the same. The winning concept has now come to London and Khattar has created an Indian dining room like no other, hence the move from Bazaar to Bizarre. Antiquities abound and one table, for example, is encased in an 18th-century four-poster bed from Calcutta. While it is worth visiting for the interior alone, the cuisine on offer gives a rare opportunity to savour Kashmiri cooking through dishes such as Yakhni – pumpkin simmered in fennel-flavoured yoghurt gravy – and Goshtaba – excellent minced lamb balls in a tangy white gravy. Open Monday to Saturday noon-3p.m. and 6-11.30p.m.

DELHI BRASSERIE NEW ENTRANT

44 Frith Street, Soho, London W1   ✆ 0171 437 8361

'It was a Saturday evening in London, what hope for a free table! To my surprise a table was available and a reservation made. This was the start of an exceptional eating experience. I was greeted at the door and ushered immediately to my table in the packed restaurant. The decor was a superb, warm colour and lighting very cosy, and the music was mellow. I was given the menu which was well presented, easy to understand and very informative. The choice: chicken wings to start followed by a medium-spiced lamb curry, washed down with a bottle of house red. The courses came quickly although at no time was I rushed. The food was excellent with portions of a sensible size so that you could have dessert if required. The service was of the highest standard: even at the height of the rush, the waiters had time to be individual and gave an air of control and the appearance of enjoying their work,' C.M.G.

GOLDEN ORIENT   ©

61 Berwick Street, W1   ✆ 0171 437 1817

Abdul Majid's been doing his thing since 1971, daily from noon-midnight, his thing being competent Bangladeshi curries. 'We have had so many mediocre curries in this part of London that it was nice to find one well above average. The Chilli Chicken Bayang stood out, littered with green chillies,' C.T. Price check: Papadom 40p, CTM £5.95, Fish Masala £4.95, Pullao Rice £1.40. Minimum charge £5. Service charge 10%.

GOPAL'S OF SOHO

12 Bateman Street, W1   ✆ 0171 434 1621

Chef N.T. Pittal's golden touch brought first the Lal Qila then the Red Fort to currinary prominence. Such were his talents that it was not surprising that he went solo in Soho, using his nickname, Gopal, to christen his venture. That was in 1990. It was a justifiable success and always attracted satisfied reports. Until recently. Our reliable London reporter, H.C., visits regularly and said 'it seemed better than ever'. But we were hearing of poor service in this otherwise excellent restaurant, confirmed by H.C. not long afterwards. 'We were shown to the smallest, most cramped table in a totally empty restaurant. Asked if we could move to a nearby table as we wanted to look through a few business papers. The waiter didn't say a word, and fetched the manager who asked if there was a problem. On repeating the request for a larger table he replied very haughtily, "That is a table for four people, are you going to pay for four meals?" I know restaurants have to juggle tables and diners but they don't have to speak to people like that. The restaurant was never more than a third full that lunchtime, and the service was very unfriendly for the rest of the meal, reinforcing the feeling that we had made a nuisance of ourselves. A great shame as this restaurant has always been marvellous and the food is really good, as it was on this occasion,' H.C. Kick it back into shape, Gopal! Reports, please.

GURKHA BRASSERIE   ©

23 Warren Street, W1   ℂ 0171 383 4985

'Genuine Nepalese restaurant. Superb decor with Gurkha photos on the walls (including owner Hari K.C.'s father with the Queen at a regimental do). The thatched hut decor transports you straight to Nepal, as does the food. Nepalese food is very different and must be sampled. Momos (spicy dumplings) are highly recommended as are all the dishes,' G.H. 'Try the Choala – cold lamb with garlic ... hmmm!' D.L. Branch: 756 Finchley Road, NW11.

INDIAN YMCA CANTEEN

41 Fitzroy Square, W1   ℂ 0171 387 0411

This is one of my favourite eating holes, decidedly unlicensed. It's the downstairs canteen for the Y.M.C.A. residents, many of whom are Asian students. The food is basic, unsophisticated curry, school-dinner style. I've been using it for years. Outsiders are welcome, but only now at lunchtimes from 12.30-1.30p.m. daily, prompt! Take a plastic tray, join the always busy queue. Point to your choice of curry which is unceremoniously dolloped onto your plate. Top up with chupatties, tea or coffee, and pay at the till, cash only. It's absurdly cheap – it's hard to exceed £4. Then jostle for space at a formica table. The food may not be brilliant, but the company can be, when you share your table with talkative, friendly students. Highly recommended. 'A star for years,' C.J. Strict hours: lunch 12.30-1.30p.m. No bookings, no licence, no BYO and no nonsense!

KANISHKA   ©

161 Whitfield Street, W1   ℂ 0171 388 0860

Owner Jagdish Vitish's Kanishka is very smart and very Indian, with goodies from all over the country. On two floors, ground and basement, it is as busy at lunch as at dinner, so booking is essential. A.S. found helpful staff and loved the food, but 'for the price the portions were not large enough'. R.A. felt the tables were too close together, and she too finds it expensive, 'but considering the ingredients used and the quality of the dishes, we felt the price was reasonable. I ordered the turnip dish as a dare, and it was outstanding ... easily the best dish on the table.'

THE LANCERS NEW ENTRANT

34 Brook Street and
1-4 South Molton Street, W1   ✆ 0171 629 6555

Situated in his basement territory – the smartly appointed Lancers – chef Kuldeep Makhni is a genial man who, given a chance, will tell you himself that he is a 'royally appointed chef'. Apparently he was personal chef to the kings of Nepal and Butan, but there's more. It seems he was given a midnight royal summons to Buck Pal, for a takeaway, he says, for H.M. herself. Since herself isn't known to be a curryholic and was probably tucked up asleep at such an hour, it was more likely for the likely lads, Ed and Andy ... But who knows and, just in case, could I have a report next time, Ma'am, please! We hear of very good food and service at predictable Mayfair prices (and you can opt for a free limo pick-up!). Reports, please, royal or otherwise!

MAHARANI

77 Berwick Street, W1   ✆ 0171 437 8568

'It's become my German colleague's local, its unprepossessing decor failing to do the food quality justice. The Lobster Vindaloo was excellent (though not "lobster"). The Goan Chicken was hotter and even tastier. Heinz was the only customer one time, and the one "aged" staff member took the order, cooked his meal with much banging and clattering, producing a meal only loosely related to the order, but which was, I am assured, extremely good, then entertained him with the philosophy of life throughout,' M.W.S.

MANDEER TOP 100   √ ©

21 Hanway Place, W1   © 0171 323 0660

There are two parts to Mr and Mrs Ramesh Patel's veteran vegetarian
downstairs Mandeer – the no-frills canteen, packed with lunchtime
office workers (no booking, long queues but worth it for speed, value
and quality) and the Ravi Shankar, the smart place alongside, decorated like little India, where you go to linger over Chef Daudbhai's food.
'From the moment the papadoms arrived, we knew we were in for a
veritable sensation of a meal. We were not disappointed. It was fantastic,' A.S. We do hear of some over-lingering, i.e., long waits in the
restaurant, and erratic service, but we are happy to keep the inexpensive Mandeer in our Top 100. It is licensed and takes credit cards.

MINARA   √

1 Hanway Street,
off Tottenham Court Road, W1   © 0171 636 5262

Another Hanway haven of vegan and vegetarian delights, formerly the
Hare Krishna. The mantras and orange-faded image may have gone but
the food lives on with careful, home-style cooking. There are
garlic/onion-free dishes, as eaten by those of the rare Jain religious
sect, but useful to know anyway. Lunch and dinner. Licensed and
accepts credit cards. Closed Sundays.

NEEL AKASH   ©

2 Hanway Street,
off Tottenham Court Road, W1   © 0171 580 9376

This Hanway haven has been serving formula Bangladeshi delights
since 1975, under Sheiks Ashique Miah and Rahman. Price check:
Papadom 35p, CTM £5.20, Pullao Rice £1.60. Lunch from £2.75, dinner from £8.30. Chef Raja's deluxe dinner £13.50.

NEW DIWAN-I-AM

60-62 Blandford Street, W1   © 0171 935 3955

Long-standing curry house serving competent food to a loyal following.

PALMS OF GOA NEW ENTRANT

12 Charlotte Street, W1   ✆ **0171 636 1668**

Since the demise of the Jamdani, a few doors down, this area has been devoid of a good 'Indian'. Now it has a very rare treat, even for London. It's a 40-seat Goan restaurant, run by the affable Eugene Dias. He offers a range of other Indian dishes, but the *cognoscenti* tell of superb Goan treasures like Pork Vindaloo (yes, the traditional pork, garlic, chilli dish, pronounced vin dar-loo, and as far removed from the curry house version as you can get), Peri Peri (Goan crab and fish) and Xacutti Chicken (all around £5). Ask for things to be fired up to Goan chilli levels, if that's your bag, otherwise it's a bit bland, we hear. Good value. Average meal price £12. Set lunch buffet £6.95. Lunch and dinner every day except Sundays.

LA PORTE DES INDES NEW TO OUR TOP 100 BEST INDIAN

32 Bryanston Street, W1   ✆ **0171 224 0055**

This is the really big newcomer since our last Guide. And I mean big (it has 350 covers), and big in budget. It cost £2.5 million to bring designer Yves Burton's concept to fruition, to convert the enormous former Mayfairia ballroom. Its entrance is unremarkable, tucked away one block behind the Marble Arch Odeon. Parking can be hell, though there's an N.C.P. down the street. The reception area is deceptive, too. It's attractive enough, with its dark, polished wood floor, but it gives you no hint of what is to come. But prowl around and you begin to see where the money went. Go down the nearest stairs into the bar. It is made of cane, with bamboo furniture and palms in beaten copper pots, and it's OK but still not breathtaking. There's a sandstone arch and a 40-foot waterfall, too, but take a good look at the sweeping staircase and make a point of going up and down it. It is made of white marble with pink sandstone balustrades, imported especially from India's pink city, Jaipur. Airy, domed skylights enhance La Porte's daytime atmosphere, making it a different place in darkness. There is a forest of jungle plants, a wealth of Indian artefacts, and antiques. Ask to see the adorable antique bronze coconut scraper, and the range of eating rooms, including the tiny private dining rooms, seating 12 and 24 respectively, to areas of 60-plus.

La Porte purports to present cuisine from Pondicherry. For the record, the French were the last Europeans to occupy India. Their arrival there, in 1664, posed a century-long threat to the British, until their defeat at Plassey in 1757 put paid to further French ambitions of conquest though, like the Portuguese, their presence in India thereafter was 'tolerated' by the Raj. Pondicherry, south of Madras, was their main settlement until they handed it back to India in 1954. What little 'French' that remains is described by travel writer Louise Nicholson as an 'eerie ghost town, with closed colonial shutters … decaying and deserted'. She refers to some cobbled streets, with French names (currently being Indianized), at the centre of which is a square and Hotel de Ville, with a Jeanne d'Arc statue in the park. True, the Indian police still wear French red kepi hats and belts. But if you hope to find French people, there are none left. Like the Jews in Cochin, the Portuguese in Goa and the British in the hill stations, they have all gone. Even Pondicherry is changing its name to Puducherri.

So, what of La Porte's cuisine? Taj-trained chef Mernosh Mody, and his chef-trained wife, Sherin Alexander, in charge of front of house, tell us they spent time in Pondicherry, and managed to find some recipes they describe as 'French-Creole'. I thought Creole referred to the Caribbean or Louisiana. But, I confess, the closest I've been to Pondicherry is 80 miles north, though our Indian travel agent, Melini, has a sister who lives there. She states there is no such thing as Pondicherry cuisine! Be that as it may, the opening section of the menu gives French names to Indian dishes, described in English. I suppose 'beignet' sounds better than 'doughnut', and 'cassoulet' more impressive than 'stew'. Boulettes (£10.50) are undoubtedly more enticing than meat balls! Demoiselles (£7.50) are unmarried females, and it's not for me to say whether referral to 'juicy scallops' is appropriate. Poulet Rouge (£10) – chicken in red, creamy sauce – sounds suspiciously like CTM to me! One or two recipes are attributed with Creole features: Rasoul (£5) is a samosa with a Creole sauce. Couside (£5) is a Creole broth. Main courses include Magret de Canard Pulivaar – Mme Lourde Swamy's Duck (£13) – and Policha Meen is Mme Blanc's Mullet (£11.75). If all this sounds a bit pretentious, all I can say is that dining out is meant to be theatre on occasions. And I guess that La Porte des Indes sounds more impressive than India Gate! And if the prices on Le Menu Français are Les Prix Très Chers, be warned, but at least they're half those of Le Gavroche!

The second section of the menu is no less costly but it drops the French and offers many other classic dishes from all over India. For those who wish to try a bit of everything there are chef selection meals at £29 per person without soup, or £34 with, minimum two people, and there is a seasonal menu changed monthly at £18. The lunch presentation of food on raised copper salvers is opulent and attractive, and you can eat your fill for £15. On Sundays it's called brunch, at the same price, with a live jazz band.

D.S. was impressed by everything and decided La Porte was better than India, whatever that means! G.C. felt it is: 'The place to go when you want something special, definitely a spend-the-whole-evening restaurant. Very large, but tables in different areas so not too "barny"'. *Tandoori Magazine* held a huge party for 300 there, and the food, always difficult on such occasions, was superb. H.C. found: 'The large choice was all very tempting. Food absolutely marvellous, everything was very good indeed, except for the service, which was very slow. A great shame, let down the otherwise almost faultless restaurant.' At a publisher's party, Malcolm Gluck was less complimentary, finding the food too un-curry house to recommend wines for it. 'When are they going to put some spices in?' he asked. And this will be a common cause of complaint from those unused to such food. The food here is authentic Indian food, as far removed from the formula as can be. The French connection may be tenuous, but Mernosh Mody has got over the trauma that openings bring and has settled into his stride. His food has become more confident, and we are so sure of this place that we are placing it high into our TOP 100, even though D.B.A.C. complains that 'there is no full-length mirror for sari-wearers in the Ladies. For a restaurant hoping to attract wealthy Indians, that's more than thoughtless.' We trust that will be noted by its owners, who also own the Thai restaurant, The Blue Elephant in sw6.

RAGAM SOUTH INDIAN TOP 100

57 Cleveland Street, W1   ✆ 0171 636 9098

Popular and small (booking advisable) with 36 seats upstairs, 20 downstairs. It does serve a range of standard curries and, good though they are, our advice is to ignore them and concentrate only on the south Indian specialities. D.B. adores the Rasam and the Dosas. J.L. adores the Kaalam (orange-coloured mango yoghurt) and the 'very hot'

Uthappam. It remains safely in our TOP 100. Branch: Sree Krishna, Tooting, SW17.

RAJ TANDOORI   ©

72 Berwick Street, W1   ℗ 0171 439 0035

'Standard menu. Service friendly and they gave me a Curry Club 10% discount, no hassles. Comfort and decor a bit on the cramped side. The tastiest Chicken Jalfrezi I've ever tasted! Lamb Bhuna the best. Well worth it,' D.P. 'I used to work at Oxford Circus and came here four times a week, when it was the Islamabad. The Methi Gosht was nice and bitter, Bhajees crisp and the Phal, hot! All ample portions and excellent value. I moved jobs and did not visit for four years but, when I did recently, I was recognized as soon as I walked in, and was given a welcoming free pint, plus a brandy at the end,' G.C.

RED FORT

77 Dean Street, Soho, W1   ℗ 0171 437 2525

One has to respect Amin Ali. He does not give up. He is a believer in doing things properly and, after some quite hard work, his constant efforts at the Red Fort are once again paying off. He needed to, following a few years in the doldrums, where customers did not fill the house at lunch and dinner, as in the early days. The kitchen brigade is led by Taj-trained S. Chakravaty, and is augmented from time to time by equally highly-trained Indian guest chefs who keep the new ideas flowing. Thus the regular food festivals are rewarding, bringing regional cuisine to the Fort and lifting the regular menu as well. We have certainly received more happy reports this time than last, although the geography of the room seems to matter here more than at other restaurants (upstairs is preferred to downstairs, and front preferred to rear – where one can feel marginalized and a bit too near the service door). But it is usually full, with many a tourist sent, no doubt, by local hotel concierges, so book early and stipulate your seating preference. At or near the front you'll witness, or partake in, the Ali cocktails dispensed by the attractive staff. Described as 'over the top' at least in price, if not in content, be prepared for high prices in this department. Ali's current food vogue, called Indian avant-garde, is fat-free cooking, which Bangladeshi friends of mine called 'strange'. Available daily at the lunch buffet (£12.50) or à la carte, evenings, with dishes from £6-£16, and a meal, without cocktails, at nearer £35. There is a pre-theatre set meal at £14.95. More reports, please. *See* Soho Spice, below.

SOHO SPICE   NEW ENTRANT ONE TO WATCH TOP 100

124-126 Wardour Street, W1   ✆ **0171 434 0808**

Amin Ali (*see* Red Fort) is no stranger to opening smart new restaurants, some of which have survived. His latest opened just as this Guide was being written (May 1997), and is almost too new to enter. But we've had a report or two, including one from the same Bangladeshis who sampled the Red Fort and thought this 200-seater restaurant, on two floors, 'stark and empty'! Red flock it is not. Wood floor, aqua blues and mint greens on the ground floor, and reds and saffron downstairs, are held together with Indian art. Neither, according to the law courts, is it a copy of Café Spice (*see* E1), which failed in its injunction to prevent use of its concept and similar name. Similarities there may be, but the differences are apparent, too. Firstly, this restaurant is, I believe, unique, in that it opens for breakfast at 7.30a.m. weekdays, with a conventional continental choice plus a range of spicy alternatives (£5.95). (Interestingly, it is not the first Indian to do this. Stanley Krett's Bengal Lancer tried it on Greek Street a decade ago, and it failed. Will Ali's early morning venture work? Watch these pages.) Soho Spice continues to stay open until midnight (giving it the longest curry opening hours in Britain – not even Brick Lane or Southall can match it). The short but intriguing menu offers all-day snacks/mini meals, with items such as chicken wings or bhajis (£2.95), with teas, coffee or bar drinks, interspersed with lunch and dinner. Set thalis (£12) need add-ons such as rice or bread (£1.50 each), and there is a three-course set meal (£14.95) which changes monthly, but I hope the super Jungli Maas – a dish with ghee and dry red chillies cooked on the hoof for hunting parties – stays permanently! Cooking is by Kuldeep Singh. It's a promising venture. On Saturdays it opens at midday, closed Sunday. Hours likely to change as it matures. I'll take a punt and give it TOP 100 status. Reports, please.

TAMARIND   TOP 100   BEST INDIAN

20 Queen Street, Mayfair, W1   © 0171 629 3561

Tamarind opened in late '94, to a blaze of publicity, little of it good. But, as we predicted, its deserved respect is gaining momentum, and it is now essential to book. I hear they now do 140 covers a night. Avid Guide readers will be pleased to note that the management changed the front door to something much grander, shortly after our remarks about it last time. The welcome is as good as ever, and the staircase down to the action is no obstacle. The dining room is spacious and the 100 seats do not feel cramped. The decor, in tones of blonde, gold, copper, brass and pine, is Mayfair not Madras, Todhunter not Tandoori, and subdued not sub-continent. The main feature is two long glass wall panels, displaying some rather plain, pallid pink sari silk. Last time I asked 'why not some exquisitely embroidered Kanchipuram silks?' One correspondent told me I had no taste, but then asked what Kanchipuram silk is. Deary me, madam, it's like criticizing a book without reading it! Kanchipuram is a town near Madras where the best, finest, softest, most tasteful sari silk in the sub-continent is produced. Every Indian I know agrees with that! Talking of saris, I also said last time that I was smitten by the specially commissioned wrought-iron chairs, until editor D.B.A.C. warned that their rough edges could easily snag nylons, skirts and saris, and she should know, with her stunning collection of saris from all over India, including Kanchipuram! I have not heard whether these edges have been smoothed down, but I expect they have. Rough edges in the kitchens have certainly been smoothed since, at the beginning, Oberoi-trained chef Atul Kochar needed all his reserve of enthusiasm to manage with his opening brigade of zero. Even with his eighteen-hour days of solo operating, followed by a 3-mile walk home, the resulting food has always been of the highest standard, with a light and delicate touch and some innovative work. Kochar refused to compromise and his time-consuming touches, such as long, individual preps for individual dishes, and home-made chutneys, make this restaurant stand out. Now, with his hand-picked team in place, the output is even better. Chicken Liver Masala (£5.50) is a spicy melt-in-the-mouth appetizer, as is Atul's Shami Kebab (£4.50). There is a choice of ten kebabs and tandooris (the making of which is on view, behind glass) culminating in the platter selection (£18 for two) and the Raan leg of lamb (£32 for two). The small selection of eight curries (from £10.25-£14) is perhaps as minimalist as the decor, with just two prawn, one fish, three chicken and two meat dishes, but this allows the kitchen to create each dish as its own entity and not from a central stock-pot. The result is a delicacy of touch found in the best Indian homes. There is a satisfactory range of vegetable dishes, including some classics (all £6.50). There's a selection of good birianis and, if you have not seen a Romali Roti – handkerchief bread (£3) – being 'thrown', ask to see it. It is a skill that takes years to learn, so is rarely found in UK restaurants. A lump of dough is spun and thrown into the air until it is as thin as silk. Service is now headed by Patrice Mossadek, and is equally silky and proficient. Of course, all of this does not come cheap. Remember where we are! Mayfair does not come cheap! Tamarind is at the top end of Indian restaurant pricing. The average dinner will cost at least £35, assisted by a 12½% service charge. That makes for free papadoms, true, but CTM (sorry, Murgh Masalam) is £10.50. And, please remember too, that I'm just the messenger. M.A., an Indian herself, said it's: 'better than Namaste, although it's very pretentious and an unjustifiable price hike!' Strong stuff, but watch out! The daily lunch (closed Saturdays) is £16.50, though be prepared for a relatively small plateful that might leave trenchermen wanting. Dinner every night. It is very high in our TOP 100.

TASTE OF MUGHAL NEW ENTRANT   ©

29 Great Windmill Street, W1   ✆ **0171 439 8044**

Sandwiched between two expensive giants in our Guide, but nearer Eros than either, is M.S. Khan and Abdul Khalam's all-day-and-everyday (noon-11.45p.m.) good, formula curry house, where the price is right, made better by the Curry Club discount. Price check: Papadom 40p, CTM £5.95, Pullao Rice £1.95. Set meal £6.95. Service charge 10%.

VEERASWAMY TOP 100 MOST PROMISING NEWCOMER

99-101 Regent Street, W1   ✆ **0171 734 1401**

I had no sooner finished collating all the reports received, few of which were glowing, and decided to delist this restaurant completely (and that would have been the second time in five Guides), when the news came through that the Veeraswamy had been purchased, lock,

stock and tandoor, by none other than Namita Panjabi, of Chutney
Mary (SW10) fame. What great news!

She has bought Britain's oldest Indian restaurant, dating from 1927,
which became a London institution. Its menu was a mirror of those of
Raj households, serving roasts and grills, pies and tarts. As a sideline,
almost, they offered one curry of the day, complete with 'side dishes'!
I know this because, in the early 1930s, my mum used to save up her
pennies as a young nurse and go every now and then to enjoy a curry
fix. Addicted from her youth in the Raj, and undoubtedly one of
Britain's first curryholics (an attribute she fortunately passed on to me
at weaning stage), it was the only place, apart from her parents' home
in Portsmouth, where she could get her fix. It cost, she thinks, 2/6d
(12½p), which then was a small fortune, plus Tube fare. My first visit
here was in 1946, when I was five! Old hands like me will remember the
Indian two-seater carved chairs, and the gold-painted, huge wooden
elephants in the bar. They lasted well into the 1980s because it was here
that I launched our Curry Club regular Friday night meetings. By then
the decor was as faded and jaded as those old Raj clubs. The food was
about as musty! It had slithered into a decline, matching that of the
British Empire, a part of which it had once so admirably represented.
Sarova Hotels of Kenya came to the rescue in 1986. Out went the relics
– staff as well as decor, and in came hotel foyer decor, and 'management'. For a while the food improved and then it went down again. I
doubt that any of the many American and Japanese tourists either
noticed or cared. Following its six-week closure for refit, it is stylish
but contemporary with modern lighting and looks. Indian exotic
colours, artefacts and etched glass take it far, far away from its early
days. So does Namita, her new managers and new brigade of top
Indian chefs, who all focus on a short menu, providing the best of
Indian regional cooking. You'll find three types of Chicken Tikka –
herbal, saffron and malai. CTM is not here, of course, but you'll find
Makhani Murgh, its classic namesake. Try Oyster Chilli Fry, or
Andhra Chicken Sixer if you like it hot. Spicy Chicken Roll, Lucknowi
Roghan Josh, Hyderabadi Usmani Lamb Korma and the Madras
Chetinand will delight the purists, and hopefully the tourists, as will
other classics from Delhi, Lucknow, Goa, Kashmir and Bombay. The
average meal price, with drink, is £26-£28, representing value for
money, and there is a lighter lunch menu with a lighter price tag. Open
daily for lunch and dinner, with pre-theatre from 5.30p.m.

This entire report was written before the re-opening. Food guide editors are supposed to wait and see, but I'll take one of my punts and, not only keep Veeraswamy in the Guide, I'll place it back high into our TOP 100.

WOODLANDS   √ ©

77 Marylebone Lane, W1   ℰ 0181 835 1799

A branch of Mr Sood's well-liked, licensed, small chain of southern Indian vegetarian restaurants (*see* SW1 and Middlesex). This one is managed by M. Ullur. Price check: Papadom £1, Mysore Masala Dosa £4.75, Pullao Rice £2.95. Set meal £5-£6.50.

W2

AKASH   NEW ENTRANT   ©

500a Edgware Road, W2   ℰ 0171 723 3651

Mohib Choudhury's small place, with Majid and Lilu, manager and chef, is a popular, friendly local. Price check: Papadom 40p, Lobster-e-Kabajpuri £9.95, CTM £5.15, Pullao Rice £1.75.

BOMBAY PALACE   TOP 100

50 Connaught Street,
Hyde Park Square, W2   ℰ 0171 723 8855

Starters include Alu Papri, thin potato crisps with yoghurt, tamarind and curry; Chooza Pakoras, spicy chicken fritters; Shammi Kebabs, succulent and superb. Main courses include the Bombay Palace's unique Murgh Keema Masala, minced chicken breast, lightly sautéed in ginger, garlic, onion, tomato, green peas, yoghurt and spices. 'Everyone in my group of nine was very pleased to be introduced to the Palace although many thought it expensive. I found that, sometimes, less than best cuts of meat had been used, and they sent vegetable dishes down automatically. This had to be stopped because, although they weren't ordered, they would be charged for. I don't like the Rice and Naan order to be done automatically either, but the waiter insisted on bringing "a selection" for the table. On the whole, the food is very good, but service pushy. (They serve Cobra Lager.)' M.D. Others are more laudatory in their reports: indeed, it is several reviewers' favourite Indian restaurant. Although we have not received any reports this time, we are happy to retain the Palace in our TOP 100. To do so, though, we really need more reports.

EVEREST NEW ENTRANT

41 Craven Road, Lancaster Gate, W2   © 0171 262 3853

This 'old' venue – opened 1961 – is new to the Guide. Owned by Mohammed Ali and managed by M. Ahmed, the Everest has been refurbished to provide a very up-market image of light decor, cane furniture and interesting framed photographs of old India. 'Papadoms and pickles, Meat Samosas (lean mince) and crisp salad were followed by Chicken Tikka Bhuna (one of the best I have had) and Paratha (very light) washed down by large bottles of Cobra. The bill was £14 for a small meal but the quality was good. Many of the diners were local residents who commented on their high regard for the Everest,' A.E. Price check: Papadom 35p, CTM £5.95, Pullao Rice £1.60. Set meal £12.95.

GANGES

101 Praed Street, Paddington, W2   © 0171 723 4096

Another Paddington veteran (1965) and still going strong. 'A small restaurant seating 30, an inexpensive pleasant meal in pleasant surroundings and good friendly service,' B.P.-D.

GOLDEN SHALIMAR   ©

6 Spring Street, W2   © 0171 262 3763

This concise report comes from regular A.E.: 'Decor traditionally ethnic, dim, small and cosy. Seats 56. Busy, good service, fast. There are 10 Indian restaurants in Paddington, this is the best. Onion Bhajia (£1.50), crispy. Tikka Bhuna (£5.65) was salty but good. Big bottles of iced Cobra.'

INDIAN CONNOISSEURS   ©

8 Norfolk Place, W2   ✆ 0171 402 3299

An easily found smart frontage reveals a bright and airy, small (46-seat) cosy interior (so booking advisable) with a 'big' menu. Yes, it has all your favourites, but it's not often you are offered Bangladeshi fish (Ayre and parrot fish) or Venison Bhoona. The even more adventurous could plump for Khashi Gazar (goat with carrot), Tandoori Pheasaeant (sic) or grouse. D.R. says the Shorisha Ayre (£5.75) is 'magnificent'. Congratulations to chef Kabir Miah for adding authenticity to the formula. Paddington sleuth A.E. found a warm haven on a cold night and was 'swiftly served with free papadom and excellent pickles. The meat thali (£9.50) was excellent value, good quality, nicely presented and very filling.' Branch: Golden Orient, 639 High Road, E11.

OLD DELHI   TOP 100

48 Kendal Street, W2   ✆ 0171 724 9580

You'll often find so-called 'Persian' dishes on the standard curry house menu. There is a centuries-long link between Persia (now Iran) and India. Dishes such as Biriani, Patia, Pullao and Dhansak had their origins in Persia. But to most curry houses these dishes are merely a modification to formula curries. Not so at the Old Delhi, whose owner is Iranian, and whose son Jay is manager. You can certainly get superbly cooked curries in its superb setting, but venture further and try at least some of the rather less spicy but authentically cooked Iranian specials. Faisenjan (chicken marinated, then cooked in a purée of pomegranate, spices and nuts) goes divinely with Saffron Rice and Doog (minty lhassi). A must for serious spicy food *aficionados*. Awarded our TOP 100 cachet.

RYATH INDIAN TANDOORI   BYO

32 Norfolk Place, W2   ✆ 0171 723 8954

'Open since 1978, it has been tastefully converted from takeaway to cosy restaurant, having good brasserie ambience, good lighting, hanging flora, crisp linen tablecloths and smartly dressed waiters. Currently unlicensed so BYO. I could hardly believe the bill: £10.60 for four

courses,' A.E. Price check: Papadom 30p, CTM £5.25, Pullao Rice £1.40.
Branches: Kensington Tandoori, W8; Chambali, WC1.

Westbourne Grove – W2 and W11

This short street, whose postcode changes midway, is well-known for
its ethnic restaurants and is home to many curry houses. These are
worthy of mention:

KARAHI TANDOORI

27 Westbourne Grove, W2   *©* **0171 727 5154**

N.S. found 'good food and good value'. Price check: Papadom 40p,
CTM £4.95, Pullao Rice £1.50.

KHAN'S   TOP 100

13-15 Westbourne Grove, W2   *©* **0171 727 5420**

The only report I got this time (though I know of many people who
have been) was from N.S. who found 'people queuing out of the door
at 11p.m. on more than one occasion!!!', so he went elsewhere. Such is
its popularity, so be warned, and in the absence of new things to say,
here's my review from last time. Khan's is the most difficult restaurant
to review. I'll explain: it's a love it or hate it place – there's no in
between. You'll probably love the decor. It's a fairyland room, whose
high, cloud-painted ceiling is supported by a forest of gilt palm trees.
There is a huge Hindi-arched mahogany bar and countless tables with
pink cloths and black bentwood chairs. It is huge (over 300 seats on
two floors) and is as full at lunchtime as dinner. Apparently it is not
unusual for them to do 1000 covers a day. And therein lies the problem. This sheer volume results in an American-style 'have-a-nice-
day/take-it-or-leave-it' attitude. Even Americans are shocked, and my
files continue to bulge with complaints mostly about the inaccurately
delivered orders and missing items, but occasionally about undesirable
cabarets such as brawling customers with the waiters joining in. As first
impressions count, we would not recommend it for a curry first-timer,
nor to demure foreign tourist groups. But, for seasoned curryholics, it
is an institution and decidedly not to be missed. Indeed, Khan's has

built up a very large customer base of regulars who frequently come from far and wide. This recent report from Colchester's D.B. is typical: 'Another enjoyable visit to Khan's – a huge busy restaurant with bags of atmosphere. Chilli Chicken Masala – excellent spicy taste – also the Lamb Bhuna Ghost. Reasonably friendly service this time, which wore off when the place got busier – we had to ask five times for our pudding! Overall Khan's represents excellent value, and is highly recommended.' And from P.D.: 'I'm a regular here and if they don't make a mistake on my order and blame me for it, I'd think I was somewhere else!' Despite all this we'll go along with the majority and retain Khan's in our TOP 100. But maybe owner, Salman Khan, usually on hand, should consider implementing operational improvements. Tell him yourself. He's articulate and funny. And tell me of your visits too, please.

KHYBER   ©

56 Westbourne Grove, W2   ✆ 0171 727 4385

Much improved since Mr Lamba took it over, we hear, so it's welcome back to these pages, though N.S. found things a bit bland. Price check: Papadom 35p, CTM £4.95, Pullao Rice £1.75. Service charge 10%. Branch: Laguna, W13.

STANDARD

23 Westbourne Grove, W2   ✆ 0171 727 4818

Standard's the apt name for the street's longest established curry house.

SULTAN TANDOORI BUFFET   ©

57 Westbourne Grove, W2   ✆ 0171 792 2565

The 150-seat Sultan opened in 1993, under Messrs Khan and Majid, with a successful eat-all-you-can 20-dish (menu changed weekly) self-serve buffet for £6.99. Included in the price are table-served Papadoms and starters. The bonhomie from all this tummy-bursting good value spreads to the waiters, who are 'always pleasant' says E.D. Talking of the tummy, as if all this isn't enough, on Tuesdays there's an added attraction – Cathy the International Belly Dancer. And as if it isn't cheap

enough already, the owners promise Curry Club members a discount.
Branches: Kebabish, Wembley; Manor Park, E12.

W3 – Acton

ACTON TANDOORI

138 Churchfield Road, Acton, W3   ✆ **0181 992 4583**

'Good Nepalese food. Corn Bhajee and Jeera Chicken huge and delicious,' M.D. 'Simply outstanding,' S.A.

HIMALCHI   NEW ENTRANT

31 High Street, W3   ✆ **0181 992 3308**

Manager Gopal Paudyal wants you to know this is the best Nepalese restaurant in west London. Agreed?

W5 – Ealing

BHAI-JAN'S BALTI   NEW ENTRANT

57 New Broadway, W5   ✆ **0181 567 5577**

Newly opened since our last Guide, Taha Hussain Ebrahim has Ealingized Balti, to the displeasure of one reporter. 'The starters were good, fresh and of a decent size. The chutneys were very hot and the pots were small. Then plates were put in front of us – a tell-tale sign that this was not real Balti. Small pots arrived with the food. They were not sizzling, and showed no signs that the food had been cooked in the pot – the food was not bonding with the metal. However, the ingredients were fresh and the Vegetable Curry and Naans were noteworthy.' Others delight in the murals, the pewter and terracotta, and mixing-and-matching their Baltis. 'Great to have such a civilized place on the doorstep. And if I want to do it "chupatti-style", I can always pop over to Southall!' D.C. Watch out, it's unlicensed.

CLAY OVEN   ©

13 The Mall, Ealing, W5   ✆ 0181 840 0313

Still one of Ealing's favourites. Go for Bhadur Chelleri's cooking and
owner Vinod Khanna's discount. Branch: Ealing Cottage, 76 Uxbridge
Road, w13.

GITANJLI OF MAYFAIR   NEW ENTRANT   TOP 100

18-19 The Mall, W5   ✆ 0181 810 0006

There was once a time, in the early 1970s, when the Geetanjli (sic) of
Mayfair brought tears of joy to the eyes of its *aficionados*, which turned
to sadness when it shut. It was then arguably the best restaurant in the
UK. In 1996, its original owner, the ebullient Jetty Singh, turned to my
once home town, Ealing, to reincarnate his same-name venture with,
curiously, different spelling. Of course, nice though she is, the queen
of the suburbs ain't Mayfair, though such aspirations of grandeur may
well appeal to current Ealingites. It is typical of Mr Singh who, having spent the intervening period running a same-name restaurant in
Spain, clearly wished to mark his return to London with a Marbella to
marble (magnolia, at that, at least on the floors and green on the bar
top) spectacular decor scheme. And those murals, my dear, done it
seems, by Jetty's wife, Jaslein! The decor must have cost a whacking
packeeto, yet the prices are not Mayfair, and that too seems to appeal
to new Ealing. Its 140 seats are filled with chattering, contented regulars. And with good reason. The Gitanjli's food has lost nothing in the
intervening years. It is classic Punjabi, aromatic and gentle in its spicing, and far removed from the formula. Jetty's signature dishes are
game, venison, partridge, pheasant and quail, from £7.75. And try the
meat pickles. The less adventurous can partake of anything tandoori,
or a small menu of curries. Vegetarians can pick their way through the
menu to pastures green. Glad to see Jetty back. He'd closed before I
could give him my accolades in my first Guide, and was wasted in the
Costa. So welcome to our TOP 100. But a word of warning, for goodness sake don't even think of saying 'Goodness gracious me' – not, that
is, unless you want Jetty to regale you with his relationship with the
late Peter Sellers. He'll show you that famous advertisement, and no
doubt open the doors to the cavernous 300-seat banqueting suite too,
named after his most famous customer. For the record, price check:

Papadom 50p, Chicken Tikka £5.05, Tandoori King Prawn Masala £10.75, Pullao Rice £1.90. Set lunch from £3.95, dinner from £15-£20.

MONTY'S   TOP 100

1 The Mall, The Broadway, Ealing, W5   ℂ 0181 567 8122

Even with the arrival of the above competition, Monty's is still ahead on points as Ealing's most popular, with a full range of standard curries, done exceedingly well, plus some Nepalese specials. 'Still my favourite,' J.W. Remains in our TOP 100.

SAMRAT   ©

52 Pitshanger Lane, Ealing, W5   ℂ 0181 997 8923

A welcome curry-hole in the Pitshanger area, and serving the full range of curry favourites.

TAJ MAHAL   ©

12 Station Parade, Uxbridge Road, Ealing Common, W5   ℂ 0181 992 2874

Mrs Zaman continues to run this long-standing curry house. Established in 1961, it was the first in west London. It soon grew out of its one-shop unit and became known for its stainless-steel frontage opposite the Underground. It was the first to give a carnation to the lady, made the more unique in that it was a lady who managed it. Ann Marie moved on to her own venue much later (*see* NW10). It was one of my locals and I welcome it back to the Guide. Price check: Papadom 50p, CTM £5.45, Pullao Rice £1.55. Set meal from £8.50.

YAK AND YETI   ©

185 South Ealing Road, Ealing, W5   ℂ 0181 568 1952

Another good Nepalese in the area. Manager M.B. Thapa and chef Rajesh Maharajar's specials are the thing to choose for something different. No Yak or Yeti on the menu but Lamb or Chicken Bhutawa or Swadilo and Momo (dumplings with tomato pickle) make a nice change.

ZAYKA INDIAN CUISINE   ©

8 South Ealing Road, Ealing, W5 ℃ 0181 566 5662

'Rafiq Karim (proprietor) and staff could not have been nicer. Their service was superb and so was their food,' M.S. Fresh Carrot Chutney with the Papadoms, tasty starters (Gurda Masala – kidney) and 'great Chicken Ginger!'

W6 – Hammersmith

ANARKALI

303-305 King Street, Hammersmith, W6 ℃ 0181 748 1760

'Good honest food and nothing too startling,' D.L. Branch: Rajdoot, 291 King Street, W6, gets the same comments from D.L.

GANDHI

116 King Street, Hammersmith, W6 ℃ 0181 748 1826

Formerly Aziz. 'Decor plain, modernish, typically Indian, Indian music. Menu fairly extensive. Prices and portions good. Service was proficient and civil but definitely not friendly. Quite a long wait for the food, no first courses ordered which may have explained the delay. Lovely and light Papadoms with six excellent relishes. Chef's Special, Chicken Kashmiri, deserved its title, the sauce was very rich and sophisticated,' H.R.C.

TANDOORI NIGHTS TOP 100   ©

319 King Street, Hammersmith, W6 ℃ 0181 741 4328

Mr Modi Udin's Tandoori Nights still gets the best-in-the-area vote from our reporters. One local couple still goes on a regular King Street curry crawl, lucky them, from time to time – a kind of bindi-bender, I suppose, taking in them all, but they always find Tandoori Nights their favourite. 'The bright white facade is as inviting as the manager, A.B. Choudhury, and his staff. The pink decor is relaxing, and the food from chef Mabul Miah is curry house at its best,' J.W. We did get one complaint (from G.M.P.) about an open credit card slip following the

10% service charge being taken, and a scene, which we are checking out as we write. Meanwhile it remains in our TOP 100 because it performs the Bangladeshi formula well in all departments. Price check: Papadom 55p, CTM £7.95, Meat Thali £11.95, Pullao Rice £2.25. Set meal average for two £24.90.

W8

KENSINGTON TANDOORI

1 Abingdon Road, W8   ✆ **0171 937 6182**

M.A. Rahim and his Kensington venue are still doing it, trolleying the tricks of the trade to its regulars, under the deft touch of chef Pan-Singh Rana. Open noon-midnight. Price check: Papadom 70p, CTM £9.10, Meat Thali £12.90, Kurzi Lamb £82.50, paid in advance, Pullao Rice £2.55. Buffet lunch £9.95. Branches: Chambali, wc1; Ryath, w2.

MALABAR TOP 100

27 Uxbridge Street, W8   ✆ **0171 727 8800**

The Italian decor and the menu haven't changed at the Malabar since it opened in 1984. After all, why change a good thing? The menu is short, yet wide-ranging: from Philouries – batter-fried prawns (£3.60) – and Hiran (venison) starters to Long Chicken – medium-hot with cloves and ginger (£4.95). J.P.L., one of our more discerning, well-travelled, frequent reporters, says: 'This is a real find, thanks to your Guide. After so many recent formula curries, it's a treat to see different offerings on the menu and all superbly cooked. The Murgh Makhani and Keema Nan are among the best I have tasted, and the "menu for two" delivers a substantial and economical feast.' Jo Chalmers has now been joined front of house by her daughter Sophie, and we hear constant praise for their customer care. Remains very high in our TOP 100. Prices are reasonable, but the Sunday lunch buffet at £6.95 is a real bargain.

W9

RAJ BRASSERIE   ©

536 Harrow Road, W9   ℂ 0181 960 4978

A. Khalique's curry house is 'thoroughly decent in all respects,' says
D.R.

W12

ASKEW TANDOORI   ©

129 Askew Road, W12   ℂ 0181 749 3379

Daya Patell owns this and the w6 Gandhi (*see* entry) just a chupatti
chuck away, both being equally popular. We hear that the Bangalore
Phal is indeed 'extra very hot' (sic).

W13 – West Ealing

LAGUNA   ©

127-129 Uxbridge Road,
West Ealing, W13   ℂ 0181 567 6211

S.K. Lamba's large Laguna continues to please West Ealing. Its 140
seats are often all taken, which says it all. Price check: Papadom 35p,
CTM £5.95, Balti Veg £3.95, Pullao Rice £1.95. Set meal from £12.95.
Branch: Khyber, W2.

SIGIRI   NEW TO OUR TOP 100   BEST SRI LANKAN

161 Northfield Avenue,
Northfields, W13   ℂ 0181 579 8000

The Sigiri is a true gem in the unlikely setting of Northfields, serving
delightful, authentic Sri Lankan food, and there are precious few such
restaurants in the whole UK. Find the corner site with its smoked glass
windows, inset in red bricks. Enter to understated elegant decor of
slate floor and green walls, and its 50 seats. Enjoy the sensible service
and its good atmosphere. The food's good, too. Try Banana Chips

(£2.60) with Pol Sambol, with Maldives fish (£1.25) followed by squid or pork (devilled they say, but if you like it hot and spicy, tell 'em – the devil is quite a mild chappie at the Sigiri). The rice-based items, Hoppers (Apa), Dosa and Uppaamas – with their glorious Coconut Chutney – are almost old hat. Regulars tell of new dishes, including peppery meat and cashew chilli chicken (around £5-£6). Leave room (Sri Lankan food is deceptively filling) for Wattalappam, a very sweet, jaggery-based Sigiri signature pudding. All good Sri Lankan Sinhalese stuff, and all at good prices (average £15), especially the nine-dish Sunday lunch and dinner buffet at £5.50. Licensed. Dinners only, Tuesdays to Saturdays. Closed Mondays and Bank Holidays. Such treasures need nurturing. Welcome to our TOP 100.

W14

KHAN SAHI BALTI HOUSE   ©

142 West Cromwell Road,
West Kensington, W14   © 0171 371 2077

N. Rafiq and K. Sheikh were quick off the mark to offer Balti to West Kensington. As in Brum, you can get Balti anything but at rather higher prices (it is Kensington, after all, and it is smart). 'All eight of us enjoyed the Baltis and Naan Breads, though service was slow,' M.D.

London WC

WC1 – Holborn

CHAMBALI   ©

146 Southampton Row, WC1   © 0171 837 3925

K. Shah and Anwar Hussain have been operating the formula successfully here since 1985, with help from chef Ram Das. Open noon-midnight, daily. Price check: Papadom 70p, CTM £7.25, Tandoori Trout £9.50, Kurzi Lamb £82.50 paid in advance, Pullao Rice £2.55. Set meal £8.95. Branches: Kensington Tandoori, w8; Lichfield Brasserie, Sheen Road, Richmond.

GANDHI'S 2 NEW ENTRANT

35 Gray's Inn Road, WC1   © 0171 831 6208

A regular curry house, with a following of regulars. Price check: Papadom 50p, CTM £5.75, Pullao Rice £1.75. Minimum charge £10. Service charge 10%.

GANPATH

372 Grays Inn Road, WC1   © 0171 278 1938

Ignore the meat/chicken north Indian food and order the south Indian vegetarian dishes for a good, inexpensive meal.

MALABAR JUNCTION NEW TO OUR TOP 100

107 Great Russell Street, WC1   © 0171 580 5230

A fair bit of trumpeting heralded the opening of this restaurant since our last edition. We met the owners of this, and its TOP 100 sister, Ragam, w1, when we were doing cooking demos at the BBC Good Food Show, Olympia, just as the restaurant opened. The scenes back-stage in the prep kitchen (shared by eight stands, all cooking their butts off) would have put the health officer onto a stretcher. We kept as clear as we could of the turmoil, as did the Malabar, but we were sustained throughout the four-day slog by wonderful unsolicited veg-etarian offerings from their stand, washed down with the curiously-named Kama Sutra lager. 'You must come to the restaurant,' they kept offering, and we did, anonymously and undetected some time later. In my experience, south Indians are much less assuming, perhaps less ostentatious, than their northern counterparts. Certainly, most such UK restaurants that we've visited can be described so. But here is taste-ful expenditure. The conservatory, the bamboo chairs, the glass-domed roof with its planters, the fountain, the colonnades, gilt pictures and pastel walls give a relaxing and comfortable welcome. So do the Keralan staff. The south Indian menu offers not only vegetarian delights of the region, it gives meat, chicken and fish dishes, too. Malabar Chicken (£7.50) is cooked with coconut, curry leaves, garlic and mustard. The Fish Mollee (£7.50) is a classic dish, so mild and gentle in its coconut base that even the Raj allowed it at table. Cochin Prawn (£7.90) with the ubiquitous coconut, this time with tomato, is another. We've had a number of reports advising you to ask them to 'up the chilli strength', and if that's your taste, the kitchen will be more than happy to oblige. Hot is the norm in Kerala. All the regular rice-based offerings are here, such as Masala Dosa (crispy, potato curry-stuffed pancake), Uthappam (an intriguing rice-flour, crisp disc, baked with a spicy topping), Vellappam (like rice noodles), Paripu, Sambar (lentil dishes) and Rasam (the peppery soup and 'national' dish of the area), and those wonderful coconut chutneys. Licensed. Daily lunch and dinner. Three-course set meal plus coffee, lunch and pre-theatre, from 6-7.30p.m., £9.50. Average à la carte meal price £18. Welcome to our TOP 100.

RED PEPPER   ©

65 Red Lion Street, WC1   ℂ **0171 405 8072**

Manager Mujeeb Sayeed's cutely-named place has a good pedigree (Chutney's, Ravi Shankar and Handi are in the same ownership). Some good, unusual dishes on offer: Pattice (spicy potato rissoles) and Shakoothi (sic) Goan chicken, with plenty of red chilli pepper, are but two.

WC2

BHATTI

37 Great Queen Street, WC2   ℂ **0171 831 0817**

Mr Puri's place is back in the Guide following up, down, and presently up reports, of which more, please.

DACCA   NEW ENTRANT

46 Bedford Street, WC2   ℂ **0171 379 7623**

'Small, very ordinary, typical, old-fashioned. Menu absolutely standard. A sandwich board on the pavement advertised a Happy Hour discount of 20% for meals ordered between 5.30 and 7.30p.m., obviously a great draw as within minutes the restaurant went from empty to full. This did put a strain on the service and that left something to be desired. Papadoms and relishes, good standard. Chicken Tikka

Masala, an eye-shattering bright red, rather mild and watery. Onion Bhajia, flat disc style, fairly good. Vegetable Biriani, absolutely first-class. Mushroom and Brinjal Bhajees very good, but hardly different from each other. Full marks for offering a Gulab Jaman. Shame the service let down the restaurant, food overall quite reasonable, but meat dishes verging on mean,' H.C.

THE INDIA CLUB TOP 100   BYO

143 The Strand, WC2   © 0171 836 0650

It hardly needs to be said, but just in case you're from planet Zog, I'll say it! London taxi-drivers know everything about everything. Even their driving test is called the 'knowledge', so when a cabbie tells our ace reporter about the India Club – 'this is the place *aficionados* go to exchange recipes' – you know the India Club's arrived! Mind you, in all the 37 years I've been going there, I've never once seen recipes exchanging hands, nor have I been asked to participate. Pity, really! But who am I to argue with a London cabbie! What does change hands, and has done since the India Club opened in 1950, is fabulous, uncompromisingly Indian food, served in unpretentious surroundings. Or, at least, it used to. There are still plenty of fans: 'Delicious. Good description in Guide. Four Asian businessmen conducting business with piles of paper over lunch added to the atmosphere,' H.M. But for the first time we've received a couple of downers. 'It is some time since I have been to the India Club and it was the first time I felt the food was slightly under par. There was a great deal of noise and laughter from the kitchen all the time I was there so I think the food was getting a little less attention than normal. The Dosa was definitely cold and soggy, the Brinjal was its usual wonderful self but the coconut beans were very different and rather uninteresting, to the point of being a different dish – change of recipe or chef? To the restaurant's credit the waiter did offer to supply replacement Dosas, but I hadn't time or enough other food left to make it worth accepting. Even though it was very early in the evening the restaurant was fairly full so I think this experience was a one-off and regulars are still satisfied with its standard,' H.C. 'Having read about the India Club in the Guide, I had to try it. So as a surprise anniversary treat for Sue, my wife, I booked a room in the hotel, bought tickets for *The Mousetrap* and awaited the meal. Just as the Guide says, both the restaurant and the hotel were very, very plain, but clean. Waiter was very attentive – rushing over with a corkscrew when our bottle of wine came out of the wife's handbag. Chose Papadoms, Onion Salad, Mango Chutney, Chicken Dupiaza, Tandoori Chicken, Pilau Rice and Chupatti. Waiter suggested Bhajis as a starter and would I perhaps prefer Korma too, as it was the special. Ordered Bhajis but declined Korma. Bhajis were inedible. Dupiaza arrived with some raw onions added. Rice was stuck in lumps. Tandoori was massive and very tasty. An interesting experience, but not one I wish to repeat,' T.N. Good though it is, it's probably not the place to take 'the wife' for 'the anniversary'.

It's a cheap café style, with laidback, friendly waiters. It's unlicensed so you can BYO. There is some nonsense about joining their club (cost £1.10) to enable you to buy Cobra lager at the so-called hotel residents' bar. We duly paid up, to the unquenchable amusement of the elderly bar waitress who, in between cackles, advised me that the waiters 'know nothing'. It's all part of the charm. The India Club has been here since 1950. Find the door-width entrance – there's a new sign, gold on black, saying 'India Restaurant and Hotel', otherwise nothing has changed since it opened, including, I do believe, the barmaid! Climb the narrow stairs. (In typical Indian style, the owners do not see the need to redecorate – it's clean enough, though.) The first floor is the hotel reception (singles £29, doubles £39). Old hands stock up with Cobra here, then proceed up another floor to the L-shaped restaurant. Flaking plaster, no tablecloths, flies a-buzzing, bare charms, pictures askew. 'Someone has been round straightening the pictures, including Gandhi's! Let us hope that this is just a prank, not official policy,' G.R. And, shortly after: 'Gandhi is askew again – thank heavens!' G.R. We greatly prefer the south Indian Rasam (served in a tea cup with saucer – hot as hell), Sambar, Masala Dosa and Coconut Chutney. Don't over-order: the portions are generous. Despite its quirks (which gives it a 'charm of its own,' says C.D.), it decidedly remains firmly in our TOP 100. The last words go to P.D.: 'Long may the Club remain open.'

MAHARAJA OF INDIA   ©

19a Charing Cross Road, WC2   ✆ **0171 930 8364**

Bazlur Rashid (Salim)'s premises in their long, narrow shape with just a row of tables down each wall are open noon-midnight (useful to know). 'Food well above average, portions good, served hot. Very large Papadoms, light and crisp. Fish Balti, small pieces of marinated fish, mild, good texture. Butter Chicken, lived up to its name, very buttery, creamy, lots of coconut and almonds. Superb Vegetable Jalfrezi, very hot, large chunks of assorted vegetables with whole small green chillies, most of which I ate. All dishes wiped clean with Naan. Two small criticisms. A waiter saw us looking at the menu on the wall outside and almost shanghaied us inside, then was too keen to offer unasked advice, treating everybody as though they had never seen an Indian menu before, very irritating. Also too quick to remove finished dishes, I suppose better than being ignored, but not relaxing,' H.C. Branches: Piccadilly Tandoor and Maharaja Tandoori, both Denman Street, W1; Iman Brasserie, Rupert Street, W1; Strand Tandoori, Bedford Street, WC2.

PUNJAB   TOP 100   ©

80-92 Neal Street, Covent Garden, WC2   ✆ 0171 240 9979

The Punjab was London's third Indian restaurant (after Veeraswamy W1, *see* entry, and Shafi, now long closed), opening in 1947 in Aldgate. Even with its move to its present site in 1951, it is still the oldest Punjabi restaurant in the UK. And for all its life, it has been in the capable hands of just two men, the late founder and now his son, Mr S. Maan. Of course, by definition, the Punjab was one of the original pioneers of the curry formula. Only here it is done as it has always been done, and as it should be. The result is unlike the newer Bangladeshi clones, and is probably what old curry hands think they remember when they say 'curry isn't like it used to be in the old days'. The food is meat-orientated, spicy, savoury and very tasty. 'It's definitive Punjabi food,' S.A. One of its former regulars used it twice a day, five days a week, for forty years, before retiring (G.L.). This astounding claim (no one has bettered it) got Geoff onto a BBC-TV Noel Edmonds programme. Such is their loyalty to the place that regulars have their own club, the 'Punjabbers'. Remains high in our TOP 100.

ROYALS

7-8 Bow Street, Covent Garden, WC2   ✆ 0171 379 1099

Sited next to the Royal Opera House, whose closure for rebuilding is affecting the area, N. Hussain's place remains busy with pre-theatre dinners (three courses for under £10) 'served swiftly and deftly', and a local trade.

SHAN

200 Shaftesbury Avenue, WC2	✆ 0171 240 3348

'Tiny Gujarati café which looked more like a kiosk. When I visited, the proprietor's wife was helping her two daughters to practise reading English – I showed them the Guide and they read that instead! Tasty food and excellent value,' G.H. Hours: noon-9.30p.m. Closed Sundays.

SITAR BALTI

149 The Strand, WC2	✆ 0171 836 3730

Formerly Aldwych Tandoori. H.C. finds the staff 'a real credit to this restaurant ... welcoming, attentive and keeping an eye out ... just good restaurant practice, but not always encountered'. She loved her crab curry (£5.95,) CTM (£6) and Vegetarian Thali (£9.99). But noted 'mean' portions on one visit. C.T. was unhappy with cold food and sent it back. This resulted in 'possibly the best Sheek Kebab I've had'. But he didn't like the Pullao Rice, nor the excess ghee in the Balti. 'However, the dishes sent back were deducted from bill.' Much patronized by the staff of India House opposite.

STRAND TANDOORI   ©

45 Bedford Street, WC2	✆ 0171 240 1333

P.J. found 'competent food and good prices' at manager S. Rashid's Tandoori.

TALE OF INDIA

19 New Row, Covent Garden, WC2	✆ 0171 240 5348

Mahtab Chowdhury has been a Covent Garden restaurateur for years. 'Had a marvellous meal. Well served, definitely above average, the next time, just ordinary. Menu has reasonable choice. Decor still quite attractive, looks tired, whole place has an air of over-use and requires decoration, menus well-handled, tatty. Staff were welcoming and friendly, service prompt and efficient. All the food was fine, nothing outstanding and nothing dismal, portions bordering on meagre. Spicing tended towards the cautious,' H.C. Branch: Taste of India, 25 Catherine Street, Covent Garden, WC2.

TANDOORI NIGHTS   ©

35 Great Queen Street,
Covent Garden, WC2   ✆ 0171 831 2558

Owner Mrs Yasmeen Rashid opened her first Tandoori Nights in
Cockfosters, Herts, in 1988, and her second in NW1 (*see* entries),
months later. In 1993 she opened this branch. We note a change of both
manager, now Salil, and chef, now Waris Miah. Only one report
received (and that very recent) since this change, which tells of service
chaos, with the old-fashioned food-hoist delivering wrong things or
nothing, to the accompaniment of 'a lot of noise and very little result.
The food when it did arrive was very good, with an absolutely marvellous CTM and Paneer Masala,' H.C. Possibly an off evening. But the
above changes mean we have to remove it from our TOP 100, we hope
temporarily. Price check: Papadom 50p, CTM £6.75, Mixed Grill
£12.95, Pullao Rice £2.15. Lunch buffet £8.95. Service charge 12½%.
Reports, please.

THALI INDIAN VEGETARIAN   NEW ENTRANT   √ ©

3-7 Endell Street, WC2   ✆ 0171 379 6493

A useful new addition in London's heartland, a noon-11.30p.m. vegetarian-only, licensed place, from N. Hussain of Royals, WC2 (*see* entry).
South Indian Dosai and Idlis rub shoulders, or is that plates, with
northern Indian Mutar Panir (sic), Samosas and Ragara Patice, a
Bombay-style potato cake. The Gujarati Thali (£6.95) is a three-course
meal, and Bhel Puri addicts will find it in the £8.95 set meal. Selection
of Indian puddings. H.C. is 'very pleased with it'. Price check: Papadom
55p, Pullao Rice £2.25. All-day eat-what-you-like 12-dish buffet £4.95.
Service charge 10% (not on buffets).

The method in this Guide is to record our entries in alphabetical
order: first the county then, within that, the town, then the restaurant. With the demise of Avon (*see* below), we now start with
Bedfordshire, the first town we record is Ampthill, and its first
restaurant is Raj Gate, and so on. Our last English county is
Yorkshire West, and Wetherby is the last recorded town.

ENGLAND

AVON

See entries for Bristol, Gloucestershire and Somerset.

BEDFORDSHIRE

Ampthill

RAJ GATE NEW ENTRANT   ©

8 Bedford Street, Ampthill   ✆ 01525 404418

Competently presented restaurant, part of Nazrul Islam's small group (branches in Arlesey and Sandy). Price check: Papadom 40p, CTM £5.95, Pullao Rice £1.65. Minimum charge £12.

Bedford

ALAMIN   ©

51-51a Tavistock Street, Bedford   ✆ 01234 327142

Judging by the reports we've received, the restaurant is maintaining good standards.

AMRAN TANDOORI   ©

53b Harpur Street, Bedford   ✆ 01234 352359

Established in 1958, with the Amran changing hands to Shabbir Raja back in 1966, it has consistently served competent and good curries ever since. It's of the old style and we're glad to see that he has not removed the red flock wallpaper and Taj Mahal pictures that adorn the walls. Precious few Indian restaurants now have that once-celebrated trademark, and it would be a pity if the Amran changed its ways, though we are delighted to see that the Amran keeps up with the trends and serves Baltis, done well by Inayat Khan Raja in the Pakistani way, including Balti Chicken Quetta Earthquake (£7.30). It uses chillies, chillies and more chillies. I wonder where Shabbir got that wicked idea from? And they give Curry Club members a super 10% discount, too. Price check: Papadom 40p, CTM £7.25 incl. rice, Pullao Rice £1.60. Minimum charge £7. Open daily, 6p.m.-midnight.

GULSHAN NEW ENTRANT   ©

69 Tavistock Street, Bedford   ℅ **01234 359566**

Tavistock Street isn't exactly Brick Lane but, of its six curry houses, our scribe J.G. tells us that Ashkir Miah manages the Gulshan 'better than well'. Price check: Papadom 60p, CTM £6.75 incl. rice, Duck Tandoor £4.75, Pullao Rice £1.45. Open daily for lunch and dinner.

MAGNA TANDOORI

50 Tavistock Street, Bedford   ℅ **01234 356960**

Our scribes also speak well of Messrs Chowdhury and Mohammed's Magna, which continues to serve consistently good curries at fair prices. Branch: 199 Bedford Road, Kempston, Bedford.

Dunstable

TASTE OF INDIA TAKEAWAY   ©

135 High Street South, Dunstable   ℅ **01582 602697**

Hello, Dunstable! Is there anyone there? How about telling us about your nine restaurants, of which most are in the High Street. Montaz and Shomshor Ali talk to us. They say their Taste of India has been in their hands for more than 27 years and they know exactly how to please. I know they do, I bought a takeaway here when it first opened, following a visit to Electrolux.

©	Curry Club discount (see p. 607)	☕	Unlicensed
√	Vegetarian	▦	Home delivery
BYO	Bring your own alcohol		service available

Leighton Buzzard

AKASH TANDOORI

60 North Street, Leighton Buzzard   ✆ 01525 372316

Two P.C.'s (not the editor) applaud the Akash; one tells us that the mango chutney is the best he's tasted. And the other says: 'The Akash is still our local after seven years, and is generally on the good side of average. Decor is good and the restaurant is air-conditioned. Service is always good, hot crisp papadoms and chutneys appearing almost instantly. The menu is limited but the Lamb Pasanda and the Methi Chicken are perennial favourites, accompanied by Niramish or the Buttery Keema Naan which have become something of a speciality.'

INDIAN OCEAN   NEW ENTRANT   ©

13 Wing Road, Linslade,
Leighton Buzzard   ✆ 01525 383251

A full range of formula curries vie for your attention on the menu at chef-owner H. Ullah's place. The Chicken Rezala (£5.20) is S.F.'s favourite, 'with a divine flavour and succulent chicken'. Price check: Papadom 40p, CTM £4.95, Pullao Rice £1.40. Open daily, 5.30p.m.-midnight.

Luton

ALANKAR   ©

276 Dunstable Road, Luton   ✆ 01582 410374

Dilip Odera's Alankar is in a beamed mock-Tudor house, complete with tower (don't expect Hampton Court, though – it's strictly 1930s). Inside, our reporters tell us, you'll find a menu with all the favourites.

MEAH TANDOORI   ©

102 Park Street, Luton   ✆ 01582 454504

Named after owner, Moklish Meah, who also owns Biggleswade's Biggles Tandoori, this is a standard curry house with a typical menu offering all the curry favourites competently. Price check: Papadom 50p, CTM £5.30, Pullao Rice £1.75.

SHALIMAR CURRY HOUSE

129 Dunstable Road, Luton	© 01582 729753

Says B.G.: 'After a hard evening's work in Luton (this must really be the town that God forgot!) we end up at the Shalimar. It is like a transport café, formica-top tables, plastic seats, glass-fronted bar. The proprietor, Mr Khan, was very pleasant. Kebabs good and well-spiced – a hot mint chutney. Chicken Curry with quite a lot of tomato but not so much chicken – meat curry was better. Naan breads were very good. Not licensed.' Maybe God did forget about Luton, but where else can you get a curry takeaway at 4a.m., seven days a week?

BERKSHIRE
Bracknell

PASSAGE TO INDIA

3 Market Place, Bracknell	© 01344 485499

More reports are requested from this area. The few we have speak well of the Passage. P.J. thinks it is 'good' (praise indeed from this much-travelled curryholic!). It has a wide-ranging menu and home delivery.

Crowthorne

VILLAGE TANDOORI   NEW ENTRANT   ©

204 Dukes Ride, Crowthorne	© 01344 780009

Babu's the manager, Haque's the chef. Both do the formula well. Price check: Papadom 50p, CTM £5.95, Pullao Rice £1.65. Minimum charge £15.

Maidenhead

JAMUNA

73 Queen Street, Maidenhead   ✆ 01628 24497

'Well-balanced menu. Outstanding quality, completely adequate portions. Relaxing and unobtrusive restaurant with friendly and efficient service,' B.H.

Newbury

CURRY GARDEN   NEW ENTRANT

18 The Broadway, Newbury   ✆ 01635 528854

'Standard curry house food. Lamb Pasanda has been ordered many times and we haven't tired of it yet. Staff very pleasant and polite. Free Papadoms and coffee on our visits,' S.O.

Reading

BINA   TOP 100   ©

21 Prospect Street, Caversham, Reading   ✆ 0118 946 2116

Since we placed the Bina high in our TOP 100 last time, we've continued to receive good reports on the place. This is largely due to the energetic management from its young Bangladeshi proprietor, Abdul Miah, and manager Ahmed, helped by a strong family connection with the UK curry trade. Here, in a few extracts, is what some of our reporters think: 'The outside is appealing and the inside continues the theme. It is clean and smart, but very comfortable. The waiters were welcoming and efficient. Surprisingly, the manager apologized for the service being slow. We didn't notice. We arrived early on Bank Holiday Monday. By 8 o'clock the restaurant was filling up. The menu offered a wide selection of starters, main courses, sundries and vegetables. The prices were a little higher than average, but the food was well worth it ... fresh, tasty and well presented. The quantities were good. The food was served in small korais and so the meal was piping hot. The

Chicken Pakoras were particularly impressive and contained large pieces of chicken and were very crispy. The Nan Breads were excellent, especially the Peshwari which was full of lovely sultanas. Overall the standard of the rest of the meal was consistently good,' s.r. 'The surroundings are very pleasant and the staff welcoming and friendly. During my last visit, I had an interesting and most enjoyable chat with the owner. The service is just about right – not too rushed yet not too slow. Most importantly, of course, the food is quite exquisite and a little hotter than the average. I would certainly recommend the Puri Path as a starter. This is the chef's own recipe of liver cooked with spices, served on a fried Indian bread. Quite delicious and worth visiting the Bina to sample this dish alone. Although the Bina is perhaps a little more expensive than other curry restaurants in the area, it is more than worth the extra. Ladies will also appreciate the rose presented to them upon leaving,' m.w. 'Both the Butter Murg and Murg Shashlick are excellent and Keema Pilau a must. Good quantities – we normally end up leaving some. We each received a Christmas card with an offer for a free bottle of wine in January or February. When redeemed we received a very acceptable bottle of Piat d'Or. Our group of diners varies from three to six people. We found the Bina by chance when we were looking for somewhere to eat one Sunday. Now it's any excuse to go there for a meal,' s.m. But out of the blue came a stinker, from a local woman, Lisa Dianne Davies, who wrote telling me (as 'Dear sir or madam'!) how disappointed she was with the place. I mention her by name because somehow she got that same letter published in the *Sunday Times!* When I took this up with Mr Miah he was deeply concerned but unable to shed light on Ms Davies' complaint. And since one complaint, no matter how bizarre, amongst much praise does not demote a restaurant, the Bina stays in our TOP 100.

EVEREST TANDOORI

**9 Meadway Precinct, Honey End Lane,
Tilehurst, Reading**   ✆ **0118 958 3429**

Says m.w.: 'Although the decor and service are nothing special, the cuisine is extremely good. The portions are enormous and you need to be careful not to over-order. Probably not a place for eating on your own – you need a few friends to help you.' And s.p. says: 'Promoted as a Nepalese restaurant, it has plenty of seating and is quite busy on midweek visits. I had papadoms for a starter with pickles. Main course Chicken Tikka Massala, really good, full rich flavour right through the meat. Vegetable curry also very good. Rice aromatic and fluffy.'

GARDEN OF GULAB

130-134 Wokingham Road, Reading   ✆ 0118 966 7979

'The food is excellent and I particularly like the Lamb Korai. For those who like it hot, the Vindaloo certainly leaves the tastebuds tingling. What makes this restaurant a particularly enjoyable place to visit, however, is the friendliness of the staff with nothing being too much trouble. Indeed, I remember one occasion when I and a few friends had enjoyed our evening so much that we had missed the last bus home. Upon asking if we could ring for a taxi, the owner said that there was no need as he would arrange for someone to take us home. A nice gesture,' M.W.

GULSHAN   NEW ENTRANT   ©

20-24 Station Hill, Reading   ✆ 0118 958 9914

Lahoor Raja is the owner-manager of this popular local. Price check: Papadom 35p, CTM £5.90, King Prawn Chaneli £9.50, Pullao Rice £1.70. Minimum charge £10.

INDIA PALACE   NEW ENTRANT   ©

83-85 Wokingham Road, Reading   ✆ 0118 962 2711

Jointly owned by Mrs L.C. Payne and chef Bhadracen, and managed by A. Ahad. The Palace, which opened in 1995, has already become a favourite with everyone, we hear, including Reading's Asian community. Price check: Papadom 60p, CTM £6.30, Haandi – 'home-cooked' – Chicken and Mushroom with Rice £6.50, Pullao Rice £1.50. Set meal £9.95.

©   Curry Club discount (see p. 607)   Unlicensed
√   Vegetarian   ⊞   Home delivery
BYO   Bring your own alcohol   service available

Slough

ANAM TANDOORI AND BALTI HOUSE ©

1a Baylis Parade, Oatland Drive, Slough   © 01753 572967

A typical competent curry house owned by Javeed Ali, open evenings only. 'Baltis are a speciality here and very tasty too,' R.E.

BARN TANDOORI

Salt Hill Park, Bath Road, Slough   © 01753 523183

We know of restaurants in old schools, fire stations, churches, garages, even Portakabins, but the Barn takes the papadom! It's in an ex-cricket pavilion in the middle of nowhere – well, a park, actually, and next to the tennis courts. Owners Khorshed and Khondaker have been here for years now, dispensing 'eccentric service from mature waiters, who don't miss a thing, in cosy, rather stark, log-cabin-style woody decor,' says A.I.E. He lives in Lancashire but he likes the Barn so much that it's his local away from home because 'it's very cosy, with lots of locals enjoying the freshly-cooked, delicious, inexpensive food'. Despite crass opposition from the local council, reported in our 1991 Guide, the Barn finally got its full licence. Price check: Papadom 50p, CTM £5.75, Pullao Rice £1.85. Set meal £10. Eat-your-fill Sunday lunch £5.95, under-12s £3.

Theale

CAFE BLUE COBRA   NEW ENTRANT TOP 100
BEST IN THE WEST

20 High Street, Theale   © 0118 930 4040

Here's a new (mid-1996) place with a real difference, in an unlikely location – a tiny, pretty village just off the M4's J12. It is owned by the enterprising Abssar Waess, whose curry connections extend to his celebrated uncle, Wali Udin, curry restaurateur and Bangladeshi Consul in Scotland. With such a pedigree, it was not surprising that Waess would want to open his own restaurant, but he decided to do something ambitious and unique. The clue is in the name. The venue opens at noon and operates, café-style, until midnight. The first-timer is struck by the coolness and fresh cleanliness of the decor. The bar area, with its marble and cane furnishings, seats 30. It leads on to the main dining area, whose 60 ormolu seats are designed to evoke airy oriental verandas. The light walls are a regularly changing 'gallery', home to the works of local professional artists. The Cobra Express Platter lunch can be advance-ordered by phone and served on arrival – useful for the busy exec. Those with less demanding timescales can choose à la carte until 2.30p.m., or simply linger in the bar over the snacks menu until 6p.m., with cappuccino, or sample some of the 16 worldwide beers, including Cobra, which are on offer. From 6p.m. the full menu comes into play, and an interesting document it is. Naturally there is a wide range of Bangladeshi and Bengali dishes, some of which will be familiar to the curry *aficionado*. Delights include Tikka (£ 3.95), Methi Saag Gosht (£6.45) and Birianis (£8.85). But there are so many other dishes and ingredients that 'it takes several visits, and we're still just learning,' M.N. There is duckling, crab, venison, veal, pomfret, ayre, surma river fish and much more.

Indeed, so far I've only touched on half the menu. The other half is Thai food. Two different master chefs have their own stations in the kitchens. The Thai operation includes some classics, such as, for starters, steamed mussels (£5.50), Chicken Sateh (£3.95) or a mixed platter (£9.95). Tom Yam soups start at £2.95, and the main courses range from Thai Green Chicken Curry (£7.50) to Ped Pad Prik – Hot Duck (£13.90) with Pad Thai noodles (£5.95). Egg-fried rice is £2.75. Expect to spend around £35 per head for a three-courser with drink and coffee. There are themed set meals from £17.90, but Waess reports that many diners happily mix and match the two cuisines. And why not? Eating has no rules other than enjoyment. Traditionalists who insist that nothing can be changed are bores. Café Blue Cobra is far from boring. Welcome to our TOP 100.

Twyford

GAYLORD ©

26 London Road, Twyford ✆ **0118 934 5511**

Says A.V.G.: 'The service is friendly and good-humoured. My companion chose Moglay Chicken, absolutely superb. A waiter even came over to ask her if the chicken was too strong — I think he meant tough — but it was perfect.' M. Ullah also owns the Maharajah in Yateley and Lightwater's Raj Rani.

MITA'S NEW ENTRANT ©

37 London Road, Twyford © 0118 934 4599

Mita's is owned by Shilu Miah and managed by M. Qayyum. It's a good, solid local, we hear. Price check: Papadom 50p, CTM £5.95, Bengal Fish £6.10, Pullao Rice £1.65. Minimum charge £15.

Windsor

SHARMIN'S OF WINDSOR NEW ENTRANT ©

41 Thames Street, Windsor © 01753 832499

Attractive, green-fronted corner site, near the theatre, attractive green inside. Price check: Papadom 50p, CTM £5.95, Kurzi Chicken for four £52 paid in advance, Pullao Rice £1.60. Set meal £6.50.

Wokingham

ROYAL INDIAN TANDOORI ©

72 Peach Street, Wokingham © 0118 978 0129

Our reporters tell us of a thoroughly competent restaurant serving standard curry house food. Last time we reported that prices were high (Wokingham is the UK's wealthiest town!) but, three years on, owner A. Khalique's Royal's prices are as good as any other restaurant out of London town.

© Curry Club discount (see p. 607)   Unlicensed
√ Vegetarian ⊞ Home delivery
BYO Bring your own alcohol service available

BRISTOL

Avon no longer exists as a county and its towns are now divided between Gloucestershire and Somerset, apart from the city of Bristol which is now a county in its own right.

LAL JOMI PAVILION   ©

2 Harcourt Road, Redland, Bristol   ℭ 0117 924 4648

'Excellent food, excellent service, though occasionally a little slow when pushed. We've never had a poor meal off their extensive menu. Try the Jalfrezi, Chicken Tikka Biriani or Makhani. I've been here many times, comfortable, usual decor but nice booths to hide in. Book at weekends,' A.W.

MEENAR   NEW ENTRANT   ©

143 Church Road, Redfield, Bristol   ℭ 0117 939 5534

New to the Guide, and quickly attracting attention. Why? Because it is owned and managed by Shaukat (Shaun) Alime and his chef-trained wife, Bushra. The food is Pakistani, cooked on view if not by Bushra then by Abdul Nasir, and it's really good value. Only 36 seats, so book. Open daily, 5p.m.-1a.m. Price check: Papadom 25p, CTM £4.20, Pullao Rice £1.80. Set meal £11.75.

THE NEW TAJ TANDOORI

404 Gloucester Road, Horfield, Bristol   ℭ 0117 942 1992

Takeaway only, evenings only. Says A.J.W.P.: 'I have been eating Indian food for 35 years, and in the last 10 years or so I thought my palate had become jaded since all the normal Indian restaurant food tended to taste the same and was indifferent in flavour, not like it used to be in the 50s and 60s. However, the New Taj has restored my faith. It is first class.' Owned and run by Parvin Rayman, a Bangladeshi Muslim woman described by all our reporters as helpful and friendly. Her take-away is spotless, decorated with flowers and serving fresh, tasty food.

PUSHPANJLI   √

217a Gloucester Road, Bristol   ℂ 0117 924 0493

'A wonderfully informal yet smart Gujarati vegetarian restaurant fitted with formica tables and plastic chairs, with all food displayed under a glass counter. All food is home-cooked, a huge variety of starters, Dhal Bhajia, Samosa, Kachori, Bateta Wada, Mogo Chips, all superb. Large assorted pickle tray offering wide choice and lovely Papads. Masala Dhosas enormous helping with Sambar and coconut chutney. Many lovely vegetable curries, rice and breads. I visit this restaurant several times a month and it is truly brilliant in all aspects listed above,' D.R. 'My number one restaurant, great vegetarian food which I cannot fault. Bhel Puri great, portions good, sweets are very indulgent. They hold buffet evenings where you help yourself for £10-£12ish, eat until you drop. A quality restaurant,'J.M.

RAJDOOT   TOP 100   ©

83 Park Street, Bristol   ℂ 0117 926 8033

Now in its 27th year, Rajdoot continues to reign supreme. The owner, Mr Des Sarda, is Indian. As most restaurants are Bangladeshi-run, Rajdoot's food may come as a surprise to some. It is much truer to the authentic food you'll find in homes in northern India. It is this very fact that leads to the disappointment which is expressed to us by a small percentage of Rajdoot's diners who simply do not find the food matching their expectations. The complaints, and I stress again that they are few but they are persistent, are that the food is bland and the prices high. It's the same at all three Rajdoot branches (see Birmingham; Dublin; Manchester). I personally continue to dine here (and at the others), and I have to say that I find it excellent on all counts. Actually, we have had fewer such reports this time. Of course, the prices are higher than average – it is easy to spend £25-£30 a head. However, there are Chef's Recommendations – set meals from about £15 per person, including a vegetarian platter. A.E.J. keeps coming back for more! – 'The cooking is good, the meals nicely spiced if a little mild for my taste. They do, however, serve delicious Indian sweets. I particularly enjoy the Gulab Jamun. Polite service, good food, atmosphere and the smell of incense are what makes it for me!! No wonder it's in your TOP 100. Go for it.' We confirm this enthusiastic view and recommend that you ask for the food to be spicy, if that's your bag. s.y. confirms it too: 'Maintains a very high standard. They are always willing to cook the meals to your particular taste, whilst maintaining the excellent Punjabi style of cooking.'

SHEESH MAHAL   ©

13a Gloucester Road, Bishopston, Bristol   ℂ 0117 942 2942

A typical curry house which has been in the same ownership since 1979 and with sufficient 'satisfied' reports to maintain its entry in the Guide.

SITAR   ©

61 High Street, Westbury-on-Trym, Bristol   ℂ 0117 950 7771

'Still providing good-quality food with a very good-value takeaway discount,' G.C.

TANDOORI NIGHTS

86 Broad Street, Staple Hill, Bristol   ℂ 0117 970 1353

A.E.-J. said of this place: 'This is where I proposed to my now fiancée!! After all that was over, we settled down to order a meal that included melt-in-the-mouth Chicken Tikka starter and Shami Kebabs. This preceded her usual CTM and my Lamb Vindaloo. Both main meals were beautifully cooked, as were the accompanying rices. First time I'd tried Banana Naan, now I can't get enough.' M.B. asked 'of what?', but since this Guide is read before 9p.m., we'll assume A.E.-J. meant the well-priced, good portions and friendly staff!

BUCKINGHAMSHIRE

Aylesbury

GOLDEN BENGAL   NEW ENTRANT   ©

1-2 Villiers Building, Buckingham Street, Aylesbury
ℂ 01296 84001

Sayed Miah took over in 1996 at this well-established venue (1976), and we hear it's the best of the town's six Indian restaurants. Price check: Papadom 35p, CTM £7.40, Korai Chicken £7.60, Pullao Rice £1.50. Minimum charge £6.50.

Beaconsfield

BUCKS TANDOORI

7 The Broadway, Penn Road,
Beaconsfield   ✆ 01494 674580

Says M.S.: 'I am a regular, and I mean most Friday nights. The food here is Nepalese-style and is freshly prepared, so do not expect to get in and out in record time. The service is comfortably good with friendly and polite waiters. Every Sunday there is a buffet — eat as much as you can for £7.50 per person. Everything that has been tried is excellent, and well worth a visit. Special events take place throughout the year. Bucks Tandoori has kept a consistently good standard of food for a number of years — so much so that you will want to tell your friends.'

MOGHAL TANDOORI   ©

8 Warwick Road, Beaconsfield   ✆ 01494 674280

Dabir Ahmed's restaurant is decorated to a very high degree of comfort. The menu is extensive and contains some unusual dishes. 'Dalbura (starter) was described by the waiter as "chicken burger", not far from the truth but very nicely spiced, very filling! All the food was very tasty, generous portions and piping hot. Will return,' D.M.

SPICE MERCHANT

33 London End Road, Beaconsfield   ✆ 01494 675474

The former Tropical Garden has been refurbished in 'non-Indian' style and renamed. 'The back room opens out onto a fair-sized garden, doors open, and is very welcoming on a hot night. They intend to erect a canopy. Food is subtly spiced. Waiters dressed in traditional costume, which gave a fine overall ambience. Prices as usual average to tops for this Thames Valley area but to be expected. Highly recommended,' D.F.

Buckingham

DIPALEE   ©

18 Castle Street, Buckingham   ✆ 01280 813925

A regular entrant in our Guide because it is a well-established (1980)
curry house under the watchful ownership of Salique Ahmed. We still
hear about people enjoying the special Khurzi Chicken or Lamb (48
hours' notice required). We also hear about other tasty dishes. 'I had
Methi Chicken in a very tasty sauce,' J.G. 'The food is always good, portions large,' M. and A.J.

Burnham

AKASH TANDOORI   ©

21 High Street, Burnham   ✆ 01628 603507

Foysol Ahmed's Akash is a regular entrant in these pages. Indeed, our
regular correspondent of many years, who still wishes to remain
anonymous, now claims to have eaten his way round the menu over 15
times – every dish at least once.

Chesham

DELHI DURBAR

131 Broad Street, Chesham   ✆ 01494 783121

S.J.W. has 'visited this restaurant on many occasions. Brilliant food,
good selection. Huge portions, small restaurant. Very friendly staff.
Mushroom Rice £2, Chicken Madras £3.75, Samosas £1.75. Staff get to
know their regulars and go out of their way to chat, joke and be
extremely pleasant.'

©	Curry Club discount (see p. 607)	☕ Unlicensed
√	Vegetarian	⊞ Home delivery
BYO	Bring your own alcohol	service available

Flackwell Heath

EMPIRE OF INDIA   ©

3a Straight Bit, Flackwell Heath   ℂ 01628 530304

Fokruz Zanel's pleasant, smallish (42 seats) curry house is open evenings only, and serves all the standard curries and tandooris competently, according to our reporters, with generous portions.

Great Missenden

TANDOORI NITE   ©

56 High Street, Great Missenden   ℂ 01494 866953

Motior Rahman's Tandoori Nite has been operating since 1986. 'A very pleasant interior, imaginatively decorated with large glass panels separating the tables. We had Lamb Kursi and Lamb Tikka Massalla, Keema Nan and rice, we were very impressed with the food, service and atmosphere. Will be revisiting, recommended,' J.L.

High Wycombe

CURRY CENTRE   ©

83 Easton Street, High Wycombe   ℂ 01494 535529

A long-standing restaurant (1970) which since 1980 has been owned by A. Musowir (manager) and M.A. Mali (chef). Whenever the owners are personally looking after front of house and kitchen respectively, you can be sure of getting their best (or at least you know who to tell if not). They also own the Indian Delight Takeaway, 189 Farnham Road, Slough.

ELACHI

188 Cressex Road, High Wycombe   ℂ 01494 510810

Elachi, as all good cooks know, means cardamom. Under the same ownership as The Bina in Reading (*see* entry). It opened February 1995.

An extremely pretty restaurant with hand-painted figures on the walls reminiscent of Michelangelo. The menu is equally interesting with quite a number of new dishes. We wish Abdul great success with his new venture. Reports are welcomed.

Little Chalfont

PUKKAH SAHIB NEW ENTRANT ONE TO WATCH

**13 Nightingale Corner, Cokes Lane,
Little Chalfont** © **01494 763144**

Recently opened, early 1997, and already full to bursting. Menu reminiscent of the Bombay Brasserie and Chutney Mary, with classic Raj and Indian dishes. M.S. tells of a long wait 'nibbling papadoms and pickles, and some confusion, made up for with free wine and profuse apologies and, above all, unusual good food. Calamari Chilli (£4.60) and Salmon Samosa (£3.95) were followed by Goan Green Chicken Curry (£8.50) and Lamb and Saffron Biriani (£8.60), cooked, layered in the pot, complete with chupatti lid (called Dum). Despite the problems, we'll eat here again.' Prices above average. Traditional items are all here if you want them. Price check: Papadom 70p, CTM £6.95, Pullao Rice £1.95.

Milton Keynes

Britain's most developed new city has gobbled up many surrounding towns, in which are some 20 curry houses, including an exceptional one (the Jaipur). Many offer a home-delivery service. Indian traveller and curry expert Brian George still wonders whether MK has become 'a city of bedridden curry addicts'. Don't know about beds, Brian, but they sure love gobbling curry, whether prone or erect (sorry, I mean up and about), judging by the many reports I get on MK. Here is the pick of the city's curry houses as rated by a good number of our contributors.

AKBAR TANDOORI   ©

10-12 Wolverton Road, Stony Stratford,
Milton Keynes   © 01908 562487

Well-established (1983), owned and managed by Messrs A. and M. Nasir Uddin (who also own the Agrabad, 67 West Street, Boston, Lincolnshire). 'Pre-booked lunch for four, accompanied by an eight-month-old baby (who brought her own food). Mr Uddin extremely friendly, especially to the baby. Chose a varied menu of starters and main courses and found the quality excellent, quantities ample and the dining room very pleasant, much more daylight than the gloomy caves resembled by some of our local Indian restaurants. Adequate car-parking space. Altogether an outing to be repeated,' D.B.

BALTI NIGHTS   NEW ENTRANT   ⊞

11 Wolverton Road, Stony Stratford,
Milton Keynes   © 01908 562295

Formerly New Tandoori Grill. Takeaway only, with a thriving home-delivery service. Service is prompt and excellent. Quality is consistently good, albeit a standard menu. 'On a tired Friday night we ordered Meat Thali (£8.20) and Sag Bhajee (£1.75). Very generous portions, including copious quantities of salad and onion. Sag Paneer(£2) is good and interestingly different with creamy sauce. Generous portions of Meat Dhansak (£3.50). It's good!' B.G.

GOLDEN CURRY   ©

4 Duncombe Street, Bletchley, Milton Keynes
© 01908 377857

MK's oldest established curry house (1971) has been under Kalamdar Ali's ownership since 1982, with Iskander as head chef. They've been dispensing competent curries for years here to the contentment of a good number of regulars.

JAIPUR   BEST BANGLADESHI TOP 100   ©

502 Elder Gate, Central Milton Keynes   © 01908 669796

Mr A. Ahad's Jaipur restaurant in the centre of MK, beside the station, has set a very high standard since it opened in 1988. We awarded it a TOP 100 cachet BEST IN CENTRAL ENGLAND AWARD in our last edition. Since then Mr Ahad has achieved his ambition to bring in a chef directly from India, in the person of Oberoi-trained Vijendra Singh Kumpawt. Working alongside the already excellent Sufian Miah, the quality of the food can only get better. And so say all of you. Because, just like last time, we have again received a veritable bombardment of good reports, and not one of them was bad. Not that is, until Dr Ho Yen's outburst about some of his staff not wishing to pay some of the bill at a Christmas do. I mention him by name since he and his story appear in the intro on page 9. Then there was another pair of doctors, M. and H.K., who found the portions small. Small! I have before me about 70 reports on the Jaipur. No one mentions small. Several say it was 'a little too much food' (F.R., Mr and Mrs J. and Mr G.) I've already asked why it is we seem to get complaints from doctors (*see* Tabaq, London SW12). But we do, and frankly this one has to be wrong. That leads such complainers to say that I am in the pocket of restaurateurs like Mr Ahad. Well, I'm not! But I know him a little better than some, because he has been my client on one of my Gourmet Groups to India. And what I know is that you will not find a restaurateur who cares more about his restaurant and his customers than Mr Ahad. One of our most regular and reliable reporters, B.G., says: 'I am a Londoner, so it never annoys me in a parochial sense that London dominates the "Best-of" lists. However, should the "best" ever move out of the capital, I can't imagine there could be a better contender than the Jaipur. It does not stand still. Additions to the menu, special functions, and now the new chef. Rosemary Conley designed an exclusive low-calorie menu for weight-watchers. Once a month there's a banquet night, and there are regular "special events" menus to celebrate festivals and anniversaries, with musicians and dancers gracing these evenings, and so it goes on. And the quality never changes. Everything from the decor to presentation is first-class. The "loos" are so clean you could eat your meal there.' We're not going quite that far but we agree they are immaculate. So too is the decor. It's very plush, in shades of pink, reflecting its namesake city – Jaipur – in Rajasthan, a city where all the buildings are made from the local pink-coloured sandstone. Walls, chairs, tablecloths, ceiling (the centrepiece of which is a chandelier) are a gorgeous pink, a colour that we know appeals to J.L., one of our most prolific restaurant reporters.

C.M. says he was 'immediately impressed with the decor. Settled at my table and started on the Papadoms. My starter of Murgir Raan arrived, again I was impressed. After this excellent starter arrived the main course: Chicken Jaipuri, Pullao Rice and the best Peshwari Nan that I have ever tasted anywhere! Would feature highly on anyone's list of favourites.' Price check: Papadom 45p, CTM £6.95, Pullao Rice £1.75. Minimum charge £9.50. Service charge 10%. 'All round, the Jaipur is an outstanding restaurant,' says B.G. We certainly agree.

JALORI   NEW ENTRANT   ©

23 High Street, Woburn Sands,
Milton Keynes   ✆ **01908 281239**

Hai and Ahad's Jalori is bigger than it looks. 'Decor and comfort good. Staff very friendly and have a good sense of humour. Chicken Chat (£2.50) very good. Prawn Patia (£4.95) good but could have had a more sweet and sour taste. My friends enjoyed their Chicken Kormas (£4.25) and Karahi Gusht (£5.75),' L.G. 'An enjoyable evening,' A.G. 'First class,' B.G. Price check: Papadom 40p, CTM £5.95, Pullao Rice £1.50. Minimum charge £8.50. Eat-your-fill Sunday buffet £6.95. Branches: Mysore, MK; Dipalee, Buckingham.

MOGHUL PALACE   ©

7 St Paul's Court, High Street, Stony Stratford,
Milton Keynes   ✆ **01908 566577**

'The location is an old monastery school where monks once beat knowledge into the sons of local gentry,' L.T. Now, the only beatings are from local curryholic gentry, who beat a path through its Gothic arch, complete with wrought-iron gate, beyond which stands the imposing clerestoric building. No clergy remaining though … your greeting will be from M. Hussain or A. Ali who, given a chance, will tell you how much they spent converting this Victorian former cigar-factory-cum-orphanage-cum-school into their Palace. But impressed you will be, with the spacious reception area with its armchairs and comfortable sofas where you wait to be seated, and the scale and height of the dining room with its tiled floor, stonework and wood panels. Be nice to the gargoyles, there to ward off bad vibes! The menu offers all the familiar curry items. 'Service and food quality were both excellent although portions were on the small side. I had my usual favourite, Chicken Zalfraji (£5.75). It was very tasty as were the Chicken Madras (£4.95), Thali Special (£9.95) – delicious – and Chicken Biryiani,' B.G. Price check: Papadom 45p, CTM £6.45, Pullao Rice £1.80. Several set meals from £12.95.

MYSORE

101 High Street, Newport Pagnell,
Milton Keynes ✆ **01908 216426**

Another MK goodie from the Ahad stable, this one operated by brother Abdul Odud, who has built its reputation up and up in its seven-year run to a high standard. The dining room, combined within two cottages, provides a number of secluded areas, which 'give a good feeling of privacy,' H.G. 'I had Vegetable Thali (£7.95), interestingly different from the usual selection – Sabji Jalfrezi, Baigan Bartha, Aloo Gobi, Bindi Bhajee, Dall Tarka, mixed Raita, Naan and Rice. It was very good – I particularly liked the Dall, but their Dall and Chapatti have always been among my favourite Indian food,' B.G.

THE NIGHT OF INDIA ⊞ ©

Agora Centre, Church Street, Wolverton,
Milton Keynes ✆ **01908 222228/322232**

We're not sure why K. Kapoor subtitles his venue The Balti Kebab Palace when Night of India sums it all up – it stays open until 1.30a.m. to please the MK night owls and, not surprisingly, it doesn't do a lunch trade. B.G. tells us his 'old favourite's home-delivery trade seems to do better than in-house'. Twenty per cent discount on takeaway orders collected (over £10). Food is good, the House Special Biriani includes lamb, chicken and prawns with salad dressing. The Dal was a delight.

PALACE ON WHEELS NEW ENTRANT

1 Stratford Road, Wolverton, Milton Keynes
✆ **01908 221324**

The former Royal Engineer Pub, in the former railway town, so this new venture has chosen an original and doubly apt title. That's because India's Palace on Wheels is a vintage train which runs round Rajasthan, with stalwart tourists paying dearly to eat and sleep and be merry on board for days on end. The MK restaurant 'retains the railway tradition. A comfortable and spacious dining room, with plenty of room around the tables, and pleasant decor. Big windows let in daylight and it has retained the original bar with its mirrors – the old saloon bar is a private function room. Extensive menu. First-class food reflects the grandeur of the Maharajahs. Quantity on the large side (though we have limited appetites). Service very prompt and friendly,' D.B. 'Has fast become one of my favourites. Chooza Zafrani (£6.50) – chicken in saffron with almonds, cashews and cream – Vegetarian Thai (£8.95) with a superb Baigan (aubergine) makes this slightly different from standard fare. Service excellent, comfortable and relaxing,' B.G.

Wendover

THE RAJ

23 Aylesbury Road, Wendover   ✆ 01296 622567

Situated in a listed building in a beautiful old street, in the picture-postcard town of Wendover. Inside are 'exposed beams, with walled partitions, dividing the 60-seat space into almost separate rooms, creating an agreeable ambience. We had Machli Biran, fish parcels (£3.10), and Chicken Tikka Balti (£9.95 incl. rice) which to our delight was served in a copper "bucket" with handle!' B.G. Price check: Papadom 50p, CTM £6.95, Pullao Rice £1.80. Sunday buffet £7.50.

CAMBRIDGESHIRE
Cambridge

CURRY QUEEN

106 Mill Road, Cambridge   ✆ 01223 351027

Opened in 1972, this 96-seat family-run business is 'often the busiest in Cambridge's curry alley. Attractive decor, Cobra lager, fresh papadoms, followed by Onion Bhajis and salad, Chicken Tikka Bhuna (lovely smoky taste) and Parathas all for under a tenner,' A.E.

GOLDEN CURRY   ©

111 Mill Road, Cambridge   ✆ 01223 329432

'Unobtrusive street-side appearance should not put off. Greeting friendly, even on a busy Saturday night, from Mr Miah. Chicken Dansak was rich and hot, and the Chicken Shashlik had a wonderful taste. Very pleasant surroundings – divided into booths. Everything piping hot – including the plate,' J.B. Price check: Papadom 40p, CTM £6.25, Pullao Rice £1.70. Minimum charge £10. Branch: Gulshan, Regent Street, Cambridge.

KOHINOOR   ©

74 Mill Road, Cambridge   ✆ 01223 323639

The Kohinoor is a regular Guide entrant. It gets the thumbs up from M.B.: 'Yes, the peacock tapestries would seem to have disappeared since the last Guide. I was shown to my table by a very polite and attentive waiter. Lamb Rogan Gosht, very tasty, Pilau Rice excellent.' P.H. thinks it is 'outstanding, beautifully presented and every dish flavoursome.' J.B. was less flattering, finding lunchtime service 'poor, with bored waiters, but most delicious Chicken Tikka'.

MEGNA BALTI HOUSE NEW ENTRANT   BYO ©

36a Mill Road, Cambridge   ✆ 01223 576266

Opened in 1995, Aibab Ali's Balti house feels fresh, with its tiled floor and hooped cane chairs, and on-view kitchen. Its useful noon-midnight hours, BYO and fair prices (from £1.40 for starters, £2.95 for main dish and £4.95 for Balti incl. Naan) make it popular with all.

TAJ TANDOORI   ©

64 Cherry Hinton Road, Cambridge   ✆ 01223 248063

S.A. Haque's Taj Tandoori has a standard heat-graded menu with all your curry favourites, plus one that caught A.B.'s eye, Tandoori Chum Chum. (No, we don't know what it is either.)

Ely

INDIA GARDEN NEW ENTRANT   ©

13 Victoria Street, Littleport, Ely   © 01353 863656

It's time for a new Ely entrant, we feel (*see* next entry), so let's hear it for Sahid Abu's place. And we do hear that it's all here, all good competent stuff. Price check: Papadom 40p, CTM £5.95, Pullao Rice £1.60.

SURMA TANDOORI

78 Broad Street, Ely   © 01353 662281

An old friend on these pages, or so we thought, having been in every edition of this Guide since we started. Teacher B.G. says: 'My annual visit to the Surma – a fieldwork trip with hundreds of vibrant students!! While they munch their sandwiches in the cathedral car park, two colleagues and I enjoy a takeaway as we supervise. A very acceptable lunch. But this time, black mark! Despite it having a Curry Club sticker on the window, certificate on the wall, and Curry Club details all over the menu, the waiter had never heard of the Curry Club and refused our discount. Embarrassing!' Wake up, please, Surma. We don't mind if you don't wish to continue to give the promised discount, but firstly tell *us* – you didn't even return your form to us. Secondly, train your staff to observe what's in their venue, or next time you're out!

Huntingdon

THE DARJEELING NEW ENTRANT

69 High Street, Huntingdon   © 01480 411097

Are its displays of photos still outside, now that former PM John Major has been displaced? D.J.S. and E.J.Y., having moved from E17, feared that the sticks might be: 'A curry-less desert. It is not. A cracking example is the Darjeeling. The prices are comparable, the only drawback is that we can't get there by Tube any more.'

Peterborough

BOMBAY BRASSERIE   ©

52 Broadway, Peterborough   ✆ 01733 65606

Opened in 1988 by Rony Choudhury and Mahbub Khan (front manager and chef respectively), we hear of a very attractive red-brick interior with a brass-work bar as a feature. R.G. finds 'the food quality very good, quantities generous, service excellent, in a comfortable restaurant with an easy atmosphere.' Others talk of the good-quality Sunday lunch buffet.

INDIA GATE   ©

9 Fitzwilliam Street, Peterborough   ✆ 01733 346485

Shah Nanaz's India Gate appeals, it seems, to a solid core of regulars, some of whom talk of the 'elegant decor full of Eastern trinkets and atmosphere'. The menu consists of a full house of curry favourites, competently cooked and served.

SHAH JEHAN

18 Park Road, Peterborough   ✆ 01733 348941

This is in the Guide because of reports like this from D.L.C.: 'My wife and I visit the place whenever we can. The decor, staff, service and food are fantastic. We cannot fault the place.' And from D.L.T.: 'The Tandoori was juicy and crisp, the Dhansak just the right spicy hot. The Bhaji was a little small but we were very hungry. You get first-class service.'

TAJ MAHAL   ©

37-39 Lincoln Road, Peterborough   ✆ 01733 348840

Mohammed Shabeer is owner and manager and Gulfraz Khan head chef. Between them since 1983 they have built up a good, solid regular trade producing competent curries.

St Ives

KUSHIARA

21 Bridge Street, St Ives   © 01480 465737

'Although we live approximately 15 miles away from St Ives, whenever we are celebrating a special occasion (such as my birthday this time) we always return to this restaurant. The manager, Ali, always remembers our names and where we live. The tablecloths are so white you can see your reflection in them and the service is excellent. Value for money is good. I will continue to visit it time and time again,' N.C..

St Neots

CURRY MAHAL   NEW ENTRANT

1-2 Longsands Parade, Longsands Road,
St Neots   © 01480 407099

'In a converted modern pub, decor good if spartan. Quantities, especially on the Thalis, exceeded those of other restaurants,' S.M.

CHESHIRE

Please note: we have adhered strictly to the official county of Cheshire. Please look also at the entries for Greater Manchester (listed under Manchester, Greater) and Merseyside for other restaurants within the former Cheshire boundary.

Chester

THE ASIA   ©

104 Foregate Street, Chester   © 01244 322595

We haven't heard whether the Asia has had a redec. M.B. said last time: 'The decor is a little on the drab and tired side, but the Shammi Kebabs were a delight, Chicken Madras one of the tastiest I've ever tasted. My colleagues sampled Chicken Tikka Masala, wonderful!!! Naan bread first class. Pilau Rice comes with the meal and was excellent. Parking a bit of a problem.' s.r.p. says: 'The menu at first was a bit of a let-down as I am a vegetarian. My first impression was that people such as myself were not well catered for. The only vegetable dish listed was Vegetable Biriani. When I ordered, I found they were prepared to have a go at anything I asked for. I found the service to be quick and pleasant as I was very soon shown to my table where the starter was already waiting. I enjoyed my evening at The Asia and would recommend it to anyone looking for good food at a fair price in a pleasant environment.'

BENGAL TANDOORI NEW ENTRANT

High Street, Saltney, Chester　　　　© **01244 371194**

r.l.h. says: 'Decor is typical, but the reception is unique. You are greeted by an English lady who is a mother personified. No disrespect, but she really makes you feel at home. Tandoori Chicken, Tikka Masala, Jalfrezi, Mushroom Pilau and Naans all done to perfection.'

CHESTER TANDOORI

39-41 Brook Street, Chester　　　　© **01244 347410**

'For sheer consistency and value for money the Chester Tandoori is the best in town,' says m.d. 'Waiters a bit obtrusive but efficient and humorous. Particular favourites are Chicken and Prawn Chats as starters. Chicken Korai and Jalfrezi is always hot, well-presented and generous.'

GATE OF INDIA

25 City Road, Chester　　　　© **01244 327131**

We welcome back Chester's second oldest (it dates from 1961), having changed hands to Moinuddin Ahmed in 1992, and doing the formula well, we hear. Price check: Papadom 60p, CTM £6.05, Pullao Rice £1.45. Evenings only but open late (1a.m. Sundays, 2a.m. weekdays, 2.30a.m. Fridays and Saturdays), which could be useful for Chester's night owls and curry-insomniacs.

Congleton

ASTBURY INTERNATIONAL NEW ENTRANT

Astbury Lake, Newcastle Road, Congleton ✆ 01260 299771

'We'd heard of this new one, and ambled up to a wooden shed. Was this it? It used to be the refreshment hut for the water sporters! With some trepidation, we walked in. It was clean, comfortable, with a peaceful lake view. My favourite food came in abundance. It was gorgeous and fresh, their Chicken Biriani and Tandoori Chicken excellent. Licensed, but only open at weekends. I will visit again and again,' c.a.

Crewe

THE BOMBAY

31 High Street, Crewe ✆ 01270 214861

'A rocky start dining in, because of a very long takeaway queue, but we eventually had an excellent meal. The portions were enormous, every other table took their extras home too. We had enough for two more meals at home via the doggy bag! (Any excuse for curry three nights running!) The Naan the size of badminton rackets! Total cost of meal £21.50!!!' s.t.

Ellesmere Port

THE AGRA FORT TOP 100 BEST IN THE NORTH

1-7 Cambridge Road, Ellesmere Port ✆ 0151 355 1516

Avid Guide readers will wonder whether we have heard from Mr F. Moan and his nine colleagues this year. Sadly, we've not, so last time's comment will have to suffice: 'It is not a normal restaurant. The owner is a complete enthusiast.' s.r. says: 'From the moment we entered this restaurant, we knew it would be good. The decor was inviting, the service was attentive. Even on one of the hottest days in the year it was cool. The whole restaurant was fresh and clean. We were particularly impressed to see the chutneys being prepared while we waited. One chutney was particularly noteworthy, it was flavoured with orange.

Some original dishes were featured on the menu, e.g., pepper stuffed with lamb and chicken as a starter. The helpings were good and the presentation excellent. The food was heated at the table as it was served. Every part of the meal complemented the rest. The staff showed a lot of interest in us and gave us a suggestion for dessert. A huge helping of Indian yoghurt and fresh fruit, for £1, finished the meal off very well. Although Ellesmere Port does not have many attractions, this restaurant is a good reason to go there. We found it similar in many ways to the Bina in Reading – another one we like to rave about. Very good value for money – £24.30 incl. drink plus 10% service.' D.B. enjoyed a 'business lunch, Onion Bhajia and Chicken Madras with boiled rice, wheeled to my table and the sauce was reheated on a burner, result was piping hot. Well-presented and superb value.' H.S.C. had: 'A good evening out, good value for money, recommended.' 'The service was friendly and efficient, the servings generous, and the food amongst the best I have ever tasted in an Indian restaurant. We ordered dishes ranging from a Vindaloo for myself, a Madras for my mother and Balti dishes for the remainder of our family. Every one of us thoroughly enjoyed the meal and thought it very good value for money – so much so that we returned shortly after and were not disappointed. My thanks to the manager, whose relaxed and humorous "patter" helped set the scene, and his staff for two most pleasant evenings. I look forward to the next occasion,' M.W. We are happy to keep this restaurant in our TOP 100 category.

Handforth

THE HILAL

90 Wilmslow Road, Handforth   ✆ 01625 524942

A papadom pitch or chupatti chuck from the Cheshire/GM border, this restaurant has been drawn to our attention by a sleuth, new to us, whose brains are being picked as I write. R.K. tells us he has visited over 100 Cheshire/Merseyside curry houses. This is one of his favourites, of which he says: 'It is exquisitely decorated, the food beyond reproach, the service excellent. A treat for the tastebuds.' Branches: 351 Stockport Road, Timperley Village; Victoria Square, Stockton Heath. More reports, please, on all three.

Lymm

THE SAHIB NEW ENTRANT

4-6 The Cross, Lymm	✆ 01925 757576

'A fine establishment, menu wide and varied. Takeaway is 15% cheaper. Quantities of food are quite vast, eating a starter and a main course is not to be undertaken lightly! Chicken Chat was outstanding. Tandoori Chicken Masala makes love to your tastebuds! King Akban Cham Cham seduces your tongue and then proceeds to nail it to the table – one for those who like a spicy kick. Balti Chicken a touch disappointing,' J.C.

Northwich

CASTLE HILL TANDOORI

18-25 Chester Road, Northwich	✆ 01606 783824

M.J.G. is a regular here. He says: 'It remains very impressive, with quick, cheerful service. My granddaughter is still made welcome and a fuss of by the waiters. Large quantities, well-presented food.' Says S.N.: 'Have their own car park around the back of the restaurant which is invaluable given the double yellow lines directly outside. Picked up a takeaway. Well-cooked curries with lots of fresh spices.'

Sandbach

THE TASTE OF THE RAJ   ©

11 High Street, Sandbach	✆ 01270 753752

This was the Sapna in our 1991 Guide, and the Takdir last time. We keep up with all this, though I'm blowed if I can explain it! Whatever he calls it, Anam Islam's restaurant, opposite a very old cobbled square which contains the Sandbach Cross, continues to serve competent curries. Price check: Papadom 40p, CTM £6.50, Pullao Rice £1.40. Minimum charge £10.50. Five-course set lunch £5. Service charge 10%. Sunday buffet £8.95. Lunch and dinner, daily, except Saturdays when it opens at 3p.m. and runs non-stop until 12.30a.m.

Winsford

KESAAN

23-24 Queens Parade, Winsford   ✆ **01606 862940**

'Location and ambience of the Kesaan is to say the least bizarre. It is upstairs in a down-market shopping mall with its entrance on the ground floor. There is a separate bar, complete with china panthers. Waitresses are non-Asian but come dressed in saris. Does not serve spicy papadoms, which is a disappointment but not a catastrophe. Good food, very large portions and friendly service,' s.n. Dr m.w. says: 'The place is spacious, light and airy and has the unusual feature of a central elevated enclosed table within the dining area. We especially enjoyed the selection of both non-vegetarian and vegetarian dishes served on a thali.'

CLEVELAND

Cleveland, like Avon and Humberside, has been swept away as a county and its former territories have been distributed between Durham and Yorkshire North.

CORNWALL

Camborne

THE NEW BENGAL TAKEAWAY

2 Cross Street, Camborne   ✆ **01209 710904**

Takeaway only, evenings only, open 5.-11.30p.m., closed Mondays. Price check: Papadom 30p, CTM £5.65, Pullao Rice £1.40. Minimum charge £3.10.

Falmouth

VICEROY OF INDIA NEW ENTRANT

1 The Moor, Falmouth	✆ 01326 211688

'Represents good value for money with pleasant service and good food,' S.N.

Helston

NEW TAJ

The Old Flora Cinema, Wendron Street, Helston	✆ 01326 562752

'Free Papadoms (three) and pickle tray. Not at all busy, but service extremely slow, although very friendly. Onion Bhajia cold and greasy with no sauce. Lamb Tikka very tasty, plentiful and hot. Chicken Chilli Massala very good but no chillies! Lamb Pasanda unbearably sweet. Very good portions with large amounts of Pilau Rice,' A.M.C. D.W. of Rotherham still says: 'Excellent food, friendly service, the Chicken Phal is quite possibly the hottest in the West! Worth a round trip of 550 miles!!'

Launceston

LAUNCESTON TANDOORI

4 Western Road, Launceston	✆ 01566 774842

A comprehensive menu with everything the curryholic needs at reasonable prices, all of which pleases P.J.

Looe

THE MOONLIGHT

Fore Street, East Looe	✆ 01503 265372

Reasonable prices and food ranging from 'a bit mild' to 'excellent'. Says C.Y.: 'The thing that stands out most, though, was the service. Quick, polite and friendly. How about this ... The waiter came to replace my cutlery after I had eaten my Nargish Kebab. I was extremely surprised to see that he had obviously noticed that I am left-handed. Without any comment he set my new cutlery out for a left-handed diner. A small thing, perhaps, but I've never come across it before, even at top restaurants.'

Newquay

THE NEW MAHARAJAH

39 Cliff Road, Newquay   ✆ 01637 877377

Vasant Maru's restaurant has the unusual distinction of having Indian (rather than Bangladeshi) chefs. One is from south India, the other from Nepal. The restaurant has 'fresh and tasty food with unusual items such as Patra (rolled leaves in batter),' c.p. Mr Maru must have heeded our advice in the last Guide because, according to m.r.s.: 'The portions are now fine. I was certainly satisfied, with my large appetite!'

Penzance

TAJ MAHAL

63 Daniel Place, Penzance   ✆ 01736 366630

Tastefully decorated in an 'olde' bow-fronted building, by Messrs Hannan and Amir. c.j., a frequent visitor, recommends it: 'With all the fish on offer to Penzance diners, it's oh no not monkfish in ginger again!' but thinks 'it isn't cheap for Cornwall'.

St Austell

EASTERN PARADISE

26 Beach Road, Carlyon Bay, St Austell   ✆ 01726 813141

New (mid-1996) and welcomed by many locals. 'Excellent food. Amazed to see the portion size,' k.h. Evenings only. Price check: Papadom 40p, CTM £5.95, Pullao Rice £1.50.

St Ives

RAJPOOT TANDOORI   NEW ENTRANT

6 Gabriel Street, St Ives   🕿 01736 795301

Your editors had a thoroughly enjoyable midwinter weekday curry at A.S. Choudhury's Rajpoot, and we weren't alone. The place soon filled up around us. Local J.D.W. seems to echo the feeling: 'We eat here regularly and find the food and service first-rate.' Evenings only. Price check: Papadom 40p, CTM £5.95, Pullao Rice £1.50. Branch: New Bengal Takeaway, Camborne.

Saltash

SHALIMAR

37 Lower Fore Street, Saltash   🕿 01752 840404

We received a lovely letter from Syed Munawar Ali, the Shalimar's proprietor. Not normally sufficient to get a Guide entry, but if he cares that much to write, we reckon, he'll care about you, and frankly we do find other Cornwall restaurants are complacent. Maybe it's the air, or is it to do with their tourist trade? Reports, please, on anything curry in Cornwall.

Truro

TAJ MAHAL

19 Old Bridge Street, Truro   🕿 01872 241330

Our well-travelled scribe, J.L., says: 'The meal was typical of what I call an every-town-should-have-one restaurant. It was a reasonable standard at reasonable prices. There was nothing very outstanding, but equally nothing was below average. The sort of place you're glad to go into.'

CUMBRIA
Barrow-in-Furness

GOLDEN VILLAGE   ©

36 Dalton Road, Barrow-in-Furness   © 01229 430033

Situated on a corner site is one of Barrow's curry houses, which has been in business since late 1991. A.F. Choudhury's now in the kitchen; the venue, formerly the Sunargaon, is now owned and managed by Janet Chesher. Price check: Papadom 45p, CTM £6.50, Pullao Rice £1.40.

MONIHAR   ©

252-254 Dalton Road, Barrow-in-Furness   © 01229 431947

Elsewhere on Dalton Road is Masud Ahmed's Monihar, of which T.P. says: 'At last, a decent curry house in Barrow.' S.G. visits 'fairly often,' and she is 'impressed by the food and hospitable staff.'

Carlisle

BALTI KITCHEN   NEW ENTRANT

21 West Tower Street, Carlisle   © 01228 599992

Situated opposite the castle, this restaurant, according to N.S. 'gives big portions (too much, really) of above-average food'.

DHAKA TANDOORI

London Road, Carleton, Carlisle   © 01228 23855

Find it on the A6 between J42, M6 and the city. Says local man N.S.: 'Fazrul Karim's Dhaka is still easily the best in town. The food is always of a very high quality and the servings are generous. The staff are always very polite and friendly. Their Chicken Jalfrezi, Lamb Pasanda is the best I have ever tasted, and their Pullao Rice is very fragrant.' Price check: Papadom 45p, CTM £5.45, Pullao Rice £1.45.

SHANA TANDOORI   NEW ENTRANT

89-91 Botchergate, Carlisle   © 001228 20050

Mrs J.T. says: 'First visit to this restaurant. The food came to £14.80, the other £8 was for sherry, house wine, Irish coffee and a Tia Maria. Did not notice a service charge,' [I'm not surprised!] 'if there was one it must have been very modest. All in all an excellent restaurant, quantities and quality second to none. I shall certainly go again.' N.S. goes there, too, for 'standard fayre'.

THE VICEROY

Rigg Street, Shaddongate, Carlisle   © 01228 590909

Several correspondents believe this is in 'pole position in the Carlisle curry house grand prix,' as A.Y. puts it. 'It's near the castle just out of the city centre and not easy to find. The outside resembles a garage workshop,' continues A.Y., 'but there is a transformation when you step inside. You start in a conservatory, where you can browse over a drink, Bombay mix, and the huge menu. There you'll find most Indian favourites, plus Balti, Thalis and Jalfrezi.' R.G.M. says it all adds up to 'Carlisle's most popular Indian with an excellent selection of vegetarian meals.' N.S. tells us he likes it, too. 'Their Rogan dishes are very good. Owner Sukar Ali's opening of Ali's takeaway, opposite, has rid the Viceroy of its endless queues.'

Cleator Moor

ANAMIKA TANDOORI   NEW ENTRANT

43 High Street, Cleator Moor   © 01946 813220

The renamed Asah in this tiny town attracts its *aficionados*: 'An exquisite range of tandooris in pleasant and relaxed surroundings,' N.W.J.

©	Curry Club discount (see p. 607)	🍵	Unlicensed
√	Vegetarian	⊞	Home delivery
BYO	Bring your own alcohol		service available

Cockermouth

KNIGHTS OF INDIA

7 Old Kings Arms Lane, Main Street,
Cockermouth   ✆ 01900 827419

A full curry house menu with a good selection of house specials makes
this a favourite of local reporter R.E., who says: 'This one is first-class.
It's a good curry restaurant – my friends agree with me. The Chicken
Tikka with garlic is superb.'

Kendal

FLAVOURS OF INDIA

20 Blackhall Road, Kendal   ✆ 01539 722711

'The menu here is so long, I can never decide what to have and usually end up having one of my favourites. We had reserved a table and it
was ready and waiting for us on arrival. Staff attentive, pulling our
chairs out for us and taking drinks orders. Lovely Papadoms with pickles and chutneys. Especially good Mushroom Bhaji and Lamb Tikka.
Chicken Tikka Jalfrezi first-class. Shahi Korma absolutely delicious,
incredibly creamy. We will be back again and again,' A.Y.

Keswick

MAHARAJAH   NEW ENTRANT

6a Herries Thwaite, off Main Street,
Keswick   ✆ 017687 74799

Once you've written off the pencil museum and lapped up the lake,
D.S. recommends the Maharajah 'to anyone who would appreciate a
really good meal'. Price check: Papadom 40p, CTM £7.50, Pullao Rice
£1.55. Set meal £11.95. Kurzi Special for two £40, paid in advance.

Penrith

CAGNEYS TANDOORI

17 King Street, Penrith   © 01768 867721

'Glad to have booked, well patronized by local regulars. Table immaculate, seating comfortable and staff courteous throughout. The older I get the more these things matter!' [They matter at any age.] 'Chutneys remained on the table throughout the meal, do members find the practice of removing them as disappointing as I do?' [Yes, they do, and so do I, especially when they are charged for!] 'Lamb Masala came up trumps, encompassing a depth and range of flavours.' Aloo Sag was mild and fragrant,' M.R. Owners Imdabul (chef) and Fazul Haque (call me Hawk!) tell us they are celebrating their decade here with an expansion plan (from the current 50 seats). Price check: Papadom 50p, CTM £6.95, Pullao Rice £1.55.

TASTE OF BENGAL

60-1 Stricklandgate, Penrith   © 01768 891700

'Beautiful decor, a romantic setting best for couples. High-quality food, Boti Kebab is a must. Chicken Makhon is a delectable mild curry with lots of flavour. Jalfrezi tremendous. Good portions,' A.Y.

Whitehaven

AKASH   NEW ENTRANT   ©

3 Tangier Street, Whitehaven   © 01946 691171

Abdug Karim opened here in 1994. We noticed the good reports last time and notice more this time, including one from a Pakistani doctor, so welcome to the Guide. The secret, it seems, is Nurul Hoque's very experienced cooking. Price check: Papadom 45p, CTM £6.25, Baltis from £5.35, Pullao Rice £1.55.

ALI TAJ

34 Tangier Street, Whitehaven   ✆ 01946 693085

The locals agree that this is a good restaurant. G.M.S. felt there was 'plenty of choice', though R.E. would like 'a few more house specialities'. It is, however, still his favourite, 'improving with age'. One Londoner (D.C.) was not only impressed with the food but with the waiters, 'who,' he says, 'are walking football encyclopedias'.

DERBYSHIRE

Ashbourne

RAJAH

1-5 Digg Street, Ashbourne   ✆ 01335 342537

'A large first-floor restaurant. Lamb Rogan Josh £4.85, Chicken Curry £4.25. Does not open lunchtimes,' B.G.

Belper

GANGES BRASSERIE

East Mill, Bridgefoot, Belper   ✆ 01773 826625

'The setting is beautiful,' says W.L.S.-S., 'as it overlooks a weir.' She goes on: 'The food is really nice, fresh and well-cooked with fresh vegetables. As we don't eat meat this is especially important to us and it makes a nice change. The service is very friendly and helpful.'

Burton-on-Trent

KASHMIR BALTI AND TANDOORI
NEW ENTRANT   BYO ©

99 Station Road, Burton   ✆ 01283 511182

Balti you name it, Balti there is, cooked the right way by Kashmiri owner Mohammed Munir. Unlicensed but BYO welcomed. Evenings only, 5p.m.-12.30a.m. Price check: Papadom 25p, CTM £4.80, Balti Kashmiri Mix £5.50, Pullao Rice £1.25. Set meal for two £17.

Castle Donington

TANDOORI NIGHTS   ⊞

43-45 Borough Street, Castle Donington   ✆ 01332 853383

It opened in 1991 and has attracted good comments. It is formula curry with a standard curry menu and free delivery service as well.

Chesterfield

GULAB   NEW ENTRANT   ©

**207 Chatsworth Road, Brampton,
Chesterfield   ✆ 01246 204612**

Rahman and Miah's Gulab has attracted attention. It's standard stuff, but scribes have praised the vegetarian menu. Price check: Papadom 40p, CTM £5.95, Butter Chicken £6.20, Pullao Rice £1.60. Minimum charge £6. Evenings only.

ISMAIL'S EASTERN INN

**57 Chatsworth Road, Brampton,
Chesterfield   ✆ 01246 558922**

M.B. says of it: 'Decor is to the very highest standard in soft pinks and reds, and soft piped non-Indian music in the background goes to make a very relaxed atmosphere indeed.' 'Friendly waiters served a nice meal,' B.C. Price check: Papadom 40p, CTM £6.50, Balti King £7.95, Pullao Rice £1.50. Minimum charge £6. Evenings only.

©	Curry Club discount (see p. 607)	🍷	Unlicensed
√	Vegetarian	⊞	Home delivery
BYO	Bring your own alcohol		service available

Derby

ABID TANDOORI

7 Curzon Street, Derby   ✆ 01332 293712

'This particular evening the food was delicious. It always is, but tonight the dishes were really on form. The dishes are always very generous and the service is always quick and the waiters are helpful. The restaurant is comfortable but by no means up-class, just right,' N.H.

ADNAN BALTI AND TANDOORI   ©

196-198 Normanton Road, Derby   ✆ 01332 360314

'Though the Naans can look sad,' says T.S., 'the Tandoori dishes reach a high standard. Lamb Jalfrezi is subtle and the quality of the chutneys is unique.' And she likes 'the personal service'. In fact we hear a lot about Tahir Malik's good Pakistani food. 'What a great dish the Chicken Kalia is (£7.50 incl. rice). It's a spicy mixture of chicken, Keema and Sheek Kebab. Worth going for that alone!' says C.P. Price check: Papadom 35p, CTM £7.20 incl. rice, Pullao Rice £1.25. Set meal for two from £20. Amazing hours: evenings only, 6p.m.-1.30a.m., 2.30a.m. Friday and Saturday.

FULLMOON TANDOORI

278 Normanton Road, Derby   ✆ 01332 298298

'I visited with a large group of people efficiently handled by the staff. Very good standard of food. I had the Fullmoon Special Biryani – delicious and nicely presented,' A.T.

Ilkeston

SHAH JAHAN   NEW ENTRANT   ©

1 Awsworth Road, Ilkeston   ✆ 0115 932 3036

The full cast of tandooris and curries are at A. Aziz's place. Price check: Papadom 30p, CTM £7.50 incl. rice and Naan, Pullao Rice £1.50. Set meal for two from £20. Evenings only.

Matlock Bath

ABID TANDOORI   ©

129 Dale Road, Matlock Bath   ✆ 01629 57400

Mohammed Bashir's Abid Tandoori is situated in the very pleasant spa town of Matlock Bath, nestling on the River Derwent in the Peak District of Derbyshire, with its many pleasant walks and even a cable car to take you to the top of the cliffs. If all that does not work up an appetite then nothing will. The Abid is quite a pleasant little restaurant with seating for approximately 70 people. It has a comprehensive menu with surprises such as Maranjee Gosht, diced lamb cooked in red wine. 'I went for Karahi Gosht, chunks of lamb, cooked with fresh garlic, ginger, tomatoes and spices, served in a karahi, which was excellent,' M.B. Evenings only.

MATLOCK BATH BALTI AND TANDOORI   ©

256 Dale Road, Matlock Bath   ✆ 01629 55069

Naveed Khaliq's evenings-only Matlock Balti, complete with Kashmiri chef, 'looks well, with rich reds against a pure white-walled background. All – from what I sampled at any rate – very tasty, served by very friendly waiters. Well worth a visit,' M.B. 'My girlfriend and I have become regulars, Murghi Masala, Tarka Dhal and Onion Bhajis being our favourites. Waiters exceptionally efficient,' J.B.

Ripley

SHEEZAN TANDOORI   ©

11 Church Street, Ripley   ✆ 01773 747472

All your usual curry and tandoori favourites are here at Mohammed Sharif's Sheezan.

©	Curry Club discount (see p. 607)	☕	Unlicensed
√	Vegetarian	▥	Home delivery
BYO	Bring your own alcohol		service available

DEVON

Barnstaple

GANGES IX

The Old Railway Station, The Strand,
Barnstaple   ✆ 01271 74297

The setting is quaint and noted by our correspondents, who find the
food OK (P.J.).

Bideford

SAGOR   NEW ENTRANT

22 Chingswell Street, Bideford   ✆ 01237 472011

'The food is of a high order, though the Chicken Korai lacked a little
spice second time. Friendly, attentive service,' C.M.

Dartmouth

SHALIMAR   NEW ENTRANT

Horn Hill Steps, 10 Fairfax Place,
Dartmouth   ✆ 01803 835050

'Being the only Indian restaurant in Dartmouth, prices reflect this.
During busier periods the quality of the food decreases, but if you
catch it when it's quiet the food is of average standard. Waiters are very
keen to help,' D.P.

Dawlish

DAWLISH TANDOORI

12 Brunswick Place, Dawlish   ✆ 01626 863144

One local regular has put in an impassioned plea for the excellence of
this restaurant. So, for Mr G.I., here it is. Do others agree?

Exeter

GANDHI NEW ENTRANT

7 New North Road, Exeter   ✆ 01392 272119

'A small restaurant with a good atmosphere and friendly staff. Usual range of dishes, quality is very high. Chicken Tikka Korai and Punjabi Thali deserve a special mention. Chana Masala is one of the tastiest I have tried,' P.J.

Ilfracombe

RAJAH   ©

5 Portland Street, Ilfracombe   ✆ 01271 863499

Ralph Wild is the owner-chef here, assisted by his son James. The menu is short but comprehensive. I got one truly blistering report about this restaurant from a Mr Malcolm (*see* intro), and I can't explain why such people are so hostile. It does not accord with our usual reports. 'Wonderful innovative cooking, unusual curries including Kenyan curry. Lovely place. Well recommended,' S.B. Price check: Papadom 40p, CTM £6.50 incl. rice and Naan, Pullao Rice £1.85. Evenings only.

Newton Abbot

THE EASTERN EYE II NEW ENTRANT

120 Queen Street, Newton Abbot   ✆ 01626 52364

S.S. finds it a perfect local: 'Staff very friendly and always remember our names. Food cannot be faulted. Has Perspex-engraved partitions and tropical fish. Xmas cards to the regulars.'

Paignton

THARIK'S   ©

379a-b Torquay Road, Preston, Paignton   ✆ 01803 664116

The change of ownership to Messrs Ullah and Ali last year has altered

the reports from average to good, saving it from the chop. 'Good crisp
and warm Poppadums. Excellent Chicken Chat. Well presented and
tasty main courses. Gave us 15% Curry Club discount which was pre-
arranged by phone,' L.W. Price check: Papadom 40p, CTM £6.15,
Akbari Chicken and Lamb £6.95, Pullao Rice £1.50. Evenings only.

Plymouth

BABA INDIAN NEW ENTRANT

---

134 Vauxhall Street, Plymouth *(C* **01752 250677**

Named after E.H. 'Baba' Laskar, founder of Devon's Ganges chain, it
ought to be good. And it is, according to S.H.: 'Comfortable, smart,
with consistently excellent food. Menu contains all the old favourites,
plus a host of unusuals. Shahi Akbari Chicken and Chicken Kahlia
(both about £5) are particular favourites, presented in copper pots. But
the nine-course, once a month banquet (£9.95) is good, but not ambitious enough for the discerning palate.' Price check: Papadom 30p,
CTM £4.95, Pullao Rice £1.50. Evenings only, Monday to Saturday;
Sundays, for £6.95 buffet, noon–6p.m.

JAIPUR PALACE NEW ENTRANT ©

---

146 Vauxhall Street, The Barbican,
Plymouth *(C* **01752 668711**

Syed Wahid's venue is building a good reputation since it opened in
1993. Price check: Papadom 45p, CTM £7.40, Murgh Makhani £7.55,
Pullao Rice £1.95.

KURBANI TOP 100 ©

---

1 Tavistock Place, Sherwell Arcade,
Plymouth *(C* **01752 266778**

Since they established the Kurbani in 1985, owner Mr A.M. Tarafder
and his energetic son (A.H.) operate a restaurant that is different
from the run of the mill curry house. Even the chef is Mrs Tarafder,
so it is truly a family business. And in many respects it attempts to
achieve a home-cooking style to a restaurant discipline. First study of

the menu reveals a full deck of favourites, so lovers of safe bets will feel at home. c.p. has never varied his choice since he first came here, declining to tell us what it is, except that he's never tried the specials! Pity, really, because there are many specials, including some quite unusual ones. Goshtaba (£5.50) is a Kashmiri meatball dish. Kuta Gosht (£5.65) is spicy pounded steak. Aam Gosht (£5.55) is beef curried with mango and Machli Ka Salan (£5.50) is salmon cutlets in tandoori sauce. Chicken Rezalah (£4.15) is cooked with yoghurt and green chilli. You'll enjoy, we hope, the freshness of the herbs and spices and the lightness of touch from Mrs Tarafder. Don't forget to request the home-made pickles. If you've left enough room for desserts, you may wish to venture into their home-made world of the Zelapi or Jalebi, an Indian crispy sweet, or Gulabzam (sic), a fried paneer ball in syrup, and Bhadam Khir, a kind of almond rice pudding, all under £1.35. I am always screaming for Bangladeshi curry houses to push the frontiers of the formula forward, and am told 'there's no demand'! More like, there's insufficient skill in the kitchen. But that's not the case at the Kurbani. And their long-standing menu proves that there is a demand for such specials. We are pleased to keep this restaurant in our TOP 100. Further price check: Papadom 40p, CTM £6.75, Pullao Rice £1.75. Set four-course meal £10.35-£15.

TAJ INDIAN   ©

49 Mayflower Street, Plymouth   ✆ 01752 669485

Syed Lutfus Rahman's Taj is one of the 'old hands' of Plymouth, being here since 1971. Such experience always tells. G.M.O. talks of 'a lovely meal with really helpful waiters'. Price check: Papadom 40p, CTM £5.95, Pullao Rice £1.70. Set lunch £3.95. Set meal £8.50.

VEGGIE PERRINS   NEW ENTRANT   √

97 Mayflower Street, Plymouth   ✆ 01752 252888

This must get the award for the silliest name – no it won't, I'm just joking! But Mrs m.j.h. isn't joking when she says: 'The food is the best I have ever had. Dishes were unusual and delicately flavoured. The Parathas were light and crispy and not at all greasy. Kachori, mixed vegetables and lentils, lightly spiced, in pastry, served with

chutney and salad £1.25. Palak Paneer £3.25, Tarka Dal £1.75. All good.'
It's a licensed, lunch and dinner, vegetarian-only restaurant. Reports,
please.

Tavistock

GANGES VI

9 West Street, Tavistock ℂ **01822 616731**

The Roman numerals tell us that this is one of the Ganges chain. R.G.
loves their Peshwari Naans and finds everything to her liking.

Tiverton

GATE OF INDIA ©

52-54 Fore Street, Tiverton ℂ **01884 252380**

Competent restaurant even if J.L. thinks the Taj Mahal arches are
'hideous'. (I wonder how you'd find the real thing then, John!) He did
find the breads, Korma and Kashmiri Gosht 'excellent'. Mr Ali Chand,
the owner-chef, will give discounts to Curry Club members.

Torquay

BELGRAVE TANDOORI ©

57 Belgrave Road, Torquay ℂ **01803 292301**

It's an evenings-only, takeaway-only place, but because long-distance
truck driver P.J. gives it the thumbs up, so do we.

DINE BANGLADESHI   NEW ENTRANT

30 Tor Hill Road, Torquay ℂ **01803 291311**

'Opened in the old Ganges premises, the manager and staff are from
the Sylhet, 63 Market Street, which is now the Sultana! Food as always
is fantastic and I find it hard to escape from the Balti Chicken. I'll stop

now before my mouth waters over this report!' says L.W. Shame they don't offer authentic Bangladeshi food, though.

PEARL OF INDIA   ©

Scarborough Road, Torquay   ✆ 01803 201220

It must be the largest curry house in the West (of England), with 200 seats.

TAJ MAHAL   ©

47 Abbey Road, Torquay   ✆ 01803 295163

Torquay's oldest Indian restaurant (1964) has been in M.A. Choudhury's hands all this time. Now celebrating its 30th year it is a safe-bet, competent curry house. L.S.D.W. finds the rice portions 'a bit small', otherwise most things are OK.

DORSET
Bournemouth

BOURNEMOUTH TANDOORI   NEW ENTRANT

8 Holdenhurst Road, Lansdowne,
Bournemouth   ✆ 01202 296204

'A tastefully decorated smallish restaurant with apricot and green colours. Booth-type seating around the walls. Papadom (50p) and pickles arrived without asking within minutes. Kingfisher lager on tap. Started with a Madouri Kebab (£3.95), new to me, diced lamb, tomato, cucumber, etc., which was succulent and tasty, with mint sauce in a jug to pour on, how sensible! Followed by one of my favourites, Chicken Jalfrezi and rice (£6.95), bread and Mushroom Bhaji (£2.15), and I would rate this one at ten out of ten, it was really excellent. Service pleasant and swift. I liked the place and can recommend the food. One of the best in Bournemouth. Not my last visit!' M.S.

THE EYE OF THE TIGER

207 Old Christchurch Road,
Bournemouth ℂ 01202 780900

'We were a bit concerned that it was empty at 7p.m. on a Saturday night, but we dived in to find a pleasant restaurant with helpful waiters. It was the best curry we'd had for many a long month. I was amused to see a machine in the male toilet selling curry-flavoured condoms! The meal (without this particular item) cost us £25 including four drinks, and by the time we left, it was packed,' c.s. Guide text editor J.S. says her 'mind boggles. Imagine a Phal-flavoured version!' Really, Jane, behave yourself — this is a respectable publication!

TAJ MAHAL

42 Poole Road, Westbourne,
Bournemouth ℂ 01202 761108

Dorset's oldest (1960), in the Miah brothers' hands since 1994 but still doing a good job with satisfied locals. Price check: Papadam 55p, CTM £7.80, Pullao Rice £1.75. Minimum charge £1. Set lunch £5.95.

Christchurch

STARLIGHT

54 Bargates, Christchurch ℂ 01202 484111

Ian Clasper and Abdul Hai's Starlight, opened in 1991, is now a firm part of Christchurch's street-scene. Price check: Papadam 60p, CTM £7.85, Pullao Rice £1.85. Minimum charge £6.60. Set lunch £5.95.

Poole

THE GATE OF INDIA NEW ENTRANT

54-56 Commercial Road,
Lower Parkstone, Poole ℂ 01202 717061

'Always happy to accommodate you at this recently refitted restaurant,'

F.C.S. 'Over the past year we have had many a splendid meal. Service is very good, waiting is cut to a minimum. Servings are generous. The Chaudhury family who run the restaurant put on a special evening for my department at Bournemouth University, about 40 staff and guests – for £8 per head. Really splendid, as much as we could eat: chicken, lamb and vegetable curries with Pilau Rice and Nan bread. I am full of praise for the immense professional trouble this outfit went to and provided an evening everyone loved. Excellent parking,' R.G.

MOONLIGHT NEW ENTRANT   ©

9 Moor Road, Broadstone, Poole   © 01202 605234

'I can strongly recommend a visit to A. Malik's Moonlight. No Balti dishes but excellent food, all the normal choices with some very interesting specials of the house,' J.L. 'Good staff, food excellent,' C.C. Price check: Papadam 45p, CTM £7.95, Pullao Rice £1.75. Minimum charge £8.50. Branch: Moonlight, 14 Poole Hill, Bournemouth.

NAWABI TANDOORI NEW ENTRANT   ©

359 Ashley Road, Parkstone, Poole   © 01202 722813

Originally the Gandhi, which closed after a fire. 'Service was slow, but the food was absolutely outstanding. Katta Gosht Masala, beef in a very spicy seasoned tomato-based sauce, it has a superb outline to the flavour which was probably lemon or lime. Lamb Pasanda and Special Curry Nawani was enjoyed by colleagues. Deserves to thrive,' R.G. 'A good old-fashioned restaurant. Food is cheap and portions large,' C. and T.F.

RAJASTHAN NEW ENTRANT TOP 100

127 Pennhill Avenue, Poole   © 01202 718966

'Reputation deservedly spreading far and wide. Always busy and very difficult to book a table at weekends. In view of the quality of its cuisine, the excellence of its service and the comfort of its accommodation, this should be no surprise. It is tasteful and very spacious, napkins are of top quality, damask. There is a spacious, well-stocked bar. The service, though brisk, is friendly. Proprietor tells me that it was his intention to offer the cuisine of his native region, authentic

Rajasthan dishes, as well as a sample of the standard high street favourites. In this he is extremely successful. My wife and I took a relative out to dinner there and enjoyed a memorable evening. My wife's Rajasthani Tava Murg – a dry curry, stir-fried marinated chicken garnished with cheese (£7.50) – was exotic, fragrant and delicious. My nephew had a splendid rich Lamb Madras Curry and my Chicken Biryani was out of this world – not the usual faked-up dish with cooked rice and a few bits of chicken, but the genuine slow-cooked classic regal dish of India. The accompanying vegetable dishes cannot be described. All the vegetables, including the Bindhi (£2.20), are fresh. This is indeed obvious. A good range of drinks, including Indian lager, is available. The accommodation is spacious, comfortable and not crowded. The waiters are charming, helpful, amiable and obliging without being obsequious. We cannot recommend the Rajasthan sufficiently. Value for money is extremely impressive,' R.G. 'General tone is highly sophisticated. I would especially praise Rajasthan Dakana – chicken drumsticks, marinated in yoghurt, spices and garnished with fried onion. Brilliant Tandoori Mixed Grill. Sabzi Pathia, hot and sour vegetables, laced with chillies and lemon lingers in my memory. Range of different rices, coconut, lemon, mushroom, pilau and beautiful breads,' J.L. Dorset has been devoid of a TOP 100 for some time now. Glad to award it here.

TANDOORI NIGHTS NEW ENTRANT ©

50 High Street, Poole © 01202 684383

A.H. Choudhury opened this one in 1994, and we hear it has quickly become popular. Regular menu. Price check: Papadam 50p, CTM £7.30, Balti £7.45, Pullao Rice £1.50. Minimum charge £2.50.

Sherborne

RAJPOOT NEW ENTRANT

The House of the Steps, Half Moon Street, Sherborne © 01935 812455

H.C. says of Mizanur Rahman's Rajpoot: 'Spacious, lots of traditional tapestry upholstery. Bar and restaurant service very slow. Onion Bhaji awful, stodgy and lukewarm. Replacements were brought but they were the same but hot. Brinjal Bhaji absolutely wonderful, ingredients chopped very fine, no sauce, no tomatoes, superb flavour, nearly had a second helping. Butter Chicken marvellous and generous. Garlic Naan very good. Ayre Jalfrezi (£6.95) – a Bangladeshi fish dish, very good and very generous.' Commendable for Bangladeshi dishes, others are Rup and pomfret. Shatkora is a tangy Bengali citrus fruit used, when available, in chicken, meat or prawn. c.c. and family say: 'A warm welcome can always be guaranteed.' A.L. and party tell of delays sufficiently long to 'spoil the evening, on a very busy night'. They complained, but paid. A couple of days later A.L. got a full refund in the post. 'Since then we are all friends.' Price check: Papadam 50p, CTM £6.20, Balti £7.45, Pullao Rice £1.80. Minimum charge £8. Branch: Akash, 134 Wareham Road, Corfe Mullen, nr Wimborne.

Wimborne

WIMBORNE TANDOORI   NEW ENTRANT

2 Leigh Road, Wimborne   *©* **01202 884034**

'Situated in the small village of Wimborne, Norzul Islam's cosy little restaurant offers excellent food and service in pleasant surroundings. The menu offers a few differences from the usual choices, Duck Tikka, curries cooked with oranges, and Chicken Tikka and Tandoori Chicken cooked in Tia Maria! My Chicken Tikka Dansak was quite hot but very tasty. Usual standard accompaniments. Our local friends visit here regularly and are always enthusiastic about the place. Therefore please include in the next Guide,' N.H.

COUNTY DURHAM

Barnard Castle

SPICE ISLAND   NEW ENTRANT

9 Market Place, Barnard Castle   *©* **01833 630575**

'A clean restaurant, seems popular with the locals. High-quality food,' D.M. Lunch and dinner. Price check: Papadam 40p, CTM £5.20, Tarana from £7.95, Pullao Rice £1.50. Branches: Darlington, County Durham; 297 High Street, Northallerton, North Yorkshire.

Bishop Auckland

THE KING'S BALTI NEW ENTRANT   ©

187 Newgate Street, Bishop Auckland   ℂ 01388 604222

Boshir Ali's evenings-only takeaway is doing the formula well, we hear. Price check: Papadam 40p, CTM £4.80, Balti Special £5.95, Pullao Rice £1.45. Minimum charge £7.50.

Crook

INDIAN COTTAGE TAKEAWAY

18 Church Street, Crook   ℂ 01388 768066

Open 5.30p.m.-midnight, seven days a week. 'Good,' says long-distance driver P.J.

Darlington

GARDEN OF INDIA

43 Bondgate, Darlington   ℂ 01325 467975

'Smart, popular restaurant with good, friendly service. Tarana dishes cooked in red or white wine, flambéed with a liqueur of your choice, served with rice or Naan (£8.10). Chicken Tikka Korahi (£5.05) brought on a sizzling iron dish. Ladies receive a carnation before they leave,' E.D. Price check: Papadam 40p, CTM £5.10, Pullao Rice £1.70.

JEWEL OF ASIA   ©

Imperial Centre, Grange Road, Darlington ℂ 01325 483998

'A jewel of a menu' at P. Singh's Jewel, according to P.J., who is a regular here when in the area.

SEEMA EXPRESS   ⊞ ✆ 01325 482100

No published address because it's a delivery service only. Evenings
5.30p.m.-12.30a.m. daily (1a.m. Friday and Saturday). For those who like
to know, D.MC. tells us it's in the kitchen of the Garden of India (*see*
entry). Price check: Papadam 30p, CTM £4.85, Tarana from £6.15,
Pullao Rice £1.30.

SHAPLA

192 Northgate, Darlington   ✆ 01325 468920

'Brilliant,' P.J. 'Excellent restaurant, also does takeaways,' D.MC.

SITAR   ©

204 Northgate, Darlington   ✆ 01325 360878

Ashok Bhagat's Sitar is a sister restaurant to Garden of India (*see*
entry). 'Decor is tastefully exotic and luxurious, the service splendid
and when it comes to the food, the menu covers a wide range of
regional dishes, including some old favourites but especially many
intriguing newcomers. Fresh Fish of the Day, marinated and pan-fried
in butter,' E.M.R. 'Food of a very high standard. Nan breads exceptional,' E.D.

SPICE ISLAND

90 Surtees Street, Darlington   ✆ 01325 365575

'Portions are expensive but large. North Indian style food rather than
Bangladeshi,' D.MC. Takeaway only. Open evenings only, 5p.m.-midnight,
12.30a.m. on Friday and Saturday. Price check: Papadam 40p, CTM
£5.20, Tarana from £7.95, Pullao Rice £1.50. Branches: Barnard Castle,
County Durham; 297 High Street, Northallerton, North Yorkshire.

©	Curry Club discount (see p. 607)	🍺	Unlicensed
√	Vegetarian	⊞	Home delivery
BYO	Bring your own alcohol		service available

Durham

MOZ'S

30 Front Street, Framwellgate Moor,
Durham   © 0191 384 3672

'Ate in and found the food satisfactory. Both eat-in and takeaway are popular. I suspect that Mr Miah also owns the adjacent fish and chip shop, the Cutty Shark, since both buildings look alike!' D.MC. 'Ample portions, Brinjal and Sag Bhaji side dishes both excellent. King Prawn Dhansak, the best I've had for ages. The owner, Moz, is very nice too,' E.D.

SHAHEEN'S

The Old Post Office, 48 North Bailey,
Durham   © 0191 386 0960

'Very prompt service in comfortable, pleasant surroundings. Complimentary Bombay Mix. Reasonable quantities of excellent food. Melt-in-the-mouth lamb,' G.P.

TANDOORI CENTRE   NEW ENTRANT

28 Front Street, Framwellgate Moor,
Durham   © 0191 384 6493

'I enjoyed the Moong dishes – in my ignorance, I expected the beans to have sprouted. The special six-course meal had a large helping of the main course, and lasted me two nights. Quality and quantity are so good that I would like to see this establishment included in the next Guide.' [Your wish, sir!] 'I would recommend those waiting for take-aways to drink in the adjacent Tap and Spile. This is the only real-ale pub I know with a no-smoking bar; T-shirts and beer-bellies are optional,' D.MC.

©	Curry Club discount (see p. 607)	🍺	Unlicensed
√	Vegetarian	⊞	Home delivery
BYO	Bring your own alcohol		service available

Hartlepool

THE DILSHAD ©

49a Church Street, Hartlepool   © 01429 272727

D.M. gives Habib Ullah's venue the thumbs up: 'Lunch was a bargain, with adequate portions and above-average taste.' Price check: Papadom 55p, CTM £5.95, Pullao Rice £1.75. Set lunch £3.05.

Shildon

RAJAH ©

100 Main Street, Shildon   © 01388 772451

Abdul Subhan's Rajah is situated on the first floor over a fish bar. 'Gives the feeling of an old Indian officers' mess, with panelled walls, old wood-framed pictures, and the occasional pair of crossed swords protecting a coat of arms. Menu fairly extensive and prices reasonable. I toyed with ordering a Vindaloo, but ordered a Chicken Madras, which was at least the strength of a Vindaloo – thank God I didn't order one. Really very tasty and nothing left. Service first-class, food on the whole wonderful,' M.B. Branch: Sabu's, 199 Newgate Street, Bishop Auckland.

Stanley

MONJU TANDOORI ©

33 Park Road, South Moor, Stanley   © 01207 283259

Mrs G. Miah has owned the Monju since 1991. It's a small restaurant seating only 35 diners. Her chef, Mr Uddin, serves all the regular favourites. Price check: Papadam 50p, CTM £5.50, Murghi Mosala £7.50, Pullao Rice £1.50. Set meal £4.95. Branch: Golden Gate, 11 South Burns, Chester-le-Street, County Durham.

Stockton-on-Tees

THE ROYAL BENGAL ©

Prince Regent Street, Stockton-on-Tees   ✆ **01642 674331**

D.M. supports this as the best in town, and it's good enough for me. It has been going since 1977, a sufficient age to give it maturity and sensible management from M. Faruque and chef-partner Abdus Subhan Khan.

STOCKTON TANDOORI NEW ENTRANT ©

52 Prince Regent Street, Stockton-on-Tees ✆ **01642 607600**

Newer on the street (1993), A. Hussain's regulars tell us he's really keen to please. Open 5.30p.m.-midnight. Price check: Papadom 50p, CTM £5.25 incl. rice, Pullao Rice £1.30. Special meals from £5.95. Minimum charge £5.

ESSEX

Part of Essex was absorbed by Greater London in 1965. We note affected boroughs with the letters GL.

Barking, GL

BENGAL LANCER NEW ENTRANT ©

84 Longbridge Road, Barking   ✆ **0181 594 9598**

We've heard that this restaurant is more popular than ever since it changed hands to F. Rahman. Price check: Papadom 40p, CTM £5.75, Garlic Chilli Chicken Bhuna £5.95, Thalis from £9.50, Pullao Rice £1.75. Branch: Raj Bilash, 68 Longbridge Road, Barking.

Benfleet

AKASH   ©

219 High Road, Benfleet   © 01268 566238

Mr L. Ali's welcoming restaurant is friendly and popular. 'I have a restrictive diet, and need my curries to be as oil-free as possible. Mokis Khan, chef, is very happy to do this for me,' L.A. Price check: Papadom 50p, CTM £6.50 incl. rice, Akash Special £5.95, Pullao Rice £1.40.

MAHARAJA

358 London Road, South Benfleet   © 01268 795633

'Large, well-decorated restaurant. Good food, service, portions quite large. Would return again. Ample parking at front,' P.E.H. Price check: Papadom 40p, CTM £5.75, Pullao Rice £1.60.

TANDOORI PARLOUR

63 Hart Road, Thundersley, Benfleet   © 01268 793786

It's all the fun of the fair at the Parlour! And why not? And with a few more reports please, it could be promoted to our list of bests. 'Another good evening out enjoyed here with entertainment and music quiz. The service, however, although good and helpful can be slow at peak times. Plentiful food, prices a little higher,' P.E.H. 'What makes it so special is the food, décor and service and entertainment. Holds about 200 people. Decor is modern and very appealing, with a polished wooden dance floor area, and a stage that holds a white grand piano. A curry house with a difference, this one not only tantalizes your tastebuds with gastronomic delights but also entertains you in the process at no extra cost! Every Friday and Saturday night, resident DJ runs a Karaoke and music quiz evening, with music to listen to whilst eating, and prizes to be won. These evenings are lively, and therefore perhaps not for those wishing to spend a quiet, intimate evening. Shar, the owner, and his team of waiters are excellent, and certainly know their job. Food is fabulous and you get loads of it, Tandoori Seafood being their speciality. A very satisfied customer,' B.O. 'Dinner dance at the weekend. Magician entertains at our table,' R.L.

Billericay

RAGLA ©

6 High Street, Billericay   ✆ 01277 624996

L. Uddin's Ragla is still the favourite of D.R. Branch: Codsall Tandoori, The Square, Codsall, Staffs.

Braintree

BRAINTREE CURRY PALACE ©

28 Fairfield Road, Braintree   ✆ 01376 320083

Mr A. Noor's well-established (1975 – first in town) restaurant, seating just 38 diners, now does evenings only, closed Mondays. Price check: Papadom 50p, CTM £5.80, Palace Special £5.80, Pullao Rice £1.50.

Buckhurst Hill, GL

BUCKHURST TANDOORI

188 Queens Road, Buckhurst Hill   ✆ 0181 505 6200

'Sited in a former major bank. Food attractively presented and is piping hot. Most enjoyable kebabs, Lamb Sag consisted of well-cooked succulent meat. Chicken dishes were substantial and their chef's speciality of Chicken Tikka Makhani is well worth a try. Balti Naan breads were large and puffy with a slight crisp base,' M.F.

Burnham-on-Crouch

POLASH ©

169 Station Road, Burnham   ✆ 01621 782233

Under the same ownership since 1984, and has been in all our Guides as a reliable safe bet. Manager, Mr S.A. Motin. Price check: Papadom 50p, CTM £6.60, Pullao Rice £1.80. Minimum charge £9.50. Branch: Polash, Shoeburyness.

Chadwell Heath, GL

BHANGRA BEAT BALTI   ©

108 High Road, Chadwell Heath   ✆ 0181 590 2503

Still very popular in Shamin Khan's trendy ownership. 'We ordered Papadoms and got just one each, however, when the main courses came they made up for the shortfall. Balti Supreme very good quantities and taste very good. We felt totally stuffed and walked the 3 miles back to Romford,' T.L. and M.R. Branch: Bhangra Beat, 17-21 Sternhold Avenue, Streatham, London SW12.

Chelmsford

SHAFIQUE

30 The Green, Writtle, Chelmsford   ✆ 01245 422228

M.A. Shafique's baby, it's a mile or three out of town and is in 'beautiful surroundings,' J.T. 'Elegant, well decorated, large restaurant. Sunday buffet, good selection of food with fair pricing,' P.E.H.

Clacton-on-Sea

BALTI HOUSE   NEW ENTRANT   ©

23 Spring Road, St Osyth, Clacton-on-Sea   ✆ 01255 822224

Many familiar curries appear on the menu, along with some choice Baltis. Price check: Papadom 45p, CTM £7.95, Balti Butter Lamb £7.95, Pullao Rice £1.80. Minimum charge £7.50. Set lunch £5.50.

EAST INDIA TAKEAWAY   NEW ENTRANT   ©

182 Old Road, Clacton-on-Sea   ✆ 01255 436445

M.A. Salam's all-year-round, evenings-only (5-11.30p.m.) takeaway-only, is a favourite with the locals, swelled by the summer tourists. Price check: Papadom 40p, CTM £4.85, Pullao Rice £1.40. Set meal from £7.35.

Colchester

ALISHAN

19 Osbourne Street, Colchester   ✆ 01206 574486

'Very clean and well presented under new management, since the old restaurant burnt down, so considerable sums spent. Air-conditioned. Menu, usual offerings. Service prompt and polite. Good quantities, outstanding quality. Chicken Tikka brilliant. The best in Colchester,' N.F. Price check: Papadom 50p, CTM £5.50, Pullao Rice £1.60. Set lunch £3.95.

CURRY INDIA   ©

119-121 Crouch Street, Colchester   ✆ 01206 762747

'Every aspect of Mr Khan's restaurant and staff is impeccable. Menu is both extensive and reasonable in price. Superbly prepared and served food,' A.M.

INDUS MAHAL BALTI HOUSE   ©

59 East Street, Colchester   ✆ 01206 860156

Well-established and popular curry house, serving competent curries and baltis.

POLASH

40 St Botolphs Street, Colchester   ✆ 01206 578791

'The drab outside could put you off, but we know the food is the best available in town. The interior is old-fashioned flock wallpaper, curry house standard, and a little dreary, although kept very neat and tidy. Chutneys and dips are delivered to your table within moments of being seated, and drinks orders are promptly attended to. We ordered Chicken Bhuna (£3.80) with Pilau Rice (£1.40), Lamb Vindaloo (£3.80), Mushroom Rice (£2.30) and Keema Nan (£1.60) with a side dish of Mushroom Bhaji (£2.30). All portion sizes are very generous, especially the Nan breads, which are almost a meal in themselves. All was superb and obviously cooked to order rather than being "doled out of a pot". This superb little restaurant really proves the old adage of not judging a book by its cover. The bill for three persons, including one round of drinks, came to £30.10 including service,' H.N.

Dagenham, GL

CURRY MAHAL

27 Gorsebrook Road, Dagenham   © 0181 592 6277

'Special Chicken Curry was medium-strength, with onions, capsicum, egg and tomatoes, highly flavoured, without being too hot. Worthy of its place in the Guide,' J.T.

SHAJHAN TAKEAWAY   ©

670 Rainham Road South, Dagenham   © 0181 592 0502

Owner-chef Abdul Jobbar's evenings-only establishment serves competent curries for takeaway only. Open 5.30–11p.m.

Halstead

HALSTEAD TANDOORI

73 Head Street, Halstead   © 01787 476271

Opened in 1977 and still in the same ownership. All the favourites served competently in this 34-seater.

Harlow

RAJ LODGE

38 High Street, Old Harlow   © 01279 626119

Opened in 1987 under the management of Faruque Harun. Seats 80 diners between two rooms. Upstairs is available for large parties. 'Tables are almost on top of each other. Good news, a new menu. Chicken Achari – a revelation, overflowing with flavour, it really lived up to its reputation,' A.S. Price check: Papadom 40p, CTM £6, Pullao Rice £1.85. Set dinner from £26.95 for two.

Hornchurch, GL

TASTE OF BENGAL ©

194 High Street, Hornchurch ✆ **01708 477850**

'Decor very swish and food surpassed expectations. Best starter, King Prawn Butterfly. The staff were really helpful and didn't mind us taking nearly three hours over our meal on a busy evening,' P.W. Owner Jamal Uddin will give a discount to Curry Club members, here and at his branch: Passage to India, 99 Upminster Road, Hornchurch.

Ilford, GL

CURRY SPECIAL NEW ENTRANT TOP 100 ©

2 Greengate Parade, Horns Road, Newbury Park, Ilford
✆ **0181 518 3005**

This is an unusual restaurant and as far from the run of the mill formula as one can go. It's family-run by G.L. and Paul Luther, who are related to the Southall Anands (*see* Madhu's Brilliant, Middlesex), and are Punjabi Kenyan Asians. This results in a different menu from the Punjabi formula, which has evolved into the Bangladeshi curry house menu. This is the real taste of the Punjab — savoury, powerful, delicious and thoroughly satisfying. Such items as Palak Lamb (£5) — 'Lamb so tender with spinach so savoury, it just blends,' D.R. 'I adore the Chicken Keema (£6.50) — minced chicken with really tasty spicing. We had it with Aloo Cholai (£3) — potatoes and chickpeas, Tinda Masala (£3), and a delicious Vegetable Biriani. The food was quite unlike any we'd experienced before,' G.T. Of course, this is exactly the reason why we hear a few whinges about this place and the Brilliant: it is because the food is different. So please do go with an open mind. Food like this is as near to Punjabi home food as you're likely to get in Britain. But there's more. The family signature dishes are Butter Chicken, Jeera Chicken and Chilli Chicken. A full portion for four is

£12-£13. Half-portion £6.50-£7. These are starters, and are huge. And the fun is to go in large parties and share each of these. That's the way the local Asians enjoy it, leaving lots of room and lots of choice for the main course. The clue to the Luthers' Kenyan lifestyle is also in the menu. Mogo Chips are fried cassava (£3) and Tilipa Masala is an African fish (starter £3, main course £6.50). A further house signature dish is Karai Mexican Mixed Vegetables. It is licensed. Try the Kenyan Tusker lager. For the record here's our standard price check: Papadom 40p, CTM £6.50, Pullao Rice £1.50. Open for lunch and dinner, Tuesdays to Fridays; evenings only, Saturdays and Sundays. Closed Mondays. We should have discovered this restaurant earlier for entry to the Guide, but we hope we'll make up for that by placing it in our TOP 100.

DIDAR   NEW ENTRANT   ©

---

686 Green Lane, Goodmays, Ilford   ℂ **0181 598 9035**

S. Miah's evenings-only, takeaway-only, place. Price check: Papadom 35p, CTM £4.95, Pullao Rice £1.40. Minimum charge £7.50. Set meal £16 for two.

HAWA BENGAL   NEW ENTRANT   ©

---

530 High Road, Seven Kings, Ilford   ℂ **0181 599 9778**

Mr Bashir Ullah is the owner-chef here, while Mr Hudda Kabir runs front of house. It's a popular formula curry house. Price check: Papadom 50p, CTM £5.80, Pullao Rice £1.50. Minimum charge £8. Open evenings only.

JALALABAD   TOP 100

---

247 Ilford Lane, Ilford   ℂ **0181 478 1285**

'Have yet to find anywhere remotely up to the Jalalabad's standard. Chicken Tikka remains unique in its quality, the vegetables crisp and fresh and the Jalfrezi excellent. The portions are still enormous,' I.B. 'Methi Gosht outstanding. Aubergine and Bhindi of the highest quality. Nans and Puris light and puffy – gorgeous,' M.F. 'Fourteen of us arrived at approximately 7.45p.m. and were cordially greeted by the manager. We had pre-booked a set meal, so our table was ready. The restaurant was pleasantly decorated and lighting just right. The starters came up: Onion Bhajia and Chicken Tikka, which were both plentiful and delicious. Some papadoms and pickles were also placed on the table, and the lager was flowing freely. The waiters were very attentive without being overloading. Our main course consisted of Chicken Madras, Meat Bhoona, Chicken Tikka Masala, Chicken Korma, Pilau Rice, Naan Bread, Mushroom Bhaji, Bombay Potato and Peshwari Naan. All of the curries were top-class. The Korma had a slight "bite", not just chicken in a creamy sauce. Chicken Tikka Masala was the best I've tasted. Bhoona was excellent, as was the Madras. All the side dishes were tasty and were being replenished as we ate. When the Peshwari Naan arrived it was the best I've had. I asked the waiter if the bread had been cooked in a tandoor, at which I was invited into the kitchen to see the giant tandoor first-hand. The kitchen was immaculate with everything laid out ready. The tandoor was at one end of the kitchen finished with tiling. I could feel the heat and was shown Naan bread suspended on the tandoor "wall" cooking. Well, we finished off with ice cream and were all totally stuffed. The bill came to just over £10 each, which had included some "extras". As I said, we had pre-booked a set meal but the variety of food was first-class. We will be returning shortly,' T.L. Comments like these keep the Jalalabad in our TOP 100.

KURRY POT ©

237 Cranbrook Road, Ilford ℂ **0181 518 2131**

This is a Malay restaurant and the food is, obviously, quite different from the formula. But the clue's in the name, and we hear kind things about such dishes as Redang and Sotto Ayam. A tiny, exclusive restaurant seating 26 diners. Owners M.S. Manku and chef Mrs Manku are on hand to explain. Open 11.30a.m.-11.30p.m.

Leigh-on-Sea

MUGHAL DYNASTY ©

1585 London Road, Leigh-on-Sea ℂ **01702 470373**

Nazram Uddin's up-market, pretty restaurant in shades of green seats 68 diners. Large chandeliers hang from the ceiling. The food is well spoken of, too. Open noon-2.30p.m. and 6p.m.-midnight. Price check: Papadom 40p, CTM £5.45, Shaugathi Chicken £5.75, Pullao Rice £1.45. Set meal from £6.95.

TAJ MAHAL   ©

77 Leigh Road, Leigh-on-Sea   © 01702 711006

The Taj is a gracious old friend of the Guide. It's been with us since we started, and they've been going since 1973. It's owned by Shams and Noor Uddin, manager and chef respectively, and despite them 'unequivocally refusing our' [Mrs D.C.'s] 'discount ... they said they had never given one' a while back, they have promised they'll honour them this time. Let's hope so, because it's a place with 'good atmosphere, good food and good service,' J.T. Price check: Papadom 50p, CTM £5.65, Tandoori King Prawn Jalfrezi £9.95, Pullao Rice £1.85. Minimum charge £9.50.

TANDOORIAN NIGHTS   NEW ENTRANT   ©

1350 London Road, Leigh-on-Sea   © 01702 713040

A. Hussain has owned the Nights, as it is known, since 1985 and we welcome it to the Guide. Price check: Papadom 30p, CTM £5.85, Pullao Rice £1.40. Set meal for two £16.

Maldon

HEYBRIDGE TANDOORI   NEW ENTRANT   ©

5 Bentall's Shopping Centre,
Heybridge, Maldon   © 01621 858566

This restaurant changed hands in 1995 to Messrs Rofik, Hannan and Islam, and we hear well of it since then. Price check: Papadom 50p, CTM £5.95, Tandoori King Prawn Special £7.95, Pullao Rice £1.60. Minimum charge £ 7.95. Set meal £7.95.

THE RAJ

24 Mill Road, Maldon   ✆ 01621 852564

Formerly Tandoori Garden of Maldon. 'Crisp Papadoms and flavourful Chicken Tikka Masala and Chicken Special,' A.S. 'A pleasant, low-
key local restaurant with prices to match, but above-average cooking,'
J.W.

SHAHJAN   NEW ENTRANT

195 High Street, Maldon   ✆ 01621 52564

I.P. tells us he's been to this takeaway-only venue weekly for more than
two years. 'So often the dish ends up swimming in ghee – and we all
know why! But not here. It's absolutely superb! The Dhansak is the
best I've ever tasted.' Starters around £2. Main meal £5.

Manningtree

INDIA VILLAGE   ©

3-5 South Street, Manningtree   ✆ 01206 394102

Manager M.M. Ali's popular local curry house, serving all the old
favourites.

Rochford

ROCHFORD TANDOORI   ©

45 North Street, Rochford   ✆ 01702 543273

J.R. says of owner Azir Uddin's venue: 'Quite a lot of original dishes
and very pleasant staff.' Seats 50.

©	Curry Club discount (see p. 607)	🍺	Unlicensed
√	Vegetarian	⊞	Home delivery
BYO	Bring your own alcohol		service available

Romford, GL

INDIA GARDEN   ©

62 Victoria Road, Romford   © **01708 762623**

Originally opened in 1970 and under the present management (Yeabor Ali) since 1975. A medium-sized restaurant seating 54 diners. Branch: Rupali, 10 Guildway, off Inchbonnie Road, South Woodham Ferrers, Essex.

Saffron Walden

NEMONTHON

18 George Street, Saffron Walden   © **01799 522739**

'Our local, producing an excellent standard of food and service,' J.H.

Shoeburyness

POLASH   ©

84-86 West Road, Shoeburyness   © **01702 293989**

The Polash and its slightly younger branch (*see* Polash, Burnham-on-Crouch) have been in our Guide since we began, which makes them old friends to these pages. But there's another reason we're happy that our reporters like them. It allows me to tell you that there's a third Polash in the same ownership. But it's not in Essex, nor even in Britain. It's in Sylhet, that Bangladeshi town where our curry house restaurateurs hail from. In fact, the Polash is the best hotel in town, and their restaurant, the Shapnil, has an item on its 200-dish menu that amazed us when we visited. Item no. 95 is no less than Chicken Tikka Masala! It is the only place in the whole of Bangladesh where it is to be found. And, says owner Sheik Faruque Ahmed, 'it sells really well!!!' His UK partner, M. Khalique, agrees. Price check: Papadom 50p, CTM £6.60, Pullao Rice £1.80. Minimum charge £9.50.

Southend-on-Sea

ANAND

363-365 Victoria Avenue,
Southend-on-Sea   ✆ 01702 333949

'Our favourite Indian, which we have frequented for years without
mishap! Decor is pleasant if rather functional. Seating is limited so
book for weekends,' P.M.

PANAHAR   ©

295 Victoria Avenue, Southend-on-Sea   ✆ 01702 348276

Seats 70 diners. Owner Syed Hassan will give discounts to Curry Club
members. Open noon-3p.m. and 6p.m.-midnight.

SOUTHEND TANDOORI

36 York Road, Southend-on-Sea   ✆ 01702 463182

'Standard Indian restaurant, decor in average condition. Staff very efficient and attentive, created a very friendly atmosphere. Food first class
at a very reasonable price. All meals were well prepared and served,'
M.J.G.

Southminster

VILLAGE TANDOORI   NEW ENTRANT

High Street, Southminster   ✆ 01621 772172

'Has been consistently excellent since Mr Abdul Kadir took over about
three years ago. Standard menu, generous portions, friendly service,'
M.P. 'We've tried most things on the menu, and have never been disappointed. The Kurzi Lamb's a dream. Customers are treated like
friends to the extent that, when one night there was no taxi available,
Mr Kadir gave my son and his girlfriend a lift home,' S.J.

South Woodham Ferrers

IZZY'S RUCHITA

Unit 1b, Guildway, Town Square,
South Woodham Ferrers   © 01245 323855

'Obliged to close for five months due to fire, I think the Ruchita is out to become the number one Indian in South Woodham again. Keema Nan very tasty. Chicken Tikka Patia superb, as was the Kashmir Fried Rice,' L.G.

Waltham Abbey

SHUHAG   NEW ENTRANT   ©

16 Highbridge Street, Waltham Abbey   © 01992 711436

Eighteen years is a long time in the curry house business, and that's how long M.H. Rashid has been going at his Shuhag. Everything from Roagan Goast (sic) to Butter Chicken (£5.75) is on the menu and, as you'd expect, it's all done with an experienced hand. Price check: Papadom 45p, CTM £5.95, Pullao Rice £1.70. Minimum charge £8. Four-course lunch £6.95, kids half-price.

Westcliff-on-Sea

MOTI MAHAL   ©

186, Station Road, Westcliff-on-Sea   © 01702 332167

'Gets my money any day. Thank heavens for the Moti Mahal,' G.C. A smallish restaurant seating 32 diners. Managing owner is Shahidur Khan.

PURBANI

387 London Road, Westcliff-on-Sea   © 01702 391947

'Small restaurant serving excellent food with fresh coriander sprinkled over most dishes which imparts a wonderful flavour and has got us thoroughly addicted to the stuff. Service is good and the waiters are friendly and helpful,' P.E.H.

GLOUCESTERSHIRE

Berkeley

BERKELEY TANDOORI

17 Canonbury Street, Berkeley   ℂ 01453 511166

'Absolutely superb,' J.G.

Cheltenham

EVEREST MOGHUL ▦

3 Portland Street, Cheltenham   ℂ 01242 221334

'A modern and clean restaurant seating 50 diners. Home-delivery service. Simply delicious Sheek Kebab followed by a first-class Lamb Rogan Josh,' M.B.

INDIAN BRASSERIE ©

146 Bath Road, Cheltenham   ℂ 01242 231350

A pretty, 56-seat restaurant decorated in pastel shades with cane furniture, managed by A. Rakib. C.S. still thinks it's the best in town, though not on one boozy night! – 'a Monday night visit with five guys from work. The food was rather bland and lifeless. It wasn't terribly bad, but it wasn't up to their usual high standard. Prices are relatively high for the area, £118 for six, although we shifted a fair bit of lager. Waiters are always very cheerful and friendly, there's a nice atmosphere.' Branch: Dilraj Tandoori, Dursley.

INDUS TANDOORI   ©

266 Bath Road, Cheltenham   ✆ **01242 516676**

'Started with Chicken Tikka, large succulent chunks. Hooray! Followed with Gosht Khatta Masala (£6.50), meat with lemon and tamarind. New to me – nice sweet and sour taste, meat a bit chewy. Not very good Brinjal Bhaji, swimming in oil. Kingfisher in bottles, Carlsberg on draught. You can see into the kitchen if you sit in certain seats so nothing to hide,' MS. R.F. complained about a very long delay on a Saturday night. Noorl Allam is owner-manager. Price check: Papadom 40p, CTM £6.50, Pullao Rice £1.50. Minimum charge £5.50. Set meal £6.95.

KASHMIR TANDOORI AND BALTI   ©

1 Albion Street, Cheltenham   ✆ **01242 524288**

The full range of curry goodies and Baltis from Messrs Anwar Hussain and Abdul Rauf. 'Menu – good selection, many Balti dishes. Very good and tasty food. Free Papadoms and chutney/pickles! Service indifferent,' J.G. 'Quality and service good, menu and decor very good, quantities OK,' R.H.A. Price check: Papadom 30p, CTM £5.25, Keema Mushroom Balti £4.25, Pullao Rice £1.50. Minimum charge £6.

SHEZAN   NEW ENTRANT   ©

4 Montpelier Street, Cheltenham   ✆ **01242 525429**

Owned by C. White, managed by N. Chaudhry, and opened in 1993, and now, we hear, a favourite among Cheltenham's 17 curry houses. Price check: Papadom 55p, CTM £5.95, Pullao Rice £1.95. Average meal £15.

Cinderford

AKASH

92 High Street, Cinderford   ✆ **01594 827770**

'A small restaurant seating about 42. Decor is to a high standard and spotlessly clean. Tasty Shami Kebabs if a little small followed by a quite excellent Meat Madras with lashings of fresh coriander,' M.B.

Cirencester

ALISHAN

1 Farrell Close, 39 Castle Street,
Cirencester   ✆ 01285 658987

A recent change from the Castle Tandoori, with new personnel who are
'extremely attentive. Their six-course lunchtime menu was stunning,
and priced from £3.95-£5.95, depending on which of eight main course
dishes you choose. The senior waiter promised us a 15% discount if we
return in the evening, so we will!' C.J.P.

RAJDOOT   ©

35 Castle Street, Cirencester   ✆ 01285 652651

Owner and manager Fozlur and Ataur Rahman's pretty green and yellow 52-seat restaurant has seen trojan work since it opened in 1982.
Price check: Papadom 35p, CTM £6.25, Pullao Rice £1.50. Set meal
from £6.95. Branch: Biplob, 12-14 Wood Street, Old Town, Swindon,
Wiltshire.

Dursley

DILRAJ

37 Long Street, Dursley   ✆ 01453 543472

D.H. continues to 'visit this restaurant once a week and have never had
anything less than an excellent meal or takeaway. Tandoori Machli followed by Chicken Madras or Dhansak with Madras Dal Sambar being
an exciting and different side dish. Rashid and Rakib play cricket with
the local club.' 'Our favourite restaurant. The food, and we have tried
most of the dishes, is always well prepared,' F.G. Branch: Indian
Brasserie, Cheltenham.

©	Curry Club discount (see p. 607)	🍽	Unlicensed
√	Vegetarian	▦	Home delivery
BYO	Bring your own alcohol		service available

Gloucester

BENGAL LANCER NEW ENTRANT

24-26 London Road, Gloucester   ✆ 01452 501731

'Just found a cracker. Seats about 80 in a light, airy room with windows the length of two walls, affording a panoramic view of the London Road's somewhat tatty buildings – well, you can't have everything, can you! It has its own car park at the back and full air-conditioning. Tables are polished black. There is a large reception area with a bar where you can relax over a cocktail or whatever while choosing from the menu. Started with the Lamb Pasanda which was light and creamy, continued with Murgh Jalfrezi which was loaded with the required green chillies, aromatic and delicious. The Pilau Rice was also very fragrant. I had a good night,' M.S. 'Cooking is truly excellent, especially the Biriani dishes. A comfortable and spacious restaurant,' P.N. However, C.S. had interminably long waits for service.

HILLTOP NEW ENTRANT

---

19 Worcester Street, Gloucester   ✆ 01452 308377

D.G.T. has been many times. 'The menu is familiar, but the tastes are different. They serve Nepalese and south Indian food. Bhajis are particularly good, so is the Aloo Masala Dosa, and the Nepalese Murgh Masala is very good. Our food for two £22 plus drink.'

Lechlade

BRITISH RAJ

Burford Street, Lechlade   ✆ 01367 252952

'Comfortable and intimate atmosphere. Friendly and efficient, no delays but sufficient time given between courses,' C. and S.R.

Lydney

MADHUMATI TANDOORI

3 Cavendish Building, Hill Street, Lydney   © 01594 842283

'This restaurant is smart and clean. Decked out in old cottage style complete with coach lamps on the walls. Chairs are well padded and very comfortable in red velvet. I think the chef got a little carried away with my Madras, it was a real fork-melter. Portions plentiful and Naan fresh and light. Prices a little high,' M.B.

Moreton-in-the-Marsh

MORETON TANDOORI

High Street, Moreton-in-the-Marsh   © 01608 650798

'An excellent meal in pleasant surroundings. Service quick and efficient. Balti Vegetable Bhoona very especially good. Decent-sized starters,' J.M.

Nailsworth

PASSAGE TO INDIA

Old Market, Nailsworth   © 01453 834063

'On entering I was met with a wonderful aroma of spices. Lamb Phal and Pilau Rice well-cooked, well-balanced but so huge, I couldn't eat it all,' A.E.J. 'A very tastefully decorated restaurant with friendly and courteous staff. Food is freshly cooked and mouthwatering. I will return,' S.T. 'A bit expensive, but worth it, food very good,' P.J.

© Curry Club discount (see p. 607)		🍺 Unlicensed
√ Vegetarian		▦ Home delivery
BYO Bring your own alcohol		service available

Stonehouse

TUDOR TANDOORI KITCHEN

High Street, Stonehouse   © 01453 792022

'Converted Tudor house, as the name suggests, food excellent, good Keema Naan, first-class staff,' P.J.

Stroud

JEWEL IN THE CROWN   ⊞ ©

22 Gloucester Street, Stroud   © 01453 765430

'A small restaurant which consistently gives excellent quality food, always white juicy breast meat and lovely deep flavours to all dishes. Service is occasionally slow and disorganized,' J.M. Home delivery service available. Owner Mohammed Yasin. Branch: Shelan Balti Palace, 73 Blackwell Street, Kidderminster.

Tewkesbury

MUNIRA   ©

69 Church Street, Tewkesbury   © 01684 294353

Remains popular and well spoken of. Branch: 60 Upper High Street, The Strand, Cheltenham.

Thornbury

MOGHUL'S BRASSERIE

High Street, Thornbury   © 01454 416187

A.E.-J. tells us he was Moghul's first customer a few years back when it opened. He tells us in his reports how much he likes it.

MUMTAZ INDIAN ©

7 St Mary's Centre, Thornbury ✆ **01454 411764**

Evenings only. The Mumtaz is on two levels. The downstairs seating area and small bar are for takeaway customers and perusal of the menu. The restaurant is situated upstairs. 'Menu not too extensive, but food extremely good and large portions. Clean European-style decor and music! Very helpful staff and friendly. Would go back,' W.W. K.B. was less enthusiastic about the decor and other reports talk of standard curries of generous proportions. A.E.-J. found the Phal too hot on one occasion and too mild on another, although his fiancée 'loves the Kormas'.

Wotton-under-Edge

INDIA PALACE NEW ENTRANT

13 Church Street, Wotton-under-Edge ✆ **01453 843628**

The former Wotton Indian is a 'welcome holiday discovery in the beautiful Cotswolds. The service efficient, if a little curt. Chicken Sagwala well flavoured, the Prawn Rogon average, the Bindi crisp and fresh, Aloo Gobi likewise. Filling meal for two, £23,' M.D.

HAMPSHIRE

Aldershot

JOHNNIE GURKHA'S ©

186 Victoria Road, Aldershot ✆ **01252 28773**

'Glad to see the restaurant is still as seedy as ever, although it's not quite so easy to accept since the prices are now as much as anywhere else. Mint sauce is excellent. Famous Dil Kusa Nan – an enormous bread topped with cherries and coconut,' P.D. 'Food is very plentiful, beautifully cooked and spiced and nothing was left!' J.W.

Alton

ALTON TANDOORI

7 Normandy Street, Alton   ✆ 01420 82154

'Food is very good and in plentiful quantities,' J.M. 'It was the hottest Madras my husband had ever had, verging on Vindaloo. Chicken Bharta was delicious,' J.W.

Andover

MUGHAL TANDOORI   NEW ENTRANT   ©

33 Andover Road, Ludgershall, Andover   ✆ 01264 790463

Owned by Towidar Rahman, managed by S. Miah, it's a typical popular local. Price check: Papadom 45p, CTM £5.95, Mughlai Kopta (fish) Dupiaza £6.10, Pullao Rice £1.50.

Ashurst

EURO ASIA INDIAN CUISINE   ©

179 Lyndhurst Road, Ashurst   ✆ 01703 292885

Managing partner Azad Miah runs the front while Mr Rahman cooks the food, which we continue to hear is fine. Price check: Papadom 55p, CTM £5.80, Kurzi Lamb for four £42.25, Pullao Rice £1.70. Evenings only. Branches: Prince of Bengal, 42 Pylewell Road, Hythe, Hampshire; Dynasty, 57 Brookley Road, Brockenhurst, Hampshire; Lal Quilla, 135-136 High Street, Lymington, Hampshire.

Basingstoke

CURRY PARADE   ©

4 Winchester Street, Basingstoke   ✆ 01256 473795

This 'old hand' originally opened in 1978 and has been under Shelim

Ahmed's careful ownership since 1985. Open noon-2.30p.m. and 6p.m.-midnight.

Fareham

FAREHAM TANDOORI

174a West Street, Fareham	✆ 01329 286646

M.S. updates us: 'The portion sizes are now below average, but the food is one of the best for curry – and that's the only food I eat!' Price check: Papadom 30p, CTM £4.95, Pullao Rice £1.30.

Farnborough

BALTI HOUSE   NEW ENTRANT

72 Farnborough Road, Farnborough	✆ 01252 541419

'Holds about 30 diners and is quite nicely decorated. The food could not be faulted, really excellent. Balti King Prawn Madras, Balti Korahi Chicken and Balti Chicken Dopiaza, with boiled and Pullao Rice, Mushroom, Cauliflower and Sag Bhajis. I had a Garlic Nan which was superb, very light. One small criticism, cold plates,' J.W. 'An aero-spatial welcome for our group of pilots before, during and after the airshow,' C.P.

POPADOMS ANGLO-INDIAN BRASSERIE
NEW ENTRANT   ©

33 Medway Drive, Cove, Farnborough	✆ 01252 376869

Sean Usher's place has attracted attention since it opened in 1996. It's evenings only, and only seats 34, so booking is advisable. It's bright and airy, with café-style polished wood floor and pine chairs under a colourful awning roof. The Anglo bit refers more to its owner and his young female waiting staff than the menu, which is a short but thorough document Cooking is done by Nepalese, apparently, though the menu does not offer enough Nepalese dishes, according to one ex-Gurkha officer. Reports, please.

RAJPUR   NEW ENTRANT

57d Mytchett Road, Mytchett,
Farnborough   ✆ 01252 542063

'You must try it. They want to get into the Guide,' P.L. They're in it. Do
they live up to it?

Fleet

GULSHAN

264-266 Fleet Road, Fleet   ✆ 01252 615910

'Were treated like royalty. Food and service excellent as usual. Though
they were spicy and hot, all the flavours were as they should be in the
King Prawn Zalpiazi and Pullao Rice. £64 for four, including drinks
and service,' J.W.

THE GURKHA SQUARE   NEW ENTRANT TOP 100   ©

327 Fleet Road, Fleet   ✆ 01252 810286

Talking of the Gurkhas (*see* Popadoms Anglo-Indian Brasserie,
Farnborough), there are precious few Nepalese restaurants in the UK,
let alone London, but it is not surprising that they abound in
Hampshire, near Church Crookham, the Gurkha base. This smallish
(44 seats) new (1996) venture, owned by A.B. Gurung, gives as good
definitive Nepalese food as you'll find. The restaurant is 'beautifully
decorated, with good carpeting and interesting photographs of
Nepalese people. Waiters all wear military-style uniform, though they
brought our main courses before serving our starters, which they rec-
tified. Absolutely delicious, beautifully spiced Tareko Chau (£2.80) –
stuffed mushrooms – and Aloo Achar (£2.80) – pickled potato.
Portions a good size. Beer expensive, pint of Tiger lager £2.90. Belgian
chocolate with the bill,' J.W. The menu contains many Nepalese specials. Other starters, all under £3, include Momo – a Keema-filled
dumpling – Sandheko Pork (or lamb or chicken) marinated with spicy
garlic and served cold, and Chatamari – a patty topped with meat or
vegetables. Main courses include a variety of chicken (Kukhara), lamb
(Kashi) or prawn (Jhingay) dishes. Swadilo is mild, Khorsani hot. Bhat

is rice. 'We chose Kukhara Bhutawa – fried chicken – (£5.50) and the Kashi Ledo Bedo (£4.20) – lamb in a Nepalese gravy – with Yogi Bhat (£4.90) and Aloo Tama Bodi (£2.70) – fermented bamboo shoots, black-eye beans and potato with sour spicing. It all transported us back to Nepal,' M.B. For those who prefer the regular list of familiar curries, they are all here, some 18 lamb, 16 chicken and 15 prawn curries, ranging from Kurma through Balti to Phal, plus an ample supporting cast of vegetable and side dishes. For the record, our standard price check: Papadom 40p, CTM £5.70, Pullao Rice £1.70. A great find, which we are pleased to bring into our TOP 100.

Gosport

DIL TANDOORI AND BALTI HOUSE NEW ENTRANT ©

73 Forton Road, Gosport ℂ **01705 521997**

Evenings only, takeaway only. Owners are Abdul Muhit and Abdul Rob. All the standard fare plus special Indian BBQs. Price check: Papadom 35p, CTM £4.95, Balti Special Meal £8.95, Pullao Rice £1.30.

TASTE OF INDIA ©

5 Bemisters Lane, Gosport ℂ **01705 601161**

Owner-manager Abdul Khalique has run this small 40-seater restaurant since 1992. Price check: Papadom 35p, CTM £5.95, Pullao Rice £1.45. Minimum charge £5.

Hamble

LAST VICEROY ©

4-7 High Street, Hamble ℂ **01703 452285**

'Still excellent food, and firmly recommended,' B.F.

Hook

HOOK TANDOORI NEW ENTRANT   ©

1 Fairholme Parade, Station Road, Hook   © 01256 764979

Syed Ahmed's 1986 venue is a favourite with a number of our scribes. Price check: Papadom 50p, CTM £8.95, Pullao Rice £1.85. Branch: Mogul, 13 London Road, Bagshot, Wiltshire.

Liss

MADHUBAN TOP 100

94 Station Road, Liss   © 01730 893363

After the last Guide, owner Lodue (Ludo) Miah engaged me as consultant on his range of chilled curry sauces, and so I have got to know him and his brothers Bedar and Dodu by name. I make no secret of such liaisons, and it does not make a difference to my opinion about a particular restaurant. Put another way, I only work for people I believe are doing a good job. As I said last time, this restaurant is one of my local haunts. Make such a statement and someone's bound to want to snipe. Take this comment ... 'Decor, service, fine, even toilets. But food – what a disappointment. Full of yuppies who don't have a clue what they are eating. Why don't you send out a few knowledgeable spies. Perhaps my problem is I spent most of my working life in curry-eating Asia!!!' I.A. Brown, Fernhurst. Well, Mr Brown, I'd like you to know that I mentioned your quote, verbatim, to 400 guests, those very 'yuppies', at the Madhuban's tenth birthday party. As perfectly normal working folk, they found your comments highly amusing and would just love to meet you! For some reason, they don't agree with you and, incidentally, for the record, we don't spy on restaurants. We rely on sensible reports from sensible people. Here are just some of those we've received about the Madhuban. 'A pretty blue restaurant with glittering chandeliers and a golden fountain, containing a resident duck. They obviously like river birds ... if you order a brandy, they serve it to you supported by a brass swan with flame!' D.B.A.C. 'At the end of a particularly bad week we decided to take off, anywhere, to try a new restaurant. After reading about the Madhuban in the Guide, we came from

London and found the restaurant easily. It was busy when we arrived at about 8.30p.m. but we were quickly accommodated and had only a short wait for a table. The decor, atmosphere and service were all excellent. It was hard to decide what to order because easily recognized dishes are lined up with some originals. What we did decide on was excellent. Some of the dishes are on the pricey side but justifiably. A worthwhile 120-mile round trip,' s.r. Another regular does a similar round trip, weekly from Kent. 'A lovely welcoming restaurant. Decor is light, pleasant and relaxing.' 'Staff are very friendly and remember your name even after some considerable time between visits. Food is the best. Jalfrezi is so good I can't bring myself to order anything else,' j.m. 'I was met at the door and welcomed in by the head waiter and was immediately struck by the decor. Service impeccable and the food the best,' j.s. 'Toilets were actually the best I have ever found, spotlessly clean,' j.o. Another j.m. thinks the food is the 'best I know. The only change I'd make is the removal of the fountain.' (So where's the duck going to go? d.b.a.c.) Though Lodue is usually out front serving in his smart waistcoated uniform, he does supervise the cooking. The menu is not over-large but there is ample choice of old favourites. Unusual items include Hyderabadi Shorba (£1.50) – a soup with chicken and potato, flavoured with coconut and lemon – and Hussaini Kebab (£2.30), meat stuffed with raisins. Dhaba Meat (£5.50) is billed as a 'roadside dish of lamb' while Ilachi Gosht (£5.50) is meat flavoured with cardamom and coriander. In addition there is a supplementary menu sheet, with some specials such as Keema-stuffed Chicken Tikka leg in a CTM creamy sauce, curry-filled pineapple, and sliced Raan. Price check: Papadom 50p, CTM £5.75, Pullao Rice £1.90. Remains in our TOP 100.

Lyndhurst

PASSAGE TO INDIA   NEW ENTRANT   ©

---

50 Romsey Road, Lyndhurst   ℭ **01703 282099**

'Highly recommended. We had a glorious meal. Chicken Patia and Mixed Grill were especially good. Excellent service with pleasant atmosphere,' c.m. Has been in Soyef Tarafder's ownership since it opened in 1983. Minimum charge £8.95.

Portsmouth

GANDHI ©

139-141 Kingston Road, North End, Portsmouth ✆ 01705 811966

K.A. Khan's huge restaurant seats 110 diners. Portsmouth Football Club eat at this establishment on a regular basis. 'Thali excellent value for money. Free popadoms and chutneys. Lamb Madras very tender, wonderful flavour,' J.C. 'Chicken Dhansak superb, well-flavoured with an excellent Sag Aloo. It was a pity to see the boring dessert menu of ice-creams,' J.H.

GULSHAN ©

128 London Road, North End, Portsmouth ✆ 01705 660045

Moklsur Rahman's well-established (1978) restaurant seats 56 diners and does the job of a curry house competently.

NEW TAJ MAHAL ©

54 Kingston Road, Buckland, Portsmouth ✆ 01705 661021

One of Portsmouth's oldest. This small restaurant, seating 40 diners, has been in Moshod Miah's hands since 1965 and, as is often the case with maturity, it's doing the job very competently.

PALASH TOP 100 ©

124 Kingston Road, North End, Portsmouth ✆ 01705 664045

I've said before of Portsmouth and Southsea that they boast an astonishing number of curry houses – currently around 40 between them! Most are average, with some described as 'garbage designed for lager louts'. Whether these are the lads from the sea or not, we neither know nor care, but we know that matelots enjoy a pint or ten before currying up. I overheard one such able body saying he couldn't contemplate eating on an empty stomach, as he lurched to the washroom! Partners Abdul Mazid, Mukith and Kadir have been going long enough to know how to exclude such custom. You have to book after 10p.m. and the staff will not admit those whose dress or behaviour is unacceptable to them. It's true all the sailors like a curry, but such is Girl Power that no longer do all the spice girls like a sailor, unless, they tell me, he's good enough for the Palash! Says Ms T.C.: 'I met my then sailor, now husband, there on a blind date with friends years ago.' D.R. vows: 'I could take my granny there. In fact, I do!' As to the restaurant, 'it does take a lot of beating,' G.D. The owners divide the roles of ownership, management and cheffing between them, achieving a formula that has worked well since the restaurant opened in 1981. We hear of great interest being taken over children, and queues of regulars at busy times. C.M. says: 'Yet another first-class restaurant. Papadoms arrived crisp and warm, and I followed with a very good Lamb Tikka. Our main course was Chicken Jalfrezi and Palash Special Rice and Chicken Tikka Biriani, which to my wife's delight contained sultanas! Service was of the highest standard and we were provided with free drinks during our meal. In addition, before paying the bill, we ordered a couple of papadoms to take home to our son, and the staff refused to take payment for them.' One dissenter, though: P.F.M. found it well below standard. Stays in our TOP 100. Reports, please. Branches: Palash Takeaway, 65 London Road, Cowplain; Bombay Express Balti House, 79 Albert Road, Southsea.

STAR OF ASIA   ©

6 Market Way, City Centre, Portsmouth   ℂ 01705 837906

Open noon-3p.m. and 6p.m.-1a.m. A small restaurant seating 40. Owner Abdul Mothen will give a discount to Curry Club members.

Ringwood

CURRY GARDEN

10 High Street, Ringwood   ℂ 01425 475075

'Very good,' P.J. Standard curry house, offering a wide range of heat-graded curries.

Southampton

KUTI'S BRASSERIE TOP 100

37-39 Oxford Street, Southampton   © 01703 333473

'Service and atmosphere exuded quality,' P.B. Smartly attired waiters 'in
Noel Coward jackets,' J.L. 'Kuti Miah's impressively decorated restaurant
is in a very salubrious part of town. The tables were laid out with plenty of space between them. We were surprised how busy the restaurant
was for a Tuesday. The restaurant offers a set menu on Monday and
Tuesday evenings for an appealing £12.50. The set menu had to be asked
for, however, and it had to be searched for by the waiter. When it did
arrive the choice was very good . . . Lemon Prawns, Garlic Chicken,
Mixed Kebab, Prawn Puri, Bombay Aloo and Mixed Vegetable Curry
with Pullao Rice. Everything was excellent. The service was brisk but
given the human touch when the boss arrived, a very genial character.
The girl on the cash desk was charming as well. We left before the traditionally dressed gentleman began playing his instruments. It would
have been good to see the place in full swing but we had to catch a ferry.
The toilets in this restaurant are worth a separate mention. They were
exquisitely clean and the attention to detail was much appreciated –
boxes of facial tissues, etc. If you're in Southampton this is a must. It's
even worth a special visit,' S.R.

   We had some reports about the closure of Kuti's other branch. 'I
am sure that you are aware that Kuti's other restaurant on London
Road has closed. We eventually ended up in Kuti's Brasserie. The manager who welcomed us apologized profusely for our inconvenience.
Apparently they have lost a lot of custom due to the London Road
entry in the Guide. He was not a happy man!! However, food was
excellent. It was nice to see a selection of venison and duck on the
menu. Starters were superb and Tandoori Jinga was beautifully presented although I'm not sure it justified paying £5.95. Onion Bhajias
were nice and crisp and the Mint Raita was superb. Venison Korai was
good and my colleagues were most impressed with the Chicken Tikka
Masala. Tarka Dal had the right texture, too. An evening to recommend,' C.T. Since Kuti's Indian Cuisine and Kuti's Brasserie were owned
by the same man, Kuti Miah, we conclude that he lost custom because
he closed the restaurant, not because it appeared in the Guide! We are
sorry he did not tell us any of this but, notwithstanding, we'll transfer

our TOP 100 award to the Brasserie, keeping it in the Kuti family, so to speak.

SUNLIGHT INDIAN TAKEAWAY NEW ENTRANT ©

67 Testwood Road, Shirley, Southampton ℂ 01703 704867

S. Rahman took on this evenings-only, takeaway-only, in 1996. Price check: Papadom 30p, CTM £4.95, Tandoori Bucket £9.95, Pullao Rice £1.25. Closed Tuesdays.

Southsea

GOLDEN CURRY ©

16 Albert Road, Southsea ℂ 01705 820262

Following a previous Guide entry we had an impassioned letter from owner Salim Ullah emphasizing that, by closing at 12.30a.m. (midnight Sundays), this 'actively discourages the after-pub trade,' and that 'we succeed in maintaining a quiet pleasant and relaxed family atmosphere.' And we're sure you are right, Mr Ullah.

INDIAN COTTAGE NEW ENTRANT

257 Albert Road, Southsea ℂ 01705 826010

Opened in June 1995. Forty-eight seater. 'Lovely decorations, apricot, green, blue, high-quality furnishings, including wood screens. Heavy silver cutlery, white crisp cotton tablecloths on dark wood polished tops. Papadoms arrived as I sat down, my Lamb Tikka starter arrived five minutes later with the chutneys! Followed with Chicken Shashlik Kebabs – two huge skewers more like swords on a bed of shredded lettuce and white cabbage. Great lumps of chicken, onion, green pepper all burnt on the edges – yummy! Kingfisher lager on draught, Cobra in bottles, coffee with real cream. Excellent food, cheerful and speedy service and good ambience,' M.S.

JEWEL IN THE CROWN NEW ENTRANT   ©

60 Osborne Road, Southsea   ℭ **01705 827787**

Shofik Miah's large, well-decorated, newish venue, already well-established in a curry city. Reports, please.

MIDNIGHT TANDOORI   ©

101 Palmerston Road, Southsea   ℭ **01705 822567**

Nazrul Islam's massive, 92-seat restaurant is divided between two floors, and it remains one of Southsea's most popular curry houses.

PURNIMA   ©

54 Albert Road, Southsea   ℭ **01705 826343**

A comprehensive range of competent curries at owner Elias Miah's Purnima.

STANDARD   ©

8 Albert Road, Southsea   ℭ **01705 811307**

D. Miah owns Southsea's oldest (1959) curry house, and it has remained ever popular with succeeding generations of curry-lovers, serving above-average food. Stays open very late (until 2.30a.m.) which pleases the natterers, night owls and the Navy.

TASTE OF BENGAL   ©

17 Albert Road, Southsea   ℭ **01705 827342**

Moklis Ali's small 40-seater restaurant is yet another of this road's good curry houses.

Waterlooville

INDIAN COTTAGE NEW ENTRANT   ©

**51 London Road, Cowplain,
Waterlooville**   ℭ **01705 269351**

D. and B.R. and L. and A.C. have been coming here as a foursome for many years. It opened in 1984 and changed hands to Sheik Shab Uddin in 1993. They say 'the food is excellent and the staff always attentive' and they plan to keep on coming. Thanks for telling us. Identifying such restaurants is what this Guide is all about. Price check: Papadom 40p, CTM £5.25, Tandoori Trout £6.25, Pullao Rice £1.75. Minimum charge £5.55. Branches: 44 The Broadwalk, Port Solent Marina, near Portsmouth; 4 The Square, Havant Road, Horndean.

Winchester

GANDHI

163 High Street, Winchester   ✆ 01962 863940

'My local. I think it's the best for food and service, even though it's a touch more expensive than the others. I go back again and again, I just can't seem to get enough curry!' P.B. 'Superb ambience. Most of the tables (50-60 covers) arranged for four in cabins, which can be partitioned by curtains – very unusual, but very nice for a young couple in need of a quick cuddle before a curry! Chicken Phal – the hottest ever! The quality and quantity of food can be one of the best,' B.P.D.

HEREFORDSHIRE

The splitting of Hereford and Worcester back to Herefordshire and Worcestershire leaves the former with few restaurants, therefore few reports, so more welcomed, please.

Bromyard

BOMBAY PALACE   ©

22 High Street, Bromyard   ✆ 01885 488668

Opened in 1992 under the ownership of Mr Sofik Miah. Seats 60 diners. Open 5.30p.m.-midnight. 'The friendliest restaurant in town. Food can only be described as first-class, a pleasure to look forward to on a night off,' R.W. 'Their food and service are excellent,' C.T.

Hereford

KAMAL   ⊞

82 Widemarsh Street, Hereford   ℂ **01432 278005**

Home-delivery service available. Open Sunday to Thursday noon-2.30p.m. and 6p.m.-midnight, Friday and Saturday 12-2.30p.m. and 6p.m.-1a.m. 'Needed a fix, Chicken Ceylon excellent,' P.J.

Leominster

JALALABAD

33 Etnam Street, Leominster   ℂ **01568 615656**

This restaurant is well promoted by the ebullient owner-manager Kamal Uddin. It's attractively decorated in greens, and owner-chef Abdul Mukith's food menu attracts regular, satisfactory praise from Leominster locals. Evenings only, lunch as well Fridays and Saturdays.

SHABAGH BALTI TANDOOR   ©

16 Burgess Street, Leominster   ℂ **01568 614500**

Mokbul Miah's Shabagh attracts local comment. Price check: Papadom 30p, CTM £1.95, Pullao Rice £1.35. Set meal £7.95. Evenings only.

Ross-on-Wye

OBILASH

19a Gloucester Road, Ross-on-Wye   ℂ **01989 567860**

A smallish restaurant seating 40. Some unusual Bangladeshi authentic dishes on the menu include Shathkora Curry and Ada Lembu Curry. Open for lunch and dinner.

HERTFORDSHIRE

Part of Hertfordshire was absorbed by Greater London in 1965. We note affected boroughs with the letters GL.

Abbots Langley

ABBOTS LANGLEY TANDOORI   ©

Langley Road, Abbots Langley   ✆ 01923 260402

Gulam Ambia's pretty 70-seater restaurant, with its hanging plants, colonial fans and large golden chandeliers and fish tank, is very smart indeed. 'Spotlessly clean and inviting. We were shown to a table close to the aquarium which was built into the adjacent wall. This immediately relaxed us after a somewhat hectic football match. Service was attentive but not pushy and they put themselves out to please and succeeded. Food beautifully prepared and cooked perfectly. Onion Bhaji was very big. My son's Chicken Tandoori was brought in hot and sizzling and tasted marvellous,' D.M. Branch: Shefford Tandoori, 8 High Street, Shefford, Bedfordshire.

VICEROY OF INDIA   TOP 100   ©

20 High Street, Abbots Langley   ✆ 01923 262163

Last time, D.M. from Marlow raved about managing partner Ronney Rahman's place. So, following two visits from us and other good reports, we promoted it to our TOP 100 for him. Since then other publications have followed with their awards but, curiously, we've not had a single report, not even from D.M., though he still tells us plenty. Since no news is good news we stay with our instincts and keep it in our TOP 100. Here's what you've said: 'A lovely restaurant, busy but we had pre-booked our table. We ate Onion Bhajees – four tiny, cute little bhajees! Hash (duck) Tikka, yummy; Lamb Bhoona, rich tasty gravy; Mushroom Rice – which wasn't on the menu, but they didn't mind whizzing it up and a Garlic Nan (I smell now!!). And the all essential mints afterwards, not the After Eights, oh no!! Suchard Twilights!!!' s.w. 'On another night we had the most disappointing meal, I think it was an off-night,' s.w. 'Decor reasonable. Layout and general cleanliness are impeccable. Always fresh carnations on the table. Highly impressed with the food. Popadoms are fresh and served within seconds as are the drinks. Level of service, my only criticism,' N.C. Reports, please.

Barnet, GL

KING TANDOORI   NEW ENTRANT   ©

92 East Barnet Road, New Barnet   ℂ 0181 441 9272

M.D. Salim opened his 46-seater in 1995 and we hear well of it, especially of the Happy Hour Half Price Meal. 'It makes me happy at that price,' N.L. Price check: Papadom 40p, CTM £5.30, Pullao Rice £1.50. Set meal £9.75. Minimum charge £6. Cover charge £1. Evenings only, except Sunday eat-your-fill buffet £5.95, lunch and dinner.

SHAPLA TANDOORI   ©

37 High Street, Barnet   ℂ 0181 449 0046

S.I. Ahmed's smart restaurant seats 50 and is popular. 'My local for four years, always very reliable. Fairly standard menu. Excellent Dhansak, generous Shashlik and very good side dishes. A clean and cosy restaurant,' C.T. Price check: Papadom 40p, CTM £4.95, Pullao Rice £1.45. Minimum charge £7.50. Branch: Curry Cottage, 7e High Street, Barnet.

Berkhamsted

AKASH   ©

307 High Street, Berkhamsted   ℂ 01442 862287

'We particularly like the level of personal service – you are greeted at the door, coats taken, napkins placed in your lap, staff are attentive without hovering, they top up your wine glass,' L.B. Open noon-2.30p.m. and 6p.m.-midnight. The owner is Foysol Ahmed.

CURRY GARDEN   ©

29 High Street, Berkhamsted   ✆ 01442 877867

'An old converted pub, lovely low beams and cosy booths. We were very impressed with everything, will most definitely be back,' s.w.

Cheshunt

RAJ VOGUE   NEW ENTRANT   ©

48 High Street, Cheshunt   ✆ 01992 641297

Khalek Quazi's Raj Vogue is popular locally, serving formula curries, tandooris and baltis. Price check: Papadom 40p, CTM £6.15, Pullao Rice £1.80. Sunday buffet £6.95.

Cockfosters, GL

TANDOORI NIGHTS   ©

27 Station Parade, Cockfosters Road,
Cockfosters   ✆ 0181 441 2131

Right at the end of the Piccadilly Line Tube is Mrs Yasmeen Rashid's good and reliable restaurant seating 60 diners. First opened in 1988, it is now managed by H. Karim and we regularly get satisfactory reports about it. Price check: Papadom 40p, CTM £6.95, Roast Quail and Kurzi Lamb dinner for four, ordered in advance, £110, Pullao Rice £2.30. Sunday buffet £6.95. Service charge 10%. Branches: 108 Parkway, London NW1; 35 Great Queen Street, London WC2.

Harpenden

DHAKA COTTAGE

1a Harding Parade, Station Road,
Harpenden   ✆ 01582 769317

Formerly the Anarkali, this is a small, smart establishment with a large modern frontage, which is home to several exotic palm and rubber plants. It seats about 40 diners. 'Amongst my very enjoyable meal was a green vegetable dish in cashew sauce. I can't remember its name (my wife says slime!) but it was composed of fresh broccoli, sprouts, chilli and an Indian leaf. The sauce was sublime – crunchy and sweetish,' P.F.M.

Hatfield

TASTE OF INDIA NEW ENTRANT   ©

33-34 Salisbury Square, Old Hatfield   ℂ 01707 276666

Owned by Mrs A. Khatun and managed by Golam Yahna, the Taste has become a popular local haunt. Price check: Papadom 40p, CTM £6.95, Duck Korai £6.95, Balty (sic) Tropical £6.50, Pullao Rice £1.40. Mondays, four-course banquet £9.95.

Hemel Hempstead

GADEBRIDGE BALTI NEW ENTRANT   ©

2 Rossgate, Gadebridge,
Hemel Hempstead   ℂ 01442 249249

Following an impassioned phone call from a Ms M.D. that her favourite restaurant had not received a form from us, and 'how could we omit them, they're so excellent', we rushed the restaurant a questionnaire by return and they duly filled it up and rushed it back. Now I find they had already done one a month earlier! Never mind, this is for you, Marina: Mr E.H. and A.H. Uddin opened in 1996 and the locals, well curried for in HH, clearly love it. Price check: Papadom 45p, CTM £5.45, Pullao Rice £1.60. Sunday eat-your-fill buffet £5.95, 1-5p.m. Wednesday banquet £9.95. Branch: Eastern Spice, Rickmansworth.

GURU TANDOORI   ©

5 Bridge Street, Hemel Hempstead   ℂ 01442 254725

The very next day after hearing from Ms M.B., we received an impassioned letter from Mr M.B.S. (*see* above, but no connection, we think) telling us that he's eaten here twice a week for twenty years, and that he always recommends it to his friends, who in turn have become satisfied customers. We don't think this is owner, Mr Rahman, because at least he'd get the address right! The Guru is one of our regulars, dating from our first Guide. Price check: Papadom 50p, CTM £7.50, Pullao Rice £1.80. Branch: Hemel Tandoori, Hemel Hempstead.

HEMEL TANDOORI   ©

51-55 Waterhouse Street,
Hemel Hempstead   **✆ 01442 242937**

'Splendid menu and one of the few to do duck,' P.J. The owner is Mr M. Rahman. Branch: Guru Tandoori, Hemel Hempstead.

PARADISE TANDOORI   ©

79-81 Waterhouse Street,
Hemel Hempstead   **✆ 01442 243595**

'The Pasanda, cooked with wine, was just divine,' M.S. A 60-seater restaurant. Open noon-2p.m. and 5.30p.m.-midnight. Owner, M. Ruez, opened this one in 1988. Branch: Raja, Hemel Hempstead.

RAJA   ⊞ ©

84 London Road, Apsley,
Hemel Hempstead   **✆ 01442 252322**

'They deliver at no extra cost and the service was fast. Food arrived piping hot within the 30 minutes. Portions were large and very tasty. Prices average for the area,' J.H. 'Surroundings both spacious and intimate. Portions were generous and waiter brought the food sizzling,' J.P. Branch: Paradise Tandoori, Hemel Hempstead.

©	Curry Club discount (see p. 607)	🍷	Unlicensed
√	Vegetarian	⊞	Home delivery
BYO	Bring your own alcohol		service available

Hertford

GURU   ⊞

6 Parliament Square, Hertford   ✆ 01992 551060

'There is always ample food to eat, always served promptly. The food is always very good quality and you can ask to inspect the kitchen at any time,' K.R. Open daily, noon-2.45p.m. and 6p.m.-midnight, including Bank Holidays. There is a free delivery service or if you can pick up your own takeaway there is a discount of 20%. Every Sunday a buffet is served from noon-6p.m.

MOYURI

15 Castle Street, Hertford   ✆ 01992 581069

'A small restaurant seating thirty diners. Popadoms were served with six chutneys – three standard and three unusual. Standard menu with some specialities. Portions enormous, struggled to finish despite not having starters. Massalla Nan was great,' K.B. 'Arrived at 11.15 to find the waiters attempting to throw out some rather drunk potential customers! Fortunately you soon learn the trick which is to appear sober when you enter an Indian restaurant! Service – like lightning. Food – excellent, quantities and quality well above average,' P.C.

Hitchin

INDIA BRASSERIE   ©

36 Bancroft Road, Hitchin   ✆ 01462 433001

Reliable food and service at proprietor-chef M.J. Choudhury's small restaurant seating 38 diners. Open noon-2.30p.m. except Friday, evenings 6-11.30p.m., Friday and Saturday open till midnight.

Letchworth

CURRY GARDEN   ©

71 Station Road, Letchworth   ✆ 01462 682820

Afiz Ullah is the head chef and owner of this large, 72-seater restaurant, which has a 'huge friendly menu,' M.T. Open noon-2.30p.m. and 6p.m.-midnight, Sunday buffet noon-5.30p.m. Branches: Curry Garden, 29 High Street, Berkhamsted; 141 Uxbridge Road, Rickmansworth; 69 Katherine Drive, Dunstable, Bedfordshire; 307 Hornchurch Road, Hornchurch, Essex.

SAGAR   ©

48 The Broadway, Letchworth   ✆ 01462 684952

Mirrors, classical Indian pictures and high-backed chairs make Motiur Rahman's Sagar attractive to Letchworth locals. So does the food, we hear. 'The Trout Masala (£8.50) is one of the best,' L.V. Price check: Papadom 50p, CTM £6.95, Pullao Rice £1.65. Service charge 10%. Lunch buffet, weekdays £5.50, Sundays £5.95. Branches: Aashiana, Broadway, Bedfordshire; Ahkbar Takeaway, Abbot's Walk, Biggleswade, Bedfordshire.

Radlett

RADLETT INDIA CUISINE

70e Watling Street, Radlett   ✆ 01923 856300

'Started with Chicken Chockro Vorty – strips of marinated chicken, grilled, served with salad – exceptional!! Jeera Kata Garlic Chicken – brilliantly tasty, no cloying curry gravies. Nan, chewy and delicious,' C.J.

©	Curry Club discount (see p. 607)	🍺	Unlicensed
√	Vegetarian	⊞	Home delivery
BYO	Bring your own alcohol		service available

Rickmansworth

EASTERN SPICE   ©

9 Penn Place, Northway, Rickmansworth   © 01923 711101

Formerly the Modhubon, but only a name change because it is still
owned by Ekbal Hussain. Popular with its local following. A small
restaurant seating 40 diners. Open noon-2.30p.m. and 6-11.30p.m. Price
check: Papadom 45p, CTM £5.45, Pullao Rice £1.60. Branch:
Gadebridge Balti, Hemel Hempstead.

Royston

BRITISH RAJ   TOP 100   ©

55 High Street, Royston   © 01763 241471

Last time I confessed that I had not visited the British Raj and I confess I still haven't. What I know of it is what you tell me, and what the
ever-exuberant owner Nazzir Uddin Choudhury tells me. And, believe
me, he tells me a lot. And as I keep on saying, I do have a soft spot for
Mr C.'s sense of humour. Firstly, the venue itself, in its Grade ii listed
building, is built on a hill and 'kind of leans, a feeling which is
enhanced when you step inside. It is small and compact, with white-
washed walls and olde black beams, with not a straight-edge in sight.
To avoid vertigo, the best thing to do is sit down and order a quick
drink!' D.R. The mini menu, as tacky as ever, says it all, and it's available free for all who want it. One complainer, obviously devoid of Mr
C.'s sense of humour, finds its 1970s pictures old-fashioned. In fact it's
been updated recently, warts and all, but at least the various Miss
Anglias from decades ago have been eased back, if not removed. That
won't suit the feminists, but that I'm sure won't deter Mr C. who
doubtless would love to entertain the Spice Girls at his idiosyncratic
venue. For those who don't know, the mini menu is a 24-page, A5-size
booklet illustrated with pictures and cartoons, and facts, some bizarre,
some straight, lifted from here, there and everywhere (including some
uncredited lifts from this Guide). As bedtime reading it will bring a
smile to your lips. And all of it's intentional: 'Royston is a nice little
blooming twin town.' 'The beautification of the High Street is now

over and it now looks exceedingly beautiful.' 'We've made it our business to put more on the menu for the Happy Eater.' 'Take him out for dinner when he's flat broke.' 'Bring the family in and loosen your belt.' 'Remember curry enhances your appetite while you eat, until unknowingly you find yourself overloaded.' 'The tastefulness is terrific.' And is it? The menu contains starters; main meals – three pages of them; and third course – desserts; fourth course – finishers (coffee/liqueurs); and the remarkable fifth course, unique to the Raj – a Hukkah (£2.55) (hubble-bubble) pipe, 'so you can smoke your way out of the meal.' Chef Junab Ali's specials include some unusual items. One is struck (or is it stuck?) by Fixed Bayonet Poussin (£9.95), a whole chicken twice-cooked with green chillies, served sizzling, Shooting Bird Bhuna (£6.75) – quail, Tandoori Duck Biriani (£9.95), Crab Rezalla (£6.95) with a yoghurt and chilli base, and Chicken Baramoza Mixed Curry (£8.95) – chicken, meat, prawn and vegetable which is, according to the menu, 'a dish of profound distinction,' whilst Meat Jaljalae is a mixture of Lamb Tikka, chilli and onion – 'a flaming dish of delight.' Balti dishes are new to the Raj and, in his inimitable way, Mr Choudhury has his own definition. Correctly he attributes it to Baltistan in (Pakistan's) northern Kashmir but, not content with that, he adds an alternative option: 'Banglastan (Bangladesh) is also its place of its origin,' thus bringing in his home lands over 1200 miles away. Banglastan, that's a new one! Patakstan more like, Mr Choudhury! Various Thalia (sic) dishes are available – ten set meals from £8.95-£15.95, plus two pre-booked feasts. Price check: Papadom 50p, CTM £6.75, Pullao Rice £1.65. Weekday set lunches – 'Bring the office and cash in on these gastronomically balanced lunches' – from £3.95. Weekend eat-your-fill buffet lunches £7.95, kids £3.95. Cover charge 25p(!).

We continue to receive many reports, mostly contented, mostly from the band of locals who enjoy Mr C. and his merry ways. 'An excellent meal and deservedly in the TOP 100. Ate chef's recommendations – a mountain of food. We left feeling bloated – our own fault. Paan Liqueur should be tried – if only for the experience!' A.S. As usual, we have received one stinker (as we have done since we first entered this restaurant in our first Guide). Prof. and Mrs K. found it 'not good or bad, the curries not very tasty, overcooked chicken, overpriced and lack-lustre decor'. Their bill came to £28 plus wine and service, which seems reasonable to me, but they did remark on loutish customer behaviour, which always discolours a visit to any restaurant.

Door-control really is crucial, Mr Choudhury. Yet again, though, I'll stick my neck out and, from one idiosyncrat to another, I'll give the British Raj our TOP 100 award for the third time. 'Children are welcome ... they get small meals.' I promise I'll visit it (unannounced, anonymously and undetected, I hope) this year. Reports, please. Branch: Tandoori Villa Takeaway, 16a Melbourne Street, Royston.

St Albans

MUMTAJ   NEW TO OUR TOP 100   ©

---

115 London Road, St Albans   © 01727 858399

Originally opened as a restaurant way back in 1962. Present owner, Muklasur Rahman, took over in 1983 and has established himself as a reliable source of Indian cuisine. Seats 44 diners in two rooms partitioned by an archway. We've had many recommendations for this one but none more interesting than from P.F.M.: 'I am lucky enough to travel widely on business, and never travel without your Guide. I aim to visit every TOP 100. I agree with all but one of those visited.' [Please tell us about the others.] 'Having visited many, many curry houses in the UK, as well as in Brussels (ugh), Amsterdam (great), Stockholm (ugh), Riyadh (ummm), and the USA (hmmm), I am always pleased to get home to St Albans and eat at my local, the Mumtaj. Its location and interior are not as grand as some but its food is sublime. Many — too many — curry houses serve their food with a general brown type gravy. Everything is coated in the same sauce. But in the Mumtaj each flavour stands out on its own. I eat in or take out there on average three times a month. It would be more if I didn't do so much travelling. When I am at home I may eat there two or three times a week. The owner's son now runs the kitchen and is front of house or in the kitchen. He loves to try out new ideas and has been experimenting for a new menu. He worked for some time in curry houses in Houston, Texas. I don't know whether the influence came from there, but he introduced sauces I have not encountered elsewhere, such as "dill weed white wine", "tarragon mushroom" and "lemon mustard and mild almond". However, our favourite dish is Karachi Kebab — sizzling Chicken Tikka in a spicy sauce, with peppers and tomatoes. This is a very commonly found dish (CTM), but none has brought it to the height that The Mumtaj has. Incidentally, the name dates from their first menu when the English printer mistook the name 'karahi' and they have kept it ever since. I propose it for elevation to the TOP 100.' Done, sir! Everyone agree? Price check: Papadom 40p, CTM £7.50 incl. rice, Pullao Rice £1.70.

Sawbridgeworth

STAR OF INDIA

51 London Road, Sawbridgeworth   ✆ 01279 726512

'Waiters were very friendly, ensuring everything was OK. Onion and Cauliflower Bhajees were superb. Special Chicken Passanda and Chicken Madras very good, but Madras could be hotter,' K.B. 'My all-time-favourite Indian restaurant. Food is average-priced but the quantities are very generous (Onion Bhajias the size of melons),' D.W.

Stevenage

SHEPHALL TANDOORI TAKEAWAY   ©

20 The Hyde, Stevenage   ✆ 01438 360520

A wide range of curries 'well done here,' P.J. Owned since 1991 by N. Hussain and A. Hoque, the former is front of house, the latter the chef behind the scenes. Open 5p.m.-midnight, till 12.30a.m Friday and Saturday. Branch: Huntingdon Indian Takeaway, 144 High Street, Huntingdon.

Tring

JUBRAJ   ©

53a High Street, Tring   ✆ 01442 825368

Many talk about the special dinners for two at Monnan Miah's large restaurant seating 90 diners, adjacent to the town car park. Open noon-2.30p.m. and 6-11.45p.m.

Ware

NEELAKASH

1-3 Amwell End, Ware   © 01920 487038

'Quantities, quality and service were good. Only one complaint, the mango chutney was like treacle!!' P.C. 'Brightly decorated, genuine carnations on the tables. The meal, Sunday buffet, was enjoyable,' A.S.

Watford

ALI BABA TANDOORI

13 King Street, Watford   © 01923 229793

'Plenty of food with each dish, Vindaloo was excellent, the freshest Nan bread I have ever had,' A.M.

BOMBAY TANDOORI   ⊞ ©

36 Market Street, Watford   © 01923 225768

Free delivery takeaway service in the Watford area. The manager is S.A. Khan. Open daily, noon-3p.m. and 6p.m.-midnight.

JAIPUR   ©

37 Market Street, Watford   © 01923 249374

Owner-manager Mohammed Abullaes' Jaipur has, you tell us, been Watford's favourite since 1989 and is now open evenings only, 6p.m.-midnight. Price check: Papadom 45p, CTM £5.50, Peshwari Lamb £5.95, Pullao Rice £1.50. Minimum charge £10. Service charge 10%. Set meal £5.95.

©	Curry Club discount (see p. 607)	🍵	Unlicensed
√	Vegetarian	⊞	Home delivery
BYO	Bring your own alcohol		service available

Welwyn Garden City

RAJ OF INDIA

16 Hall Grove, Welwyn Garden City   © 01707 373825

'Decor is light and airy. The staff are helpful and even smile and joke with you. Generous quantities of food, served promptly. Chicken Balchara including rice was loaded with flavour,' K.B.

HUMBERSIDE

The former counties of North and South Humberside have been abolished, and towns north of the River Humber have been placed into a brand new county, East Yorkshire, with those south of the river reverting to Lincolnshire.

KENT

Part of Kent was absorbed by Greater London in 1965. We note affected areas with the letters GL.

Ashford

CURRY GARDEN   ©

31 Bank Street, Ashford   © 01233 620511

'Service was very efficient and food was of a high quality, portions were ample,' J.S.K. The owner is Bajloor Rashid. Open noon-3p.m. and 6p.m.-midnight. Branch: Shapla, 36 Harbour Street, Whitstable.

TANDOORI NIGHTS   ©

9 Torrington Road, Ashford   © 01233 636681

Partner Ziaul Ahmed's Nights continues to get favourable comments. Open noon-2p.m. and 5.30-11.30p.m.

Barnehurst, GL

JHAS TANDOORI ©

158c Mayplace Road East, Barnehurst   ✆ 01322 555036

Opened in 1989 by K.S. Jhas, it's an evenings-only establishment seating 45-50 diners. Open 6-11.30p.m., till midnight on Friday and Saturday and closed all day Sunday.

Beckenham, GL

ROSE TANDOORI ©

406 Upper Elmers End Road, Eden Park,
Beckenham   ✆ 0181 650 0919

Managing partner Keenu Mul Islam's small and friendly restaurant seats just 38 diners. Serves all your favourite curries and accompaniments. Open noon-2.30p.m. and 6-11.30p.m.

Bexley, GL

ALBANY ©

44 Steynton Avenue, Albany Park,
Bexley   ✆ 0181 309 7254

Manager S. Alom's curry house is popular, especially for the really good special set lunches and set dinners on Sundays and Bank Holidays. Branch: Mahatma Tandoori, 156 Bexley Road, London SE9.

RUCHI ©

58 Steynton Avenue, Albany Park,
Bexley   ✆ 0181 300 0200

The Ruchi opened way back in 1986 and has established itself as a good, reliable and competent restaurant seating 56 diners. 'A well-organized restaurant with an enormous takeaway trade. Service was friendly. Breads were the best feature,' J.L. The owner, Madan Lal Prashar, promises again to give a discount to Curry Club members, but we have a case of a refusal. Price check: Papadom 50p, CTM £6.10, Nawabi Chicken or Chicken Nigiri, incl. rice, both £8.50, Pullao Rice £1.75. Sunday lunch £8.95. Minimum charge £7.50. Open daily for lunch and dinner.

SAGGOR   NEW ENTRANT   ©

145 Blendon Road, Bexley   ✆ 0181 303 7549

'We just have to tell you about a great new find ... Ali Uddin's Saggor. We've been a few times now, and we love the Sugati Mussala (£6.50) – chicken with coconut, the Mase-e-Masala (£5.50) – fish cooked with wine, and the Subze Tandoori (£2.80) – vegetables, marinated then tandoor-cooked,' G. and R.T. Price check: Papadom 45p, CTM £6, Pullao Rice £1.45. Minimum charge £10.

Biddenden

MAHARAJA   NEW ENTRANT   ©

5-7 Headcorn Road, Biddenden   ✆ 01580 291485

D. Hussain took over this restaurant in 1996 and we have heard 'it's OK,' D.R. Price check: Papadom 40p, CTM £5.80, Kurzi Lamb/Chicken £32 for two ordered in advance, Pullao Rice £1.35. Minimum charge £10.

Biggin Hill, GL

MEHBUBA   NEW ENTRANT

226 Main Road, Biggin Hill   ✆ 01959 570150

As far as C.D. is concerned, this is now Biggin's best: 'Decor is pleasant with each table divided by highly artistic engraved clear acrylic panels. Service pleasant, quality and value for money is good, especially the Sunday buffet lunch at £7, comprising two mild meat curry dishes, two vegetable dishes plus rice and chutneys. Starters are usually chicken wings and small onion bhajias, with fresh green salad, cucumber

raita, etc. It's nice to see waiters remove the tops of the food containers each time you go up to help yourself — far too many similar places
leave the removal of lids to the customers, which is not a good deal as
there is never anywhere to put the darned things! Usual limited selection of puds! Why don't restaurants offer barfi and the like?' 'Excellent
food, unwelcoming waiter — why don't they understand just how
important the initial greeting is? Friendly chef,' G.M. However, M.P.W.
found it all bland.

Borough Green

RAJ NEW ENTRANT   ©

31 High Street, Borough Green   ℂ **01732 882650**

'Shamsar Uddin's smart little 50-seater restaurant is in a row of shops,
well kept, with friendly staff. The standard of both food and service
above-average,' R.L.T. Price check: Papadom 45p, CTM £6.05, Pullao
Rice £1.60.

Bromley, GL

DORSHONI TAKEAWAY NEW ENTRANT   ©

453 Downham Way, Downham, Bromley   ℂ **0181 695 8777**

A. Islam's new (1996) takeaway provides low-cost nutriment to
Bromley's appreciative curryholics. Price check: Papadom 30p, CTM
£4.25, Pullao Rice £1.25. Branch: Alka Tandoori Takeaway, 62 Croydon
Road, Caterham, Surrey.

SURUCHI NEW ENTRANT   ©

466 Bromley Road, Downham, Bromley   ℂ **0181 698 8626**

S. Dey opened his Suruchi in 1979, which in curry terms makes it long-
established. This means that he and manager T. Roy know their business, and that everything that should be on the menu is here and done
competently. Price check: Papadom 45p, CTM £5.70, Kalya Galda
Mustard King Prawn £9.95, Pullao Rice £1.55. Service charge 10%.

TAMASHA TOP 100 BEST IN THE SOUTH   ©

131 Widmore Road, Bromley   ℅ 0181 460 3240

This restaurant was opened in 1993 with the arrival of a horse-drawn landau, from which emerged Queen Victoria and Prince Albert. This was apt since the large house in which the restaurant is located is Victorian. In fact, it is large enough to contain a small hotel, so if you need a decent curry, followed by a bed for the night, now you know. Tamasha means 'something worth seeing – a big event'. So far so good, and its opening ceremony was different. Even though one knew the royal couple were only well-dressed look-alikes their act was convincing enough for some of the guests to bow, and mean it! And is it worth seeing? There is ample car parking, and you enter past a smartly saluting beezer, via an awning flanked by tub plants. Once inside, there is a well-stocked bar where residents can forget the car! There's a fine selection of wines and beers including Cobra. 'It is quite a smart area with large expensive cars outside the houses. We went in after an impromptu shopping trip to Bromley, dressed in jeans! The doorman was in traditional dress, the man on reception was in a very smart suit and all the waiters were in uniform. The dining room, in two parts, is beautifully decorated in tasteful greens and pinks. There were lots of interesting artefacts to look at while ordering, with the walls adorned with old colonial prints. It was quite empty at 6p.m. but soon filled up with people dressed for an evening out. The service was excellent and very friendly,' s.r. 'Needs to be seen to be believed, it's very impressive. Decor is brilliant. The tables are well spaced and there isn't a chance of pushing your chair (dark wood-carved backs, and of quality) into someone else,' m.w.

And what of the food? A point of interest here is that this is an Indian restaurant, with Indian chefs, led by the talented Dakesh Kumar, so no Bangladeshi formula stuff here. The menu includes favourite starters such as Bhajis (Pakoras), Kebabs and Tikka, and main courses Jalfrezi and Chicken Tikka Masala, both £6.95. And good they are, too. But a little exploring can yield some treasures. Their Keema Khumb (£3.95) – mince-stuffed mushrooms – were unusual, and Sev Pappri (£3.95) – gram flour threads, with chickpeas, potato, fresh coriander and mint and tart tamarind, a type of Bel Puri (q.v.), rarely encountered and always refreshing. Goan Fish Curry (£6.95) cooked in coconut with red chillies is to be commended, as is the Raan Jaipuri

(£8.50) – marinated, roasted leg of lamb – and Tandoori Pomfret (£7.95). 'The prices were a little on the dear side, but not extortionate, and worth it for the gorgeous meal. The food was very well-presented, and arrived piping hot. We had Papadams (75p each), then Vegetable Samosa (£3.25) – very light and crispy, with Chicken Chat Chatpata (£3.95) – chicken pieces sautéed in butter, which was quite hot. This was followed by Chicken Manchoori (£7.95) – tikka-style, with spring onions and green chillies with Pilao Rice (£2.25) and a Naan (£2.25). The Maharani Thali (£12.95) was a good choice, enabling us to try a selection of vegetable dishes. We had coffee and Masala tea afterwards. The toilets were noteworthy, the pictures of the Kama Sutra were particularly interesting!' s.r. Mixed Kebab Karara (£4.25) is popular, and Abrakebabra! so is the table magician who entertains the kids during their Sunday lunch. And there's live entertainment on Monday (jazz) and Tuesday (Latin) evenings. Opinion is unanimous: 'Overall – exceptional, large portions that were well-presented and full of flavour. Service polite, precise and helpful,' m.w. The owner is Shekor Tarat and the manager is Pramod Dey. A deserving new entrant to our TOP 100. Set lunch £7.95. Service charge 12½%. Branch: Tulsi, 20 London Road, Westerham.

ZANZIBAR   ©

239 High Street, Bromley   ✆ 0181 460 7130

Ebullient owner Ken Modi opened his Carioca as far back as 1971 but changed its name because 'I got fed up with Karaoke requests'. The small exterior belies the massive interior seating 120, which includes a mock Pullman railway carriage. The menu contains the regular favourite tandooris, baltis, curries and accompaniments. 'After a morning shopping on a Saturday, we headed to the Zanzibar for a lunchtime buffet. The food is on view from the outside, as it is displayed on a warming table in the window. This sounds awful but it's actually well done, the dishes polished and spanking clean, the food, fresh. We were politely served our starters first: a fresh, crisp salad with flat Onion Bhajis and half a Naan with chutneys, raita and a Coconut Chutney which was incredible, with a slight hint of heat from its mustard seed. The service became very friendly and helpful when we were given huge warm bowls for the self-serve buffet. The dishes were explained to us: Chicken Tikka Masala (smoky flavour – great), Bhoona Gosht, Mild

Chicken Curry, Meat Madras, Bombay Aloo (excellent – new potatoes), Cauliflower Bhajee, Dal Makhani, Brinjal Bhajee, Plain and
Pullau Rice and Naan bread. After two visits to this array of food, I
was stuffed and delighted. Good food from a clean, well-decorated
restaurant,' M.P.W. Price check: Papadom 50p, CTM £5.95, Pullao Rice
£1.50. Set lunch £4.95, dinner £9.95. Closed Mondays.

Canterbury

GANDHI   ©

---

36 North Gate, Canterbury   ✆ 01227 765300

Owner Nurul Islam Khan's Gandhi continues to get the thumbs up
from our local reporters.

Chislehurst, GL

BENGAL LANCER TOP 100   ©

15 Royal Parade, Chislehurst   ✆ 0181 467 7088

Many towns have the perfect restaurant. One that is enjoyed by local
patronage and does not look for accolades outside that because it does-
n't need them. We promoted the Bengal Lancer to our TOP 100 last
time and we see no reason not to keep it there. Not only our entry, but
all reports received, are understated in detail but seem completely content in general. 'It is spot-on in all respects,' G.C. 'Always busy when we
go, but they always remember us, and serve good food superbly well,'
T.G. We've not heard from our ace J.L. for some time, so we hope he and
his daughter still find 'excellent food with vegetables "done but not
done in" as my Gran would say!' More detailed reports welcomed.

JAIPUR   NEW ENTRANT   ©

53 Chislehurst Road, Chislehurst   ✆ 0181 467 9390

Relatively new (1995) and quickly gaining respect in curry-rich
Chislehurst. Owner Abdul Mushahid and manager Abdul Hannan
have put together 'an exciting, different menu,' P.P. Starters include

Lacy Cutless (£2.95) – an Anglo-Indian Keema-stuffed potato rissole
– and Fish Roe (£2.95) breadcrumbed and deep-fried. Main courses
include a wealth of interesting items, such as Green Goan Chicken
Curry and a Sylhetti red version, both £5.95. There is a creditable selection of Bangladeshi dishes. Ayre and Roop, Bengali fish, and the super
Baingan Torkari – aubergine with tamarind cooked Sylhetti-style in
black terracotta. We put the errors on the menu down to shabby, lazy
printers who should know better. Sadly, we note this phenomenon all
too often, but it will not deter the keen diner who will enjoy the food
and the service. This is a restaurant to watch, and we'd like comments,
please. Price check: Papadom 50p, CTM £6.25, Pullao Rice £1.75.
Minimum charge £10. Open for lunch and dinner.

Deal

BENGAL DINERS   ©

53 The Strand, Walmer, Deal   ✆ 01304 363939

Azad Ali's popular local establishment continues to 'give a good deal',
H.G. Fax for a copy of their menu or book a table on 01304 368888.
Price check: Papadom 50p, CTM £6.50, Pullao Rice £1.90. Minimum
charge £9.95. Service charge 10%.

Dover

LIGHT OF INDIA

Burlington House, Town Wall Street,
Dover   ✆ 01304 241066

A pretty and large (100-plus seats) restaurant furnished with blue
upholstery and gold curtains and tablecloths. 'Menu is pretty standard
but the food is of a high quality. Portions are ample. Prawn Puri was
full of prawns, excellent value,' J.S.K.

East Peckham

RED FORT ©

14 Hale Street, East Peckham   ✆ **01622 872643**

A spacious restaurant in a tiny country village, about 6 miles south-west of Maidstone, and not, repeat not, the Peckham in London SE15. That's for the person who complained to me – phew! 'Large quantities of food served on hot plates by uniformed waiters. This is a place to take visitors, very impressive, we think so anyway and we shall return,' N.G. A huge restaurant seating 98 diners. It's been under the present ownership of managing partner, Mr Mainuzzaman, since 1989.

Farnborough, GL

VILLAGE CUISINE NEW ENTRANT ©

145 High Street, Farnborough   ✆ **01689 860077**

No clues from the name that this is a curry house, but it is and this Village is in GL Kent, not Hampshire, for that same person who complained about East Peckham (*see* Red Fort)! All your favourite items are served competently at Mr A. Miah's Village. Price check: Papadom 45p, CTM £5.95, Badshahi Chicken £7.95, Pullao Rice £1.60. Closed Sundays.

Folkestone

INDIA TOP 100 ©

1 The Old High Street, Folkestone   ✆ **01303 259155**

One regular reporter, a driver, has sent us just one report a year since chef-proprietor Ali Ashraf opened his 50-seater India in 1985. 'Chance routed me into Folkestone, rather than my usual Dover to cross the channel. Now I always use Folkestone, the arrival of the Chunnel adding spice to my choice of route, because I always spice up at the India each trip on departure and on arrival,' P.J. Mr Ashraf is a French-trained Indian chef and speaks French, too. In some cases he combines the French use of cream, wine and brandy with delicate spices to provide an original interpretation of his Indian dishes. The starters include Sabzi-ka-Soup (£2) – a freshly-made spicy vegetable soup, Sita's Dosha (£2.95) – pancake, stuffed with prawn, mushroom, crab and coriander, Crab Kochin (£3.50) – crab with a southern Indian spicing of ginger and fresh coriander. Main courses range far and wide. The Beef Hyderabadi (£4.95) is spiced with mustard seeds, and Lamb Roghan Gosht is delicately and correctly spiced with nutmeg and mace and pistachio nuts. D.P. loves the Chana Masala (£2.25) and says the Special Rice (£2.25) is 'fragrant and subtle'. N.G. still remembers his 'most delicately spiced and tasty Dhansak (not on the menu) curry I have had in years. Pullao Rice was uncoloured and garnished with coriander and coconut, Naan bread was hot and crisp!' Old hands swear by the special dishes for two, requiring 24 hours' notice and a deposit. 'With such attention, you are bound to get something even better. We've tried all three,' J.T. These are Murog Masallam (£20.95) – whole chicken in cream, with poppy, cinnamon and bay, Vath (£25.95) – duck with cashews, raisins and cardamom, and Raan (£30.95) – leg of lamb, marinated then roasted and topped with saffron, nuts and lemon. 'The portions are huge,' D.B., as are the set meals for two from £22-£27. Further price check: Papadom 50p, CTM £5.75, Badami Gosht £5.95, Pullao Rice £1.60. Closed Mondays. Remains in our TOP 100.

Gravesend

GANDHI BALTI HOUSE   NEW ENTRANT   ©

66 West Street, Gravesend   ✆ 01474 536066

Abdul Khan's restaurant serves all the regular items, including Balti. Price check: Papadom 55p, CTM £5.90, Pullao Rice £1.80. Minimum charge £15.

MEOPHAM TANDOORI   ©

**2 The Parade, Wrotham Road, Meopham,
Gravesend**   ✆ 01474 812840

Comprehensive menu with all the favourites. The managing owner (since 1985) is Jahir Ali.

Maidstone

BLUE ELEPHANT CURRY INN   ©

98 King Street, Maidstone   ✆ 01622 756094

Maidstone's oldest restaurant, opened way back in 1965, and still under the same ownership of S.T. Meah. Seats 48 diners. All-day Sunday buffet. Price check: Papadom 40p, CTM £5.65, Pullao Rice £1.60. Set meal £4.50. Branch: Joshan of Wye, 2-4 High Street, Wye, Ashford.

SHAMRAT BRASSERIE   ©

36 Upper Stone Street, Maidstone   ✆ 01622 764961

'Chicken Jalfrezi — extra hot, superbly hot. I rate this one as one of the best I have visited. It appeals to me as a fire-eater!!' B.P.-D. 'Always an excellent welcome from all the staff. Warm on a cold night. Papadoms and pickles, Dhansak with rice included, Tikka Patia again rice included, sizzling Tikka, Cauliflower Bhajia and Naan, bottomless coffee, liqueurs, orange slices, Suchard Mints, hot towels and an excellent house white wine. How do they do it?' P.S. 'The warmth of a real blazing fire and Bombay Mix helped thaw me out whilst I looked through the menu. Quality, tasty, large portions of food,' N.G.

Margate

ALI RAJ   NEW ENTRANT

65 Canterbury Road, Westbrook,
Margate   ✆ 01843 297151

'A small, 40-cover, impeccably clean, well-decorated, air-conditioned restaurant. Which has gained regular clientele with a good reputation. Staff charming and polite. A full menu at reasonable prices. Often go for complete set meals for two at £19.95 consisting of Papadoms, chutneys, Chicken and Lamb Tikka, Chicken and Meat Dupiaza, Aloo Gobi, Mushroom Bhajee, Pilau Rice and Nan breads. Can only eat the large portions if we haven't had lunch,' T.N.

Orpington, GL

THE BOMBAY TOP 100

**76 High Street, Green Street Green,
Orpington**   ✆ **01689 862906**

A large 90-seat restaurant very well settled in its local area, under the ownership of Hannan Miah and M. Ali since 1986. Our comments are much the same as those for Chislehurst's Bengal Lancer. The Bombay is equally enjoyed by its local patronage, and it too does not look for accolades outside that – it doesn't need them. What both these restaurants do is the formula, without fault, and with careful customer care. 'On each visit, we thought it very good. Unbelievable trade in take-aways. Decor above average, service ever so polite. Raita was the best, a humungous portion served in a gravy boat! Aloo Chat, lovely flavour, crisp salad and Reshmi Kebab took me by surprise – a small omelette envelope with lamb kebab inside, also with crispy salad. Lamb Vindaloo Balti, nicely hot – just right. An excellent meal,' M.P.W. 'Another excellent Chicken Tikka Biryani, accompanied by their superb bread products. My son's Chicken Tikka Masala was brilliant, too,' J.L. 'Chicken Tikka Kebabs absolutely mouthwatering. My daughter dropped her Papadom on the floor and before we'd realized it a waiter produced a fresh one,' J.L. Let's hear more from you, John, please, about your favourite, which stays in our TOP 100. Price check: Papadom 50p, CTM £5.50, Pullao Rice £1.60. Service charge 10%.

CURRY HOUSE   ©

**24 Station Square, Petts Wood,
Orpington**   ✆ **01689 820671**

If you go down to the Woods today you're sure of no big surprise … not at B. Wahab's Curry House, at any rate. It's a family business (A. Wahab is the chef) which has been trading since 1972. Twenty-five years mean experienced hands, and all the old favourites including Sik (sic) Kebab and Vinderloo (sic). Price check: Papadom 35p, CTM £5.50, Pullao Rice £1.35. Closed Mondays, except Bank Holidays.

RAJ OF INDIA   ©

4 Crescent Way, Orpington   ✆ 01689 852170

'Smart restaurant. They do me an ultra-hot Phal, which sometimes is too hot to eat in one sitting, so I have the rest for breakfast! Aubergine Bhaji is worthy of a mention,' P.W. 'Our kitchen had just been gutted and we couldn't face trying to cook. Dhansak and Lamb Tikka Masala were superb but the meat lacked quality,' J.L. Mr Muzibur Rahman is the owner-manager. Branches: Raj of India, 23-25 High Street, Swanley; Raj of India, 2 Bell Road, Sittingbourne; Raj Bari, 7 Tubs Hill Parade, London Road, Sevenoaks; Maharajah, 84 High Street, Bexley; Raj of India, 9-10 Neptune Terrace, Sheerness; Juboraj, 84 Warley Hill, Brentwood, Essex.

Ramsgate

RAMSGATE TANDOORI   ©

17 Harbour Street, Ramsgate   ✆ 01843 589134

We have received a delightful letter from Mr Razaur Rahman, proprietor of the above establishment, advising us that his restaurant, formerly Curry Palace, is now the Ramsgate Tandoori. 'Now refurbished and cleaned it up. Ample lunchtime portions and all tasted excellent,' T.N.

Rochester

BENGAL BRASSERIE   ©

356 High Street, Rochester   ✆ 01634 841930

'Reasonable portions, good flavours. We enjoyed our meal and everything was all right for us!' s. and V.P. Partner Shahin Ali is out front, while partner-chefs Shamin Ali and Abdul Roob head the kitchens. Price check: Papadom 45p, CTM £6.10, Pullao Rice £1.70. Minimum charge £15. Set meal £8.95. Branch: Viceroy of India, 77a High Street, Bexley.

SINGAPORA   ©

51 High Street, Rochester   ✆ **01634 842178**

Opened in 1990 by Dr and Mrs Shome. A huge restaurant seating 150 diners. A good range of Singaporean food including curries. Open daily 11a.m.-3p.m. and 6-11p.m., Sunday 11a.m.-10.30p.m. Reports, please. Branches: Singapore Garden, 73 Brewer Street, Maidstone; Gordon Hotel, 91 High Street, Rochester.

Sandwich

INDIAN VILLAGE NEW ENTRANT

The Old Fire Station, 11 The Butchery, Sandwich   ✆ **01304 611926**

'It really did once house horse-drawn fire-engines, giving reason for its gently uplit long, low ceilings. It is a classy 50-seater, with the restaurant name woven into the carpet and onto the seat backs. Smart, efficient waiters offer just the right amount of attentiveness. We had Papadoms and the Chutney Daba, Aloo Chat – nicely cooked and excellent flavour, completely covered with shredded lettuce, and Onion Bhaji, and for our main course, Tandoori Chicken served sizzling from the trolley, tasty Roghan, and all the business including pudding and wine for only £30 for two. Only criticism: the rice was stuck together. Otherwise good value indeed for such a quality establishment,' T.N.

Sidcup, GL

BLACKFEN TANDOORI   ©

33 Wellington Parade, Blackfen Road, Sidcup   ✆ **0181 303 0013**

A friendly, pleasant, competent 48-seat curry house, owned by Muzammil Ali since 1983.

OVAL BRASSERIE   ©

49 The Oval, Sidcup   ✆ 0181 308 0274

Ansar Miah has owned and managed the aptly-named Oval since 1988. No problems, we hear, and M.W. still rates the Samosas. Price check: Papadom 50p, CTM £5.10, Pullao Rice £1.60. Sunday lunch £7.95, £4 for kids.

Strood

SHOZNA INDIAN CUISINE   NEW ENTRANT   ©

18 High Street, Strood   ✆ 01634 710701

Since Mr J.U. Ahmed took over the Raj in 1996 and changed its name to the Shozna, we have had several good reports. Price check: Papadom 45p, CTM £5.30, Pullao Rice £1.40. Minimum charge £10.50 per person.

Swanley

BENGAL LANCER   ©

3 Station Road, Swanley   ✆ 01322 662098

Formerly Lalquila and still a popular curry house. Seats 48 diners. Owners Hiron Miah (chef behind the scenes) and Feruz Ali (front of house manager) will give a discount to Curry Club members. Open noon-2.30p.m. and 6p.m.-midnight.

GURKHA PALACE   ©

9 High Street, Swanley   ✆ 01322 663608

Formerly the Viceroy, then the Shaan, but now an exciting change, as its name indicates, to the Nepalese chef-ownership of Bhim Lal Gautam, with Jhabindra. A large restaurant seating 76 diners. There is also a large hall in the basement of the restaurant that could be hired for private buffet parties. The menu contains many favourite tandooris and curries, but the 'Nepalese touch is subtle and different,' P.P.

Tonbridge

SIMLA CUISINE   ©

---

2 Church Road, Paddock Wood,
Nr Tonbridge   ✆ 01892 834515

The Simla is a smart place, inside and out, with a good menu. Abdul
Miah, managing owner, has agreed to give a discount to Curry Club
members on Mondays only. Price check: Papadom 40p, CTM £5.60,
Pullao Rice £1.50. Set meal for two £19.50. Branches: La Lipu Cuisine,
Tunbridge Wells.

Tunbridge Wells

LA LIPU CUISINE   ©

---

69 London Road, Southborough,
Tunbridge Wells   ✆ 01892 534182

Makhan Miah's 65-seater restaurant, with its smoking and no-smoking
area, appeals to L.G. at lunch: 'Papadoms crisp and dry. Tandoor
oven not fired up, so ate Stuffed Paratha. King Prawn Vindaloo
hot and tasty.' B.P.-D. found his Onion Bhajia 'very small, no Mint
Raita,' and got hot under the collar, not from his Chicken Chilli
Masala Balti – 'very nice but again small' – but about lager! 'Choice of
Carlsberg, Carlsberg and Carlsberg. 3% lager is RUBBISH! Why no
Cobra?' Good question, Mr Miah, so if you want Brian to return,
stock Cobra!

Welling, GL

FALCON   NEW ENTRANT   ©

---

16 Falconwood Parade, The Green,
Welling   ✆ 0181 303 7219

'The menu is the usual full and thorough document, but we spotted
Chicken Indo Puri (£8.20) – marinated in cream, then cooked with Tia
Maria. Amazing!' L.M. The manager is Harun Miah. Price check:
Papadom 50p, CTM £6.50, Pullao Rice £1.70.

TAGORE NEW ENTRANT

3 High Street, Welling   © 0181 304 0433

This restaurant opened early in 1997, with a carefully constructed PR campaign by its director Jayne Walker. Manager Nur Monie, who ran a restaurant in Paris and before that the Viceroy in Farnham, Surrey, is assisted by head waiter Tapesh Majumber in the running of this relatively small 40-seater, which opens for evenings only. The chef is Bombay-trained Rajendra Kumar. Its claim to fame is Pakhtoon food, which presumably refers to the Pathan tribal people of Afghanistan and the rugged Pakistani passes, whose name for themselves is Phuktana or Pukhtun. Afghan food is pretty basic (*see* page 25), especially at tribal level, involving kebab-skewer cooking and slow-cooking in pots. This is translated at The Tagore into a select menu on which kebabs do indeed feature prominently (the £15 selection for two is popular). Indeed, shortly after opening, they ran a novel kebab festival with no less than twelve kebabs, half non-meat, with twelve naan breads. Main dishes are divided between six chicken dishes, five meat, six from the tandoor and three fish dishes. At £6, Patrani Mahi, pomfret coated in herbal chutney, leaf-wrapped and baked is a rarity to be treasured, Murgh Chennai (£5) is none other than Chicken Madras, and Koh-e-Avadh (£5.50) is Roghanjosh – lamb knuckles simmered in the dum method. Average meal £20. Very interesting, and a restaurant to watch. Reports, please.

Westerham

TULSI   ©

20 London Road, Westerham   © 01959 563397

'Formerly the Shapla, and still owned by Anil Kumar and Shekhor Tarat, it has undergone some basic refitting, which now gives the restaurant a small waiting area with tables and chairs, and an extended slightly elevated, well-decorated eating area, with a polished wooden floor. Walls covered by framed posters of Indian film stars. Ambience is good with very friendly staff and an excellent front man who oozes charm and personality – what a difference that makes in any restaurant! Waiters are well-dressed in national costume. Chicken Nilgri, so tender and excellent. Murgh Makhani was lovely and creamy. Manchoori had real "bite" from the chillies. Best of all was the Peshwari Nan which was absolutely exquisite, light and brushed with hot ghee. Shared a melon sorbet. Hot towels and mints with coffee. Service did suffer when the restaurant became full. Drinks are expensive. Sunday buffet lunch comprises the usual range of mild curries, Chicken Tikka Masala, Jhinga Shahi Korma, Bhuna Gosht, Tobro Subzi, Bombay Aloo, Kashmiri Pilau, Sada Naan with a selection of kebabs, Mixed Kebab Karara (Lamb and Nilgiri Tikka, Seekh Kebab and Chicken Wing) and Fish Balls accompanied by small Chapatis and pickles. The choice is changed at regular intervals to provide a different Sunday buffet lunch. Well recommended with good food and, above all, friendly service,' C.D. Branches: Tamasha, 131 Widmore Road, Bromley; Sharju, Adlington, Lancashire.

Westgate

REGENCY TANDOORI NEW ENTRANT   ©

---

9 Station Road, Westgate   ✆ 01843 831412

'Food was excellent. I had the tastiest Chicken Tikka, then Roghan Gosht with Chana Masala and the Memsahib declared her CTM (four large pieces on the bone) equally good. Our two friends declared their meal good too. The total bill, including drinks before and house red during, was just £48,' T.N.

West Wickham, GL

OLD CALCUTTA   ©

---

54 Croydon Road, Coney Hall,
West Wickham   ✆ 0181 462 9416

Generally good comments continue about partner Dewan Faizul Islam's restaurant.

Whitstable

SHAPLA ©

36 Harbour Street, Whitstable ℂ 01227 262454

Mr S. Rahman continues to get the best-in-town nomination from our scribes.

Wye

JOSHAN OF WYE

2-4 High Street, Wye ℂ 01233 812231

'Quantities of food – while not piled high – are on the generous side of average. A very friendly welcome and service. Value for money is outstanding,' R.C.D. One Balti dish on the menu – spelt Bhalti. In fact, there is a number of intriguing dishes on the menu. And for regulars there is their Tiffin Club, with banquets from time to time. The manager is M. Rahman. Reports, please.

LANCASHIRE

We have adhered strictly to the official county of Lancashire here. Please also refer to the entries for Greater Manchester (listed under Manchester, Greater) and Merseyside for other restaurants within the former Lancashire boundary.

Accrington

SAGAR II

217-219 Whalley Road, Clayton-le-Moors,
Accrington ℂ 01254 871700

A largish restaurant seating 90 diners. 'Have visited this restaurant many times, both sit-in and takeaway, and the food is excellent, very fresh and expertly presented, always brought to the table piping hot,' J.H. Open noon-2p.m. and 6-11.30p.m. Branches: Sagar I, 61 Church Street, Blackrod, Bolton; Sagar Premier, Clayton Brook Road, Bamber Bridge, Preston.

Adlington

SHAPLA TAKEAWAY

178 Chorley Road, Adlington   © **01257 474630**

'I have been addicted to Indian food from an early age and wonderful to have this need satisfied on my doorstep. Quality and freshness are unquestionable,' A.L. 'Menu is various and offers a wide range of food which is excellent,' A.H. Open Sunday to Thursday 4-11.30p.m., Friday and Saturday 4p.m.-midnight.

SHARJU TOP 100   ©

Church Street, Adlington   © **01257 481894**

This is an old favourite of our Guide, and of its loyal following. 'Congregation' may be a more appropriate word because this was surely the first restaurant to occupy a former church. And, yes, they've heard all the gags: from Vestry Vindaloo, R.C. Roghan, Baptistry Biriani, C. of E. Tikka to 'will they be serving papadoms with communion wine?' Now owned by Mithu Dhar, the opportunity was taken in 1984 to convert this building to its now ideal use. In fact, it is not a large room, in clerical terms, but it has made for a large number of seats in restaurant terms. Reached by an imposing staircase, the plum seats are on the balcony, which extends around the remaining three sides of the room. From here one has a view of downstairs diners.

M.K.M. says: 'It has bags of atmosphere, with its oak beams and strategically placed Indian artefacts. We go fairly regularly on the Thursday evenings for the £12.95 per person Candlelight Dinner.' Other reporters tell of the special 'royal' dishes. 'From time to time we treat ourselves to one or other of these,' K.L. Two of these are chef Faruk Ali's signature dishes – Chicken Shagorika (£10.45) and Lashuni Chicken Flambé (£12.45), both with rice. The former is tikka pieces twice-cooked in a very spicy sauce with peas, the latter consists of a tandooried long fillet of chicken breast, which is flambéed in brandy, in a creamy garlicky sauce at your table. 'Huge portions of everything. There is only one word which covers the experience – magnificent,' D.B. 'Madras is very hot but with bags of flavour right down to the last grain of excellent Pullau rice, all helped down with a Naan bread of the highest quality,' M.B. It is managed by B.B. Choudhury. Price check: Papadom 50p, CTM £7.25, Pullao Rice £1.50. Set meal from £9.25. Eat-your-fill Sunday lunch, noon-4.30p.m., £7.95, kids £3.50. Service charge 10%. Minimum charge £10. Branch: Shanti, 466 Bromley Road, Bromley, Kent. Remains in our TOP 100.

Blackburn

BALTI HOUSE   ©

1-3 High Street, Rishton, Blackburn   © 01254 887386

A massive establishment seating 120 diners and serving Balti everything and anything. 'We were well received in this very good and large restaurant. Kitchens are on view behind large glass windows, clean, full of stainless steel. Food very good indeed, rounded off by a glass of Indian liqueur,' I.S. Opened in 1982 by Mr Asab Ali. Open 5p.m.-midnight.

SHAJAN   ©

Longsight Road, Clayton-le-Dale, Mellor,
Blackburn   © 01254 813640

Mohamed (Shaju) Ali, founder of Shaju's, now Sharju, Adlington (*see* entry) is now owner-manager of this venue, which he is at pains to tell you is easily found on the A59. Resembling a residential bungalow, it has 136 seats. 'Our favourite dishes are the Chicken Shajan (£8.50) – whole poussin marinated, barbecued and served with Keema Pullao, and a mushroom sauce, and Fish Jhol (£7.95) – cod, spiced the Bengali way, served with Prawn Bhaji, special rice and curry sauce.' Price check: Papadom 30p, CTM £5.95, Pullao Rice £1.55. Minimum charge £6.45. Sunday lunch buffet £7.95. Open Monday to Thursday, noon-2p.m. and 5.30-11.30p.m., Friday and Saturday till midnight, Sunday 1-11p.m.

Blackpool

BOMBAY NEW ENTRANT

227 Dickson Road, Blackpool   © 01253 296144

Askor Ali opened the small, 30-seat Bombay in 1996. 'The Chilli Masala is just fabulous but, good though it is, I don't think anyone's Roghan Josh originated in Rangoon!' R.T. Price check: Papadom 40p, CTM £6.90, Pullao Rice £1.50. Set meal £4.95. Open daily, lunch and dinner, Fridays and Saturdays till 1a.m. For home delivery, you pay for the taxi.

FAYEZ TANDOORI AND BALTI HOUSE

82 Victoria Road West, Cleveleys,
Blackpool   © 01253 853562

'Food as great as always. Papadoms, warm and crisp and a selection of pickles. Maharajah Fort Special – superb, huge portion of off-the-bone Chicken and Lamb Tandoori Masala served with excellent vegetable Pullao Rice garnished with strips of tomato, cucumber, cress and coconut. The manager resembles a Pakistani George Michael!' B.R. Open noon-2.30p.m. and 6p.m.-midnight, Friday and Saturday till 1a.m. and Sunday noon-midnight. There is also a taxi food-delivery service.

SUNAM NEW ENTRANT

93 Redbank Road, Blackpool   © 01253 352572

Good stuff, so we hear at Dudu Miah's Sunam. 'I had to try the Special Masala (£8.90) – a unique, I think, Tikka Masala Curry, containing a mixture of Tandoori Chicken, Chicken and Lamb Tikka, Sheek Kebab cooked in a sauce. With all this meat in the air, my boyfriend opted for the Vegetable Thali (£8.50), and by sharing we had a super, well-balanced meal,' H.J. Price check: Papadom 50p with pickles, CTM £6.50, Pullao Rice £1.50. Set dinner for two £24.90, for six £64.90.

Burnley

AGRA

Horse Hill Farm, Hapton, Nr Burnley   ✆ **01282 770113**

'A most impressive converted barn in the last place you'd expect to find
a restaurant, let alone an Indian. Someone has gone to long lengths to
create a rich and comfortable Indian atmosphere. Food was as good as
the interior. Chicken Tikka and Shammi Kebabs were perfect. Chicken
Tikka Makahan and Royal Bengal Special both excellent mopped up
with a large succulent Nan. Well recommended,' M.B.

SHALAMAR   ©

56 Church Street, Burnley   ✆ **01282 434403**

A huge, well-reported restaurant seating 120 diners. The owner is A.
Majeed. Open Monday to Thursday 5.30p.m.-12.30a.m., Friday and
Saturday 5p.m.-1a.m., Sunday 5p.m.-12.30a.m.

Carnforth

FAR PAVILION

25 Bye Pass Road, Bolton-le-Sands,
Carnforth   ✆ **01524 823316**

A restaurant seating 70. 'Difficult to fault this restaurant. Decor
and welcome second to none. Service efficient and courteous,' F.S.
'Sampled my usual benchmark meal of Shami Kebab, which was
excellent, followed by Chicken Madras, which was standard curry
house,' M.B.

Clitheroe

DIL RAJ   ⊞

7-9 Parsons Lane, Clitheroe   ✆ **01200 427224**

A medium-sized establishment seating 52 diners. 'Has been a favourite of ours for three years. Staff friendly and decor nice and clean. On-view kitchen makes interesting feature. Sag Gosht and Gobhi Gosht are particularly good as are tandoori dishes. Home-delivery service,' A.P.

SHAH ANAZ

35-37 Whalley Road, Clitheroe   © 01200 424999

A large restaurant seating 80 diners. 'Very polite staff. Very good food, no complaints, except for the English Spring Chicken,' s.p. Serves you right for ordering an English dish in an Indian restaurant. Branches: Agra, Nr Burnley; Akash, 198-200 Duckworth Street, Darwen; Akash Takeaway, 87 Whalley Road, Accrington.

Darwen

ANAZ

110-112 Duckworth Street, Darwen   © 01254 703357

'We chose from the very extensive menu, Chicken Sambar, which is tender juicy chicken cooked in a very spicy lentil sauce and absolutely delicious. Lightest of Naans. First-class,' M.B.

SHANTEE

161-163 Duckworth Street, Darwen   © 01254 774335

'Very good family-run restaurant. Very friendly caring team. High-quality food at reasonable prices,' J.N. Open seven days a week.

SONALI NEW ENTRANT

144 Bolton Road, Darwen   © 01254 702122

A. Hannan's Sonali has been brought to our attention, simply because it has been doing a 'good job for 14 years. I first went as a student, and I take the kids now,' says s.a. Everything is heat-graded, as you'd expect from the formula curry house, but the hottest, with a six-star grading, isn't Phal but a mysterious Samber! Price check: Papadom 40p, CTM £5.40, Pullao Rice £1.20.

Fleetwood

MANZIL

3 Poulton Street, Fleetwood   ℂ 01253 772580

'Very small, 30 seats. Very clean, as you'd expect, and tastefully decorated. Fresh and crisp Papadoms. Lamb Tikka Badami excellent, mild, rich, lovely tender lamb in sauce with ground almonds and whole peanuts. Chicken Jalfrezi – hot! Waiter brought in a karahi, crackling, spluttering, smoking and steaming – the Jalfrezi that is, not the waiter! First-rate Sag Paneer,' B.R.

Greenhalgh

ASHIANA

Fleetwood Road, Greenhalgh,
Nr Kirkham   ℂ 01253 836187

'In a large imposing building, conveniently next to the pub. A smart establishment on which no expense has been spared,' M.B. 'Very busy, need to book well ahead. Lovely decor, varied menu. Starters crisp and delicious, curries, rice, and chupatis faultless. One criticism: too many tables make it rather cramped,' T.E. Price check: Papadom 40p, CTM £6.95. Pullao Rice £1.80. Lunch and dinner, Monday to Saturday; Sunday, noon-midnight.

Haslingden

SUNAR GAW   NEW ENTRANT   ©

16 Regent Street, Haslingden   ℂ 01706 212137

Owner-manager N.A. Malik and owner-chef A. Quddus share ownership and roles at this popular 1987, evenings-only restaurant. R.K. says: 'The Kyber Murghi Maladari (£5.50) – chicken cooked with ginger, green chilli, onion, garlic and coriander – was out of this world. Brinjal Bhaji delicate. It's another gem.' Price check: Papadom 30p, CTM £6.90, Mixed Tikka Balti £8.50, Pullao Rice £1. Open 4.30p.m.-midnight. Branch: Sunar Gaw, Bolton, Greater Manchester.

Lancaster

NAWAAB

32 Parliament Street, Lancaster   © 01524 847488

'Of exceptional quality, serving wonderful food,' D.B.

Leyland

INDIAN COTTAGE   ©

115 Towngate, Leyland   © 01772 457236

Opened in 1987 by Rojob Ali. Seating 46 diners. Open noon–2.30p.m. and 6p.m.–midnight, Friday and Saturday till 1a.m. and Sunday 4.30p.m.–midnight. Manager Hir Miah has promised to give a special deal to Curry Club members on Sundays – if you would like to dine between 4.30p.m. and 8p.m. and you order two main courses, he will only charge for one. What a great deal that is, so go along and take up his offer.

MUGHAL

Thornlees, Wigan Road, Leyland   © 01772 622616

'Very tastefully decorated with no-smoking area. Will go again and again. Menu superb. Free Papadoms with dishes of onion and spices. Food of a very high standard,' K.P.

VICEROY TANDOORI AND BALTI   ©

3 Golden Hill Lane, Leyland   © 01772 621031

A good Balti house serving all your favourites in a restaurant seating 80 diners. The proprietor is Makhlisur Rahman.

Longridge

POLASH

23-33 Berry Lane, Longridge   © 01772 785280

'Tropical fish tank. Food excellent, Shammi Kebabs, Chicken Madras and Pullao Rice all first-class. The Nan was a little on the crispy side. Extensive menu with Balti dishes, 146 dishes and accompaniments. There is something for everyone,' M.B. Open 5.30p.m.-midnight, Sunday 3p.m.-midnight. Fully licensed and air-conditioned. Branch: Polash, 67-71a Curzon Street, Burnley.

Morecambe

MORECAMBE TANDOORI

47 Marine Road West, Morecambe   ✆ 01524 832633

A good standard restaurant seating 45 diners. You will be happy to find all your favourite tandooris and curries on the menu.

Nelson

MADHUBON

62 Manchester Road, Nelson   ✆ 01282 691282

Previously the Shabana. 'Service excellent, decor very pleasant. Food an absolute delight. Lamb Sambar (very good lemon-flavoured sauce), Chicken Darjeeling (came with onion rings). Very hot towels and orange slices finished off a great meal,' A.S.

Ormskirk

PASSAGE TO INDIA

Moor Street, Ormskirk   ✆ 01695 578979

'Small, tastefully decorated, impeccably clean restaurant serves a decent range of dishes cooked and presented with above-average care,' A.G.J.

Preston

DILSHAD

121-122 Friargate, Preston   ✆ 01772 250828

'Has built itself a good reputation. Very modern and tastefully decorated for around 60 people. Sampled Nargis Egg for starters, which was excellent. Tandoori Mixed Grill again excellent, served with a curry sauce, which was a little over the top with garlic. I didn't mind, but it kept my work colleagues well away,' M.B.

LAL-VINA NEW ENTRANT   ©

**43 Cannbridge Street (A 675),
Higher Walton, Preston**   ℂ **01772 698999**

Evenings-only (from 4.30-11.30p.m., 365 days a year), friendly takeaway run by chef M. Abdul Mujid and manager M. Abdul Kalam. Price check: Papadom 30p, CTM £5.45, Pasanda, cooked with red wine in rice £5.45, Pullao Rice £1.20. Children's portions smaller and cheaper. Set meals from £7.95.

NAAZ

Club Street, Bamber Bridge, Preston   ℂ **01772 626695**

A large restaurant seating 100 with two bars and alcove seating. 'Baltis first-class,' M.B. 'Large parties now assemble to enjoy the ambience, especially the performance of the cheerful waiters doing "wheelies" with the serving trollies!' A.E. 'Food second to none – specialities Hasina Kebab and Chicken Tikka Shahee, but my favourite Chicken Tikka followed by a Madras,' J.W. Open Monday to Friday noon-2.30p.m. and 6.30-11.30p.m, Saturday and Sunday noon-midnight. The other branch is a takeaway: Naaz, School Lane, Bamber Bridge

---

NEW KISMET   ©

20 Derby Street, Preston   ℂ **01772 251880**

A deceptively large restaurant seating 76 diners. Decorated in pale blues. Seating is arranged in partially screened off booths for four. Colonial fans, suspended ceiling with spotlights, blue chintz Austrian blinds and Indian paintings. 'Six of us from work decided to give it a try. Although the food was on the whole excellent, the service was abysmal and there were no plate-warmers,' M.B. Open 5p.m.-3a.m., obviously for insomniacs. The owner is S.N. Ahmed. Branch: Shiraz, 23 Berry Lane, Longridge.

PRACHEE

Preston New Road, Newton, Preston   © 01772 685896

'Had a takeaway, service good. Chicken Madras, very hot and spicy, very large juicy pieces of chicken,' J.H.

SAGAR PREMIER

Clayton Brook Road, Bamber Bridge,
Preston   © 01772 620200

'Seats 120 people and is "THE BUSINESS". Very smart and very comfortable and gets very busy. Tried Kahari Chicken on waiter's recommendation, first-class,' M.B. 'Six visits have confirmed they are consistent for excellent service, fine cuisine and value for money,' T.E. Branches: Sagar I, 61 Church Street, Blackrod, Bolton; Sagar II, Accrington.

SANGAM   NEW ENTRANT

14-15 Hope Terrace, Lostock Hall, Preston   © 01772 628616

The new management has injected some fire here: 'Wings of Fire were – wow! The main course dish, Tava Chicken Lahori, was great, as was the Pullao Rice. We didn't know whether to eat it or climb it, so big was the portion! Luckily they supplied doggy bags!' R.K.

Rawtenstall

BAAZIGAR   NEW ENTRANT   ©

93-95 Bacup Road, Rawtenstall   © 01706 224075

Mohammed Abdullah opened this 50-seater in 1994, and has built up an adoring following (there's no other word), who impress upon me to tell him not to change a thing, and I doubt that he will. 'Huge quantities of first-class food. Fourteen-course banquet (£11.95 – 24-hour notice required) takes all night to eat. Excellent,' S.B. 'Where else can you get Fillet Steak Masala (£7.65) – a delicious Indianized variation of the pepper steak?' D.E. Price check: Papadom 60p, CTM £6.75, Pullao Rice £1.75. Eat-your-fill Sunday 10-course banquet £8.95, kids

£3.95. Wednesday special 8-course £7.95, kids £3.75. Open evenings only, from 6-11p.m., except Sunday when open for lunch.

SAMRAT   NEW ENTRANT   ©

13 Bacup Road, Rawtenstall   ℂ 01706 216183

Alkas Ali is owner-chef here, and he's proud of his cooking – so proud, in fact, that you can ring him on his mobile on 0973 328426 and he'll explain about his dishes. A unique service, we believe. So is his Chicken Tikka Masala with Cherries. Price check: Papadom 30p, CTM £5.50, Pullao Rice £1.55. Set meal £21.95. Minimum charge £3.50. Open 5p.m.-midnight, 365 days a year.

St Annes

MOGHUL   ©

12 Orchard Road, St Annes   ℂ 01253 712114

M. Liaquat Ali owns and presides over a very sunny, friendly 60-seat restaurant, decorated in pastels and pine, serving all the usual Dansak, Madras, Vindaloo, Baltis and Karahis. We hear well of the Moghul Jeera Chicken (£5.90), with cumin flavour predominating, and Keema Patila (£5.90), a tasty mince curry, which one couple enjoy for takeaway – and they also like the special box provided. Price check: Papadom 40p, CTM £6.10, Pullao Rice £1.50. Minimum charge £5.90.

Whalley

TRISHNA

25 King Street, Whalley   ℂ 01254 822394

'Very nice restaurant, bigger inside than it first appears (seats 72 diners). Food absolutely gorgeous – could not fault it. Biggest Naan bread ever seen! Polite service. On leaving, ladies get a flower, men a lollipop,' S.P.

LEICESTERSHIRE

Although bureaucracy's latest county fiddle has divested Leicestershire of an amount of territory by re-establishing Rutland, it has made no difference to either county's curry restaurant reportage. Rutland is once again Britain's smallest county – it is geographically smaller than the city of Birmingham – and its reappearance no doubt delights its few inhabitants, unless they happen to be curryholics. We know of only a couple of Indian restaurants in Rutland but, as yet, we have no Guide entries for these (reports, please), which prompts D.Mc. to enquire 'whatever do they eat with their pints of Ruddles?'

Leicester

Leicester is home to a good number of Gujaratis from India. In addition, many of its Asian community settled there in the 1970s when they became exiled from Africa, specifically Kenya and Uganda, where they had lived for generations, having been taken there as clerks and semi-skilled plantation labour by the British. Most contemporary Leicester Asians have little concept of the Indian sub-continent, few having ever visited it, but you would not know this from the quality of the food, particularly in the cheap and cheerful cafés, snack bars and sweet shops all over town. The first curry house, the Taj Mahal, opened in 1961 and is still there! I dined there that year, and when I asked for chilli pickle the anxious owner appeared and spent half an hour counselling me against eating hot food! (To no avail, I might add!) Now there are over 80 'Indian' restaurants on our database which, with a city of around 300,000 population, is a ratio of one 'Indian' restaurant per 3,750 people, making Leicester our second most densely curry-housed city in the UK (*see* Bradford, West Yorkshire).

AKASH   ©

159 London Road, Leicester   ℂ 0116 255 9030

Owner B. Uddin and manager S. Haque describe their Akash as 'the price busting restaurant', with a Special Meal Deal: an eat-as-much-as-you-like lunch at £5, Mondays to Saturdays, Sundays £12 per couple, plus one child under 12 free. The à la carte menu has a full cast of goodies, too. 'No sooner than we were seated, the menus and free Popadoms arrived complete with obligatory mango chutney, onion salad and a delicious red sauce. Onion Bhaji very delicately spiced, excellent Pakuras (sic), crunchy and more flavoursome. Service was hotter than a Phal. Waiters were quick, enthusiastic and very attentive,' G.R. 'We love the Akash,' J. and P.R. Price check: Papadom 60p, CTM £4.95, Pullao Rice £1.25.

BOBBY'S GUJARATI VEGETARIAN

154 Belgrave Road, Leicester   © **0116 266 2448**

'Busy restaurant and takeaway. Cafeteria-type atmosphere, you pay (cash please) at the till. Unlicensed. Good breads, excellent service,' K.F. 'Very good,' D.G.

CURRY FEVER TOP 100   ©

139 Belgrave Road, Leicester   © **0116 266 2941**

Opened in 1978 by Sunil and Anil Anand, cousins of the owners of Madhu's Brilliant and The Brilliant in Southall, Middlesex, the Curry Craze, Wembley, Middlesex, and Curry Special, Ilford, Essex. This gives them and their menu a particular pedigree, since their style derives from one man, a Punjabi, who practised his trade for decades as an owner chef-caterer in Kenya before arriving in England, with family, in the 1970s, and it is to these places that sons, daughters, nephews and nieces have spread. Since we explain at considerable length about their food in the Ilford and Southall entries, we refer you to those for fuller details. Suffice to say here that, despite some natural exuberant family jesting about each one's venue being better than the others', the differences are really marginal. Last time's refurb has now settled in, and 65 diners find it 'fantastic – the best,' G.K.G. 'The menu is very extensive, and the service was very good, after I informed the manager that I was a member of the greatest club in the world (Curry Club!). The air-conditioning was welcoming, and the decor just right. I had a beautiful Chicken Bhoona, and the Garlic Naan was completely smothered in garlic (yum). It also served up the world's best Aloo Chana Chaat. Well done, the Guide, you've done it again,' D.P. The three unmissable chicken signature dishes are Pili Pili, Jeera and Butter,

as huge starter portions (£6.70), or for main course. If you adore
Punjabi flavours, the most typical are Methi and Sag dishes, in the
Karai, and the Keema curry is always a favourite, all from £6.50. Unlike
its southern cousins, the Curry Fever shows its Midlands roots with
'some mean Baltis,' H.M. Wash all this down with Cobra or Tusker lager.
We are glad you agreed that this is TOP 100 and have pleasure keep-
ing it there. Price check: Papadom 45p, CTM £6.50, Pullao Rice £1.90.
Service charge 10%. Open noon-2.30p.m. and 6-11.30p.m., Friday and
Saturday till midnight. Closed Sunday lunchtime and all day Mondays,
except Bank Holidays.

CURRY HOUSE   ©

63 London Road, Leicester   © 0116 255 0688

'Food absolutely superb, served by very friendly waiters eager that you
enjoy. Sheek Kebabs served on a bed of fresh salad with fresh tangy
yoghurt sauce. Really excellent Chicken Vindaloo and Pullao Rice full
of flavour. Mandatory Naan was simply perfect,' M.B. Chief cashier,
Mrs Lipinski, promises a discount to Curry Club members. Open
11a.m.-2p.m. and 6-11.45p.m. Branch: The Jewel in the Crown, 98-100
Leicester Road, Wigston Magna.

FRIENDS TANDOORI TOP 100   ©

41-45 Belgrave Road, Leicester   © 0116 266 8809

Opened in 1982 by T.S. Pabla. The interior is attractive in peach and
midnight blue, with its mahogany spiral staircase, enormous 'hookah'
and works of art. It is a massive restaurant seating over 110 diners, with
a separate upstairs drinks lounge in which to peruse the menu or to
relax over a coffee after your meal. As to that menu, first-timers will
need time to peruse it. It's practically a book! It begins with starters,
ordinary enough with Tikkas (£3.75), Kebabs (£3.75) and Bhajis (£3.25).
Tandoori main meals start at £7.50 with Tikka, while amongst 'Friends
Favourites' CTM is £6.95 and King Prawn Goanese £9.95, in a coconut
and chilli base. Vegetarians are catered for with a decent selection of
dishes. Odd moments of Pabla wit come to the fore in the menu. Here
are some in descending order of wit: Gulab Jamun is 'the missing holes
out of doughnuts'; Kulfi is 'a legend in its own lunchtime'; Bhindi
Masala is 'fresh okra (Winfrey!)'; and it gets worse: Roti is 'Pavarotti –

I mean 'ave a roti – Tandoori Roti.' Since I do the funnies in this Guide, I'd go for 'Pablarotti' – and you can 'ave that one on me, Mr Pabla! But don't think I've not noticed your snipe at Balti being 'down-market', and at best 'an animal fodder bucket'. He goes on: 'In half-decent Indian-authored (sic) cookery books, the word Balti does not appear.' It's not surprising, since Balti is from Pakistan. Even so, I have a new Indian cookbook, published in 1995 by Lustre Press, New Delhi, called *Step by Step Indian Recipes – Balti*, and even Madhur Jaffrey has done a full-frontal U-turn and now acknowledges its existence. But who am I to argue? Mr Pabla wants it known as Karahi cooking (Chicken or Lamb at £6.25 and Tandoori Mixed Grill Karahi £9.95), so if you want to stay friends with him, stick to that at Friends! And I am certainly not going to fall out about his food. I have a file full of reports which glow about the cooking by Delhi-trained master chef V.K. Gautam, son Bobby Pabla and their brigade. 'The Baingan Bartha (£4.95), aubergines mashed with peas, has that mysterious, haunting smoky taste that few restaurants can achieve,' G.H. 'We regularly drive over from curry-rich Brum just for the food at this restaurant,' F.L. 'If competition is a good thing, it's proved here on Belgrave Road at Friends,' T.F.

Getting back to the menu, the wine list is clearly a labour of love, apparently of son Manjit Pabla, and is probably as good an exposition of wines which go well with spicy food as you'll find anywhere. Fourteen pages are given over to very professional explanations though these, too, are not immune from Pabla humour. What getting his hands on Brigitte Bardot (mentioned twice) has to do with wine, ask him, not me, but there are 109 very interesting wines, ranging in price from £6.95 (house red or white) to £39.95 (a delicious Deuxième Grand Cru Classe red from St Estephe). Excellent though this is, there is another list, unique, I believe, to the Indian restaurant trade, and rare in any restaurant. It is a 22-strong malt whisky list, which Pabla calls his 'collection'. Prices go from £2 for Glenfiddich to £5.25 for a rare Laphroaig 1968, although the 100%-proof Macallan, said to 'cure all ills', will certainly create some if you don't stagger home by taxi! Talking of staggering, whisky is the favourite tipple in India, in the form of a chota peg (two-finger measure), topped up with still water, and no ice. At all the parties, at all the best homes, this is what you drink for a couple of hours until the food comes. Nothing is drunk with the actual meal itself, and then you go (staggering) home!

Friends is a caring restaurant that deserves to remain in our TOP

100. Minimum charge £8.50. Takeaway 15% off above prices. Open for lunch and dinner daily.

GRAND DURBAR   ⊞ ©

294 Melton Road, Leicester   ℂ 0116 266 6099

Opened in 1988 and seating 80 diners. Free home-delivery service available within a 5-mile radius. The manager is Kibria Wahid. Open noon–2.30p.m. and 6p.m.–midnight.

KHYBER   ©

116 Melton Road, Leicester   ℂ 0116 266 4842

A. Raval's small restaurant, seating 40, opened in 1984 and has built up a good and reliable reputation among its local customers. Open noon–2p.m. and 6.30–11.30p.m.

MONSOON   NEW ENTRANT

194 Elvington Road, Leicester   ℂ 0116 273 9444

Mokhtar Hussain opened here in 1995, and his menu offers some unusual items. Halim (sic) soup (£2.30) is a meat- and lentil-based spicy broth, Haash Masala (£8) is half a duck, on the bone, marinated and deep-fried, and Roup Chanda Bhaza (£7.50) is Bangladeshi fish, marinated and pan-fried. With 24 hours' notice and a deposit, you can have Shagorana (£35), a feast for two, with, amongst other things, mussels, crab, lobster and Bangladeshi vegetables. Price check: Papadom 40p, CTM £5.95, Pullao Rice £1.75. Open daily for lunch and dinner, closed Mondays.

NAMASTE   NEW ENTRANT

65 Hinckley Road, Leicester   ℂ 0116 254 1778

C.R.M.'s favourite of all time and, since he visits curry restaurants up and down the land, we'll oblige him by entering it in the Guide. He says: 'I had not visited for some time and was greeted by the manager and was reminded by him that we had not visited for around a year. How's that for memory! Nothing had changed – the staff, service was as friendly, attentive as ever, and they are interested in you as people, not just customers, and the food was still out of this world!' Price check: Papadoms 45p, CTM £7.05 incl. rice, Pullao Rice £1.50. Set lunch £3.99.

NASEEB BALTI HOUSE ©

20 Melton Road, Leicester ✆ **0116 266 9047**

Opened in 1985 by Surinder Singh. A small and cosy restaurant seating 34 diners, so on weekends be sure to book your table so as not to be disappointed. All the usual curries and Baltis on the standard curry house menu. And the infamous 'Tropical Balti' – a huge combination of chicken, meat and prawns. Also a vegetarian version – Chana, Saag, mushroom and corn – sounds delicious. Open 6p.m.-1a.m., seven days a week.

NILA PALACE NEW ENTRANT

61 London Road, Leicester ✆ **0116 255 6161**

'We came hoping to be impressed, and were not not disappointed. Smartly decorated with individual cabins along the two main walls. Hasina Kebab (£2.75), probably the best that I have tasted anywhere. Onion Bhaji (£2.25), excellent served with fresh salad. Warm Popadoms were accompanied by more chutneys, pickles and sauces than you could shake a stick at! Chicken Jalfrezi (£6.95), Tikka Garlic Bhoona (£6.95) and Tikka Mirch Masala (£6.95) were all first-class. Another highly recommended restaurant,' C.R.M.

RISE OF THE RAJ ©

6 Elvington Road, Leicester ✆ **0116 255 3885**

Somehow Abdul Abdal's Rise fell from our previous Guide but you've asked to see it back, so here it is. 'It is smart yet not overawing, its pinks, burgundy and maroon colour scheme seeming to relax you as you enter,' F.H. The regular cast of favourites appears on the menu. Price check: Papadom 50p, CTM £6.25, Thali from £9.95, King Prawn Karahi £10.95, Pullao Rice £1.70. Set meal £8.95. Minimum charge £9.95.

SHARMILEE VEGETARIAN   √ ©

71-73 Belgrave Road, Leicester   © 0116 261 0503

Opened way back in 1973 by Gosai brothers (manager, L.K. Goswami), this is a two-part venue. The sweet mart serves a rich assortments of Indian sweets, and such delightful items as Vegetable Samosas, Pakoras and Dahi Vadia, from 9.30a.m.-9p.m., daily, except Mondays. The restaurant does all vegetarian starters, puds and gorgeous vegetable curries. Paneer Tikka Masala (£5.30) – home-made Indian cheese, tandooried and second-cooked in a rich sauce, the vegetarian equivalent of CTM, is a popular house special, as is Handi Biriani (£3.95) – plentiful vegetables cooked with basmati rice, served in the Handi pot. Price check: Papadom 40p, Pullao Rice £1.50. Set meal £7.50. Minimum charge £5.50. Licensed, the restaurant is open Tuesdays to Thursdays, noon-2.30p.m. and 6-9.30p.m.; Fridays, Saturdays and Sundays, noon-9.30p.m.

THE TIFFIN   NEW ENTRANT

1 De Montfort Street, Leicester   © 0116 247 0420

It changed in 1990 from a wine bar to a colonial-style Indian, as the name suggests. Tiffin was, of course, the endless luncheon which could take the Raj until sunset to eat. This Tiffin plies its wares after sunset too, of course, being open for lunch and dinner. Reports, please.

Loughborough

AMBER TANDOORI

5a High Street, Loughborough   © 01509 215754

'Decor is pleasant and clean. Food and service always good and prompt,' M.G. Open noon-2.30p.m. and 5.30p.m.-12.30a.m, till 1.30a.m. on Fridays and Saturdays.

©	Curry Club discount (see p. 607)	☕	Unlicensed
√	Vegetarian	⊞	Home delivery
BYO	Bring your own alcohol		service available

Market Harborough

SHAGORIKA   ©

16 St Mary's Road, Market Harborough   ✆ 01858 464644

Ala and Ablas Uddin have been trading successfully here since 1980, and are not new to our Guide, so welcome back. It's a standard curry house with a long enough track record to ensure that everything is competent. Price check: Papadom 40p, CTM £6.15, Pullao Rice £1.60. Open 6p.m.-midnight.

Melton Mowbray

PARI TANDOORI   ⊞ ©

38 Leicester Street, Melton Mowbray   ✆ 01664 410554

Home-delivery service available at Babul Ali's Pari. Menu offers all the usual curries, tandooris and Baltis. Open 6p.m.-midnight.

LINCOLNSHIRE

This county has now regained its former territory, following the recent abandonment of South Humberside.

Barton-upon-Humber

GANDHI TANDOORI

28 High Street, Barton-upon-Humber   ✆ 01652 634890

'Tandoori dishes are excellent, with Chicken Tikka worth singling out. Curries are distinctive and aromatic,' B.T.

Boston

STAR OF INDIA TOP 100 ©

110-112 West Street, Boston ℭ **01205 360558**

Owned by Tanvir Hussain and seats 52 diners. 'Very pleasant decor, typical Indian restaurant style enhanced by large numbers of cotton flowers. Service attentive but not intrusive. Balti Chicken was quite delicious. Keema Naan was piping hot and filled with ample quantity of minced meat. Highly recommended,' M.S.-R. 'Best-ever Tandoori Chicken starter followed by superb Dhansak,' A.G. We have regularly placed this restaurant in our TOP 100 and it continues to get plentiful one-liners of satisfaction. No less than twelve people nominated it among their top three in our 'list your favourite' slot on our report forms. 'Service welcoming and friendly. Adequate to generous quantities. Decor fairly spartan, but I'd rather pay for good food than expensive decor. Overall above-average,' F.B.McM. Such repeated praise keeps the Star in our TOP 100. Open noon-2.30p.m. and 6p.m.-midnight. Other branches which are both takeaways and fast-food outlets: Chilli Master, 2 Red Lion Street, Stamford; Chilli Master, 11 Winsover Road, Spalding.

TASTE OF BOMBAY NEW ENTRANT ©

53 West Street, Boston ℭ **01205 359944**

Messrs Faluk and Khan run the Taste, which we hear is a good contender for a good curry. Price check: Papadom 45p, CTM £6.25, Pullao Rice £1.45. Branch: Bombay Brasserie, 24 Railway Road, King's Lynn, Norfolk.

Bourne

PRINCE OF KASHMIR ⊞ ©

8 Abbey Road, Bourne ℭ **01778 393959**

It's double As all the way at the Prince, with co-owners Ali Ashker, Ali Akbar (chef), Ali Arshad and Ali Amjad, and if you're a Guide reader you're sure of a double-A welcome here. The Alis tell me they have made a lot of new customer friends since they appeared in the Guide last time, and they really welcome Curry Club members for their discount, so get booking and enjoy all your favourites, reliably done. New are Baltis from £4.35. Chilli Naan (£1.40) is still unique to this restaurant, unless you know better. Price check: Papadom 40p, CTM £5.95, Pullao Rice £1.35. Set meal for two from £24. Dial-a-curry takeaway service with free delivery within 10 miles. Free bottle of wine with takeaway orders over £20. Open 5.30p.m.-midnight, Friday and Saturday till 12.30a.m.

Cleethorpes

AGRAH

7-9 Seaview Street, Cleethorpes   ℗ 01472 698669

A 65-seater restaurant owned by Bashir Miah since 1979. A well-established and reliable curry house. Open noon-2.30p.m. and 6p.m.-midnight. Branches: Helal Tandoori, Louth; Shaki Mahal Takeaway, 6 Pinfold Lane, Grimsby.

TASTE OF PUNJAB

9-11 Market Street, Cleethorpes   ℗ 01472 603720

'An easy-to-read and comprehensive menu, which the owner, Mr Sagoo, is only too happy to help you with. From the initial Papadoms to the final coffee, the quantities are just right,' H.C.

Grimsby

ABDUL'S TANDOORI   ©

152 Victoria Street, Grimsby   ℗ 01472 356650

'I have been using the place for years every time I'm in town, and have never had a bad meal. It's absolutely brilliant,' P.J. Owner is Abdul Salique. Open seven days a week, noon-2.30p.m. and 6p.m.-midnight, Friday and Saturday till 12.30a.m. Branch: Eastern Delights, 43 Market Place, Cleethorpes.

Lincoln

RAJ DOUTH

7 Eastgate, Lincoln   © 01522 548377

'In a quaint building in the exclusive part of town. Restaurant comprises several rooms, linked together by the reception area. You get a special offer for birthdays: one main course free upon proof of birth! We decided to give it a whirl. We ordered Papadoms and chutneys (hot, mango and onion), Mixed Kebab and Chicken Chat for starters followed by Meat Madras and Chicken Dhansak, which was OK except meat was a bit tough,' L.W.

Louth

HELAL TANDOORI

1 Mercer Row, Louth   © 01507 607960

Well-established (1975), huge (100 seats) restaurant. 'An attractive restaurant if rather dimly lit. Friendly service. Meal was very good indeed. Each dish had its own characteristics with delicious gravies. Chicken Tikka Dopiaza was outstanding,' D.C.G. 'Good value,' C.P.

Scunthorpe

RAHMAN'S TANDOORI

143 Frodingham Road, Scunthorpe   © 01724 841238

'They serve first-class food and service,' S.R.

THE TAJ   NEW ENTRANT   ©

159 Frodingham Road, Scunthorpe   © 01724 862220

Rehman Rahman's takeaway-only has been trading successfully since 1989. Evenings only, 5.30-11.30p.m., closed Tuesdays. Price check: Papadom 35p, CTM £4.95, King Prawn Delight £7.95, Veg Malai Kofta £1.95, Pullao Rice £1.45.

Sleaford

AGRA   ©

99 East Road, Sleaford   ✆ 01529 414162

'This is a very fine curry house, offering a vast choice, and they will
even cook what you want. Chef specialities are both good value and
nice to see, Chicken Tikka Masala and Madras are very good,' R.T.
Managing director, Leeneth Karim, has promised to give a discount to
Curry Club members, which especially pleases Ms L.McM. because it's
her 'favourite restaurant'.

Spalding

CHILLI MASTER   ▥

11 Winsover Road, Spalding   ✆ 01775 762221

A hot and spicy restaurant, offering Pizza (make your own, toppings
45p and 55p each – garlic and chilli free!), Curry, Balti, Tandoori,
Doner Kebabs, Southern Fried Chicken and Burgers. Fast and free
delivery service available locally. Open 5p.m.-1a.m., Friday and Saturday
till 3a.m. Branch: Chilli Master, 2 Red Lion Street, Stamford.

SHAHEEN

2 Pinchbeck Road, Spalding   ✆ 01775 767852

'Quantities vary from adequate to very generous and the quality very
good. Coffee pot is never-ending and we recommend a visit,' M.S

Stamford

BOMBAY COTTAGE   NEW ENTRANT   ©

52 Scotgate, Stamford   ✆ 01780 480138

Opened in 1992 and taken over in 1994 by Akhtar Hussain, with manager Habibur Rahman, it gets the thumbs up, particularly for the
specials Achar-Gosht-Ka-Salan (£6.10) – meat simmered in a pickled
spice base, and Shorshe-Bata-Prawns (£6.50) – with mustard seeds.

Price check: Papadom 50p, CTM £6.90, Pullao Rice £1.80. Set meal £15.80 for two.

RAJ OF INDIA ©

2 All Saints Street, Stamford © 01780 753556

Owner Rohom Ali has been running the Raj since 1982, and such experience shows. 'Excellent evening out, good and attentive service. Nicely decorated and furnished. Food well-presented, hot and good portions. Lamb Tikka Masala particularly good,' J.A.G. Price check: Papadom 50p, CTM £7.20, Pullao Rice £1.90. Set meal £18 for two. Minimum charge £10.

Woodhall Spa

INDIA VILLAGE NEW ENTRANT

6 The Broadway, Woodhall Spa © 01526 352223

Wasn't this the Dam Busters' HQ? Not the India Village, though the chaps would have loved it – the actual village, I mean. I know that Scampton, which is relatively near, was their base. Anyway, Ms L.N. found it 'a little slow, but the food OK'. Price check: Papadom 55p, Green Herbal Chicken Kebab £5.80, CTM £5.95, Very Hot Pili Pili Chicken £5.95, Pullao Rice £1.85.

GREATER MANCHESTER

Although Greater Manchester was introduced as a county in 1965, it is still disregarded by many of its residents who prefer to refer to the counties that Greater Manchester gobbled up, e.g., parts of Lancashire and Cheshire. We have adhered strictly to the official current Greater Manchester territory for town locations in this Guide.

©	Curry Club discount (see p. 607)	💺	Unlicensed
√	Vegetarian	🏢	Home delivery
BYO	Bring your own alcohol		service available

Altrincham

MUGHAL ©

86 Park Road, Timperley, Altrincham   ℭ **0161 973 4513**

M. Hoque's popular Tondori Royale became the Mughal in 1994 and remains just as popular. Open 5p.m.-midnight. Branch: Tondori Royale, Manchester, M19.

SHERE KHAN

Old Market Place, Altrincham   ℭ **0161 926 8777**

'Situated next to the Orange Tree Pub (CAMRA award-winner). An up-market restaurant matched by up-market prices. Restaurant on two floors. Dhansak sauce rich and creamy, Chupatis nice and large,' S.N. Branches: Mister Khan, 36 Wilmslow Road, Manchester, M14; Shere Khan, 52 Wilmslow Road, Manchester, M14.

Ashton-under-Lyne

INDIAN OCEAN ⊞ ©

83 Stamford Street East, Ashton   ℭ **0161 343 3343**

'A home-made taste to the food. What really made the place was the sizeable and beautiful room they called the wine bar with extensive bar counters, good beer and satellite TV,' R.H. 'Huge portions served by very helpful waiters. The Chicken Pathia is the best I have ever tasted – hot, sweet and sour. The Pasanda is superb and so was my girlfriend's Chicken Korma Sashlic,' S.N. Price check: Papadom 45p, CTM £6.50, Pullao Rice £1.60. Open Monday to Thursday, 5-11p.m.; Saturday, noon-2.30p.m. and 5p.m.-midnight; Sunday, 4-10.30p.m. Free delivery service.

JALAL-ABAD

24-26 Cotton Street East, Ashton   ℭ **0161 343 4844**

'Sizeable portions. Quality of food was outstanding. A small restaurant, comfortable and tastefully decorated,' C.B. Open Monday to

Thursday noon-2.30p.m. and 5-11.30p.m., Friday, Saturday and Sunday noon-midnight, Sunday family lunch noon-5p.m.

Atherton

SAVAR

39-41 Mealhouse Lane, Atherton   ℭ **01942 875544**

'We simply cannot contain ourselves any longer, we must tell you about our favourite restaurant in the whole wide world, the Savar in Atherton. My hubby and myself have eaten in numerous restaurants throughout Europe – 50% at least were of the Indian variety and we cannot find a meal to equal – indeed, approach – the quality, flavour, texture and total experience of the Savar's Balti dishes. Good-quality meat and vegetables wallow in a variety of thick, rich, tangy sauces, delicately suffused with a multitude of fragrant spices and lavishly strewn with fresh coriander. The Naan breads are as light as clouds and as large as duvets, the portions reach well halfway up the side of the washing-up-bowl-sized Balti dishes – and you must try the special red sauce that arrives with the pickles and starters. The Savar is a pleasant, unassuming restaurant, situated in a converted chapel. The staff are lovely – especially Ranu, the chatty manager. The prices are extremely modest. All in all, this is an experience not to be missed,' I.F.-E. 'Has a Balti chef from Birmingham, so we expected authenticity – and we got it. Portion quantities were just about right, and the quality was superb thanks to the liberal use of fresh ingredients. King Prawn Puri quite delicious. Balti Lamb Jalfrezi was mind-blowing – love those chillies! I'm going to enjoy being a regular here,' M.S.

Billinge

BALTI KING NEW ENTRANT

191 Main Street, Billinge   ℭ **01744 607707**

'Tastefully decorated, with bare stone walls and exposed beams. They must be the friendliest staff I've ever met. Ask them to do home-cooking (not on the menu). You won't be disappointed,' R.K.

Bolton

ANAZ TAKEAWAY

138 St Helens Road, Bolton   ✆ **01204 660114**

'The shop is absolutely spotless, service first-class and I was offered a fresh cup of coffee whilst I waited. Very extensive menu, Shami Kebab, Chicken Madras, rice and chips with Naan. All done perfectly. Only fault no yoghurt sauce,' M.B.

HILAL TANDOORI   NEW ENTRANT

296 Chorley Old Road, Bolton   ✆ **01204 842315**

This one was opened in 1975 by Surat Ali, and he's still here with Anor Liiah as manager. Such longevity ensures smooth-running and competence. A nice touch is the free liqueur at the end of the meal. Price check: Papadom 40p, CTM £6.05, Pullao Rice £1.20. Minimum charge £5. Open evenings only, 6p.m.-2a.m., Fridays and Saturdays till 3a.m.

LEENA

131-133 Bradshawgate, Bolton   ✆ **01204 383255**

'Gets rave reviews locally. Called in for Sunday lunch. Shami Kebab and Onion Bhajee for starters, Kebabs made the textbook way with lentils, really tasty. Lamb Rogan Josh, first class, full of flavour, peppers, pimentos and tomatoes in a rich creamy sauce – excellent!!' M.B.
'Myself and six other colleagues, who were working for Sky Sports covering the football, had a meal there. Service was a little slow – there was only one other couple there when we arrived. Dishes were very bland, needed more spices, no cardamoms, cassia bark, etc. We asked for coffee at the end and were alarmed to see the head waiter put a spoonful of Nescafé into a gold-framed cafetiere, which he then "plunged" at the table! Overall, we thought it was average,' R.M. Reports, please.

THE SPICE ISLAND   NEW ENTRANT   ©

87 Tonge Moor Road, Bolton   ✆ **01204 361678**

Your favourites are on offer here at Mohammed Mehbub's Spice

Island. What's more, he's the chef as well as the boss and he cooks some intriguing unusuals. I've never seen Ekuri (£2.10) served anywhere else. It is spicy scrambled egg, served with Puri, and it's delicious. Palak Shira (£1.35) is a tasty spinach-based soup. Reporters tell of good Baltis, maybe because Mehbub professes to like them himself, especially the Garlic Special Balti, which he describes on the menu as 'recommended if you are going vampire-hunting' – presumably missable if you want to impress a new partner who's not shared your indulgence, but in all respects mind-blowing and breath-blowing! The Bangladeshi Speciality Dishes are also in demand, we hear. Shandus Baja (£4.25) is chicken or meat, roasted, then stir-fried with bamboo shoots, fresh hot chillies and other delights. Joynal is the manager. Price check: Papadom 35p, CTM £4.10, Pullao Rice £1.10. Sunday Thali £4.60. Open 5-11.30p.m. Monday to Thursday, 4.30p.m.-midnight Friday and Saturday, 4-11.30p.m. Sunday.

SUNAR GAW   ©

310 Manchester Road, Bolton   ℭ 01204 364915

Formerly Taj Mahal. Sunar Gaw means 'golden village'. Opened in 1992 by Abdul Shahid and Abdul Hannan, the former is the manager front of house, the latter the chef behind the scenes. Seats 44 diners so do book for weekends because it's popular, having won the local newspaper's best restaurant award. Open 6p.m.-midnight. Price check: Papadom 35p, CTM £6.50, Pullao Rice £1.30. Set meal for two £25.95. Minimum charge £7. Branch: Sunar Gaw, Lancashire.

Bury

TANDOORI NIGHTS

135 Rochdale Road, Bury   ℭ 0161 761 6224

'This little takeaway is brilliant. You can see them cooking the food – open counter – very friendly and free chutney,' P.J. Open 5.30-11.20p.m., Friday and Saturday till 12.30a.m., Sunday 4-11p.m.

Dukinfield

INDIA COTTAGE

Foundry Street, Dukinfield   ✆ 0161 343 5961

'A huge restaurant seating 120 and it could take more. Situated in a modern brick building, previously a nightclub. Roomy waiting area near the bar with large bowls of Bombay Mix. Service excellent. Food excellent, satisfied with portions, Garlic Chicken particularly good,' B.G. 'Best Lamb Tikka ever. Lal Qila is delicious. Lamb Tikka Dupiaza is superb! For the fire-eaters try the Jalfrezi – full of green chillies and ginger – mind-blowing! Quantities huge, one meal could be enough for two,' D.P.

Manchester City

The postcodes of Manchester and its surrounding suburbs were recently changed. For the purpose of this Guide we have included M postcodes in all our Manchester City entries, and have divided the area into Central, East, South, West and North, using major roads as our arbitrary boundaries.

Manchester Central M1 to M4

GAYLORD   TOP 100   ©

Amethyst House, Spring Gardens,
Manchester, M2   ✆ 0161 832 6037

'I looked at my watch. It was 12.45p.m., sudden pain flashed through my stomach, I needed a fix and fast. I looked round to get my bearings. I was on Brown Street. I looked up, there was a street sign pointing to the Gaylord. Sweat started to ooze from my forehead, running down my face in long cool rivulets. I staggered up the short street and into Marriots Court; I could see the entrance, would I make it? The pain was worse so I quickened my stride and into the restaurant area. I was aware of a person standing next to the bar at the top of the stairs;

I looked up. God, I thought, I must be mad, I'm hallucinating, Henry Kissinger has come to meet me.

"'Are you OK, sir?" a voice enquired.

"'Henry," I said, "quick! I need a fix."

"'Henry? I'm not Henry! I'm Raman Kapoor, the manager. I'll show to your seat, sir. You have got it bad ..."

'He hurried off to return a few minutes later with a fresh Papadom and a tray full of the most wonderful chutney you've ever tasted. This was followed in no time at all by a sizzling Sheek Kebab, the taste of which was out of this world. Next I sampled from the regular menu a dish of Chilli Chicken. Again, the taste was unbelievable. This was accompanied by Pillau Rice and a fresh Naan which I watched the chef prepare through the glass wall into the kitchen. Suitably fixed, I found myself back on the street. How lucky we are, having one of the best restaurants in the country right here in Manchester,' M.B.

Mike's remarkable hallucinatory story is too good to leave out this time, and we are still flooded with reports praising the Gaylord. We are pleased to restore it to our TOP 100.

KAILASH

34 Charlotte Street, Manchester, M1   © 0161 236 6624

Nepalese restaurant situated in the basement. 'As you descend the steps you are met with the most wonderful spicy smells imaginable. Tandoori Fish for starters, the only way to eat fish as far as I'm concerned. Specialities of the house include Rogan Josh and Jalfrezi which are first-class. Perfect rice and bread. Parking a nightmare as this restaurant is in Chinatown,' M.B.

KIEZMAT

25-29 Great Ducie Street, Manchester, M3 © 0161 834 1088

'A very spacious restaurant, up-market with comfortable seating. Food is good, standard curry house stuff. All the staff from the old Kismet have moved to this establishment,' M.B.

NAWAAB

47 Rochdale Road, Manchester, M4   *©* 0161 839 0601

Formerly the Al Khayyam, this restaurant is now part of the Nawaab chain (*see* entries for Bradford and Huddersfield, Yorkshire West). 'Very comfortable and smacks of class. First-class standard curry house food. Service very friendly and attentive,' M.B. 'An excellent restaurant with quick, friendly service. Tandoori Mixed starter is a very substantial meal. Shahi Passanda, Chicken Jalfrezi and Buttered Chicken were rich and satisfying. Prices are higher but worth every penny,' B.H.B.

RAJDOOT   TOP 100   ©

Carlton House, 18 Albert Square,
Manchester, M2   *©* 0161 834 2176

The Rajdoot is the 1966 creation of architect Des Sarda who also owns the Rajdoot in Bristol, Birmingham, Dublin and of all places, Fuengirola, Spain. The Rajdoot is noticeable for its authentic, elegant and exotic atmosphere; indeed, it was one of the first to present itself in an up-market and attractive way, and Mr Sarda's architect's training shows with the Indian arts and crafts, colour styles and general layout. This restaurant, along with the other three Rajdoots in this group, offers Curry Club members a discount. 'Still up there amongst the very best. Exceptionally well-presented and comfortable. The stools in the waiting area may be uncomfortable for tall people, but this would soon be forgotten whilst you dip into bowls of fresh Bombay Mix. Extensive menu with emphasis on Moghul cuisine. No standard curry but, what the hell, who needs it with food like this? Shish Kebab excellent, Lamb Rogan Josh first-class, really tasty, kept me going,' M.B. We are happy to keep this restaurant in our TOP 100.

USMAN CAFE   NEW ENTRANT   BYO

6 Lena Street, Off Dale Street, Piccadilly,
Manchester, M1   *©* 0161 237 5392

The former Tandoori Cuisine, despite its new name, is still 'gloriously cheap and gloriously tatty. Not the place to take anybody to impress, but if the curry fever strikes you at around dinnertime it will do the trick. I introduced it to a work colleague who loves curry and has given it the thumbs up. Onion Bhajis were 40p, had been positively soaked in that red food-colouring stuff, "Goodness gracious, great balls of fire!" but were quite tasty. Vegetable Masala £2.75. I would recommend it to a person I knew well,' A.G. And we'd recommend it to all curry-holics. 'Limited menu, superb Chicken Naan for £2 and Meat Palak £2.75. Very good value, very good food,' B.H. Lots of Asian customers. Cheap, cheerful, jugs of water, and soft drinks, and BYO.

Manchester East Including M11, M18, M34, M35, M40, M43

LA MIRAGE TANDOORI

67-69 Kenyon Lane, Moston, M40   © 0161 681 9373

'After being a regular customer here for many years and never been disappointed, I feel La Mirage should be given recognition for its excellent curries and tandoori dishes. The decor is not brilliant, but the meals, service and prices are. The best Madras in Manchester,' B.T.

Manchester South Including M12, M17, M19, M21, M32, M33

GREAT KATHMANDU

140 Burton Road, West Didsbury, M20   © 0161 434 6413

'Service excellent if bordering somewhat on the irritating side – I was asked by at least five waiters whether I wanted a drink or any Papadoms to which I answered that I had ordered a pint of lager when I came in. I still had to ask for it again after all that. I chose from a fairly extensive menu, Shami Kebabs which were excellent followed by, yes, you've guessed it, Chicken Madras (for a change), which was really tasty as was the Pullao Rice. Naan was fresh, light and extremely big,' M.B. Branch: 198 Mauldeth Road, Burnage, Manchester, M19.

KHANDOKER ©

812 Kingsway, East Didsbury, M20   ℂ 0161 428 4687

An evenings-only establishment (5p.m.-12.30a.m.), owned by Khandoker Sufi Miah, seating 60. Popular, it seems, with students and locals.

SONAGRA

2691 Barlow Moor Road,
Chorlton-cum-Hardy, M21   ℂ 0161 861 0334

'Our local is an absolute jewel! You are greeted with olde-world charm and made to feel special. Tastefully decorated. Food is divine,' v.h.

TONDORI ROYALE ©

628-629 Burnage Lane, Burnage, M19   ℂ 0161 432 0930

This huge (110-seat) restaurant, owned by M. Hoque and Miss M. Choudhury, is very well-established (1980) and very well spoken of by the locals. 'It was packed! It is not difficult to work out why when you taste the cuisine. Atmosphere is electric and food well worth the 40-mile trip,' m.b. It has distinguished itself with a full house of familiar dishes plus some great Bangladeshi specials. Fish dishes include Boal and Ayre. n.w.'s favourite is Zhal Golda Chingri – king prawn cooked with chilli and ginger, while e.f. loves the Jeera Chicken. i.k.p. still says 'it's very good indeed'. Price check: Papadom 30p, CTM £5.50, Pullao Rice £1.25. Set meal £10.75. Minimum charge £6. Open 6p.m.-1.30a.m. Branch: Mughal, Altrincham.

Wilmslow Road, Rusholme – M14

Wilmslow Road extends for nearly 6 miles south from Manchester Centre. It passes through Rusholme, Manchester's main Asian area. To get there from the city centre it's best to walk – parking is normally a joke. Face south on the Oxford Road, with the BBC on your left, and go for about 800 metres, passing the Uni and then the Royal Infirmary. At the Moss Lane East junction, Rusholme and Little India starts. In the last five years the expansion has been amazing and is continuing unabated. Now, in the 600 metres from Moss Lane to Claremont Road, there are no less than 35 curry eateries – Indian snack and sweet shops, cafés and restaurants. As if that's not enough, there are numerous pubs, offies, chippies, Chinese, pizza joints, kebab houses and burger bars, Asian grocers and halal butchers. Some of the cheap and cheerful all-day cafés allow BYO (but always ask – it can offend some Muslims). Some are quite expensive licensed restaurants, the largest of which seats 150 and is planning an expansion to 400! A conservative estimate on curry consumption is 50,000 curries a week here. We believe this to be the curry record for a district. Any challenges? Go a further 900 metres along Wilmslow Road and there are some 30 more curry eateries, making this a genuine Golden Mile. With such rapid growth, we'd love full details on this phenomenon from all our scribes. Maybe it will merit a special extended feature in the next Guide. Meanwhile, here are some of your favourites:

EASTERN TOUCH   BYO

76 Wilmslow Road, Rusholme, M14   © 0161 224 5665

'My favourite. Lino floor and glass-topped tables – more a café, really. Warm Papadoms, chutney and sauces are brought to the table immediately – free to all diners. Standard but comprehensive menu. Kebabs cooked freshly over charcoal in the corner of the restaurant, piping hot, highly spiced and juicy, served with a large plate of tomatoes, onion and lettuce. Chicken Madras, prime quality, tender and succulent, very hot, sauce is rich and fiery, perfect for mopping up with a meaty Keema Naan. Not licensed, I bring my own,' P.W.

LAL HAWELI   NEW ENTRANT   ©

68-72 Wilmslow Road, Rusholme, M14   © 0161 248 9700

One of the road's early restaurants (1973), it has been in Mohammad Choudhury's hands since 1980. The menu has an interesting assortment of Pakistani and Nepalese dishes with good cooking from Imran Nayer and Jessy Singh Jatt. Price check: Papadom complimentary, CTM £4.95, Pullao Rice £1.10. Open 12.30p.m.-1a.m. Branches, all on Wilmslow Road: Nasib, no. 90; New Tabak, no. 199; Pan House Balti, no. 35.

SANAM

215 Wilmslow Road, Rusholme, M14   ✆ 0161 224 8570

'On two levels. The waiter could have done with a clean shirt but apart from that the place was spotless. You can see your meals being cooked in the open kitchen. The food is brilliant, Papadoms were fresh and crisp and came with a tray of various onions and chutneys. Colleague swore blind he had the best Chicken Tikka Masala. Not licensed,' M.B.

SANAM SWEET HOUSE

145-151 Wilmslow Road, Rusholme, M14   ✆ 0161 224 8824

Despite A.Q. Akhtar's restaurant being huge (seating 160, plus a further 200-seat function room), it is so popular locally that it's often full, with queues waiting to be seated. Open noon-midnight. Branches: Abdul's, 121 and 318 Wilmslow Road, and 298 Oxford Road.

SANAM TAKEAWAY

167 Wilmslow Road, Rusholme, M14   ✆ 0161 257 3557

'More of a kebab-style takeaway than a restaurant, serving only starters. Easily missed, as the frontage covers no more than about 10 feet. Dingy decor and formica tables belie the standard of the food. Samosas, both meat and vegetable, are the best I've ever eaten. Shikh Kebabs (three to a portion) are superb. All served on a metal dish with no cutlery but a warm, large and deliciously moist Naan. Not the place to impress a new girlfriend, maybe, but a must for those late nights out with the boys,' D.B.

SANGAM

13-15 Wilmslow Road, Rusholme, M14   ✆ 0161 257 3922

'Up-market, bright and clean. Licensed. Lamb Chop Tikka, one of the best and most filling starters I have had. Will visit again,' R.C.

SHERE KHAN

52 Wilmslow Road, Rusholme, M14   ✆ 0161 256 2624

Opened in 1987 and has built up a regular clientele in this 'Curry

Golden Mile'. Fully licensed and air-conditioned. Open noon-midnight. Branches: Mister Khan, 36 Wilmslow Road; Shere Khan, Altrincham.

SHEZAN

119 Wilmslow Road, Rusholme, M14   © 0161 224 8168

A massive restaurant seating 120 diners, owned by Masued Ahmed. 'Yet another brilliant and fairly cheap restaurant. Service was a little on the slow side, but the food was quite superb,' M.B. Open noon-1a.m.

TABAK

199-201 Wilmslow Road, Rusholme, M14   © 0161 257 3890

'Another of those little gems. A large restaurant seating over 200 people. Karahi Nawabi Bataire, quails. Afghani Bashyan, tender juicy lamb chop marinated in cream, spices and barbecued — not to be missed,' M.B.

TANDOORI KITCHEN   BYO

131-133 Wilmslow Road, Rusholme, M14   © 0161 224 2329

'Not licensed, no objection to bringing your own. Glass-topped tables. Shamee Kebab made with lentils, served with plenty of salad and chutney. Chicken Madras very tasty and plenty of it. Service good,' M.B.

Manchester West Including M5, M7, Salford, M27, M31, M38, M41, M44, M46

Cadishead, M44

SUNDORBON   ©

40 Liverpool Road, Cadishead, M44   © 0161 775 2812

An early starter (1970), and in Iqbal Uddin's ownership since 1975, this restaurant is fairly large, seating 80 diners. All the old favourites are on the menu. Price check: Papadom 40p, CTM £6.75, Sundorbon Special Chicken £6.75, Pullao Rice £1.20. Open 6p.m.-12.30a.m.

Eccles, M30

PASSAGE TO INDIA ©

16 Monton Road, Monton, Eccles, M30   ✆ 0161 787 7546

Opened in 1988 by M. Hassan Choudhury and H. Uddin, a large establishment seating 90 diners. Serves all the formula curries. Open noon-11.30p.m. Branch: Gate of India, Swinton.

Urmston, M41

STANDARD

2-4 Victoria Parade, Higher Road,
Urmston, M41   ✆ 0161 748 2806

A largish restaurant seating 76 diners. 'Interior is well above average – not standard. Comfortable seating. Service I received was beyond reproach, nothing was too much trouble. Sheek Kebab must rate as the biggest I've ever had and one of the tastiest. Portions were so large that it would have been impossible to eat it all in one session, so I took half home with me. Restaurant prepares its own mango chutney, which they sell along with a variety of pickles, chutneys and curry pastes. Nothing is standard about this restaurant, except its name. Well worth a visit,' M.B. Open noon-2p.m. and 5.30-11.30p.m.

©	Curry Club discount (see p. 607)	☕	Unlicensed
√	Vegetarian	▦	Home delivery
BYO	Bring your own alcohol		service available

Manchester North Including M8, M9, M24 (Middleton), M25 (Whitefield), M25 (Prestwich), and M26 (Radcliffe)

Middleton, M24

RHODES TANDOORI TAKEAWAY

606 Manchester Old Road, Rhodes,
Middleton, M24   © 0161 655 3904

'Very friendly. Chicken Malaya enjoyed as well as the Bhindi Bhaji which was well sized with lots of okra,' s.n. and r.a. Open 4p.m.-midnight every day. Branch: Lees Tandoori, 54 High Street, Lees, Oldham.

Prestwich, M25

GARDEN OF INDIA   ©

411 Bury Old Road, Prestwich, M25   © 0161 773 7784

An 88-seat restaurant, opened in 1984 by Hafizur Rahman and managed by A. Quyum. 'Chicken Samber, very reminiscent of a Dhansak, hot, but not as sweet, which was a very pleasant change and one which I shall look out for again. Chicken Paneer met with total approval,' s.n. and r.a. 'Have visited several times and have always found it quite acceptable,' m.b. t.t. likes the Fish Kufta Masala – fish balls in a creamy sauce. Price check: Papadom 30p, CTM £6.20, Pullao Rice £1.70. Service charge 10%. Cover charge £1.25. Open 5.30-11.30p.m.

Radcliffe, M26

ALISHAN

21-23 Church Street, Radcliffe, M26   © 0161 725 9910

'Madras, one of the best. This little 40-seater restaurant continues to get good reports locally, and not without good reason. We've been here several times and have yet to fault it. Chicken Sambar, first-class,' M.B.

RADCLIFFE CHARCOAL TANDOORI

Blackburn Street, Radcliffe, M26   © 0161 723 4870

'Very smart, up-market restaurant with alcoves. Bar has large ornamental built-in fish tank. Chicken Madras and Pullao Rice were perfect, so were the Chupatis. Cheerful and efficient service,' M.B.

SHAHBAAZ NEW ENTRANT   ©

Old Barn, Radcliffe Moor Road,
Radcliffe, M26   © 0161 724 0000

F.A. Syed and Capt. N.I. Moshin opened this restaurant in 1989 (as the Curry Cottage) with its easy-to-remember phone number and address. Even the postcode is apt – OWL. In fact, Mr Syed should have renamed it the Owl Tandoori at the Old Barn! But we hear that the food is memorable, too, with the regular choice of favourites. Price check: Papadom 25p, Karai Chicken £4.95, CTM £5.50, Pullao Rice £1.30. Set meal from £12.50. Open 4-11p.m. weekdays, till midnight Fridays and Saturdays, 1-11p.m. Sundays and Bank Holidays. Branch: Shahbaaz, 13 Stansfield Centre, Boothstown, Worsley, Salford.

Whitefield, M25

AKRAM'S NEW ENTRANT

Sefton Street, off Bury New Road,
Whitefield, M25   © 0161 796 0412

The decor is really striking. It is set in a spacious former Methodist hall, now decorated in a minimalist way. Our scribes tell of good à la carte food and set meal bargains, especially the set lunch at £4.95 and the enormous Sunday buffet at £6.95. Open noon-2p.m. and 6-11.30p.m, Sunday noon-11.30p.m.

DAWAT TAKEAWAY

184 Bury New Road, Whitefield, M25   ✆ 0161 796 5976

M.G. Mustafa's takeaway-only establishment opened in 1986. 'Shami Kebabs best in the UK. Despite many hours of grilling' [is that a joke, Mike?] 'for the recipes to no avail, and many hours experimenting in my own kitchen, I'm afraid that the unique flavour is just out of reach. Same applies to their curries, a unique flavour and consistent. Baltis first-class,' M.B. Price check: Papadom 25p, CTM £4.40, Pullao Rice £1.10.

FORTS OF INDIA   ©

7-11 Radcliffe New Road, Whitefield, M25 ✆ 0161 766 5873

Opened by Abdul Haris and seating 70 diners and 20 in the lounge. 'Decor is very much up-market. Staff dressed in traditional costume. Cheap it is not, but nevertheless the food is absolutely wonderful and well worth the cost. Parking is not a problem,' M.B. Open noon-2.30p.m. and 6-11p.m., Sundays 1-11p.m.

KIPLINGS INDIA

24 Elm Square, Bury New Road,
Whitefield, M25   ✆ 0161 796 0557

A very impressive up-market restaurant from the outside, plate-glass windows with Austrian blinds. Inside, white linen, Chippendale-style chairs, large bar and plants hanging from suspended ceilings. 'Menu is quite extensive with all the favourites and a selection of Balti dishes. Extremely tasty and delicately spiced Shish Kebab followed by a Chicken Madras — what else! — which for me personally was perfect as I like the bite. Service could have been a little smoother and quicker. If you are looking for somewhere to celebrate something special, then look no further,' M.B.

©	Curry Club discount (see p. 607)		Unlicensed
√	Vegetarian		Home delivery
BYO	Bring your own alcohol		service available

Oldham

BRITISH RAJ   NEW ENTRANT   ©

185-187 Lees Road, Oldham   ✆ **0161 624 8696**

Oldham's oldest, once Deans, then the Prince and now, since 1997, the British Raj. Owned by Atik Miah and Aysha Khanom and managed by S. Rahman. 'The place has been transformed into an extremely adventurous establishment. The decor is tasteful, right down to the Union Jacks embroidered into the chairbacks. The food is really good. The Shan Special Chicken and Bombay Chicken were both like a dream – hot and spicy and unlike the normal formula stuff. Pullao Rice exceptionally light and perfumed. The meal was finished off with hot towels and orange segments. The manager then brought us two free tall cocktails to finish off with. They do special evenings with home-cooking, food as eaten by Bangladeshi families. One to return to,' R.K. Price check: Papadom 30p, CTM £4.50, Pullao Rice £1.30. Open 5.30p.m.-12.30a.m., weekdays, Fridays and Saturdays till 2a.m., Sundays 3p.m.-midnight. Reports, please.

LIGHT OF BENGAL   ©

114 Union Street, Oldham   ✆ **0161 624 4600**

Large restaurant seating 80. Opened in 1980 by Abdul Hannan who is also front of house manager, in order to see that things go smoothly. Open Sunday to Thursday 5.30p.m.-1a.m., Friday and Saturday, till 1.30a.m. Branch: Bengal Brasserie, 31-33 Milnrow Road, Shaw, Oldham.

MILLON RESTAURANT   NEW ENTRANT   ©

Westwood Business Centre,
Featherstall Road South, Oldham   ✆ **0161 620 6445**

Abdul Momin and Ashik Ullah opened their Millon in 1993 in a purpose-built, elegant building. The inside is as smart as the outside. There is a bar and a 100-seat dining room, with alcoves and pillars and smart upholstery. The menu contains all the things one expects and, since the chef is Mr Momin, the food is of a high standard, so we hear. Price check: Papadom 45p, CTM £6.75 incl. rice, Pullao Rice £1.60. Set meal from £22 for two. Minimum charge £8.50. Open weekdays 5-11.30p.m., Fridays and Saturdays till 12.30a.m., Sundays 4-11p.m.

PANAHAR TANDOORI

175 Park Road, Oldham   © 0161 773 7784

'Service excellent in small, intimate restaurant. Specialities, particularly the Lamb Pasanda, are wonderful – dip your Naan!' J.H.

Ramsbottom
Known to residents as 'Rammy'.

EASTERN EYE

38 Bolton Street, Ramsbottom   © 01706 823268

'Have dined here on many occasions and have never had a bad meal yet. Indeed, the only complaint is that the restaurant is quite small with low ceilings which allow it to get a little warm when it gets busy. Though licensed, you may be asked to visit the pub over the road whilst your table is cleared and prepared. Chicken Tikka absolutely perfect,' M.B.

MOGHUL DYNASTY TOP 100

51 Bolton Street, Ramsbottom   © 01706 821510

'Superb, high ceilings, pillars and hanging baskets. Friendly, attentive service. First-class food, generous amounts,' J.N. 'Chilli Massala Tandoori Chicken was out of this world, absolutely full of the most wonderful flavour. Washed down with wonderful Cobra lager,' M.B. We gave it our TOP 100 award last time just for our ace reporter M.B. Everyone who has tried it since agrees that it's the formula at its best.

© Curry Club discount (see p. 607)	Unlicensed
√ Vegetarian	Home delivery
BYO Bring your own alcohol	service available

Rochdale

DERAJ BALTI CROWN   NEW ENTRANT   ©

244 Yorkshire Street, Rochdale   **② 01706 358649**

Opened in 1976 and taken over by Abdul Bhuiyan in 1996 and renamed (it was the Everest). We hear that this 45-seater has become a popular local haunt again. Price check: Papadom 30p, CTM £6.15, Pullao Rice £1.20. Minimum charge £12. Open every day except Monday, 5p.m.-midnight.

LA TANDOOR   NEW ENTRANT   ©

Unit A7, Bamford Shopping Precinct,
Martlett Avenue, Bamford, Rochdale   **② 01706 715949**

'A superb restaurant, and be warned – book a table, as it gets very busy. Samir, the manager, took pity on us as we'd arrived on spec from Liverpool and squeezed us in. We had Nargis Kebab and Vegetable Chaat for starters – a dream – and we followed with a main-course choice of Chicken Tikka Biriani and Chilli Chicken Balti, with a side dish of Malayee Kufta (vegetable balls in a coconut sauce with pineapple and peaches), Pullao Rice and Chupattis. It was all excellent, followed by ice cream, face towels, a free drink and after-meal sweets. All this cost us just £26.45. They then asked us to sign the visitors' book. We'd eat there every day if we were locals!' R.K.

Standish

TASTE OF BENGAL   NEW ENTRANT   ©

11 High Street, Standish   **② 01257 473119**

One correspondent raves on about owner-manager G. Uddin's Korai Coriander and Chilli Fish (£4.90 incl. rice). 'Fish is so good for you. We have it with Balti Dopiaza Sag (£4 incl. Naan) – spinach and lashings of onion, served in the iron pot – a double dose of iron, and our meal for two is barely a tenner,' N.M. Price check: Papadom 40p, CTM £6.60 incl. rice or Naan, Pullao Rice £1.45. Open daily, 5p.m.-midnight. Branch: Wigan Tandoori Takeaway, 50 Frog Lane, Wigan.

Stockport

ATITHI TAKEAWAY

43 London Road South, Poynton,
Stockport   ✆ 01625 858090

'Open kitchens, very clean. Free coffee and Bombay Mix while waiting.
Quality consistent and generous. Chicken Tikka Sambar very good.
For garlic/chilli-lovers – North Indian Garlic Chicken is superb,' E.F.
Open 4-11p.m.

KUSHOOM KOLY   ©

6 Shaw Road, Heaton Moor, Stockport   ✆ 0161 432 9841

Owned by Mrs Kulsum Uddin and in the same family since it opened
in 1971, with Fakuk front of house and Kashim in the kitchens.
The Kushoom Koly, meaning 'flowerbud', has had a recent refurb,
giving it a bow-front window and an open kitchen. 'The food is
plentiful and if you like garlic then this is the place to go,' G.C. 'The
menu features the usual range of favourites. Jalfrezi cooked the way
I prefer it, very spicy and liberal use of green chillies,' P.H. Home-
delivery service. Price check: Papadom 40p, CTM £5.20, Pullao Rice
£1.60. Set meal from £5.90. Open daily, noon-2p.m. and 6p.m.-1a.m.
Branch: Kaya Koly Takeaway, 70 Heaton Road, Heaton Moor,
Stockport.

MARPLE MASSALLA   ©

105 Stockport Road, Marple, Stockport   ✆ 0161 427 2558

Formula reports from manager, A. Choudhury's, core of locals, tell of
a contented formula here. Open 5p.m.-11.30p.m., Friday and Saturday
till midnight.

MEGHNA INDIAN   ©

55 Dairyground Road, Bramhall,
Stockport   ✆ 0161 440 9464

Opened in 1989 by Mohammed Abdul Ashik, who can be found managing front of house in this 60-seater restaurant, making sure things

run smoothly for all his curryholic regulars. Open 5-11.30p.m., Sundays 3-11.30p.m. 10% discount on takeaway meals.

PHOOLBAGH   ©

345 Edgeley Road, Cheadle Heath,
Stockport   ✆ **0161 427 3496**

Gous Miah opened this restaurant in 1977, quite some time ago now, so he has proven himself in running a good, competent restaurant offering all your favourite curries and a few specialities thrown in for the more adventurous. But be sure to book at weekends as it is a small restaurant seating only 40. Open 6p.m.-1a.m.

ROMILEY TANDOORI

6-7 The Precinct, Romiley, Stockport   ✆ **0161 430 3774**

'A very plush establishment, clean and serves excellent food. Shami Kebab very tasty, served with red mango chutney and yoghurt sauce. Mild but tasty Chicken Madras. Service polite and attentive.' M.B.

Wigan

AJMEER MANZIL   ©

76 Market Street, Wigan   ✆ **01942 235910**

Opened in 1970 by G. Uddin and seats 72 diners. A reliable restaurant serving good reliable curries, Baltis and Korais with all your favourite accompaniments. An unusual bread on the menu – Pyaaz Puri – fried, thin bread with spicy onion. Open 5p.m.-1a.m. Branch: Bombay Duck Takeaway, 50 Frog Lane, Wigan; Taste of Bengal, 11 High Street, Standish, Wigan.

SUHANA

81 High Street, Golborne, Wigan   ✆ **01942 717730**

Previously in the Guide as the Samundar, and new decor too of pinks, greens and gold, although the personnel at Feroze Ali's restaurant are the same, with Bashir Uddin as the chef. 'Supreme food. Onion Bhaji light and tasty. Chicken Asfana – dry and packed full of chillies and flavour. One let-down – the pink plastic tablecloth. A good meal for two cost us £22.75,' R.K. Open 5.30p.m.-midnight.

MERSEYSIDE

Formby

JEWEL IN THE CROWN

126-128 Church Road, Formby   ℗ 01704 873198

'We feel privileged to have such a fine curry house so close. We have never been disappointed,' D.G. Open noon-2p.m. and 5.30p.m.-midnight, till 12.30 a.m. Friday and Saturday, Sunday 6p.m.-midnight.

Liverpool

ALLERTON TANDOORI   ©

79 Allerton Road, Mossley Hill,
Liverpool, L22   ℗ 0151 722 1940

Opened in 1985 by Mr A. Rahman and seating 62 diners. In the intervening years he has built up a good trade, serving the locals reliably with good curries with all their favourite accompaniments. Minimum charge £7.50. Open 5.30p.m.-1a.m.

ARONG   NEW ENTRANT

22 South Road, Waterloo,
Liverpool, L22   ℗ 0151 928 6790

No-frills takeaway-only opened by Joshuma Dean in 1994. Price check: Papadom 35p, CTM £4.60, Balti £3.65, Boal Machli (Bangladeshi Fish) £4.70, Pullao Rice £1.05. Minimum charge £4. Whatever is that for at a takeaway-only joint? – supposing I only want an Onion Bhaji? Set meal £14.95 for two. Open daily, 4.30-11.30p.m. Branch: Arong II, 51 Warbeck Moor, Liverpool, L9.

GULSHAN NEW TO OUR TOP 100

544-546 Aigburth Road,
Liverpool, L19   € 0151 427 2273

A previous Guide entrant, which has been owned by M. and S. Rahman since it opened in 1986. One look at the three-shop-wide frontage tells you that it is likely to be good. Its distinctive feature is a long white facia, supported by twelve pillars, above each of which resides an attractive uplighter resembling an ice cream cone. Between each light is a small canopy that crowns each of the tinted, partially-curtained windows below, beyond which one can see an inviting restaurant scene. Inside, it is equally smart, with a relaxing lounge complete with leather sofas, alongside which is the 70-seater dining room with equally impressive leather-backed dining chairs. The toilets are very expensively fitted out and they're spotless. The 'ladies' powder room' contains hair-spray, perfumes, deodorants, hand-creams, cotton-buds and, if no powder, at least it has its very own resident and resplendent black elephant. Sorry, chaps, no can see, not even if you're Lily Savage in full drag. D.R. says 'you could eat your dinner in there' – you're welcome, Denise, and we get your drift, but the Toilet Tikka has limited appeal, no matter how long the queue.

The waiters wear distinctive, striped waistcoats, and the tables are all well-dressed too, with crisp linen and decent cutlery. 'Even before we started to study the menu, complimentary Papadoms and chutneys were discreetly served ... why doesn't every Indian restaurant do that?' asks G.B. The menu has all the standard formula items, but one correspondent draws our attention to the Gulshan Special (£5.75) – a mild dish containing king prawn, Chicken Tikka, Lamb Tikka, tomatoes, coconut and mushrooms in a cream and wine sauce, topped with egg soufflé and cheese. Another refers to the 'luscious' Chicken Zeera (£4.95) – chicken chunks cooked with cumin. The Green Balti Massala (£4.95) contains puréed coriander, tamarind, green chilli and green herbs, and the Mustard Balti (£4.95) is cooked with mustard and wine. The imaginative use of wine is rare in Indian restaurants and, done well as it is here by owner-chef M. Rahman, it gives traditional dishes an unexpected and subtle lift. This is clearly a caring restaurant. They give a nuts-warning where relevant and, we hear, are great with kids. Several regulars have remarked on these points, and the fact that the prices have hardly varied in several years, and they want us to know that the Gulshan is now probably the best Indian in Liverpool. P.S. agrees: 'Our group of ten ordered the set menu. I mentioned that I prefer hot and spicy meals and, without saying a thing, they very kindly provided me with a free bowl of Vindaloo sauce – great stuff. Buttered Prawns with Puri were very good, nice and hot. The whole meal was declared superb. Well worth a visit.' Everything points to the Gulshan being in our TOP 100. We're thrilled that Merseyside has at last joined this elite group. Everyone agree? Price check: Extra Papadom 60p, CTM £6.75, Pullao Rice £1.95. Set meal from £10.40. Open daily, 5-11p.m.

JEWEL OF INDIA ©

9-11 Allerton Road, Woolton,
Liverpool, L22 ✆ **0151 421 1264**

Very popular establishment which, though newish, knows the business of curry. Owner Mr D. Miah has promised to give a discount to Curry Club members. Open noon-2p.m. and 5.30p.m.-midnight.

TAJ MAHAL

57 South Road, Waterloo,
Liverpool L1 ✆ **0151 928 7050**

'Superb restaurant – noted as being one of the best in north Liverpool. Pleasant decor and surroundings though the background music can be rather intrusive at times. Service rather slow but the food makes up for it,' P.S. 'Papadoms were very light and crispy. Vegetarian Thali very good,' G.F. Open noon-2.30p.m. and 5.30p.m.-midnight, till 2a.m. Friday and Saturday, Sunday 2p.m.-1a.m.

Newton-le-Willows

TASTE OF INDIA   NEW ENTRANT ©

56 Market Street, Newton-le-Willows ✆ **01925 228458**

Akhlaqul Ambia opened his Taste in 1986, and it is managed by F. Islam. 'Menu wide-ranging without being too long. Decor, very smart and cosy. Service, exceptionally polite and attentive. Food, quantities were very generous. Balti Exotic (£8.50) contained chicken, lamb and tiger prawns,' s.r.t.-f. Price check: Papadom 40p, CTM £6.25, South Indian Thali £9.95, Pullao Rice £1.50. Minimum charge £5. Open daily, 5.30p.m.-midnight. Branch: Haydock Tandoori, 17a Kenton Lane, Haydock.

Southport

LAL QILA NEW ENTRANT   ©

---

35 Bath Road, Southport   ✆ **01704 544991**

B. Miah has been owner-chef here since 1984, leaving front management to Ismail Choudhury. A full menu offers all the favourites. Price check: Papadom 40p, CTM £6.75, Pullao Rice £1.40. Minimum charge £10. Set meal £4.95. Open daily, noon-2p.m. and 5.30-11.30p.m., Sunday open all day. Branch: Lal Qila, 5 Red Lion Buildings, Liverpool Road, Maghull, L31, Lancashire.

Wirral

The Wirral is neither a town nor a county and, until 1965, was part of Cheshire. Since then the northern part — a small, digit-like, curry restaurant-rich peninsula between the rivers Mersey and Dee — has been part of Merseyside. Ellesmere Port (q.v.) remains in the Wirral but is in Cheshire. Here are the Merseyside Wirral towns in alphabetical order:

Egremont

TANDOORI MAHAL

24-26 King Street, Egremont, Wirral   ✆ **0151 639 5948**

Our regular here, D.B., calls it: 'An up-market Balti house. Again treated like a long-lost friend on arrival. Waiter remembered that Jacqui drinks Kingfisher and that she wanted an omelette with her Biryani and a mild curry sauce. The Biryani and sauce were superb. The sauce was more of a Bhuna than the usual Korma and was really tasty. Chicken Tikka Roghan Josh was excellent but maybe too many tomatoes. Vindaloo Sauce very hot, Chicken Tikka excellent. Service always superb.' On another occasion he said: 'CTM disappeared without a trace in double-quick time, even before I managed to get a dip! Tikka was done to perfection and superb sauce was hot. Food back to its best after a period of inconsistency.'

Heswall

HESWALL TANDOORI

52 Pensby Road, Heswall, Wirral   © 0151 342 8614

A cosy establishment seating only 32 diners. Essential to book on Friday and Saturday nights. 'Standards in this small restaurant remain consistently high. Dishes have a distinctive taste and one can always be sure of enjoyable food and attentive service,' Dr p.a.w.w. Open Sunday to Thursday, 6-11.30p.m., Friday and Saturday, 5.30p.m.-midnight.

RAJ BALTI   ©

513 Pensby Road, Thingwall, Nr Heswall,
Wirral   © 0151 648 5949

Mr Miah's small restaurant seats only 48 diners and we hear it gets busy, so be sure to book a table or you will miss out on all your favourite curries with accompaniments. Mr Miah has promised to give a discount to Curry Club members. Open 5-11.30p.m. Branches: Dilshad Balti, 132 Hagley Road, Oldswinford, Stourbridge; Dilshad Balti, Unit 6, Penkridge Retail Park, Wolverhampton Road, Penkridge.

Moreton

SURMA TANDOORI   NEW ENTRANT

271-273 Hoylake Road, Moreton, Wirral   © 0151 677 1331

'Decor and service very good, but we were the only lunchtime customers. Started with Popadoms and chutneys, which were good,

Tandoori Mixed Kebab, excellent, served on a sizzling-hot plate. Shamee Kebab could have been more spicy. Large portions of Pullau Rice left us stuffed but a special mention for the Mushroom Pullau which was superb,' D.B.

New Brighton

MAGIC SPICES

225 Seabank Road, New Brighton,
Wirral   © 0151 691 1919

Formerly in the Guide as the Khanum. Its rename and new staff have revived its fortunes. 'Nothing too much trouble. Meat Samosa light and flavourful. Chicken Jalfrezi probably the best I've ever tasted, and I've had a few,' R.K. He has, too – at the time of writing (April 1997) he has been to 186 different curry restaurants. He wants this one promoted to our TOP 100. Anyone agree? Our other Merseyside roving reporter, D.B., says: 'Asked the waiter to choose the starters, we couldn't make up our mind and were going to share anyway. Eight of us consumed a mountain of fresh Popadoms and chutneys while we waited. Impressive Onion Bhaji – good and spicy, Prawn Puri – excellent, Shish Kebab and Samosa – good, but the star was Stuffed Pepper – magnificent. Chicken Tikka Rogan Josh – superb, Chicken Tikka Bhuna a little too hot. Portions were a bit on the small side. I recommend a visit.' Reports, please.

Upton

UPTON HALAL BALTI HOUSE
NEW ENTRANT   BYO ©

167-169 Ford Road, Upton Village,
Wirral   © 0151 604 0166

Shofiul Miah's venture opened in 1996 and is not licensed, so BYO is a big attraction. Price check: Papadom 35p, CTM £6.80, Pullao Rice £1.60. Minimum charge £5. Set meal £9.50. Open every day except Tuesday, 5-11.30p.m. Branch: Manzil, 73 Grange Road East, Birkenhead.

Wallasey

GATE OF INDIA   NEW ENTRANT

5 Seaview Road, Wallasey, Wirral	✆ 0151 346 9676

'Comfort, service and decor excellent. Popadoms crisp and warm, chutneys were good but mango a bit runny. Mixed Kebab starter (Lamb Tikka, Chicken Tikka and Shammee Kebab) good. Balti Murgh Tikka very tasty, though too much sauce,' D.B.

SURUCHI TAKEAWAY   NEW ENTRANT

105 Wallasey Road, Wallasey, Wirral	✆ 0151 639 9404

We notice that the menu offers small and large portions and prices for all main dishes. What a great idea! D.B. may have the local attendance record here. Can anyone beat it (and prove it)? He has come here for a takeaway every Thursday evening, most Fridays and occasionally Saturdays since it opened. That's around 100 times a year, he tells us! And his girlfriend likes it too (just as well!) And he still visits other restaurants, and finds time to send us plentiful reports on them. We need more like you, Dave. 'Chicken Biryani (£3.70 small, £4.75 large) is excellent – ask for the omelette. Chicken Dhansak Madras-strength (£2.60 small, £3.60 large) is absolutely superb. CTM is thick and creamy, and when done to Madras-strength is exquisite. It's frequented by the cricket club. Owner Raj bends over backwards to ensure your meal is exactly what you require. Can't recommend highly enough,' D.B. Price check: Papadom 35p, CTM £2.95 small, £4.25 large, Pullao Rice £1.15. Open every day except Monday, 4p.m.-midnight, but open on Bank Holiday Mondays.

MIDDLESEX

Greater London

The county of Middlesex is very ancient. It once contained most of London, though this distinction became diminished when central London became autonomous during Victorian times. What was left of the county (located west and north of London) was completely 'abolished' when Greater London was formed in 1965, a move unpopular with Middlesex residents. Confusion exists because the Post Office still use Middlesex as a postal county. Postcodes add to the confusion. Enfield, for example, is EN1, 2, 3 in postal Middlesex but is in (Hertfordshire) GL county. Potters Bar EN6 is the same. Barnet is in postal Hertfordshire with EN4 and 5 codes. It used to be in geographical Middlesex but is now a GL borough! There is talk of reviving the county of Middlesex. It would certainly help beleaguered guide editors!

Edgware

SHREE GANESHA VEGETARIAN   √

**4 The Promenade, Edgwarebury Lane,
Edgware**   © 0181 958 2778

This superb vegetarian restaurant was opened in 1990 by Pamchandra Tiwari, with his wife Hemantika supervising the kitchen staff, making sure only the best was served from it. Bombay street food, such as Bhel Poori with tamarind chutney, features on the menu along with south Indian delights – Masala Dosa (wafer-thin pancake wrapped around potato curry made from lightly spiced curry leaves, sautéed onions, mustard seeds and turmeric) served with home-made coconut chutney – delicious. Unusual and tasty curries such as pumpkin are also a delight. Open 6-10.30p.m. Open for Sunday lunch.

Enfield

ALBANY TANDOORI   NEW ENTRANT

569 Hertford Road, Enfield   © 0181 805 3027

'It was a cold, breezy, rainy night. Autumn was here, never mind the season of mists and mellow fruitfulness. I was cold! To top it all the central heating had broken down and was in no danger of being fixed this century. There was no other course of action, we decided to have a takeaway and, even better, have it delivered. We chose: Chicken Tikka

Biriani, Sag Prawn, Pullao Rice and two Naans. It was lovely. The Naan was so soft you could have laid down and slept on it. Chicken Tikka had lots of white meat, Vegetable Curry was creamy and not too spicy,' Mr and Mrs S.

Feltham

INDIAN PALACE II   ©

414 Staines Road, Bedfont, Feltham   ✆ 0181 751 5822

Managed by Mr Tula Miah. Licensed, with Bangladeshi curries on the menu. House special: Chicken Chinta Puree £6.95. Price check: Papadom 40p, CTM £5.55, Pullao Rice £1.20. Minimum charge £7.95. Open noon-2.30p.m. and 6-11.30p.m.

Greenford

SUNDARBAN   NEW ENTRANT

**3 Odeon Parade, Sudbury Heights Avenue,
Greenford   ✆ 0181 900 0988**

Opened in 1984 by Mr Abdul. Bangladeshi curries on the menu. Open noon-2.30p.m. and 6-11.30p.m. Branch: Pinner Tandoori, Pinner.

Harrow

JHUPDI   NEW ENTRANT   √

235 Station Road, Harrow   ✆ 0181 427 1335

Licensed, vegetarian restaurant. 'Friendly, with no frills. Plenty of assistance with menu, varied choice, 18 starters, Kachoris, Mogo Chips and Bombay Tiffin. Masala Dosa, huge portion, best I've tasted,' D.D.

EASTERN EYE   ©

20 Station Parade, Northolt Road,
Harrow   © 0181 422 5323

Featured in our previous Guide and still a reliable source of good, tasty curries with all the usual accompaniments. Open noon-2.30p.m. and 6p.m.-midnight.

Hayes

THAMOULINEE   ©

128a Uxbridge Road, Hayes   © 0181 561 3723

Owned and run by husband and wife team Mr Anthony Pilla (front of house) and Mrs Jasmine Hyacinth (cook). Sri Lankan and south Indian curries served in this establishment. Plain or Masala Dosa or String Hoppers (£2.85) are good choices. Kothu Rotti (£4.10) is a chopped rotti bread with spicy vegetables. Choose, for a good starter, the Mixed Special (£2.50) — vadai, mutton roll, crab claw, prawns all deep-fried, accompanied by home-made coconut and tomato chutneys. Open for lunch daily except Tuesday and Sunday noon-2.30p.m. and for dinner daily except Tuesday 6p.m.-midnight.

Heathrow Airport

NOON OF TASTE OF INDIA   NEW ENTRANT

Mezzanine Floor, Terminal 1, Landside Area,
Heathrow Airport

No phone here because you don't book at airports, you just turn up and get a seat or queue. It's a 90-seater, open 16 hours a day, 7 days a week. The name Noon is nothing to do with lunchtime, nor is it high noon, because it's on the mezzanine. The owner is G.K. Noon, owner of a vast state-of-the-art factory in Greenford, which makes curry ready-meals for the likes of Sainsbury's and Waitrose, as well as under its own name of Noon. The Heathrow venture started up in 1996 and is a pilot (excuse the pun) for many more such outlets at airports, railway stations and motorway service stations. The idea is sound, and anyone reading these pages knows that such places are crying out for decent curry catering. The venture opened to a flourish of publicity, with the media implying that the restaurant would give tourists a first/last taste of the Great British curry. Of course that notion is nonsense, since this outlet is located at the hub of the British business air travelling network. Consequently it is more likely to be used by our readers – people who regularly eat such food around the country – rather than novice tourists. Future branches sited airside in international terminals will doubtless reach the tourists.

Meanwhile, what of this pilot branch? The place opens at 7a.m. for breakfast. For £4.95 you can have juice, tea or coffee, Masala Dosa or Idli with Sambar. Snacks and meals are available until 11p.m. The Shami Kebab Burger (£3.75) and the CTM burger (£3.50) both come in a sesame bun with thick-cut potatoes. Tandoori Raan Sandwich (£4.25) is spicy slices of roast lamb in bread slices on a salad, and Paneer Kebab Sandwich (£2.75) provides the vegetarian with lightly grilled cheese topped with mint. More substantial offerings give plenty of choice. Cooking is by Noon's exec chef, Ashok Kaul. I have known him since he was in charge of Air India's London cooking (1000 meals a day served in the air), and his qualifications are impeccable. This is an interesting venture. Your reports will be welcomed.

Hillingdon

HILLINGDON TANDOORI ©

6 Byron Parade, Uxbridge Road,
Hillingdon   ✆ 0181 561 7055

Mr Islam Uddin opened his Tandoori in 1985. He has proved himself in operating a competent and reliable curry house. All the usual formula curries and accompaniments on the menu, but good food nonetheless. Open noon-2.30p.m. and 6p.m.-midnight.

©	Curry Club discount (see p. 607)		Unlicensed
√	Vegetarian		Home delivery
BYO	Bring your own alcohol		service available

Hounslow

ASHNA   √

368 Staines Road, Hounslow   ✆ 0181 577 5988

A pure vegetarian restaurant. Try the specials, they are truly pleasurable. Masala Dosa and Bhel Poori are also on the menu.

HOUNSLOW BRASSERIE   NEW ENTRANT

47-49 Spring Grove Road, Hounslow   ✆ 0181 570 5535

'New owner Mr Naveed. The menu had changed but the chef had been retained – what a relief! Meat Samosas (£1.50) are absolutely outstanding, the pastry recipe, uniquely spiced, lean minced lamb and careful cooking create a perfect result – the holy grail of samosas! Chicken Tikka Bhuna (£5.40), Karahi Murgh (£4.95) and Lamb Bhuna (£4.40) with Pilau Rice and Bombay Alu (£2.75) did not last long – all superbly cooked and retained on hot plates,' T.E. Licensed. Price check: Papadom 40p, CTM £4.95, Pullao Rice £1.65. Open noon-2p.m. and 6p.m.-midnight.

KARAHI MASTER LAHORE TANDOORI CUISINE
NEW ENTRANT   ⊞ ©

795 London Road, Hounslow   ✆ 0181 572 2205

Situated opposite Hounslow Bus Garage since 1996. Proprietor S. Butt, and manager H. Dar, provide Pakistani and northern Indian food. Meat Karahi (£3.95) is a popular house special. Licensed. Price check: Papadom 25p, CTM £4.50, Pullao Rice £1.50. Open noon-11p.m., till midnight Friday and Saturday. Home delivery service on orders over £10.

Isleworth

REGALE INDIA CUISINE   ©

545 Twickenham Road, Isleworth   ✆ 0181 744 3118

Owned by Aziz Ahmed. A smallish restaurant with all your favourites on the menu, no surprises but still good, scrumptious, curries.

Northolt

EMPRESS OF INDIA   ©

40-42 Church Road, Northolt   ✆ **0181 845 4361**

Celebrating its 20th year in the restaurant trade. 'Congratulations, Ali, Zaman and Khan. You have proved yourselves to be successful restaurateurs, serving Britain's most popular formula curries,' s.w.

Northwood

RUCHITA   ©

19 Joel Street, Northwood   ✆ **01923 825546**

One of Northwood's local curry houses. Owner, M.A. Matlib, runs an efficient curry house, with no surprises but good for that curry-fix. Open noon-2.30p.m. and 6p.m.-11.30p.m., till midnight Friday and Saturday.

VICEROY   ©

48 High Street, Northwood   ✆ **01923 827856**

A well-managed and pleasant curry house, serving formula curries and accompaniments. Managing proprietor, Mofiz Miah, is a welcoming host. Open daily noon-2.30p.m. and 6p.m.-midnight.

Pinner

BALTI HUT   NEW ENTRANT   BYO

**435 Alexandra Avenue, Rayners Lane,
Pinner**   ✆ **0181 868 0007**

Unlicensed, but bring your own, no corkage. Authentic Baltis served in this simply decorated café-restaurant. Open 5-11.30p.m., till midnight Friday and Saturday.

PINNER TANDOORI NEW ENTRANT   ©

141 Marsh Road, Pinner   ℂ 0181 866 5474

A snug little (32-seat) restaurant, opened in 1993 by Mr Abdul. No surprises, formula curries on the menu. Worthy food at reasonable prices. A suitable venue for a night out. Open noon-2.30p.m. and 6-11.30p.m. Branch: Sundarban, Greenford.

VILLAGE TANDOORI   ©

426b Rayners Lane, Pinner   ℂ 0181 866 7363

Agreeable food and prices served at Lipu Miah's popular formula curry house. Open 6p.m.-midnight, till 12.30a.m. at weekends.

Ruislip

RUISLIP TANDOORI   ▦ ©

115 High Street, Ruislip   ℂ 01895 632859

Owned by K.B. Raichhetri, who enjoys explaining about his Nepalese house specials on the menu. Worth trying, since there are very few Nepalese restaurants in the British Isles. Open noon-2.30p.m. and 6p.m.-midnight. Home delivery service on orders over £12 within a 3-mile radius.

Southall

From a single acorn (*see* Maharaja), there is an ever-growing number of sweet/snack centres, cafés and restaurants to be found in Southall. Most are on the Uxbridge Road, called The Broadway as it passes through Southall. Others are on South Road and the Green. These places, and others around, cater largely for their indigenous Asian population. This may inhibit others from entering. It should not. In our experience everyone is treated equally and all are welcome. However, if you are looking for lush decor, candlelight, carnations for the lady, etc., etc., you will not find them in most Southall venues. Neither will you find 'haute cuisine' and an alcohol licence. But you will find good, authentic cuisine in straightforward, functional eating houses usually with formica-topped tables. The food is served fast, whether in self-service cafés or in sit-down restaurants. Below we examine our (and our correspondents') favourite eating holes. The indigenous population is largely Sikh and Punjabi, resulting in a fascinating and generally peaceful mix of Indian and Pakistani carnivores, enhanced by East African Asians. PS I'm still waiting to hear whether Sue Lawley would let me take Southall to her Desert Island as my luxury.

ADCHAY VIHAAR NEW ENTRANT

80 South Road, Southall ℭ 0181 574 9209

The recent changes of ownership give the clue that this restaurant is not widely frequented by the local Punjabi population. This is a pity, because they simply don't know what they are missing. Formerly the Bhararth, then the Sahaana, now the Adchay Vihaar, and all three serving Sri Lankan and south Indian food. And despite a tempting display of Samosas, Pakoras, and sweets, the place is rarely full. Nevertheless, new owners Mr and Mrs Kalanthar Shamsudeen persevere. Says D.B.A.C.: 'It is a small, café-style restaurant. Takeaway counter in the front of the shop and a tiny, simply decorated restaurant at the back. Licensed. We always order two large bottles of Cobra as we peruse the menu, but I always know exactly what I'm going to eat, it never changes. Pat, however, always has to know what the seafood specials are. If crab is on the blackboard that stands outside, he can hardly get the security locks on the car, wanting desperately to scramble into the restaurant. We always sit at the same table, too, by the small bar, right at the back and next to the large TV, sitting on the bar, which is usually playing Hindi/Sri Lankan movies or their equivalent to *Top of the Pops*. It never matters to me that I don't speak their language, I always know what's going on, who is in love with who, who is the villain. We order plain Papadoms with delicious home-made Coconut Chutney. Unlike Bangladeshi-run operations, it seems that Papadoms are only cooked to order, so there is always a small wait while we sip the Cobra. My usual order is Rasam, with curry leaves and flakes of fresh garlic floating on top, but lurking at the bottom are chillies and I get hiccups every time, so resort to my upside-down-with-a-glass-of-water trick – works every time! Followed by Masala Dosa and Sambar with more home-made Coconut Chutney. After that lot – portions are good –

I'm completely stuffed. Pat also chooses Rasam, it goes down without touching the sides and he helps me with mine, by picking up my chillies. On two separate occasions, he has had their blackboard daily special – Crab Curry. The first one was cooked by the proprietor's wife, the second by the proprietor himself. They were both delicious, but Mrs Shamsudeen had the upper hand. We do see her sometimes, she pops out of the kitchen to say hello and we thank her for a wonderful meal – cost, incidentally, under £20 for two. Cash or cheques only. Very highly recommended.' Open for lunch daily except Tuesday 11.30a.m.-3p.m. and 6p.m.-midnight.

BABU TANDOORI

156 The Broadway, Southall   ℂ **0181 574 1049**

Reasonably-priced food with friendly staff make for a good night out at this formula curry house.

BRILLIANT   BEST PUNJABI RESTAURANT TOP 100   ©

72-74 Western Road, Southall   ℂ **0181 574 1928**

This restaurant was established in 1975, when one Mr Anand settled in the UK, having been forced to flee from troubled Kenya. He brought with him a large energetic family, of which more later, and a tradition of catering going back generations.

Mr Anand and family deliver authentic Kenyan Asian Punjabi curries in their cheerful restaurant. Changes are afoot here, with expansion plans having added a well-decorated upstairs dining room. And still the place is full to bursting. So much so, in fact, that even more expansion plans will soon add the next-door venue onto the main room. The Brilliant has always been popular with Asians as a family restaurant. The tables are large, and groups of 10 to 20 are the norm. Half of these will be kids, and Asian kids are always well-behaved at the restaurant, loving the experience as much as their parents. Says D.B.A.C.: 'It is decorated in burgundy and I always think it's rather like being in someone's home, a large dinner party, but with formica tables. Nephew Gulu is always there to welcome his guests. There is also a large photograph of him with Prince Charles! The last time we ate here, we had just picked up my twin sister Helena and her two children (Lucas aged four, Harry aged one) from the airport, they had been skiing.

Thinking of an early light dinner, I had thrown two frozen pizzas into the boot of the car, but since their flight had arrived two hours late, the pizzas were not going to suffice. So, I suggested that we went for a curry and Pat said 'BRILLIANT'. We had not booked, but the restaurant was not full (yet). Asians like to eat late, making a night out of their entertainment, so we were lucky. Lucas was tired and being difficult. Gulu offered the upstairs room for him to rest, but he said no. Fortunately, after he had a quick nibble on a Butter Chicken leg, he went to sleep and we could enjoy our meal in peace. Warm Papadoms with their famous and unique mint (with a hint of chilli) chutney and pickled carrots. We ordered huge portions of Butter Chicken and Jeera Chicken (both on the bone), served with a heap of salad and tackled them very well indeed, including Harry. Next came the Keema Paneer and Murgh Karahi, strongly spiced with fenugreek and cumin. Pat ordered something chilli-hot with prawns, all served in beaten copper detchis, carefully balanced on their own individual heaters. Rice and hot, soft Nan and Roti breads accompanied. All this was washed down by Cobra lager and a bottle of house wine. When we left, there wasn't a table left.' 'Being an *aficionado* of Indian food I eat at this restaurant,' A.M. 'First visit to this renowned TOP 100. Impressed by the range of dishes offered which I'm sure led to a severe case of over-ordering. Having said that, it was good to sample such delights as Karahi Gosht (£6), Masala Chicken (£5), Meat Samosa (£1.40), Bhindi (£3.50), Rice, Naan, etc., not forgetting the awesome Karahi Mexican Mix (£4.50). Standard of service good, will definitely return,' D.B. 'Had to return to this restaurant as soon as possible. My fellow curryholics were impressed with the excellent Palak Chicken, superb Karahi Chicken and astounding Masala Fish (Talapia), a Kenyan-style dish – not one I would have chosen but in my opinion was the best dish of the meal. Lives up to its name,' B.D. Service charge 10%. Decidedly remains in our TOP 100. Open Tuesday to Sunday noon-3p.m. and 6-11p.m. The upstairs party room, with its own bar, is available for hire.

KARAHI TANDOORI KABAB CENTRE

161 The Broadway, Southall   ℂ **0181 574 3571**

Walking past A.F. Choudhury's restaurant, you are immediately attracted to the display cabinets containing all sorts of tempting snacks such as Pakora, Tikki, Samosa, Indian sweets, etc. The restaurant – café-style with formica tables – seats 66 diners. It is clean and waiter-served. Fabulous Tandooris, Kebabs and breads, cooked by the chefs on show. Curries are also cooked in front of you and are quite delicious. Gaining ground in Southall are street foods such as Bhel Poori and Gol Goppas with Jeera Pani (cumin water). 'If you have never had a Gol Goppa – go for it! They can be an acquired taste, since black salt is used and the best description of that is sea water with a touch of sewage. Sounds gruesome I know, but once you have the taste for it, there's no going back. The Gol Goppas served at Karahi Tandoori are – I think – rather mild, but lovely nevertheless. The first and best ones I have ever had were in Bombay, in a dirty little restaurant just off Collaba (the main drag of Bombay). Pat and I were staying at the Taj Mahal Intercontinental and were in Burlington's (posh boutique). I was just in the process of getting a salwar kameez made when who should walk in with her Harrods carrier bag but Namita Panjabi, owner of London's Chutney Mary and now Veeraswamy. She, of course, immediately took charge of the situation, instructing the ancient tailor in colour, design, etc. She decided we all ought to go for lunch. She knew a wonderful place – "Don't tell my mother, it's so dirty, she'll be horrified." It wasn't dirty, it was filthy. We stood outside, a stream of murky water ran past us in the gutter. Namita negotiated the choice with the chap behind the counter, while we negotiated the gutter. We all watched the – well, you can call him the cook. He was the assembler of the Bhel Poori. This is a small, deep-fried disc, sitting on top is finely-chopped potato and onion, a blob of thick spicy tamarind chutney and a flick of thick, creamy home-made natural yoghurt. After a few of those, you move to the next assembler for a Gol Goppa. He picks up one of the puffed balls, breaks a hole in it, fills it up with a very watery but spicy Imli chutney (looks rather like what's in the gutter) and pops it into your katuri. There is only one way to eat this and that is to open your mouth wider than at the dentist and all at once. I wonder if Gob Stopper (those huge, coloured balls that we all had as children) is some sort of derivation,' D.B.A.C. Great prices and gets very busy since it is immensely popular with the young trendy Asians at weekends. Unlicensed. Open 9a.m.-midnight.

LAHORE KARAHI AND TANDOORI   ⊞ BYO

162-164 The Broadway, Southall   ℰ 0181 813 8669

A huge plate-glass window with sliding doors dominates this frontage. The kitchen is open and stainless steel, and runs down one side, the tandoor oven being in view from the street. You sit at simple tables towards the front of the restaurant, or at the back in more glamorous ones with high-backed padded seats. At the simple café-style open kitchen, you can watch the chefs prepare your food. 'Better to order something from the tandoor – e.g., Reshmi Kebabs with Nan Bread, this is where they excel. There is also another counter with Bhel Poori, Paan and sweets which make an interesting change. On our last trip we tried the Bhel Poori with Dhai Vada (one of Pat's favourites). It was good but, for me, nothing beats Bombay (India that is, not the name of a takeaway on the high street!)' [*See* previous entry.] 'Waiters have a leisurely approach to service but are happy about it,' D.B.A.C. Home delivery service is free locally.

MADHU'S BRILLIANT BIGGEST EVENT AWARD
TOP 100   ©

39 South Road, Southall   ℰ 0181 574 1897

Opened in 1980 by J.K., K.K., Sanjay and Sanjeev Anand, nephews of the great Mr Anand of the Brilliant (*see* entry). You will often find Sanjay in the restaurant, welcoming diners, and as old friends you will know which one he is, because of his very distinctive laugh. Our Guide was the first to recognize this restaurant, back in 1984, and at that time the clientele was mostly Asian. Today, and dozens of awards later, there are as many non-Asians as Asians enjoying the food and ambience here. The latter is rather basic, though the company is always animated, the Asians sitting on large tables in family groups, kids and all, the Brits in twos and fours and more reticent, but enjoying it nonetheless. The food is typical Punjabi and far removed from the Bangladeshi curry house formula. Cooking is led by brother Sanjeev (affectionately called Mint). The Anand signature dishes, Butter and Jeera Chicken (both £6.60 for half and on the bone), are an absolute must when dining here. The restaurant seats 104 on two floors, the upper floor, toilets and second bar being reached by a large spiral staircase at the front of the restaurant. 'Sanjay and his wife Reena came to India with us last September, and Sanjay divulged Mint's secret recipe for Jeera Chicken in front of our Gourmet Group in a small hotel, called Shikarbadi (hunting lodge). This hotel is beautiful but with paper-thin walls. Sanjay found this out belatedly, and still blushes over what was said in his room, when he thought no one could hear, but that's another story!' D.B.A.C. 'We were soon sitting with a bottle of good French wine, well-chilled, with two very thin, very crispy Popadoms with three chutneys. Jeera Chicken tasted just as it had in the garden at the Shikarbadi but we missed the sunshine!! Makhani Chicken, Masala Fish, Pilau Rice with Peas and fried Bhatura (very light and crispy). Impressed,' G.M. 'Onion Bhajias £2.50 (huge portion) are in fact onion rings, coated in a lightly spiced batter and fried, crispy and wonderful. Ask for Pakorian Raitha (£2),' D.M. 'Had to wait for the doors to open, but well worth it. Karahi Mexican Mix (£4.50) highly recommended, Karahi Chicken (£6.50) full of flavour. Karahi Gosht, lamb a little tough. Peshwari Nan (£2) and freshly cooked Rotis (£1) complemented the meal. Friendly service,' D.B. 'The restaurant may not be to everyone's taste, especially if you are expecting curry house food – you won't get it, they specialize in Punjabi cuisine, with curries such as Pakal Lamb in a rich gravy. Have been many times and enjoy their food,' A.M. Sanjay (the entrepreneur of the family) and Mint run the biggest Asian wedding outside-catering business in the country, with two or three engagements a week – 1000 guests is not uncommon. It is no mean feat, but they have developed techniques to make it look easy. Definitely a TOP 100 restaurant. Price check: Papadom 50p, CTM £6.50, Pullao Rice £2. Three-course set menu £15. Open daily except Tuesday 12.30-3p.m. and 6-11.30p.m.

MAHARAJA

171-173 The Broadway, Southall   © **0181 574 4564**

In a remarkable coincidence, I met an old Punjabi the other day who told me something more about Southall's Asian history. Retired now – he is in his nineties – he had been employed, as were a number of other Punjabis, at the now defunct local AEC bus factory in 1937, and naturally he lived nearby, in Southall. But there were no 'ethnic' restaurants then, and getting spices required a trip by trolley bus to Shepherd's Bush, then on by Tube to Tottenham Court Road, to go to Grafton Way, where London's only Asian grocery, the Bombay Emporium, had been established a few years earlier. I used to visit this wonderful shop myself in the early 1950s. It has long gone, though its descendant is the huge manufacturer B.E. with their Rajah brand. But, to this day, people ask me if the shop is still there. My Punjabi friend also told me that he went to Southall's very first Indian restaurant on its opening day in 1955. It was owned then, and now, by his nephews Tesgor Veper and Ramadan Mogadon, and they named it after their local Maharaja, back home in Kanchnipur. This makes it amongst the first handful of curry houses to have opened in Britain, let alone being the original curry restaurant in Southall. I first dined here myself way back in the 1950s, but it declined somewhat during the 1970s. I am delighted to say that, quite by chance, we discovered recently that it has revived, and is way above average now. Says D.B.A.C.: 'My social worker sister Rachael was in town and joined us on a provisioning trip to Southall. She's been with us before, and we assumed she liked its ethnicity. But Rachael's a fussy eater. She doesn't like this and she doesn't like that. Meat is in; veg is out. For most carnivores, Southall is a haven. But not for our Rach. After loading the car with spices and stores, we felt hungry. "Sagoos OK?", I said. "Isn't there anywhere else we could go?" asked Rachael. "What's wrong with Sagoos?" It turned out that she was shocked that her Sagoos chicken curry had a bone, and that there was no Chicken Korma. She was not impressed by the lack of G&T and Chardonnay and there were certainly no obsequious waiters running round after her. Pat remembered that the Maharaja did curry house food, though we'd not been there for years. The menu outside got the thumbs up from Rachael: it had the golden word – Korma. An even bigger smile appeared on her face when she saw it had a large bar, stocking everything conceivable. She may not have noticed the lovely stained glass peacock behind the bar, nor the smart redec in blues and greys, while she nibbled contentedly on her Papadom. It was early in the evening, but already the waiting area was busy with whites collecting takeaways. There was plenty of seating, which filled up rapidly with Asian families. Rachael's Korma came and went – she almost licked the plate clean. I got one taste – it was nutty, not sickly. My CTM and Pat's Prawn Madras were decidedly good, and the Bombay Potato was magical, so unlike the formula method where it is enrobed in onion and capsicum. Here potato cubes are lightly fried in cumin seed. Even carnivorous R. actually liked it. In two phrases, I'd describe the Maharaja as the formula done better, and an ideal starting place for those unsure about the delights of Southall. Our meal for three with drinks cost £42.' Open noon-3p.m. and 6-11.30p.m.

MOTI MAHAL

94 The Broadway, Southall   ⓒ **0181 574 7682**

A busy, unlicensed café-style restaurant. Great spicy curries on the menu.

OMI'S TOP 100

1 Beaconsfield Road, Southall   ⓒ **0181 571 4831**

Situated off South Road on a side street. The shop front stands slightly back from the pavement, making room for the parking of vehicles. A short menu above the counter describes what is on offer, along with the Specials of the Day. Mykesh Kharbanda is the owner-chef. Since we were taken here years ago by Indian journalist K.N. Malik ('I want to show you Indian food at its best'), we can safely say this is the Indian's Indian restaurant. We love his food and adore Mykesh's idiosyncrasies. The place doubles for van-hire. So one phone call can order you lovely, soft, delicious Garlic Naan and noisy diesel-fumey Transit Van! With just 42 seats, it gets harder to find a space, especially in the evenings. It has the usual plastic tables and chairs, making for a clean and tidy restaurant, but it's the freshly-cooked food you go for. Open 10.30a.m.-9p.m., till 9.30p.m. Friday and Saturday. Closed on Sunday. Remains in our TOP 100.

POORIMA

16 South Road, Southall   ⓒ **0181 813 8424**

'A snack bar rather than a restaurant. Decor non-existent, surroundings typically bare and plain with long glass display counter, piled high with Indian sweets, then Samosas and similar snacks. Then containers of dhal, curry, vegetables and daily specials. Reasonable choice of food all at rock-bottom prices. Helpful staff. Absolutely outstanding food, quite the best home-style Indian food. Paratha was so delicious I ate the lot,' H.C.

©	Curry Club discount (see p. 607)		Unlicensed
√	Vegetarian	⊞	Home delivery
BYO	Bring your own alcohol		service available

SAGOO AND THAKHAR ASIAN TANDOORI
CENTRES TOP 100   BYO

The Roxy, 114 The Green, Southall	ℂ 0181 574 2579
157 The Broadway, Southall	ℂ 0181 574 3476

Owners Mr Sagoo and Mr Thakhar (but who is who?) opened their restaurants to serve the local community morning, noon and night. Strategically located at either end of Southall. 'Clientele is predominantly Asian, you do see a few whites now and again (me, for example). The Roxy is the larger, but they both serve identical food (almost). The Broadway branch is two shops deep, there is plenty of seating. The Roxy has two shop-fronts, one with delicious Indian sweets piled high in the window, the other is for dining in, but a lot of customers come to collect takeaways. When you enter, there may be a queue even outside the door, so join it (it's not like Haslemere Somerfield who can make a queue from one customer) – it really doesn't take long before it is your turn. Long glass counters display tempting savoury snacks (Bhajias, Kebabs, Samosas, Aloo Tikki, Dahi Vasa, etc.), curries (Murgh Masala – on the bone, Bombay Potato, Sag Paneer, Sag Gosht and more, all cold but will be reheated in the microwave on request), Channa Dhal, Rice (Plain, Pullao and Biryani) and breads. Pick up a tray and tell the chap behind the counter what you want and whether you are eating in or taking out. Portions are generous and I have to restrain myself from over-ordering. When you have paid (cash or cheques only), take your tray to the other room and seat yourself,' D.B.A.C. 'The absolute curry experience – should be compulsory for all members to visit! Sample the vast range of dishes on offer – all authentic and served up in a no-nonsense style. We ate vast quantities of food, including Pakoras, Dall (black bean), Chicken and Meat Curries, Rotis and rice. Service with a smile, staff friendly. Highly recommended – must be very high in the TOP 100,' D.B. They also serve a wonderful chutney, sticks of carrot, slices of onion, embalmed in a tamarind and yoghurt sauce – delicious, I can't get enough of it. You can BYO as far as we know, which all makes for a great meal out. Fresh fruit juice and Lassi are available. The Roxy is licensed for lager. If Sue Lawley won't let me take Southall, may I please take the Roxy? Open 10a.m.-10.30p.m., till 11p.m. on Friday, Saturday and Sunday. It is high in our TOP 100.

SHAHANSHAH VEGETARIAN   🍵 √ ©

60 North Road, Southall   ℂ 0181 574 1493

Opened in 1994 by partners B.S. Gill and S.S. Johl. They specialize in
vegetarian cooking from north and south India. Indian sweets are
made on the premises, so you can be sure they are fresh. The dining
area seats 22 and is unlicensed. House delights include Cheese and
Tomato Pakoras. Price check: Papadom 50p, no CTM here, Pullao
Rice £1.50. Minimum charge £3. Open daily except Tuesday 10a.m.-
8p.m. Branch: Shahanshah Vegetarian, 17 South Road, Southall.

TANDOORI EXPRESS ON JALEBI JUNCTION

93 The Broadway, Southall   ℂ 0181 571 6782

Opened in 1986 by Abdul Chaudhury who wanted to open a restaurant that would appeal to the local young and trendy population. It
is a bright and colourful venue which does indeed attract the young. It
is often full of chattering, bright young Asians babbling on in animated Southall cockney accents. A richly painted and decorated rickshaw
can be seen outside on the wide pavement which enhances the environment. Also a cook makes Jalebis, those crispy, deep-fried squiggles,
immersed in syrup, right there on the pavement. So if you've not seen
it done, here's the only place in Britain we know of that does it on view.
Great Pakistani curries and fresh breads are a big pull, along with
snacks such as Samosas, Pakoras, etc. There is also a vast sweet counter
to pile on the pounds (weight that is, not the bill). Good prices as is
the norm in Southall. Open 9a.m.-11p.m.

TANDOORI KABAB CENTRE

163 The Broadway, Southall   ℂ 0181 571 5738

Owned by Dalawar Chadhuri in 1965 and can claim to be one of the
first Pakistani restaurants. Pakistani food cooked at its best, the Punjabi
way, with lots of meat dishes (anything that comes out of the tandoor)
being specialities. Frequented mostly by Asians with a few whites. A
busy, friendly establishment. When I recently filmed in Southall with
the BBC for their show *Good Food*, the crew insisted on eating here "cos
of its buzz'. Director Nichola Silk and I, however, stayed loyal to
Sagoos, where we'd also been filming. Crew verdict on both was excel-

lent. Free home delivery service on orders over £10 and within a 5-mile radius. Branch: Tandoori Express on Jalebi Junction, Southall.

Stanmore

PASSAGE TO INDIA   NEW ENTRANT   ©

---

905 Honeypot Lane, Stanmore   ✆ **0181 952 9151**

Licensed restaurant for 42 diners, serving northern Indian food, CTM being a house special. Owned by S. Miah and managed by S. Rahman. Price check: Papadom 45p, CTM £5.35, Pullao Rice £1.50. Set menu £4.95. Open noon-2.30p.m. and 5.30p.m.-midnight. Branch: Balti Paradise, Sunbury-on-Thames, Surrey; Romna, 132 Seymour Place, London w1.

Sudbury

GANGES   ▦ ©

---

769 Harrow Road, Sudbury   ✆ **0181 904 0011**

Fully air-conditioned and licensed restaurant seating 45. Opened by Mr Haque in 1985 with Naz running front of house. A Bangladeshi-style curry house with all the usual curries and accompaniments, from Korma to Madras. Nepalese dishes also feature. Price check: Papadom 40p, CTM £5.95, Pullao Rice £1.60. Set menu £5.95. Open noon-2.30p.m. and 6p.m.-midnight. Home delivery on orders over £12.

Teddington

BILAS   ©

---

4 Broad Street, Teddington   ✆ **0181 977 1529**

'Offers all the usual things one expects from a well-run restaurant. Good range of dishes including Balti. Good quality of food at reasonable prices, service friendly and we were not hurried,' D.B. Owner Z.T. Froki.

Twickenham

RAWALPINDI TANDOORI GRILL   NEW ENTRANT   ⊞ ©

62 King Street, Twickenham   ℭ 0181 892 3082

Opened in 1962 by Ashad Miah. Serving Bangladeshi and Pakistani (halal) curry house food. Moghlai delicacies and Persian dishes feature highly on their menu. Price check: Papadom 45p, CTM £6.50, Pullao Rice £1.85. Open noon-2.30p.m. and 6p.m.-midnight. Home delivery free on orders over £15 and within a 3-mile radius. Under £15, £2.50 delivery charge.

SHEESH MAHAL   NEW ENTRANT

London Road, Twickenham   ℭ 0181 892 3303

'The only good thing I can say is the service was friendly and attentive and the place had a clean, comfortable feel,' v.mcc.

STANDARD TANDOORI   ©

68 Heath Road, Twickenham   ℭ 0181 892 7072

Owned by A. Moin. He opened his 'standard' curry house way back in 1975. Good food at reasonable prices, you will not be disappointed. A reliable night out. Open noon-2.30p.m. and 6p.m.-midnight.

Wembley

Rapidly gaining ground as the second Southall. Unlike Southall, its large Gujarati/East African population gives Wembley food a different (predominantly vegetarian) taste from Southall. As with Southall, there are many good sweet/snack shops/cafés and restaurants crammed with Indian goodies. Here are your favourites:

CHETNA'S BHEL PURI   TOP 100   √

420 High Road, Wembley   ℭ 0181 903 5989

A vegetarian restaurant with vegan dishes. 'You often have to queue here. We waited on the pavement until they called out our number, but it is well worth it. They do deluxe Masal Dosas, and a great Vegetarian Thali main course. Their Bhel Puri is gorgeous, with its crispy, crunchy textures, and its tart, hot and savoury tastes, and there is a variant called Alloo Papdi Chaat. Strangely enough serves pizzas alongside curries from south India,' J.M. 'Pat was impressed to see Pau Bhaji on the menu, which he last ate in Delhi at the Taj Palace, but it was considerably more than £2.10,' D.B.A.C. Open noon-3p.m. and 6-10.30p.m.

CURRY CRAZE TOP 100 ©

8-9 The Triangle, Wembley Hill Road, Wembley © 0181 902 9720

Owned by Mr and Mrs S.K. Malhorta, she is also the head chef, specializing in East African/Punjabi food. See the Brilliant (above) for more information. Opened in 1980 and proving to be a reliable restaurant. 'Excellent, each year there is a conference for diving instructors in London, for the past two years it has been in Wembley and both times our party has gone to the Curry Craze – we have not been disappointed yet. After eating our fill of Papadoms, we started the proceedings with full Jeera Chicken (£6.50 for half) between seven. Good value in terms of standard of cooking,' S.N. When there is a concert or football match at the Stadium, a set dinner buffet is provided. 'Dishes were full of spices. The Methi Chicken (£3.75) was of above-average quality. Pilau Rice was fluffy and the Tandoori Naan (£1.20) excellent. Service was very friendly. Certainly worth its place in the TOP 100,' M.F. Price check: Papadom 50p, CTM £6.25, Pullao Rice £1.95. Service charge 10%. Open daily except Tuesday 6-11p.m. Stays in our TOP 100.

GEETANJAI NEW ENTRANT

16 Court Parade, Watford Road, Wembley © 0181 904 5353

From the outside, it looks nothing more than a typical curry house, but you would be wrong to pass it by. A well-decorated, stylish restaurant, linen tablecloths, copper serving bowls, high-backed padded chairs and plants a-plenty. If you usually order an Onion Bhaji, go for the Corn version instead – served with chutney for £2.90, it makes a refreshing change. Open noon-3p.m. and 6p.m.-midnight.

KARAHI KING   BYO

213 East Lane, Wembley   ✆ 0181 904 2760

Following a fire, everything is back to normal at the Karahi King in
Wembley. Fabulous food — fabulous tandoori (including the breads),
curries for meat-eaters and vegetarians. Served up by the same staff.
Open noon-midnight. No credit cards. Unlicensed, no corkage, so
BYO.

KARAHI RAJA   NEW ENTRANT   BYO

195 East Lane, Wembley   ✆ 0181 904 5553

Opened in 1993 by M. Ahmad. He runs an unlicensed restaurant, seating 45. He welcomes his guests to bring a bottle with them for their
enjoyment of a night out. Northern Indian curries are on the menu
with Nihari (spring lamb) being a house special. Price check: Papadom
30p, CTM £4.95, Pullao Rice £1.60. Open noon-midnight.

MARU'S BHAJIA HOUSE   √

230 Ealing Road, Alperton, Wembley   ✆ 0181 903 6771

Another family from East Africa, bringing their unique style of vegetarian cooking with them. This restaurant, opened by Maru over 20
years ago, provides superior vegetable curries and accompaniments.
Their Bhajias are the real thing, and they are even spelt correctly, rather
than the formula Bhaji. Try their Potato Bhajias, besan-batter-coated,
deep-fried and served with tamarind (imli) chutney for a real treat to
die for. Open noon-8.45p.m., till 9.45p.m. on Friday and Saturday,
closed Monday. It is unlicensed, alcohol is not permitted, which is a
shame because this policy alienates some clientele.

MARUTI BHEL PURI   √

238a Ealing Road, Wembley   ✆ 0181 903 6743

A vegetarian restaurant serving melt-in-the-mouth delights, such as
Dosas with Sambar and, of course, the namesake Bhel Puri. Try their
Karahi Corn-on-the-Cob. 'All fantastic stuff for the lucky residents of
Wembley. I wish I lived nearer,' D.B.A.C. Open daily except Tuesday
noon-10p.m. Fully licensed.

PALM BEACH NEW ENTRANT

17 Ealing Road, Wembley   ✆ 0181 900 8664

A Sri Lankan and south Indian restaurant, but this doesn't mean there is no meat on the menu. Alongside the Dosas, Vadias and Hoppers, you will find Mutton Ceylon Curry – tender lamb, steeped in a richly spiced, meaty, juicy gravy. Decorations are relaxed, with batiks and wood carvings. Open daily except Tuesday noon-3p.m. and 6-11.30p.m. Branch: Palm Beach, 18 The Avenue, Ealing, London W13.

RAJBHOG NEW ENTRANT   BYO

140 Ealing Road, Alperton, Wembley   ✆ 0181 903 9395

A similar establishment to Sakoni (*see* entry below), selling Bombay street food and other snacks such as Bhajias. South Indian dishes – Idli (white, sponge-like UFO), Dosa (wafer-thin lentil pancake stuffed with potato curry lightly spiced with mustard seeds and curry leaves) and Sambar (a watery, yellow-coloured curry, thickened with lentils, medallions of carrot and potato with fingerlike pieces of drumstick) are must-haves, because they are quite delicious. Open 11a.m.-10p.m., till 10.30p.m. on Friday, Saturday and Sunday.

SAKONI NEW ENTRANT

119-121 Ealing Road, Alperton,
Wembley   ✆ 0181 903 9601

Says D.B.A.C.: 'Not licensed, it is not allowed, so that will have some customers marching straight to Rajbhog, including me. When Pat and I visit India, we have a little ritual. Air India always lands at some hideous hour like midnight, so by the time we get to the hotel it's the small hours. On a recent trip to Delhi we stayed at the Imperial, which is a lovely old grand hotel, if a little run-down. After dumping our luggage, it's time for our ritual – to go to the 24-hour coffee shop and order Samosas and Pakoras, and two large, brown, pint-sized bottles of Indian beer. The 24-hour coffee shop had three problems. Firstly, no staff – the manager had to prod them out of bed. Secondly, when they sleepily arrived, they told us no Indian food is served at that time, only club sandwiches, burgers and chips and, as for the beer, it's only served from room service. Asked if we could get our food served by room service, they replied, "No, sir. Food after midnight only in 24-hour coffee shop." Their silly rules didn't stop there. The next day our friend Greta Chana took me to have my hands painted with henna. We returned to the hotel for a lunchtime chota peg, and I sat on the terrace in the sun, waiting for my hands to dry. Did they now have Samosas and Pakoras? Yes, they did, but for food you must sit at an adjacent table on the lawn, only drinks are allowed to be consumed at the tables on the terrace! We gave up and changed to the Taj Hotel.' So no drink at the Sakoni, but there's no problem getting authentic Indian food. It serves only: 'Real Indian vegetarian snacks in a pleasant and informal atmosphere. Service good and quick. Run by Gujaratis who know about the food and tradition. Generous portions. Chutneys freshly prepared and are not removed from the tables every few minutes, which makes a change from most other Indian restaurants. No alcohol, but it is not needed with Indian food. Lassi is excellent,' b.h. (b.h. must know the Imperial.) Tell that to our Indian friends, who are all partial to a large Black Label or three before dinner! Open 11a.m.-11.30p.m. Branch: Sakoni, 129 Ealing Road, Wembley.

TASTIEY LAND   NEW ENTRANT

537 High Road, Wembley   © 0181 900 9919

Sri Lankan and south Indian curries feature highly on the menu in this restaurant. The set meals are good value, offering good and varied food. Egg Godhamba Rotti, Veechu Rotti, Katta Sambol, Mutton Curry all for £3.95 including a free Papadom. Open 6-11p.m.

WEMBLEY COTTAGE   NEW ENTRANT   ©

305 Harrow Road, Wembley Triangle   © 0181 902 4039

One of the few Nepalese restaurants, even fewer on the ground than south Indian ones. Opened in 1995 by Mr T. Moniz with Baban in the kitchen cooking up all those unusual delights which include Chicken Chowla or Bhutuwa. 'This Nepalese restaurant has been recommended to me by so many of my colleagues,' c.t. Price check: Papadom 40p, CTM £5.95, Pullao Rice £1.80. Open noon-2.30p.m. and 6-11.30p.m.

West Drayton

PALACE TANDOORI NEW ENTRANT

Station Road, West Drayton   © 01895 431206

'As undeniable curryholics, my wife and I found our food paradise.
The food was the best we had ever tasted – could not find a single
fault. Free Pakora was delicious, while we waited for our starters,
Murgh Chat and Prawn Puri, mouthwatering. Jeera Chicken, Murghi
Massalla, Sag Aloo, Mushroom Rice and Keema Nan, portions so
large, got the better of us. I only wish I lived next door and not 120
miles away!' A.D.W.

Whitton

JOLLY'S TANDOORI NEW ENTRANT

2 Hounslow Road, Whitton   © 0181 894 3122

Particularly stylish decor, bright and chintzy. Good basic menu.
Extremely willing to accommodate individual requests.

NORFOLK

Diss

DISS TANDOORI   ©

1-3 Shelfanger Road, Diss   © 01379 651685

Opened in 1986 by Mobashir Ali (front) and Jalal Khara (chef) and
seats 52 diners. J.S. and R.S.P. visited at about the same time, but presumably they are not acquainted. J.S. thought it 'expensive, busy and
ordinary, with clean tables, but the spaces between are cramped. The
portions were small to medium, and the service adequate – the waiter
seeming to hover.' But he got an amazing £7 discount off the £30 bill
as a Curry Club member. R.S.P. says: 'Though it is not very big, one
does not feel cramped, as the tables are set far enough apart to gener-

ate a feeling of spaciousness. Our meal for two was £36.' [No mention of a discount.] 'Everything was delicious, full of flavour and tastefully served in quantities that were more than generous. Service was deft, efficient and friendly without being familiar. Unreservedly enjoyable and good value.' Make of this what you will, my gentle readers! There must be easier jobs than being a Guide editor ... lion-taming, perhaps? Price check: Papadom 6op, CTM £6.25, Pullao Rice £1.85. Open daily for lunch and dinner.

Great Yarmouth

BOMBAY NITE   NEW ENTRANT   ©

25a King Street, Great Yarmouth   © 01493 331383

Raza is the owner and Louise Hughes is manager. It has been open since 1985 and is one of those restaurants to have escaped our net. Question from P.J.: 'Whyever don't you mention our favourite restaurant?' Answer: because no one had ever told us about it. (See comment in previous entry.) We hear well of the Roast Chicken Massala (£6.25) and the Sylhet Supreme (£5.95). Price check: Papadom 4op, CTM £5.95, Pullao Rice £1.50. Minimum charge £12.50. Service charge 10%. Open daily 6p.m.-midnight.

King's Lynn

INDIA GATE   ©

41 St James Street, King's Lynn   © 01553 776489

Owned and managed by D.S. and A.S. Pabla, this 50-seater (which opened in 1992) is now a well-patronized local. 'Decor pastel blues and pinks with ornate plaster coving round the ceiling and ornate plaster frames round the Indian picture scenes. Food absolutely first-class throughout. Value for money,' M.B. Curry Club discounts at lunchtimes only. Price check: Papadom 4op, CTM £6.05, Pullao Rice £1.60. Minimum charge £7.50. Open daily for lunch and from 6p.m.-midnight.

North Walsham

PRINCE OF BENGAL   ©

13a Mundesley Road, North Walsham   ✆ 01692 500119

'I even talked my mother in-law into going, and she was adamant she
did not like curry. She had a mild Shahi Korma and is looking forward
to returning for a hotter dish! We hope to keep on going there for
many years,' c.b. 'I have been going there about once a week since it
opened some five years ago. The standard of food is unfailingly superb,
and the general ambience of the establishment is warm and friendly.
The owner, Mr Folik Miah Choudhury, can be found in the restaurant
welcoming guests in for their meal, and always finds time for a chat
with his guests. As a measure of my regard for this establishment, I
continued to go there by bicycle – a round trip of 13 miles – when pre-
vented from driving for six months because of failing eyesight. I am
happy to say that, since having a cataract operation, I am now able to
go by car,' Dr w.f.c. Open noon-2.30p.m. and 6-11.30p.m. Branches:
Prince of Bengal, 40 Cromer Road, Sheringham; Prince of Bengal, 13a
Mundesley Road, North Walsham; Prince of India, 32 High Street,
Princes Risborough, Buckinghamshire; Prince of India, 7 Upper High
Street, Thame, Oxfordshire.

Norwich

Norwich has a number of attractions, including d.b.a.c.'s sister. For the
curryholic, there's the dubious distinction of the curry price-wars that
have been plaguing Norwich for years. Twelve curry houses and a population of 127,000 is not a remarkably high ratio of restaurants to people (*see* Bradford, West Yorkshire) but, by virtually halving prices, many
seem to have achieved full houses, unlike Bristol, whose price-war
resulted in numerous bankruptcies. Whilst everyone likes a bargain,
price-wars are best left to giant corporations, such as supermarkets.
Meanwhile, make Methi while the restaurants last, and tell us about it.

BOMBAY RESTAURANT   ©

12-14 Magdalen Street, Norwich   ✆ 01603 666874

New (1996) management at Norwich's Bombay restaurants (owner
Shaheed Choudhury, manager Abdul Kadir) brings it back into the
Guide. It is not immune from the price-war mentioned above, but we
are getting much more positive reports now, and we'd like more. Price
check: Papadom 40p, CTM £3.55, Pullao Rice £1.20. Open daily 4.30-
11.30p.m. Branch: Bombay, 43 Timber Hill, Norwich.

NAZMA   NEW ENTRANT   ©

15 Prince of Wales Road, Norwich   ✆ 01603 616101

In 1996 Mohabbat Ali was brave enough to open his Nazma venture
on a site long-established with Indian restaurants (a Bombay, and more
recently the short-lived Lal Toofan were there). But his branch seems
to thrive, as does this one so, like his locals, we wish Mr Ali well. Price
check: Papadom 35p, CTM £3.05, Pullao Rice £1.40. Minimum charge
£5. Open daily for lunch and dinner. Branch: Nazma Brasserie, 15
Magdalen Street, Norwich.

NORWICH TANDOORI   ©

98 Magdalen Street, Anglia Square,
Norwich   ✆ 01603 621436

Kuti Meah is the managing owner. His 50-seater restaurant has: 'A
straightforward comfortable interior. Lamb Pasanda best tried so far in
the city. Chicken Tikka Pasanda, mildly creamy, cooked with butter,
almonds and sultanas, exceeded expectations,' T.W. Open noon-3p.m.
and 6p.m.-midnight.

PRINCE OF INDIA

19 Prince of Wales Road, Norwich   ✆ 01603 616937

This is undoubtedly one of the city's most popular restaurants, judging by the correspondence we receive. 'Beamed ceilings and divided
alcoves to give a cosy atmosphere. Food is quite good. When ordering
Papadoms, be sure to ask for the chutneys and onions, or you'll end up
with nothing. Shami Kebabs quite delicious as is the Madras. Service

slow when empty,' M.B. 'We found the food to be tasty and competently spiced and presented. Service was good considering the restaurant was packed to capacity. Noticed at least 15 people in the "Bombay Mix Zone" waiting to be seated,' G.R. 'Food was very good and my colleague enjoyed his Chicken Tikka Masala although it was vibrant with food colouring. Rice was good and Naan excellent. Meal unfortunately marred by the service. It was efficient, but intolerant,' C.T. Service seems to be this restaurant's Achilles heel. I recently published a piece in *Tandoori Magazine* (the curry restaurant's trade magazine) about an incident embarrassing to the few customers present shortly after opening time (6p.m.) on a quiet weekday. Mr Bashir unreasonably refused entrance to a blind customer because his trained guide dog was 'unacceptable'. But this elicited no response from him. (Watch these pages in the unlikely event that it does.) Price check: Papadom 35p, CTM £3.40, Pullao Rice £1.05. Set meal £10.25. Open noon-3p.m. and 6p.m.-midnight. Branch: Passage to India, 45 Magdalen Street, Norwich.

Thetford

NEMI INDIAN CUISINE ©

17 White Hart Street, Thetford ℘ 01842 761260

A snug restaurant seating 48 diners, owned and managed by Abdul Rouf. 'For starters I sampled Nargis Kebab, a hard-boiled egg covered with spicy mincemeat, unbelievably tasty. Methi Murgh, Bombay Potato and Pullau Rice, absolutely terrific. Well worth a visit,' M.B. 'Had been booked into Center Parc for a weekend break – sort of middle-class Butlins where, instead of donkey rides and funfairs, there is all manner of "healthy" activities. A peep through Nemi's window worried us as only four people were eating in on a Saturday night. Usual discussions about whether or not to eat here, a major argument was swiftly averted much to relief of our rumbling stomachs. We had come for a takeaway. Service was polite and efficient. The food was brown gravy variety, competently prepared and spiced, and certainly good value,' G.R. Price check: Papadom 30p, CTM £5.75, Pullao Rice £1.60. Open noon-2p.m. and 6p.m.-midnight. Branch: Naima, 11 Exchange Street, Attleborough, Norfolk.

NORTHAMPTONSHIRE

Brackley

THE RAJ TANDOORI NEW ENTRANT   ©

36 Market Place, Brackley   ✆ **01280 703265**

Described as a welcome addition to the town, owner A. Hussain and
manager A. Ahmed opened here in 1994 and have established a local
following. Price check: Papadom 40p, CTM £5.95, Pullao Rice £1.45.
Open every day except Monday, 5.30-11.30p.m.

Corby

BOMBAY DYNASTY NEW ENTRANT   ©

76 George Street, Corby   ✆ **01536 400660**

Sunafor Ali's Dynasty is a decade old (1987) and Corby likes it, according to our scribes. Price check: Papadom 40p, CTM £5.80, Pullao Rice
£1.60. Minimum charge £7.50. Set meal £9.50. Service charge 10%.
Open daily for lunch except Friday noon-2p.m., and daily for dinner
5.30p.m.-midnight.

Daventry

SPICE DELIGHT NEW ENTRANT

22a High Street, Daventry   ✆ **01327 312883**

A. Afsar is the owner and M.A. Khan the manager of the new (1996)
Spice. It's delighted the locals, they tell me, partly because they like the
name, replacing the short-lived Al-Siraaj at the same site. They also tell
me that it's Kashmiri cooking, with really authentic Brum-style Baltis,
the pick of which are to be had on Tuesdays or Wednesdays for just
£4.95 – for a Balti of your choice, plus any side dish, a Naan or Roti
and a soft drink! Price check: Papadom first one free then 45p, CTM
£4.90, Pullao Rice £1.70. Open daily 6-11.30p.m.

Irthlingborough

EASTERN SPICE

56-60 High Street, Irthlingborough   ✆ **01933 650044**

Manager Golam Sarwar's menu lists all the curry house favourites with a few additions. Our attention is drawn to Kalmi (chicken) Kebab (£2.20), Murgh Bemisall (£5.60) – Chicken Tikka with onion, ginger, garlic, tomato and coriander – and Murgh La Jawab (£5.60) – tandoori chicken chunks in a thick gravy. Price check: Papadom 40p, CTM £5.85, Pullao Rice £1.50. Minimum charge £7.95. Set meal £7.95. Sunday eat-your-fill buffet £5.95, under 10s half-price. Open noon-2.30p.m. (extended to 4p.m. Sundays) and 6-11.30p.m.

TANDOORI NIGHTS   ©

48 Station Road, Irthlingborough   ✆ **01933 652675**

Chef-owner Moyna Miah's small but cosy restaurant was established in 1989 in an old Tudor building, and seats just 35 diners. Usual curry house menu, serving all your favourite dishes with accompaniments, and we've been told about some interesting specials. Stuffed Murgh Mossolla (£6.95) – breast of chicken, stuffed with spicy, tangy potato, onion and peas, and served with a curry sauce. Chicken Shah Rukh (£5.95) – chicken, cooked with Keema, topped with an egg. The Veg Thali (£8.90) is popular, as is the Sunday eat-your-fill buffet at £5.95, under 10s half-price. Price check: Papadom 40p, CTM £5.30, Pullao Rice £1.60. Open noon-2.30p.m. and 6-11p.m., till midnight Friday and Saturday, noon-11p.m. Sunday.

Kettering

THE RAJ   ▦ ©

50 Rockingham Road, Kettering   ✆ **01536 513606**

The Raj, owned by Goyas Miah and managed by Lisu Miah, is becoming increasingly popular since it opened in 1991. 'Bhindi Bhaji (£1.65) fresh and nicely cooked. Excellent Pasanda and Madras, beautiful Chupattis. Attentive and informative service,' T.P. Separate Balti menu with every different combination including Balti Shahjahan (£5.45) – chicken, mincemeat, almonds, coconuts and sultanas. Home-delivery service (minimum order £7.50). Sunday eat-your-fill buffet £5.55, under 12s half-price. Price check: Papadom 50p, CTM £6.95, Pullao Rice £1.60. Minimum charge £10 per head. Set meal £24.95 for two. Open noon-2p.m. and 5.30p.m.-midnight, every day except Sundays when open noon-11p.m. Branch: The Ancient Raj, Long Buckby.

RED ROSE   ▦ ©

1 George Street, Kettering   © 01536 510120

Opened in 1991 and seats 80 diners. Tandooris, Tikkas, Korai (sic), Kormas and Jal-Frezi (sic) are on the menu, including a satisfactory section on Balti. Manager is Matin Rashid. Open noon-2.30p.m. and 6p.m.-midnight, till 12.30a.m. Friday and Saturday. Free delivery service.

Long Buckby

THE ANCIENT RAJ   ▦ ©

12 High Street, Long Buckby   © 01327 842193

Nothing ancient about this restaurant. It opened in 1993 and is popular. Manager is Raj Miah. Home-delivery service (minimum order £7.50). Price check: Papadom 50p, CTM £6.95, Pullao Rice £1.60. Minimum charge £10 per head. Set meal £24.95 for two. Sunday eat-your-fill buffet at £5.55, under 12s half-price. Open noon-2p.m. and 5.30-11p.m., daily except Sunday when open noon-11p.m. Branch: The Raj, Kettering.

Northampton

FAR COTTON TANDOORI   NEW ENTRANT   ©

111 St Leonards Road, Far Cotton,
Northampton   © 01604 706282

'Far out' wrote a local scribe (I.M.), when this place opened in the southern outskirts of town. He also tells of the 'open kitchen where you can watch the above-average food being cooked'. Price check:

Papadom 35p, CTM £4.95, Pullao Rice £1.25. Open noon-2p.m. and 5-10.30p.m. daily. Branch: Gate of India, 19 Spencer Bridge Road, Northampton.

IMRAN BALTI HUT NEW ENTRANT BYO

285 Wellingborough Road,
Northampton ✆ 01604 22730

'If you can get inside the door of this extremely popular restaurant and push through the crowds of people to try and get a seat you are guaranteed an excellent meal. Always best to book. At the weekend people queue out of the door! Simply decorated, pleasant waiters. A large vegetarian choice. After papadoms and chutneys, don't order starters unless you have a particularly huge appetite, though a must is the family Naan – 2 feet long by 18 inches wide – a highlight. Can bring your own drink for a small corkage charge,' s.s. Reports, please.

RAJPUT BALTI NEW ENTRANT ©

224a Wellingborough Road,
Northampton ✆ 01604 37336

One of the town's earlier curry houses, the 1974 Northampton Tandoori, became the Rajput Balti in 1996 when it changed hands to Shabab Uddin and his manager Ala. It serves standard formula curries and Baltis but is a popular place, by all accounts. Price check: Papadom 25p, CTM £4.50, Jinga Prawn Masalader £6.95, Pullao Rice £1.50. Set meal £7.95. Open noon-2p.m. and 6p.m.-midnight.

STAR OF INDIA ©

5 Abington Avenue, Northampton ✆ 01604 30664

Opened in 1982 by Abdul Noor and seats 40 diners. Manager, Bodrul Islam, ensures you'll find everything from Tandoori and Tikka to Madras and Vindaloo, and everything in between, at this reliably good curry house. Open noon-2.15p.m. and 6p.m.-midnight, till 1.30a.m Friday and Saturday.

TAJ MAHAL

7 Marefair, Northampton   © 01604 31132

This restaurant has maintained its position in the Guide for two reasons. First, because it is Northampton's oldest, having opened in 1952
– indeed, that ranks it among the country's first ten Indian restaurants.
Second, its hours of opening on Friday and Saturday nights are
remarkable, closing at 3a.m. This is typical curry house, nothing more
and nothing less. With over 45 years in the business, you would expect
them to be good at the job. I can't imagine why they find it necessary
to stay open till 3a.m., but for those who pound up and down the M1
(yes, there are some of us who do it in the wee hours) they are just a
hop and a jump away from junctions 15 and 16. Anything is better than
motorway food, any time of the day or night. As for the quality of the
food, it's fine, but who cares at that hour of the morning?

Rushden

CURRY GARDEN   NEW ENTRANT

24 Church Street, Rushden   © 01933 314121

Komor Uddin, the proprietor of the Curry Garden, opened in 1989
and has established a good local trade. Price check: Papadom 45p,
CTM £5.35, Pullao Rice £1.40. Kurzi Lamb meal £26.50 for two. Open
daily for lunch and from 6p.m.-midnight.

Wellingborough

AKASH TANDOORI

36 Cambridge Street, Wellingborough   © 01933 227193

'Papadoms crispy and Tikka tender. Chicken Shashlik, fresh and spicy
with a Naan bread. Restaurant clean and service good,' D.D.C. Menu
says: 'Dining without wine is like a day without sunshine.' And so say
all of us!

NORTHUMBERLAND

Alnwick

ALNWICK TANDOORI   ©

17 Clayport Street, Alnwick   ✆ **01665 510772**

Owned by Abdul Khalique and Abdul Tahid. Mr Khalique can be
found in the restaurant welcoming guests and Mr Tahid can be found
in the kitchen cooking up all our favourite curries and accompaniments. Open daily 5.30-11.30p.m.

Berwick-upon-Tweed

MAGNA   ©

39 Bridge Street, Berwick-upon-Tweed   ✆ **01289 302736**

The Magna has been in our Guide since we started it in 1984. 'And no
wonder,' says Curry Club member Michael Fabricant, MP. It's a family business headed by Jahangir Khan. The food, which is the standard
formula stuff beloved by all curryholics, is as well described on the
menu as it is cooked. It's a port in a storm right there on the A1-
Scottish border, with the ghosts of Lindisfarne not far behind. Open
noon-2.30p.m. and 6p.m.-midnight, closed for Sunday lunch.

Corbridge

CORBRIDGE TANDOORI   NEW ENTRANT

8 Market Square, Corbridge   ✆ **01434 633676**

Cor blimey, have I caused a stir at Corbridge. Well, I hope I have. Dr
M.H. wants us to know that he dines here regularly (although he lives
in Wales) and that: 'It is as good or better than the Valley,' [*see* entry]
'and I go to both. If you want excellent decor and different dishes, then
go to the Valley. If you want excellent "standard" dishes, go to the
Corbridge. It has only two drawbacks: it is small and can get stuffy and
hot when busy, and it does get busy, especially at weekends. I cannot

recommend it highly enough, and I always visit when I can. Oh yes, it's a small restaurant hidden above a shop. Please tell everybody.' OK, OK, Doc, we've got the message, and we don't think you're the owner S.M. Shahjahan (who took over in 1996) writing under a pseudonym. Anyone else agree with the doc? Price check: Papadom 50p, CTM £6.40, Pullao Rice £1.95. Set meal £38 for two. Open daily 6-11.30p.m.

THE VALLEY TOP 100 ©

The Old Station House, Corbridge © 01434 633434

It is a pleasure to report on something quite unique, and probably un-copyable on the Indian restaurant scene. It's Syed Nadir Aziz's Valley restaurant. Known universally as Daraz, he has been involved in curry restaurants in the north-east since 1973 (including Newcastle's Moti Mahal and Daraz). In 1991 he came across the Corbridge station building in the beautiful Tyne valley. Built in 1835 for Stephenson's railway, it is no longer used as a station although it is on the important Newcastle-to-Carlisle railway line. Indeed, trains stop at Corbridge station throughout each day but passengers do not use the old building any more. That is, not until Daraz breathed new life into it. He turned it into a stylish, up-market Indian restaurant. Its USP (unique selling proposition), which has attracted wide media attention, is its location and the fact that the restaurant offers a unique train service that is ideal for a celebration or special treat. Uniformed restaurant staff welcome you at Newcastle Central Station and escort you by train to The Valley Restaurant to enjoy a meal that you have chosen while sitting on the train – the order is telephoned through to the restaurant via a mobile. This service is for parties of 10 or more. 'It beats ordering a taxi,' G.M. Of course, individuals can make their own way here and back by scheduled train – but beware a fairly early last train. One wag tells me that he books his takeaway by phone and collects it en route without leaving the train on his way home from work!

As for the restaurant, there is a reception room and seventy seats in four connecting rooms (one of which opens onto the eastbound platform). Decor is lush and Indian in feel (turquoise and gold predominate). And the food? The menu is extensive and all the currinary correct favourites are there. Chef Abdul Khalick's specials are much in demand. We hear of the creamiest Shah Jahani Pasanda and Luari Mangsho – lamb with fresh herbs and spices – a dish 'unique to the

Valley', according to Daraz. We have placed this restaurant in our TOP 100 for originality and flair as well as for food. Open 6-11p.m., closed on Sundays. Branch: Moti Mahal, 14 Maple Avenue, Dunston, Gateshead, Tyne and Wear. Daraz is talking of opening a further branch in a train. Watch these pages.

Cramlington

LAL QILA ©

Dudley Lane, Cramlington © **01670 734268**

Opened in 1987, Muhit and Miah's restaurant continues to satisfy its regulars, according to reports received. Seats 54 diners and serves everything from Karahi to Balti and all in between. Manager, Sabu Miah, will give a discount to Curry Club members at weekday lunchtimes. Price check: Papadom 50p, CTM £5.50, Special King Prawn £7.50, Pullao Rice £1.60. Minimum charge £8 per person. Open noon-2.30p.m. and 6-11.30p.m., Sunday 7-11.30p.m.

Hexham

ABBEY TANDOORI ©

28 Priestpopple, Hexham © **01434 603509**

Miah Sahid's 44-seat Abbey restaurant is plainly decorated but neat and tidy. A good selection of tandoori dishes on the menu with, as they call them, 'supporting dishes' and four different Naans. 'We found ourselves snowbound in Hexham en route to Essex from Scotland. Naturally we had our trusted *Good Curry Guide* in the car, and found the Abbey Tandoori. Meal was superb. King Prawn Vindaloo and Chicken Pathia. Naan bread one of the best I've tasted, crispy on the outside but beautifully light and fluffy on the inside. Too few king prawns in my Vindaloo. I'd have happily paid more for a few extra prawns,' s. and k.t. Open noon-2p.m. and 6-11.30p.m., Sunday 6-11p.m. only.

Morpeth

TANDOORI MAHAL   ©

---

17 Bridge Street, Morpeth   ✆ **01670 512420**

This restaurant opened in 1980 and is now owned by Afruz Miah. It serves all the favourites and its menu gives very good descriptions of every dish. 'An absolutely first-class establishment. Prices fair, service good, decor of a very high standard, parking no problem,' M.B. Manager Surot Miah has promised to give a discount to Curry Club members at lunchtimes. Price check: Papadom 50p, CTM £6.05, Pullao Rice £1.50. Minimum charge £7 per person. Open noon-2.30p.m. and 6p.m.-midnight, Sunday 7-11.30p.m. only.

NOTTINGHAMSHIRE

Mansfield

MODHU MITHA

11-15 Ratcliffe Gate, Mansfield   ✆ **01623 651203**

Decorated in cool greens and seats around 70. Extensive menu with standard curry house stuff. 'Food quite delicious and always plenty of it. Fresh Bhindi in the Bhajee,' M.B.

Newark

ASHA

---

2 Stodman Street, Newark   ✆ **01636 702870**

'Decor, very wine-bar. Chicken Tikka Masala pleasant but lacked the creaminess that I am used to, though still well recommended,' D.H.

Nottingham

BEESTON TANDOORI   ©

150-152 High Road, Beeston, Nottingham ✆ **0115 922 3330**

A small but cosy restaurant seating 40 diners. Chef recommendations include Uri and Muki Special, which are described as fairly dry but well-spiced. You are advised to book your table for Friday and Saturday evenings. Owner is S. Choudhury. Open noon-2.30p.m. and 6p.m.-midnight.

CHAND   NEW TO OUR TOP 100   ©

---

31 Mansfield Road, Nottingham   ✆ **0115 947 4103**

The Chand has been relocated across the street since our last Guide, and is now jointly owned by Mohammed Shanaz, who looks after front of house, and chef Mohammed Riaz. The new restaurant is small with just 38 seats, so booking is essential. The menu is largely unchanged and contains a very good selection both in quality and quantity of vegetarian dishes. Dhava Thaum (£2.20) – garlic mushrooms served on a thin bread, and Mixed Vegetable Karahi (£5.15). 'We come for quiet meals on our own, and at other times we bring our friends, covering an age range from 15 to 67, some of whom are vegetarians. We all love it,' H. and M.W. There are plenty of meat, fish and fowl dishes, too. Balti dishes are also on the menu. 'We've probably tried 90% of the menu. Our favourites are the Jalfrezi and Biriahi dishes, and the Keema Vindaloo, not on the menu. The rice is always excellent – don't you just hate it when it isn't just right? We always feel comfortable – which can be a problem when you arrive with a two-year-old,' K.A. 'Since the move, we have to say that the food has become even more of a delight. Where else could you get more nuts and honey on your Peshwari Naan?' C.H. and F.R. 'Myself, family and friends have been dining at the Chand for many years. The new place is less spacious, but the welcome is as warm, the portions as very large, and the food is still the best. I hope to dine with them for many years to come. Prices are very reasonable,' B.H. Price check: Papadom 50p, CTM £7, Paradise Balti £7.50, Pullao Rice £1.50. Minimum charge £6.50. Set four-course lunch £5.95. Open 5.30p.m.-12.30a.m. weekdays, till 1a.m. at weekends. We are impressed with the level of customer care here, and are awarding the Chand our TOP 100 cachet.

THE INDIAN   ©

7 Bentinck Road, Nottingham   ✆ 0115 942 4922

The pretty black beams, white frontage and inviting curtained windows of Naj Aziz's restaurant suggest up-market decor. The high standard continues inside. Cream walls, ornate white plasterwork, tiled floor, large palms in white pots and carpets hanging from walls. We hear that the food is family-style. 'Aubergine Paneer and Garlic and Mushroom Baji for starters, served with crisp salad. Murgh Makhani, Chicken Tikka cooked with garlic, coriander and brandy, and I can honestly say it was among the best curries I have ever eaten. Rice portions were large. Staff extremely friendly and food is outstanding,' c.y. Price check: Papadom 75p, CTM £7.20, Pullao Rice £1.90. Minimum charge £10. Open Tuesday to Sunday 6p.m.-midnight. Closed Mondays, and they take a week off at Christmas and two weeks in the summer.

KASHMIR   ©

60 Maid Marian Way, Nottingham   ✆ 0115 947 6542

A large restaurant seating between 90 and 100 diners. Opened in 1988 by A.D. Satti, and serving the formula menu with competence. Open 6p.m.-1a.m., till 2.30a.m. (for all you night owls!) Friday and Saturday.

LAGUNA

43 Mount Street, Nottingham   ✆ 0115 941 1632

'Serves the rice that I judge all others by – always fluffy and *al dente* and never sticky. Decor well above average, chairs are comfortable. Starter prices a bit steep. Lamb Badam Pasanda was rich and tasty. As Arnie says, "I'll be back!"' p.r. 'Cobra lager available. Overall excellent-quality food and big portions. Praised for its authenticity by my Asian friends,' a.t.

MAHARANI   ©

7 Hockley Street, Nottingham   ✆ 0115 950 6785

Well-established tandoori curry house, owned and managed by Mr Bashir. 'It just goes quietly about its business, doing things the way it has always done, and the way I always like,' r.k.

MEHRAN II ©

948-950 Woodborough Road, Mapperley, Nottingham © 0115 955 1005

All the Mehran branches belonging to managing owner, Akram Dhareeja, have an identical pretty and informative menu, with some interesting and unique dishes. Sommerkhand is lamb, chicken or prawn, etc., cooked with strawberries, cherries, fresh cream and pistachios. Sassi is cooked with bananas, pineapple and fresh cream. Awami is cooked with Keema, fresh tomatoes and omelette. Siaherr is cooked with tomatoes, garlic and green peppers in mustard oil. All these are from £6.30. Balti and Karahi dishes are also featured on the menu. Their Tikka Masala Curry (either lamb or chicken £8.50 incl. rice and salad) must be unique to the trade, and I must try cooking it this way – it is cooked with red wine and flambéed at your table with brandy. 'Portions were generous and extremely tasty. Fabulous choice of main meals. Selected two unknowns – Meat Sassi, which my husband loved, and Chicken Khacksan which was good, hot and tasty. Our meal cost £20.70,' L.W. Price check: Papadom 55p, CTM £8.50 (*see* above), Pullao Rice £2.10. Open Monday to Sunday 6p.m.-1a.m., till 2a.m. Friday and Saturday. Branches: Mehran, 2 Cromford Road, Langley Mill, Derbyshire; Mehran Takeaway, 245 Nottingham Road, Somercotes, Derbyshire.

MILAAP TANDOORI NEW ENTRANT ©

67 Chilwell Road, Beeston, Nottingham © 0115 925 4597

Pervaz Iqbal has owned this tiny (28-seat) restaurant since 1987. It is managed by Perwaise Ayoub and the cooking, by Noman Khan, is Pakistani and covers all the favourite things you'd expect at a curry house. Price check: Papadom complimentary, CTM £5.90, Pullao Rice complimentary. Minimum charge £8.50. Open daily 6p.m.-midnight.

MOGAL E AZAM ©

7-9 Goldsmith Street, Nottingham © 0115 947 3826

The Mogal was opened in 1977 by Mr S.N. Miah, and has long been a Nottingham favourite. 'Cosy decor, excellent cuisine. Big bottles of Cobra, well-chilled. Food well-chillied. Recommended,' T.E. 'Visited several times over the past two years, consistently good food and attentive service. My friend amused the waiters by ordering the hottest curry on the menu and then spent the evening with sweat streaming down his face. In fairness they warned him against it!' A.T. 'The restaurant has a wall gallery of stars — autographed photos of artists from the nearby theatre, thanking him for his superb meals and service,' G.W. Open noon-2.30p.m. and 5.30p.m.-1.30a.m.

MOUSHUMI   ©

124 Derby Road, Stapleford, Nottingham   ℂ **0115 939 4929**

A tastefully decorated restaurant decked out in sea greens and stained wood. Large and expensive engraved glass panels divide the restaurant. Proprietor Sanawor Ali is a romantic soul. His Valentine's Night at £25 per couple, with free cocktails for her and champagne for him, sounds good. Any proposals? Price check: Papadom 40p, CTM £5.75, Pullao Rice £1.50. Minimum charge £5.45. Service charge 10%. Sunday eat-your-fill £6.95. Open noon-2.30p.m. and 6-11.30p.m.. Branch: Amrit Indian Takeaway, Nottingham.

NEW KOH-I-NOOR   ©

**25-27 Bridgford Road, West Bridgford,
Nottingham**   ℂ **0115 981 1645**

A small restaurant seating 40 diners. 'I am always impressed with the freshness of the vegetables here. My mother fell in love with the Peshwari Naan,' P.R. Managing owner is Mr Ibrahim. Open 5.30p.m.-12.30a.m., seven days a week. Branch: Plaza Tandoori, 15 Main Road, Gedling.

PAPPADUM BALTI   ©

207 Radford Road, Nottingham   ℂ **0115 978 0972**

A cute little restaurant seating just 24. Tariq Mahmood, owner, manager and creator of curries in the kitchen, promises to give discounts to Curry Club members. Open Sunday to Thursday 6p.m.-1a.m., Friday and Saturday 6p.m.-3a.m. (for curry insomniacs).

SAAGAR TOP 100   ©

**473 Mansfield Road, Sherwood,
Nottingham**   ✆ **0115 962 2014**

Mohammed Khizer opened his Saagar in 1984. Front of house is managed by Imtiaz Ahmed, leaving Mr Khizer to do his thing in the
kitchen, assisted by Amjaid Parvaiz. From the abundant correspondence we receive, the Saagar does its thing really well. Its 90 seats are
split between two floors, and it is smart. 'After reading about this restaurant in your TOP 100, I took some friends there to find out if it is as
good as people make it out to be. The place was very busy, but we got
our booked table at once, and the pops and picks were gorgeous. My
Mixed Kebabs (£4.90) were tasty. Chicken Kaallan (£9.10) was very
sweet, yet very sour too, with tender chicken cooked in a south Indian
style, with mango, coconut and yoghurt. My girlfriend was brave
enough to tackle Chilli Chicken Tikka Masala (£9.50 incl. rice), and our
Garlic and Tomato Naan (£1.95) was excellent, covered in fresh tomato
chunks. Everyone felt the food had been made freshly, and it was
cooked to perfection. It makes a nice change to come to a decent restaurant which has the edge over others because of little things that just
make a difference, like fresh flowers at every table, proper lemon-
squeezers, spotless toilets, etc. It is expensive at the Saagar, but you get
exactly what you pay for,' N.H. Price check: Papadom 40p, CTM £9.10
incl. rice, pops and picks, Pullao Rice £2.10. Open noon-2.30p.m. and
5.30p.m.-12.30a.m. Remains in our TOP 100.

SHABAZ

142 Alfreton Road, Nottingham   ✆ **0115 979 0061**

'Food is always of the highest quality. My favourite,' L.W. Open 6p.m.-
3a.m., Friday and Saturday 6p.m.-4a.m. Insomniacs, take note.

SIMLA NEW ENTRANT   ©

32 Lower Parliament Street, Nottingham ✆ **0115 924 2405**

Nottingham's two Simlas (*see* entry below) have similar names and sim-
ilar-looking business cards, but they are no longer connected, so owner
Mohammed Riaz wishes us to know. This one opened in 1994, with 50
seats, and it is a good local haunt for curries, baltis, tandooris and

masalas. Price check: Papadom 50p, Pullao Rice £1.40. Minimum charge £8. Open 6p.m.-midnight daily.

SIMLA II NEW ENTRANT   ©

5 James Street, Kimberley, Nottingham   ✆ 0115 945 9350

Owned by chef Mohammed Ayub, and managed by Nadeem Iqbal, the 30-seat Simla II is a good local haunt. Our attention is drawn to Nawabi Chicken Tikka (£6.95), topped with cheese and tomato passata, served with rice and a curry sauce, and Indian-style fish (£6.50) – marinated in tangy spices, baked and momentarily grilled in sunflower oil to seal in the flavours, and also served with rice and a curry sauce. Price check: Papadom 50p, CTM £6.75, Pullao Rice £1.40. Minimum charge £7. Open daily 6p.m.-midnight.

Southwell

SANAM BALTI HOUSE NEW ENTRANT   ©

15-17 King Street, Southwell   ✆ 01636 813618

Khalid Mahmood is both the owner and the chef, and we hear well of his Kashmiri-Pakistani cooking, with authentic Brum-style Baltis. Price check: Papadom 50p, CTM £6.90, Pullao Rice £1.20. Open daily 6p.m.-12.30a.m.

Sutton-in-Ashfield

BEKASH   ©

83 Outram Street, Sutton-in-Ashfield   ✆ 01623 559955

Friendly, competent food and service at Masuk Miah's Bekash. We reported last time that they adore children here. Judging by reports received, adults adore the Bekash too.

OXFORDSHIRE

Abingdon

PRINCE OF INDIA   ©

10 Ock Street, Abingdon   ℂ 01235 523033

We hear good things about manager, A. Sulman's Prince, especially the Sunday lunch buffet. 'It always used to be Sunday lunch at the pub. Now, with the kids the curry buffet cannot be beaten. It's always good, always cheap, and always a blow-out for the four of us aged eight to thirty-eight!' C.E. Open noon-2.30p.m. and 6p.m.-midnight. Branch: Prince of India, 31 High Street, Wallingford.

Banbury

MOGHUL

58 Parsons Street, Banbury   ℂ 01295 264177

'I have used this place for years when in town (keeps the same chef), lovely inside, good food, first-class service,' P.J. 'Located in one of the more pleasant and interesting shopping areas of Banbury. A compact restaurant, pleasant decor, seating is efficient but cosy, not cramped. Exquisitely tender Chicken Korai, sauce full of flavour. The chef-owner was concerned for our enjoyment. Heartily recommended,' Dr J.C.C.

SHEESH MAHAL   ©

45 Bridge Street, Banbury   ℂ 01295 266489

M. Khalid is the owner-chef here, and has been since 1986. It's a 70-seater, managed by M. Manwar, and it serves standard formula curries. 'Decided to visit on a friend's recommendation. Tandoori Fish for starters, very good. Chicken Moghlai, excellent, Naan breads were massive. Coffee pot and cream were left on our table so we could help ourselves,' J.S.K. Price check: Papadom 40p, CTM £6.75, Pullao Rice £1.55. Minimum charge £4.55. Open 5p.m.-midnight.

Bicester

SAHANA   ©

15 Market Square, Bicester	✆ 01869 245170

'Having visited every Indian restaurant in Oxford and surrounding area in the past 10 years, this must rate highly. The menu is wide and varied. The friendly and efficient service is second to none. Decor is basic but clean and tidy,' C.F.B. 'Entering the restaurant gave one a feeling of comfort, with the lights dimmed to the right level. Sheek Kebab very good and Samosa was thoroughly cooked. Dansak was of good consistency, an excellent sweet and sour taste. Good food at an affordable price,' R.C. Proprietor is A. Uddin. Open noon-2.30p.m. and 6-11.30p.m.

Chipping Norton

ANARKALI   ©

6 West Street, Chipping Norton	✆ 01608 642785

'Good selection on menu, good-sized portions. Best-ever Naans, light and fluffy. Onion Bhajees out of this world. Bank Holiday weekend and was busy but manager still had time to talk to us,' P.A. Proprietor is A. Uddin. Open noon-2.30p.m. and 6-11.30p.m. Branch: Moreton Tandoori, Moreton-in-the-Marsh, Gloucestershire.

Faringdon

AZAD TANDOORI AND BALTI   NEW ENTRANT   ©

14 Coxwell Street, Faringdon	✆ 01367 244977

Mrs Rabia Ali owns this tiny (30-seater) with Ahad Ali the manager and Arman Ali the chef. It is popular in town, we hear. Price check: Papadom 50p, CTM £6.25, Pullao Rice £1.70. Set meal £26.50 for two. Open daily 5-11.30p.m.

Henley-on-Thames

GAZAL   ©

53-55 Reading Road, Henley-on-Thames   ✆ 01491 574659

Anwer Naseem named his restaurant after gentle Indian love songs, for
that's what Gazal means. It has nothing to do with guzzling. I hope
that puts one reporter right, who told me that's why he came here in
the first place – to get big portions! You greedy slob, P.J.! He loves the
place, though, visiting whenever he's in town. Open noon-2p.m. and 6-
11p.m.

VICEROY

40 Hart Street, Henley-on-Thames   ✆ 01491 577097

A large restaurant seating 100. A good and reliable establishment serving all the usual curries and accompaniments with a few specials
thrown in, such as Chingri Jhol (king prawns served in a skillet) and
Karahi Kebab Khyberi from the Khyber Pass.

Kidlington

OVISHER TANDOORI

11- 13 Oxford Road, Kidlington   ✆ 01865 372827

It is a smart 80-seater, opened in 1983 by M. Bari. Brown wooden arches are offset against panelled windows and a white frontage. The
interior carries the same colours and design, with high-backed
mahogany chairs, discreet lighting and booths. It is 'one of my
favourite restaurants,' Dr J.C.C. 'I have a customer who insists on
eating here, and who am I to resist? Last time we had Dhansak, Moglai
Chicken, Madras, Sag Aloo, Chana Mussla and Pasware Naan (both
their spellings), rice and drinks all for £36.15 for three. The food was
delicious and far too much. I can't think of a better place to do
business,' M.S. Price check: Papadom 50p, CTM £6.25, Pullao Rice
£1.90.

ALCAZAR

1 The Parade, Windmill Road, Headington, Oxford   ✆ 01865 760309

'A smallish restaurant serving Balti food. My wife and I both had Balti Mughlai, an elegant, subtly-flavoured dish as good as anything we have ever had in an Indian restaurant. Pullao Arasta Deluxi, very finely-flavoured rice. Service was efficient, courteous and good-humoured. Impressed,' Dr G.G. 'Mediterranean-feel decor, white walls and tiled floor. Boasts a cushioned area, one can languish upon thick cushions and enjoy a relaxed and unique feast,' D.H.

AZIZ   TOP 100

230 Cowley Road, Oxford   ✆ 01865 794945

Named after its owner, Azizur (Aziz) Rahman, this restaurant is 'one of Oxford's best', says M.S. And we know that to be true. Mr Aziz is one of the spearhead founder members promoting Bangladeshi cuisine, and we were delighted when he opened Britain's first restaurant devoted to authentic Bengali and Bangladeshi cuisine, the Khansana, shortly after our last Guide was published. We are saddened that it closed within months. I took BBC Radio 4's *Food Programme* guru Derek Cooper there, and he liked it enough to do a programme from there. But close it did. It is significant that all the top restaurants serving authentic Indian food are, indeed, Indian. There is no reason I can think of why there should not be one specializing in authentic Bangladeshi cuisine. That country's capital, Dacca, has a few superb restaurants, most acclaimed of which is the Kastoori. Perhaps the location must be London, but sooner or later it must happen. And there are few better qualified restaurateurs than Mr Aziz and his ambitious colleagues. Meanwhile the Aziz is one place where you will find the Bangladeshi curry house formula done as well as it can be. 'Tastefully simple decor, airy and bright. Ada Gosht superbly flavoured and most delicious. Korai Murgh was tender and tasty, and both served in ample quantity. Outstanding Pullao Rice in texture and fragrance. Service was slow, excusable because the restaurant was well attended,' Dr J.C.C. 'Excellent quality, charming service. Very comfortable and relaxing atmosphere,' R.T. 'Decoration immediately impressed. Tables simply but elegantly set with crisp white linen. Good vegetarian selection on menu. Generous quantities and delicately flavoured. Emphasis on subtlety. A splendid meal,' W.C. 'My no. 1 favourite,' Dr J.C.C. A worthy entry in our TOP 100.

DHAKA BRASSERIE   NEW ENTRANT

186 Cowley Road, Oxford   ✆ **01865 200203**

Formula stuff here. 'Of particular note is the Vegetable Moglai,' says J.C.

JAMAL'S

108 Walton Street, Oxford   ✆ **01865 310102**

'My Vindaloo was not a good tingle but a bit of a volcano! Very good portions, Chapatis lovely and moist. Highly recommended,' G.H. 'Very comfortable restaurant, pleasing decor. Food absolutely delicious! We'll go again,' J.W. 'Good value with delicious food,' C.M.E. 'A very good place,' J.C.

KASHMIR HALAL   ©

64 Cowley Road, Oxford   ✆ **01865 250165**

Opened in 1970 by Said Meah and seats 50 diners. A comprehensive menu listing all your favourite curries and accompaniments. Price check: Papadom 40p, CTM £5.45, Pullao Rice £1.60. Open daily noon-3p.m. and 6p.m.-midnight.

MOONLIGHT

58 Cowley Road, Oxford   ✆ **01865 240275**

Dr J.C.C.'s no. 2 favourite, and popular with students, too, for its Pakistani food, no doubt because of the good quality and large portions.

©	Curry Club discount (see p. 607)	🍷	Unlicensed
√	Vegetarian	⊞	Home delivery
BYO	Bring your own alcohol		service available

OXFORD TANDOORI   ©

209 Cowley Road, Oxford   ✆ 01865 241493

A small establishment seating 44 diners. A good, reliable curry house serving competent curries. Proprietor is Tosir Ali. Open noon-2.30p.m. and 6p.m.-midnight.

POLASH TANDOORI   TOP 100   ©

25 Park End Street, Oxford   ✆ 01865 250244

Dr J.C.C. rates it his no. 3. J.C. (not the same person) says: 'This is quite the best in Oxford. Polash dishes are light and intriguing. Rather than the overly-sauced route, the chefs here prepare their dishes with distinctive spicings. It also has the best vegetarian menu for miles. We have yet to tire of it. The starters vary slightly in taste depending on chef, which makes it rather pleasing.' 'We were impressed by the very polite waiters and speed of service. Our table (reserved) was really too small for two plate-warmers, wine, breads, rice and three dishes. Confusion over the order, but was sorted out quickly. Not overly expensive,' M.S. 'Cannot fault the food, but consider it expensive for the small portions,' C.M.E. 'Capacious restaurant is bright, simply attractive and welcoming. A truly extensive menu and bar facilities offer all one could wish. Food is excellently prepared, Parathas clean and tasty. Passanda Gosht creamy and spicy with tender lamb. Highly recommended,' Dr J.C.C. 'I had a Murgh Jalfrezi which was ridiculously hot with green chillies in abundance – to be fair the manager did warn me. Staff were very courteous and apologetic when we were stranded with Papadoms but no pickle tray,' N.D. The cooking by Mohana Pilliai is well above average and some of the specials are unusual, featuring duck, venison, pheasant and chitol and buaal – Bangladeshi fish. We are happy to retain the Polash in our TOP 100. Manager Gous Uddin will give a discount to Curry Club members. Open noon-2.30p.m. and 6-11.30p.m.

SHEMON'S INDIAN CUISINE   NEW ENTRANT   ©

135 High Street, Oxford   ✆ 01865 242062

Shemon's has been on the High Street since 1976, and is now owned and managed by Abdul Kashem. It's all standard stuff, with a good selection of dishes and meals for vegetarians. Price check: Papadom 50p, CTM £8.50 incl. rice, Pullao Rice £1.90. Minimum charge £5. Set meal £12.50. Open daily for lunch and dinner.

TAJ MAHAL

16 Turl Street, Oxford   ✆ 01865 243783

The Taj Mahal has been on the first floor above Whites in the middle of a beautiful part of Oxford since 1937. It was only the third curry restaurant in England at the time and the first outside London, and has always attracted the *cognoscenti* from don to student. 'Varied menu, we chose from the specials. Massive quantities of quality food. Waiter was happy to explain dishes to an American lady sitting at the next table,' J.F. 'A smart, comfortable restaurant with splendid views. Karahi Chicken – exceptional, Methi Gosht and Vegetable Curry – very good. We rate them pretty highly,' Dr G.G. 'Birianis remain outstanding. Huge portions,' Dr A.G.J. 'For location and low price, you can't beat the Taj. But it is very standard high street curry style. It's really nothing special,' J.C.

Thame

DE WANI SHAH'S   NEW ENTRANT   ©

8 Swan Walk, Thame   ✆ 01844 260066

Nural Isam is owner and chef at his De Wani (which means 'hall of assembly'), found behind the Swan Hotel. D.K. liked the 'leave-it-to-us' set meal at £9.99. Price check: Papadom 40p, CTM £5.50, Pullao Rice £1.65. Open daily 5-11.30p.m.

Wallingford

PRINCE OF INDIA   ⊞

31 High Street, Wallingford   ✆ 01491 835324

Miah Ishaque manages Mr Abdul's Prince – a standard curry house seating 40 diners and serving all the usual tandooris and curries . They also do a free home-delivery service, minimum order £10. Open noon-2.30p.m. and 6p.m.-midnight.

Witney

CURRY PARADISE   ©

39 High Street, Witney   ✆ 01993 702187

House specials include Makhnee (sic) (Chicken Tikka Masala), Shak Shu-Ka (sic) (a mild mince dish) and Achaar Lamb (pickled). Korai dishes are also to be found here but no Baltis as yet. Head chef M. Uddin is so eager that you try his wonderful curries that he has promised to give Curry Club members a discount at his quieter moments in the kitchen. Open noon-2.30p.m. and 6-11.30p.m.

SHROPSHIRE
Bridgnorth

EURASIA

21 West Castle Street, Bridgnorth   ✆ 01746 764895

The Eurasia is well-established, having opened in 1975. It changed hands in 1987 to Azadur Rahman, who will be found front of house dispensing competent curries. Price check: Papadom 35p, CTM £7.80 incl. rice, Fish Mosala £6.95, Pullao Rice £1.75. Set meal £5.75 Sundays only. Open daily for lunch and dinner, Sundays 1p.m.-midnight.

Ludlow

SHAPLA BALTI   ©

58 Broad Street, Ludlow   ✆ 01584 875153

'We were really looking forward to eating here after 2½ years, and we were delighted to discover that nothing has changed. The windows are covered in hand-written adverts and interior is basic, but an effort has been made to make it comfortable. Owner is enthusiastic and keen to help. Balti Sag was delicious – you wanted it to go on and on. Naans were massive. Price was very reasonable. The restaurant also does kebabs and cheeseburgers for philistines!' s.r. And Donner Kebabs, including a Donner Chicken Tikka Kebab (£3.25). Owned and managed by Shalim Miah. Price check: Papadom 50p, Balti CTM £5.35, Pullao Rice £1.60. Minimum charge £7. Open daily noon-midnight. Branch: Shapla Tandoori, Ludlow.

SHAPLA TANDOORI ©

17 Tower Street, Ludlow ✆ **01584 872033**

Shalim Miah has owned the Shapla since 1972. Manager is Azizur Rahman. We always hear of prompt, kindly service, and one correspondent likes the Nargis Kebab (£5.55) – kebab shaped into balls – and Scallop Bunja (£5.50) with lashings of curried onion and tomato. Our attention is also drawn to Rowgoonjus (£4.10) – 'a double preparation of Sylhet origin, with chicken or meat or prawn, with methi, tomato and onion'. On reflection, this must be the most curious spelling and explanation for Roghan Josh we've encountered. Price check: Papadom 55p, CTM £6.50, Pullao Rice £1.65. Minimum charge £8. Open daily for lunch and dinner, Sundays from noon-midnight. Branch: Shapla Balti, Ludlow.

Oswestry

SIMLA ©

42 Beatrice Street, Oswestry ✆ **01691 659880**

Sufu Miah's Simla has been trading since 1976, and seats 100. We continue to get satisfied reports about the food, prices and service. Open daily noon-midnight. Branch: Simla, 5 Grapes Hill, Llangollen, Clwyd.

©	Curry Club discount (see p. 607)		Unlicensed
√	Vegetarian	⊞	Home delivery
BYO	Bring your own alcohol		service available

Newport

SHIMLA NEW ENTRANT   ©

---

22 St Mary's Street, Newport   ✆ **01952 825322**

Set takeaway meals are excellent value at Nurul Islam's restaurant. Balti (£8.95) includes Papadom with mint sauce and onion salad, Tandoori Mix Kebab, Chicken (or Lamb) Tikka Balti, Sag Aloo, Pullao Rice (half-portion) or Naan, and sweet or coffee. Price check: Papadom 30p, CTM £5.95, Pullao Rice £1.50. Minimum charge £10. Open 6p.m.-midnight.

Shrewsbury

COPTHORNE BRASSERIE TAKEAWAY NEW ENTRANT

**39 Mytton Oak Road, Copthorne Shopping Centre,
Shrewsbury**   ✆ **01743 270336**

'First impressions are good. Atmosphere is welcoming with a large waiting area furnished with comfortable cane armchairs. Tasteful decorations, restful. My selection was conservative. Onion Bhajee, Chicken Vindaloo with Egg Fried Rice. Picture window into the kitchen, I watched the food being prepared and thought to myself that any establishment that opens its kitchen to view in this way must be confident of their product. It was a joy to watch experts at work. Two Popadoms, a bag of onion salad, a bag of lettuce salad and a pot of creamy dip were part of the package and the smell was mouth-watering. I hastened to the car and headed for home. I have to admit that the food was gorgeous. Popadoms were crisp and fresh-tasting and the dip was the perfect appetizer with only the merest hint of spice. The pieces of chicken in the Vindaloo were huge and succulent and there was a liberal sprinkling of fresh coriander in the sauce, which was aromatic, creamy, thick and wonderfully hot. Salads were crisp with none of the limpness so often associated with takeaway establishments. A delicious meal,' s.c. Open noon-midnight.

SHERAZ NEW ENTRANT

79 Wyle Cop, Shrewsbury   © 01743 351744

Shropshire's Sheraz first started trading as early as 1960, at a time when there were only a few hundred curry houses in the whole UK. Boktiar Uddin took it over in 1982 and, guess what, he too sells Rowgoonjus (£4.10) (*see* Shapla, Ludlow), although his is Balti! Price check: Papadom 55p, CTM £6.50, Pullao Rice £1.60. Set meal £12.50. Open daily 6p.m-1 a.m. Branch: Gandhi Takeaway, Shrewsbury.

Telford

MISTER DAVE'S   BYO ©

15 Burton Street, Dawley, Telford   © 01952 503955

Mister Dave's is, in fact, owned by Mr M. Kirton, who bought it in 1988. The menu is straightforward, with plenty of Balti and plenty of Pakistani curry alternatives to choose from at knock-down prices. The BYO is accepted 'in moderation' and, not surprisingly, this 72-seater is usually packed. Price check: Papadom 25p, CTM £4.50, Pullao Rice £1. Open daily 6p.m.-midnight.

Wem

SHABAB NEW ENTRANT   ©

62b High Street, Wem   © 01939 234333

Say 'Wem' to confirmed curryholic Mick Jagger, and he'll fondly remember Charlie Watkins, the father of rock and roll big sound systems, whose Watkins Electronic Music amps and speakers achieved the first ever 1000-watt outdoor system in Hyde Park in 1969. Now you can have that level of sound in your car if you want to go prematurely deaf! This has nought to do with ought, except to say that since 1993, when M. Lal opened his Shabab, with Jay Bhatti as manager, Wem has been known, locally at any rate, for its good Pakistani curries cooked by Shabir. Price check: Papadom 40p, CTM £6.75 incl. rice or Naan, Pullao Rice £1.30. Minimum charge £6.50. Open daily 5.30p.m.-midnight.

Whitchurch

BALTI KING   NEW ENTRANT   ©

9 High Street, Whitchurch   ✆ 01948 662478

Opened in 1976 as Jay's and owned by I. Hussain, with Javed Khan managing and Mushtaq Khan cooking. The recent name-change gives the clue that there are indeed Baltis on the menu, indeed in literally any combination of ingredients you care to name. Price check: Papadom 40p, Balti CTM or Jeera Chicken both £6.75 incl. rice or bread, Pullao Rice £1.30. Minimum charge £6. Open daily 6p.m.-midnight.

SOMERSET

The 1997 county changes have abolished Avon, returning the former Somerset towns, such as Bath and Weston-super-Mare, to their rightful home.

Bath

THE EASTERN EYE   ©

11 Argyle Street, Bath   ✆ 01225 422323

New ownership, to Suhan Choudhury, at this large (120-seat) restaurant, and larger portions, to please D.Y. 'Nice to see into the kitchens,' H. and M.K. Price check: Papadom 45p, CTM £6.50, Pullao Rice £1.70. Minimum charge £10.

JAMUNA   ©

9-10 High Street, Bath   ✆ 01225 464631

Beautiful upstairs views over an orange grove and Bath Abbey. Decorated in soft pinks. 'Quality of food excellent,' says J.G., adding a comment we've reported before: 'but portions were on the small side.'

RAJPOOT

4 Argyle Street, Bath   ✆ 01225 668833

A very smart restaurant, complete with doorman dressed in Indian costume, and a welter of awards. Proprietor Ahmed Chowdhury, who also has a stake in the Bengal Brasserie (32 Milson Street, Bath) and the Jamuna, did take note of the rumblings in the last Guide; enough, at any rate, to ring me to complain about our entry. So why, sir, do we still get mixed reports? J.G. 'likes the place, and had tasty food,' but notes unfriendly service, and the wrong meal, destined for another table, being served, then removed. D.Y. was less complimentary. Reports, please.

RUPOSHI TAKEAWAY   NEW ENTRANT   ©

3 Sussex Place, Widcombe Parade, Bath   ✆ 01225 337294

A safe bet, reasonably-priced lunch and dinner takeaway-only, managed by Gous Ali. Price check: Papadom 30p, CTM £4.90, Pullao Rice £1.20. Branch: Ruposhi, 110 Mount Road, Bath.

Bridgwater

SIMLA   ©

31-33 Penel Orlieu, Bridgwater   ✆ 01278 446666

P.J. calls in here for 'good food and good fun with friendly waiters, who call a Samusa (£2.25, meat or veg) a Samusa!' It's a large (100-seat) place, opened in 1976 and since 1989 has been in Farid Hassan's hands, with his manager, Abdul Hamid Ali, and chef, Mainul Hassan. Price check: Papadom 50p, CTM £5.45, Pullao Rice £1.75. Minimum charge £15. Open noon-2p.m. and 5.30p.m.-midnight daily.

©	Curry Club discount (see p. 607)	🍵	Unlicensed
√	Vegetarian	⊞	Home delivery
BYO	Bring your own alcohol		service available

Clevedon

MOGHULS TANDOORI   ©

33 Old Church Road, Clevedon   ✆ 01275 873695

Continues to provide good, competent, standard menu curries. Gives
10% discount on takeaways. Recommended as a safe bet by several correspondents including P.J. who 'adores the Pakistani Basmatic' rice (for
asthmatics perhaps?) and is amused by 'Samusas'.

Glastonbury

INDIAN OCEAN

62 High Street, Glastonbury   ✆ 01458 834175

'As you are probably aware, Glastonbury is a centre for strange religious
practices and I searched the menu hoping for something new, such as
Druid Dopiaza or Chicken Solstice, but found it to be a typical, standard curry house menu. I ordered Kingfisher but Carlsberg arrived. I
ordered King Prawn Butterfly but they had not been delivered by their
supplier (along with the Kingfisher), so I ordered Prawn Puree, followed by Chicken Jalfrezi. Service was slow, largely because of a steady
stream of takeaways, but the waiters remained cheerful. Average curry
house fare,' M.S. Owned by Iqbal Miah, with Akbul and Mannan. Price
check: Papadom 30p, CTM £4.10, Pullao Rice £1.25. Open daily noon-
2.30p.m. and 5.30-11p.m.

Midsomer Norton

SHAPLA INDIAN TAKEAWAY

42 High Street, Midsomer Norton   ✆ 01761 411887

A takeaway-only in an attractive stone-faced building. L.T. especially
liked their Dandag (sic) and had not previously heard of their
Chicken, Lamb or Prawn Dim (sic) – 'cooked with egg in a sauce'.
Neither have we!

Nailsea

TIKKA FLAME   NEW ENTRANT   ©

Unit 5-6 Ivy Court, High Street, Nailsea   ℂ 01275 855700

If it's all in the name, the Flame's a good one. Mrs S. Elahi is the owner-manager and Mohamed Hanif is the chef. The menu is clear and concise, containing everything Indian that it should, plus one nice spicy surprise from Malaya: Satay (£4.50) — marinated chicken or lamb, cooked in the traditional peanut sauce, with a hint of chilli, lemon grass and lime. Price check: Papadom 25p, CTM £6.60, Pullao Rice £1.70. Open every day except Sunday 5.30p.m. till late.

Portishead

SPICY AROMA TANDOORI   ©

Clarence House, High Street, Portishead   ℂ 01275 845413

Another Chowdhury family restaurant which has, we hear, settled in well under the management of Samad who, like me, has by now heard all the gags about pongs! So save them for later, and enjoy the good things on offer here, which include in their not over-long menu a number of unusual specialities, such as Cobra Salon. No, it's not a beer cellar — it's chicken, lamb, egg, tomatoes and mushroom and X'cutti (pronounced dja-cewt-ee) — chicken cooked in a coconut, chilli and vinegar-tamarind purée — from Goa. More reports, please.

Taunton

GANGES BALTI HOUSE

93-95 Station Road, Taunton   ℂ 01823 284967

We continue to hear from very satisfied customers telling us how satisfied they are with the Ganges, some local, some from 250 miles away (passing holiday trade). But we got a blaster from H.S., one of our regular Welsh reporters, who assures us he won't return. Coincidentally, the very next letter we opened was about this same restaurant, from

M.S., another very regular, widely travelled reporter from Buckinghamshire, who said: 'It was a class act and the best I have found in Somerset — so far!' Open daily for lunch and dinner. Reports, please, about this restaurant and all Somerset.

Wellington

TASTE OF INDIA   ©

21 North Street, Wellington   ℂ 01823 667051

Naz Choudhury's Taste is a cosy little 30-seater, which serves all the usual curries year-round to its satisfied locals, and contends with the inevitable holiday crowds in the summer. P.J. likes the Tandoori Trout. Price check: Papadom 45p, CTM £6.25, Pullao Rice £1.90. Open daily except Tuesday noon–2p.m. and 6p.m.–midnight.

Weston-super-Mare

AVON TANDOORI

16 Waterloo Street, Weston-super-Mare   ℂ 01934 622622

Shahim Miah's menu contains all the old favourites plus a few surprises including Fish Chilli Masala (£6.50) and a sprinkling of Balti dishes. Price check: Papadom 40p, CTM £7 incl. rice, Pullao Rice £1.60. Minimum charge £7.

SURMA   ©

71 Orchard Street, Weston-super-Mare   ℂ 01934 635540

Syed Hussan is not only the owner, he's the chef. Syed Ahmed runs things out front. Price check: Papadom 35p, CTM £5.30, Pullao Rice £1.80. Minimum charge £10. Branch: Nat Raj, 1148 East Reach Street, Taunton.

VICEROY

57 Whitecross Road, Weston-super-Mare   © 01934 628235

Continues to receive glowing reports about excellent food, service, decor, etc. It is A.B.'s favourite restaurant. He says: 'They make every effort to ensure satisfaction and, as regular customers, a personal touch is always given, remembering names, favourite drinks, etc. Always willing to provide dishes not on the menu.' He would perhaps prefer larger portions and G.C. was shocked to find Kingfisher lager at £3 a pint but he does enjoy the food and the pond in the restaurant, which houses a collection of Koi carp and a working fountain. This restaurant was recently visited by Anthony Hopkins of *Silence of the Lambs* fame. (Brings a whole new meaning to Chef Special.)

Wincanton

MIAH'S   ©

4 Church Street, Wincanton   © 01963 33417

We continue to hear well of Akthar Hussain's restaurant, serving good curry house food at good prices.

STAFFORDSHIRE

Burton-on-Trent

GEORGE'S TANDOORI   ©

48-49 Station Road, Burton-on-Trent   © 01283 533424

When I recently took one of our Gourmet Tours to India, I took the group to the Cobra lager brewery in Bangalore. The owner assured me we'd all get B & B. I said thanks, but the hotel arrangements are already made and paid. 'Of course they are,' he said, 'but I mean Beer and Biriani!' It has nothing to do with Davinder Gidda's George's Tandoori, except his humorous terminology reminded me of that story. For example, a G & T Naan (£1.95) is not my favourite tipple - it's a Garlic and Tomato version. And the George's Special Cocktail (£6.75) is a mix of Tandoori Chicken, Sheesh Kebab, Lamb and Chicken Tikka, prepared in the karahi with a mild sauce. Open daily 6p.m.-1a.m.

Cannock

BENGAL BRASSERIE ©

4 Market Street, Hednesford, Nr Cannock   ✆ 01543 424769

Standard competent curries at Mr Miah's Bengal. Open daily 6p.m.-midnight.

SALEEM BAGH   NEW ENTRANT

1 Abbey Street, Queen Square, Cannock   ✆ 01543 505089

Nanu Miah opened this restaurant in 1991, with Rafique Chowdhury managing. It is a large (120-seat), smartly decorated restaurant, popular locally for the full complement of curry dishes done competently. We hear well of the Monday banquet (£9.95) - a set meal 'but very good value and very filling,' D.R.

SANAM BALTI HOUSE   NEW ENTRANT   BYO

193 Cannock Road, Chadsmore, Cannock   ✆ 01543 573565

'Excellent food and very friendly service. Book or be prepared for a long wait at weekends. It allows you to BYO. Our bill for ten was £64!' Price check: Papadom 35p, Balti CTM £4.95, Pullao Rice £1.10. Open daily 5.30p.m.-1a.m., till 2a.m. Fridays and Saturdays.

Codsall

RAJPUT

The Square, Codsall   ✆ 01902 844642

Its Tudor building could fool you into thinking it's a pub. But it is a smart place, with an upstairs 'rather cramped restaurant, though the food is very good, and the service polite and friendly,' D.G.

Kingsley Holt

THORNBURY HALL RASOI NEW ENTRANT

Lockwood Road, Kingsley Holt   © 01538 750831

This unusual restaurant is approximately 10 miles east of Stoke-on-Trent in a renovated Grade II listed building, once the house of the manor. Since 1994 it has been owned and managed by Mr and Mrs Siddique, who have brought style and Pakistani food to this beautiful area. It has three public areas, including a conference room. 'Could be tricky to find, but my in-laws live close by. The main hall is very grand, but not always open. Other areas are elegant and comfortable. Service good, including some staff from the village in Pakistani dress. Excellent flavours and quality. Sensible portions,' Dr H.M. Price check: Papadom 50p, CTM £5.90, Pullao Rice £1.90. Sunday lunch buffet £8.95, kids £4.50, under 5s free. Open daily for lunch and dinner.

Kinver

SHANAJ TANDOORI NEW ENTRANT   ©

122 High Street, Kinver   © 01384 877744

Three Alis run this 56-seat restaurant. Makmad Ali owns it, Mohammad manages it and Tabaruz cooks. Price check: Papadom 45p, CTM £5.80, Pullao Rice £1.45. Set meal £14.50, veg £10.50. Kurzi Murch £21.50 for two. Open daily 5.30p.m.-midnight.

Lichfield

EASTERN EYE TOP 100   ©

19b Bird Street, Lichfield   © 01543 254399

Abdul Salam has not been sitting still since our last edition, nor is he the type of restaurateur to do so. After 10 years of operations, he has gone for a total redec in his Eastern Eye. But rather than break out the red flock (due for a revival), or the now rather clichéd skeletal leaves (due for their final harvest) and Perspex dividers, Salam has gone to town for the job. Literally, I mean. Local artist Jenny Hobbs dreamed up the idea of creating a house to be found in the Swat valley, right up in Pakistan's northern mountain ranges (just a naan nudge from Baltistan). It is famous for its forests and ornate wooden carved furniture, showing Buddhist influences going back 2000 years and predating Islam. In the restaurant, the beams, pillars and window are from Swat. The bar front is from neighbouring Afghanistan, the chairs are Rajasthani and the table tops are from 150-year-old elm. 'Count the rings,' enthuses Mr Salam. Internal decorating is by Jane Smith, with her 10-year-old daughter painting the radiators. Tracy Potts did the outside sign, and apparently she decorated the toilets, too. These are a 'must-see' on your list. The theme is Agra's Red Fort - probably India's best example of a Moghul residence. Michael Fabricant, M.P., kept his seat at the 1997 election and regularly takes his seat at the Eye as a loyal local. And since he's a member of the Curry Club, we are pleased to hear how much he rates it. Indeed, everyone we hear from rates it highly. 'It is not your standard formula stuff. It is carefully prepared, carefully spiced and thoroughly excellent,' B.M. 'Still excellent, I wish I lived closer! Each time I visit the food still amazes me. Special Patia was superb, portions are large. Faultless service in a quiet but good atmosphere. I was glad to see it is still a TOP 100,' P.J. Price check: Papadom 35p, CTM £6.95, Pullao Rice £1.50. Open 5p.m.-midnight.

LAL BAGU NEW ENTRANT   ©

9 Bird Street, Lichfield   ✆ 01543 262967

Formerly the Indus, we hear of good-quality formula Bangladeshi curries here at owner-chef A. Hussain's restaurant. Wednesday and Sunday Special Dinner £6.95 - four courses - you choose from the menu. Price check: Papadom 40p, CTM £5.25, Pullao Rice £1.40. Open Monday to Thursday 5.30p.m.-midnight, till 1a.m. Friday, noon-midnight Saturday and Sunday.

©	Curry Club discount (see p. 607)		Unlicensed
√	Vegetarian	⊞	Home delivery
BYO	Bring your own alcohol		service available

Newcastle-under-Lyme

BILASH   ©

22 Keele Road, Newcastle-under-Lyme   ✆ 01782 614549

'It's by far the plushest restaurant in town, with wood panel decor, nice cutlery and comfortable seating,' D.E. 'The food is back to form,' D.C. Manager is Abdul Matin. Open daily 5p.m.-12.30a.m. Branches: Asha Takeaway, 22a Higherland, Newcastle-under-Lyme; Monzil, 44 Broad Street, Hanley.

Perton

FLAMINGO EXQUISITE BANGLADESHI CUISINE
NEW ENTRANT   ©

7 Anders Square, Perton   ✆ 01902 745200

Perton, a village just 3 miles west of Wolverhampton, is the location for M. Miah's venture, managed by Rikki Haque. It must get points for the name, says one of our wags, though he speaks more of typical formula curries than exquisiteness. Price check: Papadom 50p, CTM £5.95, Pullao Rice £1.55. Minimum charge £12. Open daily 5.30p.m.-midnight.

Rugeley

BILASH   NEW ENTRANT

7 Horsefair, Rugeley   ✆ 01889 584234

'What a surprise! We went in unplanned on a busy night. A wide choice of dishes was available including 16 different Baltis. Murgh Tikka Rezala was hot and delicious. It is now our favourite,' N. and G.D..

GANGES   ©

5 Horsefair, Rugeley   ✆ 01889 582594

Mahub Ahmed Choudhury runs Rugeley's longest established restaurant. It has many loyal locals who like the food and everything about it. Open daily 5.30p.m.-1a.m.

Shenstone Woodend

THE LODGE   NEW ENTRANT   BYO ©

The Lodge Cottage, 24 Birmingham Road,
Shenstone Woodend   ✆ 01543 483334

Shenstone Woodend is a small Staffordshire green-belt village on the West Midlands border, about 4 miles north of Sutton Coldfield, where Jamal and Imam Uddin opened their Lodge in 1996. It is beautifully appointed, with carpet and pine floors, simple chandeliers, white ceiling-roses, arches and cornices, contrasting against magnolia walls. We hear it is a busy, popular place. 'My family eats as often as possible in this luxurious restaurant with excellent parking facilities. Smart, efficient waiters remember customer names and preferences, and they adore children. Chef Motin Miah excels with a wide variety of Indian cuisine,' R.L.P. Price check: Papadom 40p, CTM £5.45, Kasa Kalia Murgh (green herbal chicken curry) £6.25, Pullao Rice £1.70. Open daily 5.30p.m.-midnight.

Stoke-on-Trent

AL SHEIK'S   TOP 100   BYO

15 Howard Place, Shelton, Stoke-on-Trent   ✆ 01782 285583

It's BYO and it's busy. So busy that if you care to tank up at the pub across the road, they'll call you when they are ready. Then you BYO, and settle down for a cheap and cheerful, very satisfying meal. Again plenty of satisfied reports. 'This restaurant stood up very well. Baltis slightly sharper in taste than our regular Brum local, Adils. The interior is splendid and different from most Indian restaurants. The room is long and thin, about the same width as a railway carriage, and I imagine that at peak periods it can be quite hectic. Recommended. The staff had no idea they were in the Guide until I showed them their entry,' A.G. Just to put the record straight, Al Sheik's has been in our Guide since the 1991 edition. We promoted it to our TOP 100 last time, following numerous good reports from many of our regular scribes, especially S.N. and R.A. Over the years, Al Sheik's has had plentiful correspondence from us, including free window stickers and free wall certificates to put on display, to tell the world of their achievement. Of course, we can't make them do that, but it gets my goat when restaurants deny our existence. But I do believe this is the only TOP 100 that has done so. Still, it makes copy for the intro. Perhaps I should create a further Dummy of the Year Award, but as Guide entrants we'll keep on sending them our free certificate and window stickers, even if they choose to bin them. Perhaps more of their adoring fans should take time out to educate them. Or perhaps with six other branches they don't need us and our accolades. And what cometh before a fall? What do you think? Branches: Crewe, Cheshire; Nantwich, Cheshire; Shelton, Stoke-on-Trent (two branches); Stafford; Stone.

BALTI PALACE ©

39-41 Hope Street, Hanley, Stoke-on-Trent © 01782 274744

Nuruz Zamal's well-stocked menu delivers everything you want. Open weekdays 6p.m.-1.30a.m., weekends till 2a.m.

MONZIL ©

44 Broad Street, Hanley, Stoke-on-Trent © 01782 280150

A. Matin's Monzil has a massive 120 seats, and keeps on going till really late. Open daily 7p.m.-3a.m.

Uttoxeter

KOHI NOOR BYO ©

11 Queen Street, Uttoxeter © 01889 562153

S. Miah's restaurant has been ticking over nicely, in the form of happy

local reports, since 1986, though N. and G.D. have not been going as
regularly as they used to, saying it's not quite on previous form. Others
tell of a licensed place where you can BYO in moderation, making it
a reasonably-priced night out, and a place worth returning to. One of
the bees in my bonnet is just that. The law in Australia states that all
restaurants, whether licensed or not, must allow BYO. True, liquor
sales play a part in the profit margin, though with duty being so high
it is not as great as people imagine. What do create profits are regular
customers, something Mr Miah achieves with flying colours. Price
check: Papadom 50p, CTM £5.95, Kohi Noor Special Balti £9.95,
Pullao Rice £1.50. Open daily 5.30p.m.-midnight. Branch: Kohi Noor,
Shopping Centre, Swadlincote, Derbyshire.

SUFFOLK

Brandon

BRANDON TANDOORI NEW ENTRANT

17-19 London Road, Brandon   *©* **01842 815874**

Arjad Ali's Tandoori opened here in 1991, just a runway length from
USAF Lakenheath. But the roar of the F111s is drowned out here by
the roar of the tandoor, and the roar of approval from the locals. An
aero-med colonel pilot tells us he can't get his curries back home in the
Midwest corn-bowl of America. 'I've gotten my wings twice. Once on
Phantom jets, and again on the Brandon's Chicken Garlic Chilli
(£6.10). It's hotter than my bird's jet pipe!' Price check: Papadom 40p,
CTM £6.20, Pullao Rice £1.70. Minimum charge £10. Open daily
noon-2p.m. and 6-11p.m.

Bury St Edmunds

MUMTAZ INDIAN NEW ENTRANT

---

9 Risbygate Street, Bury St Edmunds   *©* **01284 752988**

New to the Guide, but an old hand (1974) in Bury, is Narul and
Kamral Haque's Mumtaz with, they say, 'probably Britain's most com-

prehensive menu'. Now there's a challenge for a Guide editor! It certainly is not the most comprehensive menu, but they do offer most of the formula and, according to our scribes, they do it very well. Price check: Papadom 50p, CTM £5.90, Pullao Rice £1.75. Minimum charge £6.50. Set meal £22 for two. Open noon-2.30p.m. and 6p.m.-midnight.

Felixstowe

BOMBAY NITE   ©

285 High Street, Felixstowe   ℭ 01394 272131

Owner, Mahbub Alam, can be found front of house greeting his customers at this friendly, competent curry house. Open noon-2.30p.m. and 6-11.30p.m. Branch: Bombay, Orwell Place, Ipswich.

Hadleigh

ROYAL BENGAL

51 High Street, Hadleigh   ℭ 01473 823744

'Small restaurant but very comfortable. Menu is quite extensive and full of old favourites. Speciality tandoori dishes are recommended,' M.B.

Halesworth

RUCHITA   NEW ENTRANT   ©

26 Market Place, Halesworth   ℭ 01986 874524

E. Miah and Z. Allam run the Ruchita, with able assistance from John Gomez in the kitchen, whose handiwork is highly regarded. Try the Chicken Patiwala (£6.20) - diced chicken cooked with cheese, yoghurt, garlic, garnished with stuffed tomato and capsicum. Price check: Papadom 40p, CTM £5.20, Pullao Rice £1.30. Set meal £22 for two. Open daily 4.30-11.30p.m.

Ipswich

SONAR BANGLA   NEW ENTRANT   ©

36-40 Grimwade Street, Ipswich   ✆ 01473 252310

The clue that owner-chef Aftab Ali's menu is Bangladeshi formula lies in the name. Management is in Harun Ali's hands. Our attention is drawn to Aftab's *pièce de résistance*, the Tandoori Murgh Mussalla (£6.80) - two chicken pieces cooked with pistachio, cream, minced meat, egg and tomato, served with Pullao Rice. There is a commendably long list of vegetarian specials. Price check: Papadom 55p, CTM £3.95, Pullao Rice £1.10. Minimum charge £6.50. Set meal £14.95, veg £11.95 for two. Open daily noon-2p.m. and 5-11.30p.m.

TAJ MAHAL   ©

40-42 Norwich Road, Ipswich   ✆ 01473 257712

Opened in 1985 and serving competent curries and accompaniments, its 60 seats are managed by Muktar Ali. Open noon-2p.m. and 6p.m.-midnight.

Lowestoft

AHMED   ©

150 Bridge Road, Oulton Broad, Lowestoft ✆ 01502 501725

Boshor Ali's cute little restaurant has just 28 seats. 'Brilliant,' says P.J. Open noon-2.30p.m. and 6-11.30p.m. Branch: Jorna Indian Takeaway, 29-33 Wherstead Road, Ipswich.

SEETA   ©

176 High Street, Lowestoft   ✆ 01502 574132

Is a 28-seater the norm round here? I don't suppose that's why M. Uddin gave his pretty establishment that name. (Groan!) Sita is the Indian goddess of beauty and love. Alternatively, the Sitar is the melodic Indian stringed instrument. Now you'll remember the name! Either way, you like the Seeta. It has the usual curries and accompaniments on the menu including, we're told, fresh scampi on request in the curries. Open daily except Tuesday noon-2p.m. and 6-11.30p.m.

Newmarket

ARIF INDIAN RESTAURANT   NEW ENTRANT

30-32 Old Station Road, Newmarket   © 01638 665888

Messrs Ahmed and Ahadi opened the Arif in 1995, and already we hear that you have to jockey for a seat on race days, in this now very popular, attractive restaurant. 'Our friends took the trouble to think ahead, and book ahead, for the Khurzi Lamb (£58 for four). It's a whole leg of lamb, apparently marinated for ever, and slowly cooked for ever in the oven, until it is too tender to believe. They do something with red wine in the cooking, but we can't fathom what. Anyway, who cares? It's a great way to be entertained by our friends. For over three hours we were stuffed full of papadoms, chutneys, starters, the magical lamb, curry side dishes, special fried rice, house wine, coffee, fabulous service and good will, at the end of which we simply roll into a taxi home, and our friends have no washing up to do!' J.McA. Price check: Papadom 50p, CTM £5.95, Pullao Rice £1.60. Open daily noon-2.30p.m. and 6p.m.-midnight.

Stowmarket

ROYAL TANDOORI   ©

16-18 Tavern Street, Stowmarket   © 01449 674392

M. Ahmed and S. Miah's 'food is gorgeous,' P.J. 'Once I got used to the idea of curry gravy with Chicken Jalfrezi, it was decidedly delicious. Keema Naans are excellent. Easily worth its place in the Guide,' L.G. Price check: Papadom 50p, CTM £6.90, Pullao Rice £1.50. Open noon-3p.m. and 6-11.30p.m.

Woodbridge

ROYAL BENGAL   TOP 100   ©

6 Quay Street, Woodbridge   ℂ **01394 387983**

We never seem to have much to say about this restaurant. Yet it remains in our TOP 100, simply because it is currinarily correct in all departments. We have never had a complaint. The venue is spotlessly clean, including the toilets. The welcome is warm. The service is efficient, friendly, accurate, and positive. The untoward is handled with experience and tact, such as late arrivals, customer ordering error, spillages and small things that can become big things, such as a corked bottle of wine, spotted by the waiter and removed before comment was needed by the clients. There is nothing over-remarkable about the items on the attractive menu. But everything is here, and everything is cooked well, and is above average. Even the departure is handled well. Customer care is uppermost, and if other restaurants modelled themselves on these simple rules there would be 9300 TOP 100 restaurants in this Guide, but then I suppose there would be no need for our Guide at all. Open noon-2.30p.m. and 6-11.30p.m.

SURREY

Parts of Surrey were absorbed by Greater London in 1965. We note affected boroughs with the letters GL.

Addington, GL

SURUCHI   NEW ENTRANT   ©

120 Headley Drive, New Addington   ℂ **01689 841998**

A standard Bangladeshi curry house, opened in 1995 by A. Miah, with manager Junel Ali. Price check: Papadom 40p, CTM £5.80, Manchurian Chicken £5.90, Pullao Rice £1.50. Minimum charge £12. Open daily 5.30-11.30p.m. Branch: Goa Tandoori, 118 Bromley Road, Catford, London SE6.

Ashford

SHAPPI OF ASHFORD NEW ENTRANT

7 Church Parade, Church Road, Ashford   ✆ 01784 423266

'Reasonably impressed with the quality and price. Onion Bhaji £1.55, Prawn Dhansak £3.65, Chicken Biryani £4.95, Pullao Rice £1.45 and Peshwari/Keema Nan £1.35. A decent local with reasonable service,' S.R.

Ashtead

MOGHUL DYNASTY   ©

1 Craddock Parade, Ashtead   ✆ 01372 274810

Manager Abdul Mannan's restaurant has been the favourite local for years. Open noon-2.30p.m. and 5.30-11p.m. Branch: Cannon Tandoori, 7 Station Parade, Cannon Park, Edgware, Middlesex.

Banstead

BANSTEAD TANDOORI   ©

6 High Street, Banstead   ✆ 01737 362757

Manager Abdul Noor's place is the one in Banstead we hear about most often. Open noon-3p.m. and 6-11.30p.m.

Bramley

CHAMPAN TANDOORI

High Street, Bramley, Nr Guildford   ✆ 01483 893684

D.B.A.C. comes here and says: 'It is a delightful little restaurant. Seating is split between two beamed rooms, the smaller one is almost like a private dining room and would be great for an exclusive party, seating about ten. I always order Chicken Tikka Masala as my benchmark and can tell you that it is superb, the chef adds puréed mango chutney which gives it a slightly sweet but tangy flavour.' 'Small but cosy. Best Chicken Murgh I've ever had - so garlicky - a new recipe, they informed me!' s.v.

Byfleet

RED ROSE OF BYFLEET   ©

148-150 High Road, Byfleet   ✆ 01932 355559

An attractively decorated restaurant, with plaster cornices and dado rails. Ivies and palms divide tables and chandeliers hang from the ceilings. King Prawn dishes are house specialities. Managing partner, Shuel Miah, appropriately gives a rose to the lady on departure. Open noon-2.30p.m. and 6-11.30p.m. Branch: Gaylord in Weybridge, Weybridge; Red Rose in Surbiton, Surbiton; Red Rose of Chessington, Chessington.

Camberley

ANCIENT RAJ

9 The Parade, Frimley High Street, Frimley,
Camberley   ✆ 01276 21503

'Very professional, decor of high standard, starched table linen. Courteous services. Food aimed at Raj period of Indian history, excellent quality, good range of specials. All chicken dishes prepared with best cuts. No bitter and the lager was very expensive,' r.v.

DIWAN EE KHASS

365 London Road, Camberley   ✆ 01276 66606

'Chicken Jalfrezi tends to be on the hot side and is usually made even hotter for me. Staff appreciate my desire for hot food - if I don't have the Jalfrezi I choose the Meat Phal. Situated in a poor location so not that busy, my dread is that they will close and leave a gaping hole in my life and stomach. Introduced a special - Islamabad Balti,' b.g.

FRIMLEY TANDOORI TAKEAWAY NEW ENTRANT ©

47 High Street, Frimley, Camberley   ✆ 01276 685537

Everything you expect to find on the menu at owner-chef Hussain Ahamed's takeaway-only, managed by Abdul Kashem with, commendably, some Bangladeshi specials. Price check: Papadom 35p, CTM £6.10 incl. rice, Pullao Rice £1.55. Open daily noon-2p.m. and 6-11.30p.m.

TARIQ'S INDIAN BRASSERIE NEW ENTRANT ⊞

369 London Road, Camberley   ✆ 01276 66422

Opened in 1995. 'Built up an excellent reputation in my eyes! Restaurant beautifully decorated with tasteful background music to add to the ambience. Staff are first-class, polite, helpful and attentive when required. Ample portions. Chicken Vindaloo (£4.20) could have been slightly more spicy for my own taste, I'll ask for that next time. Home-delivery service available,' w.p.s. Price check: Papadom 35p, CTM £6.20, Pullao Rice £1.60. Open Monday to Saturday lunch and dinner, Sunday dinner only.

Carshalton, GL

ASIA STANDARD ©

140-142 High Street, Carshalton   ✆ 0181 647 0286

Reliable, good curry house of managing owner, Abdul Hannan. Open noon-2.30p.m. and 6-11.30p.m.

CLAY OVEN TAKEAWAY ©

15a Gordon Road, Carshalton Beeches   ✆ 0181 647 9190

A takeaway-only establishment, opened in 1992 by Hermon Miah. Open 5.30-11.30p.m. Branch: Gaylord, 141 Manchester Road, Isle of Dogs, London E14.

ROSE HILL TANDOORI   ⊞ ©

320 Wrythe Lane, Rose Hill, Carshalton   ℂ 0181 644 9793

Opened in 1985 by Salequr Rahman, it seats an intimate 32 diners. The menu offers all your favourite curries and accompaniments, and on the drinks menu I see Confederates' Coffee, made with Southern Comfort – nice one! There is also a delivery service. Price check: Papadom 35p, CTM £4, Pullao Rice £1.50. Minimum charge £6. Open noon-2.30p.m. and 5.30p.m.-midnight.

Chipstead

CHIPSTEAD TANDOORI   ©

32 Station Approach, Chipstead   ℂ 01737 556401

Manager Abdul Munaim's restaurant is popular, with a loyal following and a good London pedigree (*see* branches). Open noon-2.30p.m. and 6-11.30p.m. Branches: Delhi Brasserie, 134 Cromwell Road, Kensington, London sw7; Delhi Brasserie, 44 Frith Street, London wc2.

Cobham

COPPER CHIMNEY NEW ENTRANT   ©

40 Portsmouth Road, Cobham   ℂ 01932 863666

A. Alam opened here in 1995, with P.H. Choudhry managing and Shaid Miah in the kitchens. We soon amassed a number of good reports indicating that it is a cut above the norm. 'It is an old building and is very quaint, with lots of little alcoves, wooden beams and cream walls, set off with a blue carpet and rich damask tablecloths with matching napkins, and a fresh flower on each table. My husband declared his Tandoori King Prawn Massala (£11.95) as memorable, while my Bhuna Murgh Tandoor (£7.95) - dry curried chicken - was superb. With it we had Keralan Bhuna Kaji (£2.95) - sautéed cashew nuts - wonderful - very hot temperature-wise, very crunchy and with a slightly sweet taste. We'll be back,' j.w. Others talk of Spicy Crab Cake (£3.95) and Patray (£3.95) - deep-fried leaf in gram flour batter, Duck Curried with

Apricot (£10.95 incl. rice), Roast Duck Massala (£8.95), Salmon Kedgeree (£8.95). Price check: Papadom 35p, CTM £6.50, Pullao Rice £1.95. Open daily noon-2.30p.m. and 6-11.30p.m.

Croydon, GL

AKASH NEW ENTRANT   BYO ©

79 London Road, West Croydon   ✆ **0181 686 4464**

Formerly the Jaipur, it was taken over in 1996 and renamed by Abdul Muktadir and Abdul Hussain, who look after the kitchen and the front of house respectively. Croydon's price-war makes it one of the cheapest around, made even more economical by BYO and the Curry Club discount. Price check: Papadom 30p, CTM £3.20, Balti Special £3.50, Pullao Rice £1. Set meal from £5.50. Minimum charge £5. Open daily 12.30-2.30p.m. and 6p.m.-midnight.

BANANA LEAF   ©

27 Lower Addiscombe Road, Croydon   ✆ **0181 688 0297**

Mr V. Thambi is manager of one of two good south Indian restaurants in the area, serving authentic food. Owner Mr D. Sitharaman is also the head chef, creating all your favourites, and some of his, in the kitchen. Fully licensed. Open noon-2.30p.m. and 6-11.30p.m.

THE DEANS   ©

241 London Road, Croydon   ✆ **0181 665 9192**

The Deans opened in 1993 and is named after its chef-owner Salam Ud Din and manager Zaka Ud Din. It is a massive, fully-licensed restaurant seating over 100 diners. It has some arch mosaic mirror decorations, to be found in the Moghul palaces. It has a small but typically authentic Pakistani Punjabi menu, serving tandoori items and well-spiced curries. 'Rows and rows of fairly plain tables, often packed full. What we like about it is the number of Asians in the place, probably something like 80%, which is generally a good sign of the standards and quality offered. The food comes predominantly in iron karahis or earthenware pots (handis), which makes the whole meal look that much more interesting besides helping to retain heat in the food. We enjoyed a selection of starters and main courses and several rounds of excellent ethnic beers,' c.d. Price check: Papadom 30p, CTM £5.50, Handi Aloo Chana £3.50, Dhal-stuffed Karela (bitter gourd) £5, Pullao Rice £1.50. Open noon-3p.m. and 6p.m.-midnight.

ROYAL TANDOORI 2 ⊞

226 Addington Road, Selsdon, Croydon   ✆ 0181 651 3500

An attractive restaurant decorated in green, with engraved glass panels separating diners. Restaurant is partitioned by plants, which splits up a rather large and long room. A few interesting dishes on the menu include Veal Karahi, Quail Karahi and Tandoori Trout. Home delivery is available. Open noon-2.30p.m. and 6-11.30p.m., weekends till midnight. Branch: Royal Tandoori 1, 209 Godstone Road, Whyteleafe.

RUPEES TAKEAWAY NEW ENTRANT ©

184 Wickham Road, Shirley, Croydon   ✆ 0181 655 1866

E. Karim Khan and chef Chand Miah opened their Rupees in 1996, brave fellows considering the Croydon price-wars, and hope to make rupees themselves, though the prices are very cheap at this takeaway-only venue. Price check: Papadom 35p, CTM £4.40, Pullao Rice £1.30. Set meal £7.25 veggie, £9.50 non-veggie. Open daily 5-11p.m. Branch: Shelina Takeaway, 62 Church Road, Crystal Palace.

SOUTH INDIA

16 London Road, Croydon   ✆ 0181 688 6216

Owned since 1989 by Mr Dinamani and Mr Vaman, the former (ex-Sree Krishna, London sw17) heads the kitchen and the latter is front of house manager. It's a licensed south Indian restaurant serving lovely vegetarian dishes, including your editors' favourite dishes, such as Oothappam (£2.20) - spicy pizza, Masala Dosai (£2.20) - stuffed pancake, with Iddli Sambar (£2.90) - rice cakes in spicy thin lentil gravy, Kalan (£2) - yoghurt curry with mangoes and Coconut Chutney (50p). There is enormous choice for the carnivore, though the house has no tandoor so no CTM! Try the Meat Fry (£4.90) - made dry with coconut and spicy with red chilli instead. And in-betweenies will love the Fish Curries (£4.50). Price check: Papadom 50p, Chicken Masala £4.50, Pullao Rice £1.90. Set lunch £2.95 and £4.95. Set dinner £10.90. Minimum charge £3. Open noon-2.30p.m. and 6-11p.m.

Dorking

MOGHUL

187 High Street, Dorking   ✆ **01306 876296**

The best in town, says P.W.: 'Wide choice of meals consumed, all up to usual high standards.'

East Molesey

GOLDEN CURRY   ©

19 Hampton Court Parade, East Molesey   ✆ **0181 979 4358**

Thirty years is a long time in anyone's book, and that's how long A. Aziz's Golden Curry has been going. It makes for three generations of regulars who go for a stable, quality operation and friendly service, led by head waiter Abdul Karim. Price check: Papadom 45p, CTM £5.10, Pullao Rice £1.70. Minimum charge £6. Open noon-2.30p.m. and 6p.m.-midnight.

Epsom

LE RAJ

211 Firtree Road, Epsom Downs   ✆ **01737 371371**

Owner-chef Enam Ali's cooking is light and innovative, and includes some Bangladeshi specials. For those who like things spicy, ask and you shall receive. Front of house is run by Enam's brother, Tipu. But we are perplexed. We have eaten here on more than one occasion, and we know Le Raj satisfies a large local following. It's always full, we hear, and maybe they are used to Enam's light touch. But for every good report received, there are two dissatisfied ones. 'The restaurant was empty when we arrived, but filled up by the time we left at about 8p.m. Service was good, and so was the atmosphere, even when it was empty. The food was well-presented and fresh. Exclusive dishes on the menu to make the experience interesting. Impressed,' s.r. 'Certainly not curry house formula stuff, and that makes it a place to visit for a refreshing change,' j.k. 'Unfortunately we were greatly disappointed. Summunder-Se and Tangri Kebab, both starters, were OK but unremarkable. Main courses lacked in spicing, though the Naan was cooked just as we'd asked for, and the Aloo Gobi was fresh and crunchy. The prices must be near the top of the UK's Indian restaurant trade,' a.m. 'Table booked for six people, chairs too large for table, had to forage for chairs that fitted, very little help from staff. Menu suggested special dishes, but the quantities very small, prices very high. Prawn Korma looked terrible and tasted no better. Korai Lamb and Chicken Dansak good, but small portions,' c.r.r. m.p.w.'s report ran to three pages of criticism. There is no doubt that Enam, as one of the founders of the Bangladeshi Caterers' Association, is a pioneer and a very capable owner-chef, and Tipu is a good lieutenant. But I sincerely worry that his outside interests are affecting things at the restaurant. A good tweak on the tiller is needed now. Open daily for lunch and dinner. Reports, please.

SAVAR BALTI HOUSE NEW ENTRANT   ©

21 Waterloo Road, Epsom   ✆ **01372 724167**

The 1976 Anwar changed name, and hands, to Moin Uddin in 1996. The new menu has many old favourites and one or two nice changes, such as Salmon Samosa (£3.20), Duck Muglai (£5.10) or Balti (£5.50), Bangladeshi Fish (£5.50) and Shatkora Chicken or Lamb (£3.95) - cooked with Bangladeshi citrus fruit. And, as I always say, it's worth breaking the habits of a lifetime and trying these more authentic dishes. Price check: Papadom 40p, CTM £5.10, Pullao Rice £1.50. Open daily noon-2.30p.m. and 6-11.30p.m. Branch: Savar Tandoori, Sutton.

©	Curry Club discount (see p. 607)	🍵	Unlicensed
√	Vegetarian	🏧	Home delivery
BYO	Bring your own alcohol		service available

Ewell

BOMBAY   ©

332 Kingston Road, Ewell   ✆ 0181 393 0445

A very long-standing and capable curry house, managed by F. Miah.
Open noon-2.30p.m. and 6p.m.-midnight.

CURRY HOUSE

1 Cheam Road, Ewell   ✆ 0181 393 0734

'Gosht Methi was particularly delicious and had a crunchy texture from
fresh onion. Tarka Dhal also deserves a mention, perfect for dipping
Naans into. Food was piping hot and the portions adequate,' Dr J.P.

Farnham

DARJEELING

25 South Street, Farnham   ✆ 01252 714322

Owned by A. Rahman and S. Islam. Seats 46 diners so booking, particularly at weekends, is necessary. 'Everything about this restaurant is
good. The decor is subtle, low light, tropical fish. Good carpeting and
sumptuous table linen and crockery. The menu is extensive. Service is
very good. Waiters are friendly but unobtrusive. Food is excellent, subtly spiced, generous portions, excellent quality. Continues to be our
favourite restaurant,' J.W. Price check: Papadom 55p, CTM £7.95 incl.
rice, Pullao Rice £1.75. Buffet Sunday lunch £8.95. Minimum charge
£10.50. Open noon-2p.m. and 6-11.30p.m. Branches: Banaras, 40
Downing Street, Farnham; Viceroy, 1a High Street, Hartley Wintney,
Hampshire.

SHOMRAT   NEW ENTRANT

133 Upper Hale Road, Upper Hale,
Farnham   ✆ 01252 735175

'A very up-market-looking restaurant, seating 50-60. The carpeting is sumptuous, the tables and beech chairs of high quality, topped with pink and white starched tablecloths and napkins. There are marble pillars, chintz curtains, moulded reliefs of various animals, pictures painted directly onto the walls. The lighting is shaded, there is a candle on each table and a vase of fresh flowers. The waiters are very smart and have a good knowledge of all the dishes on the menu. We had Balti Surat Chicken (£2.90), which Geoff enjoyed but I thought was a bit bland, with not much of a flavour in the batter. It was delightfully served with cucumber and lettuce and a small jug of mint sauce. We were advised not to have our usual four Papadoms and chutney as the main course we had ordered was very filling. They were right. We had Tabaq Lobster Tapa (£9.60) with Mushroom Rice (£2.45) and Cauliflower Bhaji (£2.45). It was delicious, but again I felt a little disappointed that there was not more taste of the spices, but masses of onion. However, the lobster was very plentiful. A highly recommended restaurant,' J.W.

Fetcham

FETCHAM TANDOORI

248 Cobham Road, Fetcham   ✆ **01372 374927**

'Service was pleasant, though distant. Onion Bhajia was large and crisp. Phall was tasty (I was expecting a super fire-eater experience - instead I received a Phall barely hotter than a Madras), together with the Pillau Rice, and Mushroom Bhaji plentiful. Restaurant scrupulously clean, decor predominantly green, brown, pleasantly relaxing,' B.P.-D. Open noon-2.30p.m. and 6-11p.m., till midnight Friday and Saturday.

Godalming

FARNCOMBE TANDOORI

18 Farncombe Street, Farncombe,
Godalming   ✆ **01483 423131**

'Wide menu of standard dishes. Just the right amounts of food. Very tasty Sag Aloo and Butter Chicken. Pleasant service at the right time,'

B.H. Open noon-2.30p.m. and 6-11.30p.m., till midnight Friday and Saturday. Branch: Chalfont Tandoori Takeaway, 4 Station Approach, Little Chalfont, Amersham, Buckinghamshire.

Guildford

KOHINOOR   ©

24 Woodbridge Road, Guildford   © 01483 306051

Owner-chef Azizur Rahman's Kohinoor is a bit tricky to find, being adjacent to, but not directly accessible from, the bypass, but this does not deter the locals. 'Gets busy at the weekends. Service and food are excellent and this is rapidly becoming my favourite in Guildford,' C.D. 'My wife's Pasanda was the most delicious she has ever eaten. Very reasonable prices considering the location. Tables very close to each other,' E.J.R. 'Well worth its place in the Guide, well done. A light and bright atmosphere. Had a special resembling a Madras crossed with a Jalfrezi - rich sauce and an abundance of green chillies - superb! Happy to return anytime,' R.V. Price check: Papadom 50p, CTM £6.25, Pullao Rice £1.75. Minimum charge £7.50. Open noon-2.30p.m. and 6-11.30p.m.

MERROW DYNASTY   NEW ENTRANT

261 Epsom Road, Merrow, Guildford   © 01483 562190

'A fairly new restaurant (1995) with an attractive façade and equally attractive interior, typical modern Indian. Staff, smart, welcoming and efficient. Fairly extensive menu and locals obviously support the takeaway service very well. All the food was excellent. Three different starters, four main courses, two vegetable side dishes, Bombay Duck, rice, Papadoms, etc. A pretty typical meal in quantity. We were all very happy with the restaurant and the food, definitely a "would go back" place. Has the advantage of being out of the centre of Guildford so it is easy to park nearby,' H.C. Welcome to the Guide, Mr Choudhury. However, I'm not impressed by your silly rule: cheques and credit cards accepted only for orders above £10. Bad luck on me if I want to go alone for your Tuesday evening buffet (£9.95) with no cash! (*See* intro.) Price check: Papadom 45p, CTM £6.95, Pullao Rice £1.75. Open daily noon-2.30p.m. and 5.30-11p.m.

RAJDOOT NEW ENTRANT

220 London Road, Burpham, Guildford   © 01483 451278

S. and M. Miah opened here in 1992, with an air-conditioned restaurant which 'proved to be a boon during the recent hot summers, especially since we get overheated enough with our chillies! As non-meat-eaters, we are especially taken with their Bengal Fish Massalam (£7.50) - a freshwater Bangladeshi fish, which they call bowl, but is boal, is cooked highly spiced with onion, chilli, garlic and cumin. We love it with the Bindi Bhaji, Tarka Dhal and Mushroom Rice (all £2.20),' D.C. Price check: Papadom 50p, CTM £6.50, Pullao Rice £1.80. Sunday buffet £6.50. Minimum charge £8.50. Open daily noon-2.30p.m. and 5.30-11p.m.

Haslemere

SHAHANAZ EDITOR'S CHOICE

17 Kings Road, Haslemere   © 01428 651380

The sight of the little red Fiat van driven by the chef-owner Mr Ullah whizzing around Haslemere is a familiar and reassuring sight to curryholics. He took over the Shahanaz some years ago and, shortly after that, he pioneered home-delivery in this area, and it probably transformed the restaurant's fortunes. Their tiny 25-seat restaurant is busy enough on weekdays, boosted by its takeaway trade. After a full day writing about curry (what a way to earn a living - it's better than working), both your editors look at each other and say 'We've just got to have a curry.' Sometimes, for the real thing we travel miles, to Southall, for example. But since this is a work up, and we don't always want home delivery, we just flop round to our local, usually soon after opening. It's a great time for people-watching. Weekday regulars include a number of pinstripes who nip in straight off the Waterloo to Portsmouth train. (Laughingly called an Intercity, and now the responsibility of Stagecoach - you know the one: it has narrowly avoided a £1m fine for inefficiency - so it's a stressful journey for the oft-delayed London commuter requiring a chill-out - or is that a chilli-out?) Anyway, the station is opposite, so some have pre-ordered on their mobiles and pick up their goodies straightaway. Another one pops in,

orders and asks for it to be delivered, leaves, presumably allowing him
time to shower, change and have a chota peg before his curry arrives.
Meanwhile, if the van is busy, which it usually is, the station taxi rank
supplies a driver to do the home deliveries. One of these chaps, we
observed, was being quite bossy, telling the kitchen to speed up, and
querying the contents of the bags, but the staff can handle it all ami-
ably. The free delivery radius is enormous, and we have heard of up to
four drivers doing this at the weekend. Restaurants that charge for the
privilege, such as Anwars, Bognor, at 75p a mile, should reflect that
even MPs don't get that much and they should ask, does this imposi-
tion deter business? Ask the Shahanaz perhaps, because their business
has never been healthier. Incidentally, it does formula Bangladeshi
curry house food. Like most places, it does it better on weekdays, the
Friday-Saturday pressure meaning they lack the edge. D.B.A.C. still
orders the same old thing, having no doubt written copiously in the
Guide that you must be adventurous and try this and that new thing.
'I do try new things at other places, but on my home patch I confess
that it's normally the old faithfuls: Chicken Tikka followed by CTM
or Chicken Dhansak, their Bombay Potato - wonderful, with onions
and capsicums - and their creamy Sag Paneer. Once I ordered Palak
Paneer and head waiter Mr Rouf gently told me off. "It's Sag Paneer,"
he said! "We're not from the Punjab." Naans are large and fresh.
Papadoms always crisp and light, and they do a great onion chutney.
Mr Rouf, by the way, is an avuncular "old hand". His riveting tales
about his lascar (sailor) ancestors from Sylhet, who for generations
crewed the East Indiamen ships on the Calcutta-London route until
the demise of the docks in the middle of this century got them into
the business of the British curry, appear in Pat's book *Bangladeshi
Restaurant Curries.* "After all," winks Mr Rouf, "all Bangladeshis come
from Sylhet!"' Price check: Papadom 50p, CTM £5.75, Pullao Rice
£1.75. Open daily noon-2.30p.m. and 6p.m.-midnight. Home deliveries,
evenings only.

©	Curry Club discount (see p. 607)	☕	Unlicensed
√	Vegetarian	⊞	Home delivery
BYO	Bring your own alcohol		service available

Horley

FORT RAJ BALTI RESTAURANT NEW ENTRANT

74 Victoria Road, Horley   ✆ 01293 822909

With a name like this, you'd be right to expect many Balti dishes at Ali Athar and Abdul Khan's restaurant. Our attention is drawn to one of chef Ali Mokoddus's specials, Balti Chicken or Lamb Tikka Shankapuri (£6.95), whose sauce contains coconut and red wine. 'Portions large and well-presented. Service very friendly. Decor is tasteful,' Mr and Mrs D.N.L. Price check: Papadom 50p, CTM £7.95, Pullao Rice £1.50. Set dinner £16.95. Open daily noon-2.30p.m. and 6p.m.-midnight.

Kingston upon Thames, GL

GOLDEN CURRY   ▦ ©

36-38 High Street, Hampton Wick,
Kingston upon Thames   ✆ 0181 977 1422

Mabashar Ali's menu lists all our favourite curries and accompaniments, with a few specials as well, such as Chicken Rejala - fairly hot with yoghurt and black pepper. Free home delivery service available. Open noon-2.30p.m. and 6p.m.-midnight.

MONTY'S TANDOORI   ©

53 Fife Road, Kingston upon Thames   ✆ 0181 546 1724

A modern restaurant, with a light and airy feel, owned by Kishor Shrestha. South Indian face-masks decorate the white walls and hang from cream drapes. Hand-painted silk pictures of Indian scenes cover the walls, the floor is tiled. 'Service is excellent, unobtrusive, polite and no mistakes. Food is plentiful and piping hot,' S.T. Open noon-3p.m. and 6p.m.-midnight.

Leatherhead

CURRY QUEEN

41 Church Street, Bookham, Leatherhead   ✆ 01372 457241

'Have always been impressed with the constant high standard of cooking. Delicious Chicken Tikka and Butterfly Prawns. Wonderful Naan bread. A true feast at a reasonable price,' E.J.R.

Oxted

GURKHA KITCHEN   NEW ENTRANT

111 Station Road, Oxted   ✆ 01883 722621

With the demise of Mahatma Cote, the former occupant at 111 Oxted Road, our regular reporter C.D. was devastated that his pun 'What do you call an Indian cloakroom attendant?' could no longer be used. (Oh yes it can, Colin, I'm not one to let a good corny gag go that easily, so we'll get at least one more outing with it.) He says 'So much for the restaurant with the modest claim to being the best in Surrey. It did not sustain standards, aided and abetted by very poor waiting staff. But its replacement, The Gurkha Kitchen, offers excellent Nepalese fare. We started off with Tareko Shabg (£1.95) - deep-fried vegetables - and Choyia (£2.45) - smoked chicken with spices and onion, served cold - followed by Phewa Maccha (£6.50) - pan-fried fish wrapped in crisp spinach with coriander sauce, and Gurkhali Chicken (£4.95) - marinated for hours in green chilli, ginger and Nepali herbs accompanied by Kalo Daal (£2.25) - black urid dhal in a special pot, with Tibetan herbs, Aloo Tama Bodi (£2.40), Patina Patre (£2) - unleavened bread with fresh mint, and Rashilo Bhat (£1.80) - rice cooked with bay leaf and cardamom, and garnished with Onion Tarka. All items well presented and very tasty, with strong spicing, but not in the same way as Madras, Vindaloo or Phal. We had with it Nepalese-brewed beer called Iceberg. All in all it cost two of us £38 for an interesting and different set of flavours. Interior is still first-class with a lot of attention being paid to the presentation. Good crisp white linen, decent cutlery and glassware. The staff are first-class, friendly with a good grip on English. Perhaps they are all ex-Gurkha troops - definitely the finest fighting machines in the world,' c.d. Three-course buffet lunch daily £6.99. Open weekdays noon-2.30p.m. and 6-11p.m., till 11.30p.m. Fridays and Saturdays, Sundays 1-10p.m. Of all the Nepalese restaurants whose menus we have seen (and there are precious few anywhere in the UK), this one is the most faithful to Nepalese food, with not a single item bowing to the curry formula. Long may that last, and it will if you support it. Decidedly one to watch. Many reports, please.

Purley, GL

INDIA PALACE   ©

11 Russell Parade, Russell Hill Road,
Purley   © **0181 660 6411**

Well-liked curry formula house owned by Z. Haq. 'My mother-in-law's favourite. A full menu at reasonable prices with a superb Tandoori Chicken OFF the bone, i.e., it was whole but boned,' t.n. Open noon-2.30p.m. and 6-11.30p.m.

Redhill

EXOTICA TANDOORI   NEW ENTRANT   ©

18 Cromwell Road, Redhill   © **01737 778624**

Unlike the SW London restaurant with this name, owner Sazid Ali has resisted calling his 1990 venue the Exotikka, although the menu is predictably as full of Tikka as it is of formula curries et al. On takeaway orders, two free cans of lager on orders over £12, bottle of house wine on orders over £20. Price check: Papadom 40p, CTM £5.25, Pullao Rice £1.20. Open noon-2.30p.m. and 5.30-11.30p.m.

Reigate

VILLAGE BRASSERIE   NEW ENTRANT   ©

10 West Street, Reigate   © **01737 245695**

When it was the Reigate Tandoori, you said it is: 'The best in Reigate by a wide margin. Food arrived very well presented and tasted fresh and authentic. I recommend this well-appointed restaurant, especially the Sunday buffet,' A.D. It has been in A. Rashid's ownership since 1997, with A. Ali managing. The Sunday buffet is still good value at £6.25, £3.50 kids. Price check: Papadom 50p, CTM £4.95, Pullao Rice £1.50. Minimum charge £10. Open daily 5.30-11.30p.m., Sunday also open noon 4p.m.

Richmond upon Thames, GL

INDIAN TANDOORI

113 Kew Road, Richmond upon Thames   ✆ 0181 940 4308

'Everyone gets Papadoms and chutneys while they peruse the menu. Food was excellent, just the right heat, flavours wonderful,' J.M.W. 'It's our second favourite, and we're from Hampshire. The little old boy who runs it is always delighted to see us. He knows exactly what we like, and will always suggest something new for us to try. The restaurant is not flush in its fittings, but is clean and functional. Started with Papadoms and five chutneys, which were delicious. King Prawn Madras was hot but the taste of the spices was not obliterated,' J.W.

LICHFIELD BRASSERIE NEW ENTRANT   ©

13 Lichfield Terrace, Sheen Road,
Richmond upon Thames   ✆ 0181 332 6704

The archetypal formula menu from Noor Miah and M. Choudhury. Price check: Papadom 50p, CTM £6.95, Pullao Rice £1.60. Service charge 10%. Sunday buffet £6.95, £3.95 kids. Open daily noon-2.30p.m. and 6p.m.-midnight, Sunday lunch noon-6p.m., dinner till midnight.

Q'S NEW ENTRANT   ©

135 Kew Road, Richmond upon Thames   ✆ 0181 940 5552

This just-opened venture differs from the formula, with authentic home-style Indian food and a hint of Sri Lankan, managed by R. Revantha and Nick Salt. Reports, please. Open every evening except Monday.

RANI NEW ENTRANT   √

3 Hill Street, Richmond upon Thames   ℂ 0181 332 2322

The parentage is by Sheila and Jyoti Pattni, whose London Rani (*see* entry) has been a firm favourite in our Guide since it opened in 1984. It is Gujarati and south Indian vegetarian cooking. When they expanded the seating at their London branch in 1991, the cooking took a dip for some time, but then returned to form. Richmond is a much bigger proposition and, although we've had plentiful praise for it, mostly from locals, we also have had this dampener from H.C., our number one reporter, who spends much of her eating-out time at similar vegetarian restaurants: 'Apart from the modern style with acres of polished parquet flooring and hundreds of square feet of plain walls, completely devoid of any pictures, the tables and chairs are modern canteen-style, the latter slippery to sit on, and very uncomfortable. There was no atmosphere, and Ella Fitzgerald tapes and white staff gave no feel of India. The Chef's Special Starter of the Day (£3.60), billed as potato stuffed with garlic and spices and fried, turned out to be two potatoes, coated with lukewarm, cooked-earlier batter, and the stuffing was a knife blade inserted into each potato, leaving a smear of chilli paste. The Spinach and Aubergine Curry (£4.80) and Plain Dosa were all right, but I felt being charged for a full Masala Dosa (£8.40) was a bit of a nerve. The couple nearby seemed satisfied, though. It was a good job my husband wasn't with me. He'd have thought it a complete waste of time.' On the other hand, s.b. found it 'unlike any other Indian restaurant. The chutneys were hot, the Dosa massive and wonderful value.' This so-called 'family-run' place will only allow children at the management's discretion after 7p.m. So does that mean, having climbed up to the first floor, a potentially embarrassing refusal and an exit downstairs again in front of a room full of customers, following an inquisition? Phew! Come on, Jyoti, wise up. Whatever are you thinking of? I remember your original place with bumbling service, and your Mum in the kitchen years ago cooking brilliant food. I don't recall it ever being cheap, but I remember being told that if I left a tip it would be donated to charity. I don't remember barmy rules and over-pricing. Maybe all this suits the Richmond richarati, with holes in their wallets as big as Vadai, and their kids left with the nanny or the au-pair. But can you afford to alienate real *aficionados* (who can equally afford to eat here, provided they get value for money) on whose custom, in the long run, you'll survive? As soon as the next trendy local venue opens, your butterflies will like as not flit off to be seen there. Having said all this, I know Ranis can do the job as well as anyone, and I'd like to be swamped with reports from the *cognoscenti* about both venues. And if the Pattnis write to me, be sure I'll publish their comments here. Price check: Papadom 80p, Coriander Chutney £1.40, Mango Chutney £1.40, Pullao Rice £3.70. Set meal £8.40. Minimum charge £10 on Saturday evenings only. Open daily 4.30-11.30p.m. Branch: Rani, London N3.

Staines

ANCIENT RAJ   ©

157 High Street, Staines   © **01784 457099**

'This restaurant is appropriate for all occasions, from takeaways to family celebrations. A stylish setting, pinks and creams, but not overpowering. Moghul swordsmen figures decorate the walls. We are impressed with the consistently high standard of well-presented and hot food. Reasonably priced,' S.R. Owner-chef is Syed Joynul. Open noon-2.30p.m. and 6-11.30p.m.

Surbiton, GL

AGRA TANDOORI   ©

142 Ewell Road, Surbiton   © **0181 399 8854**

Owner-manager H.K. Paul runs a good and reliable curry house, serving competent curries and their accompaniments. Open noon-2.30p.m. and 6p.m.-midnight.

AJANTA   ©

114 Ewell Road, Surbiton   © **0181 399 1262**

Head waiter Rubel Ahmad will help you to find all your usual favourite spicy starters and main courses. 'Usual favourites as the Guide says. Set meal for four, looked good value and so it proved.

Huge quantities, good selection of starters, sensitively spiced Lamb Dupioza. Restaurant comfortable with bright decor. Toilets splendid, pity no soap,' c.j.c. Open noon-2.30p.m. and 6p.m.-midnight. Branches: Shapla, 491 Bristol Road, Selly Oak, Birmingham, West Midlands; Shapla, 173a Stratford Road, Shirley, Birmingham, West Midlands.

RAJ   ©

163 Ewell Road, Surbiton   ✆ **0181 390 0251**

'More than enough to eat for very modest prices. Convivial surroundings, proprietor Aziz Miah is always very attentive and polite. Food of consistently good quality, always a pleasure to eat there,' p.j. Open noon-2.30p.m. and 6p.m.-midnight.

SARADA   ©

286-288 Ewell Road, Surbiton   ✆ **0181 399 0745**

A medium-sized restaurant seating 48 diners, owned and managed by Nani Gopal Seal. All the usual spicy dishes on the menu, including Rougan Josh (sic), Jalfrazzi (sic) and Bangalore Phal. There are not, as yet, any Balti dishes but there are Korai dishes instead. Open noon-2.45p.m. and 6p.m.-midnight.

Sutton, GL

BENGAL TANDOORI   ©

260 High Street, Sutton   ✆ **0181 643 8214**

Perusing the menu you will find Balti and Karai (sic) dishes, along with all your favourite curries and accompaniments, with owner-manager, Sufi Miah, usually on hand to help. Open noon-2.30p.m. and 6p.m.-midnight.

SAVAR TANDOORI

7 Cheam Road, Sutton   ✆ **0181 661 9395**

'Food was all freshly cooked. Specialities include fish dishes and also venison. Chicken Jalfrezi was tasty and spicy, Pullau Rice had no artificial colouring but had a good spicy and minty flavour,' J.S. Open noon-3p.m. and 6-11.30p.m., till midnight Friday and Saturday. Branch: Savar Balti House, Epsom.

Thornton Heath, GL

BEULAH ROAD TANDOORI NEW ENTRANT	©
77 Beulah Road, Thornton Heath	ℭ 0181 771 7783

M.R.A. Khan opened here in 1995 and it has, we hear from H.C., become 'Bona Bhuna at the Beulah!' Price check: Papadom 30p, CTM £4.75, Pullao Rice £1.65. Set meal £7.95. Minimum charge £10. Open daily 6-11.30p.m. Branch: Ramsgate Tandoori, Ramsgate, Kent.

Tolworth, GL

JAIPUR NEW TO OUR TOP 100	©
90 The Broadway, Tolworth	ℭ 0181 399 3619

The external decor makes this venue unmissable. Its huge pink stone pillars make it stand out, a fact not unnoticed by the local council, who in the early days spent a considerable amount of time, and presumably money, trying to force owner S.U. Ali to remove them. Fortunately bureaucracy lost, and the pillars remain; indeed, they continue inside, giving a very Indian feel to the interior. India's Jaipur is the pink city, where every building is made from pink sandstone. Naturally the Jaipur's theme is pink too, with 'an amazing sugar-pink decor, with friezes of dancing ladies seemingly sculpted out of the wall,' D.D. 'A thoroughly enjoyable restaurant,' D.R.C. 'One of my regular haunts,' P.D. Both branches join our elite TOP 100 club. We describe the food in the entry for the branch: Jaipur, Woking.

©	Curry Club discount (see p. 607)	🍴	Unlicensed
√	Vegetarian	⊞	Home delivery
BYO	Bring your own alcohol		service available

Virginia Water

VICEROY OF INDIA   ©

4 Station Approach, Virginia Water   ✆ 01344 843157

M.S. Ali's Viceroy remains very popular. A.F. says: 'The food here is really exceptional. I have eaten in hundreds of Indian restaurants over the past 20 years, including many of this Guide's TOP 100.' So why is this the only one you've written to us about then, Alan? Not that I'm ungrateful - one report is better than none at all. He goes on: 'The Chilli Chicken Masala is amazing. The Viceroy Special (chicken and mincemeat) Dansaks and Vindaloos fabulous. Regulars include many celebrities and sportsmen, to add to the ambience, and the service is as good as you'll get anywhere.' Any of those celebs or even ordinary curryholic mortals care to tell us more?

Weybridge

GOLDEN CURRY   ©

132 Oatlands Drive, Weybridge   ✆ 01932 846931

A number of good reports received about owner Enayeth Khan's golden curries. All give the thumbs up, though no one has confirmed that the green flock wallpaper is no more!

THE HUSSAIN   ©

47 Church Street, Weybridge   ✆ 01932 844720

'Garlic chicken was memorable, even next day, according to one wag,' H.C. All reports speak well of the food and the service at M. Suleman's Hussain. Price check: Papadom 40p, CTM £5.60, Pullao Rice £1.65. Open daily noon-3p.m. and 6-11.30p.m. Branch: The Curry Corner Tandoori, 90 Molesey Road, Hersham, Surrey.

Whyteleafe

CURRY GARDEN   ©

242 Godstone Road, Whyteleafe   ℰ 01883 627237

'Cool place, warm service,' reported one regular (R.M.) who referred to the air-conditioning and owner Akhlaqur Rahman's customer care. Our attention is also drawn to a popular house special: Tandoori Chicken and Mushroom Rizoti (£5.95), cooked with herbs and spices in a medium sauce, and Bamboo Shoot Bahjee (£1.90). Good reports received. Price check: Papadom 50p, CTM £5.75, Pullao Rice £1.50. Sunday lunch buffet £5.95, kids £4.50. Minimum charge £6 per head. Service charge 10%. Open daily noon-3p.m. and 6p.m.-midnight. Branch: Curry Garden, 92 St Dunstan's Street, Canterbury, Kent.

Woking

JAIPUR   NEW ENTRANT TOP 100

49 Chertsey Road, Woking   ℰ 01483 772626

This elegant restaurant is more subdued in its tones of pink than its sister branch in Tolworth (*see* entry). Talking of sisters, your editors had the privilege of meeting the Jaipur's owner, Nizam Ali, and his two delightful sisters, Reggi and Sophi, in Sylhet, during a monsoon storm a couple of years ago, when our friend there, Rashid, insisted we see their home. 'It is a Londoni house. It is very grand, and they are from Londoni,' he exclaimed. It is and they aren't. They all live and work in tatty old Woking, which ain't London but, when you're 6000 miles away, who cares? Londoni houses are those built in Sylhet by visiting curry restaurateurs. This is an exploding market, causing land prices to rise and costs to be very high, a source of some resentment to the locals, who feel left behind. Be that as it may, servants proffered soft drinks, fried snacks and hospitality, as is the norm in Bangladesh. I asked if they missed England when they were in Bangladesh, which they are regularly. 'I miss the cold,' said Reggi, understandably, since the temperature that day was in excess of 104°F, humidity 90%. 'In England, I miss the heat,' she added. Said Sophi: 'I miss Cheddar cheese - in fact we bring pounds of it with us here.' Nizam said he missed his restaurant, which is also understandable, because it is a very good place indeed, and Nizam is very popular with his loyal band of customers who come far and wide, according to a wealth of reports received. 'The ambience when you come in the door is smooth and peaceful. The bar on the right invites you to enjoy a relaxing drink, while the huge pillars make you feel that you are in India. The food is always an adventure, spiced with care and forethought by chef Rupa Kumar. This time we had Plain Papadoms (50p each) with a coconut chutney which was nice, but a bit bland for our taste. For starters we had Onion Bhaji (£1.95) - four, and they were lovely, and Jeera Chicken (£2.50) - the most succulent, juicy chicken pieces, marinated in yoghurt, I think, and tandoori-cooked, then fried in cumin seeds. Unique and delicious, and quite different from the robust Punjabi versions offered at places like Southall's Brilliant. For main courses we had the Tandoori Thali (£7.95), consisting of Lamb and Chicken Tikka, again unbelievably succulent, Sheek Kebab and a succulent King Prawn. The Plain Naan (£1.25) was fresh, hot and a bit crispy, yet soft, which was gorgeous. The Duck Chilli Jalfrezi (£9.95) - delicately spiced, tender pieces of duck breast, laced with onion, green pepper and fresh chilli. The Dall Tarka (£2.25) was outstanding. It had subtle, spicy flavours combined with the slightly burned taste a correctly caramelized Tarka should have. You can tell a lot about a chef from this dish, and I've seldom had better, even in India. The Pullao Rice (£1.75) was fragrant and fluffy, and to tie it all together we had Dahi - natural home-made yoghurt - soft and gentle and delicious, even on its own, and not acidic, unlike factory-made versions. The whole meal was outstanding,' D.B.A.C. The menu contains the formula favourites, but they are also always above-average, we hear. Decidedly this restaurant goes into our TOP 100, as does its sister. Business weekday self-serve buffet lunches £5.95, Sunday ditto £6.95, kids £3.95, eat your fill. Minimum charge £7. Open daily noon-2.30p.m. and 6-11.p.m. Branch: Jaipur, Tolworth, Surrey.

KHYBER PASS   ©

18 The Broadway, Woking   ✆ **01483 764710**

It's a standard curry house, green decor and Hindi arches. 'Food is always good. Of particular interest to us is the lime pickle on the chutney tray,' D.R.C. Manager Jafar Abdul Wahab promises to give a generous discount to Curry Club members. Branches: Khyber Pass, 12 Lower Guildford Road, Knaphill; Khyber Pass, 54 Terrace Road, Walton-on-Thames.

SUSSEX

For the purposes of this Guide we combine East and West Sussex.

Bexhill-on-Sea

ANWAR ©

2 Sackville Road, Bexhill-on-Sea   ☎ **01424 210205**

Proprietor Jamir Uddin opened his restaurant in 1989. Moghul arches complement this nicely decorated curry house. Khori Bindi Gosht at £4.50 is a house special, and at that price (all prices are very reasonable) it's a bargain. Price check: Papadom 40p, CTM £5.50, Pullao Rice £1.30. Service charge 15%. Open noon-2.30p.m. and 6p.m.-midnight.

SHIPLU ©

109 London Road, Bexhill-on-Sea   ☎ **01424 219159**

Sparkling blue and silver marble-effect decor make managing owner Abdul Kalam Azad's standard curry house stand out from the rest. 'Service couldn't be bettered, all dishes were well cooked and presented in adequate quantities,' D.J.B. Open noon-2.30p.m. and 6p.m.-midnight.

Bognor Regis

ANWAR'S TANDOORI   NEW ENTRANT   ⊞

43 Queensway, Bognor Regis   ☎ **01243 842010**

'This restaurant has been renamed and has a new chef. Prices are slightly above average for the area but worth it. Wide selection of dishes, generous quantities. Our current favourite!' J.O. Price check: Papadom 40p, CTM £5.75, Pullao Rice £1.70. Open noon-2.30p.m. and 6p.m.-midnight. Home delivery at a charge of 75p per mile. That must be a deterrent!

ELMER TANDOORI

76-78 Elmer Road, Middleton-on-Sea,
Bognor Regis   © 01243 582641

'Clean and comfortable decor, if uninspiring. Service friendly and efficient even when busy. For flavour and texture it's hard to beat,' J.D. 'On the whole, quality is very good, but the standard of the Nan bread has been known to vary. Low-price meals if one pays cash,' J.O. Open noon-2.30p.m. and 6-11p.m.

PASSAGE TO INDIA

11 The Square, Barnham, Bognor Regis   © 01243 555064

'Another lovely restaurant,' J.O. Open noon-2.30p.m. and 6-11.30p.m., till midnight Friday and Saturday.

Brighton

ANCIENT CURRY DOME TAKEAWAY   ▦ ©

6 George Street, Brighton   © 01273 670521

Opened in 1990 by Ali Hussan. Bangladeshi curries on the menu. Vegetarians and meat-eaters alike might be interested in Egg and Potato Dum (£4.70). All meals are served with Rice, Papadom and Onion Salad; if you don't want the Rice or Papadom you will be charged £1 less which sounds fair to me! Price check: Papadom 40p, CTM £5.60, Pullao Rice £1.20. Open 5.30p.m.-midnight. Home delivery service free on orders over £6.50.

©	Curry Club discount (see p. 607)	🍺	Unlicensed
√	Vegetarian	▦	Home delivery
BYO	Bring your own alcohol		service available

POLASH NEW ENTRANT

19 York Place, Brighton   ✆ **01273 626221**

'Very impressed overall. Paratha, the best I've ever tasted. Quality really first-class,' G. and M.P.

SHEZAN NEW ENTRANT

125 Western Road, Brighton   ✆ **01273 326699**

Shezan covers most options, providing a snack bar, takeaway service and a restaurant. There is a good range of vegetarian dishes and they sell a selection of Indian sweets. Unlicensed. Price check: CTM £4.50, Pullao Rice £1.45. Home delivery free, including drinks, on orders over £10.

SHIMLA TANDOORI TAKEAWAY NEW ENTRANT

92 Preston Drove, Brighton   ✆ **01273 542626**

'It's the best takeaway in Brighton. The Garlic Chilli King Prawn (£6.95) is amazing – whole cloves of garlic and whole (red hot) chilli peppers. The Chicken Tikka (£4.25) is also one of the best we've come across,' R.S. Price check: Papadom 30p, Pullao Rice £1.40. Set meal non-veggie £8.50, veggie £7. Open Sunday to Thursday 5-10.30p.m., Friday and Saturday 5-11p.m.

VICEROY OF INDIA

13 Preston Street, Brighton   ✆ **01273 324733**

Owned by Mohammed Wasid Ali who also manages front of house. Cleanly decorated in red and cream, pictures of the Taj Mahal on the walls. Bangladeshi formula and Pakistani Punjabi curries on the menu. Butter and Jeera Chicken (£4.75) a house special. Price check: Papadom 55p, CTM £4.85, Pullao Rice £1.65. Service charge 10%. Open noon-3p.m. and 6p.m.-midnight.

©	Curry Club discount (see p. 607)	☕	Unlicensed
√	Vegetarian	⊞	Home delivery
BYO	Bring your own alcohol		service available

Chichester

MEMORIES OF INDIA NEW ENTRANT

**Main Road (A259), Bosham Roundabout,
Chichester**   ✆ **01243 572234**

This restaurant, formerly the Wishingwell Tandoori, has quite an airy
feel to it. The bar area is very smart, wooden decking on the floor,
bamboo chairs and tables, natural blinds with leafy green plants for
colour. Open noon-2.30p.m. and 6p.m.-midnight. Large enclosed private car parking.

Crawley

BENGAL SPICES

71 Gales Drive, Three Bridges, Crawley   ✆ **01293 571007**

An attractive restaurant in gold and green with engraved screens to
divide diners. 'Telephone reservation was taken with efficient courtesy
(not always the case) and on arrival we were made very welcome. The
food was again exceptionally good and we were more than satisfied.
CTM absolutely wonderful, superb flavour. Balti Mushroom Fry
absolutely great, very deep tomato and green pepper sauce with large
moist whole mushrooms, perfectly cooked. Sag Panir, marvellous, dry,
very cheesy flavour. One small grumble, food does take rather a long
time to arrive, presumably the restaurant is happy that you sit all
evening over your meal. Has the cleanest and prettiest Ladies I know.
Two young men from Wales sat at the next table and both ordered
Phalls. I have never seen anybody eat this incendiary dish before, but
they ate every morsel with no sign of anything out of the ordinary –
could have been totally bland from the reaction. Must have been very
hardened Phall eaters,' H.C. Open noon-2.30p.m. and 6-11p.m.

RAJ TAKEAWAY   ©

8 Broadfield Barton, Broadfield, Crawley ✆ **01293 515425**

The Raj Takeaway was opened in 1981 by S.U. Ahmed. All the usual
curries and accompaniment are clearly listed on the menu. Curry sauce

and chips – a great favourite of children. Price check: CTM £5.95.
Open noon-2.30p.m. and 6-11.30p.m. Mr Ahmed runs a loyalty discount scheme, collect stars for a free meal.

RUBY MURRAY TAKEAWAY   NEW ENTRANT   ⊞

4 Orchard Street, Crawley   ℂ **01293 417417**

When we were doing our Fiery Food Show curry demo in Albuquerque
early in 1997, we were amazed to find no less than eight curry houses in
this chilli (or as they spell it, chile) heartland of the American
Southwest. But when I said to our friend and show producer, Mary
Jane: 'Glad to see the old ruby's doing so well here,' she earnestly told us
that the only gems they have round there are turquoise. That got me
onto the subject of cockney rhyming slang, a subject of great interest
there, it seemed. To get to the point, at last someone has called their
curry house Ruby Murray. True, it's more likely to attract *Sun* readers
than *Michelin Guide* inspectors, but what use is the latter for curryholics,
anyway? Takeaway and delivery service. The menu covers a wide range
of curries with all their accompaniments including Kebabs (Donner
£2.20 medium), Burgers (Chilli £1.70 single) and Pizzas (Bombay Mix
– curry sauce, Meat Tikka, Chicken Tikka, cheese, tomato, onion,
mushroom, sweetcorn, green peppers) £9.20 large. 'Meat Vindaloo, as
always hot, with a wonderful sauce, £3.60. Quick to arrive – free delivery in half an hour. Staff helpful and food inexpensive,' G.T. Price check:
Papadom 50p, CTM £6.50 incl. rice, Pullao Rice £1.30. Open 4p.m.-
1a.m. The Ruby Murray delivers a selection of canned and bottled
lagers, but their licence says these are strictly delivered with food to customers over the age of 18 and before 11p.m.

Crowborough

AKASH BALTI   ©

24 Crowborough Hill, Jarvis Brook,
Crowborough   ℂ **01892 661881**

M.D. Adbul Kahir will give a free Onion Salad with every takeaway
order, and free house wine with orders over £20. Balti featured on the
menu. Open noon-2.30p.m. and 6p.m.-midnight.

RAJ POOT   NEW ENTRANT

3 London Road, Crowborough   © 01892 654347

'Very good indeed, an all-rounder,' B.P.-D.

ROSE OF BENGAL   NEW ENTRANT   ©

3 Crowborough Hill, Crowborough   © 01892 662252

Opened in 1982 by Esab Ali and Moshud Ali. Bangladeshi and northern Indian curries on the menu. Exotic special – Hyrali Chicken or
Lamb Masalla – mild, cooked with sag, mint, coriander, butter and
cream (£6.15). Price check: Papadom 50p, CTM £5.95, Pullao Rice
£1.60. Minimum charge £6.95. Open noon-2.30p.m. and 6-11p.m.

East Grinstead

SHAPLA TAKEAWAY

94 Railway Approach, East Grinstead   © 01342 327655

Takeaway-only, which was opened in 1984 by A.K. Azad Chuta. Price
check: Papadom 45p, CTM £4.95, Pullao Rice £1.45. Open noon-
2.30p.m. and 5.30p.m.-midnight. Branch: Badsha, 10 West Cross,
Tenterden, Kent.

East Preston

BENGAL TANDOORI   NEW ENTRANT

116 Downs Way, East Preston   © 01903 777365

'All your favourites including wicked Phalls for the loonies. Quantities
a bit small, although I am a big eater. Polite and friendly service,' R.T.
'We have travelled abroad and round the UK and have enjoyed Indian
meals in many venues but have found none yet to compare with the
Bengal Tandoori. The menu offers a wide choice. The food is excellently prepared and served with generous portions. The various
flavours of all the different dishes are apparent. The staff are very
friendly and courteous. We have never yet had cause for dissatisfaction

as each time we go we find the meals delicious. The surroundings are very comfortable and tastefully decorated. Parking is easy – right at the door. The place is so popular that we have to book for most evenings in the week. The restaurant is never empty, and at weekends customers are prepared to wait for an hour for takeaways. Favourite dish is the Kurzi Lamb, ordered with two days' notice, serving four to five with the full meal costing around £60 – superb!' J. and K.T.

Eastbourne

INDIAN PARADISE   ⊞ ©

166 Seaside, Eastbourne   ✆ **01323 735408**

Owner A. Khalique's bright restaurant has been serving competent curries and accompaniments to a local following for the last 14 years. Open noon-2.30p.m. and 6p.m.-midnight. Delivery service available.

Goring

ASHALATA NEW ENTRANT

274 Goring Road, Goring   ✆ **01903 501659**

'Had a Meat Madras takeaway, plenty of it, competitive prices. So clean I got a wet backside from newly-washed seats, the waiter forgot to mention it!' R.T.

Hailsham

RAJ DHUTT NEW ENTRANT

48 High Street, Hailsham   ✆ **01323 842847**

Opened in 1990 by Mr A.S. Ali. Bangladeshi curries on the menu. Specialities include Chicken Silsila – Chicken Tikka cooked with fresh garlic, herbs and spices (£7.35). Balti served with Nan. Price check: Papadom 40p, CTM £5.25, Pullao Rice £1.45. Open noon-2.30p.m. and 6-11.30p.m.

Hastings

SHIPLU ©

177a Queens Road, Hastings　　　℡ **01424 439493**

'Tastefully decorated and clean. Service a little on the slow side but friendly. Popadoms warm and crisp, Onion Bhajia large, couldn't be beaten. Bangalore Phall not on the menu but asked for it and got it, very hot as it should be,' B.P.-D. Managing owner is Mr Hoque. Open noon-2.30p.m. and 6p.m.-midnight.

Haywards Heath

CURRY INN ©

58 Commercial Square, Haywards Heath　　℡ **01444 415414**

'We were warmly welcomed into this well-decorated restaurant. Really good Prawn Butterfly. Lamb Chilli Masala extra hot was superb,' J.L.G. Manager is Ahad Miah. Open noon-2.30p.m. and 6-11.30p.m.

NIZAM　NEW ENTRANT

139 South Road, Haywards Heath　　　℡ **01444 457527**

Originally opened in 1976 but under present ownership since 1985. Bangladeshi formula curries on the menu, all your usual favourites. Specials include: Badmi Kurma Chicken – Chicken Tikka in a yoghurt, pepper and onion sauce (£6.50); Methi Kalia Chicken – Chicken Tikka with spinach and lentils (£6.50). Price check: Papadom 55p, CTM £6.50, Pullao Rice £1.80. Minimum charge £12. Open noon-2.30p.m. and 6-11p.m. Branch: Nizam, 43 High Street, East Grinstead; Nupur, 122 High Street, Hurstpierpoint.

Horsham

CURRY CENTRE

43 London Road, Horsham　　　　℡ **01403 254811**

'Our regular haunt for over 20 years. Thoroughly recommended for consistent food. Excellent Niramish,' D.R.M.

Hove

AL RIAZ   ⊞ ©

244 Portland Road, Hove   ✆ **01273 722332**

Decorated in shades of grey and blue. Fabulous comfy chairs to sit in at the bar, the sort you could quite happily go to sleep in. Smartly laid tables, blue candles and crystal glasses. Towards the rear of the restaurant is a very grand conservatory, which makes summer dining so much more pleasurable. Managed by Mrs Kosser Riaz. Price check: Papadom 45p, CTM £6.95 incl. Pullao Rice, Pullao Rice £1.55. Service charge 10%. Open 5p.m.-midnight. Home delivery service which can be paid for on the phone with your credit card – great!

ASHOKA   ©

95-97 Church Road, Hove   ✆ **01273 734193**

Owned by Rafique Miah. 'Nice roomy restaurant, clean and comfortable. Onion Bhaji, small but good and tasty. Chicken Ceylon with Pilau Rice and Nan, hot, as it should be, nicely served and plenty of it! Bill allowed for 10% discount to Curry Club member, but offset by service charge.' B.P.-D.

BALI BRASSERIE   ©

Kingsway Court, First Avenue, Hove   ✆ **01273 323810**

Partner Mrs B. Calais' very modern and stylish restaurant serves Indonesian and Malaysian curries and cuisine. Delights include Indonesian Sausage – tasty sausage filled with prawns, fish and vegetables. Part of the restaurant is a glamorous bar, with slightly different hours. Open noon-2p.m. and 7.30-10.30p.m.

GANGES   NEW ENTRANT

93 Church Road, Hove   ✆ **01273 728292**

Recently taken over, with Abdul running front of house, supported by Karim in the kitchen. An attractive restaurant from the street, decorated in white and green. Pakistani- and Bangladeshi-styled curries on the menu. Poneer Shashlik £2.95. Brandy King Prawn (£13.95) sounds interesting. Price check: Papadom 55p, CTM £7.25 incl. Pullao Rice, Pullao Rice £1.75. Minimum charge £6.95. Open noon-2.30p.m. and 6p.m.-midnight.

HOVE TANDOORI ⊞ ©

175 Church Road, Hove   © 01273 737188

A bright, if slightly gaudy, curry house, owned by Sofir Ahmad, serving good curry house food (Balti also included) at reasonable prices. Open noon-2.30p.m. and 5.30p.m.-midnight. Delivery service available.

KARIM'S TANDOORI

15 Blatchington Road, Hove   © 01273 739780

'Starters are brilliant, especially Nagis Kebab. Garlic Nan very tasty. Curries delicately spiced, but small portions,' A.D.S. 'Restaurant underground, so rather cold, but food and service made up for this,' P.A. Open 6-11.30p.m. Branch: Tandoori Nights, 2 Coombe Terrace, Lewes Road, Brighton.

KASHMIR ©

71 Old Shoreham Road, Hove   © 01273 739677

Opened by Mr Subab Miah in 1978 – 29 July 1978, to be precise. When a restaurant has survived for many years, it has to be reliably good and the Kashmir is. 'I have always found the food delicious and the service courteous and friendly,' H.F. 'Have been regular customers for nine years. and have always found a consistently high standard of cooking and preparation,' J.H.W. 'Mr Miah and family have provided excellent service, good-quality food at all expectations,' C.R.C. 'I have been coming to the restaurant since it opened 18 years ago. The restaurant is well appointed, all signs of red flock wallpaper have disappeared, the seating and bar are very pleasant. They are courteous, friendly and helpful. Curries are delicately spiced and individual,' L.H. Price check: Papadom 40p, CTM £5, Pullao Rice £1.60. Open noon-3p.m. and 6p.m.-midnight.

Lewes

SHANAZ NEW ENTRANT   ©

83 High Street, Lewes   ✆ **01273 488038**

North Indian and Bangladeshi curries on the menu at Kayum Ali's establishment. Separate function room, which is available for business lunches and receptions. Shanaz specials include Lobster Rang Puri (£9.95) – sliced onions, capsicums, tomatoes, red wine, coconut powder and spices. Garlic Chicken Tikka £4.95. Fish Chutney £5.95. All takeaway orders receive a free onion salad, and if you spend £15 or more you receive a free bottle of wine. Price check: Papadom 50p, CTM £5.95, Pullao Rice £1.60. Minimum charge £8. Open noon-2.30p.m. and 6p.m.-midnight.

Newhaven

LAST VICEROY   ⊞ ©

4 Bridge Street, Newhaven   ✆ **01273 513308**

Opened in 1986 by A.S. Ahmed. Serving Bangladeshi formula and Pakistani curries including Duck Tikka (£2.50). 'Is our favourite restaurant, always offering good food and friendly service. The restaurant is divided into smoking and non-smoking. There is a separate entrance for takeaway customers. Ample portions, very enjoyable,' B.J.MCK. The restaurant has an off-licence and cigarettes can be arranged for on request. Half-price menu for children, please ask. Price check: Papadom 45p, CTM £5.75, Pullao Rice £1.60. Open noon-2.30p.m. and 6p.m.-midnight. Free home delivery service locally.

Nutley

GANGES   ©

High Street, Nutley   ✆ **01825 713287**

Proprietor M. Haque's Ganges continues to dispense good, competent formula curries. Open 6p.m.-midnight.

Petworth

VICEREGAL LODGE   ©

East Street, Petworth   ✆ 01798 343217

Owned by Joe Choudhury who tells us that, to his regular customers
(who are all, it seems, pilots and yachtsmen), his restaurant is their 19th
hole, and that it is more like a private club than an Indian restaurant.
Since Petworth is near neither the sea nor an airstrip, we are as
bemused as you are, but Joe will give you a really warm welcome whatever! Price check: Papadom 50p, CTM £6, Pullao Rice £1.80. Open
12.30-2p.m. (reservations only) and 6p.m.-midnight.

Ringmer

RINGMER TANDOORI   ©

72 Springett Avenue, Ringmer   ✆ 01273 812855

Balti dishes feature on owner, M.A. Uddin's, menu along with all our
regular favourites. Open noon-2.30p.m. and 6p.m.-midnight.

Rustington

TANDOORI NIGHTS   NEW ENTRANT   ⊞

35-37 Sea Lane, Rustington   ✆ 01903 782666

Their takeaway menu is quite amazing, quoting half-priced curries but
at 1994 prices. For example, Chicken Bhuna was £4.60 but is now
£2.30, as is Chicken Roganjosh (sic) and Meat Patia. The list is endless. King Prawn dishes receive a 20% discount on 1994 prices. 'The
prices are the most attractive feature here. Certainly good value, and
good food. Would visit again,' J.O. Price check: Papadom 25p, CTM
£3.30, Pullao Rice 95p. Open noon-2p.m. and 5.30-11.30p.m. Home
delivery service free but 20% discount on 1994 prices.

Steyning

MAHARAJA

The Street, Bramber, Steyning   ✆ 01903 812123

'Good helping of Chicken Biriani well presented. Right balance of ingredients. Nan bread light and fluffy. One of our favourites,' S.R. 'Immediately impressed with the ambience. Quality of food was excellent,' G.C. Open noon-2.30p.m. and 6-11.30p.m.

Worthing

CURRY LAND   NEW ENTRANT   ⊞

239 Tarring Road, West Worthing   ✆ 01903 504631

'Free home delivery. Very polite people. The best Vindaloo. Jeera Chicken is very spicy, very rich flavours,' N.D.

MA'HANN   NEW ENTRANT

179-181 Montague Street, Worthing   ✆ 01903 205449

A huge restaurant seating 120. Opened in 1984 by Abdul Monnan, who will be found in the kitchen of his restaurant preparing such delights as Beef Jagannath (£8.25) – well-spiced fillets cooked with capsicum, green chillies and coriander, including rice. 'Most polite and friendly, greeting regular customers like old friends. Sampled most of the dishes, an outstanding feature is the generosity of the portions, piping hot and very nicely presented,' G.V. 'One of the best, if not the best in the area,' B.G. 'I dine here whenever I wish to enjoy eastern cuisine,' A.J.E.P. 'Delicious food,' M.R.D. Price check: Papadom 40p, CTM £5.25, Pullao Rice £1.75. Open noon-2.30p.m. and 5.30p.m.-midnight.

SHAFIQUE'S   ©

42 Goring Road, Worthing   ✆ 01903 504035

Shafique Uddin's restaurant is 'another favourite of ours', say J. and K.T.

TASTE OF BENGAL TAKEAWAY   ▦ ©

203 Heene Road, Worthing   ✆ **01903 238400**

Opened in 1984 by Salik Miah. Bangladeshi food on the menu. 'We
were feeling lazy and had it delivered — Popadoms, Tandoori, Prawn
Madras with Nans, and as usual chips (for my son). Madras flavour
was perfect balance between tangy and hot. Chicken pieces decent size,
generous,' R.T. Price check: Papadom 40p, CTM £4.60, Pullao Rice
£1.50. Open noon-2.30p.m. and 5.30p.m.-midnight. Home delivery service 95p. Branch: Golden Bengal, 40 Lyndhurst Road, Worthing.

TYNE AND WEAR

Gateshead

THE LAST DAYS OF THE RAJ   ©

218 Durh Road, Shipcote, Gateshead   ✆ **0191 477 2888**

A takeaway-only establishment serving Bangladeshi curry house food.
Price check: Papadom 55p, CTM £5.95, Pullao Rice £1.75. Open noon-
2.30p.m. and 6p.m.-midnight.

THE LAST DAYS OF THE RAJ   NEW ENTRANT
TOP 100   ©

168 Kells Lane, Low Fell, Gateshead   ✆ **0191 482 6494**

An up-market and stylish Bangladeshi curry restaurant. Opened on 16
February 1997 by Athair Khan. Tastefully decorated in natural colours.
Linen cloths and napkins laid up on beautifully presented tables, brass
light-fittings, ceiling-fans, trellis-climbing plants and a grand piano
with pianist. This restaurant must have one of the biggest and most
comprehensive menus in the country, it is quite a delight. You will find
all the regular formula curries with some regional and authentic dishes including recipes from the British Raj — Country Captain (£6.55), a
dry dish cooked with chicken breast, onion, ghee, chillies, ginger, garlic, turmeric and salt. Raj Lamb and Cabbage (£6.55) is cooked with
yoghurt, poppy seeds, lemon juice, green coriander, garlic, onion, fresh

coconut, green chillies, ground coriander, ginger, cinnamon and cumin with ghee and chilli. You will also find on the menu a few dishes with an oriental flavour, such as Dim Sum (£3.10), Oriental King Prawn Rolls (£3.50) and Butterfly Breaded Prawn (£3.50), and there is also a Pizza or two – quite fabulous, definitely a TOP 100 restaurant. Price check: Papadom 70p, CTM £6.95, Pullao Rice £2.15. Set menu £5.95. Minimum charge £10. Open noon-2.30p.m. and 6p.m.-midnight. Branch: The Last Days of the Raj, 565 Durham Road, Low Fell, Gateshead.

Houghton-le-Spring

PENSHAW TANDOORI   NEW ENTRANT

13 Chester Road, Penshaw, Houghton-le-Spring	✆ 0191 512 0015

'This is my local and I visit it frequently. It is a small, licensed establishment in a village location which does considerable takeaway trade. Busy on a weekend, advisable to book, during the week usually quiet. Exception is Thursday and Sunday nights when a starter, main course with rice and coffee or ice cream is offered from a limited menu for £5.95 a head. Excellent food and prices are reasonable. My personal favourites are the Balti meals. A Naan or two Tandoori Rotis are included in the prices. The Baltis are served in an enormous karahi, if you are a man; the fairer sex always gets a smaller version, much to the indignation of my girlfriend. Baltis are excellent and contain whole spices such as cinnamon, bay leaves, cardamoms, etc. Another highlight is the Bhuna Prawn on Puri,' N.W.

Newcastle upon Tyne

BALTI HOUSE   ©

4 Waterloo Street, Newcastle upon Tyne	✆ 0191 232 7952

A 64-seater restaurant with a cocktail bar for you to make a night of it! Open 6p.m.-midnight. Proprietor is Firuzul Islam Khan. Branch: Balti House, Winlaton.

DARAZ

4 Holly Avenue West, Jesmond,
Newcastle upon Tyne   ✆ **0191 281 8431**

All your favourite curries on the menu including Karahi but no Balti as of yet. Proprietor is Imran Haider Choudhury. Open noon-2.30p.m. and 5.30-11.30p.m.

INDIANNA TAKEAWAY   NEW ENTRANT

6 West View, Forest Hall,
Newcastle upon Tyne   ✆ **0191 270 0423**

A takeaway establishment. Originally opened in 1984 under the name of Forest Hall Tandoori, but taken over by the Miah family in 1996. Sajjad Miah wrote to us to inform us that he completed a facelift to the shop which has resulted in good business. Bangladeshi and northern Indian curries are on the menu, including a special Meat Thali (£6.50). Price check: Papadom 35p, CTM £4.75, Pullao Rice £1.40. Open 5.30p.m.-midnight. Home delivery service on orders over £8 within a 5-mile radius.

RAJ   NEW ENTRANT

Bigg Market, Newcastle upon Tyne   ✆ **0191 232 1450**

'Service, quick and efficient, felt we were rushed. Could not fault Vindaloo and Pilau Rice. Chicken Dupiaza, good, nicely spiced with lashings of onion. Hot and dry Chicken Tikka Jalfrezi, a good blend of spices,' M.G. Large choice of rice dishes, such as Tandoori Keema, Mushroom, Onion, Nuts, Garlic, to mention a few. Price check: Papadom 45p (plain), CTM £5.75, Pullao Rice £1.90.

RUPALI   TOP 100

6 Bigg Market, Newcastle upon Tyne   ✆ **0191 232 8629**

Lord Latif could teach Saatchi and Saatchi a thing or two about PR. He just never stops promoting his restaurant and, of course, himself! Try his Curry Challenge – if you can eat the chef's hottest curry then you get it free. What an incentive and, can you believe it, some people (men, of course) do it. So, for all you hot-heads out there – give it a go! 'Classic curry house decor with usual curry house menu,' c.f. Price check: Papadom 50p, CTM £6.50, Pullao Rice £1.70.

SACHINS   TOP 100

Old Hawthorn Inn, Forth Banks, Newcastle upon Tyne	✆ 0191 261 9035

We always seem to have so little to say about Sachins. Actually, contented reports rain in, and so be it, Sachins stays comfortably on our TOP 100, really for being spot on, unpretentious, non-exhibitionist, and well above average. Among the popular starter and main course favourites is Paneer Pakora, curd cheese deep-fried in a gram flour batter (£3.75), Murgh Pakora, chicken pieces deep-fried in a gram flour batter (£3.95), Murgh Marchi Masala, like a Chicken Tikka Masala but with fresh green chillies to give it a bite (£6.95). 'I thoroughly enjoyed my Muglai Akbari (£5.95),' F.D. Scottish owner Liam Cunningham adds to the flair. Booking advisable. Price check: Papadom 40p, CTM £7.50, Pullao Rice £1.60.

SHIKARA   ©

52 St Andrew's Street, Newcastle upon Tyne	✆ 0191 233 0005

Seats a massive 150 diners on two floors. 'Buffet night very busy, so book a table. Great value for money,' M.S. 'Impressive menu,' D.C. Owner is Saif Ahmed. Open noon-2.30p.m. and 6-11.30p.m.

THALI   NEW ENTRANT

44 Dean Street, Newcastle upon Tyne	✆ 0191 230 2244

A tasty innovation on the starters list is Chinghri Masala, an Indian-style prawn cocktail (£3.15). For vegetarians and meat-eaters alike, go for the Chilli Bhajee, fresh mixed vegetables cooked with lots of green chillies (£4.75). Price check: Papadom 50p, CTM £6.50, Pullao Rice £2.

VUJON   TOP 100   ©

29 Queen Street, Newcastle upon Tyne	✆ 0191 221 0601

'Very stylish decor. Comfortable, well-lit and very clean. No standard curries, but starter and main courses proved interesting and a good choice,' K.D.F. Remains in our TOP 100, and gives discounts.

South Shields

INDIAN BRASSERIE   NEW ENTRANT

146 Ocean Road, South Shields   © **0191 456 8800**

All your favourite Bangladeshi formula curries and accompaniments. Price check: Papadom 30p, CTM £4.45, Pullao Rice £1.30. Open noon-2.30p.m. and 5.30p.m.-midnight, till 2a.m. Friday and Saturday.

KHANA PINA   NEW ENTRANT   ©

150 Ocean Road, South Shields   © **0191 454 4407**

Bangladeshi curry house, owned by Syed Faruk Hussain, with manager Feruz Hussain. Price check: Papadom 40p, CTM £4.95, Pullao Rice £1.45. Minimum charge £5. Open 5.30p.m.-midnight. Closed on Monday.

NASEEB

90 Ocean Road, South Shields   © **0191 456 4294**

'Immediately impressed with the layout and decor. A bright and airy restaurant. We were presented with colourful menus while we waited for the pickle tray and Papadoms. The meals arrived hot, looking great and smelling wonderful. Very good portions of Chicken Tikka Jalfrezi, Korma, Singapore, Sri Lanka and King Prawn Singapore. These were all eagerly consumed with aromatic Pilau Rice. No hesitation in recommending the Naseeb,' T.H.

STAR OF INDIA   ©

194 Ocean Road, South Shields   © **0191 456 2210**

Originally opened in 1960, owned by M. Faruque, who took over this restaurant in 1972. Must be the one of the first, if not the first, curry house in South Shields. Bangladeshi formula curries on the menu. Chillies must be very popular in South Shields, try the Chilli Pilau

(£1.95) or Beef Phal (£4.35). Price check: Papadom 40p, CTM £5.50, Pullao Rice £1.75. Set menu £3.95. Minimum charge £4.40. Open noon-2.30p.m. and 5.30p.m.-midnight. Branch: Royal Bengal Brasserie, Prince Regent Street, Stockton-on-Tees; Shapla, 192 Northgate, Darlington.

TANDOORI INTERNATIONALE

97 Ocean Road, South Shields   ✆ 0191 456 2000

'Is situated in a converted boarding house. The restaurant is the former dining room. There is a new menu which includes Balti dishes. Good ambience with tasty food, reasonably priced. I ordered Nargisi Kofta with sauce, both were good, but no trace of a boiled egg,' D.M. Price check: Papadom 50p, CTM £5.20, Pullao Rice £1.50 (takeaway prices).

Sunderland

GRANGETOWN TANDOORI KITCHEN   ⊞ ©

1 Stockton Terrace, Grangetown,
Sunderland   ✆ 0191 565 5984

A takeaway-only establishment. Balti and other favourites on the menu. Open noon-2p.m. and 5.30p.m.-midnight, till 12.30a.m. Friday and Saturday. Owner, Shofozul Islam, will give a discount to Curry Club members. Home delivery service.

RED HOT CHILLI PEPPER

27 Fawcett Street, Sunderland   ✆ 0191 567 0535

Formerly City Tandoori. 'Mainstream food. A one-course lunch for £3.95 is a bargain,' D.M. 'Extensive menu with all the old favourites (Baltis). Food well presented. Good view into the kitchen – nothing to hide – reassuring,' C.F. and A.W.

SAJAN   NEW ENTRANT   ⊞ ©

11 North Bridge Street, Sunderland   ✆ 0191 564 2637

Owned since 1996 by Ms Sharmina Begum. Bangladeshi and northern

Indian curries on the menu. Price check: Papadom 40p, CTM £5.40, Pullao Rice £1.60. Set menu £3.95 for three courses. Open noon-2.30p.m. and 6p.m.-midnight. Home delivery service within 2 miles on orders over £10. Free bottle of wine on orders over £15.

SHAGORIKA   NEW ENTRANT

3 Queen's Parade, Seaburn, Sunderland   © **0191 529 3194**

Bangladeshi curry house, established in 1980 by Shayequr Rahman. Price check: Papadom 40p, CTM £5.75, Pullao Rice £1.80. Set menu £3.95. Open 12.30-2.50p.m. and 6p.m.-midnight.

Wallsend

LIGHT OF INDIA

120 High Street East, Wallsend   © **0191 234 5556**

'Manager Mr Salik is always very helpful. Food more than enough, does an excellent Chicken Tikka Chilli Mosala (sic),' M.S. Open noon-2.30p.m. and 6p.m.-12.30a.m., closed Sunday lunch.

MODERN TAKEAWAY   NEW ENTRANT   ©

178 High Street, Wallsend   © **0191 212 4437**

Bangladeshi formula curries at this popular takeaway, owned by Mohammed Nirjash Miah who is also in charge of the cooking. Price check: Papadom 30p, CTM £4, Pullao Rice £1.35. Set menu £2.10. Minimum charge £4.50. Open noon-2p.m. and 6p.m.-midnight.

Washington

INDIAN EXPRESS TAKEAWAY   NEW ENTRANT   ©

Unit 1, Gayton Road, Sulgrave, Washington   © **0191 417 1101**

Opened in 1995 by T. Hussasin. Serving formula Bangladeshi and northern Indian curries. Reasonable prices. Price check: Papadom 30p, CTM £4.30, Pullao Rice £1.15. Open 6p.m.-midnight.

Whickham

JAMDANI   ©

3 The Square, Front Street, Whickham   ✆ 0191 496 0820

Opened in 1988 by Mr A. Miah. Bangladeshi formula curries and accompaniments on the menu. Try the Chicken Saffron (£6.95) or King Prawns (£7.50) – delicious. Price check: Papadom 40p, CTM £5.95, Pullao Rice £1.75. Open noon-2p.m. and 6-11.30p.m.

MOTIJHEEL   ©

9 Front Street, Whickham   ✆ 0191 488 0851

A takeaway establishment serving the full menu. Manager is E.H. Choudhury. Open noon-2p.m. and 6-11.30p.m.

Whitley Bay

HIMALAYA   ©

33 Esplanade, Whitley Bay   ✆ 0191 251 3629

Reliable curry house. Owner is Abdul Goffar. Open noon-2.30p.m. and 5.30p.m.-midnight.

KISMET   NEW ENTRANT   ©

177 Whitley Road, Whitley Bay   ✆ 0191 297 2028

Originally opened in 1968, but taken over by Maklisur Rahman in 1996. Pakistani Punjabi cooking and Bangladeshi formula curries on the menu. Friday night is Balti night – six courses for £7.95 – great value. Price check: Papadom 35p, CTM £5.35, Pullao Rice £1.45. Open noon-2.30p.m. and 6p.m.-midnight, closed Tuesday lunchtime. Branch: Jesmond Takeaway, 243 Jesmond Road, Newcastle upon Tyne.

SHAHENSHAH   ©

187-189 Whitley Road, Whitley Bay   ✆ 0191 297 0503

'Food first-class. Chicken Tikka terrific, full of flavour,' M.B. 'My local for a year,' S.N. 'We found the restaurant busy in a quiet and efficient way. To drink, Cobra lager, the perfect accompaniment,' P.A.P.

TAKDIR   ©

11 East Parade, Whitley Bay   ℂ 0191 253 0236

Owned by Majibur Rahman who is also the manager. Opened in 1979, a reliable 70-seater restaurant with regular locals. Bangladeshi and northern Indian food on the menu. Price check: Papadom 30p, CTM £5.10, Pullao Rice £1.50. Minimum charge £10. Open 5.30p.m.-midnight. Branch: Akash, 3 Tangier Street, Whitehaven, Cumbria; Al Mamun Takeaway, 5 John Street, Cullercoats.

Winlaton

BALTI HOUSE   ©

18a The Garth, Front Street, Winlaton   ℂ 0191 414 2223

A small restaurant seating just 34 diners. All the usual favourites plus Balti. Owner F.I. Khan has promised to increase his takeaway discount from 15% to 20% for Curry Club members. Support him – you can't get fairer than that! Open 6p.m.-midnight. Branch: Balti House, Newcastle upon Tyne.

WARWICKSHIRE

Alcester

BALTI CELLAR   ©

7 Market Place, 316 High Street, Alcester   ℂ 01789 764635

Director M.M. Hussain will give a discount to Curry Club members. Open 5.30p.m.-midnight, till 1a.m. Friday and Saturday.

ROMNA TANDOORI   ©

25 High Street, Alcester   © 01789 762252

Proprietor Rofik Ullah will give a discount to Curry Club members.
Open 5p.m.-midnight.

ROMNA II   BYO

Adjoining Somerfield Supermarket, Moorfield Road,
Alcester   © 01789 765430

'Small and very popular Balti restaurant, advisable to book in advance.
Good range of starters and Balti dishes, plus tandoor. The chef
specializes in Biryani dishes. Service excellent, huge portions of good-
quality food,' B.B.

Henley-in-Arden

ARDEN TANDOORI   ©

137 High Street, Henley-in-Arden   © 01564 792503

Opened in 1984 by partners Nanu and Angor Miah. House specials:
Nan Rathan Bhuna – succulent pieces of chicken, lamb and king
prawn, medium-spiced (£6.95). Price check: Papadom 45p, CTM
£6.25, Pullao Rice £1.65. Open noon-2.30p.m. and 5.30-11.30p.m.
Branch: Saleem Bagh, Queen Square, Cannock, Staffordshire; Saleem
Bagh, 476 Station Road, Dorridge, Solihull, West Midlands.

Kenilworth

BALTI TOWERS

Kenilworth Lodge Hotel, 149 Warwick Road,
Kenilworth   © 01926 851156

'Obviously very popular as there was a good turnaround of customers.
Staff a bit vacant but, when asked for something, they were prompt.
Not quite as good as Royal Naim but still authentic and thoroughly
enjoyable. Balti Lamb Rogon £4.10, Balti Meat with Vegetables £4.25.
Portions were good, making it good value for money,' S.R.

SUNAM BALTI HOUSE   NEW ENTRANT   BYO ©

57 Abbey End, Abbey Court, Kenilworth   ✆ **01926 863070**

Opened in 1995 by Amin Uddin. Northern Indian food on the menu. Unlicensed, but you are welcome to bring your own wines, strictly before 9.30p.m., a small charge will be added to your table. House special is Garlic King Prawns £5.95. Price check: Papadom 40p, CTM £4.60, Pullao Rice £1.40. Minimum charge £5. Open 5-11.30p.m.

Leamington Spa

ASHOKA   TOP 100

22 Regent Street, Leamington Spa   ✆ **01926 428272**

'Consistently the best. Variety and quality of food speaks for itself. Free popadoms when collecting a takeaway,' s.n. and r.a. Open 6p.m.-2a.m., opens 6.30p.m. Sunday, closes 3a.m. Friday and Saturday. Remains in our TOP 100.

BOMBAY TANDOORI   NEW ENTRANT   ©

38-40 Regent Street, Leamington Spa   ✆ **01926 420521**

Opened in 1990 by Mr Ahmed. Serves Bangladeshi and north Indian curries. House special in Karahi Lamb – whole leg of spring lamb spiced, marinated for at least eight hours, roasted tandoori-style, garnished with mincemeat and served with Vegetable Bartha and Pillao Rice – £58.50 for four. Price check: Papadom 50p, CTM £5.75, Pullao Rice £1.50. Minimum charge £7.50. Open 6p.m.-1a.m, till 3a.m. Friday and Saturday.

LEAMINGTON BALTI COTTAGE   NEW ENTRANT

50 Clarendon Street, Leamington Spa   ✆ **01926 885882.**

Opened 1 February 1997 by Ruman Ahmed. It is indeed a cottage, complete with rough plaster walls and a low beamed ceiling. Pakistani food is served to 46 covers. Try a starter of Stuffed Mushroom (£1.90), just for a change. House special is Chicken Tikka Mochammon – pieces of diced Chicken Tikka breast cooked with green beans, dressed with eggs and tomatoes (£4.95). Price check: Papadom 45p, CTM £4.95, Pullao Rice £1.50. Minimum charge £10. Open 5p.m.-1a.m.

Nuneaton

RAJDHANI NEW ENTRANT   ©

Unit 1, Cambourne Drive, Horeston Grange,
Nuneaton   ℂ 01203 352254

Proprietor is Surat Miah. Opened in 1985. For an unusual starter, order Tikka Paneer (£2.55) and for a main course Tandoori Quail (£8.95) or Trout (£6.50). Price check: Papadom 40p, CTM £6.95, Pullao Rice £1.75. Minimum charge £12. Open 5.30-11p.m. Lunch available if booked in advance.

SUNDARBON

39 Attleborough Road, Nuneaton   ℂ 01203 344243

'Very, very good,' P.J. Open 5p.m.-midnight, till 1a.m. Friday.

Rugby

DILRUBA   ©

155-157 Railway Terrace, Rugby   ℂ 01788 542262

Serving good curries and accompaniments since 1983. Owner, Liaquat Ali, will give a discount to Curry Club members. Open 6p.m.-1a.m., till 2a.m. Friday and Saturday, till 1.20a.m. Sunday.

TITASH INTERNATIONAL BALTI   ©

65 Church Street, Rugby   ℂ 01788 574433

Owned by Mashuk Ali since 1993. Bangladeshi curries and accompaniments on the menu for 58 diners. Price check: Papadom 60p, CTM £5.60, Pullao Rice £1.60. Open 5p.m.-1a.m. Branch: Titash, 2278 Coventry Road, Sheldon, Birmingham.

Stratford-upon-Avon

ALADDINS NEW ENTRANT   ©

**4 Main Road, Tiddington,
Stratford-upon-Avon**   ✆ **01789 294491**

Opened on 21 November 1994 and owned by Ala Uddin. A very attractive restaurant from the outside. The usual plate-glass windows that dominate shop-fronts have been removed and white panels with windows have been replaced. The interior is equally attractive and spacious with large pillars supporting the ceiling, accompanied by scrolling corbels, and we just adore the bar with its elephants. Menu contains all the usual Bangladeshi curries and accompaniments including some interesting extras, such as Chicken Anarkali – tandoori-baked chicken cooked with minced lamb lightly spiced, wrapped in an envelope of traditional Bangladeshi-style omelette, complemented with sauce and served with Basmati Rice (£7.50), and Jhinga La Jawab – tandoori-baked king prawns stir-fried in a medium-spiced sauce garnished with french beans, tomatoes and fresh green herbs, served with Pulau (sic) Rice (£8.50). Price check: Papadom 45p, CTM £6.25, Pullao Rice £1.90. Minimum charge £8.50. Open 5.30p.m.-midnight.

HUSSAIN'S

6a Chapel Street, Stratford-upon-Avon   ✆ **01789 205804**

'Close to all theatres, popular with actors, apparently. Delicious curries, Chicken Biriani and Chicken Tikka Masala came with veritable slabs of succulent chicken breast. Superb featherweight Pillau Rice, best we've tasted! Cosy atmosphere. Good Nan,' H.S.

LALBAGH BALTI   ©

---

3 Greenhill Street, Stratford-upon-Avon   ✆ **01789 293563**

Opened in 1989 by Abdul Aziz, who is also to be found in the kitchen as head chef. Bangladeshi and northern Indian food dominates his menu. 'Wide, if conventional menu. Excellent comfort. Well-kept decor, polite and reserved service. Papadoms served with delicious sauce and onion relish, very good. Lalbagh Special Chicken £5.95, large quantity, wholesome chicken, quality ingredients,' G. and M.P. Price check: Papadom 50p, CTM £5.25, Pullao Rice £1.70. Open 5.30-12.30p.m.

THESPIAN'S INDIAN CUISINE   NEW ENTRANT   ▦ ©

26 Sheep Street, Stratford-upon-Avon   © 01789 267187

Opened in 1996 by chef-proprietor Habibur Rahman, Air-conditioned. Bangladeshi food features on his menu. For an interesting change, try Boal Biriani for a starter (£3.25) – fillets of Bengal boal, lightly spiced. House specials include Lobster Beruda, aubergine-flavoured sauce, served with Pilau Rice (£9.75). Price check: Papadom 35p, CTM £6.50, Pullao Rice £1.70. Minimum charge £10.95. Open 5.30p.m.-midnight. Home delivery service on orders over £10 within a 3-mile radius. Branch: Knowle Indian Brasserie, High Street, Knowle, West Midlands; Stockland Balti Takeaway, 332 Marsh Lane, Erdington, Birmingham, West Midlands.

USHA BANGLADESHI STYLE CUISINE   NEW ENTRANT

28 Meer Street, Stratford-upon-Avon   © 01789 297348

Opened originally in 1967, but its current ownership under partners Achab Au and Rufa Miah began in 1995. Serves Bangladeshi and northern Indian curries. 'Attractively decorated restaurant is close to the centre of Stratford. Lamb Muchammon, smaller size chunks of lamb would have improved the digestibility. Chicken Shashlik was melt in the mouth, succulent and well marinated. It was mild and served up in equally large quantity with huge chunks of chicken, complete with salad and a whole roasted onion, but almost no sauce. Comfort was excellent. Service leisurely,' G. and M.P. 'Service was excellent, prompt and attentive. Food was presented beautifully and served piping hot. Papadoms and chutneys were offered whilst we chose from the extensive and sensibly priced menu,' J.D. Price check: Papadom 40p, CTM £6.95, Pullao Rice £1.70. Minimum charge £10. Open noon-2.30p.m. and 5p.m.-midnight.

Warwick

CASTLE BALTI NEW ENTRANT	BYO
11 St John's, Warwick	© **01926 493007**

'Asked three separate locals for their recommendation and it was recommended by all three. FAN-BALTI-TASTIC. Quality of food, service and value for money outstanding. Shami Kebab followed by Chicken Mushroom Balti with Nan – absolutely the best – superb,' C.P.

WEST MIDLANDS
Birmingham

At the hub of the county of West Midlands is Birmingham city. Unquestionably Britain's number two city, Brum has come vibrantly alive with investment in its centre. The new convention centre-concert hall-hotel complex has breathed new excitement into the city, not least by placing the buildings, and a number of new pubs and restaurants, alongside the confluence of four canals. For those unaware of what flows beneath and between Brum's busy roads, there is no better place to view this astonishing network. There are even a couple of Birmingham's other assets nearby: Balti houses. For the purposes of this Guide, we divide the city into geographical areas, in which are grouped postcode zones B1 to B48 although, as ever, there is no sequential logic to postcode numbering. We start with Birmingham Central, then go to the adjacent Balti Zone, next North, East, South East, South West, and West. Further B postcodes, B62 (Halesowen) to B93 (Solihull) follow, listed alphabetically by their suburb name.

©	Curry Club discount (see p. 607)	🍷	Unlicensed
√	Vegetarian	🏠	Home delivery
BYO	Bring your own alcohol		service available

Birmingham Central Postcodes B1 to B5 (restaurants listed in alphabetical order)

AGRA FORT NEW ENTRANT ©

14-16 Suffolk Street Queensway, Birmingham, B1 ☎ 0121 643 2230

Opened in 1995 by Jamal Chaudhuri. Serves Bangladeshi- and northern Indian-style curries. You will be unable to miss this restaurant from the street – the large plate-glass windows allow you a peep into this very smart (and large – 130 seats) restaurant which is conveniently situated next to the Alexandra Theatre. The decor is not typically Indian. Polished wooden floor, creamy-gold walls with faint murals of zebras and peacocks. Comfortable, armchair seating makes this the sort of restaurant where you can relax and spend the evening. Sunday evening eat-as-much-as-you-like buffet from 6p.m., £9.95 per person which includes a glass of house wine. Happy hour is on Monday to Thursday evenings, between 6p.m. and 7.30p.m., 10% off the bill – a good dinner arrangement if you are going to the theatre. Balti Chicken and Mushroom £6.25, Nan £1.30. House special is Aba Fado De Camaro (£11.50) – Goan dish with king prawns. Price check: Papadom complimentary, CTM £7.25, Pullao Rice £1.80. Open noon-2.30p.m. and 6-11.30p.m., till 1a.m. Saturday. Branch: Yew Tree Cottage, Birmingham, B25.

ALOKA NEW ENTRANT

6-8 Bristol Street, Birmingham, B5 ☎ 0121 622 2011

In 1960, I became a stage manager at Coventry's Belgrade Theatre. I'd not long since left home and one thing I missed was my curry. Fortunately I'd learned a little about cooking curry from my ex-Raj grandmother but, let's put it this way, I had a heck of a lot to learn. But it did not stop me from inflicting my offerings on the permanent members of the theatre company. I suppose this was the glimmerings of the Curry Club. My weekly wage, I recall, was under £7, and half went on the rent, but my occasional treat was to save up for a restaurant curry. In 1960 there were no curry houses in Coventry – not one (today we have over 40 on our database!) So two or three of us would pop on a bus to Brum, well into its massive rebuild programme, spearheaded then by its gleaming new Bull Ring. Then it was round the corner to Brum's only curry house. The meal and bus fare cost under 5 shillings (25 pence) then! I really don't remember if the curry house was called the Aloka then, but it is now. During the 1960s, the spread of the curry house was as prolific as the city's building. But I always came here. Indeed, it was not until the opening of the Maharajah that I varied my allegiance. So here's to the Aloka, a pioneer indeed. Reports, please.

BALTI SOCIETY

68 New Street, Birmingham, B2   ✆ 0121 643 9493

'Balti Society is licensed and tends to attract a younger clientele later on, but still stays true to its Balti roots with a good range of traditional dishes. My Balti Chicken Tikka Masala was mild but tasty, although this Balti house tends to make its Baltis saucier than most and certainly it was on the rich side. However, teardrop Nans were on hand to soak up the sauce,' A.M. Open Sunday to Thursday 6p.m.-1a.m., till 1.30a.m. Friday and Saturday.

THE CELEBRITY   NEW ENTRANT

Broad Street, Birmingham, B1   ✆ 0121 643 8969

'On arrival we were met by a slim young man in very casual shirt and jeans who nearly knocked us out with alcoholic fumes and who was very clearly drunk. Although he gave us a laugh this is an unforgivable situation. He could hardly write down our order. Murgh Balti, absolutely fabulous, Onion Bhajia, very good, Spinach and Mushroom Balti, excellent. Small Naan, lovely and light. We were served by a more competent young man. There was a manager present, but like last visit he spent most of the time on the phone,' H.C.

DAYS OF THE RAJ   TOP 100   ©

51 Dale End, Birmingham, B4   ✆ 0121 236 0445

Owners Kulair and Singh spared no expense when this restaurant opened in 1986, and it continues to get good reports: 'Superbly cooked meal with individual flavours coming through,' T.M.C. 'Food absolutely superb, though the service less than warm,' D.R.C. 'Excellent rice,' C.M. 'As good as ever. There is only one problem – two doors marked Officers and Ladies. I am neither, and always feel that I should use the door downstairs marked Private,' D.MC. Remains in our TOP 100.

DIGBETH BALTI TOWERS

1-2 Barn Street, Digbeth   © 0121 643 8667

'Has an excellent range of Baltis and starters all at reasonable prices. Pakora which was championship class served up superbly fresh with a spicy taste. The usual tasty dips were on hand for dunking purposes. Balti Chicken Korma served up sizzling – although it was not in the Carnation cream category it has a lot more character than some of the blander Balti Kormas I have tasted. Chicken content was excellent and the dish was well spiced whilst retaining the traditional mildness of a Korma. Fresh, doughy teardrop Nans,' A.M.

FESTIVAL BALTI   NEW ENTRANT   ©

The Arcadian Centre, Birmingham, B5   © 0121 622 6289

Opened in July 1994. Bangladeshi food on the menu. House special is Seafood Delight (£4.95), medium-spiced with fish, prawns and scampi. Balti Chicken and Mushroom £4.55, Nan £1.35. Price check: Papadom 40p, CTM £4.75, Pullao Rice £1.75. Minimum charge £5. Open 5.15-11.45p.m.

MAHARAJAH   BEST IN THE MIDLANDS   TOP 100

23 Hurst Street, Birmingham, B5   © 0121 622 2641

Continuing the story from the Aloka (*see* entry), I recall this restaurant serving Biriani topped with edible silver leaf (vark) when it first opened in the 1970s. It was the first time I'd seen it used in Britain, though traditionalists in India would not contemplate the dish without it. It was a Moghul fetish, of course, the emperor permitting a gold leaf garnish only on the food for himself and the chosen member of the harem (the dish of the day!), while his wives had to make do with silver leaf. They believed it to be an aphrodisiac. It is not for me to comment on the validity of this claim and, with the EU ban on vark (*see* intro), neither can anyone else in Britain. Certainly the Maharajah is no longer allowed to serve it, sadly. But the food is still outstanding. I came here unbooked alone one dinnertime. Despite a full to bursting room, I was seated at once and served with every care and attention. There were the usual contented groups of Asians, always a good sign of authenticity, and I was not the only loner. A young Asian woman was uncomfortably alone, peering frequently out of the window, and explaining that her friends would soon arrive. Owner N. Bhatt did his utmost to relax her with nibbles and a drink, and smiling chat, *en passant*, and eventually her uncles and father arrived, with profuse apologies. Meanwhile the waiting bookers were deftly dispatched to the downstairs bar. Such competence is rare and welcome. On two floors, it's a small place, and booking is recommended. The food is Indian, rather than Bangladeshi formula, and it is always spot on. We continue to receive plentiful reports on the Maharajah. Stays in our TOP 100, indeed I'm happy to give it our BEST IN THE MIDLANDS Award. Lunch and dinner daily. Closed on Sundays and for two weeks in the summer.

MILAN INDIAN CUISINE   ©

93 Newhall Street, Birmingham, B3   ✆ **0121 236 0671**

Dhirendra Patel opened his restaurant in 1995. It is decorated in pastel shades, giving it a light and airy feel even though it seats 120 diners. The bar area is typically Indian with beaten copper drinks tables and large coffee pots. The menu features all the usual curry house favourites from Korma to Jalfrezi but there is also an extensive vegetarian section. Paneer Tikka (£2.25), spicy paneer cooked in the tandoor. Stuffed peppers filled with coconut, potatoes and coriander (£1.95). Reshmi Mattar Paneer (£4.50), home-made cheese with herbs, spices, peas, cashews and corn. Price check: Papadom 50p, CTM £6.25, Pullao Rice £1.60. Minimum charge £8.50. Open noon-2p.m. and 6p.m.-midnight. Closed on Sunday. Fully licensed.

MOKHAM'S OF DIGBETH   ©

140 Digbeth High Street, Birmingham, B5 ✆ **0121 643 7375**

Says A.M.: 'Mokham's pride themselves on their cooking so you may have to wait as all the food is freshly prepared. Tandoori Sheeksh

Kebab is certainly one of the best I have ever tasted. Balti Exotica is meat, chicken, prawns, mushroom and pasta, without doubt unique in my experience. A very substantial dish, served up in the traditional black bowl, it was beautifully spiced and the pasta blended superbly but when combined with my Nan bread it left me feeling like Pavarotti.' Unlicensed. Open daily, noon-2.30p.m. and 6p.m. till late. Owner Naz Khan will give a discount to Curry Club members.

RAJDOOT TOP 100   ©

---

12 Albert Street, Birmingham, B4   ✆ **0121 643 8749**

Des Sarda's Rajdoot has branches in Bristol, Manchester, Dublin and Fuengirola, Spain. He opened this restaurant in 1972. It is, as are all the Rajdoots, tastefully and authentically decorated. Des is an architect and knows a thing or two about style. The chefs here are Nepalese (head chef Basu Mali) and their cooking is as delicate as you'll find. 'Absolutely superb, we find this establishment to be extremely reliable. Fish Tikka starter exquisite as usual as was the Chilli Chicken Tikka, generous portions. King Prawn Chilli Garlic was a favourite amongst our group again but I decided to try the Lamb Punjabi Massalla this time and what a good choice!! Meat extremely lean and well spiced, served in a dark onion and tomato gravy finished with balsamic vinegar and red wine. We ordered the usual side dishes, dal of the day, Bombay Allo Jeera and Sag Paneer as well as Pillau Rice and Peshwari Nan, all of which were fresh and cooked to perfection,' c.t. The Rajdoot seats 84 diners, serves northern Indian cuisine and is fully air-conditioned. Price check: Papadom free, CTM £7.20, Pullao Rice £1.80. Service charge 10%. Open noon-2.30p.m. and 6.30-11.30p.m., Sunday 6-11.30p.m.

Birmingham – Balti Zone
B10 to B13 postcodes (restaurants listed in alphabetical order)

The Balti Zone starts about 2 miles south east of the city (follow the A34), and is thickly spread around the suburbs of Small Heath,

Sparkhill, Sparkbrook and Moseley (B10 to B13). The population is largely north Pakistani, mostly from Kashmir's Mirpur, adjacent to which is Baltistan, all high up in the north Pakistani mountains. The doubters should visit K2 balti house, upon whose walls is the biggest map of the region that I've seen, and it is from there that Balti originated. But for those who prefer to say it did so in Birmingham, you are certain to get the nation's best Baltis here. Here is your pick of the bunch:

ADIL 1   BYO ©

148-150 Stoney Lane, Sparkbrook, B11   © 0121 449 0335

'My birthday and what better, after a 7.30a.m. champagne and Guinness breakfast in London's Smithfield Market, than to travel to Birmingham for a Balti at Adil's. After the initiation course of Green Chilli Bhajis (70p) we settled down to enjoy Balti Chicken Tikka Veg-Dall-Spi-Chana (£4.60), two massive Table Nans (£2.90) and two portions of rice (£1). My colleague Ian (two puddings) Hunter could not contain himself, unable to decide between Rasmali (90p), Barfi (60p) and Kulfi (£1.40), and ate all three. Simple as ABC – Adil's for Balti Curry,' D.B. 'This is my old original Balti restaurant. If I am anywhere near Birmingham I pilgrimage to Adil's. Oh! the Baltis! and so low a price. Avoid the starters, they are ordinary and the small portions make them poor value for money. Not licensed, but there is an off-licence next door run by his cousin. If you order a cab, the driver is another cousin! Family enterprise!' C.D.

ADIL 2   ©

130 Stoney Lane, Balsall Heath, B12   © 0121 449 9296

Adil's other branch is really the overflow for Adil 1. Manager is M. Ashraf. Open noon-midnight. Branch: Waterfront Balti, 127-129 Dudley Road, Brierley Hill.

ALAMGEER   BYO ©

811 Stratford Road, Sparkhill, B11   © 0121 778 2388

A small restaurant seating just 30 diners. Baltis and curries on the menu. Owned by G. Arif who is always extremely welcoming. Bring your own drinks. 'Probably my favourite Balti house, certainly the best in Birmingham. Decor and comfort are both basic but service is absolutely outstanding. Quantities are good, quality excellent. My Pakoras were delicious. In contrast to other restaurants, they sell only fresh starters and not warmed-up stale food. The Tandoori Fish (silver hake) literally crumbled in my mouth. Highly recommended,' G.P. Open 6p.m.-2.30a.m.

AL-FRASH NEW ENTRANT   BYO ©

186 Ladypool Road, Sparkbrook, B12   © **0121 753 3120**

Opened in 1994 by Mukhtar Ahmed. A Balti house seating 85. A smart and pleasantly decorated restaurant in pinks and blues with a spiral staircase. Quality high-backed chairs make for a comfortable evening. Starters include Onion Rings (65p), one of my personal favourites, with Aubergine Pakora (75p), which I usually only get on my trips to India. Balti Chicken and Mushroom £4.35, Nan 70p (small), £1.95 (medium) or £3 (large). Price check: Papadom 35p, CTM £4.80, Pullao Rice £1.30. Open 5p.m.-1a.m.

ALI BABA   BYO ©

250 Ladypool Road, Sparkbrook, B12   © **0121 449 4929**

Owned by Mr Aslam, who is also proprietor of Nirala in Moseley Road. We like the restaurant logo of a chap holding a sizzling Balti, sitting on a flying carpet (is this a new mode of transport for home delivery?) As with the Nirala, it is unlicensed and starters such as kebabs, tikka and tandoori are cooked to order on the charcoal-fired barbecue, which gives them that extra special taste. Price check: Papadom 30p, CTM £5, Pullao Rice 95p. Open noon-2.30p.m. and 4p.m. till late.

COSMOPOLITAN NEW ENTRANT   BYO ©

31 Woodbridge Road, Moseley, B13   © **0121 449 5793**

An unlicensed Pakistani establishment. Balti Chicken and Mushroom, £3.70, Nan 75p. Price check: Papadom 30p, served with dip, BCTM £4.40, Pullao Rice £1.10. Open 5.30p.m.-midnight. If you want a lunchtime party the restaurant can be privately booked.

DESI KHANA

706 Stratford Road, Sparkhill, B11   © 0121 778 4450

'Pakora, highly spiced but not overpowering, very fresh. Seekh Kebab, came sizzling hot with onion, tender, succulent. Chicken Tikka Balti, generous quantity, good quality, unusual taste,' G. and M.P.

GRAND TANDOORI

345 Stratford Road, Sparkhill, B11   © 0121 772 5610

'Very popular. If you order anything other than a Balti they get confused. Not licensed,' J. and A.McL.

I AM THE KING OF BALTI   BYO ©

230-232 Ladypool Road, Sparkbrook, B12   © 0121 449 1170

Opened in 1989 by Khalid Hussain. Pakistani- and Kashmiri-styled Baltis (the best) are on the menu. Pilau (sic) and charcoal dishes (King Kebab, £1.50) are house specialities. Balti Chicken and Mushroom £5, Nan £1, Extra Large Nan £3.50. Unlicensed, but if you bring your own wine they are very happy to chill it for you. On the bottom of the menu in minuscule type reads: 'There is a 5% charge on any payments made by credit or debit cards.' Is this legal? It's certainly unethical. Price check: Papadom 40p, CTM £6, Pullao Rice £1.60. Open 3p.m. till late, Friday and Saturday 2p.m. till late, Sunday 1p.m. till late.

IB NE GHANI   ©

264-266 Green Lane, Small Heath, B9   © 0121 772 8138

Competent curries and Baltis at Dawood Hussain's establishment. Open 5p.m.-1a.m., Friday and Saturday 4p.m.-2a.m.

IMRAN   BYO

264 Ladypool Road, Sparkbrook, B12   © 0121 449 1370

'Baltis, superb. Family Nan, unbelievable – 3 feet by 2 feet. BYO from "offy" next door. Excellent value for money,' R.S. Says A.M.: 'Imran is one of Birmingham's oldest established Balti houses and indeed is one of several that claim to have been around at the time of the first-ever splitting of the Nan bread in Birmingham. The restaurant is spacious and includes a see-through Kebab cooking area for those who like to see a Sheeksh Kebab being cooked live. Predictably, Sheeksh Kebabs and Tikkas have a tasty charcoaled flavour. My main course Balti Chicken and Mushroom was served up in a shiny bowl and had an impressively spicy kick. Nans are available in the usual range of sizes and unusually you can also get a family Chapatti. Other unusual items include the Quail Balti (a dish which has now achieved almost protected status).' Open noon-midnight.

K2 ©

107 Alcester Road, Moseley, B13   © 0121 449 3883

Owned by N. Pasha (since 1994), managed by M. Niam. This restaurant seats 58 diners, serves Kashmiri Baltis and is BBC TV producer Nicola Silk's absolute favourite. There is a huge map of Baltistan gracing one wall which gives a good feel of the Northern Territories. On checking out the starters, we like the sound of Peppered Chicken (£3.10) – sweet and sour chicken prepared with a mixture of black and green pepper, ginger, soya sauce, sugar and lime. Balti Chicken and Mushroom £5.50, Nan £1.20. Price check: Papadom served with mint sauce, 30p, CTM £6, Pullao Rice £1.30. Fully licensed. Access and Visa accepted. Open 6-11.30p.m.

KABABISH ©

29 Woodbridge Road, Moseley, B13   © 0121 449 5556

Opened originally in 1983, taken over by K.M. Yaqub in 1997. A 60-seater Pakistani restaurant serving authentic Punjab and North West Frontier curries. Balti Chicken and Mushroom £5.55, Nan 95p. Fully licensed. Price check: Papadom 30p, CTM £5.75, Pullao Rice £1.20. Minimum charge £5.50. Open noon-2.30p.m. and 6p.m.-midnight. Branches: Kababish, Hall Green, B28; Kababish, Sutton Coldfield, B73.

KASHMIR LAKE BALTI ©

127-129 Ladypool Road, Sparkbrook, B12 © 0121 440 1238

Managing owner Jabber Karim's venue serves quality food. Open noon-2.30p.m. and 6p.m. till late.

KASHMIR LODGE

132 Stratford Road, Sparkbrook, B12   © 0121 773 1632

Says A.M.: 'It is housed in a former bank – the sort of grandiose building used before such establishments became virtually an excuse for a
hole in the wall. Prices remain at a credible street level. There is a good
range of Baltis including Balti Tinda (sweet potato) and Balti Karele
(bitter gourd). Chicken and Mushroom was fairly spicy with tender
meat. The accompanying Naan was fresh and yeasty.' Licensed. Open
noon-2.30p.m. and 6p.m.-midnight.

KHYBER

365 Ladypool Road, Sparkbrook, B12   © 0121 449 5139

'One of the spit and sawdust Balti houses that proliferate in
Sparkbrook. Tandoori Chicken very tasty. Chicken Tikka absolutely
superb,' G.G.P.

KILIMANJARO

9a Walford Road, Sparkbrook, B11   © 0121 771 3994

'Bills itself as a Kenyan restaurant. Menu out of the ordinary. Kuku
Parka – half a chicken marinated in coconut milk and spices, slowly
grilled and served with saffron rice and a bread made of coconut flour.
Quite simply marvellous,' G.G.P.

KINGS NEW ENTRANT

230-232 Ladypool Road, Birmingham, B12 © 0121 449 1170

'As a fan of Indian food I highly recommend this restaurant. Great
choice of excellent food, service was first class, friendly and clean,'
A.W.

KING'S BALTI NEW ENTRANT

13-15 York Road, Kings Heath,
Birmingham, B14   © 0121 443 1114

Menu lists all the Balti house favourites including the irresistible Balti
Chicken and Mushroom £3.95, Naan 90p. A great selection of veg-

etable dishes for the veggie-fanatics and meat-eaters alike – Balti Phool Gobi Naryal (£3.95), cauliflower florets with coconut; Balti Karela Rangeen (£3.95), karela, peas and carrots in a sauce with onions and tomato. Prawn and Onion Rice (£2.15) is a new one to try. 10% discount on takeaway. Price check: Papadom 30p, CTM £4.95, Pullao Rice £1.20. Payment can be made by credit card. Open 5p.m.-12.15a.m., till 12.30 a.m. Friday and Saturday.

KING'S PARADISE   ©

321 Stratford Road, Sparkhill, B12   ✆ 0121 753 2212

Owned by Mahboob Hussain. 'Balti Tandoori Butter Chicken, very smooth-tasting, in bright red sauce with some onion in there. Peshwari Naan, large, tasty with just a hint of syrup,' G. and M.P. Mushroom Nan (£1.30) sounds great! Price check: BCTM £4.50, Pullao Rice £1.30. Open noon-2.30p.m. and 5.30p.m.-midnight. Private car parking.

KUSHI   NEW ENTRANT

58 Moseley Road, Birmingham, B12   ✆ 0121 449 7678

'Starters were of uniformly excellent standard – Reshmi Kebab 85p, Meat Samosa 70p, Pakora 70p and Tandoori Chicken £1.95. First-class main courses. Balti Chicken Tikka Shashlik Masala £5.25. Balti Chicken Tikka Mirch Masala £5.75. Ample quantities, good service,' G.P. Price check: Papadom 35p. 'All nine of us agreed that this was a magnificent Balti house,' G. and M.P.

MINAR BALTI HOUSE   BYO

7 Walford Road, Sparkbrook, B11   ✆ 0121 773 5734

Opened by a trio of Mohammeds in 1990. They are from Pakistan and cook up authentic Baltis in their own individual pans. This restaurant is unlicensed and seats 48 diners. House specials include Balti Tropical (£5). Price check: Papadom free, CTM £5. Open 6p.m.-midnight, till 11p.m. Sunday.

NIRALA

580 Moseley Road, Moseley, B12   ✆ **0121 440 7600**

Unlicensed Balti restaurant, seating 100, opened in 1982 by Mr Mohammad Aslam. A well-known feature of this restaurant is the charcoal-fired starters – Chicken Tikka, Lamb Chop, Sheeh Kebab are all cooked fresh. Balti Chicken and Mushroom £4.30, Nan 60p, Family Nan £3. House special is Balti Seafood Special (£6). Price check: Papadom 30p, CTM £4.60, Pullao Rice 95p. Open noon till very late. Branch: Alibaba, 280 Ladypool Road, Sparkbrook, Birmingham.

PEARL OF KASHMIR

310 Highgate Road, Sparkbrook, B11   ✆ **0121 772 6085**

Says A.M.: 'Deceptively small from the outside, it is surprisingly spacious and airy inside aided by several extremely efficient fans. Free dips are an ideal accompaniment to a distinctly orangey (in taste as well as colour) Pakora. Main Baltis are robustly spiced and portions are good. The Balti was a trifle oily but nevertheless very tasty. Yeasty Nan breads were an ideal accompaniment. Menu has one or two surprises.' Unlicensed. Open noon-2.30p.m. and 6p.m.-1a.m.

PLAZA TANDOORI BALTI   BYO ©

278 Ladypool Road, Balsall Heath, B12   ✆ **0121 449 4249**

Unlicensed. Northern Indian and Punjabi food is served at this large – 75 seats – and up-market establishment. The owners are R.S. Ghataora (chef) and G.S. Pank (manager), who are both Sikh; this adds a different flavour to the cooking. Price check: Papadom 30p, CTM £4.75, Pullao Rice £1.10. Open 5p.m.-midnight.

POLASH   NEW ENTRANT   BYO

11 Hobmoor Road, Birmingham, B10   ✆ **0121 766 8824**

An unlicensed Bangladeshi curry house seating just 30 diners. Opened in 1991 by Rafiqur Rahman. House special is Chicken Chilli Masala (£3.25). Price check: Papadom 25p, CTM £3.50, Pullao Rice £1. Open 5p.m.-1a.m.

PUNJABI PARADISE   BYO

377 Ladypool Road, Sparkbrook, B12   ✆ 0121 449 4110

Opened originally in 1975, taken over in 1990 by Mohammed Shabaz, who is also the manager. A clean and smart Balti house with glass-topped tables. Baltis on the menu, cooked the Pakistani way. Unlicensed, so don't forget to bring your own. Price check: Papadom 25p, CTM £5.50, Pullao Rice £1.20. Minimum charge £6. Open 5p.m.-1a.m.

ROYAL AL FAISAL   BYO

136-140 Stoney Lane, Balsall Heath, B12   ✆ 0121 449 5695

Owner-manager is Mohammed Ajaib. Smartly decorated restaurant in shades of green. Seats 150 diners, tables of four and the usual banquet-style seating. Kashmiri Baltis on the menu. This is the place to get your Kharak Nan (£3.30), absolutely huge. 'Very good Baltis,' C.D. For the adventurous try their Balti Lotus Roots (£3.50) or Balti Mustard Leaf (£3.50). Balti Chicken and Mushroom £4.30. Price check: Papadom 30p, CTM £4.60, Pullao Rice 90p. Minimum charge £6.50. Open 11.30a.m.-midnight.

ROYAL NAIM   BRITAIN'S BEST BALTI TOP 100   BYO ©

417-419 Stratford Road, Sparkhill, B11   ✆ 0121 766 7849

A massive restaurant seating 175 diners on two floors. Owned and managed by M. Nazir, with his brother. 'Authentic Balti at its best. Recommend the Balti Chicken/Vegetable/Dall/Chana (£4.95) – a glorious combination of delights. Large Naan (£3) covered the table. Washed down with a jug of Lassi. Ras Malai for pudding is hard to beat. Takeaway counter serves Samosas, Onion Bhajis just the thing for the journey home – if you live as far away as I do!' D.B. 'When my wife had to go on a course to Birmingham we took the opportunity to try the restaurant voted the Best Balti. The atmosphere was building before we found the actual restaurant because of the community in which it is situated and the numerous other Balti restaurants sur-rounding it. The basic nature emphasized the excellent food. Owner very attentive and helpful. Returned a month later, once you get the Balti in front of you and taste it you don't want it to end,' S.R. 'Visited on a busy Saturday night. Standard of service, choice, quality of food and value for money is very high. Party of eight, four adults, four children, plenty of choice for all. My children insisted I make a detour two days later on our return from Kendal to Suffolk to revisit the Royal Naim,' D.B. Perusing the menu I like the sound of Coriander Naan (£1.95). This restaurant also hand-makes its own sweets, lovely! Price check: Papadom 40p, BCTM £5.50, Pilau Rice £1.50. Open noon-1a.m., till 3a.m. Friday and Saturday. Mr Nazir produces Royal Naim frozen Baltis in his factory, a short walk from the restaurant. Perhaps you have already seen them in freezer cabinets? Branch: Royal Stirchley Tandoori and Balti House, 1526-1528 Pershore Road, Stirchley, B30.

ROYAL NAWEED

44 Woodbridge Road, Moseley, B13   *©* **0121 449 2156**

'Free Popadoms with dips. Baltis very good. Huge Naan, eventually defeated us. No frills, clean, excellent value,' M.J.G.

SANAM'S TANDOORI

80-82 Stoney Lane, Balsall Heath, B12   *©* **0121 771 4715**

'Unpretentious and simple. Complimentary Papadoms. Fish Pakora delicious. Onion Bhajia, slices of onion deep-fried. Quantities generous. Garlic Nan was garlicky indeed! Tropical Balti, sauce enhanced rather than drowned flavour of prawns. Competitive prices,' G.D.-G.

SHAHI NAN KABAB

353 Stratford Road, Sparkhill, B11   *©* **0121 772 2787**

'"Sheekh Kebabs roasting on an open fire," in the words of that famous Asian Xmas ballad. Starters include the endangered Liver Tikka, which was surprisingly quite mildly spiced, and charcoaled Kebabs. Black-bowled Baltis are served up by men in short sleeves (no posy designer gear here) and were complemented by bubbly Nans. There is an excellent range of Shahi snacks including a large Rolly Polly (three Kebabs in a Paratha with salad and chutney) — whether you get a certificate and a photograph if you finish it is another matter!' A.M. Open noon-midnight.

SHEREEN KADAH

543 Moseley Road, Balsall Heath, B12   ✆ 0121 440 4641

Says A.M.: 'The Kebabs and Tikkas are barbecued on an Olympic-style flame. In the display cabinet is a selection of Kebabs on an array of sharp skewers which look like a Zulu armoury after an attack on Rourke's Drift. Free dips are brought to the glass-topped table as the main courses are awaited. If you want to push the boat out a King Prawn Balti at £4.50 is a real catch.' Unlicensed. Open 11a.m.-midnight.

SHER KHAN   NEW ENTRANT   ©

358-360 Stratford Road, Birmingham, B11   ✆ 0121 766 8766

Managed and owned by M.R. Alam. Opened in 1980. Licensed. Currently (at the time of writing this Guide) seating 56, but is expanding to 100. Pakistani food on the menu, Baltis being a speciality. Open noon-2.30p.m. and 6p.m.-midnight, Sunday noon-midnight.

SPICE AVENUE

Moseley Road, Birmingham, B13   ✆ 0121 442 4936

'Aloo Chant, delicious, beautifully spicy, well-marinated potato. Chicken Tikka, large chunks, smoky-tasting. Chicken Pakora, delicious. Navrattan Kofta, vegetable balls, spicy, allegedly four different vegetables. Gushtabba could have been spicier. Tandoori Mixed Masala, properly marinated, spicy. Service was prompt to begin with but slow to serve main courses,' G. and M.P. The editor has dined here for lunch and dinner on several occasions and the food is very good indeed. The decor is smart and tasteful, in greens and gold. The restaurant is licensed.

©   Curry Club discount (see p. 607)   Unlicensed
√   Vegetarian   ⊞   Home delivery
BYO   Bring your own alcohol   service available

Birmingham North
B6, B7, B19 to B24, B42 to B44
(restaurants listed in alphabetical order), beyond this is Sutton Coldfield (*see* entries)

DILKUSH TANDOORI

514 Queslett Road, Great Barr, B43   ✆ 0121 325 1774

Specials on the menu include Balti and Chicken Shillong – chicken and orange curry. Open 5p.m.-12.30a.m. Branch: Dilshad, 24b Anchor Road, Aldridge.

INDIA GARDEN

992 Tyburn Road, Erdington, B24   ✆ 0121 373 9363

Owned by Gian Uddin who will be found in the restaurant welcoming diners in his 80-seat restaurant. Omar Hussain is in the kitchen cooking Bangladeshi- and northern Indian-style curries and accompaniments. Licensed. Price check: Papadom 50p, CTM £7.75, Pullao Rice £1.55. Open 5p.m.-12.30a.m. (till 1a.m. Thursday), Friday and Saturday noon-2a.m., Sunday 1p.m.-1a.m.

RAJ INDIAN   ⊞

30 Birmingham Road, Great Barr, B43   ✆ 0121 357 8368

Licensed and fully air-conditioned restaurant. Opened in 1990 (but originally in 1976) by M.A. Latif who is also the manager. Chicken and Mushroom Balti £5.50, Nan £1.30. Price check: Papadom 40p, CTM £6.50, Pullao Rice £1.70. Open 5.30p.m.-12.30a.m., till 1a.m. Friday and Saturday. Discounts available on parties of 20 or more. Home delivery service available. Branch: Arden Tandoori, Henley-in-Arden, Warwickshire.

SAMRAT TANDOORI 田 ©

710 Chester Road, Erdington, B23   © 0121 384 5900

A large menu with all our favourite curries, Baltis and accompaniments. Owner, Niresh R. Dey, will give a discount to Curry Club members. Open noon-2.30p.m. and 6p.m.-midnight. Home delivery service.

STOCKLAND BALTI ©

221 Marsh Lane, Erdington, B23   © 0121 377 8789

A takeaway establishment, managed by Noor Ali, serving competent curries to a regular crowd. Open 5p.m.-12.30a.m., till 1a.m. Friday and Saturday.

Birmingham East
B8 to B10 and B25, B26, B33, B34, B36, B37, B40 (NEC) and B46 (restaurants listed in alphabetical order)

ASHA

2250 Coventry Road, Sheldon, B26   © 0121 743 6572

'Good food, especially the Chicken Tikka Masala,' C.M.

RADLEYS BALTI HOUSE   NEW ENTRANT   田 BYO

9 The Radleys, Sheldon, B33   © 0121 743 0235

Opened in 1996 by threesome Haque (manager), Hasnath (chef) and Uddin. Bangladeshi curries and accompaniments served here. Balti Chicken and Mushroom £4.30, Nan £1.10, Family Nan £1.95. Unlicensed. Price check: Papadom 45p, CTM £4.95, Pullao Rice £1.30. Open 5.30p.m.-12.30a.m., Friday and Saturday 5.30p.m.-1.30a.m. Home delivery service free within a 4-mile radius.

SHABAR TANDOORI　　　　　　　　　　　　　©

4 Arden Oak Road, Sheldon, B26　　　　© 0121 742 0636

Owned by Mozamil Ali since 1991. Bangladeshi formula curries and side dishes on the menu. Price check: Papadom 40p, CTM £6.65, Pullao Rice £1.25. Open 5.30p.m.-midnight. Fully licensed.

TITASH INTERNATIONAL

2278 Coventry Road, Sheldon, B26　　　© 0121 722 2080

Chicken Tikka Omelette and Baranasi Nan (pineapple) on the menu along with all your favourite Baltis and curries.

YEW TREE COTTAGE　　　　　　　　　　⊞ ©

43 Stoney Lane, Yardley, B25　　　　　© 0121 784 0707

Opened in 1979 by Jamal Chaudhuri who is also the manager and knows how to keep his customers happy. Papadoms, chutneys, pickles and mint sauce are served complimentary with all meals. Tandoori Night on Wednesday, a Tandoori Mixed Grill with Nan bread for only £7.50. During the winter months, a Gourmet Night is held on Sunday and Monday, four courses from the à la carte menu for only £9.95 per person. Balti Chicken and Mushroom £4.95, Nan £1.15. Price check: Papadom free, CTM £5.75, Pullao Rice £1.70. Minimum charge £6.50. Fully licensed. Open 5p.m.-12m. till 2a.m. Friday and Saturday, Sunday 6p.m.-1a.m. Home delivery service. Branch: Agra Fort, Birmingham, B1.

Birmingham South East
B 27 and B28, beyond this is Solihull and Knowle (*see* entries)

J JAY'S

1347 Stratford Road, Hall Green, B28　　© 0121 777 3185

'Service exceptionally friendly. Boti Kebab, tender and tasty. Tandoori Chicken Masala and Karahi Chicken superbly cooked,' J.McL.

KABABISH

2 Robin Hood Lane, Hall Green, B28   ℂ 0121 745 5445

'Standard of food is very high and consistent in each of the three establishments,' R.H.A. Open noon-2.30p.m. and 6-11.30p.m. Branches: Kababish, Moseley, B13; Kababish, Sutton Coldfield, B73.

MOGHUL   NEW ENTRANT

1184 Warwick Road, Acocks Green, B27   ℂ 0121 707 6777

Fully licensed and specializing in Tandoori and Balti curries. Balti Chicken and Mushroom £4.95, Nan 95p. 'I have never had a bad meal here. I particularly like their Chicken Tikka Pathia (£3.95), Ceylon and Rezalla dishes, all of which are excellent. Rice and breads are good also,' C.M. Price check: Papadom 30p, CTM £6.50 incl. Pullao Rice, Pullao Rice £1.50. Open 5.30p.m.-12.30a.m., Friday and Saturday 5.30p.m.-1a.m., Sunday 6p.m.-midnight.

PURPLE ROOMS

1076 Stratford Road, Hall Green, B28   ℂ 0121 702 2193

Opened by Faiz Choudhury. Bangladeshi formula curry house, Baltis also included. Balti Chicken and Mushroom £4.90, Nan £1.10. 'Stuffed Peppers, excellent. Pakeeza Chicken, could taste no coconut, chicken superb. Service was prompt, but dimly lit for my liking,' G.P. Special buffet lunch gourmets – help yourself to as much as you like from the Sunday buffet – 1-4p.m., £5.95 per person. Monday and Thursday Gourmet Night – five-course dinner with wine, £6.95. For vegetarians try the Pineapple Curry (£2.20), sounds delicious! Licensed. Price check: Papadom 40p, CTM £5.30, Pullao Rice £1.60. Open 6p.m.-midnight. Branch: Regards II, 9-10 Hagley Road, Edgbaston, Birmingham.

SHAHI BALTI   NEW ENTRANT

211 Lakey Lane, Hall Green, B28   ℂ 0121 778 6499

'A pleasant restaurant decorated in turquoise. Extensive menu. Started with a Nargis Kebab (£2.45), fairly small egg served up with copious amount of salad. Excellent spicy taste. For main course, Balti Chicken

Pathoa (£3.85), large amount of hot sour sauce with good-quality chicken, excellent, accompanied by Balti Chana (£2.75), came in rich, spicy sauce, extremely tasty and a Naan (£1), just the right texture. Superb value,' G.G.P.

Birmingham South West
B14, B29 to B31, B38, B45, B47, B48, B60

AKASH

142, Pershore Road, Stirchley, B30   ✆ 0121 458 4109

'Inviting restaurant, excellent comfort with prompt and friendly service. Complimentary Papadoms. Nargis Kebabs (£2.25), good, plenty of it. Chicken Tikka Puree (£2.40), plentiful and good quality. Chicken Tikka Masala, plentiful, good quality. Peshwari Naan, no sultanas or almonds, disappointing,' G. and M.P.

AZADI INTERNATIONAL   NEW ENTRANT

27-29 York Road, off High Street,
Kings Heath, B14   ✆ 0121 444 3406

The proprietor was kind enough to send in his takeaway menu, unfortunately with no prices, but I can tell you that the menu is quite vast; there is absolutely no chance of anyone going hungry. Unusual dishes include: Balti Sag with Puri, Meat and Beansprout Curry, Tandoori Lobster, Potato Raitha. Students and nurses can apply for a special 10% discount – so get those identity cards ready. Licensed. Accepts credit cards. Open 5.30p.m.-1a.m.

BALTI BAZAAR

1267-69 Pershore Road, Stirchley, B30   ✆ 0121 459 4517

'Wide-ranging menu, all very reasonably priced. Tandoori Chicken, well-marinated, Meat Samosa, very spicy and tasty. Substantial helping of Balti Chicken Aloo Gobi, chicken came in very big lumps,' G.G.P.

A.M. says: 'Bazaar in name and bizarre in menu. Moreish aptly describes the food as well as the style of decor. Chicken Tikka Puri – the bread was crispy but moist and the Tikka was quality. I know a number of people who insist the Balti Chicken Keski is an absolute must, as is an equally tasty Balti Chicken Shim (chicken cooked with spiced green beans). The chef's special Bazaar Nan actually contains fresh fruit.' Unlicensed. Open 5p.m.-midnight.

BALTI INTERNATIONAL NEW ENTRANT

523-5 Bristol Road, Selly Oak, B29   ✆ **0121 415 5707**

'Impressive decor with good comfort. Incredibly wide menu. Service was friendly and prompt. Nargis Kebab (£1.95) excellent, served with a free Onion Bhajia. Tandoori Chicken (£1.90) very good, although a little on the small side, also served with an Onion Bhajia. Balti Chicken Tikka Masala (£4.35), good quality with french beans, eggs and tomatoes. Keema Nan (£1.45)', G.P.

DILSHAD INTERNATIONAL   ©

618-620 Bristol Road, Selly Oak, B29   ✆ **0121 472 5016**

A huge restaurant seating 100 diners managed by Zakaria Altafi. Open 5.30p.m.-3a.m., till 4a.m. Friday and Saturday. Branch: Balti Night, 1480 Pershore Road, Stirchley.

HIMALAYA   BYO

1716 Bristol Road South, Longbridge, B45 ✆ **0121 453 4336**

Extensive menu with all your favourite curries and accompaniments. Not licensed, so BYO. 'Have tried a good selection of everything and nothing has been a disappointment', M.R. Open 5.30p.m.-12.30a.m.

INDIANAS

68-9 The Green, Kings Norton, B38   ✆ **0121 451 2907**

'Another good restaurant. Decor is smart and you can watch your meal being cooked through the glass-fronted kitchen. Food is of an above-average quality and the portions are on the generous side. My favourites include the Tropical Balti, Balti Special and the Chicken

Jalfrezi. Highly recommended. Word of warning: this restaurant charges an extra 50p should you decide to have your starter served in a sizzler!' c.m. That must surely go in the 'silly rules' book.

KHAN BALTI   ©

632 Bristol Road, Selly Oak, B29   © 0121 471 3844

Get all your favourite Balti combinations here. Manager is M. Taj. Open 5p.m.-2a.m. Branch: Khanum, 510 Bristol Road, Selly Oak, Birmingham.

KHANUM   ©

510 Bristol Road, Selly Oak, B29   © 0121 471 4877

Extensive menu serving all our favourite curries. Owner is M. Suleman. Open 5p.m.-2a.m., till 3a.m. weekends. Branch: Khan's, 632 Bristol Road, Selly Oak.

RAJPOOT   ©

1831-1833 Pershore Road, Cotteridge, B30 © 0121 458 5604

A large restaurant serving 94 diners all their favourite curries and Balthis (sic). Proprietor is Watir Ali. Open 6p.m.-2a.m.

ROYAL STIRCHLEY BALTI AND TANDOORI   BYO

1526-8 Pershore Road, Stirchley, B30   © 0121 433 4320

'Smartly appointed, very spacious restaurant. Free Popadoms and dip. Shami (45p) and Sheek (50p) very spicy, good taste. Balti Chicken with Chana (£3.45), dark, sweet sauce, plenty of chicken which went well with an excellent Peshwari Naan (£1.10) which came swimming in honey,' g.p.

YASSER TANDOORI   BYO ©

1268 Pershore Road, Stirchley, B30   © 0121 433 3023

Opened in 1987 by A. Hussain (manager) and Sarwar Khan. Specializing in Pakistani and Kashmiri cooking with a full list of Baltis. Balti Chicken Tikka Mushroom Masala £5.10, Family Nan

£3.90. The famous Balti Tropical (£5.20) can be eaten here, a mix of prawn, chicken, meat and mushroom. An extensive restaurant seating 110 diners. Price check: Papadom 40p, BCTM £4.80, Pullao Rice £1.30. Minimum charge £4.50. Open 4p.m.-1a.m., till 2a.m. Friday and Saturday.

Birmingham West
B15 to B19 and B32 (alphabetical order). Beyond this is Halesowen, Smethwick, Warley, West Bromwich (*see* entries)

AZIM

106 Lozells Road, Birmingham, B19   ℂ **0121 523 5349**

Extensive Balti menu plus all the usual curries and accompaniments. 'Clean and nicely decorated. Menu under glass-topped tables. Good range of Baltis as well as traditional curry dishes. Balti Meat Spinach succulent with flavour,' G.H. Open noon-1.30a.m.

BANU   NEW ENTRANT

353 Hagley Road, Edgbaston, B17   ℂ **0121 434 3416**

Originally opened way back in 1969, present ownership, under Abdul Mizan, commenced in 1985. Bangladeshi formula curries and Baltis on the menu. Restaurant seats 50. Price check: Papadom 50p, CTM £6.50, Pullao Rice £1.75. Open 6p.m.-2a.m.

INDIA GARDEN   ©

417 Hagley Road West, Quinton, B32   ℂ **0121 421 3242**

A licensed restaurant with special Happy Hour menu – good value. Open 5p.m.-1a.m., till 2a.m. Thursday, Friday and Saturday. Branch: Balti Palace, 349 Birchfield Road, Perry Barr, Birmingham.

J JAYS

2 Edgbaston Shopping Centre,
Five Ways, B16   ✆ 0121 455 6871

'Extensive menu including wide range of vegetable dishes,' R.A.

OMAR'S KASHMIRI

167 Hagley Road, Edgbaston, B16   ✆ 0121 454 7104

'Plenty of choice, food excellent, especially Naan bread. Value for
money,' E. and O.L. Open 6.30-11.30p.m., Sunday buffet from 1p.m.

RED PALACE

1-11 Constitution Hill, Hockley, B19   ✆ 0121 236 8097

'Extensive buffet lunches served daily are superb,' R.H.A.

SHIMLA PINKS

214 Broad Street, Birmingham, B15   ✆ 0121 633 0366

'Nans the best I've had. Bhuna Chicken particularly good. Service
courteous. Plenty of space. Strange decor,' M.J.G. Branches: East Indian
Company and Varsity Blues, Stirling, Central; Killermont Polo Club,
Glasgow, Strathclyde; Shimla Pinks, Johnstone, Strathclyde.

Coventry

BENGAL DELIGHT   ©

166-168 Holbrook Lane, Coventry   ✆ 01203 686789

Opened in 1994 by Saddak Miah who is also the manager. Seats 70 and
is licensed. Bangladeshi formula curries on the menu including Royal
Murghi Mussala (£12.95), on the bone marinated chicken in minced
lamb, medium spicy sauce with egg and tomato served with basmati
rice. Price check: Papadom 45p, CTM £5.45, Pullao Rice £1.60.
Minimum charge £10. Open 5.30-11.30p.m., till midnight Friday and
Saturday.

BENGAL GARDEN NEW ENTRANT

135 Walsgrave Road, Ball Hill, Coventry ✆ 01203 652535

'Good comfort, attractive decor, excellent service. Seating for 36 people. Well-marinated Tandoori Chicken, but leg rather than breast. Aloo Keema Peas, strongly-flavoured lamb with pronounced tomato taste. They tried extremely hard and the whole meal was very satisfying,' G. and M.P.

BOMBAY PALACE   ©

64 Earlsdon Street, Earlsdon, Coventry ✆ 01203 677851

Opened in 1988 by Siraj Alo, who is also the manager. Bangladeshi food on the menu with the odd Thai dish thrown in. Restaurant seats 90, there is also a private party room and it is fully licensed. 'Plentiful and very tasty Chicken Chat. Fairly hot Chicken Ceylon, immense helpings. Service quick and pleasant,' G.G.P. House specials include Korai Moroog (£5.95). Price check: Papadom 40p, CTM £5.95, Pullao Rice £1.50. Minimum charge £5.95. Open noon-2p.m. and 6p.m.-12.30a.m., till 1.30a.m. Friday and Saturday.

THE DAYS OF THE RAJ

87-89 Radford Road, Coventry ✆ 01203 597001

'Very smart up-market decor. Shashlick Chicken was unbelievably tasty. Balti Lamb exceptionally spicy and really tasty,' P.J.

DHAKA DYNASTY NEW ENTRANT

292-294 Walsgrave Road, Coventry ✆ 01203 636615

'Starters were small in quantity but satisfactory for my wife. Balti Mixed Vegetable included carrots, onions, potato, cauliflower, tomato, peas, mushrooms with coriander, bay leaf, curry leaf, cloves, cardamom and cassia. Quantity very generous and quality outstanding. Luxurious decor with tropical fish tank dominating middle of room,' G.P.

EASTERN DINER   NEW ENTRANT

412-414 Foleshill Road, Coventry   © **01203 686700**

'Fairly basic Balti house with small menu, but they will make anything
on demand. You go to the counter to order as if in a burger restaurant.
Reasonable quality with fair quantities,' G.P.

GOLDEN GATE   NEW ENTRANT

1 Brixham Drive, Wyken, Coventry   © **01203 687308**

A small, average curry house, only 34 seats, with a restricted menu.
'Chicken Jalfrezi, large chunks of well-marinated chicken (£4.95).
Keema Nan (£1.40) was overcooked and needed more mince,' G.P.

ISTIFA BALTI   BYO

6 Hales Street, Coventry   © **01203 224311**

'The food here is good and so are the prices. There is only one thing
that is really bad about this place, and that's the music, all one tape of
it. An awful waiter is more entertainment value than frustrating and he
has special magic powers! The Balti that no one ordered magically
changes as he circles the table! Within three circuits a Chicken Rogan
has become a Chicken Dupiaza, WOW! Unlicensed,' G.R.

K2   NEW ENTRANT

124 Lower Ford Street, Coventry   © **01203 221597**

Formerly Balti Raj. 'Service prompt and friendly. Papadoms 35p each,
with chutneys £1. Started with Tandoori Chicken (£1.90), not as well
marinated as it could have been. Balti Chicken Ceylon (£4.10), good-
quality chicken, very spicy with coconutty taste. Mince Biryani
(£4.90), rice nicely done, mixed with the lamb mince and whole cumin
seeds. Peshwari Nan (£1.50), not enough syrup or sultanas,' G.G.P.

KARAHI KING   NEW ENTRANT   ▦

553 Foleshill Road, Coventry   © **01203 680620**

Fully licensed. A small menu but you will find all you need for a good
night out. We recommend you try their Chicken Wings (£2.30) for

starters followed by Karahi Lamb Chops (£3.95), back chops tenderly
marinated and cooked in rich sauce with a side dish of Paneer Sizzler
(£3.95), chunks of cheese cooked in tandoori masala with onions. 10%
discount for takeaway and students with an NUS card. Credit cards
accepted. Open 5p.m.-midnight. Free home delivery on orders over £10
and within a 3 mile radius.

KING WILLIAM IV PUB   TOP 100

1059 Foleshill Road, Coventry   © 01203 686394

We have observed in our introduction that no less than 6500 British
pubs serve curry. Not long ago, you were lucky if you could get a
decent sausage at the pub, and then only at set times. But along in 1986
came Pele and Jatinder Bains. They were already experienced publicans,
but this was a new idea. They put only authentic curries on the menu.
And guess what? From day one, it's been a resounding success. Good
ale with good curry. Roll on, I wish there were more like this. Strings
of good reports keep it in our TOP 100.

MOONLIGHT BALTI   BYO

196 Foleshill Road, Coventry   © 01203 633414

'Average menu, good food served hot and fresh. Is licensed but you can
BYO. Good value for money,' H.M. 'Onion Bhajia warm and crisp, copious salad. Balti Chicken Dupiaza, very tasty chicken, lots of sauce, big
helping. Peshwari Nan, very buttery and hot,' G.G.P.

MONSOON   NEW ENTRANT

20-21 Far Gosford Street, Coventry   © 01203 229651

'Chicken Pakora, gorgeous. Tandoori Chicken, fairly small, but very
spicy. Humungous portion of Balti Tikka Chicken Masala. Brilliant
Balti Meat with Dal. Naan – what a size! Special Fried Rice, absolutely enormous,' G.P. 'Tandoori Chicken (£1.85) – well marinated and tasty,
Chicken Pakora (£2.25) – succulent. Balti Chicken Tikka with Keema
and Chana (£4.95) – massive quantities, superb quality, very tasty and
extremely spicy. Balti Chilli Chicken Masala with Chana (£3.95) –
mouthwatering. Coriander Nan (£1.75). Quality excellent. Very prompt
and pleasant service,' G. and M.P. It's one of their favourites.

NASEEB BALTI   NEW ENTRANT

409 Foleshill Road, Coventry   ℂ 01203 682147

'Comfort acceptable if rather draughty. Meat Samosa slightly oily but tasty with good portions of salad. Chef's Special, exotic combination of chicken and lamb cooked in a very hot spicy sauce (£5.95). I would quibble with the description "very hot" as, apart from a couple of fresh green chillies, the sauce seemed of average heat to me, but the quality of the food and the lamb was particularly tasty,' G. and M.P.

PLANET BALTI   NEW ENTRANT

3e Lower Holyhead Road, Coventry   ℂ 01203 634463

'Papadom (40p), fresh, crisp, served with chutney bowl. Tandoori Chicken (£1.85), fairly small portion but very tasty, well-marinated and beautifully served with salad. Very good Nargis Kebab (£1.85). Balti Chicken Tikka Bangladesh (£3.95), well-balanced, egg, aubergine, chicken, nice texture of sauce. Balti Chicken Tikka Bhuna (£3.95), good-sized portion, well-spiced. Superb service in very pleasant surroundings,' G.G.P.

PRINCE WILLIAM HENRY PUB   NEW ENTRANT

252 Foleshill Road, Coventry   ℂ 01203 687776

This is a branch of the aforementioned William IV pub, with a formula that works, only here it is good ale with Baltis. 'Typical Balti house menu. Chicken Tikka, sizeable portion, large chunks, nicely spiced, served with salad. Tandoori Chicken, well done. Huge serving of Balti Chilli Chicken Tikka Masala, enormous lumps of chicken tikka, far bigger helping than usual. Substantial Naan. Very prompt service,' G.P.

QUICK STOP BALTI   NEW ENTRANT   BYO

80 Far Gosford Street, Coventry   ℂ 01203 632578

'Unlicensed and unpretentious restaurant. A reasonable range of Balti dishes plus a few others. Quantities were substantial, good-quality food. Papadom 40p. Started with Tandoori Chicken (£1.75), well-marinated, very spicy, a good-size portion with plenty of meat. Balti Chicken Mushroom (£3), spicy. Balti Chicken Pathia (£3), excellent, good rich sauce. Peswari Nan £1.45, Pilau Rice £1.10,' G.P.

RAJAH NEW ENTRANT

25 Cross Cheaping, Coventry   ✆ 01203 222397

'Subdued, pleasant decor. Conventional menu, two Popadoms £1.20 – extortionate. Balti Chicken Tikka Masala – large chunks of chicken with a thick sauce. Keema Naan – huge with large amount of mince. Substantial portion of Pilau Rice. Certainly couldn't complain about the quantities, but food was heavy,' G.P.

RAJDOOT

29 City Arcade, Coventry   ✆ 01203 223195

'Wide and varied menu, quantities generous. Very tasty Chicken Hakime (chef's invention), with green chillies and a hot and sour sauce,' G.G.P.

RED HOT CHILLI PEPPER NEW ENTRANT

118 Gosford Street, Coventry   ✆ 01203 634563

'Absolutely packed, everyone taking advantage of the special price voucher in the paper. Service slow but understandable. Tandoori Fish was superb, wonderfully tasty, melt-in-the-mouth quality. Onion Bhajia was burger-style (flat), spicy. Balti Chicken Tikka Masala Jalfrezi, advertised as medium, I was surprised at how hot it was, fresh green chillies in large quantities,' G.P.

RED ROSE BALTI NEW ENTRANT   ©

31 Silver Street, Coventry   ✆ 01203 222702

A couple of Guides ago, I asked which was the first restaurant to open in Coventry in 1960. I dined there then, but can't remember its name or address. Mr Mukaddas Ali bought this place in 1993, and says this was it. But was it, and what was it called then? Anyway, today it has Bangladeshi and northern Indian curries on the menu, plus a good selection of Baltis. Balti Chicken and Mushroom £3.75, Nan £1. Price check: Papadom 45p incl. chutney, CTM £4.95, Pullao Rice £1.10. Minimum charge £4.

ROYAL BENGAL NEW ENTRANT

172 Albany Road, Coventry   © 01203 712345

'Excellent, top-quality food, very impressive,' G.P.

ROYAL INDIA NEW ENTRANT

39 London Road, Coventry   © 01203 550343

Formerly Samrat Balti. This restaurant has reopened after a complete redec, with plush carpets, etc. The menu contains all the usual curries and accompaniments. 'Papadom 50p. Aloo Chat (£1.20), delicious, spicy with potato inside a chapati. Hasina Kebab (£1.80), plenty of salad, mild lamb. Balti Chicken Dansak (£4.70), copious amount of very hot lentil-based sauce. Shahi Panir (£2), this was superb, beautifully flavoured cheese-based side dish,' G.P.

RUPALI NEW ENTRANT TOP 100

337 The Hill Lane, Coventry   © 01203 422500

'Armed with Curry Club Magazine issue 43 with "Coventry Curry Criteria", it didn't take us long to select the Rupali. Full marks to Graham Paine, his resumé was spot on. The decor is certainly opulent, and equally matched by the dress of the head waiter. Mirrored back wall gives the restaurant a sense of depth and we were fortunate to be placed next to the central water fountain. The menu is extensive with an impressive list of chef's specials but for most of us the choice was easy – the award-winning Sylheti Chicken Jalfrezi. Overall consensus was that the food was excellent. Very aromatic taste, each mouthful yielded further surprises to the tastebuds. Portions were on the adequate side rather than large, service and presentation of the meals more than made up for this as both were first class. Chicken Shashlic was a work of art on the plate after being arranged by the waiter. Not cheap, £230 for seven, including three courses and four rounds of Cobra,' S.G. FOUR rounds of Cobra? You must have crawled out, it's strong stuff! 'Stuffed Pepper (£2.95), excellent, with chunks of delicious vegetables. Korai Kebab Kofta (£6.95), very spicy, extremely tasty meatballs served in copious quantities. CTM heavy coconut base, bright red, creamy sauce with succulent chicken. Aloo Nirmisha (£2.95), fresh green chilli with potato. Pullao Rice (£1.75), perfect with all the different colours picked out, beautifully presented but quantity a little stingy,' G.P. Despite that, and for G. and M.P. and many others, we are pleased to place the Rupali in our TOP 100.

SHAHI PALACE NEW ENTRANT ©

367 Foleshill Road, Coventry ℰ 01203 688719

Formerly the Palace, Kashmir and Balti, so this is the fourth name-change in ten years! Now owned by Iqbal Hussain, it is a licensed Bangladeshi curry house seating 84. Nicely decorated in greens. 'Had a voucher for free starters. Sylhetti Fish good. Nawabi Murghi (£8.50), on the bone marinated chicken, in minced lamb, medium sauce, huge portions, very tasty, rice included,' G.G.P. Price check: Papadom 40p, CTM £5.45, Pullao Rice £1.50. Minimum charge £10. Service 10%. Open 5.30p.m.-12.30a.m.

Dudley

CLASSICAL BALTI HOUSE ©

63 Halesowen Road, Netherton, Dudley ℰ 01384 240230

A small restaurant so book for a table at the weekends. Happy Hour special menu from 6-9p.m. Manager, R. Khan, will give a discount to Curry Club members. Open 6p.m.-2a.m., till 3a.m. weekends.

TIM TANDOORI NEW ENTRANT ©

44-45 High Street, Quarry Bank, Dudley ℰ 01384 412757

'Opened in 1996 by T. Tim. Bangladeshi and Pakistani curries on the menu. Licensed. Seats 74. Price check: Papadom 30p, CTM £4.25, Pullao Rice £1.20. Open 5.30p.m.-12.30a.m.

Halesowen

AMEENA   ©

192 Hagley Road, Hasbury,
Halesowen, B63   ✆ **0121 550 4317**

Opened in 1974 by Hiron Miah. Bangladeshi curry house. Licensed.
Balti Chicken and Mushroom £5.35, Nan £1.20. Price check: Papadom
35p, CTM £5.95, Pullao Rice £1.60. Open 5.30p.m.-12.30a.m.

BALTI TOWERS   ©

85 Long Lane, Halesowen, B65   ✆ **0121 559 5118**

Good selection of Balti dishes with regular curries, too. Managing
owner, Mohammed Sadique, will give a discount to Curry Club members. Fully licensed. Open 6-11.30p.m., Sunday noon-2.30p.m. and 6-
11.30p.m.

DILSHAD INTERNATIONAL   ©

14-15 Halesowen Road, Halesowen, B62   ✆ **0121 421 6549**

Opened in 1990 and has built up a regular loyal following. Manager,
Anawarul Abaden, will give a discount to Curry Club members. Open
6p.m.-midnight. Branch: Dilshad International, Kingswinford.

RED PEPPERS

8 Hagley Street, Halesowen, B63   ✆ **0121 550 8588**

Opened in 1990 by Atiqur Rahman. Bangladeshi curry house seats 46
diners. Licensed. Order the Thalis for a good choice of dishes. Price
check: Papadom 35p, CTM £5.75, Pullao Rice £1.50. Minimum charge
£7.50. Open 5.30p.m.-midnight, till 1a.m. Friday and Saturday.

Kingswinford

DILSHAD INTERNATIONAL ©

49-51 Market Street, Kingswinford ✆ 01384 294861

A popular eating place, serving the locals all their favourite Baltis, curries and accompaniments. Owner, Mohammed Miah, will give a discount to Curry Club members. Open 6p.m.-midnight. Branch: Dilshad International, Halesowen, B62.

MR DAVE'S BALTI HOUSE BYO

847 High Street, Kingswinford ✆ 01384 400288

'Is licensed, but it ain't cheap – so bring your own. Service extremely efficient and friendly, food was of a high standard. Very reasonable prices,' D.G. 'This was great. Like a café. Absolutely delicious Balti Special, huge portions, fantastic!' M.S.

Knowle

BILASH ©

1608 High Street, Knowle ✆ 01564 773030

'Need to reserve a table. Varied selection of starters and main meals. Very good quality,' J. and A.McL. Partner, N. Ali, will give a discount to Curry Club members. Open 5.30p.m.-midnight.

KNOWLE INDIAN BRASSERIE NEW ENTRANT ©

1690 High Street, Knowle, B93 ✆ 01564 776453

Opened in 1995 by Hossain Miah. Tastefully decorated in cream and the palest of pink. Natural wood, ornate plasterwork and 36 seats. 'Malai Kebab, chicken marinated in cream with herbs and spices and baked in a clay oven – very tasty. Chicken Tikka Sylhet, boneless chicken with minced lamb and an egg cooked with spices and herbs – unusual mixture of mince and chicken, very spicy with good texture and flavours. Bombay Aloo, well-marinated potato although not as spicy as they promised in the menu. Quantities – enormous. Not as expensive as one might expect. A top-quality restaurant. Popadoms at 60p are a rip-off!' G.P. Just for you, Graham, we have included a price check of Papadoms on most of the restaurants in this Guide, but we have no idea (apart from profit!) why restaurants choose to charge their customers so much for something that we all know costs but a few pence. I can sympathize with charges for chutneys and pickles as they do cost real money and, if a restaurant makes their own, which is even more enjoyable to eat, it seems only fair to charge a little extra, since preserve-making is (and I am speaking from experience) a costly and time-consuming business. Price check: Papadom 35p, CTM £4.95, Pullao Rice £1.40. Minimum charge £10. Open 5.30-11.30p.m. Branch: Stockland Balti Takeaway, 332 Marsh Lane, Erdington, Birmingham; Thespian's Indian Cuisine, Stratford upon Avon, Warwickshire.

Sedgley

BALTI BAZAAR   ©

2 The Bull Ring, Dudley Street, Sedgley   © 01902 671759

Opened in 1986 by Syead Miah, who is also the manager. Clean and smart Bangladeshi curry house serving formula curries and Balti dishes to 46 diners. Balti Chicken and Mushroom £4.10, Nan £1.20. Price check: Papadom 35p, CTM £5.30, Pullao Rice £1.30. Open 5.30-11.30p.m. Car parking available at rear,

Solihull

DARJEELING   NEW ENTRANT

326 Stratford Road, Shirley, Solihull, B90   © 0121 733 2712

'I have visited regularly since it first opened in 1989, still remains one of Shirley's best. All items on the menu are good but I particularly like the Shami Kebab, and their Kurma is among the best that I have ever tasted. Rice and breads are all good and of decent proportions,' C.M.

JAIPUR

79 Hobs Moat Road, Solihull, B92   ✆ 0121 722 2982

Formerly Kunjon. Air-conditioned and fully licensed. Balti Chicken and Mushroom £4.75, Nan £1.20. Price check: Papadom 40p, CTM £5.65, Pullao Rice £1.45. Open 5.30p.m.-midnight.

RAJNAGAR INTERNATIONAL

256 Lyndon Road, Olton, Solihull, B72   ✆ 0121 742 8140

Fully licensed and air-conditioned. You can watch, through a glass panel, your meal being prepared by the chefs. Tandoori Lamb Spare Ribs £1.95. For that special occasion try the Rajnagar Lobster, brushed with garlic sauce and herbs, served with vegetable side dishes, £29.95 for two. Price check: Papadom 35p, CTM £5.05, Pullao Rice £1.50 (takeaway prices – which are 15% less). Open 5p.m.-12.30a.m., till 1a.m. Friday and Saturday.

SALEEM BAGH   NEW ENTRANT

476 Station Road, Dorridge, Solihull, B93   ✆ 01564 771190

'Is as good as ever. Food is of a very high standard, Pathia, Ceylon and Jalfrezi being particularly good. Portions are good and service friendly,' C.M.

SHAPLA   NEW ENTRANT

173a Stratford Road, Shirley, Solihull, B90   ✆ 0121 733 2864

'Opened around 1989. One of the best in the area. Quality of food and standard of service remains good,' C.M.

Stourbridge

BALTI BAZAAR   NEW ENTRANT   BYO

1a Pedmore Road, Lye, Stourbridge   ✆ 01384 353800

Opened in 1997 by R. Miah. Unlicensed. Bangladeshi formula and Pakistani curries on the menu. Price check: Papadom 35p, CTM £4.30,

Pullao Rice £1.20. Minimum charge £7. Open 5p.m.-midnight. Branch: Dilshad, Stourbridge; Dilshad, 6 Penkridge Retail Park, Wolverhampton Road, Penkridge, Staffordshire.

DILSHAD ©

132 Hagley Road, Oldswinford, Stourbridge ✆ 01384 372762

A 50-seater establishment serving competent curries and accompaniments to the local curry-eating population. Proprietor is R. Miah. Open 5p.m.-midnight. Branch: Balti Bazaar, Stourbridge; Dilshad, 6 Penkridge Retail Park, Wolverhampton Road, Penkridge, Staffordshire.

KAMRAN ⊞ BYO

34 High Street, Lye, Stourbridge ✆ 01384 893030

Unlicensed, so BYO, waiters will chill and serve. What service! Open 5.30p.m.-midnight. Home delivery service available.

NASEEB OF LYE

15 High Street, Lye, Stourbridge ✆ 01384 891353

Originally opened in 1985 as Mr Dave's Balti House. Taken over in 1996 by Mr Ahmed who was the manager of the former. Pakistani Balti curries on the menu. Balti Chicken and Mushroom £3.80, Nan 75p. Price check: Papadom 30p, CTM £4.30, Pullao Rice £1.10. Open 5.30p.m.-12.30a.m.

NEEL AKASH BALTI AND TANDOORI ©

2F High Street, Wollaston, Stourbridge ✆ 01384 375919

Opened in 1994 by Mujibur Rahman. Bangladeshi formula curries including Bengal Masala (£5.75) and Bhoona Shashlik (£5.75). Complimentary mint sauce and onion salad are both served with starters. Balti Chicken and Mushroom £4.75, Nan £1.20. Price check: Papadom 50p incl. chutney, CTM £5.75, Pullao Rice £1.50. Open 5p.m.-midnight, till 1a.m. Friday and Saturday. Minimum charge £5. Fully licensed.

PEPPER AND SPICE ©

4 High Street, Lye, Stourbridge ✆ **01384 893933**

Owned by Sabber Iqbal in 1996. Pakistani- and Bangladeshi-styled curries served to 50 diners. Fully licensed. Pepper Chicken (£2.25), stuffed with tandoori chicken, Balti Chicken and Mushroom £3.30, Nan 75p. Price check: Papadom 35p, CTM £4.50, Pullao Rice £1.50.

REDFORTE

**70 Bridgnorth Road, Wollaston,
Stourbridge** ✆ **01384 835555**

A takeaway establishment only, situated next door to the village bakery. Comfortable and stylish seating arrangements. Owned and managed by F.H. Shah. Price check: Papadom 30p, CTM £4.60, Pullao Rice £1.15. Open 5.30p.m.-midnight.

SPICE MERCHANT ⊞ BYO

19 High Street, Lye, Stourbridge ✆ **01384 424956**

This Bangladeshi curry house opened in 1990. Fully licensed, but you are welcome to bring your own drinks – well, isn't that nice! Balti Chicken and Mushroom £4.25, Nan £1.20. Cosy, seats 36 diners. Price check: Papadom 35p, CTM £4.85, Pullao Rice £1.65. Open 5p.m.-midnight. Home delivery service free on orders over £7. Branch: Spice Merchant Takeaway, 25 High Street, Quarry Bank, Brierley Hill.

Sutton Coldfield

ASIAN GRILL NEW ENTRANT

91 Park Road, Sutton Coldfield, B73 ✆ **0121 354 7491**

Opened way back in 1968. If you, or any other business for that matter, have survived that long, you must be good. Bangladeshi curries on the menu including Balti Chicken Tikka £5.90, Nan £1.30. Fully licensed. Seats 76 diners. Price check: Papadom 40p, CTM £7.25, Pullao Rice £1.60. Minimum charge £8. Open 5.30p.m.-midnight, till 1a.m. Friday and Saturday.

BASHUNDORA

The Guildhall, Lichfield Road,
Sutton Coldfield, B74   ✆ 0121 354 8397

'Excellent meal in quantity and quality. Relaxing and spacious decor. Helpful service. A real find, will return,' J.A.G. On checking out the takeaway menu, I see something that just has to go into the 'silly rules' book – I quote: 'One meal cannot be shared between two persons.' So, does that mean if I order a side dish of Bombay Potato, only one of us can eat it but not both of us? Price check: Papadom 55p, CTM £7.60, Pullao Rice £1.55. Open noon-2p.m. and 6p.m.-midnight.

THE CROWN

Walsall Road, Four Oaks,
Sutton Coldfield, B74   ✆ 0121 308 1258

'An Indian restaurant in a pub, surroundings excellent and clean, service same. Korai Chicken, Tikka Jalrezi, all superb. Popadoms and Kulcha Nan were the best,' D.B.

INDUS TANDOORI

11 Kings Road, New Oscott,
Sutton Coldfield, B73   ✆ 0121 355 5089

'Quality of starters very good, Sheek Kebab and Chicken Tikka as good as anywhere I have been,' R.H.A. 'Comfortable, relaxed restaurant,' B.E.

JAHED CUISINE OF INDIA

425 Birmingham Road, Wylde Green,
Sutton Coldfield, B72   ✆ 0121 382 2105

'Wide menu selection, excellent food, beautifully presented,' P.W.

KABABISH   ©

266 Jockey Road, Sutton Coldfield, B73   ✆ 0121 355 5062

Follows the same format as the others in the group. Manager is Mr M.

Sadiq. Open 5-11.30p.m. Branches: Kababish, Hall Green, B28; Kababish, Moseley, B13.

STREETLY BALTI NEW ENTRANT   BYO

188 Chester Road, Streetly,
Sutton Coldfield, B73   ✆ 0121 353 2224

'Excellent food, generous portions. Polite and attentive staff. One interesting feature, the availability of divided serving dishes allowing one to order smaller portions of two different dishes. No licence, but the off-licence is almost next door. Not open on Sundays,' B.P. 'Not only is the food excellent but the staff are most pleasant and helpful at all times,' V.Y.

Walsall

EAST END   ©

9 Hawes Close, Broadway, Walsall   ✆ 01922 614800

Opened 31 years ago, says owner Muhibur Rahman. Bangladeshi-styled curries and accompaniments on the menu. House special is Green Chilli Chicken Tikka Masala (£4.95). Balti Chicken and Mushroom £3.50, Nan 90p. Licensed. Price check: Papadom 35p, CTM £5.25, Pullao Rice £1.35. Open 5.30p.m.-midnight.

KING BALTI   BYO

89 Ablewell Street, Walsall   ✆ 01922 20376

Formerly Khan. Owned by Mozamil Khan, who invites you to bring your own wine to his establishment. Menu lists all the favourite curries from Balti to Phal. Balti Chicken and Mushroom £3.30, Nan 95p. Price check: Papadom 25p, CTM £4.25, Pullao Rice £1.25.

KISMET

20 Aldridge Shopping Precinct, Walsall   ✆ 01922 59861

All our favourite curries and accompaniments served from a comprehensive menu. Open 5.30p.m.-12.30a.m. Reports, please. Branch: Romna Takeaway, Alcester, Warwickshire.

PAPRIKA

78 Bradford Street, Walsall   ✆ 01922 29944

'A good-value restaurant which always delivers first-rate meals. Decor very simple. Advisable to book at weekends. Staff helpful,' D.G.

POLASH BALTI   ⊞

10 Anchor Parade, Aldridge, Walsall   ✆ 01922 51442

Situated behind Anchor shopping parade. Owned by Mr Rahman. Licensed. Bangladeshi curries, accompaniments and Baltis on the reasonably priced menu. Price check: Papadom 30p, CTM £5.75, Pullao Rice £1.20. Open 5p.m.-12.30a.m., Friday and Saturday 4p.m.-1.30a.m. Minimum order £5. Home delivery service free. If your order is £50 or over, you will receive a voucher for two people to dine in free.

SAFFRON   ⊞

42-43 Bradford Street, Walsall   ✆ 01922 27899

Opened in 1963. Owned by Mr Monjur Choudhury. Northern Indian food and other specialities served in this 65-seater, smart restaurant. Aromatic Shredded Duck (£12.75) – half a duck roasted in an aromatic gravy with cumin, saffron and cardamom, then shredded off the bone and served with Puri and Sag Paneer Bhaji. Balti Chicken and Mushroom £4.45, Nan £1.25. Sunday lunch eat-as-much-as-you-like buffet £6.95. Price check: Papadom 35p, CTM £5.25, Pullao Rice £1.55. Open 5.30p.m.-12.30a.m., till 1.30a.m. Friday and Saturday. Home delivery service free over £8.

SALMA BALTI KINGDOM   NEW ENTRANT   ⊞ BYO ©

41 Caldmore Green, Caldmore, Walsall   ✆ 01922 35162

Bangladeshi and Pakistani food. Opened in 1995 by Mohibur Rahman who is also the manager. Unlicensed, but you are welcome to bring your own. Price check: Papadom 25p, CTM £4.95, Pullao Rice £1.30. Open 5.30p.m.-1a.m., till 1.30 a.m. Friday and Saturday. Private parking at rear. Home delivery service free on orders over £5 within a 4-mile radius.

SHAHI GRILL ©

89 Bridge Street, Walsall ✆ **01922 24079**

Owners are Mozmil Ali (chef) and Mokous Ali (manager). Licensed. Bangladeshi curries on the menu. Price check: Papadom 35p, CTM £4.95, Pullao Rice £1.25. Minimum charge £7.50. Open 6p.m.-midnight.

Warley

AL MOUGHAL ©

**622 Bearwood Road, Smethwick,
Warley, B66** ✆ **0121 420 3987**

Book at weekends, tends to get busy. Serving competent curries to a loyal local following. Owner is Saeed Mougha. Open 6p.m.-midnight. Reports, please.

HAWELI NEW ENTRANT

509 Hagley Road, Bearwood, Warley, B66 ✆ **0121 434 4869**

Kashmiri food served at this licensed 68-seater restaurant. We like the sound of the Papadom Roll (£1.50) – crispy Indian snack stuffed with vegetables or meat and deep-fried, and the Panir Shashlik (£3) – diced home-made cheese barbecued with diced onion, tomatoes and capsicums. Not a Balti in sight but they do serve Korai dishes with Khandani Nan (£2.25), family-sized with a stuffing of lamb or vegetables. Price check: Papadom 35p, CTM £5.05, Pullao Rice £1.50. Open 6p.m.-midnight.

MARTIN'S TANDOORI ⊞

**22-24 Abbey Road, Bearwood,
Warley, B67** ✆ **0121 429 8287**

Varied menu, full of the usual curry house favourites. Balti Chicken and Mushroom £5.40, Nan £1.25. Price check: Papadom 45p, CTM £5.40, Pullao Rice £1.60. Open 6p.m.-1a.m., till 2a.m. Friday and Saturday, till midnight Sunday. Home delivery service free within a 3-mile radius.

ROWLEY VILLAGE   TOP 100

**10 Portway Road, Rowley Regis,
Warley, B65**   Ⓒ **0121 561 4463**

Owned by Mr Moin Udin. 'It is without doubt the best tandoori restaurant in the Midlands if not the whole of the UK,' D.H. 'Starters are like main courses and the main meals are, well, enormous! Everything tried on the menu, so far, has been of a very high standard. Watch out for their special mixed dishes, which represent extremely good value for money. Highly recommended,' C.M. Remains in our TOP 100. Open 5.15p.m.-midnight.

STANDARD   ⊞ ©

**2 High Street, Blackheath,
Rowley Regis, B65**   Ⓒ **0121 561 2048**

Owned by Kazi Ashafuz Zaman and Kazi Wahiduz Zaman. Licensed. Pakistani and Bangladeshi food on the menu. Price check: Papadom 50p, CTM £5.50, Pullao Rice £1.50. Set menu £3.95. Minimum charge £15. Open 6p.m.-1a.m., Friday and Saturday noon-2.30p.m. and 6p.m.-2a.m. Home delivery service free on orders over £10 within a 3-mile radius.

West Bromwich

CLOCK TOWER BALTI   NEW ENTRANT   ⊞ ©

33 Carters Green, West Bromwich, B70   Ⓒ **0121 553 4167**

Opened in 1993 by Mr H. Singh and managed by Joginder Singh. My, my, haven't you worked hard these last months, getting all your customers to write in and tell us how wonderful your establishment is? All the more remarkable since they are all on Curry Club report forms! And all in different hands, except for one thing: a different single hand has put the same membership number on nearly all of them! So, 025935, you have a lot of clones! Despite Joginder's antics, we believe the reports to be genuine. At any rate, he can now add our certificate to all those off-the-shelf ones he's got. We hear well of the Punjabi/northern Indian food on the menu. 'Clean and tidy restaurant with tiled floor giving a café feeling. Excellent service, friendly atmosphere, superb food, good choice of beverages,' F.G.M. 'Highly competent service. Good quality and pleasant restaurant, food was of high quality,' S.H. 'Food excellent, served in bright and clean environment,' K.S. 'Outstandingly good,' P.T. 'Food is delicious,' A.P. Price check: Papadom 35p, CTM £5.95, Pullao Rice £1.30. Home delivery service free on orders over £8.

PARADISE PALACE NEW ENTRANT

500 Lombard Street, West Bromwich, B70 © 0121 525 1266

Has been owned by Wasim Ali Khan since 1993. Pakistani and Bangladeshi food on the menu at reasonable prices. Licensed. Seats 120. Price check: Papadom 50p, CTM £6.50, Pullao Rice £1.50. Open 5.30p.m.-midnight.

SHALIMAR

145 High Street, West Bromwich, B70 © 0121 553 1319

'I have eaten here regularly over ten years and have been impressed by their excellent quality food. Friendly unobtrusive service. Reasonable prices,' S.C.H.

Wolverhampton

BILASH

2 Cheapside, Wolverhampton © 01902 427762

'Sampled the midweek lunch buffet, which was excellent,' M.B. 'Kitchens were visible behind a fully glazed wall and the food was superb,' I.B.

HABIB INDIAN CUISINE   ©

46 Queen Street, Wolverhampton   ✆ **01902 772155**

Serves competent curries and accompaniments from an extensive menu. Chef is Habibur Rahman. Open 6p.m.-midnight, till 2.30a.m. Friday and Saturday. Branch: Maharaja Takeaway, Highbridge Road, Sutton Coldfield.

NEELAKASH   NEW ENTRANT   ▦ ©

31 School Street, Wolverhampton   ✆ **01902 424511**

Opened in 1989 by S. Rahman. 'Staff helpful and polite, they smile as well. Papadoms warm, plates are pre-warmed and food well presented and savoury,' D.G. 'Average decor, wide if conventional menu. Chicken Rezala (£6.95) impressive and Shahi Chicken (£6.95) very good, unusual flavour, both served with Pilau Rice,' G. and M.P. Price check: Papadom 40p, CTM £5.75, Pullao Rice £1.60. Open 5.30p.m.-midnight. Home delivery service.

PURBANI   ©

41-43 Birch Street, Wolverhampton   ✆ **01902 424030**

Seats a massive 130 diners. Menu contains all our favourite curries and side dishes. A popular curry house serving competent curries to a local following. Owner, L. Hussain (since 1978) will give a discount to Curry Club members. Open 5p.m.-12.30a.m. Branch: Raj Balti, 66 Bradford Street, Walsall.

WILTSHIRE
Chippenham

AKASH TANDOORI AND BALTI

19 The Bridge, Chippenham   ✆ **01249 653358**

Opened in 1979 by Mr N.H. Islam, and an old friend of this Guide, having been in our first edition. It serves the formula menu, though tandoori items are only served in the evenings. Price check: Papadom 50p, CTM £6.70, Pullao Rice £2.20. Open noon–2p.m. and 6p.m.–midnight, 6p.m.–12.30a.m. Friday and Saturday.

TAJ MAHAL NEW ENTRANT ©

51 The Causeway, Chippenham ✆ 01249 653243

Opened in 1989 by Mr Arju Miah, serving Bangladeshi curries to 50 diners. Mr Miah tells us that, 'it always takes time to prepare good food, why not try a few of our starters while you wait?' Lobster Butter Fried (£4.50) and Tandoori Lobster (£5.10) sound delicious – so we'll try them! Price check: Papadom 50p, CTM £6.50, Pullao Rice £1.75. Minimum charge £4.50. Open noon–2p.m. and 6p.m.–midnight.

Devizes

DEEDAR

2 Sidmouth Street, Devizes ✆ 01380 720009

Owned by Joshim Ahmed. Restaurant seats 24 diners and serves Bangladeshi formula cuisine. 'Kitchen is in full view of a basic restaurant. Portions smaller than we are used to, gravies slightly stronger, trying very hard. Will return,' J. and B.W. House special: Chutney Deedar (£4.50), chicken, lamb or prawn cooked with mango chutney and lime pickle. Price check: Papadom 30p, CTM £4.80, Pullao Rice £1.30. Minimum charge £15. Open noon–2p.m. and 5.30–11.30p.m.

Everleigh

GOA BALTI HOUSE NEW ENTRANT

Everleigh Filling Station, Everleigh, Nr Tidworth ✆ 01264 850850

'An enterprising restaurant, building up a substantial local reputation. The pumps for the petrol station actually remain in the forecourt. A fine small bar, comfortable restaurant. A good sign is the genuine linen napkins. Extensive menu. All the vegetables are fresh and it shows.

Bindi Bhaji (£2.45), an education in what this dish really should be. Sashlik Chicken (£4.95), spicy marinated chicken served with ample fried capsicum, tomato and onion. Cucapaka (£4.75), well-spiced tandoori-baked chicken and minced meat. Goa Special (£5.95), tandoori-baked chicken cooked with almond, sultana, coconut and cashew nuts with a creamy, yoghurt sauce. Service is swift, amiable and obliging. Staff are clearly determined that you should have a good time. Generous portions and moderate prices. Ample parking and you can eat outside when the weather is warm. This is a filling station indeed,' R.G. Open noon-2.30p.m. and 6p.m.-midnight. Prices quoted are takeaway, which is 15% cheaper.

Marlborough

ASIAN GRILL   NEW ENTRANT

8 London Road, Marlborough   ✆ 01672 512877

'Place was busy, staff courteous and pleasant. Drinks and nibbles brought quickly and order taken, then read back to confirm everything and delivered piping hot. Dansak very pleasant with extra sauce being offered if required. Madras hot and sour with plenty of meat. Sag Bhajee should be renamed Sag and garlic, it was excellent – definitely no vampires visiting that night!' C.L. Open noon-2.30p.m. and 6p.m.-midnight.

Melksham

MELKSHAM TANDOORI   ©

26 Church Street, Melksham   ✆ 01225 705242

Bangladeshi formula food served at Mr Mahammed Mayna's restaurant. 'Adjacent to car park in an attractive Cotswold stone building. Long narrow room with bar/reception at one end. About 50 comfortable seats. Asked for a Papadom and got three (not charged). Chicken Tikka, great lumps, very well cooked, nice and succulent. Lovely mint sauce. Lamb Jalfrezi with Sag Aloo and Nan Bread, which I just about consumed although touch and go at the end! Sauce rich and loads of green chillies lurking in there for the unwary – I love 'em. Portions huge, cooking great and amazing value. Recommended,' M.S. Price check: Papadom 30p, CTM £5.50, Pullao Rice £1.50. Open 6p.m.-midnight. Branch: Saadi Takeaway, 8 Silver Street, Bradford on Avon.

Salisbury

ASIA

90 Fisherton Street, Salisbury   © 01722 327628

The Asia opened in 1963, which makes it a very early bird, especially so far from London. It also makes it an experienced venue, and we have constantly heard, since our first Guide, that it is above average. 'A thriving business – it's always packed. Service extremely fast, very efficient and absolutely charming. Kashmiri Chicken, beautifully done. Sag Bhaji was the best I have had – very spicy with guts and edge,' R.G.

Swindon

BHAJI'S TAKEAWAY   NEW ENTRANT   ©

76 Thames Avenue, Swindon   © 01793 533799

Opened in 1997 by Iqbal Shishir, serving Nepalese and Bangladeshi curries and accompaniments. House special is Tandoori Garlic Chilly Chicken or Meat (£5.25). Price check: Papadom 45p, CTM £4.95, Pullao Rice £1.50. Set menu £7.95. Open 5p.m.-midnight. Branch: Simla Takeaway.

BIPLOB   NEW ENTRANT   ©

12-14 Wood Street, Swindon   © 01793 490265

Opened in 1993 by Rokib Alo and Fozlur Rahman. Bangladeshi and northern Indian cuisine on the menu. House specials include Begun Bahar (£5.95). Restaurant seats 60 diners, with a separate lounge/bar area seating 20. Price check: Papadom 45p, Masala 50p, CTM £5.95, Pullao Rice £1.50. Minimum charge £10. Open noon-2.30p.m. and

6p.m.-midnight. Branch: Raja Takeaway, Cheltenham, Gloucestershire; Rajdoot, Cirencester, Gloucestershire.

CURRY GARDEN   ©

90 Victoria Road, Swindon   ✆ **01793 521114**

Opened on 14 May 1979 by Mr R. Khan. A large restaurant seating 80 diners, Pakistani and Bangladeshi curries on the menu. 'Swindon is a dump but it *has* got the Curry Garden, definitely the best Indian restaurant that I know of. Although the menu is not unusual, the food is the best quality, especially the starters like the Prawn Puree and Aloo Chat. Mmmm,' R.S. Before you Swindonites start writing in to me, I should say that opinions expressed in this Guide are not necessarily those of the editor – and I'm saying it because, of course, Swindon's a wonderful place ... It houses W.H. Smith's HQ, and they buy lots of my books. Crawl, crawl! House special is Butter Chicken (£4.95). Price check: Papadom 50p, CTM £5.85, Pullao Rice £1.60. Minimum charge £6. Open noon-2.30p.m. and 5.30p.m.-midnight.

GOLDEN DELIGHT   ©

47 High Street, Cricklade, Nr Swindon   ✆ **01793 750303**

Opened in 1990 by Makram Ali, who also manages front of house. House special is Taranan Chicken, Lamb or King Prawn (£6.90), their own invention – cooked with potato, egg, green chilli, red wine, a hot and spicy dish. Price check: Papadom 60p, CTM £6.25, Pullao Rice £1.75. Minimum charge £10. Open noon-2.30p.m. and 6-11.30p.m., till midnight Friday and Saturday.

GULSHAN   NEW ENTRANT   ©

122 Victoria Road, Old Town, Swindon   ✆ **01793 522558**

Opened in 1995 by Mr A. Noor, who has promised 10% off your bill to Curry Club members. House special is Ashiana Special (£6.90 takeaway), your choice of lamb or chicken cooked with cucumber, cauliflower, brandy, green chilli with spicy hot sauce. Price check: Papadom 50p, CTM £6.90, Pullao Rice £1.50. Minimum charge £12.50. Open noon-2.30p.m. and 6p.m.-midnight, till 1a.m. Friday and Saturday,

Sunday noon-12.30a.m. Buffet £6.90 which includes either a glass of house wine or half a pint of lager – great value!

MAHARAJAH NEW ENTRANT ©

6 High Street, Purton, Swindon ℂ 01793 770253

Opened by Abdul Khalique Ali. Pakistani-styled curries on the menu, including Lobster Tikka or Butterfly, both £3.95. For vegetarians, Beans Bhajee (£2.25). Set meals are good value – Maharajah Feast £18 per person. Price check: Papadom 50p, CTM £6.25, Pullao Rice £1.75. Minimum charge £10. Open 5.30p.m.-midnight. If you would prefer lunch, the restaurant will open for you, by prior arrangement, for parties of 10 or more.

RAFU'S TANDOORI

29-30 High Street, Highworth, Swindon ℂ 01793 765320

Opened in 1982 by Mr Rafu as the Biplob. Thank you, Mr Rafu, for inadvertently contributing for the second time to the introduction to this Guide. For that alone we will keep you in the Guide. But if you send us any more phoney reports, you'll be out altogether. It makes all the reports we've received on you suspect, since none are from our known reporter list. And it certainly will *not* make you a top restaurant! Price check: Papadom 45p, CTM £6.95, Pullao Rice £1.60. Set menu £6.95. Open noon-3p.m. and 6p.m.-midnight.

Warminster

AGRA NEW ENTRANT

32 East Street, Warminster ℂ 01985 846941

This 50-seater originally opened in 1979. It's been under the current ownership of Mr M. Rahman since 1984, and it appeared in our first Guide. It is a useful watering hole in an area otherwise devoid of curry. Price check: Papadom 30p, CTM £7.95, Pullao Rice £1.95. Minimum charge £9. Open noon-2.30p.m. and 6-11.30p.m. Branch: Assam Takeaway, 58 East Street, Warminster.

Wootton Bassett

SALIK'S NEW ENTRANT

21 High Street, Wootton Bassett   ✆ 01793 852365

Situated opposite the Curriers' Arms! 'Bhajia £1.95 and Samosa £1.95, freshly made, nicely presented and delicious! Fragrant, fluffy Pullao Rice. Lots of meat in Keema Nan (£1.65). Massive portion of Chicken Biryani (£4.95). Chicken Tikka Bhuna (£4.65), lots of well-marinated breast meat,' T.E. 'This little gem deserves a mention. Providing extra-ordinary food, quality and service at a low price,' A.E. Price check: Papadom 40p, CTM £5.25, Pullao Rice £1.55. Open noon-2.30p.m. and 6p.m.-midnight, till 1a.m. Fridays and Saturdays. Home delivery service free on orders over £10.

WORCESTERSHIRE
Bewdley

THE RAJAH

8 Load Street, Bewdley   ✆ 01299 400368

'Food is excellent and the people extremely friendly, offering a high standard of customer service,' S.H.

Droitwich

MOGHUL

17 St Andrews Street, Droitwich   ✆ 01905 794188

Opened in 1992 by Abdul Matin. Serves Pakistani, Bangladeshi and north Indian curries and accompaniments. House specials include Tikka Green Masala (£6.25), Kufta Curry (£5.50) and Zalfrezi (£5.50). Price check: Papadom 40p, CTM £6.25, Pullao Rice £1.75. Open 5p.m.-midnight, till 1a.m. Friday and Saturday.

Kidderminster

EURASIA TAKEAWAY NEW ENTRANT ©

Unit 1, Stourbridge Road, Kidderminster ✆ 01562 825861

This takeaway is really tastefully decorated in terracotta and beige with plaster cornices and crystal chandelier. The service bar is made from natural wood and is simply stained and varnished. Must be the most sophisticated takeaway in the country! House special is Chicken Jafalong (£4.50). Price check: Papadom 30p, CTM £4.50, Pullao Rice £1.20. Open 5p.m.-midnight.

NEW SHER E PUNJAB ©

48 George Street, Kidderminster ✆ 01562 740061

Evenings only at Puran Singh's restaurant which has been open a long time (since 1971). Satisfactory reports generally. More reports welcomed.

Malvern

ANUPAN

85 Church Street, Malvern ✆ 01684 573814

'Friendly efficient service, decor pleasant and comfortable. Chicken Tikka Masala, excellent flavour, not too hot, good-sized portion. Chicken Patia, not on menu, was also excellent,' D.R.

Malvern Link

AJANTA NEW ENTRANT

243 Worcester Road, Malvern Link ✆ 01684 569820

'Chicken Tikka Masala and Chicken Jalfrezi both excellent, especially the Jalfrezi with the use of lemon, gave an exquisite dimension, eaten with Naan. Finished off with Kulfi and washed down with the best chai I've ever had,' J.F.M. Price check: Papadom 45p, CTM £5.95, Pullao Rice £1.75.

Pershore

SHUNARGA   ©

44 High Street, Pershore   ✆ 01386 555357

Owned by Mosnul Haq. 'Decor, standard curry house, but comfortable, warm welcome and Bombay Mix on arrival. Starter, Chicken Bhuna on Puree (£2.20) – house special – very good and spicy, served with salad and mint sauce. Chicken Vindaloo (£4.25), good, nice and hot, still not overpowered, with plenty of taste. Pullao Rice was watery. Nan bread (£1.10), very good and piping hot,' M.G. Price check: Papadom 35p, CTM £4.95, Pullao Rice £1.45. Open 12.30-2p.m. and 6p.m.-midnight. Credit cards are not acceptable on meals under £10!

Redditch

AKASH   ©

31-33 Unicorn Hill, Redditch   ✆ 01527 62301

Opened in 1979 by Akil Choudhury. A reliable and well-established restaurant, serving Bangladeshi curries and Cobra lager. Tastefully decorated in pale pink, Moghul arches around pictures of India. Price check: Papadom 50p, CTM £7.25 incl. rice, Pullao Rice £1.50. Minimum charge £5.50. Open noon-2.30p.m. and 5.30p.m.-midnight. Branch: Balti Desh Takeaway, Alvechurch, Birmingham, West Midlands; Balti Raj Takeaway, 41 Unicorn Hill, Redditch; Tilla Balti Takeaway, 1242 Evesham Road, Astwood Bank, Redditch.

DHAKA   ⊞

19 Beoley Road West, Redditch   ✆ 01527 61815

Takeaway/delivery service only. Evenings only. 'Waiting area for takeaway is warm and comfortable where we can relax and enjoy spicy Bombay Mix whilst watching TV or reading magazines. The staff are very friendly and always helpful. Our tastes vary each week but we particularly like their Tandoori Chicken Masala,' D.W.

MAHARAJAH TANDOORI AND BALTI   ©

17-21 Unicorn Hill, Redditch   ✆ 01527 64594

A wide range of curries and Baltis at Sheikh Elahee's 60-seater restaurant. Open Sunday to Thursday 6p.m.-midnight, Friday and Saturday 6p.m.-1a.m. Will give discounts to Curry Club members.

Tenbury Wells

SHAMRAJ BALTI HOUSE   ©

28 Cross Street, Tenbury Wells   ✆ 01584 819612

Manager Lokon Miah's Shamraj seats 50 diners, and is reported as being fair-priced and competent. Open noon-2.30p.m. and 6p.m.-midnight. Other branches: Shapla Balti, Ludlow, Shropshire; Shapla Tandoori, Ludlow, Shropshire.

Worcester

ASHLEY'S BALTI HOUSE   ©

11 The Tything, Worcester   ✆ 01905 611747

Owner M. Ashfaq's Baltis are 'the talk of the town', says E.M. Open 5.30p.m.-midnight, till 1a.m. Friday and Saturday. Sunday buffet lunch noon-5p.m.

BOMBAY PALACE   NEW ENTRANT   ©

38 The Tything, Worcester   ✆ 01905 613969

A Bangladeshi curry house seating 40 diners. Owned by Abdul Rob. Price check: Papadom 40p, CTM £5.20, Pullao Rice £1.35. Minimum charge £12. Open 6p.m.-midnight.

PURBANI   NEW ENTRANT   ©

27 The Tything, Worcester   ✆ 01905 23671

Managing partner Abdul Haie's Purbani was established in 1979 and continues to earn a strong reputation with its regulars. Open noon-2p.m. and 6p.m.-midnight.

YORKSHIRE

Until 1965 there was one county of Yorkshire, and it was Britain's biggest. It was then divided into three new counties: North, South and West Yorkshire, with a part north of the River Humber called North Humberside. The 1997 county changes have abandoned that county and created a 'new' Yorkshire county – East Yorkshire. Because the area is so large, we are dealing with these four counties in compass order, N, E, S, W or, as D.B.A.C. remembers it, Never Eat Shredded Wheat!

North Yorkshire
Harrogate

RAJ RANI TAKEAWAY   NEW ENTRANT

---

235 Skipton Road, Harrogate   © 01423 529295

We have received a lovely letter from Mr Ahad Miah, the proprietor of this takeaway, which he opened in late 1995. He is offering Monday and Tuesday customers 15% discount on their collected takeaways over £15. A generous offer. Take (away) him up on it, and tell us about it. Price check: Papadom 30p, CTM £4.95, Pullao Rice £1.25. Open from 5.30p.m. Home delivery service for orders over £7.50 within a 4-mile radius.

SHABAB   NEW ENTRANT   TOP 100

---

1 John Street, Harrogate   © 01423 500250

This restaurant originally opened in 1975 but was taken over by its present owner, Arshad Javed and family, in 1985. It is part of a chain of four, serving Punjabi, Pakistani and Kashmiri food. The lounge area is richly decorated with wooden screens, gold embroidered cushions, silk paintings and huge brass trays as drinks tables. The main restaurant is adorned with Moghul arches, brass lanterns with stained glass and some really fabulous hand-made Indian chairs with little tinkly bells. A full description of the food, with its caveat, appears under the Leeds, West Yorkshire branch. We welcome all four back to the Guide, and believe our joint TOP 100 cachet is well deserved. Price check: Papadom 20p, CTM £5.70, Pullao Rice £1.50. Buffet £5.50. House specials include Jalfrezi and Karahi dishes. Open 11.30a.m.-2.30p.m. (till 5p.m. Sunday) and 6-11.45p.m., Saturday 6-11.45p.m only. Home delivery service. Branches: Bradford, Halifax and Leeds, all West Yorkshire.

Malton

RAJ TANDOORI   NEW ENTRANT
---
21 Church Street, Norton, Malton   ✆ 01653 697337

'Has been a satisfying experience following their progress, to what is now a very good restaurant. It is small (about 20 seats) and friendly. They are always very welcoming and had a special Christmas menu. Malton is a small market town and this is my six-year-old daughter's favourite eating establishment,' A.T. Price check: Papadom 30p, CTM £4.60, Pullao Rice £1.20. Open lunchtime only by reservation Wednesday, Thursday, Saturday and Sunday. Open 5.50p.m.-midnight Tuesday to Sunday. Closed Monday except for Bank Holidays.

Middlesbrough

CLEVELAND TANDOORI   NEW ENTRANT   ©
---
289 Linthorpe Road, Middlesbrough   ✆ 01642 242777

Owner-chef Abid Hussain's menu is formula stuff but there are some Pakistani gems. Shalgum Gosht (£3.70) is meat with turnip and Lahori Gosht (£3.90) is meat with okra. Evenings only (till 2a.m., Friday and Saturday). Price check: Papadom 30p, CTM £5.80, Pullao Rice £1.40. Special buffet Sunday, Monday and Tuesday.

KHAN'S BALTI HOUSE ©

349 Linthorpe Road, Middlesbrough   ✆ **01642 817457**

Mr K. Khan's three venues have been in the Guide in the past. They are now doing Baltis (which should be good since the owner and chef are from Pakistan). Try the three-course (Tuesday) Balti meal (£8.50), and tell us about it, please. Price check: Papadom 30p, CTM £6.50, Pullao Rice £1.20. Open 6p.m.-1a.m. Branches: 42 and 417 Linthorpe Road, Middlesbrough.

Richmond

RICHMOND TANDOORI

32a Market Place, Richmond   ✆ **01748 850338**

Well-established with a loyal local following. Open 6p.m.-midnight, Saturday and Sunday 3p.m.-midnight. Branch: Sultan Takeaway, 62 Front Street, Winlaton, Tyne and Wear.

Ripon

MOTI RAJ   ⊞ ©

18 High Skellgate, Ripon   ✆ **01765 690348**

Owned by Abdul Malik since 1995. He assures us that '... the only path to good food, like good wine, is time.' Price check: Papadom 40p, CTM £5.25, Pullao Rice £1.35. Open 5.30p.m.-midnight. Delivery service available, ring 602030.

Scarborough

TANDOORI NIGHTS   NEW ENTRANT

St Helens Square, Scarborough   ✆ **01723 375227**

'Service was good and meal highly enjoyable. We both had a Chicken Madras which was absolutely fantastic, shared a Pilau Rice which was a bit stuck together in places and a Keema Naan each,' C.P.

Settle

GOLDEN GATE TANDOORI   NEW ENTRANT

Fern Cottage, Market Square, Settle   ✆ **01729 822901**

Opened in 1993 by Abdul Rashid. A restaurant seating 40 diners. House specials include Chicken Tikka Shashlik (£7.95), which Ali, the manager, insists is the 'best' and Chicken Tikka Dal Masala (£6.95). Price check: Papadom 40p, CTM £6.30, Pullao Rice £1.50. Set menu £11.95 for two, Sunday only. Open 5p.m.-midnight.

Skipton

AAGRAH   BEST RESTAURANT CHAIN TOP 100   ©

**4 Unicorn House, Devonshire Place,
Keighley Road, Skipton**   ✆ **01756 790807**

This is one of a chain of six Aagrah restaurants, all of which are good enough to be awarded a collective TOP 100 cachet. Since the decor and menu are identical at each branch, a full description appears under the first branch to open – Shipley, West Yorkshire (*see* entry). Comments on the Skipton branch are many: 'Always been very pleased. Nothing is too much trouble and children are well catered for. Menu has expanded, especially vegetarian and Balti dishes. Quality food. Highly recommended,' A.P. 'Exceptionally pleased with both the food and the service. Vegetarian menu is most innovative and varied,' J.H. 'Ample portions and reasonable prices,' E.D. 'Complimentary Popadoms. Food was absolutely superb with many dishes that I hadn't encountered,' I.S. Open 6p.m.-midnight, till 11p.m Sunday. Branches: Doncaster, South Yorkshire; Garforth, West Yorkshire; Pudsey, West Yorkshire; Shipley, West Yorkshire; Tadcaster, North Yorkshire.

RAJ BALTI HOUSE   ©

11 Keighley Road, Skipton   ✆ **01756 795697**

Owner-manager Mastab Ali's restaurant seats 42. House specials include Chicken or Lamb Hawally (palace), £7.50. Price check:

Papadom 40p, CTM £6.10, Pullao Rice £1.60. Set menu £24.95. Open noon-2.30p.m. and 6p.m.-midnight, Sunday 5.30-11p.m.

ROYAL BENGAL   ©

21 Keighley Road, Skipton   ✆ 01756 792473

Owner, Raza Miah, has a good regular following, we hear. Open noon-2p.m. and 6-11.30p.m. Branch: Prince of Bengal, 1b Court Lane, Skipton.

Tadcaster

AAGRAH   NEW ENTRANT BEST RESTAURANT CHAIN
TOP 100   ©

York Road, Steeton, Tadcaster   ✆ 01937 530888

This, the newest of six Aagrahs, opened in 1996 and at once became as packed and popular as the others in the group. (*See* Skipton entry above for fuller comment.) All the six Aagrahs are rated with a collective TOP 100 cachet. Branches: Doncaster, South Yorkshire; Garforth, West Yorkshire; Pudsey, West Yorkshire; Shipley, West Yorkshire; Skipton.

Yarm

BALTI HOUSE

49 High Street, Yarm   ✆ 01642 788998

In the mid-1960s I used to fly over tiny Yarm, landing RAF jets at Middleton St George, now Teesside Airport, but there wasn't a curry house there then, nor indeed anywhere within a 50-mile radius. Now there are over 100 in that area, and even this one at Yarm. Reports, please. Price check: Papadom 40p, CTM £6.95, Pullao Rice £1.45. Minimum charge £5.95.

York

AKASH NEW ENTRANT   ©

10 North Street, York   ✆ **01904 633550**

This 38-seater competent curry house is managed by Barik Miah. Price check: Papadom 40p, CTM £5.85, Pullao Rice £1.40. Open noon-2.30p.m. and 6p.m.-midnight, Sunday 6p.m.-midnight only.

GARDEN OF INDIA   ©

5 Fawcett Street, York   ✆ **01904 645679**

Opened in 1992 by Mr Alom. His restaurant seats 40 diners and introduces you to a wide selection of tandoori and Indian dishes presented in a traditional style. It is conveniently situated next to the Barbican Centre. Price check: Papadom 40p, CTM £6.60 incl. rice, Pullao Rice £1.60. Open noon-2.30p.m. and 6p.m.-midnight.

JINNAH BALTI   ©

105-107 Micklegate, York   ✆ **01904 659999**

This humungous restaurant, owned by Saleem Akhtar, seats 135, but if everyone breathes in an extra 15 people can be seated. Price check: Papadom 45p, CTM £6.95, Pullao Rice £1.95. Open noon-2.30p.m. and 6p.m.-midnight. Branch: Jinnah, 845 York Road, Leeds, West Yorkshire; Jinnah Takeaway, 18 The Village, Haxby; Taj Mahal, York; Viceroy of India, 26 Monkgate, York.

RISE OF THE RAJ

112 Micklegate, York   ✆ **01904 622975**

'Three of us entered at about 11p.m. on Friday and found it surprisingly quiet. An average menu with nothing special. We munched our way through the Popadoms and pickles and then had our starters which were Mixed Kebabs, very tasty. Chicken Madras, I must say I enjoyed this, superb, best ever,' C.P.

TAJ MAHAL

4 Kings Staith, York   © 01904 653944

'Food and prices excellent,' A.A. Open noon-2.30p.m. and 6p.m.-midnight. Branch: Jinnah, 845 York Road, Leeds, West Yorkshire; Jinnah Balti, York; Jinnah Takeaway, 18 The Village, Haxby; Viceroy of India, 26 Monkgate, York.

East Yorkshire

This is a new 1997 county, transferring the territory and towns from the former North Humberside into East Yorkshire. Prior to 1974 this was, in any case, part of Yorkshire.

Beverley

NASEEB NEW ENTRANT   ©

9-10 Wednesday Market, Beverley   © 01482 861110

Owner Abdul Muzir's and Ashik Uddin's Naseeb is our new find. It's R.K.'s favourite (he's visited 203 curry houses in a year) in the former county of Humberside. He says: 'It's top-notch, rather smart and up-market, with prices to match, but well worth it. Sabzi Pakora a dream, followed by Rosmoon-eh-Mirchi Murgh — a hot chicken curry. Chupattis light, not like some you can sole your shoes with.' We hear of a refurbishment coming. Reports, please. Price check: Papadom first one free then 40p, CTM £7 incl. rice, Pullao Rice £1.60. 10% discount on takeaways. Evenings only, 6-11.30p.m.

Bridlington

BRIDLINGTON TANDOORI

124 St John Street, Bridlington   © 01262 400014

'BEST Chicken Madras that I've EVER tasted, expertly spiced with a most delightful lemony flavour,' M.B. Open noon-2.30p.m. and 6p.m.-

midnight. Branch: Wold Tandoori, 81 Middle Street South, Driffield, West Yorkshire.

Hessle

LIGHT OF INDIA NEW ENTRANT   ©

27 The Weir, Hessle   ✆ 01482 649521

Farahd Tarafder's takeaway-only Light of India is under the shadow of the fabulous bridge, and does 'fabulous takeaways', according to K.Y. Open 5p.m.-midnight, till 1a.m. Friday and Saturday. Price check: Papadom 30p, CTM £4.60, Garlic Chilli Chicken Tikka £4.30, Pullao Rice 90p. Set dinner £16.95.

Hull

BALAKA   ©

133 Chanterlands Avenue, Hull   ✆ 01482 442119

A medium-sized restaurant seating 54 diners. Balti specials on the menu. Managing owner is A. Hamid. Open noon-2p.m. and 6p.m.-midnight, till 1a.m. Friday and Saturday.

JEWEL OF ASIA NEW ENTRANT   ©

328 Beverley Road, Hull   ✆ 01482 445469

Owner Syed Ali and manager Asrob Ali always 'make you welcome at their Jewel', B.D. Open 5p.m.-midnight, till 1a.m. Friday and Saturday. Price check: Papadom 30p, CTM £6.50, Tandoori Salmon £10.95, Garlic Chilli Chicken £6.50, Pullao Rice £1.20. Set dinner £22.95 for two.

MAHARAJAH NEW ENTRANT

245 Holderness Road, Hull   ✆ 01482 224647

Well-spoken of by R.K. 'It's smart, air-conditioned, with quality service, matched by quality food.'

NEW EASTERN NEW ENTRANT

618 Holderness Road, Hull   ✆ 01482 701917

Another very competent restaurant, getting good marks from R.K.

TANDOORI MAHAL   ©

589 Anlaby Road, Hull

Abu Maksud and Mizanur Tarafder's 64-seat restaurant is one of R.K.'s favourites, and we know it has a pack of loyal supporters, although C.T. tells of bland food and the annoyance of nearly all main dishes priced with rice when he only wanted bread. I'd have thought they could do either/or, without charging extra. Open 6p.m.-midnight. Price check: Papadom 40p, CTM £4.60, Garlic Chilli Chicken Tikka £7.85 incl. rice, Thalis £8.95, Pullao Rice £1.10. Kurzi Lamb £45. Set dinner £16.95.

Pocklington

TANDOORI MAHAL

Railway Street, Pocklington   ✆ 01759 305027

'One of our two favourites. Lamb Pasanda is mild but tasty and their Zalfrezi is also worth a special mention,' B.T.

South Yorkshire

Barnsley

INDIAN GARDENS

16 Peel Square, Barnsley   ✆ 01226 282612

'Staff are very polite and attentive – perhaps because the place is always quiet. Bombay Mix is provided free whilst a choice is made from the menu. The prices of the specials are only marginally more expensive than the standards, but they are significantly better dishes of a superior quality. A separate Balti menu is also offered with Naan bread included in the price, these are excellent. They are served in stainless steel karahis and feature copious amounts of whole garlic with lashings of green coriander. Naan breads are wonderfully light, but on the small side. Personal favourite is Chicken Karahi, comes to the table sizzling in a blackened cast-iron karahi on a wooden base,' N.W. Evenings only.

JALSA ©

7 Pitt Street, Barnsley ℂ **01226 779114**

A popular restaurant, opened in 1992 by Mr Rahman, perhaps suffering from its own success. Chef's special, Chicken Tikka Shirazi (CTM with banana), £4.80, sounds great. 'Always teeming on a weekend and booking is an absolute requirement. Despite having booked, when we arrived we were told we would have to wait, no one asked us if we would like a drink. I had to go to the bar where the staff ignored me for a good while. We ordered a single starter to share – Tandoori King Prawn (£3.20). When this came it was definitely on the small side. For main course we ordered Chicken Dopiaza (£3.95) and a Prawn Biryani (£5.70) with a Garlic Naan (£1.60). We had been overcharged by £10. No apology was offered. It cannot be denied that the Jalsa is a very popular establishment. Maybe they were having a bad night,' N.W. What this restaurant needs is a good, experienced manager to handle and oversee the staff. Price check: Papadom 40p, CTM £6.40, Pullao Rice £1.70. Open 6-11.30p.m. Branch: Dilshad, Sheffield.

K2

5 Royal Street, Barnsley ℂ **01226 299230**

'Unlicensed. Excellent Chicken Pakoras and Mushroom Bhajias. Chicken Karahi with a very tasty Peshwari Nan,' T.H.

©	Curry Club discount (see p. 607)		Unlicensed
√	Vegetarian	⊞	Home delivery
BYO	Bring your own alcohol		service available

AAGRAH NEW ENTRANT BEST RESTAURANT CHAIN
TOP 100 ©

Great North Road, Woodlands, Doncaster ✆ 01302 728888

Opened in 1995 and is the fifth of the Aagrah chain of restaurants. Owned by Mr M. Sabir and brothers. Decorated in cream and green, high ceiling, chandelier and colonial fans. The exquisite hand-painted chairs are green and yellow. Seats 70 diners. 'This one is well up to standard, I would put it at no. 1 in Doncaster, and there's a lot of competition. The starter, Mixed Tandoori for two, is excellent and good value for money – a meal in itself,' J.F. (*See* Shipley branch for fuller description.) Price check: Papadom 30p, CTM £6.20, Pullao Rice £1.30. Open 6-11.30p.m., till midnight Friday and Saturday, till 11p.m. Sunday. In our TOP 100. Branches: Garforth, West Yorkshire; Pudsey, West Yorkshire; Shipley, West Yorkshire; Skipton, North Yorkshire; Tadcaster, North Yorkshire.

GANDHI'S BALTI AND INDIAN TAKEAWAY ⊞
NEW ENTRANT ©

Unit 3, York Building, Edlington Lane, Edlington, Doncaster ✆ 01709 860889

Proprietor and chef Yasin Din opened Gandhi's in 1996. Price check: Papadom 25p incl. free onion salad, CTM £5.50 incl. Pullao Rice or Nan bread, Pullao Rice £1.20. Open 5.45p.m.-12.30a.m. Home delivery service on orders over £8, within a 5-mile radius, otherwise add 50p per mile. 10% discount on orders over £35. Branch: Gandhi's Balti and Indian Takeaway, 1 Hunt Lane, Bentley, Doncaster.

INDUS ©

24-26 Silver Street, Doncaster ✆ 01302 810800

Owned since 1968 by partners Nayeem and John Din. Seats 185 diners. 'A sophisticated restaurant for special occasions or whenever you deserve a treat – which is all the time – right!' D.C. Price check: Papadom 70p, CTM £8.40, Pullao Rice £1.90. Open noon-2p.m. and 7p.m.-midnight. Branch: Grand St Leger Hotel, Doncaster.

SARADA NEW ENTRANT   ©

17 Hallgate, Doncaster   ℰ 01302 326406

This 60-seater restaurant, owned by Mr and Mrs Talukder, serves
Bangladeshi curries cooked by Mr R. Gupta. Price check: Papadom
30p, CTM £5.95, Pullao Rice £1.35. Set menu £4.95 lunchtime.
Minimum charge £5. Open noon-2p.m. and 7p.m.-1a.m.

Penistone

TASTE OF INDIA

56, Bridge Street, Penistone   ℰ 01226 766951

A standard curry house serving standard curries and accompaniments
at reasonable prices. Open noon-2.30p.m. and 6p.m.-midnight.

Rotherham

SHAHJAHAN NEW ENTRANT   ⊞

28-32 Westgate, Rotherham   ℰ 01709 829223

Opened in 1994 by S. Loonat, serving northern Indian food and a
whole heap of fabulous extras. Are you ready? Southern Fried Chicken
with Chips £2.40 to £6.25, Coleslaw 40p, Sweetcorn 40p, Donner
£2.30, Garlic Nan Donner £3.20, Donner Meat and Chips £2.50, Nan
Tikka Sandwich £3.50, Onion Bhaji £1, including Korma £3.30, Madras
£3.40 and Vindaloo £3.50. Main courses are served with three
Chappaties, boiled rice, a Nan or chips. The restaurant is fully air-conditioned and has ample parking. Price check: Papadom 20p (takeaway
15p – must be the cheapest ever), CTM £5.50, Pullao Rice £1.50. Open
6p.m.-midnight. Home delivery service on orders over £5, within a 3-
mile radius, 6p.m.-1a.m.

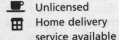

© Curry Club discount (see p. 607)	🍺 Unlicensed
√ Vegetarian	⊞ Home delivery
BYO Bring your own alcohol	service available

BALTI KING NEW ENTRANT ⊞ ©

216 Fulwood Road, Broomhill, Sheffield © 0114 266 6655

Owned by Hanif Hussain (known as Tony to his regulars) since February 1994. He also manages front of house. The restaurant seats 105 and serves Pakistani food. If it is your birthday Hanif presents his guest with a bottle of Bucks Fizz and a birthday card. Price check: Papadom 35p, CTM £5.70, Pullao Rice £1.30. House special Tropical Balti (£7.90) consists of (hope you're feeling hungry) chicken, lamb, prawn, mushroom, potatoes, channa, pineapple and fruit cocktail, cooked with tomatoes and onion, garnished with fresh coriander leaves. Sounds like starter, main course and pudding mixed into one! Open noon-3a.m., Sunday noon-1a.m. Home delivery service free within a 3-mile radius, 5p.m.-1a.m.

BILASH TAKEAWAY NEW ENTRANT

347 Sharrow Vale Road, Sheffield © 0114 266 1746

Established by Abdul Jahir in 1986. Price check: Papadom 35p, CTM £3.95, Pullao Rice £1. Open 5p.m.-midnight.

DILSHAD NEW ENTRANT ©

96-98 The Dale, Woodseats, Sheffield © 0114 255 5008

Opened in 1995 by Mr Zaman and serves Bangladeshi cuisine to 48 diners. Try the Bangladeshi Roast – it's the house special. Price check: Papadom 40p, CTM £6.40, Pullao Rice £1.50. Open 6p.m.-midnight. Branch: Jalsa, Barnsley.

NEW INDIA GARDEN NEW ENTRANT

659-661 London Road, Heeley, Sheffield © 0114 250 0059

'This restaurant is our benchmark. I have eaten here over the last three years and the quality has never dipped. Over that time it has built up a large and steady clientele and now it is rarely empty on any night of the week. What this restaurant lacks in decor and refinement it makes up for in the quality of the food. Onion Bhajias are wonderful in texture and taste. Try also the Prawn Puree either as a starter or a main course. The Baltis are authentic and compare well with the taste of those in Birmingham. A large appetite is needed for a starter and a main course, the portions are big,' A.G.

West Yorkshire

Batley

BOMBAY PALACE   NEW ENTRANT   BYO ©

3 St James Street, Batley   © **01924 444440**

Opened in 1992 by G. Maniyar and A. Akudi, who promise large portions at affordable prices. Unlicensed, manager Shahid Akudi says 'bring your own bottle!' We will, thank you. 'Balti restaurant in an old converted mill. Excellent and friendly service, but not rushed. Superb food which is consistently good, huge Nans. Prawn dishes are first-class, particularly fine Tikka Masala sauce,' J.W. Price check: Papadom 20p, CTM £5.90 (takeaway) £7.50 (eat in), Pullao Rice £1.50. Open 6p.m.-midnight. Home delivery service on orders over £10 within a 3-mile radius.

SPICE GARDEN   BYO ©

2 Market Place, Birstall, Batley   © **01924 471690**

Opened in 1991 by Mr N.A. Hussain and serves Pakistani food to a restaurant seating 100 diners. Mr Hussain told us – 'no licence, bring your own wine, very popular!' I'm sure it is and we will, thank you. House specials include Balti dishes and the 'Grand Slam' – sounds interesting, doesn't it? I wonder what it is; somebody please write in and tell me. Mr Hussain also tells us that he is TOP 100 material. Well, is he? Reports, please. Price check: Papadom 30p, CTM £4.75, Pullao Rice £1.40. Open 5.30p.m.-midnight.

Bradford

With its Asian population largely Pakistani, and very well established, Bradford has a more than interesting curry background, although the restaurants, sweet shops and cafés are much more widely spread around than, say, Southall. They are unmissable for the curryholic, of course, giving excellent, uncompromising ethnic food at real value-for-money prices. With more such establishments (160 restaurants) per head of the population (475,000) than in any other city in Britain, the ratio is 1:2968. Bradford remains Curry City UK (*see* Leicester and Glasgow). Here are your favourites:

AMEER   ©

415 Thornton Road, Thornton, Bradford   ✆ 01274 833673

A 60-seater establishment serving good, standard curries. Licensed. Owner, P. Qureshi, will give a discount to Curry Club members. Open 5.30p.m.-1a.m.

ASHA   ©

31 Cheapside, Bradford   ✆ 01274 729358

Special Feast Night on Sundays and Thursdays at owner Abdul Anwar's Asha. Open 6p.m.-midnight.

BENGAL BRASSERIE   NEW ENTRANT   ©

198-200 Keighley Road, Frizinghall,
Bradford   ✆ 01274 543350

A 48-seat restaurant owned, since 1983, by Sher Ali. Decorated in blues. Has a spiral staircase, shamiania (Indian tent) and two massive coffee pots. Murgh Sagarana – serves two – £29.95. Throughout the centuries this has served the role of the traditional wedding feast. Consumed only by the bride and groom, it was always thought to have had special romantic, potent powers. The dish consists of a whole spring chicken, barbecued and stuffed with eggs and mincemeat. Served on a platter of Akhni Pilou, which is tender chunks of lamb and fine grains of basmati rice. The dish is garnished with a fresh crisp salad. Sounds

delicious! Price check: Papadom 25p, CTM £6.75, Pullao Rice £1.45.
10% discount on takeaway meals.

BOMBAY BRASSERIE

1 Simes Street, off Westgate, Bradford ✆ **01274 737564**

This building was a place of worship and makes a fantastic venue for
a restaurant. It is quite huge, seating 120 diners. 'A large building well
decorated and impressive. Service was excellent, I was the only customer. Found Popadoms and chutneys on my table which were warm
and crisp. Ordered Onion Bhajia, moist and crisp, excellent. Chicken
Biryani, superbly tender with Madras Sauce. Rice was bright red and
yellow, tired and flat,' D.B. Price check: Papadom 30p, CTM £5.90,
Pullao Rice £1.20. Set menu £4.95. Open noon-2p.m. and 6p.m.-mid-
night. Closed for Sunday lunch.

BOMBAY TANDOORI

3b Wilton Street, Bradford ✆ **01274 721879**

'Decor simple but very clean. Shown to a spacious table. Service excellent, friendly and unobtrusive. Bombay Murgh E Special – absolutely
superb, flavours delighted my tastebuds,' J.P. Open 5p.m. till late.

HANSA'S GUJARATI VEGETARIAN √

44 Great Horton Road, Bradford ✆ **01274 730433**

A vegetarian restaurant. 'Spinach and Potato Curry was lovely, leaving
a taste that developed for many hours after the meal – first-class. Well
worth another visit for a taste of something different,' G.H.

INTERNATIONAL TANDOORI ©

**40-42 Manville Terrace, off Morley Street,
Bradford** ✆ **01274 721449**

'Pleasant surroundings and waiters. Meat Vindaloo has plenty of meat
in a thick gravy, hot enough without blowing my head off,' G.H. 'Up-
market but prices are good,' R.S. Manager, Raja Yasin Khan, will give a
discount to Curry Club members. Open noon-3.30a.m.

K2   ©

116 Lumb Lane, Bradford   ℭ **01274 723704**

A popular local curry house serving good curries at reasonable prices, managed by Abdul Ghafoor. Open 11.30a.m.-midnight. Branches: Kasher Kashmiri, 119-121 Oak Lane, Bradford; Aftab Takeaway, Gleadless, Sheffield.

KARACHI

15-17 Neal Street, Bradford   ℭ **01274 732015**

'Have visited over a number of years and the food has never varied, it is always excellent. The menu never changes, but covers all the favourite curries. For several years the menu has displayed a series of new dishes available – which have remained unchanged. The waiter, Ali, knows exactly what we are going to order. Included in the price is a yoghurt, onion and tomato side salad as well as three Chupatties. Naan bread has never been available (don't ask me why). My favourite, Chicken Karahi, is the best I have ever tasted, as good if not better than the fashionable Balti. The meal is sizzling when brought to the table, served on a wooden platter. Two types of rice available, plain-boiled or fried, portions are generous. The kitchens are open and you can observe your meal being cooked and sometimes be entertained when the staff have a minor dispute. Decor has been upgraded although still maintains its "transport café" style. Finally we come to the toilets, definitely a black mark, they have to be seen to be believed. The Gents smells like a horse box – enough said. However, all this is an eating experience, cheap, good-quality food, but absolutely no frills – a real curryholic's delight,' J.P.

KASHMIR   ©

27 Morley Street, Bradford   ℭ **01274 726513**

Mohammed Latif's Kashmir seats a massive 200 diners. 'Meat and Mushroom Vindaloo acceptable, Chuppatis only warm,' R.S. We have received a letter from one of our members telling us that the proprietor, Mr Latif, refused to acknowledge the Curry Club Discount Scheme. Well, for this edition of the Guide he has once again ticked the box and signed underneath to authorize participation, so let's see what happens this time. 'Meal was excellent and the value is fantastic,' R.B. 'Meat Spinach Curry was tasty and thick-textured,' G.H. Open 11a.m.-3a.m. Branch: Taj Mahal, 25 Morley Street, Bradford.

KHADIM'S ©

103 Carlisle Road, Bradford   ℂ 01274 541699

A small and friendly restaurant seating just 26 diners. Popular curries on the menu. Proprietor is Khadim Hussain. Open noon-midnight.

KHYBER

6 The Green, Idle   ℂ 01274 613518

Menu lists all the favourite curries and accompaniments at reasonable prices. Open 4-11.30p.m.

MOGHAL ©

790 Leeds Road, Bradford   ℂ 01274 733324

Another small and friendly establishment, seating 28 diners. All your favourites including Balti. Owner is Mohammed Akbar. Open 10a.m.-2a.m.

MUMTAZ PAAN HOUSE

386-396 Great Horton Road, Bradford   ℂ 01274 571861

A large restaurant seating 150 diners. 'Masala Fish, the best starter I've ever had. Portions are plentiful. Alcohol-free zone. Service is slow, be patient, it's worth it,' R.B. 'Decor is fantastic, with fans to keep you cool. Excellent quality and consistent flavour,' K.I. Open 11a.m.-1a.m.

NAWAAB   TOP 100

32 Manor Row, Bradford   ℂ 01274 720371

'Impeccable service. Large pickle tray waiting on each table, Popadoms crisp. So many excellent main dishes to choose from, we have been through most of them, every one being of a very high standard. It isn't the cheapest but for the quality who can complain,' N.D.M. Open noon-

2p.m. and 6p.m.-12.30a.m. Branch: Nawaab, Huddersfield. Both branches get a TOP 100 award.

RAWAL ©

3 Wilton Street, off Morley Street,
Bradford   © 01274 720030

'Metallic-blue decor. Open kitchen. Chicken Tikka starter would have made a good main course. Wonderful Lassi,' D.S. Head waiter, Mobin Iqbal, will give a discount to Curry Club members. Open 5.30p.m.-2a.m., till 3a.m. Friday and Saturday.

SABRAAJ

20 Little Horton Lane, Bradford   © 01274 724316

'Relaxed, friendly, speedy service. Excellent quality, food prepared with fresh herbs and spices,' N. and M.I.

SHABAB TOP 100

15 Manor Row, Bradford   © 01274 737399

This restaurant is part of a chain of four which opened in 1975, but was taken over by its present owner, Arshad Javed and family, in 1985. It serves Punjabi, Pakistani and Kashmiri food. The lounge area is richly decorated with wooden screens, gold embroidered cushions, silk painting and huge brass trays as drinks tables. The main restaurant is adorned with Moghul arches, brass lanterns with stained glass and fabulous hand-made chairs with their tinkling bells. A full description of the food, with its caveat, appears under the Leeds, West Yorkshire, branch. We welcome all four back to the Guide, and believe our joint TOP 100 cachet is well-deserved. Price check: Papadom 20p, CTM £5.70, Pullao Rice £1.50. Buffet £5.50. House specials include Jalfrezi and Karahi dishes. Open 11.30a.m.-2.30p.m. (till 5p.m. Sunday) and 6-11.45p.m., Saturday 6-11.45p.m only. Home delivery service. Branches: Harrogate, North Yorkshire; Halifax, West Yorkshire; Leeds, West Yorkshire.

SHABINA   ©

258 Great Horton Road, Bradford   ℂ 01274 737212

Opened originally in 1983, Mr Nazir Zaman took over this 64-seater restaurant in 1993. He has kindly offered a discount on Chef Specials. Take him up on his offer and take the kids, too, they'll love the Chicken Tikka and Chips £3.20. Price check: Papadom 20p, CTM £5.50, Pullao Rice £120. Minimum charge £2.50. Open 5p.m.-3a.m.

SHAH JEHAN

30 Little Horton Lane, Bradford   ℂ 01274 390777

Formerly Eastern Delight. 'Onion Bhaji (£1.50) above average. Seekh Kebab (£2) was very nice. Tasty Kashmiri Murgh (£6.50) and Lamb Tikka Makkhani, both very tender. Mushroom Rice (£1.70) fresh and flavoursome. Nan (£1.50) fresh and crisp. Although the portions were small, they were well above average quality. Expensive for Bradford but, judging by customers present, it's popular,' N.S. Price check: Papadom 30p, CTM £6.50, Pullao Rice £1.50.

SHIRAZ   BYO ©

133 Oak Lane, Bradford   ℂ 01274 490176

Owned by Mohammed Gulbahar, with Mohammed Aslam managing front of house and Mohammed Afzal in the kitchen. Price check: Papadom 30p, CTM £4.60, Pullao Rice £1.50. Open 11.30a.m.-3.30a.m., closed Christmas Day and for Muslim festivals. Unlicensed.

SHISH MAHAL   ©

6 St Thomas Road, Bradford   ℂ 01274 723999

A 54-seater establishment, serving popular curries and accompaniments. Owner is Mohammed Taj. Open 4p.m.-3a.m.

TAJ MAHAL   ©

25 Morley Street, Bradford   ℂ 01274 724947

A large restaurant seating 80 diners. 'Very cheap,' R.S. Owner is

Mohammed Latif. Open 5p.m.-3a.m. Branch: Kashmir, 27 Morley Street.

TANDOORI NIGHTS   NEW ENTRANT

53 North Parade, Bradford   ℭ 01274 305670

Formerly Al Sabah. Abdul Ghafoor Malik, former manager and chef at K2 on Lumb Lane, has taken over this establishment. He cooks Kashmiri-style curries and accompaniments, such as Goshtabay (£6.95) – from the valleys of Kashmir – thinly-sliced lamb fillets soaked in plain yoghurt overnight, crushed a special way to produce a mince form to make meat balls. They are cooked in creamy yoghurt sauce enhanced with flavours of Kashmiri Mirch (capsicum), lychees, spices and herbs. Garnished with fresh coriander, pistachios and almonds. A fine example of Kashmiri cuisine. 'Quality excellent and the prices are reasonable, well worth a visit,' N.H. Price check: Papadom 30p, CTM £4.80, Pullao Rice 90p. Minimum charge £10. Open noon-2p.m. and 6p.m.-midnight. Branch: Allerton Tandoori Takeaway, 288 Allerton Road, Bradford 15.

TASTE OF BENGAL   NEW ENTRANT   ©

79 Bradford Road, Idle, Bradford   ℭ 01274 618308

This cosy restaurant, situated in a small village, seats just 28 diners. Abdul Qayum runs front of house with Uddin Khan in the kitchen serving Bangladeshi curries. Balti and Bengal Specialities feature on the menu with a Dine Bangladeshi-Sylhet Special (£4.95) – cooked in a thick blend of spicy succulent sauce with king prawns, mixed vegetables and (more) prawns, highly recommended to fish-eaters. Price check: Papadom 25p, CTM £4.95, Pullao Rice £1.10. Minimum charge £5.50. Licensed. Open 6p.m.-midnight. Branch: Moghul, Horsforth, Leeds, West Yorkshire; Moghul, Ilkley, West Yorkshire.

© Curry Club discount (see p. 607)	☕	Unlicensed
√ Vegetarian	⊞	Home delivery
BYO Bring your own alcohol		service available

Brighouse

THIPTI   ©

6 Huddersfield Road, Brighouse   © **01484 719818**

'Decor good. Not expensive,' B.G. Proprietor, Mokaddas Ali, will give a discount to Curry Club members. Open 6p.m.-midnight, till 1a.m. Friday and Saturday.

Castleford

PARADISE TANDOORI   NEW ENTRANT

154 Redhill Drive, Castleford   © **01977 557937**

'A takeaway with delivery service. Castleford used to have just one restaurant and it was good. Now it has about six takeaway-delivery places and no restaurant. For an establishment that does pizzas, kebabs and burgers, it does the most excellent Indian food. Chicken Pakoras huge. Vegetable Korma was divine with coconut and ginger. Jalfrezi had chillies,' B. and J.W.

Dewsbury

GULSHAN

Northgate House, Northgate, Dewsbury   © **01924 456289**

'An incredible eating experience. Basic, service is via a counter, where the kitchen can be seen. Cooking is undertaken by Asian women who are veiled. Food is great. Chicken Dhansak, highly recommended. The sanitary facilities – upstairs through a room of sleeping people (Asians), we won't tell the Health Dept because we want the Gulshan to stay as it is,' I.D. Home delivery service. Open 10a.m.-2p.m. and 5p.m.-2a.m.

SANAM ©

28 Wellington Road, Dewsbury ✆ 01924 454248

A family-run restaurant seating 60 diners, managed by Mohammed Shiraz. Open 6p.m.-midnight. Branch: Paradise, 1 Fields Street, Batley.

Garforth

AAGRAH BEST RESTAURANT CHAIN TOP 100 ©

Aberford Road, Garforth ✆ 0113 287 6606

Opened in 1993 as the fourth Aagrah restaurant. Decorated in shades of cream and brown. A stylish and up-market restaurant. Ornate plaster ceiling-roses and chandeliers. Yellow linen with block print in red and green and those fabulous hand-made, hand-painted red lacquered chairs with the bells, especially commissioned in Pakistan. You will definitely feel like a royal Nizam dining in this restaurant. Owned by Mohammed Sabir and brothers, who say: 'We pride ourselves on our consistent standards of food in all our restaurants, and whichever one you visit you will be sure of a very warm welcome.' Seating 110 diners, separate bar, reception, and no-smoking area. Free parking. Open 6-11.30p.m., Friday and Saturday 5.30-11.30p.m. Branches: Doncaster, South Yorkshire; Pudsey; Shipley, West Yorkshire; Skipton, North Yorkshire; Tadcaster, North Yorkshire.

Halifax

KAMRAN BALTI HOUSE NEW ENTRANT

27a Union Street, Halifax ✆ 01422 345777

A licensed Pakistani restaurant seating 56 diners. Owned by Mr P. Khan. Menu includes all the usual curries and Chapel Kebab, minced lamb mixed with fresh onion, coriander and spices shaped like a burger and lightly fried, served with salad (£1.40). Balti dishes a house speciality. Price check: Papadom 20p, CTM £4.50, Pullao Rice £1.20. Minimum charge £6. Three-course business lunch £3.20. Open 11.30a.m.-2p.m. and 5p.m.-12.30a.m, till 2.30 a.m. Thursday, Friday and

Saturday. Home delivery service free on orders over £6 within a 4-mile radius. Orders under £6, £1 charge.

SHABAB   NEW ENTRANT   TOP 100   ⊞

25 Union Street, Halifax   © **01422 345655**

This restaurant is part of a chain of four which opened in 1975, but was taken over by its present owner, Arshad Javed and family, in 1985. It serves Punjabi, Pakistani and Kashmiri food. The lounge area is richly decorated with wooden screens, gold embroidered cushions, silk painting and huge brass trays as drinks tables. The main restaurant is adorned with Moghul arches, brass lanterns with stained glass and those fabulous hand-made chairs with the bells. A full description of the food, with its caveat, appears under the Leeds, West Yorkshire branch. We welcome all four back to the Guide, and believe our joint TOP 100 cachet is well deserved. Price check: Papadom 20p, CTM £5.70, Pullao Rice £1.50. Buffet £5.50. House specials include Jalfrezi and Karahi dishes. Open 11.30a.m.-2.30p.m. (till 5p.m. Sunday) and 6-11.45p.m, Saturday 6-11.45p.m only. Home delivery service. Branches: Bradford, West Yorkshire; Harrogate, North Yorkshire; Leeds, West Yorkshire.

Haworth

RAJ MAHAL   NEW ENTRANT   . ©

51 Mill Hey, Haworth   © **01535 643890**

Opened in 1990 by Raj Mohammed, with Javed Iqbal in the kitchen, cooking up Pakistani curries and accompaniments. Fully licensed restaurant seating 36 diners. House specials include Chicken Zafrani (£6.50) and Murgh Hyderabadi (£5.95). Price check: Papadom 35p, CTM £5.50, Pullao Rice £1.15. Open 5.30p.m.-midnight.

©	Curry Club discount (see p. 607)	🍺	Unlicensed
√	Vegetarian	⊞	Home delivery
BYO	Bring your own alcohol		service available

Huddersfield

MAHARAJA

274 Bradford Road, Huddersfield   ℃ 01484 535037

Formerly The Banyan Tree. 'Is huge, beautiful and very, very clean. We were invited into the kitchen and greatly impressed; it was spotless. King Prawns very hot, very tasty. Definitely a must,' M.M.

NAWAAB TOP 100

35 Westgate, Huddersfield   ℃ 01484 422775

'The food was simply superb. Starters included an exquisite Shami Kebab as well as Channa Chaat which was served in yoghurt delicately soured with tamarind and lemon juice. Garlic and Aloo Kebab were also outstanding. All our main courses were equally stunning but I think that the Garlic Chicken deserves a mention on its own. Tender pieces of chicken, marinated in oil and garlic, served in a sauce of caramelized onion and garlic cooked with a touch of vinegar. This is one of the best Indian dishes I've ever tasted. Sadly, despite the food, I must say that the service was absolutely appalling. We visited on a Saturday night and, upon our arrival, despite booking a table the day before and confirming again on the day, we were told that we would have to stand at the bar for 15 minutes or so; in fact we sat down some 30 minutes later. The manager apologized but pointed out that the problem was because there were only seven of us instead of nine as originally booked – they were very busy!! After waiting a further 10 minutes or so we noticed that we were lucky enough to be seated right next to the menus so we helped ourselves. The Papadoms were served just before the main courses despite the chutney trays arriving before the starters – coleslaw instead of onion salad, is that authentic? Our wine was left at the table unopened which, despite attempts to attract the waiter's attention, we eventually opened ourselves. Even worse, they served us three different red wines (due to shortage) that they claimed to be the same – we noticed the cheaper wine straightaway. However, when the bill arrived we were still charged for the more expensive wine. This was deducted upon discussion with the manager! In short, the restaurant was superb and deserves to be placed well towards the top of your 100. However, we think it has become a victim of its own success and needs a damn good kick up the Aloo Chaat!' C.T. Other good reports have kept this restaurant in our TOP 100, but we need more reports, please.

SHABAB

37-39 New Street, Huddersfield   ℂ **01484 549514**

'Lunchtime buffet available at £4.95 a head, looked good value. Chicken Madras excellent — rich and spicy — not too hot. Jinha Pakoras nicely spiced. Prawn Korma, rather odd orange colour but tasty. In fact everything was very brightly coloured. Bombay Aloo a very odd red. Everything very enjoyable and nicely presented. Decor good. Service excellent,' A.H.

Ilkley

ILKLEY TANDOORI   NEW ENTRANT   ©

10 Church Street, Ilkley   ℂ **01943 607241**

Opened in 1995 by Shah Marshal Alam. A Bangladeshi formula restaurant. Price check: Papadom 30p, CTM £5.95, Pullao Rice £1.25. Open 6p.m.-midnight.

MOGHUL   NEW ENTRANT   ▦

**111 Main Street, Burley in Wharfedale,
Ilkley**   ℂ **01943 864403**

A licensed Bangladeshi curry restaurant opened in 1990, by Mr Hamis and Mr Qayum. Seats 40 diners. Simple menu but you will find all your favourite curries and accompaniments. Price check: Papadom 35p, CTM £5.90, Pullao Rice £1.30. Minimum charge £5.50. Open 6p.m.-midnight. Delivery service available. Branches: Moghul, Horsforth, Leeds; Taste of Bengal, Idle, Bradford.

SABERA

9 Wells Road, Ilkley   ℂ **01943 607104**

Ilkley's Sabera is an old friend of the Guide. 'For once I was not the only luncher but was joined by several middle-aged, local regulars. It is a small, clean restaurant with pine panelling and seats. I enjoyed my Kalajee Gurda Dil and will return to try some of their other dishes. If standards are maintained, it will be a strong candidate for inclusion in the fifth edition,' D.M.

Knottingley

JEWEL IN THE CROWN

110 Weeland Road, Knottingley   ℭ **01977 607233**

'Provides excellent food at reasonable prices. Service friendly and efficient. Recommend the Mixed Grill,' I.B. Open 6p.m.-midnight.

Leeds

DARBAR TOP 100

16-17 Kirkgate, Leeds   ℭ **0113 246 0381**

'When I arrived the place was almost empty and I was served quickly. Before I left two prosperous pre-booked parties had arrived and the place was almost full. I confirm the position in the TOP 100. Prices have increased, even so £4.99 for the buffet was a bargain. I applaud this restaurant,' D.M. 'Has a very impressive interior. Room is large and the décor promotes the Indian Palace feeling, spacious yet warm and elegant. We sat down and perused the menu while helping ourselves to their pre-meal nibbles. What a shame it was to have to get up and leave. There was no way, as hungry as we were, that we were going to pay a 10% service charge, TOP 100 or not. If we have to pay for service on top of that we will fetch it from the kitchens ourselves,' A.G. I think you are very brave to get up and leave. You are not alone in your experience. I have been in restaurants where a service charge is automatically added to the bill and then they have still left my credit card slip open for an additional service charge. This is, quite frankly, an outrageous practice. The other one I don't understand is, when parties of say six or more book, they are charged an 'extra' service charge. Why?

DAWAT

4-6 Leeds Road, Kippax, Leeds   ✆ 0113 287 2279

This 54-seater restaurant is owned and run by Mr and Mrs Arora, with Mr Arora running front of house and his wife cooking up all kinds of northern Indian specialities in the kitchen. House specials include Malli Kofta Curry (£5.95). Price check: Papadom 20p, CTM £5.95, Pullao Rice £1.40. Open 6.30-11p.m.

HANSA'S GUJARATI VEGETARIAN TOP 100   √ ©

72-74 North Street, Leeds   ✆ 0113 244 4408

'I particularly enjoyed the crunchy, spicy flavour of the Shrikhand,' D.M. 'As a non-vegetarian I went with an open mind. Food was fine but portions small,' D.B. 'Exquisite Lassi, portions small,' D.O'R. Proprietors, Mr and Mrs Dabhi, will give a discount to Curry Club members. Open noon-2p.m. on Thursday and Friday only, 6-11p.m. on Monday to Thursday, till 11.30p.m. Friday and Saturday. Remains in our TOP 100 but bigger portions, please.

KASHMIR NEW ENTRANT   BYO ©

162a Woodhouse Lane, Leeds   ✆ 0113 245 3058

Unlicensed, 72-seater restaurant, managed by T. Mahmood. Price check: Papadom 20p, CTM £4.60, Pullao Rice 95p. Open noon-3a.m.

MOGHUL

8 The Green, Town Street, Horsforth,
Leeds   ✆ 0113 259 0530

'Seats 45 people at tables of four. Decor clean, as was the cutlery. Were served very quickly with plain Popadoms, slightly warm but not cold. Onion Bhajias (£1.95) with nicely spiced minty Raitha. Masala Dhansak (£4.35) and Dupiaza (£4.45), nicely spiced with good portion of Pilau Rice and one Chapati (40p) each,' J.P. Price check: Papadom 30p, CTM £6.40, Pullao Rice £1.20. Branches: Moghul, Burley in Wharfedale, Ilkley; Taste of Bengal, Idle, Bradford.

NAFEES NEW ENTRANT

69a Raglan Road, Nr Woodhouse Moor, Leeds   ✆ 0113 245 3128

'Slightly out of town, simple and clean. Staff were friendly and help-ful and most importantly the food was of a good standard. Recommended,' A.G. Open noon–3a.m., till 4 a.m. Friday and Saturday and till 2a.m. Sunday. Fully licensed.

POLASH NEW ENTRANT

103 Town Street, Stanningley, Leeds   ✆ 0113 256 0989

'Has all the qualities of the Maharaja and the starters are the best we have tasted anywhere. The staff are wonderful, deserves to be in the next Guide,' M.M.

SHABAB NEW ENTRANT TOP 100   ▦ ©

2 Eastgate, Leeds   ✆ 0113 246 8988

This restaurant originally opened in 1975 but was taken over by its pre-sent owner, Arshad Javed and family, in 1985. It is part of a chain of four, all with similar gorgeous decor, which we have described in the Harrogate, North Yorkshire, entry. The food is authentic Punjabi, Pakistani and Kashmiri. It is far removed from the Bangladeshi for-mula, which gives it a difference in taste that some people find not to their liking. In fact this is closer to real authentic Indo-Pak home food, and is delicious. Anyone who grazes in the rich pastures of Bradford's caféland will recognize such tastes, albeit served at the Shababs in much more sophisticated surroundings, and at a rather higher price tag. The menu is shorter than formula versions but contains many favourites, such as Onion Bhajis and Samosas, both £2.10. But there are other unusual items, such as Chucha Yakhni (£1.70) – chicken soup with almonds, or Machlee Pasinda (£3.50) – pan-fried rainbow trout fillets. Kachi Pakki Kaleeji (£2.30) – spicy chicken liver – is popular. There is a sensible selection of tandoori items, and our attention is drawn to excellent karahi dishes from £6. One correspondent always orders the Gosht Champ (£6.50) – lamb chops marinated in spicy yoghurt and tandoor-cooked – which she always has with the cutely-named Bindian (£2.80) – okra fried with onion, tomatoes and coriander. Mention is made of the Shabab lunch buffet, which is 'self-served from really elegant domed containers, with assistance from the smartly uniformed waiters'. Weekday buffet (no lunch Saturdays) £5.50, Sunday buffet £7.90 – one child under twelve per parent eats free. Ask them about their cooking demonstrations. We welcome all the Shababs back to the Guide, and believe our joint TOP 100 cachet is well deserved. Price check: Papadom 20p, CTM £5.70, Pullao Rice £1.50. Open 11.30a.m.-2.30p.m. (till 5p.m. Sunday) and 6-11.45p.m., Saturday 6-11.45p.m. Home delivery service. Branches: Bradford, West Yorkshire; Halifax, West Yorkshire; Harrogate, North Yorkshire.

Pontefract

ROTI   NEW ENTRANT

North Baileygate, Pontefract   ✆ **01977 703915**

Opened in May 1995. Seats for 110 diners, including in a conservatory area, serving Pakistani food. Owned by Mr Arshad Mahmood. 'We have built up a solid reputation for the quality of food and service in the restaurant during the last two years.' Price check: Papadom 50p, CTM (Kerhaay Choosa Makhan) £6.95, Pullao Rice £1.75. Evenings only. Reports, please.

VICEROY 1   NEW ENTRANT   ⊞ ©

6 Front Street, Pontefract   ✆ **01977 700007**

Taken over in 1994 by Mr Akram Hussain Lohn, who has cleaned up this restaurant to its present standard and cooks Pakistani food. Managed by Susan Ruckladge. Price check: Papadom 30p (25p takeaway), CTM £5.25, Pullao Rice £1.50 (£1.20 takeaway). Open 5p.m.-1a.m., till 2a.m. weekends. Home delivery service on orders over £6 within a 3-mile radius.

©	Curry Club discount (see p. 607)	🍵	Unlicensed
√	Vegetarian	⊞	Home delivery
BYO	Bring your own alcohol		service available

Pudsey

AAGRAH BEST RESTAURANT CHAIN TOP 100   ©

---

483 Bradford Road, Pudsey   ℭ **01274 668818**

Opened in 1986 this, the second of the Aagrah restaurants, has 70 seats. High ceiling with ornate plaster ceiling roses and cornices, crystal chandelier and colonial fans and, of course, those fabulous hand-painted black and red lacquered chairs. Free parking available. *See* next entry. Open 6-11.30p.m., till midnight Friday and Saturday, Sunday 12.30-11p.m. Branches: Doncaster, South Yorkshire; Garforth, West Yorkshire; Shipley, West Yorkshire; Skipton, North Yorkshire; Tadcaster, North Yorkshire.

Shipley

AAGRAH BEST RESTAURANT CHAIN TOP 100   ©

---

27 Westgate, Shipley   ℭ **01274 594660**

It was here in July 1977 that the first Aagrah restaurant was opened. Owned then, as it is now, by Mohammed Sabir, Mohammed Aslam and Zafar Iqbal. This branch is the smallest, with seats for 50 diners. But since this is the first branch, and its menu is the same at all the other branches, we describe it briefly in this entry only. The menu is extensive and carries all the items one would expect to find at the curry house. However, the food is Pakistani rather than formula Bangladeshi. As well as the normal range of starters, our attention is drawn by many regulars to such items as Yahknee (£1.80) – a spicy chicken soup – and Panir Pakora (£2.20) – Indian curd cheese fritter. Balti Liver (£5.90) is a main-course dish, with garlic, ginger, chillies, tomatoes and coriander. And there are many meat, chicken and fish dishes. Vegetarians have a good choice too, with a wide range of curries. Price check: Papadom 30p, CTM £6.20, Pullao Rice £1.30. Minimum charge £10. Average spend £14. Open 6-11.30p.m., till midnight Friday and Saturday. Branches: Doncaster, South Yorkshire; Garforth, West Yorkshire; Pudsey, West Yorkshire; Skipton, North Yorkshire; Tadcaster, North Yorkshire.

Wakefield

RAJ POOT

134 Kirkgate, Wakefield   ℂ 01924 371215

Opened in 1983 by Mr Ashik Miah. Serves northern Indian food to 42 diners. 'I ate the Gurda Kaleja which does not feature on the takeaway menu. This was excellent although slightly different from the Ilkley version. I was brought up to appreciate offal and I am pleased to see it is included in Indian cuisine. Worthy of its entry,' D.M. House specials include their Thali (£6.75). 'Standard menu and fare. Service was good and food preparation very acceptable. Quality and portions above average. But I like to see what I am eating and I feel that there was an excess of coloured bulbs. Expensive,' A.D.K. Price check: Papadom 35p, CTM £5.50, Pullao Rice £1.20. Open 5.30p.m.-midnight. Branch: India Palace, 36 Smyth Street, Wakefield.

Wetherby

JAFLONG TANDOORI

31 High Street, Wetherby   ℂ 01937 587011

'A small restaurant. Food very good indeed, service first-class,' D.C.O'D.

THE ISLES AND ISLANDS

When he failed to capture our island nation, Napoleon dismissed the British Isles as a nation of shopkeepers. Were he around today, it would not escape his notice that many of those isles have their fair share of Indian restaurants. He might observe that we are now a nation of curry house keepers. Some isles and islands, of course, including Lundy, the Isles of Scilly, Uist, Mull, etc., have no curry houses but others do and, for neatness, we group them together. For those who delight in collecting useless information, Lerwick, capital of the Shetland Isles, contains the nation's most northerly curry house (and probably that of the whole globe). It is 800 miles from London and 1000 miles from our most southerly curry house in St Helier, capital of Jersey.

Channel Islands
Guernsey
L'Eree

TASTE OF INDIA ©

Sunset Cottage, L'Eree ℂ 01481 64516

Owned and managed by the Fernandes family. 'Two Popadoms waited at the table which was neatly laid out. Fish Tikka, marinated in a sauce, very succulent. First-rate Methi Gosht with highly-flavoured sauce,' J.T. Open noon-2p.m. and 6-11p.m. Branch: Taste of India, St Peter Port.

St Peter Port

TAJ MAHAL ©

North Esplanade, St Peter Port ℂ 01481 724008

Opened in 1993 by Mujibul Hussain, with Raj Hussain managing front of house. 'Popadoms, onion salad and mint sauce waiting on the table. Sampled Sardines on Puree, rich. A clean and well-decorated restaurant, service good,' J.T. House special is Bengal Chicken (£7.95). Price check: Papadom 40p, CTM £7.95, Pullao Rice £1.90. Set menu £8.95. Minimum charge £8.95.

TASTE OF INDIA ©

2 Mill Street, St Peter Port ℂ 01481 723730

Owned and managed by the Fernandes family, with Batu front of house. Serving northern and southern Indian food with Bangladeshi, Goan and Gujarati specials must keep the chef, Mr Ahmed, very busy. House special is Garlic Chilli Chicken (£8.95). Price check: Papadom

35p, CTM £8.75, Pullao Rice £2.15. Set menus £14.95 and £17.95. Minimum charge £15. Open noon-2p.m. and 6-11p.m. Branch: Taste of India, St Peter Port.

Jersey

St Aubin

SHAPLA

Victoria Road, St Aubin   ✆ **01534 46495**

'Interior decor to a very high standard with rich reds, golds and blues. Hasna Kebabs, pieces of lamb marinated in yoghurt and spices and tandooried with onions, peppers and tomatoes, really very tasty indeed. Chicken Jalfrezi, aroma terrific. Simply perfect Lamb Rogan Gosht,' M.B.

St Helier

THE NEW RAJ

8 St Saviours Road, St Helier   ✆ **01534 874131**

Owned and managed by the Malik family since 1984. Price check: Papadom 40p, CTM £5.25, Pullao Rice £1.75. Set menu £5.95. Service charge 10%. Open noon-2p.m. and 6p.m.-midnight.

SHEZAN

53 Kensington Place, St Helier   ✆ **01534 22960**

'A small restaurant seating 40. Sheek Kebab to my mind almost perfect. Balti Gosht, absolutely wonderful. Expensive but worth it,' M.B.

TAJ MAHAL CENTRAL

La Motte Street, St Helier   ✆ **01534 20147**

'Classy and luxurious restaurant. You are surrounded by running water and tropical fish. Had best ever Tarka Dal,' T.M.

Isle of Man
Douglas

SAAGAR   ©

1 South View, Queens Promenade,
Douglas   ✆ **01624 674939**

Opened in 1993 by Mr and Mrs Chowdhury (he is also the manager) and Mr Jaigirdar. This 60-seater restaurant is cleanly decorated, if a little plain. 'The best I've been to and worth a mention,' R.R. House special is Kachee Biriani – 12 hours' notice is required to prepare this feast. The menu describes it as '... partially cooked Basmati rice layered over meat marinated in spices, yoghurt and herbs then cooked in the oven – perfumed with saffron ...' £25 for two or £48 for four. Kurzi Lamb – 24 hours' notice is required for this extravaganza. For £70 the menu promises 'a whole leg of lamb marinated in fresh ground spices with lamb mince meat cooked in the oven.' Mixed starters, side dishes, rice and breads for four are also included. Sounds like a good deal to me! They allegedly sold a takeaway which was flown, with two chefs, to Spain for a party of four, costing a staggering £2995! Makes the Kurzi Lamb look a snip. Price check: Papadom 70p, CTM £6.55, Pullao Rice £1.95. Open noon-2.30p.m. and 6p.m.-midnight.

TAJ MAHAL

3 Esplanade Lane, Douglas   ✆ **01624 674741**

'"Welcome" the sign said. What it didn't say was, "Britain's most expensive restaurant" – Chutney Mary was cheaper. But it was worth it. All very tasty and well presented. Friendly staff,' M.B.

Ramsey

SPICE OF LIFE

8 Peel Street, Ramsey   ✆ **01624 816534**

'Sensationally good. Sauces excellent – we got the impression someone has been on a curry cooking course – and passed! Prices ridiculously high. Bizarre note on the door, "We do not serve drunks", D.McC.

Scottish Isles
Isle of Bute
Rothesay

INDIAN PAVILION

---

7 Argyle Street, Rothesay, Isle of Bute   ℭ **01700 504988**

Owned and managed by the Gidda family since 1992. Serves northern Indian, southern Indian and Goan food. Price check: Papadom 50p, CTM £7.25, Pullao Rice £1.20. Minimum charge £6. Open 5p.m.-midnight. Home delivery service 75p.

Isle of Lewis
Stornoway

ALI'S

---

24 South Beach, Stornoway   ℭ **01851 706116**

Menu includes all the favourites. 'Had a good, sound meal,' D.MCK.

Isle of Skye
Portree

GANDHI

Bayfield Road, Portree   ℭ **01478 612681**

'Don't be put off by the horrendous tartan carpet that awaits your entrance. Food took a long time to come. When it did come, however, it was excellent,' S.N. 'Pleasant surprise. Bank Holiday and was packed, we were seated promptly, a bit of a delay but service friendly. Delicious food. Gobi Panir – spicy cauli-cheese – unusual,' E.O'D. 'I have eaten better food on the mainland, but inclusion in the Guide is an absolute must to make visitors aware of the opportunity. On a rough head-count I would say that diners were 50% local and 50% visitors,' D.M.

Orkney Islands
Birsay

HEIMDALL

Earls Palace, Birsay

'Operates from a farmhouse kitchen, with an adjoining three-table café area. Humble menu. Portions are handsomely ample and reveal a scintillating flavouring only arrived at by using fresh spices and herbs,' E.S. Open Friday, Saturday and Sunday 5-10p.m.

Kirkwall

MUMTAZ

7 Bridge Street, Kirkwall　　　　　　　© 01856 873537

'Comfortable and modern restaurant. All food very tasty. Service good and efficient,' P.A.W.W. Open noon-midnight.

Shetland Islands
Lerwick

RABA INDIAN

26 Commercial Road, Lerwick

'Warm decor. Well-cooked Indian cuisine at reasonable prices. Samosas, Bhajia and Chicken Tikka Masala were all delicious,' A.I.E.

Isle of Wight

Though technically part of Hampshire, it's a ferry-ride away from the mainland so we put it in this section. There are 10 curry houses dotted around the island. However, M.M. has been telling us for years that she and her husband do a three-hour round trip to Portsmouth for a 'serious curry'! For those with less stamina, or who need a quick fix, these are the three you've talked about.

Cowes

BOMBAY PALACE

10a Shooters Hill, Cowes   © 01983 280942

'Decor quite plain, very cramped and tight inside. Waiter didn't seem happy, and rushed us. Very expansive menu, I'd never heard of some of the dishes. Ordered Achari Gosht Ka Salon, very very tasty and very very hot!! I'd definitely return, but suggest they change the miserable waiter!' D.P.

COWES TANDOORI ©

40 High Street, Cowes   © 01983 296710

Ashid Ali's Tandoori seats 64 diners. A good selection of curries and side dishes on the menu along with some specials such as Podina Gusht and Garlic Chicken. Open noon-2.30p.m. and 6p.m.-midnight.

Newport

NABAB PALACE ©

84 Upper Street, James Street, Newport   © 01983 523276

Seats 54 diners. Serves good, competent curries and accompaniments at reasonable island prices. Owner, Jila Miah, will give a 10% discount to Curry Club members. Open noon-2.30p.m. and 6p.m.-midnight.

NORTHERN IRELAND

With just 25 curry houses in Northern Ireland we cannot pretend that this is a curryholic's haven. However, the good news is that this is a doubling in three years, particularly into towns that have never had curry before. Here are the ones you like. We'd like more reports, please.

Belfast

ARCHANA NEW ENTRANT

13 Amelia Street, Belfast   © 01232 323713

'Menu very comfortable. Vindaloo very hot, excellent. Balti Chicken Chilli, also excellent. Decor and comfort good. Service poor, but improving all the time. Value for money,' J.P.

BITHIKA TAKEAWAY NEW ENTRANT   ⊞

135 Lisburn Road, Belfast   © 01232 381009

Price check: Papadom 50p, CTM £5, Pillau Rice £1.25. Open 5p.m.-2a.m., Sunday till midnight. Home delivery service. Branch: Jharna, Belfast; Tamarind, Carrickfergus.

GANDHI NEW ENTRANT

70c Lisburn Road, Belfast   © 01232 666833

'I would like to recommend strongly this restaurant. I am concerned about them because whenever my girlfriend and I go there, the restaurant is nearly always completely empty. Perhaps it has something to do with their location. It has nothing to do with the quality of the food and service, both are exemplary. Some typical prices: Onion Bhajia £1.40, Lamb Tikka £2.40, Chicken Korma £4.55, Pilau Rice £1.10 and Bombay Potato £2.25,' M.G. Branch: Himalaya, Lisburn.

JHARNA

133 Lisburn Road, Belfast   © 01232 381299

A good place for a party, seats for 110 diners. Air-conditioned.

Tandoori Crayfish sounds delicious at £11.95. Price check: Papadom complimentary, CTM £8.95 incl. Pullao Rice, Pullao Rice £1.50. Set menu £4.95 (three courses). Minimum charge £8. Open noon-2p.m. and 5.30-11.30p.m. Branch: Tamarind, Carrickfergus; Bithika Takeaway, Belfast.

Carrickfergus

TAMARIND NEW ENTRANT

32-36 West Street, Carrickfergus ℭ 01960 355579

Popular with its locals, we hear. Price check: CTM £5.95, Pillau Rice £1.20. Open noon-2p.m. and 5.30-1.30p.m., Sunday 5.30-11p.m. only. Home delivery service.

Lisburn

HIMALAYA NEW ENTRANT

1 Bachelors Walk, Lisburn ℭ 01846 660044

Owned by Feroz Talukder. Chef specials include Jalfrazi (£6.95). Price check: Papadom 40p, CTM £6.95, Pullao Rice £1.45. Set menu £4.95. Open noon-2p.m. and 5-11.30p.m. Branch: Gandhi, Belfast.

SCOTLAND

As with England, the Guide goes alphabetically in county order. We retain the former regions which provide a convenient geographical division of the Scottish mainland. We wish we could elicit a bigger response from Scotland as a whole. The largest concentration of curry restaurants is, of course, in Edinburgh (Lothian) and Glasgow (Strathclyde). Elsewhere, curry still seems thin on the ground. A big thank you to those Scottish restaurants that could be bothered to spend a few minutes completing their forms, and to the diners who wrote to us telling of their experiences, both good and bad. More please, much more.

Borders
Kelso

SWAGAT

Inch Road, Kelso   ✆ 01573 225159

'This tiny restaurant is difficult to find. Mr Kumar, the proprietor, has converted his garage into a restaurant. Sounds awful, doesn't it? Well, it isn't. The food, service, prices are all excellent, I cannot commend this little place enough,' J.R.

Central
Bridge of Allan

ASHOKA

---

23 Henderson Street, Bridge of Allan   ✆ 01786 833710

'Food good in all aspects, especially the Garlic Nan and side dishes. Service is friendly, attentive and quick. Seating is uncomfortable,' A.G.J.

Dunblane

INDIA GATE

Fourways, Perth Road, Dunblane   ✆ 01786 825394

'Exceedingly large portions, everyone was feeling full after the starters! Very large Naans. To sum up this restaurant, "lots" to eat, "lots" of taste, but not "lots" of price,' S.H.

Falkirk

MEHRAN   ⊞ ©

4 Weir Street, Falkirk   ✆ **01324 622010**

All our favourites on the menu including some extras, Nehari, Nantara and Achari. Chicken and Mushroom Samosa sounds good, too. Partner, Arif Shakir, will give a discount to Curry Club members. Open noon-2p.m. and 5p.m.-midnight, till 1.30a.m. Thursday to Sunday. Home delivery service.

Larbert

GULNAR TANDOORI   NEW ENTRANT   ⊞

50-64 Main Street, Larbert   ✆ **01324 562189**

Mr Singh took ownership of the Gulnar in 1997; he also manages front of house. All the usual Korma, Biryani and Tandoori dishes with some uncommon extras such as Masaladear and Nentara. House specials include Parsee Fish (£7.75), Achari Gosht – meat cooked in pickle (£7.35). Price check: Papadom 45p, CTM £7.25 incl. rice, Pullao Rice £1.15. Open 5p.m.-midnight, till 1a.m. Friday and Saturday. Home delivery service free on orders over £10.

Stirling

BAGHDAD   ⊞ ©

16-18 Barnton Street, Stirling   ✆ **01786 472137**

A huge restaurant seating 140 diners. Balti Night is every Monday, Buffet Night every Wednesday. Manager, Rauinder Singh Purba, will give a discount to Curry Club members. Open noon-midnight, Sunday 3.30p.m.-midnight. Home delivery service.

EAST INDIAN COMPANY and VARSITY BLUES   ⊞

7 Viewfield Place, Stirling   ℂ 01786 471330

'Down a flight of stairs to a dark oak-panelled room, a fire burning brightly, walls huge with pseudo paintings. We sat at a highly-polished mahogany reproduction table. We found no argument with their claim that, "The key to our success is a delicacy of flavour",' p.w. Home delivery service. Branch: Killermont Polo Club, Glasgow, Strathclyde; Shimla Pinks, Birmingham, B15, West Midlands; Shimla Pinks, Johnstone, Strathclyde.

TAJ MAHAL   ©

39 King Street, Stirling   ℂ 01786 470728

A large restaurant seating 100 diners. 'The humble Sleek Cobweb deserves a special mention. Chef makes Naan bread to demand in front of the customer,' D.L. Head waiter is Neil Ambasana. Open noon-midnight.

Dumfries & Galloway

Dumfries

JEWEL IN THE CROWN   ©

48-50 St Michael Street, Dumfries   ℂ 01387 264183

'A perfectly satisfactory meal as regards quality. The menu was fairly standard. Service was attentive, but a definite feeling of being rushed. The restaurant was very busy and as soon as we had completed the main course the bill arrived. The restaurant has a good reputation locally,' N.D. Manager is Mr A. Muhit. Open noon-2.30p.m. and 5.30-11.30p.m.

©	Curry Club discount (see p. 607)	☕	Unlicensed
√	Vegetarian	⊞	Home delivery
BYO	Bring your own alcohol		service available

Fife

Cupar

SHAH JAHAAN   NEW ENTRANT   BYO ©

42 Bonnygate, Cupar   ✆ **01334 655559**

A takeaway-only, serving Pakistani food. House specials include Laziz Chicken at a very reasonable £4.90. Price check: Papadom 50p, CTM £6.25 incl. rice and salad (and makes a very good-value meal indeed), Pullao Rice £1.30. Open 4.30p.m.-midnight.

Dumfermline

KHAN'S   ©

33 Carnegie Drive, Dumfermline   ✆ **01383 739478**

Owner-manager Ismail Khan's venue seats a massive 160 diners. 'Good value for money. Portions are large and they also make a mean Phal! Balti is included on the menu along with delights such as Bombay Tiffin, served with tamarind chutney,' L.R. Open noon-2.30p.m. and 5.30-11.30p.m.

Glenrothes

NURJAHAN   ©

Coslane, Woodside Road, Glenrothes   ✆ **01592 630649**

A large establishment seating 110. Decorated in pinks to a very high standard. Roomy carver-chairs at all the tables. A restaurant for a special occasion. Striking menu with photographs of spices, dishes of curry and breads. Proprietor is Manirul Islam. 'A truly magnificent meal. Decor tastefully outstanding and spotless. More than generous quantities. The best quality we have ever tasted. Delighted to hear we were Curry Club members and gave us an unsolicited discount of 10%. A superior restaurant in every aspect,' M.A.J.F. Open noon-2p.m. and 5-11p.m.

Kinross

RAJ MAHAL　NEW ENTRANT

132-4 High Street, Kinross	✆ 01577 864884

Owner-chef, Abdul Gafur, has a very unusual house special – Raj Mahal Rooflifter (£9.95). I wonder what it is! Please will someone write in and tell me. Price check: Papadom 45p, CTM £6.85, Pullao Rice £1.75. Set menu £5.95. Open 5-11.30p.m.

Rosyth

TASTE OF INDIA

130 Admiralty Road, Rosyth	✆ 01384 413844

'Restaurant decor good and spacious. Starters set a high standard of promises to come - the main courses let down. Raita that accompanies the Pakoras was made with yoghurt, mint and mango, very tasty,' N.S.

St Andrews

BABUR　　　　　　　　　　　　　　　　　　　　　　　　Ⓤ

89 South Street, St Andrews	✆ 01334 477778

A large restaurant seating 105 diners. 'The decor is splendid and I speak as an architect, ideally arranged for an intimate meal. We ordered the Emperor's Mid-day Feast, ate well and demolished several bottles of Cobra lager,' P.L.S. Manager is Tony Hussain. Open noon-3p.m. and 5p.m.-midnight. Fax (on same line) for a copy of their menu.

NEW BALAKA BANGLADESHI　TOP 100

3 Alexandra Place, St Andrews	✆ 01334 474825

An up-market and sophisticated restaurant, decorated in pinks. Palms divide tables and Indian art hangs from the walls. Unusual dishes on the menu include Mas Bangla – salmon marinated in lime, turmeric and chilli, fried in mustard oil, garlic, onion, tomato and aubergine. A unique feature at this restaurant is the huge kitchen garden in which Mr Rouf grows all his own herbs and vegetables. Still in our TOP 100. Mr Rouf continues to provide outstanding food in superb surroundings. There is pressure on seating at the weekends, so please book. Here are a few comments: 'My husband remembered this restaurant as Kate's Bar while at St Andrews University in the 1950s. Menu extensive and comprehensive. Quantity sufficient. Quality very good. Lacked the little touches that complement a meal, only plain Popadoms and no spoon in the Raita,' M.A.J.F. 'Food was outstanding and good value. I enjoy Indian food and have tried it in many countries, this was the best I have ever tasted,' J.D.S. 'How much we enjoyed our dinner. Service was excellent and the food exceptional – the entry in the *Good Curry Guide* is richly deserved. We have not had such a good meal in any of the London "recommended" restaurants. A very memorable evening,' G.E.-H. Price check: Papadom 60p, CTM £7.85, Pullao Rice £2.55. Open Sunday to Thursday 5.30p.m.-1a.m., Friday and Saturday noon-1a.m.

Grampian

We have received a letter from N.C. saying that the first Indo-Pak restaurant to open in Aberdeen, in 1963, was called Asia Kathon, Holburn Junction. Does anyone else remember it? Reports, please.

Aberdeen

JEWEL IN THE CROWN

145 Crown Street, Aberdeen   © 01224 210288

'A small but elegant restaurant in an old converted house. Extensive vegetarian menu. Substantial and tasty Onion Bhajee and Vegetable Pakora. Jeera Murgh, tasty, tender chicken but small. Excellent value for money,' N.H. We reported on small portions in our last edition, so that hasn't changed!

LIGHT OF BENGAL   NEW ENTRANT

13 Rose Street, Aberdeen   ✆ 01224 648224

'Very good menu and food. Madras Meat and Keema Nan of good quality. Place is warm and comfortable. Expensive, as are all Aberdeen restaurants,' N.C.

NAZMA   NEW ENTRANT

62 Bridge Street, Aberdeen   ✆ 01224 211296

'This is one for the TOP 100 – in my opinion. Always try to eat here when I see the family. Relaxing atmosphere with attentive waiters. Menu – great choice. Piazo – deep-fried dumplings – fantastic. South Indian Garlic Chilli Chicken – superb. Brinjal Patlia is wonderful, with Lacha Paratha to mop up with. Not cheap but worth a visit. Highly recommended,' R.K. Branches: Nazma, Peterhead; Nazma Takeaway, Inverurie.

POLO CLUB   NEW ENTRANT

18 Holburn Street, Aberdeen   ✆ 01224 575685

Seats 54 diners. Serves Bangladeshi and Pakistani food. On the take-away menu, two Kormas are mentioned, one 'Bombay Style' with fresh cream and chickpeas, the other 'Ceylonese Style' with fresh cream and coconut. Sounds interesting! Price check: Papadom 50p, CTM £0.75, Pullao Rice £1.90. Open 5p.m.-midnight.

Elgin

NASEEB   ©

54 High Street, Elgin   ✆ 01343 550250

Good curries at reasonable prices in pleasant surroundings. Owner is Nemat Ali. Open 5p.m.-midnight. Branch: Nemat, 52 West Church Street, Buckie.

QISMAT

202-204 High Street, Elgin   ✆ 01343 541461

'Service polite and prompt. Large portions from extensive menu. Tried Chicken Balti for the first time, with extra chilli. Offers good food in good surroundings,' A.M. Open noon-2p.m. and 5p.m.-midnight, Sunday 5p.m.-midnight only.

Ellon

NOSHEEN   ▦ ©

5 Bridge Street, Ellon   ✆ 01358 724309

Opened in 1989 by Tariq Mahmood. A large restaurant seating 82, serving northern Indian and Pakistani food. A stylish restaurant decorated with green marble, brass, chandeliers and large china 'cats'. Price check: Papadom 40p, CTM £7.95, Pullao Rice £1.90. Minimum charge £5. Open 5-11.30p.m., till midnight Friday and Saturday. Home delivery service on orders over £12 in Ellon, £18 outside Ellon. They also have an off-licence and can deliver wine, beer and cider. Branch: Shish Mahal, 48 Union Street, Aberdeen.

Forres

PRINCE OF INDIA   ©

64 High Street, Forres   ✆ 01309 673475

Opened in 1985 and has built up a good loyal following for serving good curries at sensible prices. Manager is Harunur Rashid. Open noon-2p.m. and 5p.m.-midnight. Branch: Prince of India, Station Road, Pitlochry, Tayside.

©   Curry Club discount (see p. 607)   ☕   Unlicensed
√   Vegetarian   ▦   Home delivery
BYO   Bring your own alcohol   service available

Inverurie

ALO CHAYA   ©

56 Market Place, Inverurie   ℂ **01467 624860**

A well-established restaurant, owned since it was opened in 1987 by
Syed Mujibul Hoque. 'Waiters efficient and friendly. Buffet night is
worth a visit,' A.MCW. Open noon-2.30p.m. and 5.30-11.30p.m.

NAZMA TAKEAWAY   NEW ENTRANT

42 West High Street, Inverurie   ℂ **01467 629100**

A takeaway-only establishment. 'Has a large TV as you enter, so you
can see what's going on in the kitchen. Spotless,' R.K. Branches: Nazma
Tandoori, Peterhead; Nazma, Aberdeen.

Peterhead

NAZMA TANDOORI   NEW ENTRANT

22a Queen Street, Peterhead   ℂ **01779 478898**

'Our local favourite. Have been visiting for five years. Comprehensive
menu. Service courteous and efficient. Food of consistently high standard. Excellent value. Thoroughly recommended,' D.I. Branches.
Nazma, Aberdeen; Nazma Takeaway, Inverurie.

Stonehaven

TANDOORI HAVEN   ©

54 Allardice Street, Stonehaven   ℂ **01569 762793**

Owner-manager Shofiqul Hoque has a special menu for children
which includes Herby Fish Fry, Indian-style fish and chips. Price
check: Papadom 50p, CTM £7.20, Pullao Rice £1.90. Open noon-
2p.m. and 5-11.30p.m. Branches: Currymount Indian Deli, 112
Rosemount Place, Aberdeen; Tandoori Port, Unit 8, The Green,
Portlethen.

Highlands

Aviemore

ASHA

43 Grampian Road, Aviemore   ✆ 01479 811118

'Our first impression of the menu was that it seemed expensive, but most main courses included rice. Katta Murgh Masala was very tasty with a tang of lime,' E.O'D. Open noon-2p.m. and 5.30-11.30p.m.

Fort William

INDIAN GARDEN

88 High Street, Fort William   ✆ 01397 705011

'Service slow but the food's good,' G.M. This restaurant has been under the present ownership for 10 years and seats 60 diners.

Inverness

RAJAH INTERNATIONAL

2 Post Office Avenue, Inverness   ✆ 01463 237190

A spacious restaurant seating 60 diners. H.B. says: 'The best curry experience in over 10 years.' Open noon-midnight.

ROYAL TANDOORI   NEW ENTRANT   ⊞

99 Castle Street, Inverness   ✆ 01463 712224

Moosa Kutty took over ownership of this restaurant in 1996. Serves all the usual favourites. Price check: Papadom 40p, CTM £6.50, Pullao Rice £1.60. Open noon-2.30p.m. and 5.30p.m.-midnight. Free home delivery on orders over £10.

Nairn

AL RAJ ©

25 Harbour Street, Nairn, Inverness　　　✆ 01667 455370

Opened in 1984 by Mobarok Ali and has built up a good reputation for good curries and accompaniments at reasonable prices. Even Nick Nairn himself has been seen here, escaping from his own restaurant. It seats 70 diners and has a private party room. Open noon-2p.m. and 5-11p.m.

Lothian

Hooray for Lothian restaurant owners and diners. You have all worked very hard and consequently we have a lot to say!

Edinburgh

BALLI'S TANDOORI ©

89 Hanover Street, Edinburgh　　　✆ 0131 226 3451

Balti and Nentara on the menu. Owner is A. Rarwaizon. Open 11a.m.-2p.m. and 5p.m.-midnight.

BANGALORE TANDOORI ©

52 Home Street, Edinburgh　　　✆ 0131 229 1348

Opened in 1984 by Mr R. Khan. Seats 100. 'Had a good Chicken Biriani,' P.B. Price check: Papadom 60p, CTM £6.75, Pullao Rice £2.05. Set menu £7.95. Open noon-12.30a.m.

BOMBAY BICYCLE CLUB　NEW ENTRANT

6a Brougham Place, Edinburgh　　　✆ 0131 229 3839

Price check: Papadom 60p, CTM £6.95, Pullao Rice £1.95. Set menu £6.95. Open noon-2.30p.m. and 5.30-11p.m.

CHILLI CONNECTION NEW ENTRANT

47 South Clerk Street, Edinburgh   ✆ 0131 668 1171

'We had a very good feed for £9.95. Chicken Bhuna, Lamb Madras (perfect marinated meat), two very good Nans and a rice, extra £1.50 for extra mileage, we were out of the area. Must have been a 12-mile round trip,' N.C.

EASTERN MASSALA NEW ENTRANT   ⊞ ©

191 Dalry Road, Edinburgh   ✆ 0131 337 3249

Opened by Jalal Uddin, who tells us he opened the first takeaway in Edinburgh. Price check: Papadom 40p, CTM £4.95, Pullao Rice £1.50. Open 5p.m.-midnight, till 1a.m. Friday and Saturday. Home delivery service free on orders over £12 within a 2-mile radius. Branches: Ravi Shankar, 26 Marchmont Road, Edinburgh; Saffron, 9 Pentland View Court, Currie, Edinburgh.

GULNAR'S PASSAGE TO INDIA   ©

46 Queen Charlotte Street, Leith,
Edinburgh   ✆ 0131 554 7520

'Complimentary Popadoms while you were ordering. Chicken Dupiaza delicious, not too many onions,' A.G. Manager is Mohammad Saleh.

GURU NEW ENTRANT   BYO

Dundee Terrace, Edinburgh   ✆ 0131 221 9779

'Very, very good. Good menu, food, comfort, decor and service. Meat well-marinated, fresh. BYOB (bring your own booze). Very friendly, our fourth or fifth visit – usual party, two kids, 11 and 12 years but both 5ft 7ins, my wife and I and my mother-in-law (91 years). ALL very experienced in spotting a good Indo-Pak restaurant,' N.C.

INDIA GATE

23 Brougham Place, Edinburgh   ✆ 0131 229 1537

Boal fish and Nentara on the menu of this popular Indian restaurant.

INDIAN CAVALRY CLUB

3 Atholl Place, Edinburgh   ✆ 0131 228 3282

'Smart up-market restaurant on two floors. The Officers' Mess is on the ground floor, and the tent-canopied Club is downstairs. Service quick, though waiter forgot side plates. Food excellent. The hottest Jalfrezi I have tasted. Prices high but on the whole worth it,' E.M. For vegetarians and other diners try the Pineapple Samber, pineapple in a lentil and tamarind sauce. 'Ate an excellent Bharatiya buffet. This establishment thoroughly justifies its place in the Guide,' D.M. Open daily for lunch and dinner.

JAIPUR MANSION

10 Newington Road, Edinburgh   ✆ 0131 662 9023

Opened in 1995. Very up-market. Wonderful menu with wonderful food. Tessrio, mussels seasoned with coriander, turmeric, garlic, cumin and lightly fried. Bhari Hui Simla Mirch, lean minced lamb or boneless chicken pieces with an amalgam of traditional herbs and spices. Once cooked, stuffed into a fresh bell pepper and shallow-fried. Balti Karahi and Nentara are also on the menu. Wine list is very impressive, too. Open noon-midnight.

KALPNA   √

2-3 St Patrick's Square, Edinburgh   ✆ 0131 667 9890

This vegetarian restaurant, established in 1983, remains very popular, under the auspices of owner-chef Ajay Bhartdwaj. It serves a mix of Gujarati, Bombay and south Indian items, such as Bhel Puri and Dosas (*see* glossary), with some distinctive Moghul non-meat items too, such as Aloo Dom - Kashmiri stuffed potatoes. Lunch £4.50. Wednesday evening buffet £8.50. Open noon-2p.m. and 5.30-10.30p.m., opens at 6p.m. Sunday.

KHUSHI'S   NEW ENTRANT   BYO

16 Drummond Street, Edinburgh   ✆ 0131 556 8996

'Nice short menu, good helpings, very good meat, perfectly marinated. Fair service, nice Italian waiter. Clean, light-painted decor, very clean

toilets. Good comfort on padded benches and formica tables.
Excellent big starters. No alcohol, but most people brought big jugs
(2-3 pints) of beer from the pub next door. Regret – over-spiced
Madras was now a Vindaloo; Bhuna and Korma could have been a
Madras,' N.C. Branch: Khushi's of West Lothian, Mid Calder.

KINGS BALTI   NEW ENTRANT

79 Buccleuch Street, Edinburgh   ✆ **0131 662 9212**

Unlicensed. A huge restaurant seating 100. Price check: Papadom 40p,
CTM £6.25, Pullao Rice £1.95. Set menu £4.95. Open noon-2p.m. and
5p.m.-midnight, noon-midnight Friday and Saturday.

LANCERS BRASSERIE   TOP 100   ▦ ©

5 Hamilton Place, Edinburgh   ✆ **0131 332 3444**

First opened in 1985. Wali Udin's beautifully decorated and stylish
restaurant has pink suede on the walls, tiled floor, highly polished
tables and is a really smart eating atmosphere for business lunches and
special occasion dinners. Downstairs is a private dining room for
approximately a dozen diners. Chippendale-style furniture, banquet-
style. Prints of times gone by of the Raj decorate the walls. Great for
a special treat, such as a birthday party. A small but selective menu.
Manager, Alok Saha, will give a discount to Curry Club members at
lunchtimes only. Price check: Papadom 60p, CTM £6.95, Pullao Rice
£2.25. Set menus £7.95 and £9.95 – three courses. Open noon-2.30p.m.
and 5-11.30p.m. Home delivery service free on orders over £15. Branches:
Maharajah's, Edinburgh; Suruchi, Edinburgh; Verandah, Edinburgh.

MAHARAJAH'S   ©

17-19 Forrest Road, Edinburgh   ✆ **0131 220 2273**

A modern and luxuriously decorated restaurant in salmon pinks and
subtle greys. Great swags of material hang from the ceiling, giving a
tented effect. Partner Razu Khan's menu offers all the favourite things,
measured in eight degrees of heat. Open noon-2p.m. and 5.30-11.30p.m.
Branches: Lancers Brasserie, Edinburgh; Suruchi, Edinburgh;
Verandah, Edinburgh.

MONSOON VILLAGE

13 Dalry Road, Haymarket, Edinburgh   © 0131 346 0204

A small restaurant seating 42. Well-established and well-liked.

RAJ

91 Henderson Street, Leith, Edinburgh   © 0131 553 3980

Down by the water, Tommy Miah's restaurant retains its Victorian architecture and has the potential to be a very stylish and up-market restaurant. Most tables are on a large raised floor section. Good food, portions and prices. His own mango chutney is served with Papadoms and starters and can be bought at the restaurant along with other own-labelled products.

SHAMIANA   BEST CHEF AWARD   TOP 100

14 Brougham Street, Edinburgh   © 0131 228 2265

The Butt family own and run this restaurant and have done so since 1989. The restaurant originally opened in 1977. 'My husband, myself and two friends have been going twice a month for 20 years. It has always been the best Indian restaurant in Edinburgh in our opinion. The food has always varied and is of a high standard. The restaurant has changed hands twice during this period but has always been run well. The present owners are ideal hosts and make everyone feel very welcome. We have no hesitation in recommending it to you for a high place in your ratings.' M.Mc¹ Mohammed runs the kitchen, with northern Indian and Kashmiri food influencing his style. One of his specialities is Shahi Murgh (£30), which the menu describes as 'spiced whole roast chicken created in the kitchens of the great Maharajas of India, served with salad, rice, nan and side dishes.' It is good to see Kulfi Pista, Gulab Jaman and Garjar Halwa on the dessert menu. I had the priviledge of judging Mohammed at a recent Indian chef competition cutely named Spindian because it was promoted by a spinach grower (W. Emmett) and Tesco. Mohammed's Kashmiri Chaman Gosht (lamb and spinach with peppers – a Sag Gosht variant) was undoubtedly the best dish there. He deserves to be our CHEF OF THE YEAR, and I hope his cooking continues to prosper. Price check: Papadom 50p, CTM £7.70, Pullao Rice £1.95. Minimum charge £10. Service charge 12.5%. Open 6-10p.m.

SINGAPORE SLING   ©

69 North Castle Street, Edinburgh   ✆ 0131 538 7878

Opened in 1984 by Mr C. Pang, he is also the head chef. Malay and Singaporean dishes appear on the menu so it's not a curry restaurant but there is a curry or two on the menu. A smallish restaurant, seating 45, gets busy at weekends, so book a table. Proprietor, C. Pang, will give a discount to Curry Club members. Specialities include Chicken, Beef, King Prawn or Tofu, marinated, skewered and char-grilled, served with a delicious peanut sauce (five sticks), £5.90. Open noon-2.30p.m. and 6-10.30p.m. Branch: Singapura, 69 North Castle Street, Edinburgh.

SURUCHI   √ ©

14a Nicolson Street, Edinburgh   ✆ 0131 556 6583

Suruchi means, in most Indian languages, good taste. Restaurant decor has been imported from India, and is clean and smart. Jaipur blue/turquoise tiles adorn the walls. Table linen is vegetable-dyed pink and tablewear is beaten coppered brass. It's a vegetarian-only restaurant, serving real Indian food. Owned and managed by Herman Rodrigues who is also a photographer – his many works of art appear on the walls. Well-situated for a pre-theatre (which is opposite) curry dinner. Regular food festivals make this an interesting restaurant. Price check: Papadom 50p, CTM £7.25, Pullao Rice £2.50. Three-course set menu £4.95. Open noon-2p.m. and 5.30-11.30p.m. Branches: Lancers Brasserie, Edinburgh; Maharajah's, Edinburgh; Verandah, Edinburgh.

TANDOORI LAND   ©

63 Clerk Street, Edinburgh   ✆ 0131 667 1035

What a title! A small restaurant seating 32, owned by S. Chowdhury and serving - yes, you guessed it! Open 5p.m.-midnight. Branch: Morningside, 128 Morningside Road, Edinburgh.

TIPPOO SAHIB   NEW ENTRANT   ©

129a Rose Street, Edinburgh   ✆ 0131 226 2862

A Pakistani restaurant opened in 1982 by A. Parvez. The menu includes Chicken Nentara and Massalidat Gosht, which we know are favourites of Edinburgh diners. Price check: Papadom 60p, CTM £6.95, Pullao Rice £1.95. Set menu £11.95. Minimum charge £10. Open noon-2p.m. and 5-11.30p.m. Branches: Ballis, 89 Hanover Street, Edinburgh; West End Balti House, 29 West Maitland Street, Edinburgh.

VERANDAH TOP 100   ⊞ ©

17 Dalry Road, Edinburgh   ✆ 0131 337 5828

Opened in 1981 by Wali Tasar Uddin, MBE, JP, and his nephew, Foysol Choudhury. A very popular and well-established restaurant, serving northern Indian and Bangladeshi cuisine. A pretty and relaxing restaurant with cane chairs to sit on and bamboo-slatted blinds covering the walls, a clever and effective illusion. House specials include Amer Murghi (£6.95) and Chilli Garlic Chicken (£6.95). Price check: Papadom 60p, CTM £7.25, Pullao Rice £2.25. Set menus £5.95 and £6.95 for lunch and £16.95 for dinner. Open noon-2.15p.m. and 5p.m.-midnight. Home delivery service free on orders over £15. Branches: Lancers Brasserie, Edinburgh; Maharajah's, Edinburgh; Suruchi, Edinburgh.

Linlithgow

KISMET NEW ENTRANT   ©

88 High Street, Linlithgow   ✆ 01506 671811

This 38-seater restaurant is managed by Mahbub Hussain Khan. All the usual favourites including Baltis. House specials include Chahat King Prawns (£8.50). Price check: Papadom 40p, CTM £5.75, Pullao Rice £1.45. Set menu £4.95. Open noon-2.30p.m. and 5p.m.-midnight.

Mid Calder

KHUSHI'S OF WEST LOTHIAN
NEW ENTRANT   ⊞ BYO ©

11 Bank Street, Mid Calder   ✆ 01506 884559

Opened in 1994 by Mr Islam Mohammed and serving Pakistani and northern Indian cuisine to 35 diners. Unlicensed, so BYO. Price check:

Papadom free (20p if ordered as part of a takeaway), CTM £5.75, Pullao Rice £1.30. Set menu £9.95. Open daily except Monday 5-11p.m. Home delivery service free on orders over £15 in local area. Branch: Khushi's, Edinburgh.

Musselburgh

SHISH MAHAL

63a High Street, Musselburgh   ✆ **0131 665 3121**

Opened in 1979 by Idris Khan. Pakistani and northern Indian food influence the cooking style of Tariq (head chef) in this restaurant. House special is Balti Murgh (£7.50). Price check: Papadom 65p, CTM £6.95, Pullao Rice £1.75. Minimum charge £10. Open 5p.m.-midnight. Home delivery service. Branch: Shezad, 175 Gorgie Road, Edinburgh.

North Berwick

JOYPUR NEW ENTRANT   ©

114 High Street, North Berwick   ✆ **01620 895649**

A huge restaurant seating 100 diners. 'At the opening night reception, management played it safe with Tandoori Chicken and Lamb Bhoona, Chicken Tikka Masala, vegetables and rice. Truly excellent. Prices are very reasonable and decor is great, friendly staff,' I.P. Price check: Papadom 45p, CTM £5.50, Pullao Rice £1.80. Set menu £4.95. Minimum charge £8. Open noon-2p.m. and 5.30-11.30p.m.

Strathclyde

Ardrossan

SANGEET   ©

51 Glasgow Street, Ardrossan   ✆ **01294 601191**

An intimate restaurant seating 36 diners. Owner, Fawad Khan, will give a discount to Curry Club members. Open noon-2p.m. (Thursday to Friday only) and 5p.m.-12.30a.m.

Coatbridge

PUNJAB EXPRESS NEW ENTRANT ⊞ ©

---

22 West Canal Street, Coatbridge © 01236 422522

Opened in 1993 by the Dhanda brothers, Kally and Tari. The Punjab Express is part of the former Coatbridge Central Station House. Built in 1899, the building still has many of the period features. The station was closed by Lord Beeching in 1963 and the restaurant is situated in what used to be the station master's accommodation. Downstairs, in the former ticket office, is the Pullman Lounge. Price check: Papadom 70p, CTM £6.95, Pullao Rice £1.50. Minimum charge £15. Home delivery service but with delivery charge.

Glasgow

We get a fair bit of mail from expat Glaswegians (those working in England) who are at pains to tell us that Glasgow curries are the real thing, the best anywhere … 'everywhere else is a pale imitation, especially the pakoras', writes one person frequently. The other thing they lay claim to is that Glasow is the curry city of the world! As to the first claim, what they've got, lucky people, is a largely Pakistani Asian population, and this means gutsy, spicy Punjab-style curries, as are found in Southall and Bradford, which are quite removed from the Bangladeshi curry house formula. Put it another way, Glasgow's curries are the authentic thing, once tasted, never forgotten. As to curry city, sorry lads and wee lassies, you are still number two, measured by the number of curry restaurants to the number of citizens. At 132 to 700,000 (1:4375), this puts you behind Bradford. But Glasgow has a supremely good selection of curry restaurants, nonetheless, including, for the first time, our BEST IN SCOTLAND.

ALI BABA'S BALTI BAR

51 West Regent Street, Glasgow   © 0141 332 6289

'Going by building alterations, the real Balti was downstairs but I think that the Bombay Bistro was being utilized for the time being. First-class starters. Samosa with Chana (£1.95), Aloo Tikki with Chana (£1.95) very tasty but so large. Not much room for main courses. Aloo Matter Balti (£2.50) and Lamb Kofta Achaari (£3.95), very good and oh, so tasty, oozing Garlic Nan (£1.50),' M.J.G.

ALISHAN TANDOORI   ©

250 Battlefield Road, Battlefield   © 0141 632 5294

Opened in 1978 by M.A. Qureshi. Menu includes a good range of popular northern Indian and Pakistani curries. Price check: Papadom 60p, CTM £6.90, Pullao Rice £1.30. Set menu £3.50-£6.80. Minimum charge £6. Open noon-midnight.

AMBALA SWEET CENTRE

178 Maxwell Road, Glasgow   © 0141 429 5620

Takeaway establishment, serving a small range of competently cooked curries and snacks. 'Lamb Bhoona is amazing!' D.F. Open 10a.m.-10p.m.

ASHOKA

268 Clarkston Road, Glasgow   © 0141 637 5904

Try such house specialities as Goanese Delicacy, Mewa Massala and Kerela Chilli Chicken. Open 5p.m.-midnight. Branches: Ashoka, Johnstone; Ashoka Ashton Lane, Glasgow; Ashoka West End, Glasgow.

ASHOKA ASHTON LANE

19 Ashton Lane, Glasgow   © 0141 357 5904

'Chicken Massala Dosa was excellent, filled with strips of tandoori chicken and a massive portion of rice. A recommended oasis,' C.W. Branches: Ashoka, Glasgow; Ashoka, Johnstone; Ashoka West End, Glasgow.

ASHOKA WEST END

1284 Argyle Street, Glasgow   ✆ **0141 339 0936**

'For a Londoner who is used to saucer-sized Nans, the Ashoka's oval platters are passed on in curry folklore stories,' s.g. Branches: Ashoka, Glasgow; Ashoka, Johnstone; Ashoka Ashton Lane, Glasgow.

BALBIR'S VEGETARIAN ASHOKA   √ ©
BALBIR'S ASHOKA TANDOORI
BEST IN SCOTLAND TOP 100

108 Elderslie Street, Glasgow   ✆ **0141 221 1761**

Balbir Singh Sumal opened this, his first restaurant, in 1982. Run by Gian Singh, Vegetarian Ashoka is upstairs and serves purely vegetarian delights such as Kachoris (stuffed lentil pastry), Patra (curried lotus leaf rolls) and Bhel Poori. 'And where else can you get ten types of Pakora?' L.C. Balbir's Ashoka Tandoori is downstairs and serves meat curries, and all the accessories, the spicy Punjabi way. Try a Garam Masala curry sprinkled with green chillies. 'I can vouch for this restaurant, it is excellent,' B.S. Open 5p.m.-midnight, till 1a.m. Friday and Saturday. Branches: 141 and 149 Elderslie Street, Glasgow.

CAFE INDIA

171 North Street, Charing Cross, Glasgow ✆ **0141 248 4074**

Seats a massive 250 diners. Set menus are a speciality, and Gourmet Night Extravaganza is every Monday from 7-10.30p.m.

CAFE SHABAZ NEW ENTRANT   ⊞

366 Victoria Road, Glasgow   ✆ **0141 423 8586**

Such a big menu for such a little restaurant, seating 36 diners. Must have the biggest menu in the country, a total of 240 items, absolutely everything is here. There are 16 different types of bread, listed under the heading of Flour Mill, and then comes Kulcha (a stuffed bread), and there are 5 of those, making a total of 21. Must be a record. Price check: Papadom 50p, CTM £6.60, Pullao Rice £1.10. Open noon-2p.m.

and 5p.m.-12.30a.m., Friday and Saturday noon-1a.m. Home delivery service on orders over £5.

CHANDIGARH　NEW ENTRANT　　　　　　　⊞

28 Vinicombe Street, Glasgow　　　　ⓒ **0141 400 0483**

Opened in 1985 by Mr S. Singh, seating 42 diners. Hysterical piece from me and the Moll by 'Diner Tec' on the back of the takeaway menu. Price check: Papadom 60p, CTM £7.30, Pullao Rice £1.45. Open 5p.m.-midnight. Home delivery service.

LA CREME DE LA CREME

1071 Argyle Street, Finnieston, Glasgow　　ⓒ **0141 221 3222**

Situated in a former cinema and aiming at an up-market image, it claims to be Europe's largest Indian, with 400 seats. It isn't, of course! Some can equal it (in Southall, Birmingham and elsewhere). As for Europe! Nowhere can they match that - they can't even turn out a decent curry. But no matter, La Crème can and, what's more, no expense has been spared doing it, creating a style reminiscent of parts of London's Bombay Brasserie. Former stalls and dress circle are in use, so it is a very large restaurant. 'Food good, service poor,' B.G. 'Service superb. Prices dear, but portions large,' D.McK. 'Tried the buffet, my first experience of this type of spice inhalation. As much as you like. All reasonable,' c.w. Weekday lunch prices 20% off until 3p.m. Balcony evening buffet served 6-10p.m., £8.95 weekdays, £11.95 weekends. Open daily, noon-midnight.

INDIA DINER　　　　　　　　　　　　　　　ⓒ

1191-1193 Argyle Street, Glasgow　　　ⓒ **0141 221 0354**

Managed by Anmal Lak, it is a competent formula curry house. Open noon-2p.m. and 5p.m.-midnight.

KILLERMONT POLO CLUB

**2022 Maryhill Road, Maryhill Park, Bearsden,
Glasgow**　　　　　　　　　　　　　ⓒ **0141 946 5412**

The young go-ahead brothers Kal and Parmjit Dhaliwal opened this ultra-smart place in 1991, revealing considerable style. Firstly, it really is a polo club, and if you fancy a pukka chukka your mount awaits outside. Inside are two dining areas. One is oak-panelled with Georgian-style chairs, polished tables and polo items decorating the walls. The other is more traditional with high-backed chairs and flowing table linen. The third partner, Jas Sagoo, runs the kitchen with Balbir Farwaha, from whence comes 'good food,' L.M. Open for lunch daily except Sunday noon-1.45p.m., daily for dinner 5-10p.m. Branches: East Indian Company and Varsity Blues, Stirling, Central; Shimla Pinks, Birmingham, B15, West Midlands; Shimla Pinks, Johnstone.

KOH I NOOR

235 North Street, Charing Cross, Glasgow ℂ 0141 204 1444

'An excellent meal. Meat Samosas came with a plateful of salad and chickpeas in sweet curry sauce. It was so filling I had to leave most of my main course!' S.F. 'Starters very impressive, quantities large. Garlic Nan not for the faint-hearted: beautiful. Chicken Tikka Chasini and Chicken Nentara memorable,' H.B. 'Absolutely superb. In a class of its own,' B.S.

MOTHER INDIA CAFE BISTRO   BYO

**28 Westminster Terrace, Sauchiehall Street,
Glasgow   ℂ 0141 221 1663**

'Exciting and varied lunch. Incredible value (£4.50). Aubergine Fritter, Vegetable Pakora, Fish and Chicken Balti with rice and large Nan. Relaxed atmosphere. BYO,' P.W.

MR SINGH'S INDIA   NEW ENTRANT

149 Elderslie Street, Glasgow   ℂ 0141 204 0186

'Without question the best I have visited! Vast menu. Owner Satty Singh, brother of Bobby, and other staff wear kilts! Fantastic food, good portions. Booking a table is essential, even mid-week. If you are a brandy-drinker – beware – have a 200-year-bottle of Napoleon's brandy at £35 a shot!' G.D.

MURPHY'S PAKORA BAR

1287 Argyle Street, Glasgow   © 0141 334 1550

'The best selection of Pakoras that you are ever likely to see. How about Haggis Pakora. Beam me up, Scotty,' c.w. Open noon-midnight.

NEELIM   NEW ENTRANT   ⊞ ©

1590 Dumbarton Road, Scotstoun,
Glasgow   © 0141 959 6265

Opened by Iqbal Gill, who also owns, with partners, eleven takeaways and one restaurant, all in Glasgow. You'll never guess the names of the takeaways – Chapati 1, Chapati 2, Chapati 3 – I think we've got the message. Price check: Papadom 60p, CTM £6.50, Pullao Rice £1.35. Service charge 5%. Open 4.30p.m.-midnight. Home delivery service.

RAMANA   ©

427 Sauchiehall Street, Glasgow   © 0141 332 2528

Owner B.S. Purewal's Ramana seats 120 diners, and is well spoken of. Open noon-midnight.

SEPOY CLUB

62 St Andrews Drive, Pollokshields,
Glasgow   © 0141 427 1106

'Former Victorian house now a hotel with Indian restaurant. Exquisite decor. Amazing range of meals. Beautifully presented Pakoras but expensive. Sorbet to cleanse the palate followed by well-presented Jaipuri, Green Herb Chicken, Tikka and Tandoori. A delight,' D.F.

SHISH MAHAL   ©

66-68 Park Road, Glasgow   © 0141 334 7899

Opened way back in 1964 by managing partner, Nasim Ahmed, and once held sway here as 'it'. In fact, it had a bad patch but is back and doing well, they say. Open noon-2p.m. and 5-11.30p.m., Friday and

Saturday noon-11.30p.m., Sunday 3-11.30p.m. Branch: Shish Mahal, 1348 Maryhill Road, Glasgow.

SPICE OF LIFE

1293 Argyle Street, Glasgow   © 0141 334 0678

How about Banana Pakoras or Garlic Mussel Poori? They also serve Goanese Lamb.

TURBAN TANDOORI   ⊞ ©

2 Station Road, Giffnock, Glasgow   © 0141 638 0069

Specials include Nentara and Masaledar dishes. Proprietor, Kulbir Purewal, will give a discount to Curry Club members. Open 5p.m.-midnight. Home delivery service.

East Kilbride

ATRIUM COURT   ©

3 The Boardwalk, East Kilbride   © 013552 60681

All the usual curries and a good selection of Pakoras and specials such as Nentara, Chasini and Karahi from manager J.S. Boparai. Open noon-midnight. Branch: Taj Palace, 2 Scholar's Gate, Whitehills East Kilbride.

Greenock

ROYAL TANDOORI TAKEAWAY
NEW ENTRANT   ⊞ BYO

58 Fancy Farm Road, Greenock   01475 632845

A takeaway-only restaurant, opened on 15 June 1996. Not only do they deliver Pakistani food at exceptionally good prices, they have cornered the market on takeaway food to include Kebabs, Pizzas, Baked Potatoes and Fish and Chips. House special is Tandoori Mix (£7). Price check: Papadom 40p, CTM £4.90, Pullao Rice £1. Open 4-11.30p.m. Home delivery service. Branch: Raja, 57 Old Sneddon Street, Paisley.

Hamilton

BOMBAY COTTAGE   NEW ENTRANT

4 Lower Auchingramont Road, Hamilton   © 01698 286957

'Converted warehouse, spacious. Fresh Papadoms, generous portions of good-quality chicken and meat,' T.E..

Johnstone

ASHOKA

3 Rankine Street, Johnstone   © 01505 322430

Same menu as at the Glasgow branches. Set meals are good value for money. Branches: Ashoka, Glasgow; Ashoka Ashton Lane, Glasgow; Ashoka West End, Glasgow.

SHIMLA PINKS

4 William Street, off Houston Square,
Johnstone   © 0105 22697

Modern restaurant. Polished floors, tubular stainless steel chairs arranged round black tables. Branches: East Indian Company and Varsity Blues, Stirling, Central; Killermont Polo Club, Glasgow; Shimla Pinks, Birmingham, B15, West Midlands.

Kilwinning

17TH-21ST LANCERS

3 Oswenad Road, Kilwinning   © 01294 557244

'Our favourites are Lancers' assorted Pakora, Lamb Jaipuri, Karahi Lamb Tikka Bhuna and Shahi Korma. Decor is styled as a regimental mess,' C.A. 'Chicken Tikka was delightful. Korma came in a silver dish, sprinkled with almonds; creamy and rich consistency,' J.D.

Largs

KOH I NOOR

84 Gallowgate Street, Largs   ✆ 01475 686051

This restaurant is situated on the shorefront and has a good view. 'Varied menu, good-sized quantities, quality of meal very good,' w.w.

Paisley

KOH I NOOR   ©

40 New Sneddon Street, Paisley   ✆ 0141 889 7909

Specialities include Nentara, Lyallpuri and Masala Karahi. Owner is A. Ghafur. Open 5p.m.-midnight.

TANDOORI KNIGHT   ©

14 Moss Street, Paisley   ✆ 0141 887 7693

Seats 90 diners. Owner is Gurmakh Sing Purewall. Open noon-midnight.

Peebles

PRINCE OF INDIA

86 High Street, Peebles   ✆ 01721 724455

'A wide-ranging menu including Nentara and a superb green herb chicken. The presentation of the food matches the setting, which is classy and tastefully Asian. Mohamed Khan is the owner. Overall a restaurant which is worth travelling to in the expectation of a very good meal,' R.B.

©	Curry Club discount (see p. 607)	☕	Unlicensed
√	Vegetarian	▦	Home delivery
BYO	Bring your own alcohol		service available

Prestwick

TAJ   ©

141 Main Street, Prestwick   ✆ **01292 77318**

Seats a massive 150 diners. Owner is Rabinder Singh. Open noon-2p.m., 5p.m.-12.15a.m.

Renfrew

CAFE INDIA

43 Hairst Street, Renfrew   ✆ **0141 885 1066**

Kichori, Samosas and Puri for starters. Masaledar, Nentara, Garam Masala curries for main course along with other popular favourites.

RAJPUT BALTI AND TANDOORI
NEW ENTRANT   ⊞ ©

9 High Street, Renfrew   ✆ **0141 885 0026**

Opened in 1996 by Jameel Tahir Mohammed. He runs a VIP Privilege Card promotion, which entitles the cardholder and guests to 15% off the à la carte menu. Sounds good value. Price check: Papadom 50p, CTM £6.95, Pullao Rice £1.50. Set menu £4.95-£6.95. Minimum charge £10. Open noon-12.30a.m. Home delivery service. Branch: Asman, 22 Bath Street, City Centre, Glasgow.

Saltcoats

AKOSKA PALACE

66 Hamilton Street, Saltcoats   ✆ **01294 466713**

'Special Assorted Ralwa - chicken and lamb tikka with bhuna sauce and a sea of prawns, peppers and mince as well. Gave it the thumbs up,' c.w.

Tayside
Auchterarder

SHERAY PUNJAB   NEW ENTRANT   ▦ ©

97 High Street, Auchterarder   ✆ **01764 664277**

A small restaurant with just 28 seats – so book your table on a Friday! All the usual dishes including some interesting extras, Egyptian Chicken Kebab and Shish Kebab Turkish. Proprietor, Paul Chima, also owns Mr Jingh's in Broughty Ferry. House special is Paneer Tikka (£8.95). Price check: Papadom 75p, CTM £5.95, Pullao Rice £1.50. Minimum charge £10. Open 5-11.30p.m., till midnight Friday and Saturday. Home delivery service on orders over £40 – seems a bit steep!

Broughty Ferry

GULISTAN HOUSE   ©

Queen Street Halls, Broughty Ferry   ✆ **01382 738844**

'Impressive decor. Some meals excellent. Tandoori dishes are normally very good,' F.C. Owner is M.A. Mohammed. Open 5p.m.-midnight.

Dundee

CHAAND   ©

104 Dura Street, Dundee   ✆ **01384 456786**

Good curry house food on the menu at owner M.A. Kessar's Chaand. Open 5p.m.-midnight.

Perth

SHALIMAR

56 Atholl Street, Perth   ✆ **01738 634204**

The Shalimar first opened way back in 1983, but its current owner, Bal Krishan, took over the restaurant in 1996. 'The best I have found in years!' N.C. Price check: Papadom 75p, CTM £6.95, Pullao Rice £1.50. Minimum charge £12.

WALES

As with England, the Guide runs alphabetically in town and county order. We retain the former counties which provide a convenient geographical division of Wales.

Clwyd

Colwyn Bay

BENGAL PALACE 　　　　　　　　　　　　　　　　　©

The Clock House, 55-57 Abergele Road,
Colwyn Bay 　　　　　　　　　　　　　ℂ **01492 531683**

Manager is A.M. Khan. The seating in this large, air-conditioned restaurant is divided between two rooms, seating 85 in one and 40 in the other. Price check: Papadom 50p, CTM £5.50, Pullao Rice £1.60. Open noon-2.30p.m. and 6-11.15p.m.

Deeside

AMANTOLA INTERNATIONAL

Welsh Road, Sealand, Deeside 　　　　　ℂ **01244 811383**

'Nothing impressive from outside. Huge inside, large lounge bar. Service was very helpful throughout. Huge menu, including Chinese selections. Hot Papadoms (50p and 60p) with selection of chutneys. Lamb Bhuna (£4.95), Vegetable Mossala (sic) (£4.85) with a good portion of rice. Excellent, enjoyable, good value,' J.G.

BALTI NIGHTS 　　NEW ENTRANT

286a High Street, Connahs Quay, Deeside 　ℂ **01244 830969**

'Very polite staff. Chicken Tikka (£2.50), Chicken Tikka Jalfrezi (£5.25), Chicken Bhuna (£4.50), large Peshwari Nan (£1.40), enough for three. Very reasonable meal,' D.V.-W.

BENGAL DYNASTY BEST IN WALES TOP 100   ©

106 Chester Road East, Shotton, Deeside ℰ 01244 830455

Opened in 1991 by Mohammed Monchab Ali, with Rico managing
front of house. Serves northern Indian and Bangladeshi cuisine in luxurious surroundings. The restaurant seats 92 with an additional lounge
area seating 40. 'Immense size of the restaurant, huge. Politely greeted
and guided to bar. Chicken Chat (£2.90) excellent, served with salad
and Puri. Meat Samosa (£2.50) crisp, served on a bed of salad, not
dripping with fat. Chilli Chicken (£5.95), Meat Dansak (£5.25),
Bombay Potato (£2.05), Pillaw Rice (£1.80) and Peshwari Nan (£2.20)
all cooked without fault. Can see why this restaurant features so highly in the Guide,' M.W. 'Outstanding,' W.A.J. Price check: Papadom 60p,
CTM £6.25, Pullao Rice £1.95. Set menu £4.50–£6.95. Open noon-
2.30p.m. and 5.30–11p.m. Recipient, with its branch, of our BEST IN
WALES AWARD for a second time. Branch: Bengal Dynasty, Llandudno, Gwynedd.

Holywell

DILSHAD NEW ENTRANT   BYO

1 Whitford Street, Holywell   ℰ 01352 712022

'Menu, lots of choice. Twelve starters, seven breads, fourteen house
specials. Balti, Tandoori and all the usual curries. Good quantities,
never disappointed. Restaurant can be cold. Unlicensed, so BYO,' W.J.

Llangollen

SIMLA

4-5 Victoria Square, Llangollen   ℰ 01978 860610

'Menu is daunting and wide-ranging. The restaurant was very clean
and efficient, tastefully decorated. Staff were clean, smart, smiling
and attentive. Tandoori Chicken Biryani, with egg white laced over
the presentation, plus Vegetable Bhoona, Tarka Dal, Chicken Tikka,
Nan bread and chilli chutney. Quantities were more than enough

for us. A superb evening,' D.M.D. Open noon-2.30p.m. and 6p.m.-midnight.

SYLHET

36 Regent Street, Llangollen   © **01978 861877**

'Shami Kebab fine, Chicken Madras rubbery! Mushroom Bhaji side dish OK, rice was great. Caught them as the pub opposite was kicking out, not the place for a quiet meal,' R.K.

Wrexham

CHIRK TANDOORI   NEW ENTRANT

1-2 Station Avenue, Chirk, Wrexham   © **01691 772499**

Sunday buffet £5.95. Kulchi Lamb for four persons, £35 (takeaway), 24 hours' notice required, includes two Nans and two Special Fried Rice with salad. Price check: Papadom 50p, CTM £5.95, Pullao Rice £1.80. Minimum charge £8. Open 6-11.30p.m.

Dyfed

Aberystwyth

ROYAL PIER TANDOORI

The Pier, Marine Terrace, Aberystwyth   © **01970 624888**

'Something of a novelty, situated on the end of the pier. Served by a helpful waiter. Mixed Tikka prepared at my request without the usual salad, just tomatoes, cheerfully served. Lamb Tikka Masala spiced up for me,' J.L.

©	Curry Club discount (see p. 607)	☕	Unlicensed
√	Vegetarian	⊞	Home delivery
BYO	Bring your own alcohol		service available

Cardigan

ABDUL'S TANDOORI CUISINE NEW ENTRANT

---

2 Royal Oak, Quay Street, Cardigan   ✆ 01239 621416

'This restaurant is small, best described as "cosy", but the choice in the menu is extensive. The decor is clean and pleasant and the staff friendly and helpful. We have eaten here on a number of occasions and both the food and service have been consistently of a high standard. The quantities are not large but sufficient, we have never left still hungry,' T.V. Price check: Papadom 30p, CTM £4.80, Pullao Rice £1.20. Open 5p.m.-midnight.

Carmarthen

TAJ BALTI NEW ENTRANT   ©

---

119 Priory Street, Carmarthen   ✆ 01267 221995

Opened in 1995 by Lias Miah. Check out the Moët and Chandon at £23 - great value! 'Complimentary Masala and Garlic Papadom and dips. Chicken Jalfrezi £5.25, Lamb Badam Pasanda £5.50, Pulao Rice and Garlic Nan, excellent in every aspect. Highly recommended,' J.F. Price check: Papadom 40p, CTM £5.50, Pullao Rice £1.50. Set menu £7.95. Minimum charge £6. Sunday eat-as-much-as-you like buffet. Open 6p.m.-midnight.

Haverfordwest

TAJ MAHAL

---

2 Milford Road, Haverfordwest   ✆ 01437 763610

'Started with Nargis Khabab (sic) (£2.50), described by the waiter as a scotch egg with sauce, an enjoyable change. Lamb Tikka Masala with Pulau Rice (£6.25), Keema Nan (£1.30) and Mushroom Bhajee (£1.50), all were well prepared and very tasty. Waiter engaged on phone,' J.L.

Lampeter

SHAPLA   ©

8 College Street, Lampeter   ✆ 01570 422076

'Fairly standard menu, same stock pot curries,' J.L.

Llanelli

BENGAL LANCER   NEW ENTRANT   ©

43 Murray Street, Llanelli   ✆ 01554 749199

Opened by Mr Ahmed Ali in 1996. Restaurant seats 80 diners and
serves Bangladeshi cuisine. Price check: Papadom 40p, CTM £5, Pullao
Rice £1.40. Set menu £12. Minimum charge £12.15. Service charge 10%.
Open 6p.m.-midnight. Branch: Anarkali, Swansea, Glamorgan.

SHEESH MAHAL

53 Stepney Street, Llanelli   ✆ 01554 773773

'Food and service gets better every visit,' D.V.-W.

Glamorgan

Barry

MODERN TANDOORI TAKEAWAY   ©

290 Holton Road, Barry   ✆ 01446 746787

Mr A. Akbar opened his takeaway in 1982. Try the Staff Special - three
courses at £15.95 for two. Price check: Papadom 30p, CTM £3.95,
Pullao Rice £1.10. Minimum charge £5. Open 5-11.30p.m., till 1.30a.m.
Friday and Saturday.

ROYAL BALTI TAKEAWAY   NEW ENTRANT   ©

44 Vere Street, Barry	© **01446 421366**

Owned by Mr R.B. Miah. Price check: Papadom 30p, CTM £4, Pullao
Rice £1.20. Open 5p.m.-midnight.

SHAHI NOOR

87 High Street, Barry	© **01446 735706**

Under the heading of seafood dishes there are two types of prawn
curry, either fresh or frozen, the frozen being cheaper than the fresh.
Can you tell the difference? 'Massive portions. Excellent Onion Bhajee,
really big. Chicken Biryani (sic) lacked taste. Spinach and Chicken Balti
had a good flavour but there was too much spinach which soaked up
all the sauce. Served a plain Nan instead of Keema but was politely
replaced. Very friendly service,' H.S. 'Now doing Bangladeshi dishes.
Shangorana Massalla (sic), my friend said it was the best curry he'd
ever had! Kashmiri Balti - delicious. Food, large chunks of succulent
breast meat at no extra charge and generous portions - reigns supreme.
Wish they'd play Indian music and not pop!' H.S. Price check: Papadom
45p, CTM £5.45, Pullao Rice £1.70. Minimum charge £7. Open noon-
2.30p.m. and 5.30p.m.-12.30a.m., till 1a.m. Friday and Saturday.

Cardiff

BALTI EMPEROR   NEW ENTRANT

157 Albany Road, Roath, Cardiff	© **01222 485757**

'This was our second visit. Complimentary Papadoms and four different chutneys. Had Pakora and an excellent, generous portion of Aloo
Chat, both at £1.95. Beers quite expensive. All our main course dishes
had their own individual taste. Balti Katchori Dansak was an unusual
new dish for us, tasty and spicy. Bhindi Balti made with young okra in
a good sauce. Tarka Dal had just the right consistency with a garnish
of garlic. Fresh and hot Chapatis at 75p. Decor bright and cheerful
with fish tanks. Service attentive,' H. and M.K.

STAR OF WALES

438 Cowbridge Road East, Canton, Cardiff ✆ 01222 383222

This restaurant is an old one, first opened way back in the 1960s. Its present owner, Kadir Miah, took over the establishment in 1987. 'Place was tatty and cold. Nice and polite staff. Chiken Biryani was pleasant. Good average portions. Keema Nan especially delicious, light and fluffy,' H.S. Price check: Papadom 35p, CTM £5.75, Pullao Rice £1.45. Open 6p.m.-1a.m., till 2a.m. Friday and Saturday.

Merthyr Tydfil

NEW BALTI PALACE   ⊞ ©

1 Morlais Building, High Street,
Merthyr Tydfil   ✆ 01685 388344

Formerly Star of India. Owned by Abdul Karim. House specials include Shahi Chicken Tikka Masala (£4.75). Good prices all round. Free Papadoms and Mint Sauce with takeaway orders over £7. Price check: Papadom 35p, CTM £4.45, Pullao Rice £1.50. Minimum charge £7. Open noon-2p.m. and 6p.m.-1a.m. Home delivery service.

Penarth

TROPICAL TANDOORI

14 Glebe Street, Penarth   ✆ 01222 707555

'A popular takeaway establishment with a friendly cashier. Chicken Biryani very tasty and not at all greasy. Chicken and Spinach Balti, too hot but tasty. Keema Nans were fine with enough meat. Portions were adequate,' H.S. A takeaway establishment. Opened in 1986 and well-known for serving up reliable curries and accompaniments at reasonable prices. Open 5p.m.-midnight.

Swansea

ANARKALI NEW ENTRANT

80 St Helen's Road, Swansea   © 01792 650549

When you open this menu you will find a range of traditional dishes from India, Bangladesh and Pakistan. Price check: Papadom 40p, CTM £4.95, Pullao Rice £1.40. Open noon-2.30p.m. and 5.30p.m.-midnight, till 2a.m. Friday and Saturday, noon-5.30p.m. (buffet) and 6p.m.-midnight Sunday. Branch: Bengal Lancer, Llanelli, Dyfed.

GOWERTON TANDOORI NEW ENTRANT   ▦

93 Sterry Road, Gowerton, Swansea   © 01792 875253

Takeaway only. Price check: Papadom 30p, CTM £4.20, Pullao Rice £1.10. Minimum charge £10. Open 5.30p.m.-midnight. No credit cards. Home delivery service.

INDIAN COTTAGE

69 Herbert Street, Pontardawe, Swansea   © 01792 830208

Opened in 1985 by Abdul Razzak who is also the head chef. Serves northern Indian and Bangladeshi curries - Karahi Kebab (£5.35) and Chicken Badam Passanda (£5.85) - in this well-established 64-seat restaurant. Price check: Papadom 30p, CTM £5.20, Pullao Rice £1.35. Minimum charge £4.99. Open 5.30p.m.-midnight. Branch: Gateway to Goa, St Helen's Road, Swansea.

KILLAY TANDOORI   ©

436 Gower Road, Killay, Swansea   © 01792 297059

Taken over by Abdul Kasem in 1996. Thalis are house specials at £7, £12 and £18. Price check: Papadom 40p, CTM £5.50, Pullao Rice £1.35. Minimum charge £6. Open noon-2.30p.m. and 5.30p.m.-midnight.

© Curry Club discount (see p. 607)	🍵 Unlicensed
√ Vegetarian	▦ Home delivery
BYO Bring your own alcohol	service available

MOGHUL BRASSERIE NEW ENTRANT   ©

81 St Helen's Road, Swansea   ✆ 01792 475131

Opened in 1989 by Mr S. Uddin, who is also the chef. Sunday buffet
£7 for adults, £4 for children - eat as much as you like from the selection of lamb, chicken, prawn and tandoori delicacies and three different vegetable dishes plus bread and rice. Price check: Papadom 40p,
CTM £5, Pillau Rice £1.30. Set menu - six choices from A to E, ranging in price from £14-£22. Open noon-2p.m. and 5.30p.m.-midnight,
till 2a.m. Friday and Saturday.

NAWAB NEW ENTRANT   ©

12 Christina Street, Swansea   ✆ 01792 470770

Opened in 1984 by Mr M.T. Miah, aided by Mr Abedean who is the
manager. Price check: Papadom 30p, CTM £5.95, Pullao Rice £1.20.
Minimum charge £7.50. Open from 5.30p.m.

LAL QUILA NEW ENTRANT

480 Mumbles Road, Mumbles, Swansea   ✆ 01792 363520

Formerly Ocean View. 'Completely refurbished, now has very attractive
decor, waiters wear smart uniforms. Probably Swansea's most up-market restaurant. Everything is spotless with quick and friendly service. I
particularly like the Chicken Methi with lots of fresh fenugreek. Food
generally good, only weakness heavy, greasy Nans,' J.D.

MOONLIGHT NEW ENTRANT

590 Mumbles Road, Mumbles, Swansea   ✆ 01792 360313

'Generally the food is pretty good and well-flavoured, although the
sauces tend to be a bit oily. Very generous portions. Charcoal-flavoured
Chicken Tikkas served with lots of fried onions. Garry likes their
prawn dishes, although they taste rather too "fishy" for me. Have a fast
turnover of trainee waiters who sometimes seem confused! The boss
appears to be a woman - is this unusual? Crumpled tablecloths and carpets needs cleaning,' J.D.

RAJPUTANA

44 High Street, Gorseinon, Swansea   ✆ **01792 895883**

Seats 36 diners and serves Bangladeshi curries. Price check: Papadom 35p, CTM £4.20, Pullao Rice £1.30. Open 6p.m.-12.30a.m. Branch: Bilash, 19 Wind Street, Ammanford; Curry Villa, Port Talbot.

SEAVIEW TANDOORI

728 Mumbles Road, Mumbles, Swansea   ✆ **01792 361991**

'It has recently been redecorated, although the decor could not be described as elegant - I rather like the plants covered in flashing fairy lights. Cheap and cheerful - £5.95 to eat as much as you like. You can have a starter, main dish and rice and a Nan and a side dish. Then you can re-order main course dishes, but sharing of meals is not allowed. Portions are generous and we have never had the stamina to re-order. Popadoms and pickles cost extra. Spicing is not startling, but the food is good and I particularly like the Tandoori Chicken Tikkas. Even Garry, my husband, likes them and he is normally a chicken-hater. Service is quick and very friendly and the loos are clean but scruffy,' J.D.

Gwent

Bedwas

INDIAN COTTAGE   ⊞ ©

Bridge Cottage, The Square, Bedwas   ✆ **01222 860369**

Taken over by Mohammed Riaz Jan in April 1996. This cosy restaurant - foundations were laid around the time that Queen Elizabeth I came to the throne - seats just 28 diners and serves them Pakistani food. There is an interesting and detailed history of the building on the back of the menu. Price check: Papadom 40p, CTM £5.95, Pullao Rice £1.60. Open 6-11p.m., till midnight Friday and Saturday. Home delivery service charges: Bedwas and Trethomas 80p; Llanbradach, Caerphilly and Machen £1.20.

Cwmbran

KHAN

6 Commercial Street, Pontnewydd,
Cwmbran   ✆ 01633 867141

Siraj Khan started this takeaway-only establishment way back in 1984.
Eleven types of bread are listed under the heading of 'good compan-
ions'. Price check: Papadom 25p, CTM £4.90, Pullao Rice £1. Open
5.30p.m.-midnight, till 1a.m. Friday and Saturday. Home delivery service.

MAHRAJA BALTI   NEW ENTRANT

6 General Rees Square, Cwmbran   01633 483627

Owned by Mohammed Omar Sheik since 1992. Serves Pakistani cuisine. Price check: Papadom (Indian Crispy) 40p, CTM £6.10, Pullao
Rice £1.90. Minimum charge £7. Open noon-2.30p.m. and 6p.m.-
1.30a.m, Friday and Saturday noon-2.30a.m. Home delivery service on
orders over £8 and ordered before midnight.

Gwynedd

Bangor

MAHABHARAT

5-7 High Street, Bangor   ✆ 01248 351337

The restaurant originally opened in 1968. Mr Sholayman took over the
ownership in 1990. 'Spacious and comfortable restaurant. Standard
curry house menu. Service very efficient except for the late arrival of
the mint sauce which was supposed to accompany the starter. Portions
very generous and food of a high standard,' I.M. Free Papadoms and
dips with every takeaway order. Price check: Papadom 40p, CTM
£6.50, Pullao Rice £1.45. Minimum charge £9.

Caernarfon

GANDHI

11 Palace Street, Caernarfon   ✆ 01286 676797

'Standard menu with above-average food and service. King Prawn Butterfly followed by Lamb Tikka Masala, Pilau Rice and Keema Nan. Bombay Potato, particularly spicy - excellent. A very pleasing meal all round, good portions,' J.L. Open noon-2p.m. and 5.30-11p.m., Sunday 5.30-11p.m.

Llandudno

BENGAL DYNASTY BEST IN WALES TOP 100   ©

1 North Parade, Llandudno   ✆ 01492 878445

Llandudno is a really fabulous seaside town with gorgeous Georgian buildings running in an arch along the waterfront. Lewis Carroll wrote *Alice in Wonderland* in this seaside resort. The Bengal Dynasty is situated in one of these fine buildings. 'King Prawn Butterfly (£3.95) followed by my usual main courses. A very accomplished meal. Keema Nan (£1.90) was the highlight together with a home-made Kulfi (£1.95). Gets my vote,' J.L. 'Service was welcoming, prompt and polite. Papadoms and chutneys were fresh and crisp. Main meals were large, everything was hot and well presented. An enjoyable experience, but not outstanding,' s.k. 'Menu was wide and varied. Papadoms and chutneys excellent. Raita exceptional. All meals were served piping hot with hot plates and the portions were satisfying. Waiters were very accommodating in making changes to dishes for our individual tastes. Smart, clean and tasteful surroundings. Highly recommended,' N.C. Open noon-2.30p.m. and 5.30-11p.m. Recipient, with its branch, of our BEST IN WALES AWARD for the second time. Branch: Bengal Dynasty, Deeside, Clwyd.

©	Curry Club discount (see p. 607)	🍵	Unlicensed
√	Vegetarian	🎴	Home delivery
BYO	Bring your own alcohol		service available

Llangefni

MOONLIGHT   ©

40 High Street, Llangefni   ✆ **01248 722595**

Emdadur Rahman, the owner-manager, is offering authentic
Bangladeshi and northern Indian dishes using fresh ingredients and
spices. Tables are divided between eating in the main restaurant and
private booths for more intimate dining. Price check: Papadom 50p,
CTM £5.95, Pullao Rice £1.60. Open noon-2p.m. and 5.30-11.30p.m.
Takeaway available until midnight.

Monmouth

MISBAH

9 Priory Street, Monmouth   ✆ **01600 714940**

Proprietor, D. Miah, opened his 32-seater restaurant in 1990. A good
list of Baltis served with Nan bread ranging from King Prawn Balti at
£9.95 to Vegetable Balti at £5.50. Special four-course Sunday lunch
£6.95. Price check: Papadom 45p, CTM £6.50, Pullao Rice £1.75. Set
menu £4.50. Minimum charge £9.95. Open noon-2p.m. and 6-11p.m.

Newport

⊞

BILASH NEW ENTRANT   ©

232 Corporation Road, Newport   ✆ **01633 253692**

Taken over in 1995 by Yakub Ali, who also manages front of house,
Bilash promises unique formula curries. Price check: Papadom 50p,
CTM £5.70, Pullao Rice £2.15. Minimum charge £6.50. Open 6p.m.-
1a.m., till 2a.m. Friday and Saturday. Home delivery service for the
Newport area only on orders over £12. Branch: Jasmin Tandoori, 125
Hednesford Road, Heath Hayes; Taj Mahal Takeaway, Unit A, Varteg
Road, Varteg.

GRAND BALTI HOUSE NEW ENTRANT

84 Commercial Street, Newport   © 01633 255588

Price check: Papadom 40p, CTM £7.45, Pullao Rice £2.25. Minimum charge £15. Open 6p.m.-1a.m.

INDIAN COTTAGE TAKEAWAY NEW ENTRANT   ⊞ ©

18 Malpas Road, Newport   © 01633 821196

Managed by D. Ramzan who assures us that his dishes are clearly distinguishable from the other restaurants because of their distinctive features. House special is Chilli Garlic Chicken Massalah (£7.20). Price check: Papadom 40p, CTM £5.30, Pullao Rice £1.70. Set menu £8.50. Open 5p.m.-midnight, till 1a.m. Friday and Saturday. Home delivery service on orders over £10 in Newport and £12 in Cwmbran.

Risca

BOMBAY EXPRESS TAKEAWAY NEW ENTRANT

14 Tredegar Street, Risca   © 01633 601033

Opened in 1996 by Mohammed Yamin, who also is the head chef. Price check: Papadom 30p, CTM £4.80, Pullao Rice £1.60. Open 5.30-11.30p.m., Friday and Saturday 5p.m.-midnight.

Powys
Builth Wells

BALTI HOUSE NEW ENTRANT

11 Market Street, Builth Wells   © 01982 551131

'Pleasantly furnished and the staff most obliging and friendly. Chefs working can be viewed from the dining area. Ate there three times while on holiday and each meal was better than the last,' J.P.

Newtown

BALTI HOUSE NEW ENTRANT

2 Wesley Street, Newtown   ✆ **01686 622186**

'Exterior of building does not encourage you to enter, though once inside all is of a high standard. Lamb Madras with Pilau Rice and Garlic Nan. Quantities were very good as was the presentation. My only gripe is that the pieces of meat are so large that you have to put your bread down while you cut the meat,' J.B. Complaints like that we can handle!

List of Contributors

This Guide is possible thanks to the many Curry Club members, and others, who have sent in reports on restaurants. Especial thanks to the following regular, prolific and reliable reporters (apologies for any errors, duplications, omissions, and for the tiny print necessitated by space considerations).

A: Martin Abbott, Gloucs; Colin Adam, Kilwinning; Ray Adams, Kimberley; Meena Ahamed, London; Paul Allen, Chatham; Tony and Lesley Allen, Rugby; M.F. Alsan, Rugby; G. Amos, Wirral; Capt R. Ancliffe, BFPO 12; Karen Andras, Nottingham; Lisa Appadurai, Benfleet; Robin Arnott, Stafford; Mrs M. Asher, Woodford Green; Dave Ashton, Warrington; Jo Ashton, Elland; Allan Ashworth, York; Berry Ashworth, Compton Bassett; Michelle Aspinal, Chester; Darius Astell, Southampton; Rachael Atkinson, Cheshire; Simon Atkinson, N5; Y. Atkinson, IOM; Claire Austin, Stoke; Arman Aziz, N4.

B: John Baker, Loughton; Kim Baker, Hatfield; Mr and Mrs M.L. Banks, Enfield; Keith Bardwell, Hertford; Ian Barlex, Ilford; Trevor Barnard, Gravesend; Christopher Barnes, Ashton; Derek Barnett, Colchester; Tony Barrel, Hounslow; Joanne Bastock, Saltash; Mike Bates, Radcliffe; Shirley Bayley, Worthing; Karin and Angela, Rugby; Joyce Bearpark, Murcia Spain; Derick Behrens, Bucks; Matt Bell, Derbys; P. Bell, Carlisle; Sam Bell, Coventry; Becky Benson, Worcs; John Bentley, Northampton; Ron Bergin, Gerrards Cross; Ian Berry, Goole; Kenneth Beswick, Lincoln; D.J. Betts, Bonhill; Brian and Anne Biffin, Fleet; B.H. Birch, Hyde, Jim Birkumshaw, Derbys; James Birtles, Manchester; Chris Blackmore, Bristol; David Bolton, Lichfield; Mrs C. Bone, Norfolk; A. Boughton, SE27; L. Le Bouochon, Jersey; Robert Box, Knottingley; Alan Boxall, Burwash; Sean Boxall, Andover; F. Boyd, Stranraer; Iain Boyd, Wealdstone; Roderick Braggins, Peebles; Amanda Bramwell, Sheffield; Dave Bridge, Wallasey; Sandra Brighton, Nelson; Steve Broadfoot, Anfield; John and Susan Brockington, Sutton Coldfield; Robert Brook, London; David Brown, Leeds; I.A. Brown, Fernhurst; Mark Brown, Scunthorpe; Steve Brown, Twickenham; D.A. Bryan, York; R.C. Bryant, Witney; Robert Bruce, Thornaby; Heather Buchanan, Inverness; Dr T.M. Buckenham, SW11; Mrs J. Buffey, Sutton Coldfield; L.G. Burgess, Berkhamsted; A. Burton, Weston-super-Mare.

C: D. Cadby, Swindon; Barry Caldwell, Chesterfield; Stan Calland, Kingsley; Hugh Callaway, Cleethorpes; Duncan Cameron, Fordoun; Frank Cameron, Dundee; H.S. Cameron, Wirral; Alex Campbell, Hartley Wintney; Mrs E. Campbell, Harrogate; N. Campbell, Edinburgh; Josephine Capps, Romford; L. Carroll, Huddersfield; Peter Cash, Liverpool; T.M. Chandler, Farnborough;

John Chapman, Leics; Paul Chapman, Leighton Buzzard; Desmond Carr, N8; J. Carr, Birkenhead; D.L. Carter, Huntingdon; Mrs M. Carter, Colchester; Madeline Castro, Bury St Edmunds; Dr W.F. Cavenagh, Norfolk; Neil Chantrell, Warrington; Hilary Chapchal, Fetcham; Rajender Chatwal, Bicester; Paul Chester, Cuffley; Sqn Ldr P.F. Christopher, Ferndown; Alexis Ciusczak, Capistrano Beach, CA; Peter Clyne, SW11; V.A. Coak, Penzance; C.H. Coleman, Sussex; Billy Collins, Wirral; Mrs J. Collins, Portsmouth; C.J. Comer, Basingstoke; Rhys Compton, Cheltenham; A. Conroy, Durham; Joseph Coohil, Oxford; Neil Cook, Royston; Kim Cooper, Basildon; D.W. Cope, Whitchurch; Dr J.C. Coppola, Woodstock; Will Coppola, Oxford; Nigel Cornwell, Orpington; John Costa, Tunbridge Wells; M.J. Cotterill, Bristol; Steve Cowling, Shropshire; Julie Cozens, Oxon; Dr A.M. Croft, Cornwall; Roderick Cromar, Buckie; C. Cross, Poole; Yasmin Cross, Huddersfield; Major & Mrs F.J.B. Crosse, Salisbury; Robert Crossley, Huddersfield; Frank and Elizabeth Crozier, Redruth; R. Cuthbertson, Southampton.

D: S. Daglish, Scarborough; P. Dalton, Wirral; Jan Daniel, Felpham; Mr & Mrs P.E. Dannat, Eastleigh; Martin Daubney, Hitchin; Gary Davey, W4; Alasdair Davidson, Heswall; Adrian Davies, NW3; Gwyn Davies, Wirral; Mrs J.C. Davies, Leeds; Josephine Davies, Swansea; Paul Davies, Chiddingfold; Mrs G. Davies-Goff, Marlow; Colin Davis, Tatsfield; Ian Dawson, Mirfield; D.M. Day, Preston; Michael Day, West Bromwich; Peter Deane, Bath; David Dee, Ruislip; Elizabeth Defty, Co. Durham; R. Dent, Bishop Auckland; Les Denton, Barnsley; Richard Develyn, St Leonards; Nigel Deville, Uttoxeter; Ken Dewsbury, Somerset; Richard Diamond, Romsey; R.C. Dilnot, Broadstairs; Graham Divers, Glasgow; James Dobson, Burscough; S. Dolden, Rochester; R. Dolley, W11; Clive Doody, Surrey; Keith Dorey, Barnet; Neil Downey, Worthing; Sarah Dowsett, Swindon; Anna Driscoll, Cape Province; Mrs J. Driscoll, BFPO; Diane Duame, Wicklow; Eric Duhig, Hornchurch; Sheila Dunbar, Pinner; James Duncan, West Kilbride; Mark Dunn, London E18; Robin Durant, Brighton; Martin Durrant, Chester.

E: A. Edden-Jones, Bristol; Bruce Edwards, Norwich; Dave Edwards, Rugeley; C.M. Eeley, Witney; Rod Eglin, Whitehaven; Wendy Elkington; P.T. Ellis, W'rtn; Mrs G. Elston, Woodley; Anthony Emmerton, Chorley; Mark Evans, Caersws; Brian Exford, Derbys.

F: Gary Fairbrother, Crosby; Hazel Fairley, Guildford; Chris Farrington, Cherry Hinton; John Fearson, Bucks; Denis Feeney, Glasgow; Kevin Fenner, Rothley; Stephen Field, Norton; Duncan Finley, Glasgow; Maureen Fisher, Woodford Green; Bernard Fison, Holmrook; John Fitzgerald, Great Missenden; Merly Flashman, TN12; Colin and Toni Fleet, Dorset; Dr Cornel Fleming, N6; K.D. Flint, Kempsey; Fiona Floyd, Truro; Stephen & Elizabeth Foden, Lynton; Chris Fogarty, Enfield; Gareth Foley, Porthcawl; Neil Foley, Essex; I. Folkard-Evans, Manchester; S.R. Tracy Forster, Beds; Rod Fouracres, Glos.; Rosemary Fowler, Midhurst; John W. Fox, Doncaster; Linda Foye, Barry; Theresa Frey, Fareham; Chris Frid, North Shields; Steve Frost, Kingston; Alan Furniss, Bucks; Mrs M.A.J. Fyall, Dyfed.

G: Stephen Gaines, Middlesex; M.J. Gainsford, Burbage; Leo Gajsler, Geneva; Mrs F.E. Gaunt, Stonehouse; Brian George, Wolverton; C.M. Gerry, Cyprus; G. Gibb, SE21; Robert Giddings, Poole; Andrew Gillies, Edinburgh; A.V. Glanville, Windsor; Ms D. Glass, Liverpool; A. Glenford, Lincoln; Nick Goddard, Stevenage; Andrew Godfrey, Seer Green; Matthew Goldsmith, Burgess Hill; John Goleczka, Bristol; Michael Goodband, Perhore; Bryn Gooding, Corfu; Dr G. Gordon, Kidlington; Ian Gosden, Woking; Bill Gosland, Camberley; David Gramagan, Formby; D.C. Grant, Enfield; Kathryn Grass, Wigan; Alan Gray, Erskine; D.R. Gray, SW11; A. Greaves, Chesterfield; Andrew Greaves, Derbyshire; Rachel Greaves, Tavistock; Denise Gregory, Nottinghamshire; Jonathan Green, Cathays, Michael Green, Leicester; Nigel Green, Orpington; Richard Green, Gerrards Cross; Sheila Green, Barrow; A. Gregor, Boston; Frank Gregori, NW10; Andrew Grendale, Ingatestone; A. Griffiths, Milton Keynes; M. Griffiths, Northampton; Dave Groves, Walsall; Louis Gunn, Chelmsford.

H: Karen Haley, Telford; John Hall, Cullercoats; Andrew Halling, Leigh; Stephen Hames, Bewdley; Alan Hamilton, Wakefield; Tina Hammond, Ipswich; Geoff & Janet Hampshire-Thomas, Kirkland; Neil Hancock, Derby; Ray Hancock, Chester; Dorothy Hankin, Fordingbridge; Sharon Hanson, Derby; Glynn Harby, Knaresborough; Martyn Harding, Powys; Roger Hargreaves, Stoke; J. Harman, Brentwood; Dawn Harris, Dubley; Paul Harris, BFPO; David Harrison, Dursley; Patrick Harrison, Cambridge; David Harvey, SE24; S. Harwood, Lewes; John K. Hattam, York; John Haynes, Saffron Walden; D.I. Hazelgrove, West Byfleet; M. Hearle, Tunbridge Wells; Kevin Hearn, Newcastle; Bernice Heath, Nottingham; Andy Hemingway, Leeds; Terry Herbat, Barnsley; Georgina Herridge, W9; J. & J. Hetherington, Preston; Victoria Heywood, Burton; Roger Hickman, N1; Pat & Paul Hickson, Chorley; Janet Higgins, Blackburn; Mrs S. Higgins, Blackburn; Mrs B. Higgs Cotty; Alec Hill, Wigan; Carolyn Hill, Nottingham; Barry Hills, Surrey; Bharti Hindocha, Richmond; Mrs M.J. Hirst, Kent; S.C. Hodgon; Daniel Hodson, Abingdon; Peter Hoes, Bingley; P. Hogkinson, Sheffield; Duncan Holloway, Windsor; Kevin Hooper, St Austell; Linda Horan, Wirral; Peter Hornfleck, Farnborough; Jerry Horwood, Guildford; Neil Houldsworth, Keighley; P. Howard, Hornchurch; Mrs J Howarth, Oldham; Kathy Howe, Carlisle; Simon Howell, Gillingham; Bruce Howerd, Tongham; Jan Hudson, Hemel Hempstead; Tom Hudson, Jarrow; Chris Hughes, Wraysbury; Paul Hulley, Stockport; S.P. Hulley, Reddish; Paul Hunt, Essex; Roger Hunt, Sidmouth; Vince Hunt, Manchester; Penny Hunter, Brighton; Sheila Hunter, Dundee; Dr M. Hutchinson, Gwynedd; Mrs V. Hyland, Manchester.

I: D.M. Ibbotson, Sheffield; Nick & Mandy Idle, Ossett; Ken Ingram, Leeds; G. Innocent, Dawlish; Mrs G. Irving, Redditch; Robert Izzo, Horsham.

J: Dr A.G. James, Wigan; O. Jarrett, Norwich; Sue Jayasekara, Essex; Sally Jeffries, Heathfield; L. Jiggins, Dagenham; G. John, Wirral; Maxine & Andrew Johnson, Leiden; Peter Johnson, Droitwich; Paul Jolliffe, Clyst Hydon; C.M.L. Jones, St Albans; Gareth Jones, Tonypandy; Kate Jones, Leiden; R.W. Jones,

N9; Shirley Jones, SE13; W.A. Jones, Flints; Wendy Jones, Clwyd; Michael Lloyd Jones, Cardiff; Esther Juby, Norwich.

K: A.D. Kantes, Northants; Chris Keardey, Southampton; Anthony Kearns, Stafford; Russ Kelly, Liverpool; Prof. and Mrs Kemp, Royston; David Kerray, Akrotiri; John Kettle, Dover; J.S. Kettle, Banbury; Stephen Kiely, N16; David King, Biggleswade; Alyson Kingham, Oldham; Peter Kitney, Banbury; J. & P. Klusiatis, Reading; Drs Heather & Mark Knight, Oxford.

L: Caz Lack, Kent; Martin Lally, Chester; Alan Lathan, Chorley; Cass Lawson, Swindon; Jonathan Lazenby, Littlehampton; D.H. Lee, Waltham Abbey; Jackie Leek, Dartford; David Leslie, Aberdeen; A. Lewis, Sherborne; Margaret Ann Lewis, Ashford; R. Lewis, Rayleigh; Pat Lindsay, Hampshire; David Lloyd, Oswestry; Eleanor & Owen Lock, Geneva; J. Longman, Bodmin; John Loosemore, Orpington; D.A. Lord, Hove; Julia & Philip Lovell, Brighton; A.P. Lowe, Tolworth; Mr and Mrs D.N. Luckman, Horley; Jeremy Ludlow, Dorset; Mrs H. Lundy, Wallasey; Graeme Lutman, Herts; Tim Lynch, Romford.

Mac/Mc: David Mackay, Twickenham; David Mackenzie, Darlington; Lin Macmillan, Lincoln; Deb McCarthy, E6; Patrick McCloy, N8; Vanessa McCrow, Teddington; David McCulloch, NW11; Michael McDonald, Ellesmere Port; David McDowell, Telford; B.J. McKeown, Seaford; Ian McLean, Brighton; Dr and Mrs J. McLelland, Mid Calder; Alan & Jean McLucas, Solihull; Dr F.B. McManus, Lincolnshire; Alan McWilliam, Inverurie.

M: Chris Mabey, Swindon; Richard Manley, Wirral; Cherry Manners, Hatfield; E. Mansfield, Camberley; Clive Mantle; J.F. Marshall, Bedford; Geraldine Marson, Winsford; Colin Martin, Nuneaton; Derek Martin, Marlow; P.R. Martin, Southend; D.H. Marston, Southport; D.J. Mason, Cleveland; L.J. Mason, Leeds; John Maundrell, Tunbridge Wells; Gilian May, Bromley; Peter F. May, St Albans; Simon Mayo, Farnborough; Simon Meaton, Andover; John Medd, Nottingham; Tim Mee, Harrow; Sue & Alf Melor, Hanworth; Nigel Meredith, Huddersfield; H. Middleton, Coventry; Simon Mighall, St Neots; P.J.L. Mighell, Canterbury; Robert Miles, Hertfordshire; Catherine Millar, BFPO; D.R. Millichap, Horsham; B.W. Milligan; A.J. Millington, Woodford; Mr & Mrs P. Mills, Mold; Mary Mirfin, Leeds; Al Mitchell, Belfast; Jonathon Mitchell, Alton; F. Moan, Cuddington; Jon Molyneaux, Peterborough; Mrs S.E. Monk, Gisburn; A.V. Moody, Portsmouth; Christy Moore, London; D.M. Moreland, Willington; S. Morgan, Feltham; Ian Morris, Gwynedd; Peter Morwood, Wicklow; A. Moss, Colchester; Caroline Moss, Solihull; Mrs L. Muirhead, Glasgow; David Muncaster, Stoke; Andy Munro, Birmingham; Joan Munro, Leyburn; Annette Murray, Thornton Cleveleys; R.G. Murray, Carlisle; Drs Heather & Harry Mycook.

N: Simon Nash, Cheshire; Mrs P.G. Naylor, Salisbury; Hugh Neal, Kent; Jeff Neal, Bolton; A. Nelson-Smith, Swansea; Liam Nevens, Stockton; Tony Newman, Margate; Rebecca Newman, Hayes; Clive Newton, Northwich; P. & D. Nixon, Basildon; Mrs D.A. Nowakowa, Tiverton; Robert Nugent, SE31; Canon Peter Nunn, Gloucestershire; Jody Lynn Nye, Illinois.

O: Beverley Oakes, Essex; A.M. O'Brien, Worthing; Eamon O'Brien, Holland; Pauline O'Brien, London; D.C. O'Donnell, Wetherby; Elise O'Donnell, Wolverhampton; Mary O'Hanlon, Helensburgh; Sheila Openshaw, Hampshire; David O'Regan, Leeds; Jan Ostron, Felpham; Judith Owen, sw6; William & Sue Oxley, Southampton.

P: Trevor Pack, Rushden; R.H. Paczec, Newcastle; Graham Paine, Coventry; Keith Paine, Tilbury; G.J. Palmer, Gainsborough; R.S. Palmer, Norfolk; John M.F. Parker, North Yorks; Bill Parkes-Davies, Tunbridge Wells; Angela Parkinson, Clitheroe; M. Parsons, Fareham; Roy Parsons, Richmond; G.M. Patrick, London; Mrs P.A. Pearson, Bristol; Mrs G. Pedlow, Hitchin; J. Penn, Southampton; A.J.W. Perry, Bristol; Ian Perry, Essex; M.J. Perry, E17; Ian Pettigrew, Edinburgh; Christopher Phelps, Gloucester; Diane Phillips, Hyde; Steve Phillips, Wokingham; Colin Phipps, Scarborough; Sara Pickering, Northolt; Jack Pievsky, Pinner; Mike Plant, Essex; Susan Platt, Bury; D. Pool, SE2; K. Pool, Leyland; S.R. Poole, Runcorn; Tony Pope, Derbyshire; Steve Porter, Walsall; R.L. Power, Sutton Coldfield; Dave Prentice, Devon; Steve Prentice, Devon; Tim Preston, Barrow; Alison Preuss, Glencarse; Jeff Price, Bristol; J. Priest; Dr John Priestman, Huddersfield; D. Pulsford, Marford; Janet Purchon, Bradford; Steve Puttock, Chatham; Julie Pyne, County Down.

Q: Sheila Quince, E11.

R: Diane Radigan, Welling; Clive Ramsey, Edinburgh; K.J. Rayment, Hertford; R.C. Raynham, Chelmsford; C.R. Read, Epsom; Mark Read, Romford; Debbie Reddy, W12; Francis Redgate, Nottingham; Steven Redknap, Ashford; I. Reid, Fife; Lorraine Reid, Edinburgh; Duncan Renn, Dursley; Derek Richards, Bewdley; Sean Richards, Dover; Simon Richardson, Gainsborough; Mathew Riley, SE3; Lindsay Roberts, Lancaster; Margaret Roberts, Rubery; Peter Roberts, Shipston; Stewart & Anne Robertson, Leamington; J. & P. Rockery, Leicester; K.G. Rodwell, Harston; R. Ronan IOW; John Roscoe, Stalybridge; Brian Rorton, Pontefract; John Rose, Hull; WJ Rowe, Steve Rowland, Matlock; Mrs E.M. Ruck, Darlington; D.C. Ruggins, Chalfont; J.A. Rumble, Rochford; Paul Rushton, Nottingham; Bob Rutter, Blackpool; E.J. Ryan, Effingham; N. Ryer, Mansfield.

S: M.B. Samson, Hertfordshire; Pauline Sapsford, Milton Keynes; M.R. Sargeant, Cornwall; Mark Sarjant, Guildford; GM Saville, Egremont; Mike Scotlock, Rayleigh; Mike Scott, Holmer Green; M.J. Scott, SE26; Nicky & Don Scowen, Romford; Tim Sebensfield, Beeston; M. Seefeld, W5; Patrick Sellar, Maidstone; Philip Senior, Liverpool; N. Sennett, Hull; David Sewell, Aldershot; Mrs D.A. Seymour, Burnham-on-Sea; Richard Shackleton, Wakefield; Brian Shallon, Camberley; Jeane Sharp, St Albans; Mark Shaw, Swindon; Michelle Shaw, Ilford; Deborah Shent, Nottingham; Barrie Shepherd, Bishopston; Theresa Shilcock, Derbyshire; Ewan Sim, Leeds; Jennifer Singh, Enfield; Jeff Slater, E6; William P. Sloan, Camberley; Else & Harald Smaage, Sauvegny; David Smith, Norwich; Denis Smith, Swindon; E.K. Smith, Edinburgh; Gillian Smith, St Andrews; Hazel Smith, Llandrinio; Howard Smith, S. Glamorgan; Jim Smith, Cork; L.P. & A. Smith, Gibraltar;

Mark Smith, Lancashire; Nora Smith, Cardiff; R.B. Smith, BFPO; Sue Smith, Northampton; Susan Smith, Devon; Colin Snowball, Cheltenham; Tim Softly, Leigh; Robert Solbe, Surrey; Peter Soloman, Middlesbrough; M. Somerton-Rayner, Cranwell; Maurice Southwell, Haddenham; Gill Sparks, Halifax; Andrew Speller, Harlow; G.D. Spencer, Stonehaven; Mrs P. Spencer, Norwich; Andy Spiers, Brighton; R. Spiers, Wolverhampton; Chris Spinks, Ilford; John Spinks, Hainault; Martin Spooner, Wallsend; D.J. Stacey, Cambridge; Mrs W.L. Stanley-Smith, Belper; John Starley, Birdingbury; Nigel Steel, Carlisle; Avril Steele, Crossgar; Bob Stencill, Sheffield; John Stent, Liss; Ian Stewart, Potters Bar; Tim Stewart, Norfolk; Barry Strange, Kent; Rob Struthers, Brighton; Mrs M.B. Such; F.D. Sunderland, Plympton; F.C. Sutton, Poole; Carolyn Swain, Leeds; Gary Swain, Coventry; D.L. Swann, Parbold; Frank Sweeney, Middlesbrough; Gill & Graham Swift, Beeston; M.S. Sykes, Dorrington.

T: Steve Tandy, Cleveleys; Bernard Tarpey, Failsworth; Andrew Tattersall, North Yorks; C.B. Taylor, Wolverhampton; Colin Taylor, Preston; Ken Taylor, Sevenoaks; Philip & Vivien Taylor, Cromer; Roger Taylor, Hamela; Len Teff, Whaddon; R.L. Terry, Kent; Christopher Thomas, Barnet; D.G. Thomas, Gloucestershire; D.L. Thomas, Peterborough; Mrs J. Thomas, Cumbria; Alan Thompson, Clwyd; Richard Thompson, Rainham; Bill Thomson, Ramsgate; Paul Thomson, Salford; J. Thorne, South Benfleet; Mrs B.M. Clifton Timms, Chorley; Joan and Ken Timms, West Sussex; Mrs M. Tindale, Beverley; Alan Tingle, Hampshire; Graham Todd, Crawley; Alex and Sarah Torrence, Cleveland; S.R. Tracey-Forster, Bronham; Bernard Train, Barton; R. Trinkwon, Ferring; Kevin and Sarah Troubridge, Chelmsford; Dr J.G. Tucker, SW17; Don Turnball, Geneva; Mrs S.M. Turner, Stroud; R. Twiddy, Boston; S. Twiggs, Lower Kingswood; Jeremey Twomey, Leamington; John Tyler, Romford.

V: David Valentine, Forfar; Alan & Lesley Vaughan, Paington; D. Vaughan-Williams, Penyffordd; Mrs B. Venton, Chipstead; Richard Vinnicombe, Camberley; Mr and Mrs T. Vlismas, Crymyoh; Sarah Vokes, Dorking; Gordon Volke, Worthing.

W: Phil Wain, Merseyside; R. Waldron, Oxon; Alison Walker, Droitwich; Andrew Walker, Aklington; Dr J.B. Walker, Burnham; John Walker, Chorley; Dr P.A.W. Walker, Wirral; William Wallace, West Kilbride; Alison Walton, North Shields; Mrs J. Ward, Wakefield; Pamela Ward, Birmingham; John Warren, Lancs; Nicholas Watt, Houghton; R.G. Watt, Bromyard; Andy Webb, Aberdeen; Peter Webb, West Byfleet; T.G. Webb, Peterborough; Nick Webley, Llandeilo; Dave Webster, Gateshead; Harry and Marina Webster, Nottingham; Andrew Wegg, SW16; Michael Welch, Reading; J. Weld, Eastleigh; Dave Weldon, Hale; John Wellings, Edinburgh; A.D. West, Leicestershire; Laurence West, Torquay; Joyce Westrip, Perth, Australia; Sarah Wheatley, Leavesden; George Whilton, Huddersfield; Andy Whitehead, Swindon; Mr & Mrs D.W. Whitehouse, Redditch; George Whitton, Huddersfield; Peter Wickendon, East Tilbury; Jennette Wickes, Fleet; P.M. Wilce, Abingdon; Chris Wilkinson, Cumbria; Geoffrey Wilkinson, Orpington; Babs Williams, Bristol; Mark P.

Williams, Bromley; P. Williams, St Austell; Ted Williams, Norwich; David Williamson, NW3; B.P. and J. Willoughby, Devizes; Bob & Eve Wilson, NW2; Dr Michael Wilson, Crewe; Major Mike Wilson, BFPO 140; John Wirring, Swindon; Mrs A.C. Withrington, Hindhead; W. Wood, Hornsea; John Woolsgrove, Enfield; Geof Worthington, Handforth; Mrs C. Wright, Glasgow; Clive Wright, Halesowen; D. Wright, Rotherham; John D. Wright, St Ives; Georgina Wright, Nottingham; Lynn Wright, Newark.

Y: Stephen Yarrow, NW11; E.J. Yea, Cambrideshire; Rev. Can. David Yerburgh, Stroud; Andy Young, Penrith; Mrs B. Young, Basildon; Carl Young, Nottingham; Mrs E. Young, Ilmington.

What We Need to Know

We need to know everything there is to know about all curry restaurants in the UK. And there is no one better able to tell us than those who use them. We do not mind how many times we receive a report about a particular place, so please don't feel inhibited or that someone else would be better qualified. They aren't. Your opinion is every bit as important as the next person's.

Ideally, we'd like a report from you every time you dine out – even on a humble takeaway. We realize this is hard work so we don't mind if your report is very short, and you are welcome to send in more than one report on the same place telling of different occasions. You can even use the back of an envelope or a postcard, or we can supply you with special forms if you write in (with an S.A.E., please).

If you can get hold of a menu (they usually have takeaway menus to give away) or visiting cards, they are useful to us too, as are newspaper cuttings, good and bad, and advertisements.

So, please send anything along with your report. Most reports received will appear, in abbreviated form, in the Curry Magazine (the Curry Club members' quarterly publication). They are also used when preparing the next edition of this Guide.

We do not pay for reports but our ever-increasing corps of regular correspondents receive the occasional perk from us. Why not join them? Please send us your report after your next restaurant curry.

Thank you.

Pat Chapman
Founder, THE CURRY CLUB

CURRY CLUB MEMBERS' DISCOUNT VOUCHER SCHEME SAVE POUNDS ON DINING!

To make big savings on your curry meals or takeaways, you must become a Curry Club member. It's easy: contact us at the address below. Members get, amongst other things, a quarterly magazine in which there are four vouchers. So you get sixteen vouchers a year.

Each voucher is valid at any one of the restaurants that have agreed to participate in this scheme. To identify them, look for the © sign at the top right hand of the restaurant's entry.

The actual discount each restaurant is willing to give varies from restaurant to restaurant. Some will give a free bottle of wine, or free starters, others 5% off the bill, and some are offering as much as 10%, or even more.

We have agreed with the restaurant owners that these discounts are available at the discretion of the restaurant, at their quieter times, and that each Curry Club member will book in advance when using a DISCOUNT VOUCHER.

To find out how much discount you can get, and when they will give it to you, please PHONE THE MANAGER. (Where possible we have given the name of the individual owner or manager who has agreed to give the discount in the participating restaurant's entry.) Then please BOOK.

There is no limit to the number of people Curry Club members may take. One voucher is valid for a discount on one meal, and must be handed over when paying the bill.

REMEMBER, YOU MUST BE A MEMBER OF THE CURRY CLUB TO GET YOUR VOUCHERS. SO JOIN NOW TO SAVE POUNDS.

More information about the scheme and the Club from:

THE CURRY CLUB
PO BOX 7, HASLEMERE
SURREY GU27 1EP

Please send an S.A.E.